T0128005

Get the eBook FREE!

(PDF, ePub, Kindle, and liveBook all included)

We believe that once you buy a book from us, you should be able to read it in any format we have available. To get electronic versions of this book at no additional cost to you, purchase and then register this book at the Manning website.

Go to https://www.manning.com/freebook and follow the instructions to complete your pBook registration.

That's it!
Thanks from Manning!

Learn Kubernetes in a Month of Lunches

ELTON STONEMAN

MANNING
SHELTER ISLAND

For online information and ordering of this and other Manning books, please visit
www.manning.com. The publisher offers discounts on this book when ordered in quantity.
For more information, please contact

Special Sales Department
Manning Publications Co.
20 Baldwin Road
PO Box 761
Shelter Island, NY 11964
Email: orders@manning.com

Manning Publications Co.
20 Baldwin Road
PO Box 761
Shelter Island, NY 11964

Development editor:	Becky Whitney
Technical development editor:	Kris Athi
Review editor:	Ivan Martinovic
Production editor:	Lori Weidert
Copy editor:	Pamela Hunt
Proofreader:	Keri Hales
Technical proofreader:	John Guthrie
Typesetter:	Dennis Dalinnik
Cover designer:	Leslie Haimes

ISBN: 9781617297984
Printed in the United States of America

This is the second book to come out of my barn in Gloucestershire, England. Last time, I dedicated it to my wife, Nikki, and our children, Jackson and Eris. They're still fantastic, but this time I want to say thank you to some friends, too— Andrew Price, who showed me that IT professionals can be entertainers, and Mark Smith, who helped me to stop overthinking.

contents

preface xiii
acknowledgments xiv
about this book xv
about the author xix

PART 1 FAST TRACK TO KUBERNETES 1

1 Before you begin 3

    1.1   Understanding Kubernetes 4

    1.2   Is this book for you? 8

    1.3   Creating your lab environment 8

*Download the book's source code 9 ▪ Install Docker Desktop 9
Install Docker Community Edition and K3s 10 ▪ Install the
Kubernetes command-line tool 11 ▪ Run a single-node Kubernetes
cluster in Azure 12 ▪ Run a single-node Kubernetes cluster in
AWS 12 ▪ Verify your cluster 13*

    1.4   Being immediately effective 13

2 Running containers in Kubernetes with Pods and Deployments 15

2.1   How Kubernetes runs and manages containers   15

2.2   Running Pods with controllers   21

2.3   Defining Deployments in application manifests   28

2.4   Working with applications in Pods   32

2.5   Understanding Kubernetes resource management   36

2.6   Lab   39

3 Connecting Pods over the network with Services 40

3.1   How Kubernetes routes network traffic   40

3.2   Routing traffic between Pods   45

3.3   Routing external traffic to Pods   49

3.4   Routing traffic outside Kubernetes   53

3.5   Understanding Kubernetes Service resolution   59

3.6   Lab   63

4 Configuring applications with ConfigMaps and Secrets 65

4.1   How Kubernetes supplies configuration to apps   65

4.2   Storing and using configuration files in ConfigMaps   69

4.3   Surfacing configuration data from ConfigMaps   75

4.4   Configuring sensitive data with Secrets   82

4.5   Managing app configuration in Kubernetes   89

4.6   Lab   91

5 Storing data with volumes, mounts, and claims 92

5.1   How Kubernetes builds the container filesystem   92

5.2   Storing data on a node with volumes and mounts   97

5.3   Storing clusterwide data with persistent volumes and claims   105

5.4   Dynamic volume provisioning and storage classes   115

5.5   Understanding storage choices in Kubernetes   120

5.6   Lab   120

6 Scaling applications across multiple Pods with controllers 122

6.1 How Kubernetes runs apps at scale 122

6.2 Scaling for load with Deployments and ReplicaSets 128

6.3 Scaling for high availability with DaemonSets 137

6.4 Understanding object ownership in Kubernetes 143

6.5 Lab 146

PART 2 KUBERNETES IN THE REAL WORLD 147

7 Extending applications with multicontainer Pods 149

7.1 How containers communicate in a Pod 149

7.2 Setting up applications with init containers 156

7.3 Applying consistency with adapter containers 162

7.4 Abstracting connections with ambassador containers 167

7.5 Understanding the Pod environment 171

7.6 Lab 175

8 Running data-heavy apps with StatefulSets and Jobs 176

8.1 How Kubernetes models stability with StatefulSets 176

8.2 Bootstrapping Pods with init containers in StatefulSets 180

8.3 Requesting storage with volume claim templates 185

8.4 Running maintenance tasks with Jobs and CronJobs 190

8.5 Choosing your platform for stateful apps 198

8.6 Lab 199

9 Managing app releases with rollouts and rollbacks 201

9.1 How Kubernetes manages rollouts 201

9.2 Updating Deployments with rollouts and rollbacks 205

9.3 Configuring rolling updates for Deployments 213

9.4 Rolling updates in DaemonSets and StatefulSets 220

9.5 Understanding release strategies 226

9.6 Lab 227

10 Packaging and managing apps with Helm   228

10.1   What Helm adds to Kubernetes   228

10.2   Packaging your own apps with Helm   233

10.3   Modeling dependencies in charts   243

10.4   Upgrading and rolling back Helm releases   248

10.5   Understanding where Helm fits in   253

10.6   Lab   254

11 App development—Developer workflows and CI/CD   255

11.1   The Docker developer workflow   255

11.2   The Kubernetes-as-a-Service developer workflow   260

11.3   Isolating workloads with contexts and namespaces   266

11.4   Continuous delivery in Kubernetes without Docker   271

11.5   Evaluating developer workflows on Kubernetes   276

11.6   Lab   278

PART 3 PREPARING FOR PRODUCTION 281

12 Empowering self-healing apps   283

12.1   Routing traffic to healthy Pods using readiness probes   283

12.2   Restarting unhealthy Pods with liveness probes   288

12.3   Deploying upgrades safely with Helm   294

12.4   Protecting apps and nodes with resource limits   301

12.5   Understanding the limits of self-healing apps   308

12.6   Lab   309

13 Centralizing logs with Fluentd and Elasticsearch   310

13.1   How Kubernetes stores log entries   310

13.2   Collecting logs from nodes with Fluentd   315

13.3   Shipping logs to Elasticsearch   321

13.4   Parsing and filtering log entries   325

13.5   Understanding logging options in Kubernetes   330

13.6   Lab   331

14 Monitoring applications and Kubernetes with Prometheus 332

14.1 How Prometheus monitors Kubernetes workloads 332

14.2 Monitoring apps built with Prometheus client libraries 337

14.3 Monitoring third-party apps with metrics exporters 344

14.4 Monitoring containers and Kubernetes objects 349

14.5 Understanding the investment you make in monitoring 354

14.6 Lab 356

15 Managing incoming traffic with Ingress 357

15.1 How Kubernetes routes traffic with Ingress 357

15.2 Routing HTTP traffic with Ingress rules 363

15.3 Comparing ingress controllers 369

15.4 Using Ingress to secure your apps with HTTPS 378

15.5 Understanding Ingress and ingress controllers 383

15.6 Lab 384

16 Securing applications with policies, contexts, and admission control 385

16.1 Securing communication with network policies 385

16.2 Restricting container capabilities with security contexts 394

16.3 Blocking and modifying workloads with webhooks 398

16.4 Controlling admission with Open Policy Agent 406

16.5 Understanding security in depth in Kubernetes 412

16.6 Lab 414

PART 4 PURE AND APPLIED KUBERNETES......................415

17 Securing resources with role-based access control 417

17.1 How Kubernetes secures access to resources 417

17.2 Securing resource access within the cluster 424

17.3 Binding roles to groups of users and service accounts 433

17.4 Discovering and auditing permissions with plugins 441

17.5 Planning your RBAC strategy 445

17.6 Lab 446

18 **Deploying Kubernetes: Multinode and multiarchitecture clusters 447**

18.1 What's inside a Kubernetes cluster? 447
18.2 Initializing the control plane 451
18.3 Adding nodes and running Linux workloads 455
18.4 Adding Windows nodes and running hybrid workloads 461
18.5 Understanding Kubernetes at scale 469
18.6 Lab 471

19 **Controlling workload placement and automatic scaling 472**

19.1 How Kubernetes schedules workloads 472
19.2 Directing Pod placement with affinity and antiaffinity 477
19.3 Controlling capacity with automatic scaling 484
19.4 Protecting resources with preemption and priorities 491
19.5 Understanding the controls for managing workloads 497
19.6 Lab 498

20 **Extending Kubernetes with custom resources and Operators 500**

20.1 How to extend Kubernetes with custom resources 500
20.2 Triggering workflows with custom controllers 506
20.3 Using Operators to manage third-party components 512
20.4 Building Operators for your own applications 522
20.5 Understanding when to extend Kubernetes 528
20.6 Lab 529

21 **Running serverless functions in Kubernetes 530**

21.1 How serverless platforms work in Kubernetes 530
21.2 Triggering functions from HTTP requests 537
21.3 Triggering functions from events and schedules 543
21.4 Abstracting serverless functions with Serverless 548
21.5 Understanding where serverless functions fit 554
21.6 Lab 555

22 *Never the end* 556

22.1 Further reading by chapter 556

22.2 Choosing a Kubernetes platform 559

22.3 Understanding how Kubernetes is built 560

22.4 Joining the community 561

index 563

preface

As I was finishing *Learn Docker in a Month of Lunches*, I knew that the sequel had to be about Kubernetes. For most people, that will be the next stage in their container journey, but learning Kubernetes is not easy. That's partly because it's such a powerful platform, with a huge feature set that is always evolving. But it's also because it needs a reliable guide that teaches at the right level—going deep enough on the technical knowledge but keeping the focus on what the platform can do for you and your applications. I hope *Learn Kubernetes in a Month of Lunches* will be that guide.

Kubernetes is a system that runs and manages applications in containers. It's the most popular way to run containers in production, because it's supported by all the major cloud platforms and runs equally well in the data center. It's a world-class platform used by companies like Netflix and Apple—and you can run it on your laptop. You have to make an investment to learn Kubernetes, but the payback is a skill you can take to any project in any organization, confident that you'll hit the ground running.

The investment you need to make is *time*. It takes time to become familiar with everything that Kubernetes can do and how you express your applications in the Kubernetes modeling language. You bring the time, and *Learn Kubernetes in a Month of Lunches* will provide the rest. There are hands-on exercises and labs that will get you experienced in all the platform features and also in the working practices and the ecosystem of tools around Kubernetes. This is a practical book that gets you ready to use Kubernetes for real.

acknowledgments

This is my second book for Manning, and it's been just as much a pleasure to write as the first. A lot of people have worked hard to get this book out and to help me make it better. I'd like to thank the publishing team for all their feedback.

To all the reviewers, Alex Davies-Moore, Anthony Staunton, Brent Honadel, Clark Dorman, Clifford Thurber, Daniel Carl, David Lloyd, Furqan Shaikh, George Onofrei, Iain Campbell, Marc-Anthony Taylor, Marcus Brown, Martin Tidman, Mike Lewis, Nicolantonio Vignola, Ondrej Krajicek, Rui Liu, Sadhana Ganapathiraju, Sai Prasad Vaddepally, Sander Stad, Tobias Getrost, Tony Sweets, Trent Whiteley, Vadim Turkov, and Yogesh Shetty, your suggestions helped make this a better book.

I'd also like to thank everyone in the review cycles and the early-access program who tried all the exercises and let me know when things didn't work. Thank you all for your time.

about this book

Who should read this book

I want you to get an authentic Kubernetes experience from this book. When you've read all the chapters and completed the exercises, you should be confident that the skills you've learned are how people really use Kubernetes. This book contains a lot of content, and you'll find a typical lunch hour won't be enough for many of the chapters. That's because I want to give every topic the coverage it deserves, so you really get a complete understanding and finish the book feeling like a seasoned Kubernetes professional.

You don't need any understanding of Kubernetes to start your journey with this book, but you should be familiar with core concepts like containers and images. If you're new to the whole container space, you'll find some chapters of my other book, *Learn Docker in a Month of Lunches* (Manning, 2020), as appendices in the ebook version of this book—they will help to set the scene.

Kubernetes experience will help you further your career whether you're in engineering or operations, and this book doesn't make any assumptions about your background. Kubernetes is an advanced topic that builds on several other concepts, but I give an overview of those topics when we get to them. This is very much a practical book, and to get the most out of it, you should plan to work through the hands-on exercises. You don't need any special hardware: a Mac or Windows laptop, or a Linux desktop, will be fine.

GitHub is the source of truth for all the samples I use in the book. You'll download the materials when you set up your lab in chapter 1, and you should be sure to star the repository and watch for notifications.

How to use this book

This book follows the Month of Lunches principles: you should be able to work through each chapter in your lunchbreak and work through the whole book within a month. "Work" is the key here, because you should look at putting aside time to read the chapter, work through the try-it-now exercises, and have a go at the hands-on lab at the end. You should expect to have a few extended lunchbreaks because the chapters don't cut any corners or skip over key details. You need a lot of muscle memory to work effectively with Kubernetes, and practicing every day will really cement the knowledge you gain in each chapter.

Your learning journey

Kubernetes is a vast subject, but I've taught it for years in training sessions and workshops, both in-person and virtual, and built out an incremental learning path that I know works. We'll start with the core concepts and gradually add more detail, saving the most complex topics for when you're more comfortable with Kubernetes.

Chapters 2 through 6 jump in to running apps on Kubernetes. You'll learn how to define applications in YAML manifests, which Kubernetes runs as containers. You'll understand how to configure network access for containers to talk to each other and for traffic from the outside world to reach your containers. You'll learn how your apps can read configuration from Kubernetes and write data to storage units managed by Kubernetes and how you can scale your applications.

Chapters 7 through 11 build on the basics with subjects that deal with real-world Kubernetes usage. You'll learn how you can run containers that share a common environment and how you can use containers to run batch jobs and scheduled jobs. You'll learn how Kubernetes supports automated rolling updates so you can release new application versions with zero downtime and how to use Helm to provide a configurable way to deploy your apps. You'll also learn about the practicalities of building apps with Kubernetes, looking at different developer workflows and continuous integration/continuous delivery (CI/CD) pipelines.

Chapters 12 through 16 are all about production readiness, going beyond just running your apps in Kubernetes to running them in a way that's good enough to go live. You'll learn how to configure self-healing applications, collect and centralize all your logs, and build monitoring dashboards to visualize the health of your systems. Security is also in here, and you'll learn how to secure public access to your apps as well as how to secure the applications themselves.

Chapters 17 to 21 move into expert territory. Here you'll learn how to work with large Kubernetes deployments and configure your applications to automatically scale up and down. You'll learn how to implement role-based access control to secure access to Kubernetes resources, and we'll cover some more interesting uses of Kubernetes: as a platform for serverless functions and as a multiarchitecture cluster that can run apps built for Linux and Windows, Intel, and Arm.

By the end of the book, you should be confident about bringing Kubernetes into your daily work. The final chapter offers guidance on moving on with Kubernetes with further reading for each topic in the book and advice on choosing a Kubernetes provider.

Try-it-now exercises

Every chapter of the book has many guided exercises for you to complete. The source code for the book is all on GitHub at https://github.com/sixeyed/kiamol—you'll clone that when you set up your lab environment and use it for all the samples, which will have you running increasingly complex applications in Kubernetes.

Many chapters build on work from earlier in the book, but you do not need to follow all the chapters in order, so you can follow your own learning journey. The exercises within a chapter do often build on each other, so if you skip exercises, you may find errors later on, which will help hone your troubleshooting skills. All the exercises use container images, which are publicly available on Docker Hub, and your Kubernetes cluster will download any that it needs.

This book contains a lot of content. You'll get the most out of it if you work through the samples as you read the chapters, and you'll feel a lot more comfortable about using Kubernetes going forward. If you don't have time to work through every exercise, it's fine to skip some; a screenshot showing the output you would have seen follows each exercise, and every chapter finishes with a wrap-up section to make sure you're confident with the topic.

Hands-on labs

Each chapter ends with a hands-on lab that invites you to go further than the try-it-now exercises. These aren't guided—you'll get some instructions and some hints, and then it will be up to you to complete the lab. Sample answers for all the labs are in the sixeyed/kiamol GitHub repository, so you can check what you've done—or see how I've done it if you don't have time for one of the labs.

Additional resources

Kubernetes in Action by Marko Lukša (Manning, 2017) is a great book that covers a lot of the administration details that I don't cover here. Other than that, the main resource for further reading is the official Kubernetes documentation, which you'll find in two places. The documentation site (https://kubernetes.io/docs/home/) covers everything from the architecture of the cluster to guided walk-throughs and learning how to contribute to Kubernetes yourself. The Kubernetes API reference (https://kubernetes .io/docs/reference/generated/kubernetes-api/v1.20) contains the detailed specification for every type of object you can create—that's a site to bookmark.

Twitter is home to the Kubernetes @kubernetesio account, and you can also follow some of the founding members of the Kubernetes project and community, like Brendan Burns (@brendandburns), Tim Hockin (@thockin), Joe Beda (@jbeda), and Kelsey Hightower (@kelseyhightower).

I talk about this stuff all the time, too. You can follow me on Twitter @Elton-Stoneman; my blog is https://blog.sixeyed.com; and I post YouTube videos at https://youtube.com/eltonstoneman.

About the code

This book contains many examples of source code both in numbered listings and in line with normal text. In both cases, source code is formatted in a `fixed-width font like this` to separate it from ordinary text. Sometimes code is also **in bold** to highlight code that has changed from previous steps in the chapter, such as when a new feature adds to an existing line of code.

In many cases, the original source code has been reformatted; we've added line breaks and reworked indentation to accommodate the available page space in the book. In rare cases, even this was not enough, and listings include line-continuation markers (➥). Additionally, comments in the source code have often been removed from the listings when the code is described in the text. Code annotations accompany many of the listings, highlighting important concepts.

The code for the examples in this book is available for download from the Manning website at https://www.manning.com/books/learn-kubernetes-in-a-month-of-lunches, and from GitHub at http://github.com/sixeyed/kiamol.

liveBook discussion forum

Purchase of *Learn Kubernetes in a Month of Lunches* includes free access to a private web forum run by Manning Publications where you can make comments about the book, ask technical questions, and receive help from the author and from other users. To access the forum, go to https://livebook.manning.com/#!/book/learn-kubernetes-in-a-month-of-lunches/discussion. You can also learn more about Manning's forums and the rules of conduct at https://livebook.manning.com/#!/discussion.

Manning's commitment to our readers is to provide a venue where a meaningful dialogue between individual readers and between readers and the author can take place. It is not a commitment to any specific amount of participation on the part of the author, whose contribution to the forum remains voluntary (and unpaid). We suggest you try asking the author some challenging questions lest his interest stray! The forum and the archives of previous discussions will be accessible from the publisher's website as long as the book is in print.

about the author

ELTON STONEMAN is a Docker Captain, a multiyear Microsoft MVP, and the author of dozens of online training courses with Pluralsight and Udemy. He spent most of his career as a consultant in the Microsoft space, designing and delivering large enterprise systems. Then he fell for containers and joined Docker, where he worked for three furiously busy and hugely fun years. Now he works as a freelance consultant and trainer, helping organizations at all stages of their container journey. Elton writes about Docker and Kubernetes at https://blog.sixeyed.com and on Twitter @EltonStoneman and runs a regular YouTube live stream at https://eltons.show.

Fast track to Kubernetes

Welcome to *Learn Kubernetes in a Month of Lunches*. This first section gets you using Kubernetes straight away, focusing on the core concepts: Deployments, Pods, Services, and volumes. You'll learn how to model your applications using the Kubernetes YAML specification and how Kubernetes provides abstractions over compute, networking, and storage. By the end of the section, you'll have lots of experience in all the fundamentals, and you'll have a good understanding of how to model and deploy your own applications.

Before you begin

Kubernetes is big. Really big. It was released as an open source project on GitHub in 2014, and now it averages 200 changes every week from a worldwide community of 2,500 contributors. The annual KubeCon conference has grown from 1,000 attendees in 2016 to more than 12,000 at the most recent event, and it's now a global series with events in America, Europe, and Asia. All the major cloud services offer a managed Kubernetes service, and you can run Kubernetes in a data center or on your laptop—*and they're all the same Kubernetes.*

Independence and standardization are the main reasons Kubernetes is so popular. Once you have your apps running nicely in Kubernetes, you can deploy them anywhere, which is attractive for organizations moving to the cloud, because it enables them to move between data centers and other clouds without a rewrite. It's also very attractive for practitioners—once you've mastered Kubernetes, you can move between projects and organizations and be productive quickly.

Getting to that point is hard, though, because Kubernetes is hard. Even simple apps are deployed as multiple components, described in a custom file format that can easily span many hundreds of lines. Kubernetes brings infrastructure-level concerns like load balancing, networking, storage, and compute into app configuration, which might be new concepts, depending on your IT background. In addition, Kubernetes is always expanding—new releases come out every quarter, often bringing a ton of new functionality.

But it's worth it. I've spent many years helping people learn Kubernetes, and a common pattern arises: the question *"Why is this so complicated?"* transforms to *"You can do that? This is amazing!"* Kubernetes truly is an amazing piece of technology.

The more you learn about it, the more you'll love it—and this book will accelerate you on your journey to Kubernetes mastery.

1.1 *Understanding Kubernetes*

This book provides a hands-on introduction to Kubernetes. Every chapter offers try-it-now exercises and labs for you to get lots of experience using Kubernetes. All except this one. :) We'll jump into the practical work in the next chapter, but we need a little theory first. Let's start by understanding what Kubernetes actually is and the problems it solves.

Kubernetes is a platform for running containers. It takes care of starting your containerized applications, rolling out updates, maintaining service levels, scaling to meet demand, securing access, and much more. The two core concepts in Kubernetes are the *API*, which you use to define your applications, and the *cluster*, which runs your applications. A cluster is a set of individual servers that have all been configured with a container runtime like Docker, and then joined into a single logical unit with Kubernetes. Figure 1.1 shows a high-level view of the cluster.

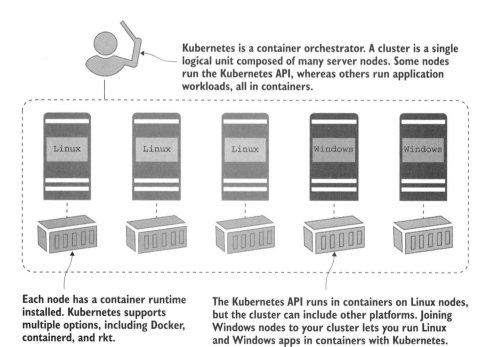

Kubernetes is a container orchestrator. A cluster is a single logical unit composed of many server nodes. Some nodes run the Kubernetes API, whereas others run application workloads, all in containers.

Each node has a container runtime installed. Kubernetes supports multiple options, including Docker, containerd, and rkt.

The Kubernetes API runs in containers on Linux nodes, but the cluster can include other platforms. Joining Windows nodes to your cluster lets you run Linux and Windows apps in containers with Kubernetes.

Figure 1.1   A Kubernetes cluster is a bunch of servers, which can run containers, joined into a group.

Cluster administrators manage the individual servers, called *nodes* in Kubernetes. You can add nodes to expand the capacity of the cluster, take nodes offline for servicing, or roll out an upgrade of Kubernetes across the cluster. In a managed service like Microsoft

Azure Kubernetes Service (AKS) or Amazon Elastic Kubernetes Service (EKS), those functions are all wrapped in simple web interfaces or command lines. In normal usage you forget about the underlying nodes and treat the cluster as a single entity.

The Kubernetes cluster is there to run your applications. You define your apps in YAML files and send those files to the Kubernetes API. Kubernetes looks at what you're asking for in the YAML and compares it to what's already running in the cluster. It makes any changes it needs to get to the desired state, which could be updating a configuration, removing containers, or creating new containers. Containers are distributed around the cluster for high availability, and they can all communicate over virtual networks managed by Kubernetes. Figure 1.2 shows the deployment process, but without the nodes because we don't really care about them at this level.

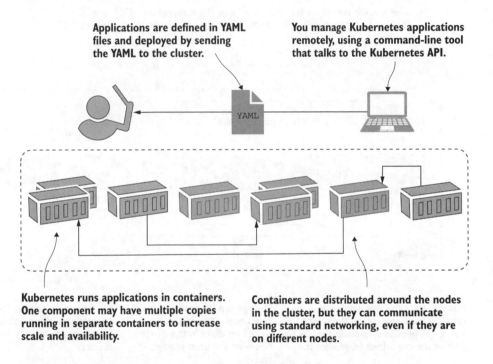

Applications are defined in YAML files and deployed by sending the YAML to the cluster.

You manage Kubernetes applications remotely, using a command-line tool that talks to the Kubernetes API.

Kubernetes runs applications in containers. One component may have multiple copies running in separate containers to increase scale and availability.

Containers are distributed around the nodes in the cluster, but they can communicate using standard networking, even if they are on different nodes.

Figure 1.2   When you deploy apps to a Kubernetes cluster, you can usually ignore the actual nodes.

Defining the structure of the application is your job, but running and managing everything is down to Kubernetes. If a node in the cluster goes offline and takes some containers with it, Kubernetes sees that and starts replacement containers on other nodes. If an application container becomes unhealthy, Kubernetes can restart it. If a component is under stress because of a high load, Kubernetes can start extra copies of the component in new containers. If you put the work into your Docker images and Kubernetes YAML files, you'll get a self-healing app that runs in the same way on any Kubernetes cluster.

Kubernetes manages more than just containers, which is what makes it a complete application platform. The cluster has a distributed database, and you can use that to store both configuration files for your applications and secrets like API keys and connection credentials. Kubernetes delivers these seamlessly to your containers, which lets you use the same container images in every environment and apply the correct configuration from the cluster. Kubernetes also provides storage, so your applications can maintain data outside of containers, giving you high availability for stateful apps. Kubernetes also manages network traffic coming into the cluster by sending it to the right containers for processing. Figure 1.3 shows those other resources, which are the main features of Kubernetes.

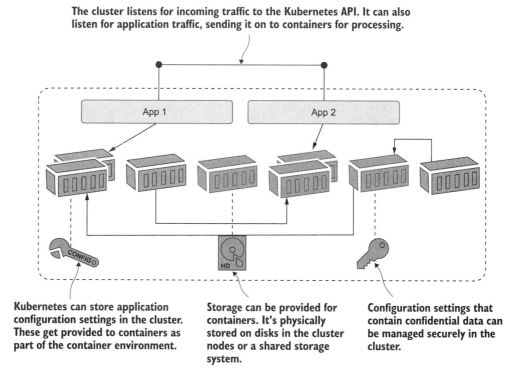

The cluster listens for incoming traffic to the Kubernetes API. It can also listen for application traffic, sending it on to containers for processing.

Kubernetes can store application configuration settings in the cluster. These get provided to containers as part of the container environment.

Storage can be provided for containers. It's physically stored on disks in the cluster nodes or a shared storage system.

Configuration settings that contain confidential data can be managed securely in the cluster.

Figure 1.3 There's more to Kubernetes than just containers—the cluster manages other resources, too.

I haven't talked about what those applications in the containers look like; that's because Kubernetes doesn't really care. You can run a new application built with cloud-native design across microservices in multiple containers. You can run a legacy application built as a monolith in one big container. They could be Linux apps or Windows apps. You define all types of applications in YAML files using the same API, and you can run them all on a single cluster. The joy of working with Kubernetes is that it adds a layer of consistency on top of all your apps—old .NET and Java mono-liths and new Node.js and Go microservices are all described, deployed, and managed in the same way.

That's just about all the theory we need to get started with Kubernetes, but before we go any further, I want to put some proper names on the concepts I've been talking about. Those YAML files are properly called *application manifests,* because they're a list of all the components that go into shipping the app. Those components are Kubernetes *resources;* they have proper names, too. Figure 1.4 takes the concepts from figure 1.3 and applies the correct Kubernetes resource names.

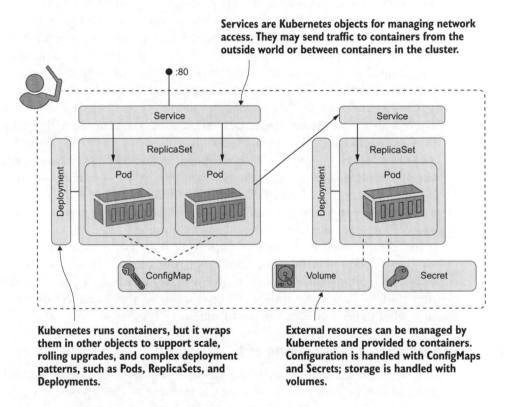

Services are Kubernetes objects for managing network access. They may send traffic to containers from the outside world or between containers in the cluster.

Kubernetes runs containers, but it wraps them in other objects to support scale, rolling upgrades, and complex deployment patterns, such as Pods, ReplicaSets, and Deployments.

External resources can be managed by Kubernetes and provided to containers. Configuration is handled with ConfigMaps and Secrets; storage is handled with volumes.

Figure 1.4   The true picture: these are the most basic Kubernetes resources you need to master.

I told you Kubernetes was hard. :) But we will cover all of these resources one at a time over the next few chapters, layering on the understanding. By the time you've finished chapter 6, that diagram will make complete sense, and you'll have had lots of experience in defining those resources in YAML files and running them in your own Kubernetes cluster.

1.2   *Is this book for you?*

The goal of this book is to fast-track your Kubernetes learning to the point where you have confidence defining and running your own apps in Kubernetes, and you understand what the path to production looks like. The best way to learn Kubernetes is to practice, and if you follow all the examples in the chapters and work through the labs, then you'll have a solid understanding of all the most important pieces of Kubernetes by the time you finish the book.

But Kubernetes is a huge topic, and I won't be covering everything. The biggest gaps are in administration. I won't cover cluster setup and management in any depth, because they vary across different infrastructures. If you're planning on running Kubernetes in the cloud as your production environment, then a lot of those concerns are taken care of in a managed service anyway. If you want to get a Kubernetes certification, this book is a great place to start, but it won't get you all the way. There are two main Kubernetes certifications: Certified Kubernetes Application Developer (CKAD) and Certified Kubernetes Administrator (CKA). This book covers about 80% of the CKAD curriculum and about 50% of CKA.

There's also a reasonable amount of background knowledge you'll need to work with this book effectively. I'll explain lots of core principles as we encounter them in Kubernetes features, but I won't fill in any gaps about containers. If you're not familiar with ideas like images, containers, and registries, I'd recommend starting with my book, *Learn Docker in a Month of Lunches* (Manning, 2020). You don't need to use Docker with Kubernetes, but it is the easiest and most flexible way to package your apps so you can run them in containers with Kubernetes.

If you classify yourself as a new or improving Kubernetes user, with a reasonable working knowledge of containers, then this is the book for you. Your background could be in development, operations, architecture, DevOps, or site reliability engineering (SRE)—Kubernetes touches all those roles, so they're all welcome here, and you are going to learn an absolute ton of stuff.

1.3   *Creating your lab environment*

A Kubernetes cluster can have hundreds of nodes, but for the exercises in this book, a single-node cluster is fine. We'll get your lab environment set up now so you're ready to get started in the next chapter. Dozens of Kubernetes platforms are available, and the exercises in this book should work with any certified Kubernetes setup. I'll describe how to create your lab on Linux, Windows, Mac, Amazon Web Services (AWS), and Azure, which covers all the major options. I'm using Kubernetes version 1.18, but earlier or later versions should be fine, too.

The easiest option to run Kubernetes locally is Docker Desktop, which is a single package that gives you Docker and Kubernetes and all the command-line tools. It also integrates nicely with your computer's network and has a handy Reset Kubernetes button, which clears everything, if necessary. Docker Desktop is supported on

Windows 10 and macOS, and if that doesn't work for you, I'll also walk through some alternatives.

One point you should know: the components of Kubernetes itself need to run as Linux containers. You can't run Kubernetes in Windows (although you can run Windows apps in containers with a multinode Kubernetes cluster), so you'll need a Linux virtual machine (VM) if you're working on Windows. Docker Desktop sets that up and manages it for you.

And one last note for Windows users: please use PowerShell to follow along with the exercises. PowerShell supports many Linux commands, and the try-it-now exercises are built to run on Linux (and Mac) shells and PowerShell. If you try to use the classic Windows command terminal, you're going to run into issues from the start.

1.3.1 *Download the book's source code*

Every example and exercise is in the book's source code repository on GitHub, together with sample solutions for all of the labs. If you're comfortable with Git and you have a Git client installed, you can clone the repository onto your computer with the following command:

```
git clone https://github.com/sixeyed/kiamol
```

If you're not a Git user, you can browse to the GitHub page for the book at https://github.com/sixeyed/kiamol and click the Clone or Download button to download a zip file, which you can expand.

The root of the source code is a folder called `kiamol`, and within that is a folder for each chapter: `ch02`, `ch03`, and so on. The first exercise in the chapter usually asks you to open a terminal session and switch to the `chXX` directory, so you'll need to navigate to your `kiamol` folder first.

The GitHub repository is the quickest way for me to publish any corrections to the exercises, so if you do have any problems, you should check for a README file with updates in the chapter folder.

1.3.2 *Install Docker Desktop*

Docker Desktop runs on Windows 10 or macOS Sierra (version 10.12 or higher). Browse to https://www.docker.com/products/docker-desktop and choose to install the stable version. Download the installer and run it, accepting all the defaults. On Windows, that might include a reboot to add new Windows features. When Docker Desktop is running, you'll see Docker's whale icon near the clock on the Windows taskbar or the Mac menu bar. If you're an experienced Docker Desktop user on Windows, you'll need to make sure you're in Linux container mode (which is the default for new installations).

Kubernetes isn't set up by default, so you'll need to click the whale icon to open the menu and click Settings. That opens the window shown in figure 1.5; select Kubernetes from the menu and select Enable Kubernetes.

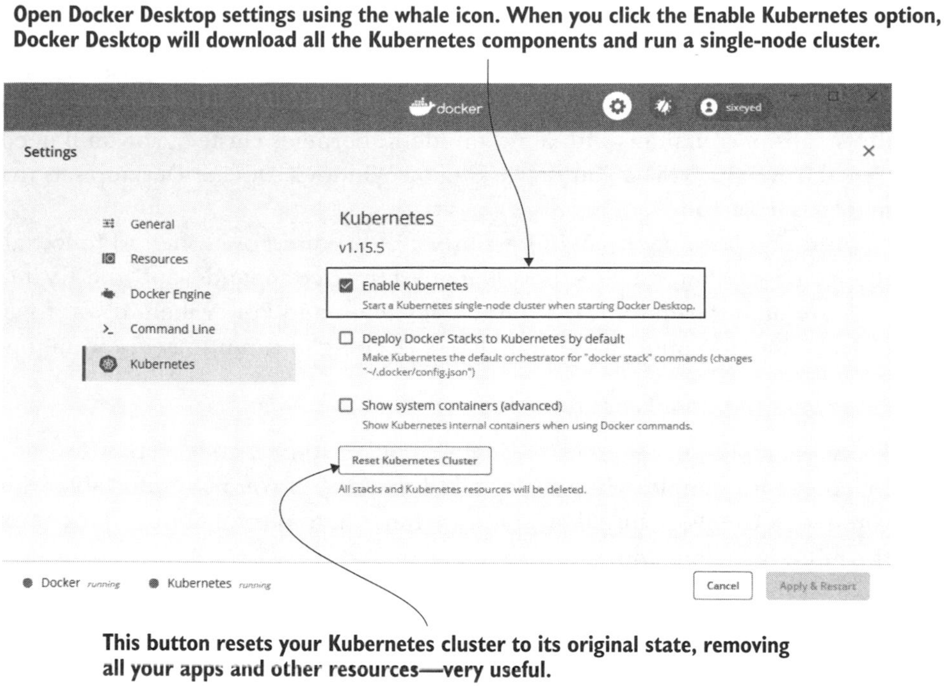

Open Docker Desktop settings using the whale icon. When you click the Enable Kubernetes option, Docker Desktop will download all the Kubernetes components and run a single-node cluster.

This button resets your Kubernetes cluster to its original state, removing all your apps and other resources—very useful.

Figure 1.5   Docker Desktop creates and manages a Linux VM to run containers, and it can run Kubernetes.

Docker Desktop downloads all the container images for the Kubernetes runtime—which might take a while—and then starts up everything. When you see two green dots at the bottom of the Settings screen, your Kubernetes cluster is ready to go. Docker Desktop installs everything else you need, so you can skip to section 1.4.7.

Other Kubernetes distributions can run on top of Docker Desktop, but they don't integrate well with the network setup that Docker Desktop uses, so you'll encounter problems running the exercises. The Kubernetes option in Docker Desktop has all the features you need for this book and is definitely the easiest option.

1.3.3   *Install Docker Community Edition and K3s*

If you're using a Linux machine or a Linux VM, you have several options for running a single-node cluster. Kind and minikube are popular, but my preference is K3s, which is a minimal installation but has all the features you'll need for the exercises. (The name is a play on "K8s," which is an abbreviation of Kubernetes. K3s trims the Kubernetes codebase, and the name indicates that it's half the size of K8s.)

K3s works with Docker, so first, you should install Docker Community Edition. You can check the full installation steps at https://rancher.com/docs/k3s/latest/en/quick-start/, but this will get you up and running:

```
# install Docker:
curl -fsSL https://get.docker.com | sh

# install K3s:
curl -sfL https://get.k3s.io | sh -s - --docker --disable=traefik --write-
    kubeconfig-mode=644
```

If you prefer to run your lab environment in a VM and you're familiar with using Vagrant to manage VMs, you can use the following Vagrant setup with Docker and K3s found in the source repository for the book:

```
# from the root of the Kiamol repo:
cd ch01/vagrant-k3s

# provision the machine:
vagrant up

# and connect:
vagrant ssh
```

K3s installs everything else you need, so you can skip to section 1.4.7.

1.3.4 *Install the Kubernetes command-line tool*

You manage Kubernetes with a tool called kubectl (which is pronounced "cube-cuttle" as in "cuttlefish"—don't let anyone tell you different). It connects to a Kubernetes cluster and works with the Kubernetes API. Both Docker Desktop and K3s install kubectl for you, but if you're using one of the other options described below, you'll need to install it yourself.

The full installation instructions are at https://kubernetes.io/docs/tasks/tools/install-kubectl/. You can use Homebrew on macOS and Chocolatey on Windows, and for Linux you can download the binary:

```
# macOS:
brew install kubernetes-cli

# OR Windows:
choco install kubernetes-cli

# OR Linux:
curl -Lo ./kubectl https://storage.googleapis.com/kubernetes-
    release/release/v1.18.8/bin/linux/amd64/kubectl
chmod +x ./kubectl
sudo mv ./kubectl /usr/local/bin/kubectl
```

1.3.5   *Run a single-node Kubernetes cluster in Azure*

You can run a managed Kubernetes cluster in Microsoft Azure using AKS. This might be a good option if you want to access your cluster from multiple machines or if you have an MSDN subscription with Azure credits. You can run a minimal single-node cluster, which won't cost a huge amount, but bear in mind that there's no way to stop the cluster and you'll be paying for it 24/7 until you remove it.

The Azure portal has a nice user interface for creating an AKS cluster, but it's much easier to use the az command. You can check the latest docs at https://docs .microsoft.com/en-us/azure/aks/kubernetes-walkthrough, but you can get started by downloading the az command-line tool and running a few commands, as follows:

```
# log in to your Azure subscription:
az login

# create a resource group for the cluster:
az group create --name kiamol --location eastus

# create a single-code cluster with 2 CPU cores and 8GB RAM:
az aks create --resource-group kiamol --name kiamol-aks --node-count 1 --
node-vm-size Standard_DS2_v2 --kubernetes-version 1.18.8 --generate-ssh-keys

# download certificates to use the cluster with kubectl:
az aks get-credentials --resource-group kiamol --name kiamol-aks
```

That final command downloads the credentials to connect to the Kubernetes API from your local kubectl command line.

1.3.6   *Run a single-node Kubernetes cluster in AWS*

The managed Kubernetes service in AWS is called the Elastic Kubernetes Service (EKS). You can create a single-node EKS cluster with the same caveat as Azure—that you'll be paying for that node and associated resources all the time it's running.

You can use the AWS portal to create an EKS cluster, but the recommended way is with a dedicated tool called eksctl. The latest documentation for the tool is at https:// eksctl.io, but it's pretty simple to use. First, install the latest version of the tool for your operating system as follows:

```
# install on macOS:
brew tap weaveworks/tap
brew install weaveworks/tap/eksctl

# OR on Windows:
choco install eksctl

# OR on Linux:
curl --silent --location
"https://github.com/weaveworks/eksctl/releases/download/latest/eksctl_$(uname
-s)_amd64.tar.gz" | tar xz -C /tmp
sudo mv /tmp/eksctl /usr/local/bin
```

Assuming you already have the AWS CLI installed, eksctl will use the credentials from the CLI (if not, then check the installation guide for authenticating eksctl). Then create a simple one-node cluster as follows:

```
# create a single node cluster with 2 CPU cores and 8GB RAM:
eksctl create cluster --name=kiamol --nodes=1 --node-type=t3.large
```

The tool sets up the connection from your local kubectl to the EKS cluster.

1.3.7 Verify your cluster

Now you have a running Kubernetes cluster, and whichever option you chose, they all work in the same way. Run the following command to check that your cluster is up and running:

```
kubectl get nodes
```

You should see output like that shown in figure 1.6. It's a list of all the nodes in your cluster, with some basic details like the status and Kubernetes version. The details of your cluster may be different, but as long as you see a node listed and in the ready state, then your cluster is good to go.

**Kubectl is the Kubernetes command-line tool.
You use it to work with local and remote clusters.**

```
PS>kubectl get nodes
NAME             STATUS    ROLES    AGE    VERSION
docker-desktop   Ready     master   49d    v1.18.3
```

**This command prints basic details about all the nodes in the cluster.
I'm using Docker Desktop, so I have a single node.**

Figure 1.6 If you can run kubectl and your nodes are ready, then you're all set to carry on.

1.4 Being immediately effective

"Immediately effective" is a core principle of the Month of Lunches series. In all, the focus is on learning skills and putting them into practice, in every chapter that follows.

Each chapter starts with a short introduction to the topic, followed by try-it-now exercises where you put the ideas into practice using your own Kubernetes cluster. Then there's a recap with some more detail, to fill in some of the questions you may have from diving in. Last, there's a hands-on lab for you to try by yourself, to really gain confidence in your new understanding.

All the topics center on tasks that are genuinely useful in the real world. You'll learn how to be immediately effective with the topic during the chapter, and you'll finish by understanding how to apply the new skill. Let's start running some containerized apps!

Running containers in Kubernetes with Pods and Deployments

2

Kubernetes runs containers for your application workloads, but the containers themselves are not objects you need to work with. Every container belongs to a Pod, which is a Kubernetes object for managing one or more containers, and Pods, in turn, are managed by other resources. These higher-level resources abstract away the details of the container, which powers self-healing applications and lets you use a desired-state workflow: you tell Kubernetes what you want to happen, and it decides how to make it happen.

In this chapter, we'll get started with the basic building blocks of Kubernetes: Pods, which run containers, and Deployments, which manage Pods. We'll use a simple web app for the exercises, and you'll get hands-on experience using the Kubernetes command-line tool to manage applications and using the Kubernetes YAML specification to define applications.

2.1 How Kubernetes runs and manages containers

A container is a virtualized environment that typically runs a single application component. Kubernetes wraps the container in another virtualized environment: the Pod. A Pod is a unit of compute, which runs on a single node in the cluster. The Pod has its own virtual IP address, which is managed by Kubernetes, and Pods in the cluster can communicate with other Pods over that virtual network, even if they're running on different nodes.

You normally run a single container in a Pod, but you can run multiple containers in one Pod, which opens up some interesting deployment options. All the containers in a Pod are part of the same virtual environment, so they share the same

15

network address and can communicate using localhost. Figure 2.1 shows the relationship between containers and Pods.

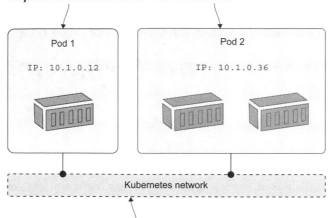

Every pod has an IP address assigned. All containers in the Pod share that address. If there are multiple containers in the Pod, they can communicate on the localhost address.

Pods are connected to the virtual network managed by Kubernetes. They can communicate by IP address, even if they are running on different nodes in the cluster.

Figure 2.1   Containers run inside Pods. You manage the Pods, and the Pods manage the containers.

This business of multicontainer Pods is a bit much to introduce this early on, but if I glossed over it and talked only about single-container Pods, you'd be rightfully asking why Kubernetes uses Pods at all instead of just containers. Let's run a Pod and see what it looks like to work with this abstraction over containers.

> **TRY IT NOW**   You can run a simple Pod using the Kubernetes command line without needing a YAML specification. The syntax is similar to running a container using Docker: you state the container image you want to use and any other parameters to configure the Pod behavior.

```
# run a Pod with a single container; the restart flag tells Kubernetes
# to create just the Pod and no other resources:
kubectl run hello-kiamol --image=kiamol/ch02-hello-kiamol --restart=Never

# wait for the Pod to be ready:
kubectl wait --for=condition=Ready pod hello-kiamol

# list all the Pods in the cluster:
kubectl get pods

# show detailed information about the Pod:
kubectl describe pod hello-kiamol
```

You can see my output in figure 2.2, where I've abridged the response from the final `describe pod` command. When you run it yourself, you'll see a whole lot more obscure-sounding information in there, like node selectors and tolerations. They're all part of the Pod specification, and Kubernetes has applied default values for everything that we didn't specify in the `run` command.

Creates a Pod named `hello-kiamol` running a single container, using the image called `kiamol/ch02-hello-kiamol` from Docker Hub

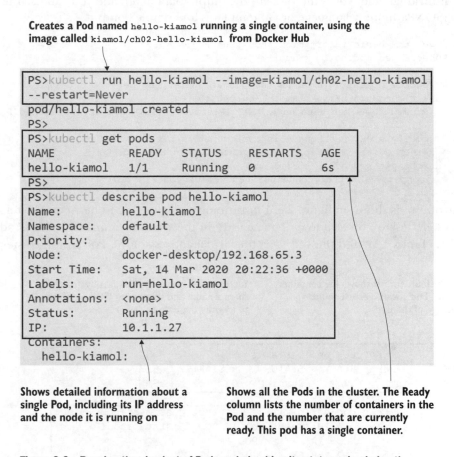

```
PS>kubectl run hello-kiamol --image=kiamol/ch02-hello-kiamol
--restart=Never
pod/hello-kiamol created
PS>
PS>kubectl get pods
NAME            READY    STATUS      RESTARTS    AGE
hello-kiamol    1/1      Running     0           6s
PS>
PS>kubectl describe pod hello-kiamol
Name:          hello-kiamol
Namespace:     default
Priority:      0
Node:          docker-desktop/192.168.65.3
Start Time:    Sat, 14 Mar 2020 20:22:36 +0000
Labels:        run=hello-kiamol
Annotations:   <none>
Status:        Running
IP:            10.1.1.27
Containers:
  hello-kiamol:
```

Shows detailed information about a single Pod, including its IP address and the node it is running on

Shows all the Pods in the cluster. The Ready column lists the number of containers in the Pod and the number that are currently ready. This pod has a single container.

Figure 2.2   Running the simplest of Pods and checking its status using kubectl

Now you have a single application container in your cluster, running inside a single Pod. If you're used to working with Docker, this is a familiar workflow, and it turns out that Pods are not as complicated as they might seem. The majority of your Pods will run single containers (until you start to explore more advanced options), and so you can effectively think of the Pod as the mechanism Kubernetes uses to run a container.

Kubernetes doesn't really run containers, though—it passes the responsibility for that to the container runtime installed on the node, which could be Docker or containerd or something more exotic. That's why the Pod is an abstraction: it's the resource that Kubernetes manages, whereas the container is managed by something outside of Kubernetes. You can get a sense of that by using kubectl to fetch specific information about the Pod.

TRY IT NOW   Kubectl returns basic information from the get pod command, but you can request more by applying an output parameter. You can name individual fields you want to see in the output parameter, and you can use the JSONPath query language or Go templates for complex output.

```
# get the basic information about the Pod:
kubectl get pod hello-kiamol

# specify custom columns in the output, selecting network details:
kubectl get pod hello-kiamol --output custom-
   columns=NAME:metadata.name,NODE_IP:status.hostIP,POD_IP:status.podIP

# specify a JSONPath query in the output,
# selecting the ID of the first container in the Pod:
kubectl get pod hello-kiamol -o
   jsonpath='{.status.containerStatuses[0].containerID}'
```

My output is shown in figure 2.3. I'm running a single-node Kubernetes cluster using Docker Desktop on Windows. The node IP in the second command is the IP address of my Linux VM, and the Pod IP is the virtual address of the Pod in the cluster. The

The default output shows the container count, Pod status, restart count, and the age of the pod.

You can specify custom columns by giving them a name and then using JSON notation to identify the data to return.

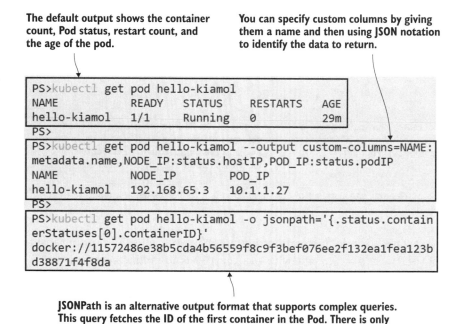

JSONPath is an alternative output format that supports complex queries. This query fetches the ID of the first container in the Pod. There is only one in this case, but there could be many, and the first index is zero.

Figure 2.3   Kubectl has many options for customizing its output for Pods and other objects.

container ID returned in the third command is prefixed by the name of the container runtime; mine is Docker.

That may have felt like a pretty dull exercise, but it comes with two important takeaways. The first is that kubectl is a hugely powerful tool—as your main point of contact with Kubernetes, you'll be spending a lot of time with it, and it's worth getting a solid understanding of what it can do. Querying the output from commands is a useful way to see the information you care about, and because you can access all the details of the resource, it's great for automation too. The second takeaway is a reminder that Kubernetes does not run containers—the container ID in the Pod is a reference to another system that runs containers.

Pods are allocated to one node when they're created, and it's that node's responsibility to manage the Pod and its containers. It does that by working with the container runtime using a known API called the Container Runtime Interface (CRI). The CRI lets the node manage containers in the same way for all the different container runtimes. It uses a standard API to create and delete containers and to query their state. While the Pod is running, the node works with the container runtime to ensure the Pod has all the containers it needs.

> **TRY IT NOW** All Kubernetes environments use the same CRI mechanism to manage containers, but not all container runtimes allow you to access containers outside of Kubernetes. This exercise shows you how a Kubernetes node keeps its Pod containers running, but you'll only be able to follow it if you're using Docker as your container runtime.

```
# find the Pod's container:
docker container ls -q --filter
   label=io.kubernetes.container.name=hello-kiamol

# now delete that container:
docker container rm -f $(docker container ls -q --filter
   label=io.kubernetes.container.name=hello-kiamol)

# check the Pod status:
kubectl get pod hello-kiamol

# and find the container again:
docker container ls -q --filter
   label=io.kubernetes.container.name=hello-kiamol
```

You can see from figure 2.4 that Kubernetes reacted when I deleted my Docker container. For an instant, the Pod had zero containers, but Kubernetes immediately created a replacement to repair the Pod and bring it back to the correct state.

It's the abstraction from containers to Pods that lets Kubernetes repair issues like this. A failed container is a temporary fault; the Pod still exists, and the Pod can be brought back up to spec with a new container. This is just one level of self-healing that Kubernetes provides, with further abstractions on top of Pods giving your apps even more resilience.

Kubernetes applies a Pod name label to containers, so I can filter my Docker containers to find the Pod container. The ID returned from the `Docker` command is the same ID kubectl returned in figure 2.3.

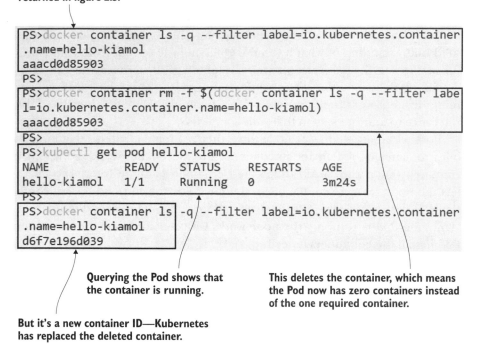

Querying the Pod shows that the container is running.

This deletes the container, which means the Pod now has zero containers instead of the one required container.

But it's a new container ID—Kubernetes has replaced the deleted container.

Figure 2.4   Kubernetes makes sure Pods have all the containers they need.

One of those abstractions is the Deployment, which we'll look at in the next section. Before we move on, let's see what's actually running in that Pod. It's a web application, but you can't browse to it because we haven't configured Kubernetes to route network traffic to the Pod. We can get around that using another feature of kubectl.

TRY IT NOW Kubectl can forward traffic from a node to a Pod, which is a quick way to communicate with a Pod from outside the cluster. You can listen on a specific port on your machine—which is the single node in your cluster—and forward traffic to the application running in the Pod.

```
# listen on port 8080 on your machine and send traffic
# to the Pod on port 80:
kubectl port-forward pod/hello-kiamol 8080:80

# now browse to http://localhost:8080

# when you're done press ctrl-c to end the port forward
```

My output is shown in figure 2.5, and you can see it's a pretty basic website (don't contact me for web design consultancy). The web server and all the content are packaged

Port forwarding is a feature of kubectl. It starts listening for traffic on your local machine and sends it to the Pod running in the cluster.

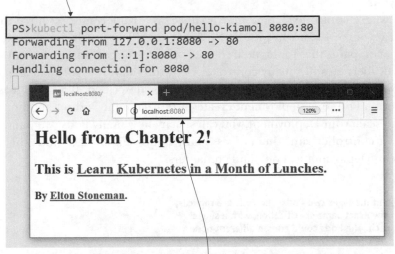

Browsing to localhost sends the request to my Pod. The Pod container processes it and sends the response, which is this exciting web page.

Figure 2.5 This app isn't configured to receive network traffic, but kubectl can forward it.

into a container image on Docker Hub, which is publicly available. All the CRI-compatible container runtimes can pull the image and run a container from it, so I know that for whichever Kubernetes environment you're using, when you run the app, it will work in the same way for you as it does for me.

Now we have a good handle on the Pod, which is the smallest unit of compute in Kubernetes. You need to understand how that all works, but the Pod is a primitive resource, and in normal use, you'd never run a Pod directly; you'd always create a controller object to manage the Pod for you.

2.2 Running Pods with controllers

It's only the second section of the second chapter, and we're already on to a new Kubernetes object, which is an abstraction over other objects. Kubernetes does get complicated quickly, but that complexity is a necessary part of such a powerful and configurable system. The learning curve is the entrance fee for access to a world-class container platform.

Pods are too simple to be useful on their own; they are isolated instances of an application, and each Pod is allocated to one node. If that node goes offline, the Pod is lost, and Kubernetes does not replace it. You could try to get high availability by running several Pods, but there's no guarantee Kubernetes won't run them all on the same node. Even if you do get Pods spread across several nodes, you need to manage them yourself. Why do that when you have an orchestrator that can manage them for you?

That's where controllers come in. A *controller* is a Kubernetes resource that manages other resources. It works with the Kubernetes API to watch the current state of the system, compares that to the desired state of its resources, and makes any changes necessary. Kubernetes has many controllers, but the main one for managing Pods is the Deployment, which solves the problems I've just described. If a node goes offline and you lose a Pod, the Deployment creates a replacement Pod on another node; if you want to scale your Deployment, you can specify how many Pods you want, and the Deployment controller runs them across many nodes. Figure 2.6 shows the relationship between Deployments, Pods, and containers.

This deployment manages two Pods. The Pods are replicas, created with the exact same specification, with a single container in each. The Pods could run on different nodes.

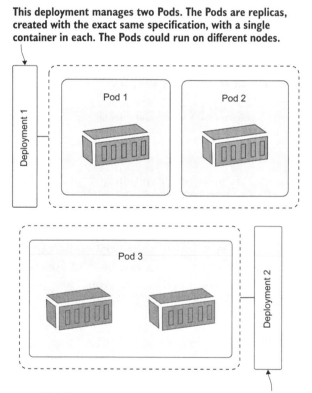

This Deployment manages a single Pod. The Pod is running two containers, but a Pod can't be split, so both containers will run on the same node.

Figure 2.6   Deployment controllers manage Pods, and Pods manage containers.

You can create Deployment resources with kubectl, specifying the container image you want to run and any other configuration for the Pod. Kubernetes creates the Deployment, and the Deployment creates the Pod.

TRY IT NOW Create another instance of the web application, this time using a Deployment. The only required parameters are the name for the Deployment and the image to run.

```
# create a Deployment called "hello-kiamol-2", running the same web app:
kubectl create deployment hello-kiamol-2 --image=kiamol/ch02-hello-kiamol

# list all the Pods:
kubectl get pods
```

You can see my output in figure 2.7. Now you have two Pods in your cluster: the original one you created with the kubectl run command, and the new one created by the Deployment. The Deployment-managed Pod has a name generated by Kubernetes, which is the name of the Deployment followed by a random suffix.

Creates a Deployment named `hello-kiamol-2`**. The number of replica Pods to run isn't specified, and the default is one, so this controller will manage a single Pod.**

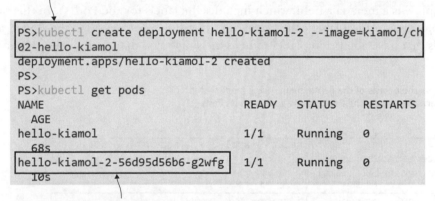

The Deployment-managed Pod is created with a naming scheme that begins with the controller name and ends with a random suffix.

Figure 2.7   Create a controller resource, and it creates its own resources— Deployments create Pods.

One important thing to realize from this exercise: you created the Deployment, but you did not directly create the Pod. The Deployment specification described the Pod you wanted, and the Deployment created that Pod. The Deployment is a controller that checks with the Kubernetes API to see which resources are running, realizes the Pod it should be managing doesn't exist, and uses the Kubernetes API to create it. The exact mechanism doesn't really matter; you can just work with the Deployment and rely on it to create your Pod.

How the deployment keeps track of its resources does matter, though, because it's a pattern that Kubernetes uses a lot. Any Kubernetes resource can have labels applied that are simple key-value pairs. You can add labels to record your own data. For example, you might add a label to a Deployment with the name *release* and the value *20.04* to indicate this Deployment is from the 20.04 release cycle. Kubernetes also uses labels to loosely couple resources, mapping the relationship between objects like a Deployment and its Pods.

TRY IT NOW   The Deployment adds labels to Pods it manages. Use kubectl as follows to print the labels the Deployment adds, and then list the Pods that match that label:

```
# print the labels that the Deployment adds to the Pod:
kubectl get deploy hello-kiamol-2 -o
    jsonpath='{.spec.template.metadata.labels}'

# list the Pods that have that matching label:
kubectl get pods -l app=hello-kiamol-2
```

My output is shown in figure 2.8, where you can see some internals of how the resources are configured. Deployments use a template to create Pods, and part of that template is a metadata field, which includes the labels for the Pod(s). In this case, the Deployment adds a label called *app* with the value *hello-kiamol-2* to the Pod. Querying Pods that have a matching label returns the single Pod managed by the Deployment.

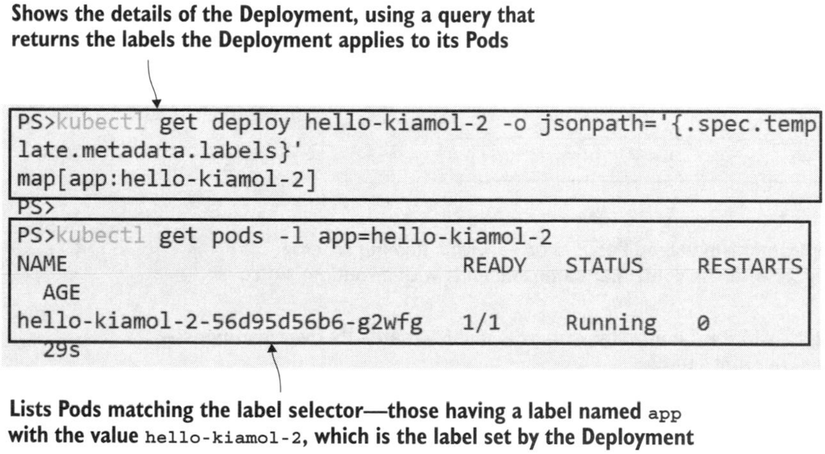

Shows the details of the Deployment, using a query that
returns the labels the Deployment applies to its Pods

```
PS>kubectl get deploy hello-kiamol-2 -o jsonpath='{.spec.temp
late.metadata.labels}'
map[app:hello-kiamol-2]
PS>
PS>kubectl get pods -l app=hello-kiamol-2
NAME                                      READY   STATUS    RESTARTS
   AGE
hello-kiamol-2-56d95d56b6-g2wfg  1/1     Running   0
   29s
```

Lists Pods matching the label selector—those having a label named `app`
with the value `hello-kiamol-2`, which is the label set by the Deployment

Figure 2.8   Deployments add labels when they create Pods, and you can use those labels as filters.

Using labels to identify the relationship between resources is such a core pattern in Kubernetes that it's worth showing a diagram to make sure it's clear. Resources can have labels applied at creation and then added, removed, or edited during their lifetime. Controllers use a label selector to identify the resources they manage. That can be a simple query matching resources with a particular label, as shown in figure 2.9.

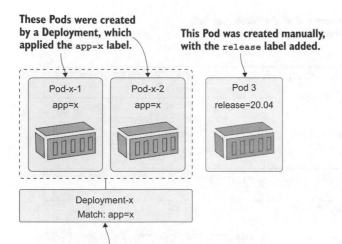

These Pods were created by a Deployment, which applied the `app=x` label.

This Pod was created manually, with the `release` label added.

The Deployment uses a label selector to find Pods. Any that match the selector are considered to be owned by the Deployment.

Figure 2.9 Controllers identify the resources they manage by using labels and selectors.

This process is flexible because it means controllers don't need to maintain a list of all the resources they manage; the label selector is part of the controller specification, and controllers can find matching resources at any time by querying the Kubernetes API. It's also something you need to be careful with, because you can edit the labels for a resource and end up breaking the relationship between it and its controller.

TRY IT NOW The Deployment doesn't have a direct relationship with the Pod it created; it only knows there needs to be one Pod with labels that match its label selector. If you edit the labels on the Pod, the Deployment no longer recognizes it.

```
# list all Pods, showing the Pod name and labels:
kubectl get pods -o custom-
    columns=NAME:metadata.name,LABELS:metadata.labels

# update the "app" label for the Deployment's Pod:
kubectl label pods -l app=hello-kiamol-2 --overwrite app=hello-kiamol-x

# fetch Pods again:
kubectl get pods -o custom-
    columns=NAME:metadata.name,LABELS:metadata.labels
```

What did you expect to happen? You can see from the output shown in figure 2.10 that changing the Pod label effectively removes the Pod from the Deployment. At that point, the Deployment sees that no Pods that match its label selector exist, so it creates a new one. The Deployment has done its job, but by editing the Pod directly, you now have an unmanaged Pod.

Shows Pods with the Pod name and all the labels. Labels
are shown with names and values separated by colons.

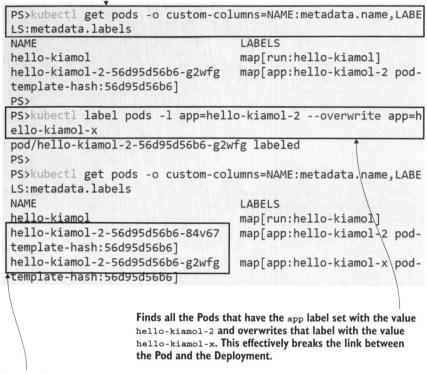

Finds all the Pods that have the `app` label set with the value
`hello-kiamol-2` and overwrites that label with the value
`hello-kiamol-x`. This effectively breaks the link between
the Pod and the Deployment.

Listing Pods again shows that the Deployment has created a
new Pod to replace the one it lost when the label was changed.

**Figure 2.10   If you meddle with the labels on a Pod, you can remove it from the control of
the Deployment.**

This can be a useful technique in debugging—removing a Pod from a controller so
you can connect and investigate a problem, while the controller starts a replacement
Pod, which keeps your app running at the desired scale. You can also do the opposite:
editing the labels on a Pod to fool a controller into acquiring that Pod as part of the
set it manages.

> **TRY IT NOW**   Return the original Pod to the control of the Deployment by set-
> ting its app label back so it matches the label selector.

```
# list all Pods with a label called "app," showing the Pod name and
# labels:
kubectl get pods -l app -o custom-
    columns=NAME:metadata.name,LABELS:metadata.labels
```

```
# update the "app" label for the the unmanaged Pod:
kubectl label pods -l app=hello-kiamol-x --overwrite app=hello-kiamol-2

# fetch the Pods again:
kubectl get pods -l app -o custom-
    columns=NAME:metadata.name,LABELS:metadata.labels
```

This exercise effectively reverses the previous exercise, setting the app label back to hello-kiamol-2 for the original Pod in the Deployment. Now when the Deployment controller checks with the API, it sees two Pods that match its label selector. It's supposed to manage only a single Pod, however, so it deletes one (using a set of deletion rules to decide which one). You can see in figure 2.11 that the Deployment removed the second Pod and retained the original.

Confirms we still have two Pods: one managed by the Deployment and one unmanaged because of the label change

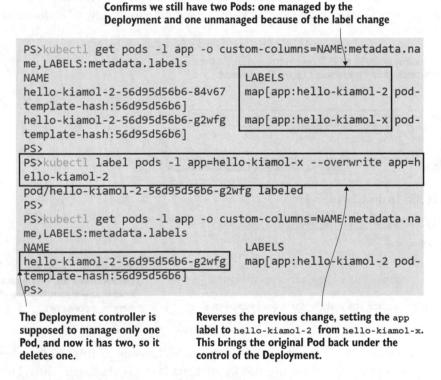

The Deployment controller is supposed to manage only one Pod, and now it has two, so it deletes one.

Reverses the previous change, setting the app label to hello-kiamol-2 from hello-kiamol-x. This brings the original Pod back under the control of the Deployment.

Figure 2.11 More label meddling—you can force a Deployment to adopt a Pod if the labels match.

Pods run your application containers, but just like containers, Pods are meant to be short-lived. You will usually use a higher-level resource like a Deployment to manage Pods for you. Doing so gives Kubernetes a better chance of keeping your app running if there are issues with containers or nodes, but ultimately the Pods are running the same containers you would run yourself, and the end-user experience for your apps will be the same.

> **TRY IT NOW**   Kubectl's `port-forward` command sends traffic to a Pod, but you don't have to find the random Pod name for a Deployment. You can configure the port forward on the Deployment resource, and the Deployment selects one of its Pods as the target.

```
# run a port forward from your local machine to the Deployment:
kubectl port-forward deploy/hello-kiamol-2 8080:80

# browse to http://localhost:8080

# when you're done, exit with ctrl-c
```

You can see my output, shown in figure 2.12, of the same app running in a container from the same Docker image, but this time, in a Pod managed by a Deployment.

Port forwarding works on different resources. For a Deployment, it sends traffic to a Pod selected by the Deployment.

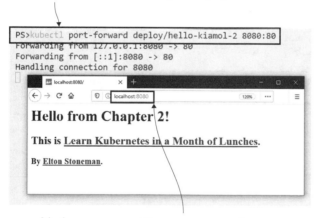

It's the same app and the same user experience.

Figure 2.12   Pods and Deployments are layers on top of containers, but the app still runs in a container.

Pods and Deployments are the only resources we'll cover in this chapter. You can deploy very simple apps by using the kubectl `run` and `create` commands, but more complex apps need lots more configuration, and those commands won't do. It's time to enter the world of Kubernetes YAML.

2.3   *Defining Deployments in application manifests*

Application manifests are one of the most attractive aspects of Kubernetes, but also one of the most frustrating. When you're wading through hundreds of lines of YAML trying to find the small misconfiguration that has broken your app, it can seem like the API was deliberately written to confuse and irritate you. At those times, remember that Kubernetes manifests are a complete description of your app, which can be versioned and tracked in source control, and result in the same deployment on any Kubernetes cluster.

Manifests can be written in JSON or YAML; JSON is the native language of the Kubernetes API, but YAML is preferred for manifests because it's easier to read, lets you define multiple resources in a single file, and, most important, can record comments in the specification. Listing 2.1 is the simplest app manifest you can write. It defines a single Pod using the same container image we've already used in this chapter.

Listing 2.1   pod.yaml, a single Pod to run a single container

```
# Manifests always specify the version of the Kubernetes API
# and the type of resource.
apiVersion: v1
kind: Pod

# Metadata for the resource includes the name (mandatory)
# and labels (optional).
metadata:
 name: hello-kiamol-3

# The spec is the actual specification for the resource.
# For a Pod the minimum is the container(s) to run,
# with the container name and image.
spec:
 containers:
  - name: web
    image: kiamol/ch02-hello-kiamol
```

That's a lot more information than you need for a kubectl run command, but the big advantage of the application manifest is that it's declarative. Kubectl run and create are imperative operations—it's you telling Kubernetes to do something. Manifests are declarative—you tell Kubernetes what you want the end result to be, and it goes off and decides what it needs to do to make that happen.

TRY IT NOW   You still use kubectl to deploy apps from manifest files, but you use the apply command, which tells Kubernetes to apply the configuration in the file to the cluster. Run another pod for this chapter's sample app using a YAML file with the same contents as listing 2.1.

```
# switch from the root of the kiamol repository to the chapter 2 folder:
cd ch02

# deploy the application from the manifest file:
kubectl apply -f pod.yaml

# list running Pods:
kubectl get pods
```

The new Pod works in the same way as a Pod created with the kubectl run command: it's allocated to a node, and it runs a container. The output in figure 2.13 shows that when I applied the manifest, Kubernetes decided it needed to create a Pod to get the current state of the cluster up to my desired state. That's because the manifest specifies a Pod named hello-kiamol-3, and no such Pod existed.

The `apply` command tells Kubernetes to apply the state described in the YAML file to the cluster. Kubectl shows the actions taken, in this case, creating a single Pod.

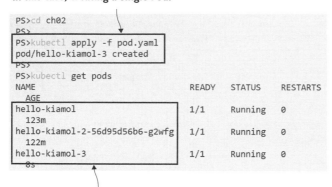

These three Pods all have the same specification and are running the same app, but they were created in different ways.

Figure 2.13   Applying a manifest sends the YAML file to the Kubernetes API, which applies changes.

Now that the Pod is running, you can manage it in the same way with kubectl: by listing the details of the Pod and running a port forward to send traffic to the Pod. The big difference is that the manifest is easy to share, and manifest-based Deployment is repeatable. I can run the same kubectl `apply` command with the same manifest any number of times, and the result will always be the same: a Pod named hello-kiamol-3 running my web container.

> **TRY IT NOW**   Kubectl doesn't even need a local copy of a manifest file. It can read the contents from any public URL. Deploy the same Pod definition direct from the file on GitHub.

```
# deploy the application from the manifest file:
kubectl apply -f https://raw.githubusercontent.com/sixeyed/kiamol/
    master/ch02/pod.yaml
```

Figure 2.14 shows the output. The resource definition matches the Pod running in the cluster, so Kubernetes doesn't need to do anything, and kubectl shows that the matching resource is unchanged.

Application manifests start to get more interesting when you work with higher-level resources. When you define a Deployment in a YAML file, one of the required fields is

The source for a manifest to apply could be a local
file or the URL to a file stored on a web server.

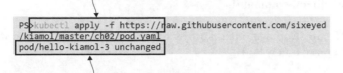

```
PS>kubectl apply -f https://raw.githubusercontent.com/sixeyed
/kiamol/master/ch02/pod.yaml
pod/hello-kiamol-3 unchanged
```

The contents of the manifest are the same as the file I previously
applied, so the state defined in the YAML matches the running state
in the cluster, and Kubernetes doesn't need to make any changes.

**Figure 2.14 Kubectl can
download manifest files from
a web server and send them
to the Kubernetes API.**

the specification of the Pod that the Deployment should run. That Pod specification is
the same API for defining a Pod on its own, so the Deployment definition is a compos-
ite that includes the Pod spec. Listing 2.2 shows the minimal definition for a Deployment resource, running yet another version of the same web app.

Listing 2.2 deployment.yaml, a Deployment and Pod specification

```
# Deployments are part of the apps version 1 API spec.
apiVersion: apps/v1
kind: Deployment

# The Deployment needs a name.
metadata:
 name: hello-kiamol-4

# The spec includes the label selector the Deployment uses
# to find its own managed resources—I'm using the app label,
# but this could be any combination of key-value pairs.
spec:
selector:
 matchLabels:
   app: hello-kiamol-4

# The template is used when the Deployment creates a Pod
template.

 # Pods in a Deployment don't have a name,
 # but they need to specify labels that match the selector
 # metadata.
  labels:
   app: hello-kiamol-4

# The Pod spec lists the container name and image
spec.
  containers:
   - name: web
     image: kiamol/ch02-hello-kiamol
```

This manifest is for a completely different resource (which just happens to run the
same application), but all Kubernetes manifests are deployed in the same way using

kubectl `apply`. That gives you a nice layer of consistency across all your apps—no matter how complex they are, you'll define them in one or more YAML files and deploy them using the same kubectl command.

> **TRY IT NOW**   Apply the Deployment manifest to create a new Deployment, which in turn will create a new Pod.

```
# run the app using the Deployment manifest:
kubectl apply -f deployment.yaml

# find Pods managed by the new Deployment:
kubectl get pods -l app=hello-kiamol-4
```

The output in figure 2.15 shows the same end result as creating a Deployment with kubectl `create`, but my whole app specification is clearly defined in a single YAML file.

The `apply` **command works the same way for any type of resource defined in the YAML file. This creates only the Deployment, and then the Deployment creates the Pod.**

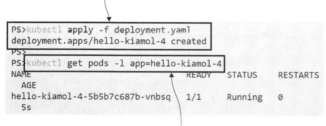

```
PS>kubectl apply -f deployment.yaml
deployment.apps/hello-kiamol-4 created
PS>
PS>kubectl get pods -l app=hello-kiamol-4
NAME                              READY   STATUS    RESTARTS
  AGE
hello-kiamol-4-5b5b7c687b-vnbsq   1/1     Running   0
  5s
```

The Deployment creates a new Pod straight away. It sets the label value defined in the manifest, and we can use that to find the Pod.

Figure 2.15   Applying a manifest creates the Deployment because no matching resource existed.

As the app grows in complexity, I need to specify how many replicas I want, what CPU and memory limits should apply, how Kubernetes can check whether the app is healthy, and where the application configuration settings come from and where it writes data—I can do all that just by adding to the YAML.

2.4   *Working with applications in Pods*

Pods and Deployments are there to keep your app running, but all the real work is happening in the container. Your container runtime may not give you access to work with containers directly—a managed Kubernetes cluster won't give you control of Docker or containerd—but you can still work with containers in Pods using kubectl. The Kubernetes command line lets you run commands in containers, view application logs, and copy files.

TRY IT NOW   You can run commands inside containers with kubectl and connect a terminal session, so you can connect into a Pod's container as though you were connecting to a remote machine.

```
# check the internal IP address of the first Pod we ran:
kubectl get pod hello-kiamol -o custom-
    columns=NAME:metadata.name,POD_IP:status.podIP

# run an interactive shell command in the Pod:
kubectl exec -it hello-kiamol -- sh

# inside the Pod, check the IP address:
hostname -i

# and test the web app:
wget -O - http://localhost | head -n 4

# leave the shell:
exit
```

My output is shown in figure 2.16, where you can see that the IP address in the container environment is the one set by Kubernetes, and the web server running in the container is available at the localhost address.

The first Pod I created is still running; it has the IP address 10.1.0.12.   **Runs a** `shell` **command inside the Pod container— the** `it` **flag connects my terminal session to the shell in the container.**

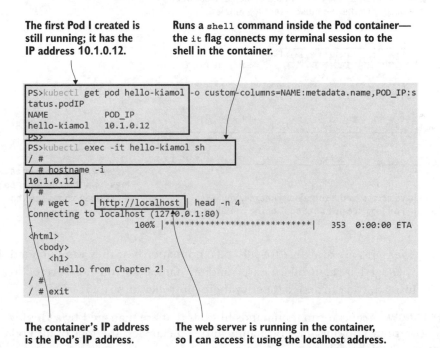

The container's IP address is the Pod's IP address.   **The web server is running in the container, so I can access it using the localhost address.**

Figure 2.16   You can use kubectl to run commands inside Pod containers, including interactive shells.

Running an interactive shell inside a Pod container is a useful way of seeing how the world looks to that Pod. You can read file contents to check that configuration settings are being applied correctly, run DNS queries to verify that services are resolving as expected, and ping endpoints to test the network. Those are all good troubleshooting techniques, but for ongoing administration, a simpler option is to read the application logs, and kubectl has a dedicated command just for that.

> **TRY IT NOW**   Kubernetes fetches application logs from the container runtime. You can read logs with kubectl, and if you have access to the container runtime, you can verify that they are the same as the container logs.

```
# print the latest container logs from Kubernetes:
kubectl logs --tail=2 hello-kiamol

# and compare the actual container logs—if you're using Docker:
docker container logs --tail=2 $(docker container ls -q --filter
    label=io.kubernetes.container.name=hello-kiamol)
```

You can see from my output, shown in figure 2.17, that Kubernetes just relays log entries exactly as they come from the container runtime.

Shows the logs written by the Pod container. The `tail` parameter
restricts the output to the two most recent log entries.

If you have access to the container runtime, you'll see
that the Pod logs are just a readout of the container logs.

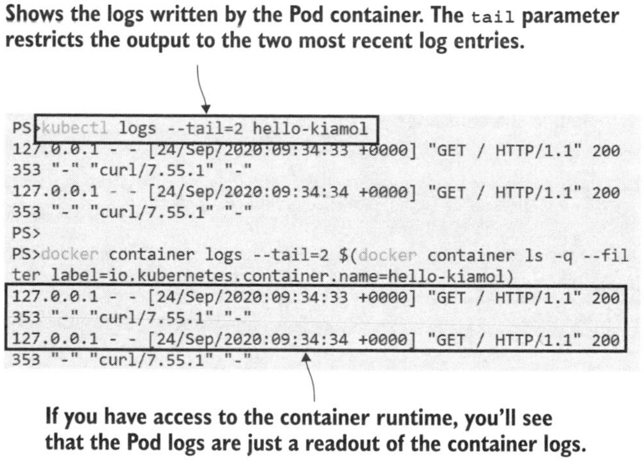

Figure 2.17 Kubernetes reads logs from the container so you don't need access to the container runtime.

The same features are available for all Pods, no matter how they were created. Pods that are managed by controllers have random names, so you don't refer to them directly. Instead, you can access them by their controller or by their labels.

> **TRY IT NOW**   You can run commands in Pods that are managed by a Deployment without knowing the Pod name, and you can view the logs of all Pods that match a label selector.

```
# make a call to the web app inside the container for the
# Pod we created from the Deployment YAML file:
```

```
kubectl exec deploy/hello-kiamol-4 -- sh -c 'wget -O - http://localhost
  > /dev/null'

# and check that Pod's logs:
kubectl logs --tail=1 -l app=hello-kiamol-4
```

Figure 2.18 shows the command running inside the Pod container, which causes the application to write a log entry. We see that in the Pod logs.

The `exec` command can target different resources. Like `port-forward`, it can operate on Pods or Deployments. This executes `wget` inside the Pod container and returns the output.

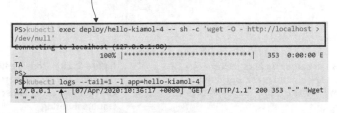

Kubectl can show logs for multiple Pods. Using a label selector means you don't need to discover the random Pod name to see its logs.

Figure 2.18 You can work with Pods using kubectl without knowing the Pod's name.

In a production environment, you can have all the logs from all of your Pods collected and sent to a central storage system, but until you get there, this is a useful and easy way to read application logs. You also saw in that exercise that there are different ways to get to Pods that are managed by a controller. Kubectl lets you supply a label selector to most commands, and some commands—like exec—can be run against different targets.

The last function you're likely to use with Pods is to interact with the filesystem. Kubectl lets you copy files between your local machine and containers in Pods.

TRY IT NOW   Create a temporary directory on your machine, and copy a file into it from the Pod container.

```
# create the local directory:
mkdir -p /tmp/kiamol/ch02

# copy the web page from the Pod:
kubectl cp hello-kiamol:/usr/share/nginx/html/index.html
  /tmp/kiamol/ch02/index.html

# check the local file contents:
cat /tmp/kiamol/ch02/index.html
```

In figure 2.19, you can see that kubectl copies the file from the Pod container onto my local machine. This works whether your Kubernetes cluster is running locally or on remote servers, and it's bidirectional, so you can use the same command to copy a local file into a Pod. That can be a useful—if hacky—way to work around an application problem.

The `cp` command copies files between Pod containers and your local filesystem. Here the source is a path in the `hello-kiamol` Pod, and the target is a local file path.

```
PS>mkdir -p /tmp/kiamol/ch02 | Out-Null
PS>
PS>kubectl cp hello-kiamol:/usr/share/nginx/html/index.html /tmp/kiamol/ch0
2/index.html
tar: removing leading '/' from member names
PS>
PS>cat /tmp/kiamol/ch02/index.html
<html>
  <body>
    <h1>
      Hello from Chapter 2!
```

Internally, kubectl uses `tar` to compress and package files. This is an information message, not an error, but if my container image didn't have the `tar` utility installed, then I would get an error.

Figure 2.19   Copying files between Pod containers and the local machine is useful for troubleshooting.

That's about all we're going to cover in this chapter, but before we move on, we need to delete the Pods we have running, and that is a little bit more involved than you might think.

2.5   Understanding Kubernetes resource management

You can easily delete a Kubernetes resource using kubectl, but the resource might not stay deleted. If you created a resource with a controller, then it's the controller's job to manage that resource. It owns the resource life cycle, and it doesn't expect any external interference. If you delete a managed resource, then its controller will create a replacement.

> **TRY IT NOW**   Use the kubectl `delete` command to remove all Pods and verify that they're really gone.

```
# list all running Pods:
kubectl get pods

# delete all Pods:
kubectl delete pods --all

# check again:
kubectl get pods
```

You can see my output in figure 20.20. Is it what you expected?

  Two of those Pods were created directly with the `run` command and with a YAML Pod specification. They don't have a controller managing them, so when you delete

I have four Pods running; the two with simple names were created directly, and the two with random suffixes were created by Deployment controllers.

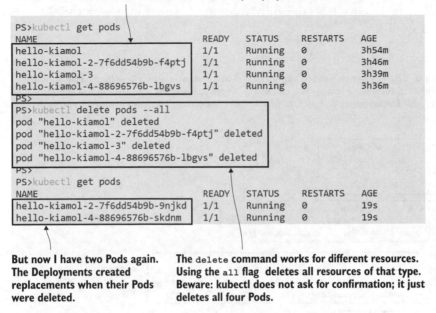

```
PS>kubectl get pods
NAME                              READY   STATUS    RESTARTS   AGE
hello-kiamol                      1/1     Running   0          3h54m
hello-kiamol-2-7f6dd54b9b-f4ptj   1/1     Running   0          3h46m
hello-kiamol-3                    1/1     Running   0          3h39m
hello-kiamol-4-88696576b-lbgvs    1/1     Running   0          3h36m
PS>
PS>kubectl delete pods --all
pod "hello-kiamol" deleted
pod "hello-kiamol-2-7f6dd54b9b-f4ptj" deleted
pod "hello-kiamol-3" deleted
pod "hello-kiamol-4-88696576b-lbgvs" deleted
PS>
PS>kubectl get pods
NAME                              READY   STATUS    RESTARTS   AGE
hello-kiamol-2-7f6dd54b9b-9njkd   1/1     Running   0          19s
hello-kiamol-4-88696576b-skdnm    1/1     Running   0          19s
```

But now I have two Pods again. The Deployments created replacements when their Pods were deleted.

The `delete` command works for different resources. Using the `all` flag deletes all resources of that type. Beware: kubectl does not ask for confirmation; it just deletes all four Pods.

Figure 2.20   Controllers own their resources. If something else deletes them, the controller replaces them.

them, they stay deleted. The other two were created by Deployments, and when you delete the Pod, the Deployment controllers still exist. They see there are no Pods that match their label selectors, so they create new ones.

It seems obvious when you know about it, but it's a gotcha that will probably keep cropping up through all your days with Kubernetes. If you want to delete a resource that is managed by a controller, you need to delete the controller instead. Controllers clean up their resources when they are deleted, so removing a Deployment is like a cascading delete that removes all the Deployment's Pods, too.

TRY IT NOW   Check the Deployments you have running, and then delete them and confirm that the remaining Pods have been deleted.

```
# view Deployments:
kubectl get deploy

# delete all Deployments:
kubectl delete deploy --all

# view Pods:
kubectl get pods

# check all resources:
kubectl get all
```

Figure 2.21 shows my output. I was fast enough to see the Pods being removed, so they're shown in the terminating state. A few seconds later, the Pods and the Deployment were removed, so the only resource I have running is the Kubernetes API server itself.

I have two Deployments. Kubectl supports abbreviated resource names—you can use `deploy` **for Deployments and** `po` **for Pods.**   **Kubectl mostly uses a consistent syntax, with a verb followed by a noun. You use the same** `delete` **command for all resource types.**

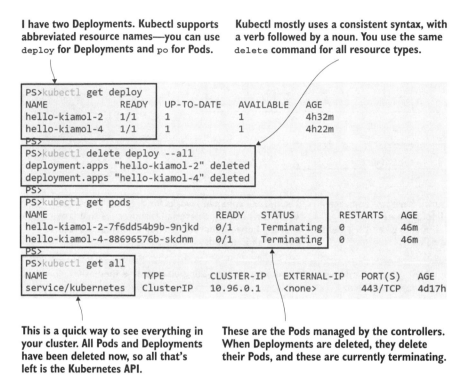

This is a quick way to see everything in your cluster. All Pods and Deployments have been deleted now, so all that's left is the Kubernetes API.   **These are the Pods managed by the controllers. When Deployments are deleted, they delete their Pods, and these are currently terminating.**

Figure 2.21   Deleting controllers starts a cascade effect, where the controller deletes all its resources.

Now your Kubernetes cluster isn't running any applications, and it's back to its original state.

We've covered a lot in this chapter. You've got a good understanding of how Kubernetes manages containers with Pods and Deployments, had an introduction to YAML specifications, and had lots of experience using kubectl to work with the Kubernetes API. We've built on the core concepts gradually, but you probably have a fair idea now that Kubernetes is a complex system. If you have time to go through the following lab, that will certainly help cement what you've learned.

2.6   *Lab*

This is your first lab; it's a challenge for you to complete yourself. The goal is to write a Kubernetes YAML spec for a Deployment that will run an application in a Pod, and then test the app to make sure it runs as expected. Here are a few hints to get you started:

- In the ch02/lab folder, there's a file called pod.yaml that you can try out. It runs the app but defines a Pod rather than a Deployment.
- The application container runs a website that listens on port 80.
- When you forward traffic to the port, the web app responds with the hostname of the machine it's running on.
- That hostname is actually the Pod name, which you can verify using kubectl.

If you find this a bit tricky, I have the following sample solution on GitHub that you can use for reference: https://github.com/sixeyed/kiamol/blob/master/ch02/lab/README.md.

Connecting Pods over
the network with Services

Pods are the basic building blocks of an application running in Kubernetes. Most applications are distributed across multiple components, and you model those in Kubernetes using a Pod for each component. For example, you may have a website Pod and an API Pod, or you may have dozens of Pods in a microservice architecture. They all need to communicate, and Kubernetes supports the standard networking protocols, TCP and UDP. Both protocols use IP addresses to route traffic, but IP addresses change when Pods are replaced, so Kubernetes provides a network address discovery mechanism with *Services*.

Services are flexible resources that support routing traffic between Pods, into Pods from the world outside the cluster, and from Pods to external systems. In this chapter, you'll learn all the different Service configurations Kubernetes provides to glue systems together, and you'll understand how they work transparently for your apps.

3.1 How Kubernetes routes network traffic

You learned two important things about Pods in the previous chapter: a Pod is a virtual environment that has an IP address assigned by Kubernetes, and Pods are disposable resources whose lifetime is controlled by another resource. If one Pod wants to communicate with another, it can use the IP address. That's problematic for two reasons, however: first, the IP address changes if the Pod is replaced, and second, there's no easy way to find a Pod's IP address—it can be discovered only using the Kubernetes API.

TRY IT NOW If you deploy two Pods, you can ping one Pod from the other, but you first need to find its IP address.

```
# start up your lab environment—run Docker Desktop if it's not running—
# and switch to this chapter's directory in your copy of the source code:
cd ch03

# create two Deployments, which each run one Pod:
kubectl apply -f sleep/sleep1.yaml -f sleep/sleep2.yaml

# wait for the Pod to be ready:
kubectl wait --for=condition=Ready pod -l app=sleep-2

# check the IP address of the second Pod:
kubectl get pod -l app=sleep-2 --output
   jsonpath='{.items[0].status.podIP}'

# use that address to ping the second Pod from the first:
kubectl exec deploy/sleep-1 -- ping -c 2 $(kubectl get pod -l app=sleep-2
   --output jsonpath='{.items[0].status.podIP}')
```

My output appears in figure 3.1. The ping inside the container works fine, and the first Pod is able to successfully reach the second Pod, but I had to find the IP address using kubectl and pass it into the ping command.

You can pass multiple files to the kubectl `apply` command. This deploys two Pods that don't do anything.

The JSONPath query here returns just the IP address of the `sleep-2` Pod.

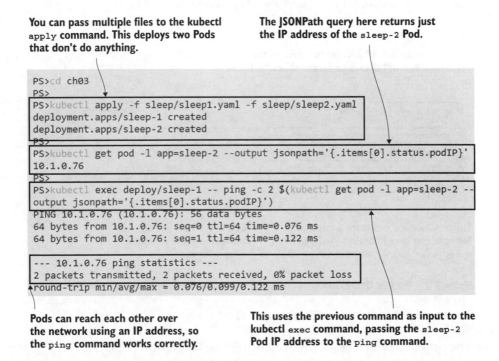

Pods can reach each other over the network using an IP address, so the `ping` command works correctly.

This uses the previous command as input to the kubectl `exec` command, passing the `sleep-2` Pod IP address to the `ping` command.

Figure 3.1 Pod networking with IP addresses—you can discover an address only from the Kubernetes API.

The virtual network in Kubernetes spans the whole cluster, so Pods can communicate via IP address even if they're running on different nodes. This example works in the same way on a single-node K3s cluster and a 100-node AKS cluster. It's a useful exercise to help you see that Kubernetes doesn't do any special networking magic; it just uses the standard protocols your apps already use. You wouldn't normally do this, because the IP address is specific to one Pod, and when the Pod is replaced, the replacement will have a new IP address.

> **TRY IT NOW**   These Pods are managed by Deployment controllers. If you delete the second Pod, its controller will start a replacement with a new IP address.

```
# check the current Pod's IP address:
kubectl get pod -l app=sleep-2 --output
   jsonpath='{.items[0].status.podIP}'

# delete the Pod so the Deployment replaces it:
kubectl delete pods -l app=sleep-2

# check the IP address of the replacement Pod:
kubectl get pod -l app=sleep-2 --output
   jsonpath='{.items[0].status.podIP}'
```

In figure 3.2, my output shows that the replacement Pod has a different IP address, and if I tried to ping the old address, the command would fail.

Pods have a static IP address for their lifetime—this
`sleep-2` **Pod will always be accessible at 10.1.0.76.**

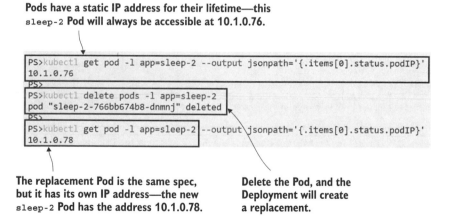

The replacement Pod is the same spec,   **Delete the Pod, and the**
but it has its own IP address—the new   **Deployment will create**
`sleep-2` **Pod has the address 10.1.0.78.**   **a replacement.**

Figure 3.2   The Pod IP address is not part of its specification; a replacement Pod has a new address.

The problem of needing a permanent address for resources that can change is an old one—the internet solved it using DNS (the Domain Name System), mapping friendly names to IP addresses, and Kubernetes uses the same system. A Kubernetes cluster has a DNS server built in, which maps Service names to IP addresses. Figure 3.3 shows how a domain name lookup works for Pod-to-Pod communication.

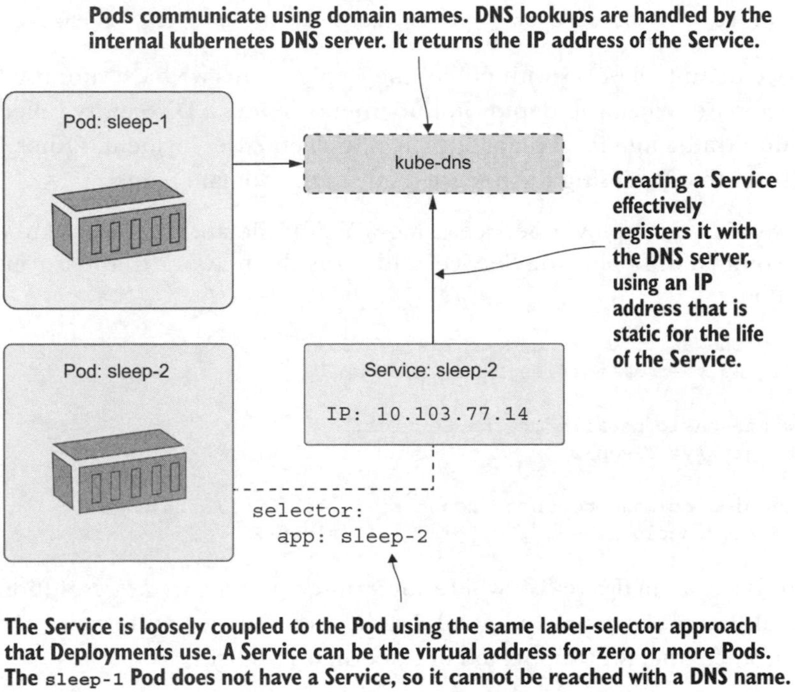

Pods communicate using domain names. DNS lookups are handled by the internal kubernetes DNS server. It returns the IP address of the Service.

Creating a Service effectively registers it with the DNS server, using an IP address that is static for the life of the Service.

The Service is loosely coupled to the Pod using the same label-selector approach that Deployments use. A Service can be the virtual address for zero or more Pods. The `sleep-1` Pod does not have a Service, so it cannot be reached with a DNS name.

Figure 3.3   Services allow Pods to communicate using a fixed domain name.

This type of Service is an abstraction over a Pod and its network address, just like a Deployment is an abstraction over a Pod and its container. The Service has its own IP address, which is static. When consumers make a network request to that address, Kubernetes routes it to the actual IP address of the Pod. The link between the Service and its Pods is set up with a label selector, just like the link between Deployments and Pods.

Listing 3.1 shows the minimal YAML specification for a Service, using the app label to identify the Pod which is the ultimate target of the network traffic.

Listing 3.1   sleep2-service.yaml, the simplest Service definition

```
apiVersion: v1     # Services use the core v1 API.
kind: Service

metadata:
  name: sleep-2    # The name of a Service is used as the DNS domain name.
```

```
# The specification requires a selector and a list of ports.
spec:
  selector:
    app: sleep-2  # Matches all Pods with an app label set to sleep-2.
  ports:
    - port: 80    # Listens on port 80 and sends to port 80 on the Pod
```

This Service definition works with one of the Deployments we have running from the previous exercise. When you deploy it, Kubernetes creates a DNS entry called sleep-2, which routes traffic into the Pod created by the sleep-2 Deployment. Other Pods can send traffic to that Pod using the Service name as the domain name.

> **TRY IT NOW** You deploy a Service using a YAML file and the usual kubectl apply command. Deploy the Service, and verify the network traffic is routed to the Pod.

```
# deploy the Service defined in listing 3.1:
kubectl apply -f sleep/sleep2-service.yaml

# show the basic details of the Service:
kubectl get svc sleep-2

# run a ping command to check connectivity—this will fail:
kubectl exec deploy/sleep-1 -- ping -c 1 sleep-2
```

My output is shown in figure 3.4, where you can see that the name resolution worked correctly, although the ping command didn't work as expected because ping uses a network protocol that isn't supported in Kubernetes Services.

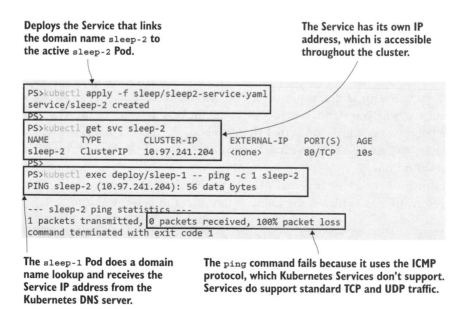

Deploys the Service that links the domain name `sleep-2` to the active `sleep-2` Pod.

The Service has its own IP address, which is accessible throughout the cluster.

```
PS>kubectl apply -f sleep/sleep2-service.yaml
service/sleep-2 created
PS>
PS>kubectl get svc sleep-2
NAME      TYPE        CLUSTER-IP     EXTERNAL-IP   PORT(S)   AGE
sleep-2   ClusterIP   10.97.241.204  <none>        80/TCP    10s
PS>
PS>kubectl exec deploy/sleep-1 -- ping -c 1 sleep-2
PING sleep-2 (10.97.241.204): 56 data bytes

--- sleep-2 ping statistics ---
1 packets transmitted, 0 packets received, 100% packet loss
command terminated with exit code 1
```

The `sleep-1` Pod does a domain name lookup and receives the Service IP address from the Kubernetes DNS server.

The `ping` command fails because it uses the ICMP protocol, which Kubernetes Services don't support. Services do support standard TCP and UDP traffic.

Figure 3.4 Deploying a Service creates a DNS entry, giving the Service name a fixed IP address.

That's the basic concept behind Service discovery in Kubernetes: deploy a Service resource and use the name of the Service as the domain name for components to communicate.

Different types of Service support different networking patterns, but you work with them all in the same way. Next, we'll look more closely at Pod-to-Pod networking, with a working example of a simple distributed app.

3.2 Routing traffic between Pods

The default type of Service in Kubernetes is called ClusterIP. It creates a clusterwide IP address that Pods on any node can access. The IP address works only within the cluster, so ClusterIP Services are useful only for communicating between Pods. That's exactly what you want for a distributed system where some components are internal and shouldn't be accessible outside of the cluster. We'll use a simple website that uses an internal API component to demonstrate that.

> **TRY IT NOW** Run two Deployments, one for the web application and one for the API. This app has no Services yet, and it won't work correctly because the website can't find the API.

```
# run the website and API as separate Deployments:
kubectl apply -f numbers/api.yaml -f numbers/web.yaml

# wait for the Pod to be ready:
kubectl wait --for=condition=Ready pod -l app=numbers-web

# forward a port to the web app:
kubectl port-forward deploy/numbers-web 8080:80

# browse to the site at http://localhost:8080 and click the Go button
# —you'll see an error message

# exit the port forward:
ctrl-c
```

You can see from my output shown in figure 3.5 that the app fails with a message stating the API is unavailable.

The error page also shows the domain name where the site is expecting to find the API—http://numbers-api. That's not a fully qualified domain name (like blog.sixeyed .com); it's an address that should be resolved by the local network, but the DNS server in Kubernetes doesn't resolve it because there is no Service with the name numbers-api. The specification in listing 3.2 shows a Service with the correct name and a label selector that matches the API Pod.

**Deploys a web application Pod and an API but no
Services, so the components aren't able to communicate**

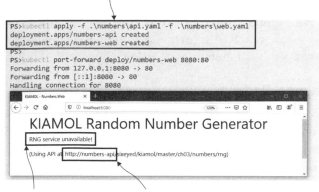

```
PS>kubectl apply -f .\numbers\api.yaml -f .\numbers\web.yaml
deployment.apps/numbers-api created
deployment.apps/numbers-web created
PS>
PS>kubectl port-forward deploy/numbers-web 8080:80
Forwarding from 127.0.0.1:8080 -> 80
Forwarding from [::1]:8080 -> 80
Handling connection for 8080
```

KIAMOL - Numbers.Web

localhost:8080

KIAMOL Random Number Generator

RNG service unavailable!

(Using API at http://numbers-api sixeyed/kiamol/master/ch03/numbers/rng)

**The error message from
the web app shows that
it can't reach the API.**

**The domain name it's using for the
API is `numbers-api`, a local domain
that doesn't exist in the Kubernetes
DNS server.**

**Figure 3.5   The web app runs
but doesn't function correctly
because the network call to
the API fails.**

Listing 3.2   api-service.yaml, a Service for the random-number API

```
apiVersion: v1
kind: Service

metadata:
  name: numbers-api      # The Service uses the domain name numbers-api.

spec:
  ports:
    - port: 80
  selector:
    app: numbers-api     #  Traffic is routed to Pods with this label.
  type: ClusterIP        #  This Service is available only to other Pods.
```

This Service is similar to that in listing 3.1, except that the names have changed and
the Service type of ClusterIP is explicitly stated. That can be omitted because it's the
default Service type, but I think it makes the spec clearer if you include it. Deploying
the Service will route the traffic between the web Pod and the API Pod, fixing the app
without any changes to the Deployments or Pods.

> **TRY IT NOW**   Create a Service for the API so the domain lookup works and
> traffic is sent from the web Pod to the API Pod.

```
# deploy the Service from listing 3.2:
kubectl apply -f numbers/api-service.yaml

# check the Service details:
kubectl get svc numbers-api
```

```
# forward a port to the web app:
kubectl port-forward deploy/numbers-web 8080:80

# browse to the site at http://localhost:8080 and click the Go button

# exit the port forward:
ctrl-c
```

My output, shown in figure 3.6, shows the app working correctly, with the website displaying a random-number generated by the API.

Deploys a Service called `numbers-api`, matching the domain name the web app uses for the API

The Service has its own IP address, but it is a front for the API Pod.

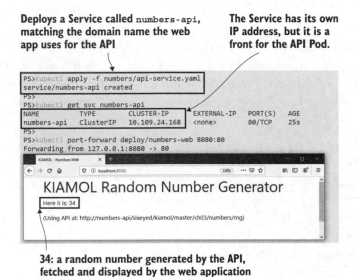

34: a random number generated by the API, fetched and displayed by the web application

Figure 3.6 Deploying a Service fixes the broken link between the web app and the API.

The important lesson here, beyond Services, Deployments, and Pods, is that your YAML specifications describe your whole application in Kubernetes—that's all the components and the networking between them. Kubernetes doesn't make assumptions about your application architecture; you need to specify it in the YAML. This simple web app needs three Kubernetes resources defined for it to work in its current state—two Deployments and a Service—but the advantage of having all these moving parts is increased resilience.

TRY IT NOW The API Pod is managed by a Deployment controller, so you can delete the Pod and a replacement will be created. The replacement is also a match for the label selector in the API Service, so traffic is routed to the new Pod, and the app keeps working.

```
# check the name and IP address of the API Pod:
kubectl get pod -l app=numbers-api -o custom-
   columns=NAME:metadata.name,POD_IP:status.podIP
```

```
# delete that Pod:
kubectl delete pod -l app=numbers-api

# check the replacement Pod:
kubectl get pod -l app=numbers-api -o custom-
  columns=NAME:metadata.name,POD_IP:status.podIP

# forward a port to the web app:
kubectl port-forward deploy/numbers-web 8080:80

# browse to the site at http://localhost:8080 and click the Go button

# exit the port forward:
ctrl-c
```

Figure 3.7 shows that a replacement Pod is created by the Deployment controller. It's the same API Pod spec but running in a new Pod with a new IP address. The IP address of the API Service hasn't changed, though, and the web Pod can reach the new API Pod at the same network address.

The original API Pod has the IP address 10.1.0.90. **The replacement Pod has the IP address 10.1.0.91.**

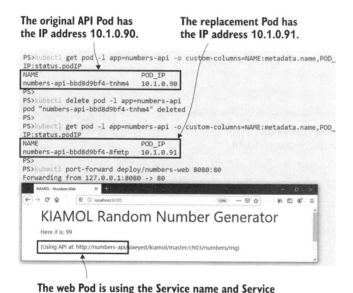

The web Pod is using the Service name and Service IP address, so the changed Pod IP doesn't affect it.

Figure 3.7   The Service isolates the web Pod from the API Pod, so it doesn't matter whether the API Pod changes.

We're manually deleting Pods in these exercises to trigger the controller to create a replacement, but in the normal life cycle of a Kubernetes application, Pod replacement happens all the time. Anytime you update a component of your app—to add features, fix bugs, or release an update to a dependency—you're replacing Pods. Any time a node goes down, its Pods are replaced on other nodes. The Service abstraction keeps apps communicating through these replacements.

This demo app isn't complete yet because it doesn't have anything configured to receive traffic from outside the cluster and send it in to the web Pod. We've used port forwarding so far, but that's really a trick for debugging. The real solution is to deploy a Service for the web Pod, too.

3.3 Routing external traffic to Pods

You have several options to configure Kubernetes to listen for traffic coming into the cluster and forward it to a Pod. We'll start with a simple and flexible approach, which is fine for everything from local development to production. It's a type of a Service called LoadBalancer, which solves the problem of getting traffic to a Pod that might be running on a different node from the one that received the traffic; figure 3.8 shows how it looks.

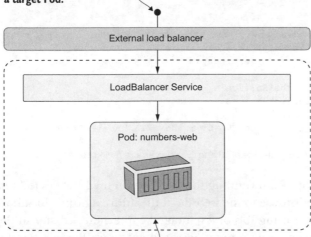

A LoadBalancer Service integrates with an external load balancer, which sends traffic to the cluster. The Service sends the traffic to a Pod, using the same label-selector mechanism to identify a target Pod.

The Service spans the whole cluster, so any node could receive traffic. The target Pod could be running on a different node from the one that received the request, and Kubernetes routes it seamlessly to the correct node.

Figure 3.8 LoadBalancer Services route external traffic from any node into a matching Pod.

It looks like a tricky problem, especially because you might have many Pods that match the label selector for the Service, so the cluster needs to choose a node to send the traffic to and then choose a Pod on that node. All that trickiness is taken care of by Kubernetes—that's world-class orchestration for you—so all you need to do is deploy a LoadBalancer Service. Listing 3.3 shows the Service specification for the web application.

```
apiVersion: v1
kind: Service
metadata:
  name: numbers-web
spec:
  ports:
    - port: 8080          # The port the Service listens on
      targetPort: 80      # The port the traffic is sent to on the Pod
  selector:
    app: numbers-web
  type: LoadBalancer      # This Service is available for external traffic.
```

This Service listens on port 8080 and sends traffic to the web Pod on port 80. When you deploy it, you'll be able to use the web app without setting up a port forward in kubectl, but the exact details of how you reach the app will depend on how you're running Kubernetes.

TRY IT NOW   Deploy the Service, and then use kubectl to find the address of the Service.

```
# deploy the LoadBalancer Service for the website—if your firewall checks
# that you want to allow traffic, then it is OK to say yes:
kubectl apply -f numbers/web-service.yaml

# check the details of the Service:
kubectl get svc numbers-web

# use formatting to get the app URL from the EXTERNAL-IP field:
kubectl get svc numbers-web -o
    jsonpath='http://{.status.loadBalancer.ingress[0].*}:8080'
```

Figure 3.9 shows my output from running the exercise on my Docker Desktop Kubernetes cluster, where I can browse to the website at the address http://localhost:8080.

The output is different using K3s or a managed Kubernetes cluster in the cloud, where the Service deployment creates a dedicated external IP address for the load balancer. Figure 3.10 shows the output of the same exercise (using the same YAML specifications) using the K3s cluster on my Linux VM—here the website is at http://172.28.132.127:8080.

How can the results be different with the same application manifests? I said in chapter 1 that you can deploy Kubernetes in different ways and *it's all the same Kubernetes* (my emphasis), but that's not strictly true. Kubernetes contains a lot of extension points, and distributions have flexibility in how they implement certain features. LoadBalancer Services represent a good example of where implementations differ, suited to the goals of the distribution.

- Docker Desktop is a local development environment. It runs on a single machine and integrates with the network stack so LoadBalancer Services are available at

LoadBalancer Services also create a cluster IP, so the Service is available to other Pods using the Service name.

LoadBalancer Services listen on an external IP address to route traffic to the cluster. The address is provided by the cluster. I'm using Docker Desktop, which routes using the localhost address.

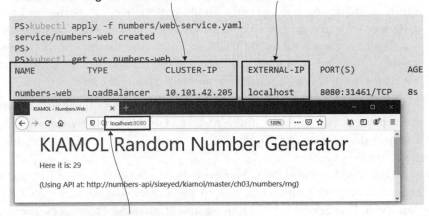

Now I can access the web application running in the Pod without needing a port forward from kubectl.

Figure 3.9 Kubernetes requests an IP address for LoadBalancer Services from the platform on which it's running.

Here, I'm running the same exercise on a K3s cluster, which I created using the setup described in chapter 1.

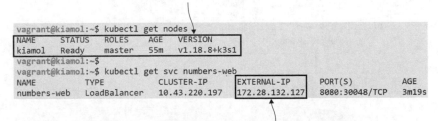

The LoadBalancer Service is created with a real IP address. This is a local cluster, so it's not a public IP address, but if I ran this same exercise in an AKS or EKS cluster, the Service would have a public address assigned by the cloud provider.

Figure 3.10 Different Kubernetes platforms use different addresses for LoadBalancer Services.

the localhost address. Every LoadBalancer Service publishes to localhost, so you'll need to use different ports if you deploy many load balancers.

- K3s supports LoadBalancer Services with a custom component that sets up routing tables on your machine. Every LoadBalancer Service publishes to the IP address of your machine (or VM), so you can access Services with localhost or from a remote machine on your network. Like Docker Desktop, you'll need to use different ports for each load balancer.

- Cloud Kubernetes platforms like AKS and EKS are highly available multinode clusters. Deploying a Kubernetes LoadBalancer Service creates an actual load balancer in your cloud, which spans all the nodes in your cluster—the cloud load balancer sends incoming traffic to one of the nodes and then Kubernetes routes it to a Pod. You'll get a different IP address for each LoadBalancer Service, and it will be a public address, accessible from the internet.

This is a pattern we'll see again in other Kubernetes features where distributions have different resources available and different aims. Ultimately, the YAML manifests are the same and the end results are consistent, but Kubernetes allows distributions to diverge in how they get there.

Back in the world of standard Kubernetes, there's another Service type you can use that listens for network traffic coming into the cluster and directs it to a Pod—the NodePort. NodePort Services don't require an external load balancer—every node in the cluster listens on the port specified in the Service and sends traffic to the target port on the Pod. Figure 3.11 shows how it works.

NodePort Services have each node listening on the Service port. There's no external load balancer, so traffic is routed directly to the cluster nodes.

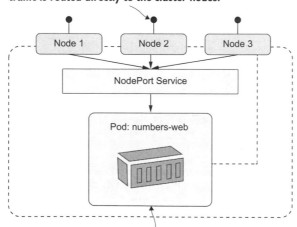

The Service works in a similar way to a LoadBalancer Service once the traffic is inside the cluster: any node can receive a request and direct it to Node 3, which is running the Pod.

Figure 3.11   NodePort Services also route external traffic to Pods, but they don't require a load balancer.

NodePort Services don't have the flexibility of LoadBalancer Services because you need a different port for each Service, your nodes need to be publicly accessible, and you don't achieve load-balancing across a multinode cluster. NodePort Services also have different levels of support in the distributions, so they work as expected in K3s and Docker Desktop but not so well in Kind. Listing 3.4 shows a NodePort spec for reference.

```
apiVersion: v1
kind: Service
metadata:
  name: numbers-web-node
spec:
  ports:
    - port: 8080        # The port on which the Service is available to
                        # other Pods
      targetPort: 80    # The port on which the traffic is sent to on
                        # the Pod
      nodePort: 30080   # The port on which the Service is available
                        # externally
  selector:
  app: numbers-web
  type: NodePort        # This Service is available on node IP addresses.
```

There isn't an exercise to deploy this NodePort Service (although the YAML file is in the chapter's folder if you want to try it out). This is partly because it doesn't work in the same way on every distribution, so this section would end with lots of if branches that you'd need to try to make sense of. But there's a more important reason—you don't typically use NodePorts in production, and it's good to keep your manifests as consistent as possible across different environments. Sticking with LoadBalancer Services means you have the same specs from development up to production, which means fewer YAML files to maintain and keep in sync.

We'll finish this chapter by digging into how Services work under the hood, but before that, we'll look at one more way you can use Services, which is to communicate from Pods to components outside of the cluster.

3.4   Routing traffic outside Kubernetes

You can run almost any server software in Kubernetes, but that doesn't mean you should. Storage components like databases are typical candidates for running outside of Kubernetes, especially if you're deploying to the cloud and you can use a managed database service instead. Or you may be running in the datacenter and need to integrate with existing systems that won't be migrating to Kubernetes. Whatever architecture you're using, you can still use Kubernetes Services for domain name resolution to components outside the cluster.

The first option for that is to use an ExternalName Service, which is like an alias from one domain to another. ExternalName Services let you use local names in your application Pods, and the DNS server in Kubernetes resolves the local name to a fully qualified external name when the Pod makes a lookup request. Figure 3.12 shows how that works, with a Pod using a local name that resolves to an external system address.

ExternalName Services create a domain name alias. Here the Pod can use the local cluster name db-service, which the Kubernetes DNS server resolves to the public address app.mydatabase.io.

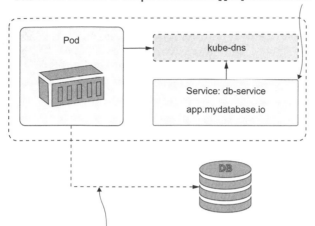

The Pod actually communicates with a component outside of the cluster, but that's transparent. The domain names it uses are local.

Figure 3.12   Using an ExternalName Service lets you use local cluster addresses for remote components.

The demo app for this chapter expects to use a local API to generate random numbers, but it can be switched to read a static number from a text file on GitHub just by deploying an ExternalName Service.

> **TRY IT NOW**   You can't switch a Service from one type to another in every version of Kubernetes, so you'll need to delete the original ClusterIP Service for the API before you can deploy the ExternalName Service.

```
# delete the current API Service:
kubectl delete svc numbers-api

# deploy a new ExternalName Service:
kubectl apply -f numbers-services/api-service-externalName.yaml

# check the Service configuration:
kubectl get svc numbers-api

# refresh the website in your browser and test with the Go button
```

My output is shown in figure 3.13. You can see the app works in the same way, and it's using the same URL for the API. If you refresh the page, however, you'll find that it always returns the same number because it's not using the random-number API anymore.

ExternalName Services can be a useful way to deal with differences between environments that you can't work around in your app configuration. Maybe you have an app component that uses a hardcoded string for the name of the database server. In

Changing the type of a Service involves
deleting and recreating it, so the Service
is unavailable while the change is deployed.

The new Service points to GitHub.
The demo app uses a URL for the
API that matches a file path on GitHub.

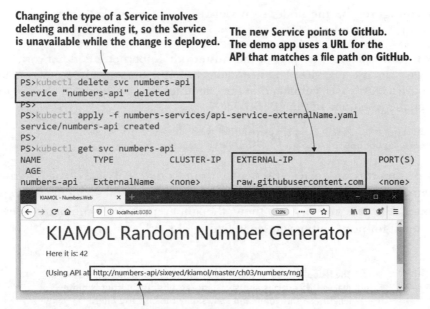

The web app is unchanged and uses the same API
address, but now it resolves to a static text file,
so the "random" number is always the same.

Figure 3.13 ExternalName Services can be used as a redirect to send requests
outside of the cluster.

development environments, you could create a ClusterIP Service with the expected
domain name, which resolves to a test database running in a Pod; in production
environments, you can use an ExternalName Service that resolves to the real domain
name of the database server. Listing 3.5 shows the YAML spec for the API external
name.

Listing 3.5 api-service-externalName.yaml, an ExternalName Service

```
apiVersion: v1
kind: Service
metadata:
  name: numbers-api    # The local domain name of the Service in the cluster
spec:
  type: ExternalName
  externalName: raw.githubusercontent.com    # The domain to resolve
```

Kubernetes implements ExternalName Services using a standard feature of DNS—
canonical names (CNAMEs). When the web Pod makes a DNS lookup for the numbers-
api domain name, the Kubernetes DNS server returns with the CNAME, which is
raw.githubusercontent.com. Then the DNS resolution continues using the DNS

server configured on the node, so it will reach out to the internet to find the IP address of the GitHub servers.

TRY IT NOW   Services are part of the clusterwide Kubernetes Pod network, so any Pod can use a Service. The sleep Pods from the first exercise in this chapter have a DNS lookup command in the container image, which you can use to check the resolution of the API Service.

```
# run the DNS lookup tool to resolve the Service name:
kubectl exec deploy/sleep-1 -- sh -c 'nslookup numbers-api | tail -n 5'
```

When you try this, you may get scrambled results that look like errors, because the Nslookup tool returns a lot of information and it's not in the same order every time you run it. The data you want is in there, though. I repeated the command a few times to get the fit-for-print output you see in figure 3.14.

The Nslookup tool is installed in the sleep container image—it makes DNS queries and shows the results. The output is quite lengthy, so this command shows only the final five lines.

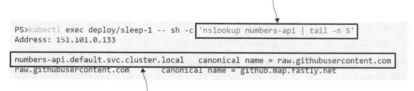

```
PS>kubectl exec deploy/sleep-1 -- sh -c 'nslookup numbers-api | tail -n 5'
Address: 151.101.0.133

numbers-api.default.svc.cluster.local    canonical name = raw.githubusercontent.com
raw.githubusercontent.com     canonical name = github.map.fastly.net
```

The local cluster name numbers-api resolves to the GitHub address (which in turn resolves to a Fastly address). The sleep Pod has no logical use for the random-number API, but the service is clusterwide so any Pod can access any Service.

Figure 3.14   Apps aren't isolated by default in Kubernetes, so any Pod can do a lookup for any Service.

There's one important thing to understand about ExternalName Services, which you can see from this exercise: they ultimately just give your app an address to use, but they don't actually change the requests your application makes. That's fine for components like databases, which communicate over TCP, but it's not so simple for HTTP services. HTTP requests include the target host name in a header field, and that won't match the actual domain from the ExternalName response, so the client call will probably fail. The random-number app in this chapter has some hacky code to get around this issue, manually setting the host header, but this approach is best for non-HTTP services.

There's one other option for routing local domain names in the cluster to external systems. It doesn't fix the HTTP header issue, but it does let you use a similar approach to ExternalName Services when you want to route to an IP address rather than a domain name. These are *headless Services*, which are defined as a ClusterIP Service type but without a label selector so they will never match any Pods. Instead, the service is deployed with an *endpoint* resource that explicitly lists the IP addresses the Service should resolve.

Listing 3.6 shows a headless Service with a single IP address in the endpoint. It also shows a new use of YAML, with multiple resources defined, separated by three dashes.

> **Listing 3.6   api-service-headless.yaml, a Service with explicit addresses**

```
apiVersion: v1
kind: Service
metadata:
  name: numbers-api
spec:
  type: ClusterIP      # No selector field makes this a headless Service.
  ports:
    - port: 80
---
kind: Endpoints        # The endpoint is a separate resource.
apiVersion: v1
metadata:
  name: numbers-api
subsets:
  - addresses:         # It has a static list of IP addresses . . .
      - ip: 192.168.123.234
    ports:
      - port: 80       # and the ports they listen on.
```

The IP address in that endpoint specification is a fake one, but Kubernetes doesn't validate that the address is reachable, so this code will deploy without errors.

> **TRY IT NOW**   Replace the ExternalName Service with this headless Service. It will cause the app to fail because the API domain name now resolves to an inaccessible IP address.

```
# remove the existing Service:
kubectl delete svc numbers-api

# deploy the headless Service:
kubectl apply -f numbers-services/api-service-headless.yaml

# check the Service:
kubectl get svc numbers-api

# check the endpoint:
kubectl get endpoints numbers-api

# verify the DNS lookup:
kubectl exec deploy/sleep-1 -- sh -c 'nslookup numbers-api | grep
  "^[^*]"'

# browse to the app—it will fail when you try to get a number
```

My output, shown in figure 3.15, confirms that Kubernetes will happily let you deploy a Service change that breaks your application. The domain name resolves the internal cluster IP address, but any network calls to that address fail because they are routed to the actual IP address in the endpoint that doesn't exist.

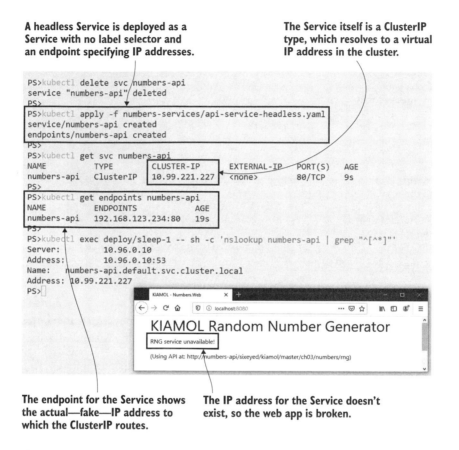

A headless Service is deployed as a Service with no label selector and an endpoint specifying IP addresses.

The Service itself is a ClusterIP type, which resolves to a virtual IP address in the cluster.

The endpoint for the Service shows the actual—fake—IP address to which the ClusterIP routes.

The IP address for the Service doesn't exist, so the web app is broken.

Figure 3.15   A misconfiguration in a Service can break your apps, even without deploying an app change.

The output from that exercise raises a couple of interesting questions: How come the DNS lookup returns the cluster IP address instead of the endpoint address? Why does the domain name end with .default.svc.cluster.local? You don't need a background in network engineering to work with Kubernetes Services, but it will help you track down issues if you understand how Service resolution actually works—and that's how we'll finish the chapter.

3.5 *Understanding Kubernetes Service resolution*

Kubernetes supports all the network configurations your app is likely to need using Services, which build on established networking technologies. Application components run in Pods and communicate with other Pods using standard transfer protocols and DNS names for discovery. You don't need any special code or libraries; your apps work in the same way in Kubernetes as if you deployed them on physical servers or VMs.

We've covered all the Service types and their typical use cases in this chapter, so now you have a good understanding of the patterns you can use. If you're feeling that there's an awful lot of detail here, be assured that the majority of times you'll be deploying ClusterIP Services, which require little configuration. They mostly work seamlessly, but it is useful to go one level deeper to understand the stack. Figure 3.16 shows that next level of detail.

Domain name lookups from Pod containers are resolved
by the Kubernetes DNS server. For Kubernetes Services,
it returns a cluster IP address or an external domain name.

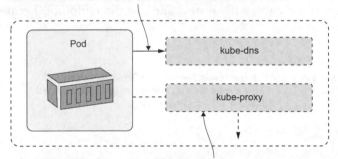

All communication from the Pod is routed by a network proxy, another
internal Kubernetes component. A proxy runs on each node. It maintains
an updated list of endpoints for each Service and routes traffic using a
network packet filter from the operating system (IPVS or iptables on Linux).

Figure 3.16   Kubernetes runs a DNS server and a proxy and uses them with
standard network tools.

The key takeaway is that the ClusterIP is a virtual IP address that doesn't exist on the network. Pods access the network through the kube-proxy running on the node, and that uses packet filtering to send the virtual IP to the real endpoint. Kubernetes Services keep their IP addresses as long as they exist, and Services can exist independently of any other parts of your app. Services have a controller that keeps the endpoint list updated whenever there are changes to Pods, so clients always use the static virtual IP address and the kube-proxy always has the up-to-date endpoint list.

TRY IT NOW   You can see how Kubernetes keeps the endpoint list immediately updated when Pods change by listing the endpoints for a Service between Pod changes. Endpoints use the same name as Services, and you can view endpoint details using kubectl.

```
# show the endpoints for the sleep-2 Service:
kubectl get endpoints sleep-2

# delete the Pod:
kubectl delete pods -l app=sleep-2

# check the endpoint is updated with the IP of the replacement Pod:
kubectl get endpoints sleep-2

# delete the whole Deployment:
kubectl delete deploy sleep-2

# check the endpoint still exists, with no IP addresses:
kubectl get endpoints sleep-2
```

You can see my output in figure 3.17, and it's the answer to the first question— Kubernetes DNS returns the cluster IP address and not the endpoint, because endpoint addresses change.

The sleep-2 Service has a single
endpoint, which is the IP address
of the current sleep-2 Pod.

When the Pod is deleted, the Deployment controller
creates a replacement, and the endpoint is updated
with the new Pod's IP address.

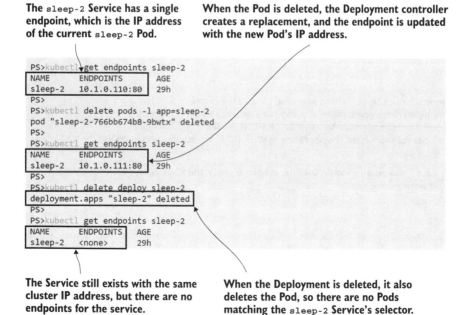

The Service still exists with the same
cluster IP address, but there are no
endpoints for the service.

When the Deployment is deleted, it also
deletes the Pod, so there are no Pods
matching the sleep-2 Service's selector.

**Figure 3.17   The cluster IP address for a Service doesn't change, but the endpoint list is
always being updated.**

Using a static virtual IP means clients can cache the DNS lookup response indefinitely (which many apps do as misguided performance-saving), and that IP address will continue to work no matter how many Pod replacements occur over time. The second question—about the domain name suffix—needs to be answered with a sideways step to look at Kubernetes *namespaces.*

Every Kubernetes resource lives inside a namespace, which is a resource you can use to group other resources. Namespaces are a way to logically partition a Kubernetes cluster—you could have one namespace per product, one per team, or a single shared namespace. We won't use namespaces for a while yet, but I'm introducing them here because they have a part to play in DNS resolution. Figure 3.18 shows where the namespace comes into the Service name.

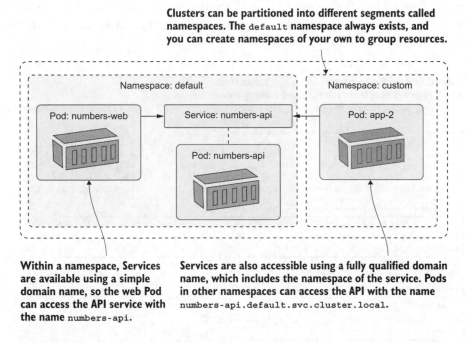

Clusters can be partitioned into different segments called namespaces. The `default` namespace always exists, and you can create namespaces of your own to group resources.

Within a namespace, Services are available using a simple domain name, so the web Pod can access the API service with the name `numbers-api`.

Services are also accessible using a fully qualified domain name, which includes the namespace of the service. Pods in other namespaces can access the API with the name `numbers-api.default.svc.cluster.local`.

Figure 3.18 Namespaces logically partition a cluster, but Services are accessible across namespaces.

You already have several namespaces in your cluster—all the resources we've deployed so far have been created in the `default` namespace (which is the default; that's why we haven't needed to specify a namespace in our YAML files). Internal Kubernetes components like the DNS server and the Kubernetes API also run in Pods in the `kube-system` namespace.

TRY IT NOW   Kubectl is namespace-aware—you can use the namespace flag to work with resources outside of the default namespace.

```
# check the Services in the default namespace:
kubectl get svc --namespace default

# check Services in the system namespace:
kubectl get svc -n kube-system

# try a DNS lookup to a fully qualified Service name:
kubectl exec deploy/sleep-1 -- sh -c 'nslookup numbers-
    api.default.svc.cluster.local | grep "^[^*]"'

# and for a Service in the system namespace:
kubectl exec deploy/sleep-1 -- sh -c 'nslookup kube-dns.kube-
    system.svc.cluster.local | grep "^[^*]"'
```

My output, shown in figure 3.19, answers the second question—the local domain name for a Service is just the Service name, but that's an alias for the fully qualified domain name that includes the Kubernetes namespace.

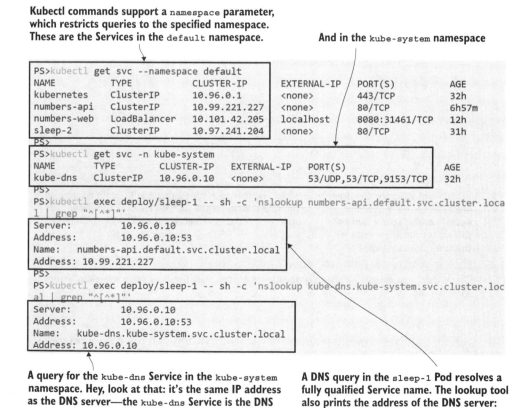

Kubectl commands support a `namespace` parameter, which restricts queries to the specified namespace. These are the Services in the `default` namespace.

And in the `kube-system` namespace

A query for the `kube-dns` Service in the `kube-system` namespace. Hey, look at that: it's the same IP address as the DNS server—the `kube-dns` Service is the DNS server address for the cluster.

A DNS query in the `sleep-1` Pod resolves a fully qualified Service name. The lookup tool also prints the address of the DNS server: `10.96.0.10`.

Figure 3.19   You can use the same kubectl commands to view resources in different namespaces.

It's important to know about namespaces early in your Kubernetes journey, if only because it helps you see that core Kubernetes features run as Kubernetes applications too, but you don't see them in kubectl unless you explicitly set the namespace. Namespaces are a powerful way to subdivide your cluster to increase utilization without compromising security, and we'll return to them in chapter 11.

For now we're done with namespaces and Services. In this chapter, you've learned that every Pod has its own IP address, and Pod communication ultimately uses that address with standard TCP and UDP protocols. You never use the Pod IP address directly, though—you always create a Service resource, which Kubernetes uses to provide Service discovery with DNS. Services support multiple networking patterns, with different Service types configuring network traffic between Pods, into Pods from the outside world, and from Pods to the world outside. You also learned that Services have their own life cycle, independent of Pods and Deployments, so the last thing to do is clean up before we move on.

> **TRY IT NOW** Deleting a Deployment also deletes all its Pods, but there's no cascading delete for Services. They're independent objects that need to be removed separately.

```
# delete Deployments:
kubectl delete deploy --all

# and Services:
kubectl delete svc --all

# check what's running:
kubectl get all
```

Now your cluster is clear again, although, as you can see in figure 3.20, you need to be careful with some of these kubectl commands.

3.6 Lab

This lab is going to give you some practice creating Services, but it's also going to get you thinking about labels and selectors, which are powerful features of Kubernetes. The goal is to deploy Services for an updated version of the random-number app, which has had a UI makeover. Here are your hints:

- The lab folder for this chapter has a deployments.yaml file. Use that to deploy the app with kubectl.
- Check the Pods—there are two versions of the web application running.
- Write a Service that will make the API available to other Pods at the domain name numbers-api.
- Write a Service that will make version 2 of the website available externally, on port 8088.
- You'll need to look closely at the Pod labels to get the correct result.

Deleting Deployments also deletes Pods. There's no namespace parameter, so this deletes resources only in the default **namespace.**

Services need to be explicitly deleted. Using the all **parameter means I've accidentally deleted the Kubernetes API, which lives in the** default **namespace. Oops.**

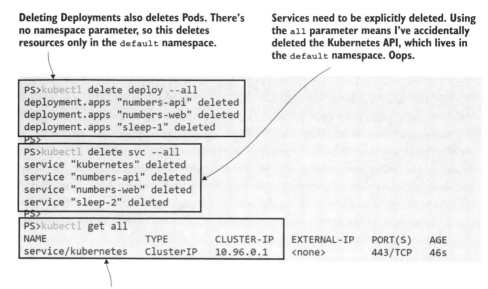

```
PS>kubectl delete deploy --all
deployment.apps "numbers-api" deleted
deployment.apps "numbers-web" deleted
deployment.apps "sleep-1" deleted
PS>
PS>kubectl delete svc --all
service "kubernetes" deleted
service "numbers-api" deleted
service "numbers-web" deleted
service "sleep-2" deleted
PS>
PS>kubectl get all
NAME                  TYPE         CLUSTER-IP    EXTERNAL-IP   PORT(S)    AGE
service/kubernetes    ClusterIP    10.96.0.1     <none>        443/TCP    46s
```

Luckily there's a controller in the kube-system **namespace that manages the API Service and recreates it.**

Figure 3.20   You need to explicitly delete any Services you create, but watch out with the all **parameter.**

This lab is an extension of the exercises in the chapter, and if you want to check my solution, it's up on GitHub in the repository for the book: https://github.com/sixeyed/ kiamol/blob/master/ch03/lab/README.md.

Configuring applications with ConfigMaps and Secrets

One of the great advantages of running apps in containers is that you eliminate the gaps between environments. The deployment process promotes the same container image through all your test environments up to production, so each deployment uses the exact same set of binaries as the previous environment. You'll never again see a production deployment fail because the servers are missing a dependency that someone manually installed on the test servers and forgot to document. Of course, differences do occur between environments, and you provide for that by injecting configuration settings into containers.

Kubernetes supports configuration injection with two resource types: ConfigMaps and Secrets. Both types can store data in any reasonable format, and that data lives in the cluster independent of any other resources. Pods can be defined with access to the data in ConfigMaps and Secrets, with different options for how that data gets surfaced. In this chapter, you'll learn all the ways to manage configuration in Kubernetes, which are flexible enough to meet the requirements for any application.

4.1 How Kubernetes supplies configuration to apps

You create ConfigMap and Secret objects like other resources in Kubernetes—using kubectl, either with `create` commands or by applying a YAML specification. Unlike other resources, they don't do anything; they're just storage units intended for small amounts of data. Those storage units can be loaded into a Pod, becoming part of the container environment, so the application in the container can read the data. Before we even get to those objects, we'll look at the simplest way to provide configuration settings: using environment variables.

TRY IT NOW   Environment variables are a core operating system feature in Linux and Windows, and they can be set at the machine level so any app can read them. They're commonly used, and all containers have some, which are set by the operating system inside the container and by Kubernetes. Make sure your Kubernetes lab is up and running.

```
# switch to the exercise directory for this chapter:
cd ch04

# deploy a Pod using the sleep image with no extra configuration:
kubectl apply -f sleep/sleep.yaml

# wait for the Pod to be ready:
kubectl wait --for=condition=Ready pod -l app=sleep

# check some of the environment variables in the Pod container:
kubectl exec deploy/sleep -- printenv HOSTNAME KIAMOL_CHAPTER
```

You can see from my output shown in figure 4.1 that the hostname variable exists in the container and is populated by Kubernetes, but the custom Kiamol variable doesn't exist.

Deploys a simple Pod with just a container image specified and no additional configuration settings

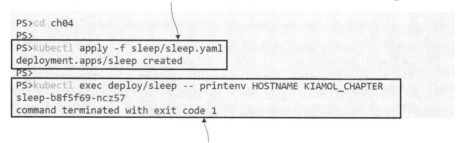

printenv **is a Linux command that shows the value of environment variables. The** HOSTNAME **variable exists in all Pod containers and is set by Kubernetes to be the Pod name. The** KIAMOL_CHAPTER **variable doesn't exist, so the command exits with an error code.**

Figure 4.1   All Pod containers have some environment variables set by Kubernetes and the container OS.

In this exercise, the application is just the Linux printenv tool, but the principle is the same for any application. Many technology stacks use environment variables as a basic configuration system. The simplest way to provide those settings in Kubernetes is by adding environment variables in the Pod specification. Listing 4.1 shows an updated Pod spec for the sleep Deployment, which adds the Kiamol environment variable.

Listing 4.1   sleep-with-env.yaml, a Pod spec with environment variables

```
spec:
  containers:
    - name: sleep
      image: kiamol/ch03-sleep
      env:                          # Sets environment variables
      - name: KIAMOL_CHAPTER        # Defines the name of the variable to create
        value: "04"                 # Defines the value to set for the variable
```

Environment variables are static for the life of the Pod; you can't update any values while the Pod is running. If you need to make configuration changes, you need to perform an update with a replacement Pod. You should get used to the idea that deployments aren't just for new feature releases; you'll also use them for configuration changes and software patches, and you must design your apps to handle frequent Pod replacements.

> **TRY IT NOW**   Update the sleep Deployment with the new Pod spec from listing 4.1, adding an environment variable that is visible inside the Pod container.

```
# update the Deployment:
kubectl apply -f sleep/sleep-with-env.yaml

# check the same environment variables in the new Pod:
kubectl exec deploy/sleep -- printenv HOSTNAME KIAMOL_CHAPTER
```

My output, in figure 4.2, shows the result—a new container with the Kiamol environment variable set, running in a new Pod.

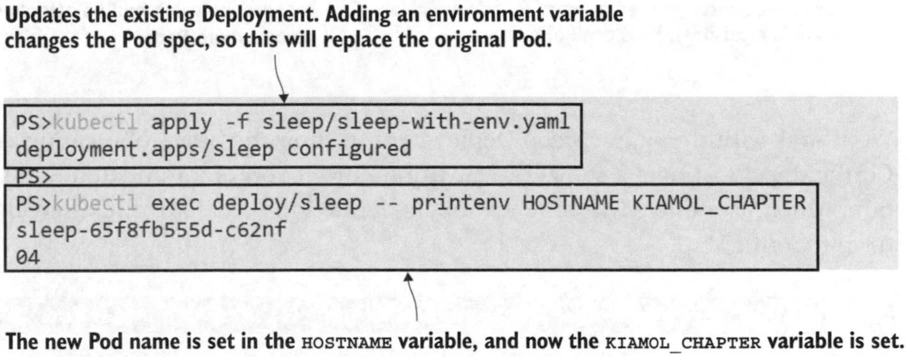

Updates the existing Deployment. Adding an environment variable
changes the Pod spec, so this will replace the original Pod.

```
PS>kubectl apply -f sleep/sleep-with-env.yaml
deployment.apps/sleep configured
PS>
PS>kubectl exec deploy/sleep -- printenv HOSTNAME KIAMOL_CHAPTER
sleep-65f8fb555d-c62nf
04
```

The new Pod name is set in the HOSTNAME variable, and now the KIAMOL_CHAPTER variable is set.

Figure 4.2   Adding environment variables to a Pod spec makes the values available in the Pod container.

The important thing about the previous exercise is that the new app is using the same Docker image; it's the same application with all the same binaries—only the configuration settings have changed between deployments. Setting environment values inline in the Pod specification is fine for simple settings, but real applications usually have more complex configuration requirements, which is when you use ConfigMaps.

A ConfigMap is just a resource that stores some data that can be loaded into a Pod. The data can be a set of key-value pairs, a blurb of text, or even a binary file. You can use key-value pairs to load Pods with environment variables, text to load any type of config file—JSON, XML, YAML, TOML, INI—and binary files to load license keys. One Pod can use many ConfigMaps, and each ConfigMap can be used by many Pods. Figure 4.3 shows some of those options.

Pods load ConfigMaps into the container environment as environment variables or files.

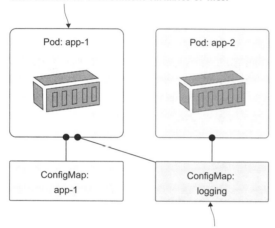

ConfigMaps can be used for app-specific settings or shared settings used in many Pods. ConfigMap data is read-only; Pods can't alter it.

Figure 4.3   ConfigMaps are separate resources, which can be attached to zero or more Pods.

We'll stick with the simple sleep Deployment to show the basics of creating and using ConfigMaps. Listing 4.2 shows the environment section of an updated Pod specification, which uses one environment variable defined in the YAML and a second loaded from a ConfigMap.

Listing 4.2   sleep-with-configMap-env.yaml, loading a ConfigMap into a Pod

```
env:                            # The environment section of the container spec
- name: KIAMOL_CHAPTER
  value: "04"                   # This is the variable value.
- name: KIAMOL_SECTION
  valueFrom:
    configMapKeyRef:            # This value comes from a ConfigMap.
      name: sleep-config-literal # Names the ConfigMap
      key: kiamol.section       # Names the data item to load
```

If you reference a ConfigMap in a Pod specification, the ConfigMap needs to exist before you deploy the Pod. This spec expects to find a ConfigMap called `sleep-config-literal` with key-value pairs in the data, and the easiest way to create that is by passing the key and value to a kubectl command.

> **TRY IT NOW**   Create a ConfigMap by specifying the data in the command, then check the data and deploy the updated sleep app to use the ConfigMap.

```
# create a ConfigMap with data from the command line:
kubectl create configmap sleep-config-literal --from-
   literal=kiamol.section='4.1'

# check the ConfigMap details:
kubectl get cm sleep-config-literal

# show the friendly description of the ConfigMap:
kubectl describe cm sleep-config-literal

# deploy the updated Pod spec from listing 4.2:
kubectl apply -f sleep/sleep-with-configMap-env.yaml

# check the Kiamol environment variables:
kubectl exec deploy/sleep -- sh -c 'printenv | grep "^KIAMOL"'
```

We won't use kubectl `describe` commands much in this book because the output is usually verbose and would use up most of a chapter, but it's definitely something to experiment with. Describing Services and Pods gives you a lot of useful information in a readable format. You can see my output in figure 4.4, which includes the key-value data shown from describing the ConfigMap.

Creating ConfigMaps from literal values is fine for individual settings, but it gets cumbersome fast if you have a lot of configuration data. As well as specifying literal values on the command line, Kubernetes lets you load ConfigMaps from files.

4.2 *Storing and using configuration files in ConfigMaps*

Options for creating and using ConfigMaps have evolved over many Kubernetes releases, so they now support practically every configuration variant you can think of. These sleep Pod exercises are a good way to show the variations, but they're getting a bit boring, so we'll just have one more before we move on to something more interesting. Listing 4.3 shows an environment file—a text file with key-value pairs that can be loaded to create one ConfigMap with multiple data items.

> **Listing 4.3   ch04.env, a file of environment variables**

```
# Environment files use a new line for each variable.
KIAMOL_CHAPTER=ch04
KIAMOL_SECTION=ch04-4.1
KIAMOL_EXERCISE=try it now
```

The details of the ConfigMap (using the alias cm) show it has a single data item.

Creating a ConfigMap from a literal value—the key kiamol.section is set with the value 4.1 in the command parameters.

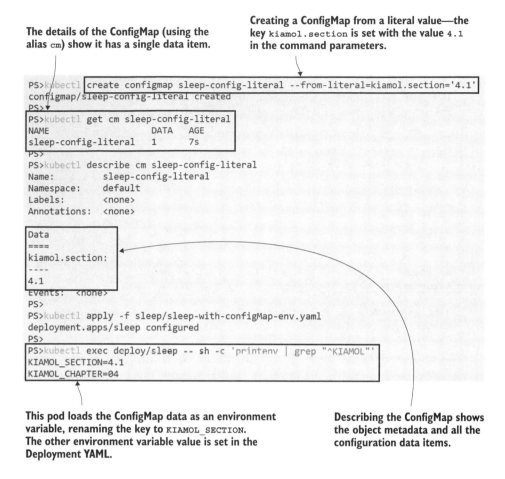

```
PS>kubectl create configmap sleep-config-literal --from-literal=kiamol.section='4.1'
configmap/sleep-config-literal created
PS>
PS>kubectl get cm sleep-config-literal
NAME                   DATA   AGE
sleep-config-literal   1      7s
PS>
PS>kubectl describe cm sleep-config-literal
Name:          sleep-config-literal
Namespace:     default
Labels:        <none>
Annotations:   <none>

Data
====
kiamol.section:
----
4.1

Events:   <none>
PS>
PS>kubectl apply -f sleep/sleep-with-configMap-env.yaml
deployment.apps/sleep configured
PS>
PS>kubectl exec deploy/sleep -- sh -c 'printenv | grep "^KIAMOL"'
KIAMOL_SECTION=4.1
KIAMOL_CHAPTER=04
```

This pod loads the ConfigMap data as an environment variable, renaming the key to KIAMOL_SECTION. The other environment variable value is set in the Deployment YAML.

Describing the ConfigMap shows the object metadata and all the configuration data items.

Figure 4.4   Pods can load individual data items from ConfigMaps and rename the key.

Environment files are a useful way to group multiple settings, and Kubernetes has explicit support for loading them into ConfigMaps and surfacing all the settings as environment variables in a Pod container.

TRY IT NOW   Create a new ConfigMap populated from the environment file in listing 4.3, then deploy an update to the sleep app to use the new settings.

```
# load an environment variable into a new ConfigMap:
kubectl create configmap sleep-config-env-file --from-env-
  file=sleep/ch04.env

# check the details of the ConfigMap:
kubectl get cm sleep-config-env-file

# update the Pod to use the new ConfigMap:
kubectl apply -f sleep/sleep-with-configMap-env-file.yaml
```

```
# check the values in the container:
kubectl exec deploy/sleep -- sh -c 'printenv | grep "^KIAMOL"'
```

My output, in figure 4.5, shows the printenv command reading all the environment variables and showing the ones with Kiamol names, but it might not be the result you expect.

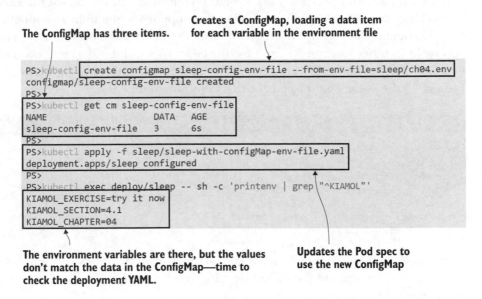

The ConfigMap has three items.

Creates a ConfigMap, loading a data item for each variable in the environment file

```
PS>kubectl create configmap sleep-config-env-file --from-env-file=sleep/ch04.env
configmap/sleep-config-env-file created
PS>
PS>kubectl get cm sleep-config-env-file
NAME                     DATA   AGE
sleep-config-env-file    3      6s
PS>
PS>kubectl apply -f sleep/sleep-with-configMap-env-file.yaml
deployment.apps/sleep configured
PS>
PS>kubectl exec deploy/sleep -- sh -c 'printenv | grep "^KIAMOL"'
KIAMOL_EXERCISE=try it now
KIAMOL_SECTION=4.1
KIAMOL_CHAPTER=04
```

The environment variables are there, but the values don't match the data in the ConfigMap—time to check the deployment YAML.

Updates the Pod spec to use the new ConfigMap

Figure 4.5 A ConfigMap can have multiple data items, and the Pod can load them all.

This exercise showed you how to create a ConfigMap from a file. It also showed you that Kubernetes has rules of precedence for applying environment variables. The Pod spec you just deployed, shown in listing 4.4, loads all environment variables from the ConfigMap, but it also specifies explicit environment values with some of the same keys.

Listing 4.4   sleep-with-configMap-env-file.yaml, multiple ConfigMaps in a Pod

```
env:                                # The existing environment section
- name: KIAMOL_CHAPTER
  value: "04"
- name: KIAMOL_SECTION
  valueFrom:
    configMapKeyRef:
      name: sleep-config-literal
      key: kiamol.section
envFrom:                            # envFrom loads multiple variables
- configMapRef:                     # from a ConfigMap
    name: sleep-config-env-file
```

So the environment variables defined with env in the Pod spec override the values defined with envFrom if there are duplicate keys. It's useful to remember that you can override any environment variables set in the container image or in ConfigMaps by explicitly setting them in the Pod spec—a quick way to change a configuration setting when you're tracking down problems.

Environment variables are well supported, but they only get you so far, and most application platforms prefer a more structured approach. In the rest of the exercises in this chapter, we'll use a web application that supports a hierarchy of configuration sources. Default settings are packaged in a JSON file in the Docker image, and the app looks in other locations at run time for JSON files with settings that override the defaults—and all the JSON settings can be overridden with environment variables. Listing 4.5 shows the Pod spec for the first deployment we'll use.

> ### Listing 4.5   todo-web.yaml, a web app with configuration settings

```
spec:
  containers:
  - name: web
    image: kiamol/ch04-todo-list
    env:
    - name: Logging__LogLevel__Default
      value: Warning
```

This run of the app will use all the default settings from the JSON configuration file in the image, except for the default logging level, which is set as an environment variable.

TRY IT NOW   Run the app without any additional configuration, and check its behavior.

```
# deploy the app with a Service to access it:
kubectl apply -f todo-list/todo-web.yaml

# wait for the Pod to be ready:
kubectl wait --for=condition=Ready pod -l app=todo-web

# get the address of the app:
kubectl get svc todo-web -o
    jsonpath='http://{.status.loadBalancer.ingress[0].*}:8080'

# browse to the app and have a play around
# then try browsing to /config

# check the application logs:
kubectl logs -l app=todo-web
```

The demo app is a simple to-do list (which will be distressingly familiar to readers of *Learn Docker in a Month of Lunches*). In its current setup, it lets you add and view items, but there should also be a /config page we can use in nonproduction environments to view all the configuration settings. As you can see in figure 4.6, that page is empty, and the app logs a warning that someone tried to access it.

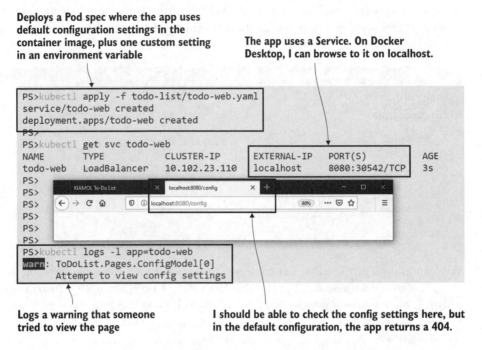

Deploys a Pod spec where the app uses default configuration settings in the container image, plus one custom setting in an environment variable

The app uses a Service. On Docker Desktop, I can browse to it on localhost.

Logs a warning that someone tried to view the page

I should be able to check the config settings here, but in the default configuration, the app returns a 404.

Figure 4.6 The app mostly works, but we need to set additional configuration values.

The configuration hierarchy in use here is a very common approach. If you're not familiar with it, appendix C in the ebook is the chapter "Application Configuration Management in Containers" from *Learn Docker in a Month of Lunches,* which explains it in detail. This example is a .NET Core app that uses JSON, but you see similar configuration systems using a variety of file formats in Java Spring apps, Node.js, Go, Python, and more. In Kubernetes, you use the same app configuration approach with them all.

- Default app settings are baked into the container image. This could be just the settings which apply in every environment, or it could be a full set of configuration options, so without any extra setup, the app runs in development mode (that's helpful for developers who can quickly start the app with a simple Docker run command).
- The actual settings for each environment are stored in a ConfigMap and surfaced into the container filesystem. Kubernetes presents the configuration data as a file in a known location, which the app checks and merges with the content from the default file.

- Any settings that need to be tweaked can be applied as environment variables in the Pod specification for the Deployment.

Listing 4.6 shows the YAML specification for the development configuration of the to-do app. It contains the contents of a JSON file, which the app will merge with the default JSON configuration file in the container image, with a setting to make the config page visible.

Listing 4.6   todo-web-config-dev.yaml, a ConfigMap specification

```
apiVersion: v1
kind: ConfigMap                      # ConfigMap is the resource type.
metadata:
  name: todo-web-config-dev          # Names the ConfigMap.
data:
  config.json: |-                    # The data key is the filename.
    {                                # The file contents can be any format.
      "ConfigController": {
        "Enabled" : true
      }
    }
```

You can embed any kind of text configuration file into a YAML spec, as long as you're careful with the whitespace. I prefer this to loading ConfigMaps directly from configuration files because it means you can consistently use the kubectl `apply` command to deploy every part of your app. If I wanted to load the JSON file directly, I'd need to use the kubectl `create` command for configuration resources and `apply` for everything else.

The ConfigMap definition in listing 4.6 contains just a single setting, but it's stored in the native configuration format for the app. When we deploy an updated Pod spec, the setting will be applied and the config page will be visible.

TRY IT NOW   The new Pod spec references the ConfigMap, so that needs to be created first by applying the YAML, then we update the to-do app Deployment.

```
# create the JSON ConfigMap:
kubectl apply -f todo-list/configMaps/todo-web-config-dev.yaml

# update the app to use the ConfigMap:
kubectl apply -f todo-list/todo-web-dev.yaml

# refresh your web browser at the /config page for your Service
```

You can see my output in figure 4.7. The config page loads correctly now, so the new Deployment configuration is merging in the settings from the ConfigMap to override the default setting in the image, which blocked access to that page.

This approach needs two things: your application needs to be able to merge in the ConfigMap data, and your Pod specification needs to load the data from the ConfigMap

Deploy a ConfigMap with app settings and an updated Deployment to use the ConfigMap.

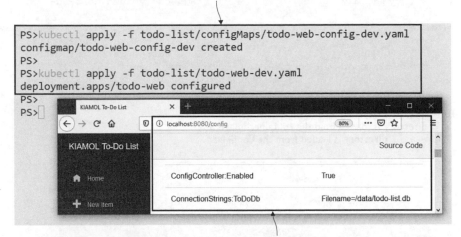

The Service hasn't changed, but the same external IP is pointing to a new Pod, which loads the JSON config file from the ConfigMap and enables the page.

Figure 4.7　Loading ConfigMap data into the container filesystem, where the app loads config files

into the expected file path in the container filesystem. We'll see how that works in the next section.

4.3　*Surfacing configuration data from ConfigMaps*

The alternative to loading configuration items into environment variables is to present them as files inside directories in the container. The container filesystem is a virtual construct, built from the container image and other sources. Kubernetes can use ConfigMaps as a filesystem source—they are mounted as a directory, with a file for each data item. Figure 4.8 shows the setup you've just deployed, where the data item in the ConfigMap is surfaced as a file.

Kubernetes manages this strange magic with two features of the Pod spec: *volumes*, which make the contents of the ConfigMap available to the Pod, and *volume mounts*, which load the contents of the ConfigMap volume into a specified path in the Pod container. Listing 4.7 shows the volumes and mounts you deployed in the previous exercise.

Listing 4.7　todo-web-dev.yaml, loading a ConfigMap as a volume mount

```
spec:
  containers:
    - name: web
      image: kiamol/ch04-todo-list
      volumeMounts:              # Mounts a volume into the container
        - name: config           # Names the volume
```

```
        mountPath: "/app/config"    # Directory path to mount the volume
        readOnly: true              # Flags the volume as read-only

    volumes:                        # Volumes are defined at the Pod level.
      - name: config                # Name matches the volume mount.
        configMap:                  # Volume source is a ConfigMap.
          name: todo-web-config-dev # ConfigMap name
```

The container filesystem is constructed by Kubernetes. The
/app directory is loaded from the container image; the
/app/config directory is loaded from the ConfigMap.

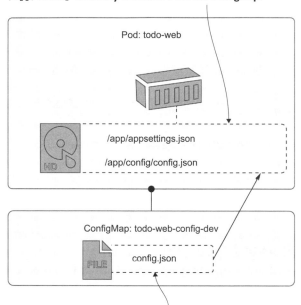

The container filesystem appears...

The ConfigMap is surfaced as a directory inside the Pod
container, and the data item config.json is loaded as a file.

Figure 4.8   ConfigMaps can be
loaded as directories in the
container filesystem.

The important thing to realize here is that the ConfigMap is treated like a directory, with multiple data items, which each become files in the container filesystem. In this example, the application loads its default settings from the file at /app/appsettings .json, and then it looks for a file at /app/config/config.json, which can contain settings to override the defaults. The /app/config directory doesn't exist in the container image; it is created and populated by Kubernetes.

TRY IT NOW   The container filesystem appears as a single storage unit to the application, but it has been built from the image and the ConfigMap. Those sources have different behaviors.

```
# show the default config file:
kubectl exec deploy/todo-web -- sh -c 'ls -l /app/app*.json'
```

```
# show the config file in the volume mount:
kubectl exec deploy/todo-web -- sh -c 'ls -l /app/config/*.json'

# check it really is read-only:
kubectl exec deploy/todo-web -- sh -c 'echo ch04 >>
  /app/config/config.json'
```

My output, in figure 4.9, shows that the JSON configuration files exist in the expected locations for the app, but the ConfigMap files are managed by Kubernetes and delivered as read-only files.

This is the default app configuration file, loaded from the container image. It has the file permissions, which are set in the image.

```
PS>kubectl exec deploy/todo-web -- sh -c 'ls -l /app/app*.json'
-rw-r--r-- 1 root root 333 Apr 16 14:55 /app/appsettings.json
PS>
PS>kubectl exec deploy/todo-web -- sh -c 'ls -l /app/config/*.json'
lrwxrwxrwx 1 root root 18 Apr 16 20:13 /app/config/config.json -> ..data/config.json
PS>
PS>kubectl exec deploy/todo-web -- sh -c 'echo ch04 >> /app/config/config.json'
sh: 1: cannot create /app/config/config.json: Read-only file system
command terminated with exit code 2
PS>
PS>kubectl exec deploy/todo-web -- sh -c 'readlink -f /app/config/config.json'
/app/config/..2020_04_16_20_13_07.024335099/config.json
```

The file appears to have read-write permissions, but the path is actually a link to a read-only file, as you can see when you try to edit the file.

This is the environment config file, loaded from the ConfigMap.

Figure 4.9   The container filesystem is built by Kubernetes from the image and the ConfigMap.

Loading ConfigMaps as directories is flexible, and you can use it to support different approaches to app configuration. If your configuration is split across multiple files, you can store it all in a single ConfigMap and load it all into the container. Listing 4.8 shows the data items for an update to the to-do ConfigMap with two JSON files that separate the settings for application behavior and logging.

Listing 4.8   todo-web-config-dev-with-logging.yaml, a ConfigMap with two files

```
data:
  config.json: |-                        # The original app config file
    {
      "ConfigController": {
        "Enabled" : true
      }
    }
  logging.json: |-                       # A second JSON file, which will be
    {                                    # surfaced in the volume mount
```

```
    "Logging": {
      "LogLevel": {
        "ToDoList.Pages" : "Debug"
      }
    }
  }
```

What happens when you deploy an update to a ConfigMap that a live Pod is using? Kubernetes delivers the updated files to the container, but what happens next depends on the application. Some apps load configuration files into memory when they start and then ignore any changes in the config directory, so changing the ConfigMap won't actually change the app configuration until the Pods are replaced. This application is more thoughtful—it watches the config directory and reloads any file changes, so deploying an update to the ConfigMap will update the application configuration.

> **TRY IT NOW**   Update the app configuration with the ConfigMap from listing 4.9. That increases the logging level, so the same Pod will now start writing more log entries.

```
# check the current app logs:
kubectl logs -l app=todo-web

# deploy the updated ConfigMap:
kubectl apply -f todo-list/configMaps/todo-web-config-dev-with-
  logging.yaml

# wait for the config change to make it to the Pod:
sleep 120

# check the new setting:
kubectl exec deploy/todo-web -- sh -c 'ls -l /app/config/*.json'

# load a few pages from the site at your Service IP address

# check the logs again:
kubectl logs -l app=todo-web
```

You can see my output in figure 4.10. The sleep is there to give the Kubernetes API time to roll out the new configuration files to the Pod; after a couple of minutes, the new configuration is loaded, and the app is operating with enhanced logging.

Volumes are a powerful option for loading config files, especially with apps like this, which react to changes and update settings on the fly. Bumping up the logging level without having to restart your app is a great help in tracking down issues. You need to be careful with your configuration, though, because volume mounts don't necessarily work the way you expect. If the mount path for a volume already exists in the container image, then the ConfigMap directory overwrites it, replacing all the contents, which can cause your app to fail in exciting ways. Listing 4.9 shows an example.

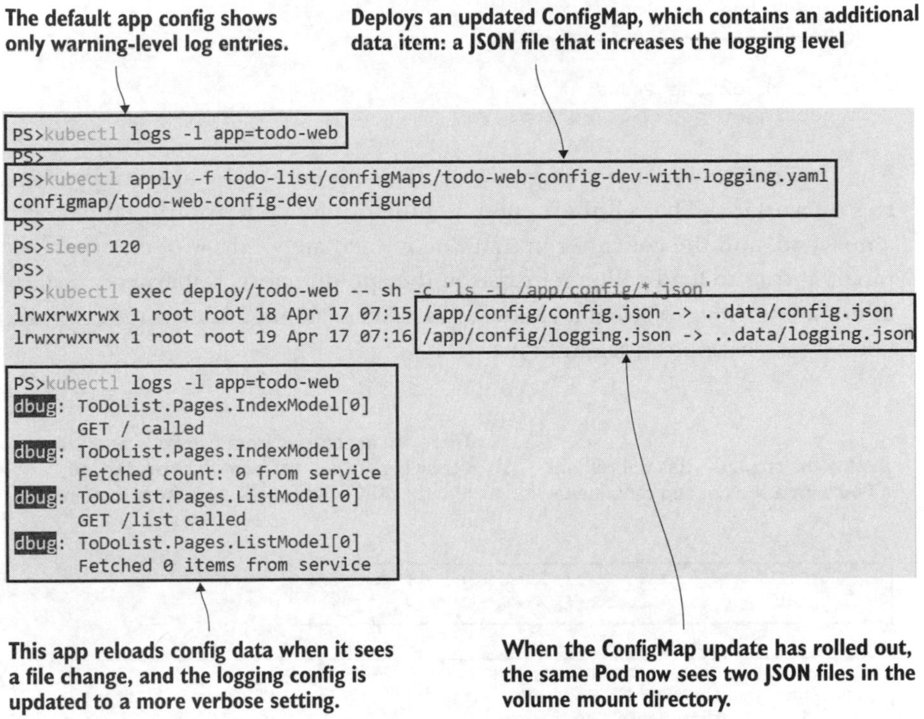

The default app config shows only warning-level log entries.

Deploys an updated ConfigMap, which contains an additional data item: a JSON file that increases the logging level

```
PS>kubectl logs -l app=todo-web
PS>
PS>kubectl apply -f todo-list/configMaps/todo-web-config-dev-with-logging.yaml
configmap/todo-web-config-dev configured
PS>
PS>sleep 120
PS>
PS>kubectl exec deploy/todo-web -- sh -c 'ls -l /app/config/*.json'
lrwxrwxrwx 1 root root 18 Apr 17 07:15 /app/config/config.json -> ..data/config.json
lrwxrwxrwx 1 root root 19 Apr 17 07:16 /app/config/logging.json -> ..data/logging.json
PS>kubectl logs -l app=todo-web
dbug: ToDoList.Pages.IndexModel[0]
      GET / called
dbug: ToDoList.Pages.IndexModel[0]
      Fetched count: 0 from service
dbug: ToDoList.Pages.ListModel[0]
      GET /list called
dbug: ToDoList.Pages.ListModel[0]
      Fetched 0 items from service
```

This app reloads config data when it sees a file change, and the logging config is updated to a more verbose setting.

When the ConfigMap update has rolled out, the same Pod now sees two JSON files in the volume mount directory.

Figure 4.10   ConfigMap data is cached, so it takes couple of minutes for updates to reach Pods.

Listing 4.9   todo-web-dev-broken.yaml, a Pod spec with a misconfigured mount

```
spec:
  containers:
    - name: web
      image: kiamol/ch04-todo-list
      volumeMounts:
        - name: config                    # Mounts the ConfigMap volume
          mountPath: "/app"                # Overwrites the directory
```

This is a broken Pod spec, where the ConfigMap is loaded into the /app directory rather than the /app/config directory. The author probably intended this to merge the directories, adding the JSON config files to the existing app directory. Instead, it's going to wipe out the application binaries.

TRY IT NOW   The Pod spec from listing 4.9 removes all the app binaries, so the replacement Pod won't start. See what happens next.

```
# deploy the badly configured Pod:
kubectl apply -f todo-list/todo-web-dev-broken.yaml

# browse back to the app and see how it looks
```

```
# check the app logs:
kubectl logs -l app=todo-web

# and check the Pod status:
kubectl get pods -l app=todo-web
```

The results here are interesting: the deployment breaks the app, and yet the app carries on working. That's Kubernetes watching out for you. Applying the change creates a new Pod, and the container in that Pod immediately exits with an error, because the binary it tries to load no longer exists in the app directory. Kubernetes restarts the container a few times to give it a chance, but it keeps failing. After three tries, Kubernetes takes a rest, as you can see in figure 4.11.

Deploy the change—this will roll out a Pod with a broken app container.

There are log entries from two Pods here: the debug log entries are from the original Pod, and the SDK failure message is from the new Pod.

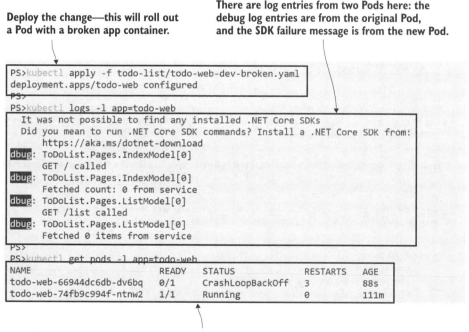

Two Pods match the Deployment label. The `Running` Pod is the original, and the new Pod has had three restarts. Kubernetes will wait before restarting the container again, which is the `CrashLoopBackOff` status.

Figure 4.11   If an updated deployment fails, then the original Pod isn't replaced.

Now we have two Pods, but Kubernetes doesn't remove the old Pod until the replacement is running successfully, which it never will in this case because we've broken the container setup. The old Pod isn't removed and still happily serves requests; the new Pod is in a failed state, but Kubernetes periodically keeps restarting the container in the hope that it might have fixed itself. This is a situation to watch out for: the apply command seems to work, and the app carries on working, but it's not using the manifest you've applied.

We'll fix that now and show one final option for surfacing ConfigMaps in the container filesystem. You can selectively load data items into the target directory, rather than loading every data item as its own file. Listing 4.10 shows the updated Pod spec. The mount path has been fixed, but the volume is set to deliver only one item.

Listing 4.10   todo-web-dev-no-logging.yaml, mounting a single ConfigMap item

```
spec:
  containers:
    - name: web
      image: kiamol/ch04-todo-list
      volumeMounts:
        - name: config                     # Mounts the ConfigMap volume
          mountPath: "/app/config"         # to the correct direcory
          readOnly: true
  volumes:
    - name: config
      configMap:
        name: todo-web-config-dev          # Loads the ConfigMap volume
        items:                             # Specifies the data items to load
        - key: config.json                 # Loads the config.json item
          path: config.json                # Surfaces it as the file config.json
```

This specification uses the same ConfigMap, so it is just an update to the deployment. This will be a cascading update: it will create a new Pod, which will start correctly, and then Kubernetes will remove the two previous Pods.

TRY IT NOW   Deploy the spec from listing 4.10, which rolls out the updated volume mount to fix the app but also ignores the logging JSON file in the ConfigMap.

```
# apply the change:
kubectl apply -f todo-list/todo-web-dev-no-logging.yaml

# list the config folder contents:
kubectl exec deploy/todo-web -- sh -c 'ls /app/config'

# now browse to a few pages on the app

# check the logs:
kubectl logs -l app=todo-web

# and check the Pods:
kubectl get pods -l app=todo-web
```

Figure 4.12 shows my output. The app is working again, but it sees only a single configuration file, so the enhanced logging settings don't get applied.

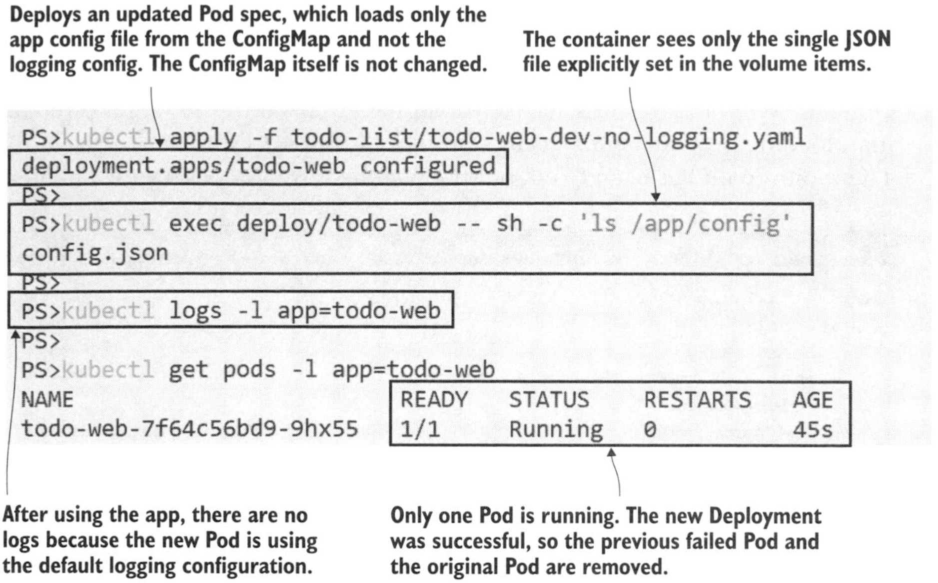

Deploys an updated Pod spec, which loads only the
app config file from the ConfigMap and not the
logging config. The ConfigMap itself is not changed.

The container sees only the single JSON
file explicitly set in the volume items.

```
PS>kubectl apply -f todo-list/todo-web-dev-no-logging.yaml
deployment.apps/todo-web configured
PS>
PS>kubectl exec deploy/todo-web -- sh -c 'ls /app/config'
config.json
PS>
PS>kubectl logs -l app=todo-web
PS>
PS>kubectl get pods -l app=todo-web
NAME                             READY   STATUS    RESTARTS   AGE
todo-web-7f64c56bd9-9hx55        1/1     Running   0          45s
```

After using the app, there are no
logs because the new Pod is using
the default logging configuration.

Only one Pod is running. The new Deployment
was successful, so the previous failed Pod and
the original Pod are removed.

Figure 4.12   Volumes can surface selected items from a ConfigMap into a mount directory.

ConfigMaps support a wide range of configuration systems. Between environment variables and volume mounts you should be able to store app settings in ConfigMaps and apply them however your app expects. The separation between the configuration spec and the app spec also supports different release workflows, allowing different teams to own different parts of the process. One thing you shouldn't use ConfigMaps for, however, is any sensitive data—they're effectively wrappers for text files with no additional security semantics. For configuration data that you need to keep secure, Kubernetes provides Secrets.

4.4   *Configuring sensitive data with Secrets*

Secrets are a separate type of resource, but they have a similar API to ConfigMaps. You work with them in the same way, but because they're meant to store sensitive information, Kubernetes manages them differently. The main differences are all around minimizing exposure. Secrets are sent only to nodes that need to use them and are stored in memory rather than on disk; Kubernetes also supports encryption both in transit and at rest for Secrets.

Secrets are not encrypted 100% of the time, though. Anyone who has access to Secret objects in your cluster can read the unencrypted values. There is an obfuscation layer: Kubernetes can read and write Secret data with Base64 encoding, which isn't really a security feature but does prevent accidental exposure of secrets to someone looking over your shoulder.

TRY IT NOW You can create Secrets from a literal value, passing the key and data into the kubectl command. The retrieved data is Base64 encoded.

```
# FOR WINDOWS USERS—this script adds a Base64 command to your session:
. .\base64.ps1

# now create a secret from a plain text literal:
kubectl create secret generic sleep-secret-literal --from-
    literal=secret=shh...

# show the friendly details of the Secret:
kubectl describe secret sleep-secret-literal

# retrieve the encoded Secret value:
kubectl get secret sleep-secret-literal -o jsonpath='{.data.secret}'

# and decode the data:
kubectl get secret sleep-secret-literal -o jsonpath='{.data.secret}' |
    base64 -d
```

You can see from the output in figure 4.13 that Kubernetes treats Secrets differently from ConfigMaps. The data values aren't shown in the kubectl describe command,

Adds a `base64` command, which is needed only for Windows users, because Linux and macOS have their own commands

Creates a Secret with the key `secret` from a literal value in the command

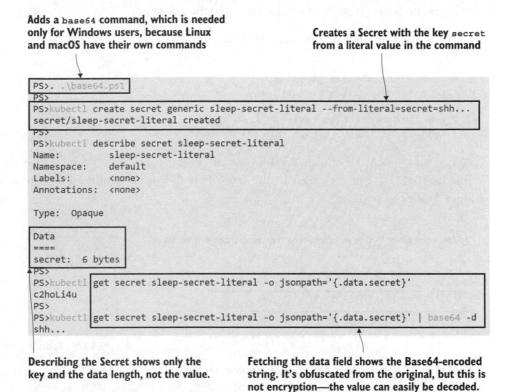

Describing the Secret shows only the key and the data length, not the value.

Fetching the data field shows the Base64-encoded string. It's obfuscated from the original, but this is not encryption—the value can easily be decoded.

Figure 4.13 Secrets have a similar API to ConfigMaps, but Kubernetes tries to avoid accidental exposure.

only the names of the item keys, and when you do fetch the data, it's shown encoded, so you need to pipe it into a decoder to read it.

That precaution doesn't apply when Secrets are surfaced inside Pod containers. The container environment sees the original plain text data. Listing 4.11 shows a return to the sleep app, configured to load the new Secret as an environment variable.

> **Listing 4.11   sleep-with-secret.yaml, a Pod spec loading a Secret**

```
spec:
  containers:
    - name: sleep
      image: kiamol/ch03-sleep
      env:                               # Environment variables
      - name: KIAMOL_SECRET              # Variable name in the container
        valueFrom:                       # loaded from an external source
          secretKeyRef:                  # which is a Secret
            name: sleep-secret-literal   # Names the Secret
            key: secret                  # Key of the Secret data item
```

The specification to consume Secrets is almost the same as for ConfigMaps—a named environment variable can be loaded from a named item in a Secret. This Pod spec delivers the Secret item in its original form to the container.

TRY IT NOW   Run a simple sleep Pod that uses the Secret as an environment variable.

```
# update the sleep Deployment:
kubectl apply -f sleep/sleep-with-secret.yaml

# check the environment variable in the Pod:
kubectl exec deploy/sleep -- printenv KIAMOL_SECRET
```

Figure 4.14 shows the output. In this case the Pod is using only a Secret, but Secrets and ConfigMaps can be mixed in the same Pod spec, populating environment variables or files or both.

Updates the sleep Pod to add the Secret as an environment variable

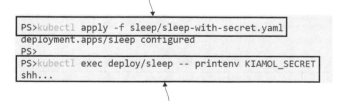

```
PS>kubectl apply -f sleep/sleep-with-secret.yaml
deployment.apps/sleep configured
PS>
PS>kubectl exec deploy/sleep -- printenv KIAMOL_SECRET
shh...
```

The Pod container sees the original plain text value of the Secret.

Figure 4.14   Secrets loaded into Pods are not Base64 encoded.

You should be wary of loading Secrets into environment variables. Securing sensitive data is all about minimizing its exposure. Environment variables can be read from any process in the Pod container, and some application platforms log all environment variable values if they hit a critical error. The alternative is to surface Secrets as files, if the application supports it, which gives you the option of securing access with file permissions.

To round off this chapter, we'll run the to-do app in a different configuration where it uses a separate database to store items, running in its own Pod. The database server is Postgres using the official image on Docker Hub, which reads logon credentials from configuration values in the environment. Listing 4.12 shows a YAML spec for creating the database password as a Secret.

> **Listing 4.12   -todo-db-secret-test.yaml, a Secret for the database user**

```
apiVersion: v1
kind: Secret                           # Secret is the resource type.
metadata:
  name: todo-db-secret-test            # Names the Secret
type: Opaque                           # Opaque secrets are for text data.
stringData:                            # stringData is for plain text.
  POSTGRES_PASSWORD: "kiamol-2*2*"     # The secret key and value.
```

This approach states the password in plain text in the `stringData` field, which gets encoded to Base64 when you create the Secret. Using YAML files for Secrets poses a tricky problem: it gives you a nice consistent deployment approach, at the cost of having all your sensitive data visible in source control.

In a production scenario, you would keep the real data out of the YAML file, using placeholders instead, and do some additional processing as part of your deployment—something like injecting the data into the placeholder from a GitHub Secret. Whichever approach you take, remember that once the Secret exists in Kubernetes, it's easy for anyone who has access to read the value.

TRY IT NOW   Create a Secret from the manifest in listing 4.12, and check the data.

```
# deploy the Secret:
kubectl apply -f todo-list/secrets/todo-db-secret-test.yaml

# check the data is encoded:
kubectl get secret todo-db-secret-test -o
  jsonpath='{.data.POSTGRES_PASSWORD}'

# see what annotations are stored:
kubectl get secret todo-db-secret-test -o
  jsonpath='{.metadata.annotations}'
```

You can see in figure 4.15 that the string is encoded to Base64. The outcome is the same as it would be if the specification used the normal data field and set the password value in Base64 directly in the YAML.

To use that Secret as the Postgres password, the image gives us a couple of options. We can load the value into an environment variable called `POSTGRES_PASSWORD`—not

Creates a Secret from a manifest, which
stores the data item in plain text

The data is Base64 encoded in the same
way as for Secrets created as literals.

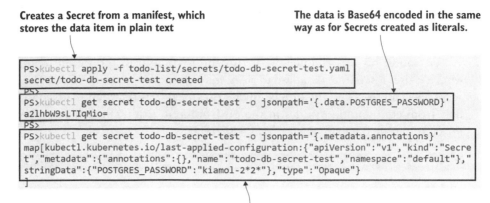

```
PS>kubectl apply -f todo-list/secrets/todo-db-secret-test.yaml
secret/todo-db-secret-test created
PS>
PS>kubectl get secret todo-db-secret-test -o jsonpath='{.data.POSTGRES_PASSWORD}'
a2lhbW9sLTIqMio=
PS>
PS>kubectl get secret todo-db-secret-test -o jsonpath='{.metadata.annotations}'
map[kubectl.kubernetes.io/last-applied-configuration:{"apiVersion":"v1","kind":"Secre
t","metadata":{"annotations":{},"name":"todo-db-secret-test","namespace":"default"},"
stringData":{"POSTGRES_PASSWORD":"kiamol-2*2*"},"type":"Opaque"}
]
```

But the original plain text is also stored in an annotation. Annotations are
used for notes about the Deployment, and this stores the whole contents.

Figure 4.15   Secrets created from string data are encoded, but the original data is also stored in
the object.

ideal—or we can load it into a file and tell Postgres where to load the file, by setting
the POSTGRES_PASSWORD_FILE environment variable. Using a file means we can control access permissions at the volume level, which is how the database is configured in
code listing 4.13.

Listing 4.13   todo-db-test.yaml, a Pod spec mounting a volume from a secret

```
spec:
  containers:
    - name: db
      image: postgres:11.6-alpine
      env:
      - name: POSTGRES_PASSWORD_FILE          # Sets the path to the file
        value: /secrets/postgres_password
      volumeMounts:                           # Mounts a Secret volume
        - name: secret                        # Names the volume
          mountPath: "/secrets"
  volumes:
    - name: secret
      secret:                                 # Volume loaded from a Secret
        secretName: todo-db-secret-test       # Secret name
        defaultMode: 0400                     # Permissions to set for files
        items:                                # Optionally names the data items
        - key: POSTGRES_PASSWORD
          path: postgres_password
```

When this Pod is deployed, Kubernetes loads the value of the Secret item into a file at
the path /secrets/postgres_password. That file will be set with 0400 permissions, which
means it can be read by the container user but not by any other users. The environment

variable is set for Postgres to load the password from that file, which the Postgres user has access to, so the database will start with credentials set from the Secret.

TRY IT NOW   Deploy the database Pod, and verify the database starts correctly.

```
# deploy the YAML from listing 4.13
kubectl apply -f todo-list/todo-db-test.yaml

# check the database logs:
kubectl logs -l app=todo-db --tail 1

# verify the password file permissions:
kubectl exec deploy/todo-db -- sh -c 'ls -l $(readlink -f
   /secrets/postgres_password)'
```

Figure 4.16 shows the database starting up and waiting for connections—indicating it has been configured correctly—and the final output verifies that the file permissions are set as expected.

Creates a ClusterIP Service for the database and a Deployment that loads the password Secret as a file into the Pod container

Postgres is ready to receive client connections, so it has been correctly configured using the environment variable and Secret.

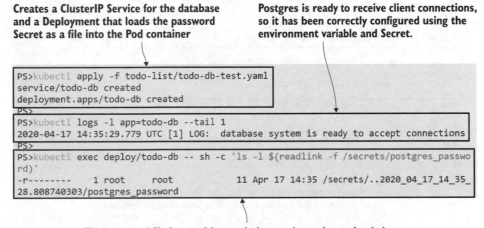

The password file is set with permissions so it can be read only by the container user. The `readlink` command gets the actual location of the file; Kubernetes uses aliases (symlinks) for the mounted files.

Figure 4.16   If the app supports it, configuration settings can be read by files populated from Secrets.

All that's left is to run the app itself in the test configuration, so it connects to the Postgres database rather than using a local database file for storage. There's lots more YAML for that, to create a ConfigMap, Secret, Deployment, and Service, but it's all using features we've covered already, so we'll just go ahead and deploy.

TRY IT NOW   Run the to-do app so it uses the Postgres database for storage.

```
# the ConfigMap configures the app to use Postgres:
kubectl apply -f todo-list/configMaps/todo-web-config-test.yaml
```

```
# the Secret contains the credentials to connect to Postgres:
kubectl apply -f todo-list/secrets/todo-web-secret-test.yaml

# the Deployment Pod spec uses the ConfigMap and Secret:
kubectl apply -f todo-list/todo-web-test.yaml

# check the database credentials are set in the app:
kubectl exec deploy/todo-web-test -- cat /app/secrets/secrets.json

# browse to the app and add some items
```

My output is shown in figure 4.17, where the plain text contents of the Secret JSON file are shown inside the web Pod container.

The full app configuration is supplied from the ConfigMap and the Secret—one stores app settings, and the other stores sensitive database credentials.

```
PS>kubectl apply -f todo-list/configMaps/todo-web-config-test.yaml
configmap/todo-web-config-test created
PS>
PS>kubectl apply -f todo-list/secrets/todo-web-secret-test.yaml
secret/todo-web-secret-test created
PS>
PS>kubectl apply -f todo-list/todo-web-test.yaml
service/todo-web-test created
deployment.apps/todo-web-test created
PS>
PS>kubectl exec deploy/todo-web-test -- cat /app/secrets/secrets.json
{
  "ConnectionStrings": {
    "ToDoDb": "Server=todo-db;Database=todo;User Id=postgres;Password=kiamol-2*2*;"
  }
}
```

Inside the container filesystem, the Secret is presented as plain text JSON, with the database connection details.

Figure 4.17   Loading app configuration into Pods and surfacing ConfigMaps and Secrets as JSON files

Now when you add to-do items in the app, they are stored in the Postgres database, so storage is separated from the application runtime. You can delete the web Pod; its controller will start a replacement with the same configuration, which connects to the same database Pod, so all the data from the original web Pod is still available.

This has been a pretty exhaustive look at configuration options in Kubernetes. The principles are quite simple—loading ConfigMaps or Secrets into environment variables or files—but there are a lot of variations. You need a good understanding of the nuances so you can manage app configuration in a consistent way, even if your apps all have different configuration models.

4.5 Managing app configuration in Kubernetes

Kubernetes gives you the tools to manage app configuration using whatever workflow fits for your organization. The core requirement is for your applications to read configuration settings from the environment, ideally with a hierarchy of files and environment variables. Then you have the flexibility to use ConfigMaps and Secrets to support your deployment process. You have two factors to consider in your design: do you need your apps to respond to live configuration updates, and how will you manage Secrets?

If live updates without a Pod replacement are important to you, then your options are limited. You can't use environment variables for settings, because any changes to those result in a Pod replacement. You can use a volume mount and load configuration changes from files, but you need to deploy changes by updating the existing ConfigMap or Secret objects. You can't change the volume to point to a new config object, because that's a Pod replacement too.

The alternative to updating the same config object is to deploy a new object every time with some versioning scheme in the object name and updating the app Deployment to reference the new object. You lose live updates but gain an audit trail of configuration changes and have an easy option to revert back to previous settings. Figure 4.18 shows those options.

App-1 loads a ConfigMap into a volume mount. The ConfigMap can be updated, and the app will see the changed data, supporting live configuration updates.

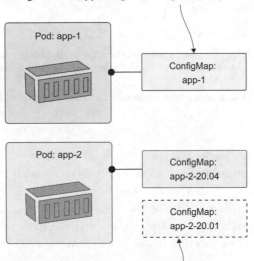

App-2 deploys a new ConfigMap for every update with a version scheme in the name. The Pod spec needs to be updated to use the new ConfigMap, so this approach doesn't support live updates, but it does give you an audit trail of configuration settings.

Figure 4.18 You can choose your own approach to configuration management, supported by Kubernetes.

The other question is how you manage sensitive data. Large organizations might have dedicated configuration management teams who own the process of deploying configuration files. That fits nicely with a versioned approach to ConfigMaps and Secrets, where the configuration management team deploys new objects from literals or controlled files in advance of the deployment.

An alternative is a fully automated deployment, where ConfigMaps and Secrets are created from YAML templates in source control. The YAML files contain placeholders instead of sensitive data, and the deployment process replaces them with real values from a secure store, like Azure KeyVault, before applying them. Figure 4.19 compares those options.

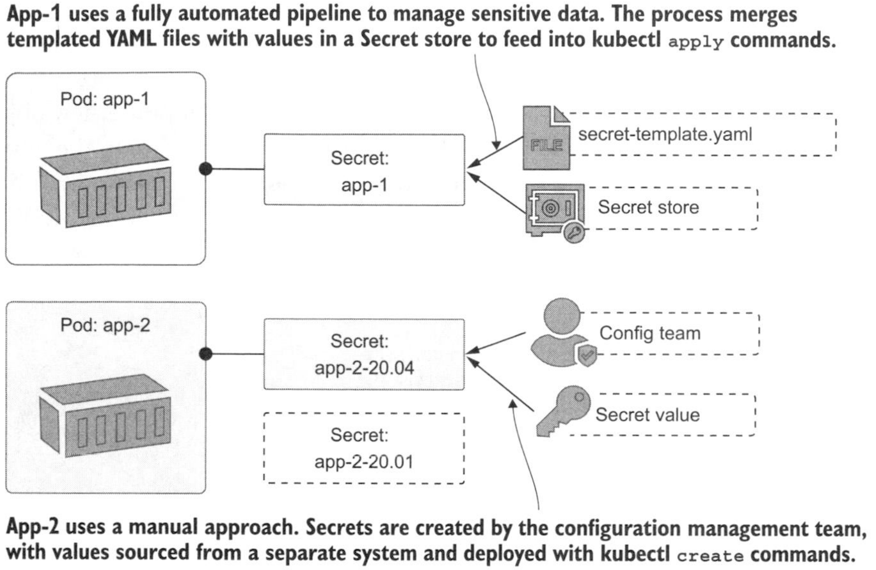

App-1 uses a fully automated pipeline to manage sensitive data. The process merges templated YAML files with values in a Secret store to feed into kubectl `apply` commands.

App-2 uses a manual approach. Secrets are created by the configuration management team, with values sourced from a separate system and deployed with kubectl `create` commands.

Figure 4.19   Secret management can be automated in deployment or strictly controlled by a separate team.

You can use any approach that works for your teams and your application stacks, remembering that the goal is for all configuration settings to be loaded from the platform, so the same container image is deployed in every environment.

It's time to clean up your cluster. If you've followed along with all the exercises (and of course you have!), you'll have a couple of dozen resources to remove. I'll introduce some useful features of kubectl to help clear everything out.

TRY IT NOW   The kubectl `delete` command can read a YAML file and delete the resources defined in the file. And if you have multiple YAML files in a directory, you can use the directory name as the argument to `delete` (or `apply`), and it will run over all the files.

```
# delete all the resources in all the files in all the directories:
kubectl delete -f sleep/
kubectl delete -f todo-list/
kubectl delete -f todo-list/configMaps/
kubectl delete -f todo-list/secrets/
```

4.6 *Lab*

If you're reeling from all the options Kubernetes gives you to configure apps, this lab is going to help. In practice, your apps will have their own ideas about configuration management, and you'll need to model your Kubernetes Deployments to suit the way your apps expect to be configured. That's what you need to do in this lab with a simple app called Adminer. Here we go:

- Adminer, a web UI for administering SQL databases, can be a handy tool to run in Kubernetes when you're troubleshooting database issues.
- Start by deploying the YAML files in the ch04/lab/postgres folder, then deploy the ch04/lab/adminer.yaml file to run Adminer in its basic state.
- Find the external IP for your Adminer Service, and browse to port 8082. Note that you need to specify a database server and that the UI design is stuck in the 1990s. You can confirm the connection to Postgres by using postgres as the database name, username, and password.
- Your job is to create and use some config objects in the Adminer Deployment so that the database server name defaults to the lab's Postgres Service, and the UI uses the much nicer design called price.
- You can set the default database server in an environment variable called ADMINER_DEFAULT_SERVER. Let's call this sensitive data, so it should use a Secret.
- The UI design is set in the environment variable ADMINER_DESIGN; that's not sensitive, so a ConfigMap will do nicely.

This will take a little bit of investigation and some thought on how to surface the configuration settings, so it's good practice for real application configuration. My solution is posted on GitHub for you to check your approach: https://github.com/sixeyed/kiamol/blob/master/ch04/lab/README.md.

Storing data with volumes, mounts, and claims

Data access in a clustered environment is difficult. Moving compute around is the easy part—the Kubernetes API is in constant contact with the nodes, and if a node stops responding, then Kubernetes can assume it's offline and start replacements for all of its Pods on other nodes. But if an application in one of those Pods was storing data on the node, then the replacement won't have access to that data when it starts on a different node, and it would be disappointing if that data contained a large order that a customer hadn't completed. You really need clusterwide storage, so Pods can access the same data from any node.

Kubernetes doesn't have built-in clusterwide storage, because there isn't a single solution that works for every scenario. Apps have different storage requirements, and the platforms that can run Kubernetes have different storage capabilities. Data is always a balance between speed of access and durability, and Kubernetes supports that by allowing you to define the different classes of storage that your cluster provides and to request a specific storage class for your application. In this chapter you'll learn how to work with different types of storage and how Kubernetes abstracts away storage implementation details.

5.1 How Kubernetes builds the container filesystem

Containers in Pods have their filesystem constructed by Kubernetes using multiple sources. The container image provides the initial contents of the filesystem, and every container has a writable storage layer, which it uses to write new files or to update any files from the image. (Docker images are read-only, so when a container updates a file from the image, it's actually updating a copy of the file in its own writable layer.) Figure 5.1 shows how that looks inside the Pod.

Each container in a Pod has its own filesystem, which is constructed by Kubernetes.

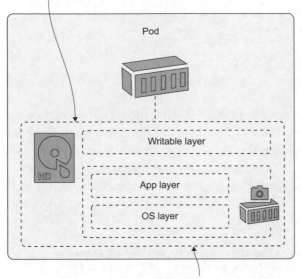

The filesystem can be built from multiple sources—at a minimum, the layers from the container image and the writable layer for the container.

Figure 5.1 Containers don't know it, but their filesystem is a virtual construct, built by Kubernetes.

The application running in the container just sees a single filesystem to which it has read and write access, and all those layer details are hidden. That's great for moving apps to Kubernetes because they don't need to change to run in a Pod. But if your apps do write data, you will need to understand how they use storage and design your Pods to support their requirements. Otherwise, your apps will seem to be running fine, but you're setting yourself up for data loss when anything unexpected happens—like a Pod restarting with a new container.

TRY IT NOW If the app inside a container crashes and the container exits, the Pod will start a replacement. The new container will start with the filesystem from the container image and a new writable layer, and any data written by the previous container in its writable layer is gone.

```
# switch to this chapter's exercise directory:
cd ch05

# deploy a sleep Pod:
kubectl apply -f sleep/sleep.yaml

# write a file inside the container:
kubectl exec deploy/sleep -- sh -c 'echo ch05 > /file.txt; ls /*.txt'

# check the container ID:
kubectl get pod -l app=sleep -o
   jsonpath='{.items[0].status.containerStatuses[0].containerID}'
```

```
# kill all processes in the container, causing a Pod restart:
kubectl exec -it deploy/sleep -- killall5

# check the replacment container ID:
kubectl get pod -l app=sleep -o
    jsonpath='{.items[0].status.containerStatuses[0].containerID}'

# look for the file you wrote—it won't be there:
kubectl exec deploy/sleep -- ls /*.txt
```

Remember two important things from this exercise: the filesystem of a Pod container has the life cycle of the container rather than the Pod, and when Kubernetes talks about a Pod restart, it's actually referring to a replacement container. If your apps are merrily writing data inside containers, that data doesn't get stored at the Pod level—if the Pod restarts with a new container, all the data is gone. My output in figure 5.2 shows that.

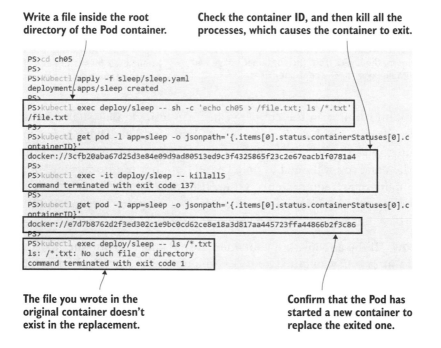

Write a file inside the root directory of the Pod container.

Check the container ID, and then kill all the processes, which causes the container to exit.

The file you wrote in the original container doesn't exist in the replacement.

Confirm that the Pod has started a new container to replace the exited one.

Figure 5.2   The writable layer has the life cycle of the container, not the Pod.

We already know that Kubernetes can build the container filesystem from other sources—we surfaced ConfigMaps and Secrets into filesystem directories in chapter 4. The mechanism for that is to define a volume at the Pod level that makes another storage source available and then to mount it into the container filesystem at a specified path. ConfigMaps and Secrets are read-only storage units, but Kubernetes supports many other types of volume that are writable. Figure 5.3 shows how you can design a Pod that uses a volume to store data that persists between restarts and could even be accessible clusterwide.

The container filesystem can be expanded with other sources, like ConfigMaps and Secrets, which are mounted to a specific path in the container.

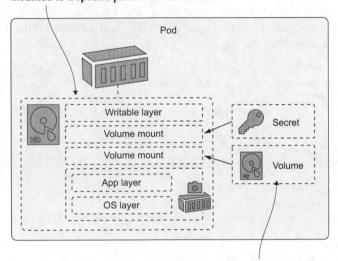

Volumes are another source of storage. They're defined at the Pod level, can be read-only or editable, and can be backed by different types of storage, from the disk on the node where the Pod is running, to a networked filesystem.

Figure 5.3 The virtual filesystem can be built from volumes that refer to external pieces of storage.

We'll come to clusterwide volumes later in the chapter, but for now, we'll start with a much simpler volume type, which is still useful for many scenarios. Listing 5.1 shows a Pod spec using a type of volume called EmptyDir, which is just an empty directory, but it's stored at the Pod level rather than at the container level. It is mounted as a volume into the container, so it's visible as a directory, but it's not one of the image or container layers.

Listing 5.1   **sleep-with-emptyDir.yaml, a simple volume spec**

```
spec:
  containers:
    - name: sleep
      image: kiamol/ch03-sleep
      volumeMounts:
        - name: data                   # Mounts a volume called data
          mountPath: /data             # into the /data directory
```

```
volumes:
  - name: data                    # This is the data volume spec,
    emptyDir: {}                   # which is the EmptyDir type.
```

An empty directory sounds like the least useful piece of storage you can imagine, but actually it has a lot of uses because it has the same life cycle as the Pod. Any data stored in an `EmptyDir` volume remains in the Pod between restarts, so replacement containers can access data written by their predecessors.

> **TRY IT NOW**   Update the sleep deployment using the spec from listing 5.1, adding an `EmptyDir` volume. Now you can write data and kill the container and the replacement can read the data.

```
# update the sleep Pod to use an EmptyDir volume:
kubectl apply -f sleep/sleep-with-emptyDir.yaml

# list the contents of the volume mount:
kubectl exec deploy/sleep -- ls /data

# create a file in the empty directory:
kubectl exec deploy/sleep -- sh -c 'echo ch05 > /data/file.txt; ls /data'

# check the container ID:
kubectl get pod -l app-sleep -o
    jsonpath='{.items[0].status.containerStatuses[0].containerID}'

# kill the container processes:
kubectl exec deploy/sleep -- killall5

# check replacement container ID:
kubectl get pod -l app=sleep -o
    jsonpath='{.items[0].status.containerStatuses[0].containerID}'

# read the file in the volume:
kubectl exec deploy/sleep -- cat /data/file.txt
```

You can see my output in figure 5.4. The containers just see a directory in the filesystem, but it points to a storage unit which is part of the Pod.

You can use `EmptyDir` volumes for any applications that use the filesystem for temporary storage—maybe your app calls an API, which takes a few seconds to respond, and the response is valid for a long time. The app might save the API response in a local file because reading from disk is faster than repeating the API call. An `EmptyDir` volume is a reasonable source for a local cache because if the app crashes, then the replacement container will still have the cached files and still benefit from the speed boost.

`EmptyDir` volumes only share the life cycle of the Pod, so if the Pod is replaced, then the new Pod starts with, well, an empty directory. If you want your data to persist between Pods, then you can mount other types of volume that have their own life cycles.

Deploy a Pod that mounts an `EmptyDir` **volume into the container filesystem.**

Write a file in the `EmptyDir` **directory mount.**

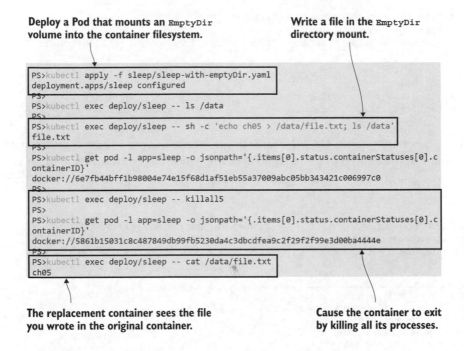

```
PS>kubectl apply -f sleep/sleep-with-emptyDir.yaml
deployment.apps/sleep configured
PS>
PS>kubectl exec deploy/sleep -- ls /data
PS>
PS>kubectl exec deploy/sleep -- sh -c 'echo ch05 > /data/file.txt; ls /data'
file.txt
PS>
PS>kubectl get pod -l app=sleep -o jsonpath='{.items[0].status.containerStatuses[0].c
ontainerID}'
docker://6e7fb44bff1b98004e74e15f68d1af51eb55a37009abc05bb343421c006997c0
PS>
PS>kubectl exec deploy/sleep -- killall5
PS>
PS>kubectl get pod -l app=sleep -o jsonpath='{.items[0].status.containerStatuses[0].c
ontainerID}'
docker://5861b15031c8c487849db99fb5230da4c3dbcdfea9c2f29f2f99e3d00ba4444e
PS>
PS>kubectl exec deploy/sleep -- cat /data/file.txt
ch05
```

The replacement container sees the file you wrote in the original container.

Cause the container to exit by killing all its processes.

Figure 5.4 Something as basic as an empty directory is still useful because it can be shared by containers.

5.2   *Storing data on a node with volumes and mounts*

This is where working with data gets trickier than working with compute, because we need to think about whether data will be tied to a particular node—meaning any replacement Pods will need to run on that node to see the data—or whether the data has clusterwide access and the Pod can run on any node. Kubernetes supports many variations, but you need to know what you want and what your cluster supports and specify that for the Pod.

The simplest storage option is to use a volume that maps to a directory on the node, so when the container writes to the volume mount, the data is actually stored in a known directory on the node's disk. We'll demonstrate that by running a real app that uses an `EmptyDir` volume for cache data, understanding the limitations, and then upgrading it to use node-level storage.

TRY IT NOW   Run a web application that uses a proxy component to improve performance. The web app runs in a Pod with an internal Service, and the proxy runs in another Pod, which is publicly available on a LoadBalancer Service.

```
# deploy the Pi application:
kubectl apply -f pi/v1/

# wait for the web Pod to be ready:
kubectl wait --for=condition=Ready pod -l app=pi-web
```

```
# find the app URL from your LoadBalancer:
kubectl get svc pi-proxy -o
   jsonpath='http://{.status.loadBalancer.ingress[0].*}:8080/?dp=30000'

# browse to the URL, wait for the response then refresh the page

# check the cache in the proxy
kubectl exec deploy/pi-proxy -- ls -l /data/nginx/cache
```

This is a common setup for web applications, where the proxy boosts performance by serving responses directly from its local cache, and that also reduces load on the web app. You can see my output in figure 5.5. The first Pi calculation took more than one

Deploy a Pi-calculating app that uses a proxy to cache responses from a web application.

Browse to the app. Computing Pi to 30,000 decimal places takes over a second. Refresh the browser, and the response will be much faster.

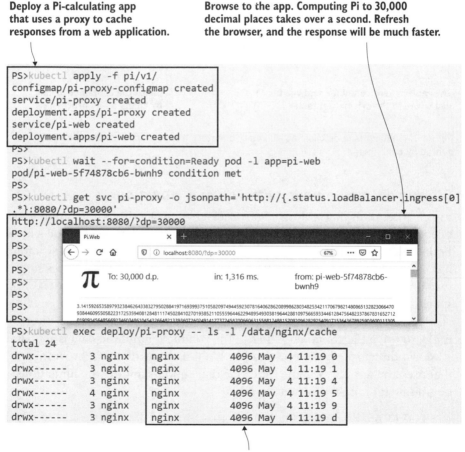

That's because the proxy cached the response from the first call and served it for the second call, bypassing the web app. This is the directory structure the proxy cache uses, which is an `EmptyDir` **mount.**

Figure 5.5   Caching files in an `EmptyDir` **volume means the cache survives Pod restarts.**

second to respond, and the refresh was practically immediate because it came from the proxy and did not need to be calculated.

An `EmptyDir` volume could be a reasonable approach for an app like this, because the data stored in the volume is not critical. If there's a Pod restart, then the cache survives, and the new proxy container can serve responses cached by the previous container. If the Pod is replaced, then the cache is lost. The replacement Pod starts with an empty cache directory, but the cache isn't required—the app still functions correctly; it just starts off slow until the cache gets filled again.

> **TRY IT NOW** Remove the proxy Pod. It will be replaced because it's managed by a deployment controller. The replacement starts with a new `EmptyDir` volume, which for this app means an empty proxy cache so requests are sent on to the web Pod.

```
# delete the proxy Pod:
kubectl delete pod -l app=pi-proxy

# check the cache directory of the replacement Pod:
kubectl exec deploy/pi-proxy -- ls -l /data/nginx/cache

# refresh your browser at the Pi app URL
```

My output is shown in figure 5.6. The result is the same, but I had to wait another second for it to be calculated by the web app, because the replacement proxy Pod started without a cache.

Deleting the Pod means the Deployment controller starts a replacement—the new Pod has a new `EmptyDir` volume.

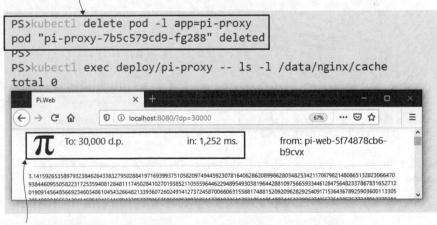

Replacing the Pod means the original proxy cache is lost, so when I refresh the browser, I get the same response, but it takes another second to calculate.

Figure 5.6 A new Pod starts with a new empty directory.

The next level of durability comes from using a volume that maps to a directory on the node's disk, which Kubernetes calls a HostPath volume. HostPaths are specified as a volume in the Pod, which is mounted into the container filesystem in the usual way. When the container writes data into the mount directory, it actually is written to the disk on the node. Figure 5.7 shows the relationship among node, Pod, and volume.

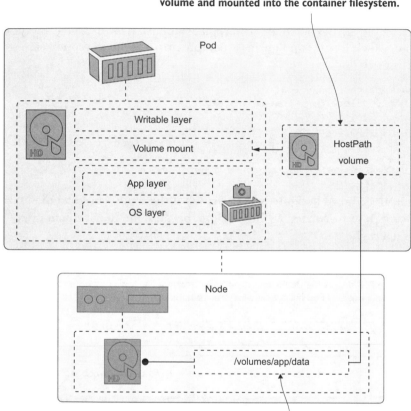

A HostPath volume is defined in the Pod spec like any volume and mounted into the container filesystem.

The data in the volume is actually stored in a directory on the host node's filesystem. If the pod is replaced, it will have access to the files, but only if it runs on the same node.

Figure 5.7   HostPath volumes maintain data between Pod replacements, but only if Pods use the same node.

HostPath volumes can be useful, but you need to be aware of their limitations. Data is physically stored on the node, and that's that. Kubernetes doesn't magically replicate that data to all the other nodes in the cluster. Listing 5.2 shows an updated Pod spec for the web proxy that uses a HostPath volume instead of an EmptyDir. When the proxy container writes cache files to /data/nginx/cache, they will actually be stored on the node at /volumes/nginx/cache.

Listing 5.2   nginx-with-hostPath.yaml, mounting a HostPath volume

```
spec:                  # This is an abridged Pod spec;
  containers:          # the full spec also contains a configMap volume mount.
   - image: nginx:1.17-alpine
     name: nginx
     ports:
        - containerPort: 80
     volumeMounts:
        - name: cache-volume
          mountPath: /data/nginx/cache     # The proxy cache path
  volumes:
    - name: cache-volume
      hostPath:                            # Using a directory on the node
        path: /volumes/nginx/cache         # The volume path on the node
        type: DirectoryOrCreate            # creates a path if it doesn't exist
```

This method extends the durability of the data beyond the life cycle of the Pod to the life cycle of the node's disk, provided replacement Pods always run on the same node. That will be the case in a single-node lab cluster because there's only one node. Replacement Pods will load the HostPath volume when they start, and if it is populated with cache data from a previous Pod, then the new proxy can start serving cached data straight away.

> **TRY IT NOW**   Update the proxy deployment to use the Pod spec from listing 5.2, then use the app and delete the Pod. The replacement responds using the existing cache.
>
> ```
> # update the proxy Pod to use a HostPath volume:
> kubectl apply -f pi/nginx-with-hostPath.yaml
>
> # list the contents of the cache directory:
> kubectl exec deploy/pi-proxy -- ls -l /data/nginx/cache
>
> # browse to the app URL
>
> # delete the proxy Pod:
> kubectl delete pod -l app=pi-proxy
>
> # check the cache directory in the replacement Pod:
> kubectl exec deploy/pi-proxy -- ls -l /data/nginx/cache
>
> # refresh your browser
> ```

My output appears in figure 5.8. The initial request took just under a second to respond, but the refresh was pretty much instananeous because the new Pod inherited the cached response from the old Pod, stored on the node.

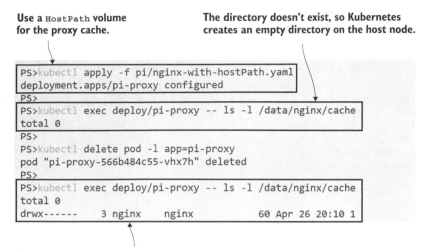

Use a `HostPath` volume for the proxy cache.

The directory doesn't exist, so Kubernetes creates an empty directory on the host node.

Using the app populates the cache volume. The replacement Pod runs on the same node and uses the same volume, so it has access to the cache written by the previous Pod.

Figure 5.8   On a single-node cluster, Pods always run on the same node, so they can all use the `HostPath`.

The obvious problem with `HostPath` volumes is that they don't make sense in a cluster with more than one node, which is pretty much every cluster outside of a simple lab environment. You can include a requirement in your Pod spec to say the Pod should always run on the same node, to make sure it goes where the data is, but doing so limits the resilience of your solution—if the node goes offline, then the Pod won't run, and you lose your app.

A less obvious problem is that method presents a nice security exploit. Kubernetes doesn't restrict which directories on the node are available to use for `HostPath` volumes. The Pod spec shown in listing 5.3 is perfectly valid, and it makes the entire filesystem on the node available for the Pod container to access.

Listing 5.3   sleep-with-hostPath.yaml, a Pod with full access to the node's disk

```
spec:
  containers:
    - name: sleep
      image: kiamol/ch03-sleep
      volumeMounts:
        - name: node-root
          mountPath: /node-root
  volumes:
    - name: node-root
      hostPath:
        path: /                   # The root of the node's filesystem
        type: Directory           # path needs to exist.
```

Anyone who has access to create a Pod from that specification now has access to the whole filesystem of the node where the Pod is running. You might be tempted to use a volume mount like this as a quick way to read multiple paths on the host, but if your app is compromised and an attacker can execute commands in the container, then they also have access to the node's disk.

TRY IT NOW Run a Pod from the YAML shown in listing 5.3, and then run some commands in the Pod container to explore the node's filesystem.

```
# run a Pod with a volume mount to the host:
kubectl apply -f sleep/sleep-with-hostPath.yaml

# check the log files inside the container:
kubectl exec deploy/sleep -- ls -l /var/log

# check the logs on the node using the volume:
kubectl exec deploy/sleep -- ls -l /node-root/var/log

# check the container user:
kubectl exec deploy/sleep -- whoami
```

As shown in figure 5.9, the Pod container can see the log files on the node, which in this case includes the Kubernetes logs. This is fairly harmless, but this container runs as the root user, which maps to the root user on the node, so the container has complete access to the filesystem.

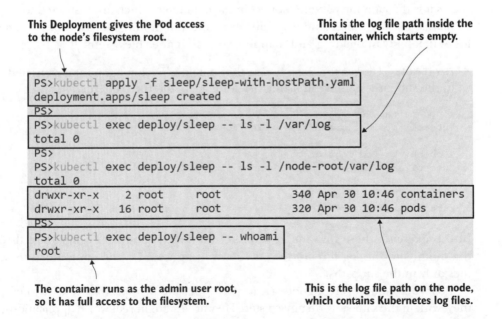

This Deployment gives the Pod access to the node's filesystem root.

This is the log file path inside the container, which starts empty.

The container runs as the admin user root, so it has full access to the filesystem.

This is the log file path on the node, which contains Kubernetes log files.

Figure 5.9　Danger! Mounting a HostPath can give you complete access to the data on the node.

If this all seems like a terrible idea, remember that Kubernetes is a platform with a wide range of features to suit many applications. You could have an older app that needs to access specific file paths on the node where it is running, and the HostPath volume lets you do that. In that scenario, you can take a safer approach, using a volume that has access to one path on the node, which limits what the container can see by declaring subpaths for the volume mount. Listing 5.4 shows that.

> **Listing 5.4   sleep-with-hostPath-subPath.yaml, restricting mounts with subpaths**

```
spec:
  containers:
    - name: sleep
      image: kiamol/ch03-sleep
      volumeMounts:
        - name: node-root              # Name of the volume to mount
          mountPath: /pod-logs         # Target path for the container
          subPath: var/log/pods        # Source path within the volume
        - name: node-root
          mountPath: /container-logs
          subPath: var/log/containers
  volumes:
    - name: node-root
      hostPath:
        path: /
        type: Directory
```

Here, the volume is still defined at the root path on the node, but the only way to access it is through the volume mounts in the container, which are restricted to defined subpaths. Between the volume specification and the mount specification, you have a lot of flexibility in building and mapping your container filesystem.

TRY IT NOW   Update the sleep Pod so the container's volume mount is restricted to the subpaths defined in listing 5.4, and check the file contents.

```
# update the Pod spec:
kubectl apply -f sleep/sleep-with-hostPath-subPath.yaml

# check the Pod logs on the node:
kubectl exec deploy/sleep -- sh -c 'ls /pod-logs | grep _pi-'

# check the container logs:
kubectl exec deploy/sleep -- sh -c 'ls /container-logs | grep nginx'
```

In this exercise, there's no way to explore the node's filesystem other than through the mounts to the log directories. As shown in figure 5.10, the container can access files only in the subpaths.

HostPath volumes are a good way to start with stateful apps; they're easy to use, and they work in the same way on any cluster. They are useful in real-world applications, too, but only when your apps are using state for temporary storage. For permanent storage, we need to move on to volumes which can be accessed by any node in the cluster.

Updates the Pod using the same `HostPath` **volume
but with subpaths defined in the volume mounts**

```
PS>kubectl apply -f sleep/sleep-with-hostPath-subPath.yaml
deployment.apps/sleep configured
PS>
PS>kubectl exec deploy/sleep -- sh -c 'ls /pod-logs | grep _pi-'
default_pi-proxy-566b484c55-d4kzq_8757483a-2d00-4729-806a-2abc2f6fe47
9
default_pi-proxy-7b5c579cd9-wpzmg_d0dae7ca-e9eb-445e-8d1f-6ce81189a7f
a
default_pi-web-5f74878cb6-b9cvx_27db66ea-523c-4524-8e8a-c7c96aa87eca
PS>
PS>kubectl exec deploy/sleep -- sh -c 'ls /container-logs | grep ngin
x'
pi-proxy-7b5c579cd9-wpzmg_default_nginx-e8d3a14d349f72c826625bea3fa4a
3ba16081bb71f545cafef97015232ce34ad.log
```

**The Pod container can still access files on the
host node but only from the specified subpaths.**

Figure 5.10　Restricting access to volumes with subpaths limits what the container can do.

5.3　Storing clusterwide data with persistent volumes and claims

A Kubernetes cluster is like a pool of resources: it has a number of nodes, which each have some CPU and memory capacity they make available to the cluster, and Kubernetes uses that to run your apps. Storage is just another resource that Kubernetes makes available to your application, but it can only provide clusterwide storage if the nodes can plug into a distributed storage system. Figure 5.11 shows how Pods can access volumes from any node if the volume uses distributed storage.

Kubernetes supports many volume types backed by distributed storage systems: AKS clusters can use Azure Files or Azure Disk, EKS clusters can use Elastic Block Store, and in the datacenter, you can use simple Network File System (NFS) shares, or a networked filesystem like GlusterFS. All of these systems have different configuration requirements, and you can specify them in the volume spec for your Pod. Doing so would make your application spec tightly coupled to one storage implementation, and Kubernetes provides a more flexible approach.

Pods are an abstraction over the compute layer, and Services are an abstraction over the network layer. In the storage layer, the abstractions are PersistentVolumes (PV) and PersistentVolumeClaims. A PersistentVolume is a Kubernetes object that defines an available piece of storage. A cluster administrator may create a set of PersistentVolumes, which each contain the volume spec for the underlying storage system. Listing 5.5 shows a PersistentVolume spec that uses NFS storage.

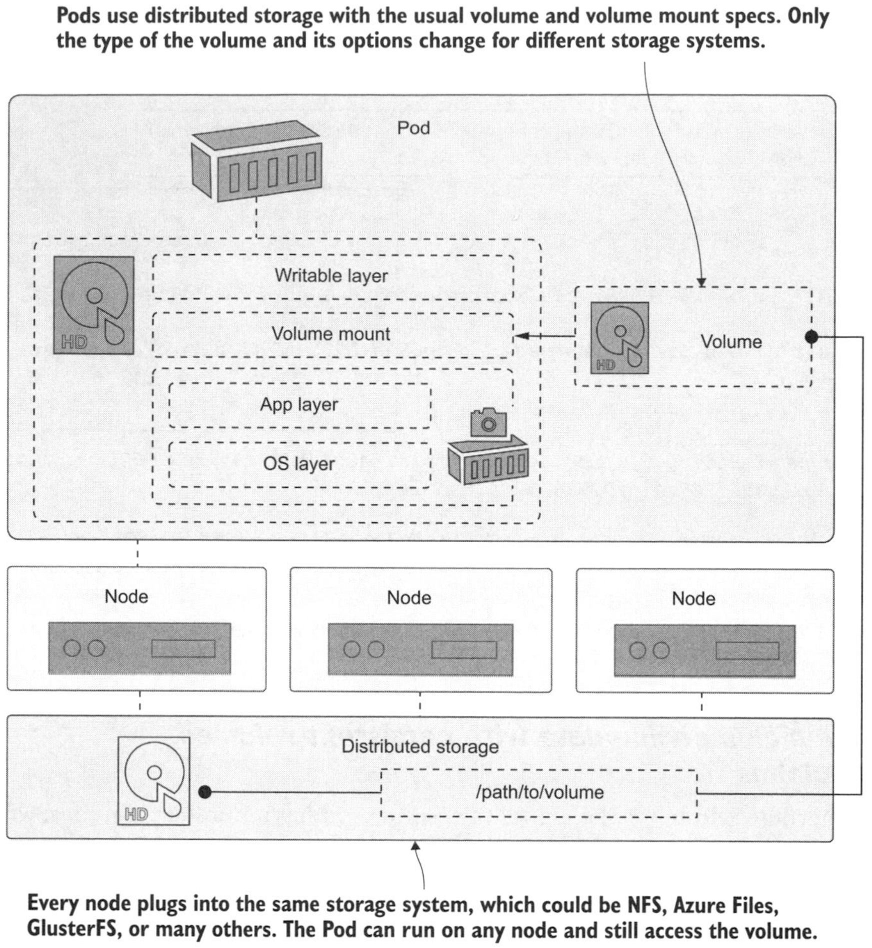
Pods use distributed storage with the usual volume and volume mount specs. Only the type of the volume and its options change for different storage systems.
Pod
HD
Writable layer
Volume mount
App layer
OS layer
HD
Volume
Node
Node
Node
HD
Distributed storage
/path/to/volume
Every node plugs into the same storage system, which could be NFS, Azure Files, GlusterFS, or many others. The Pod can run on any node and still access the volume.

Figure 5.11 Distributed storage gives your Pod access to data from any node, but it needs platform support.

Listing 5.5 persistentVolume-nfs.yaml, a volume backed by an NFS mount

```
apiVersion: v1
kind: PersistentVolume
metadata:
  name: pv01                 # A generic storage unit with a generic name

spec:
  capacity:
    storage: 50Mi            # The amount of storage the PV offers
  accessModes:               # How the volume can be accessed by Pods
    - ReadWriteOnce          # It can only be used by one Pod.
```

```
nfs:                                  # This PV is backed by NFS.
  server: nfs.my.network              # Domain name of the NFS server
  path: "/kubernetes-volumes"         # Path to the NFS share
```

You won't be able to deploy that spec in your lab environment, unless you happen to have an NFS server in your network with the domain name nfs.my.network and a share called kubernetes-volumes. You could be running Kubernetes on any platform, so for the exercises that follow, we'll use a local volume that will work anywhere. (If I used Azure Files in the exercises, they would work only on an AKS cluster, because EKS and Docker Desktop and the other Kubernetes distributions aren't configured for Azure volume types.)

TRY IT NOW Create a PV that uses local storage. The PV is clusterwide, but the volume is local to one node, so we need to make sure the PV is linked to the node where the volume lives. We'll do that with labels.

```
# apply a custom label to the first node in your cluster:
kubectl label node $(kubectl get nodes -o
  jsonpath='{.items[0].metadata.name}') kiamol=ch05

# check the nodes with a label selector:
kubectl get nodes -l kiamol=ch05

# deploy a PV that uses a local volume on the labeled node:
kubectl apply -f todo-list/persistentVolume.yaml

# check the PV:
kubectl get pv
```

My output is shown in figure 5.12. The node labeling is necessary only because I'm not using a distributed storage system; you would normally just specify the NFS or Azure Disk volume configuration, which is accessible from any node. A local volume exists on only one node, and the PV identifies that node using the label.

Now the PV exists in the cluster as an available storage unit, with a known set of features, including the size and access mode. Pods can't use that PV directly; instead, they need to claim it using a PersistentVolumeClaim (PVC). The PVC is the storage abstraction that Pods use, and it just requests some storage for an application. The PVC gets matched to a PV by Kubernetes, and it leaves the underlying volume details to the PV. Listing 5.6 shows a claim for some storage that will be matched to the PV we created.

Listing 5.6 postgres-persistentVolumeClaim.yaml, a PVC matching the PV

```
apiVersion: v1
kind: PersistentVolumeClaim
metadata:
  name: postgres-pvc          # The claim will be used by a specific app.
spec:
  accessModes:                # The required access mode
    - ReadWriteOnce
```

```
resources:
  requests:
    storage: 40Mi          # The amount of storage requested
storageClassName: ""       # A blank class means a PV needs to exist.
```

Add a label to a node in the cluster. This is used to identify where the volume is stored, and it's necessary only because I don't have distributed storage in my cluster.

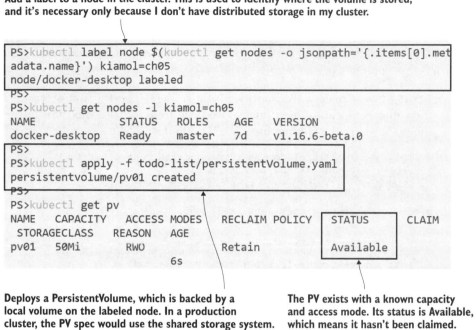

```
PS>kubectl label node $(kubectl get nodes -o jsonpath='{.items[0].met
adata.name}') kiamol=ch05
node/docker-desktop labeled
PS>
PS>kubectl get nodes -l kiamol=ch05
NAME              STATUS    ROLES     AGE    VERSION
docker-desktop    Ready     master    7d     v1.16.6-beta.0
PS>
PS>kubectl apply -f todo-list/persistentVolume.yaml
persistentvolume/pv01 created
PS>
PS>kubectl get pv
NAME     CAPACITY     ACCESS MODES    RECLAIM POLICY    STATUS       CLAIM
  STORAGECLASS    REASON    AGE
pv01     50Mi         RWO             Retain            Available
                               6s
```

Deploys a PersistentVolume, which is backed by a local volume on the labeled node. In a production cluster, the PV spec would use the shared storage system.

The PV exists with a known capacity and access mode. Its status is Available, which means it hasn't been claimed.

Figure 5.12   If you don't have distributed storage, you can cheat by pinning a PV to a local volume.

The PVC spec includes an access mode, storage amount, and storage class. If no storage class is specified, Kubernetes tries to find an existing PV that matches the requirements in the claim. If there is a match, then the PVC is bound to the PV—there is a one-to-one link, so once a PV is claimed, it is not available for any other PVCs to use.

TRY IT NOW   Deploy the PVC from listing 5.6. Its requirements are met by the PV we created in the previous exercise, so the claim will be bound to that volume.

```
# create a PVC that will bind to the PV:
kubectl apply -f todo-list/postgres-persistentVolumeClaim.yaml

# check PVCs:
kubectl get pvc

# check PVs:
kubectl get pv
```

My output appears in figure 5.13, where you can see the one-to-one binding: the PVC is bound to the volume, and the PV is bound by the claim.

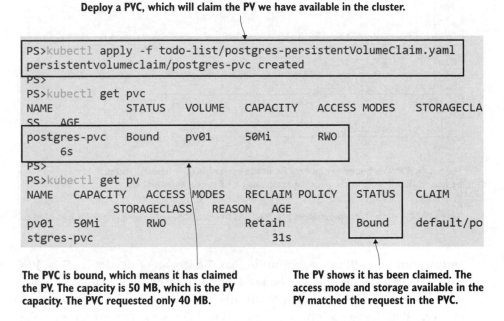

Deploy a PVC, which will claim the PV we have available in the cluster.

```
PS>kubectl apply -f todo-list/postgres-persistentVolumeClaim.yaml
persistentvolumeclaim/postgres-pvc created
PS>
PS>kubectl get pvc
NAME             STATUS    VOLUME    CAPACITY    ACCESS MODES    STORAGECLA
SS   AGE
postgres-pvc     Bound     pv01      50Mi           RWO
     6s
PS>
PS>kubectl get pv
NAME    CAPACITY    ACCESS MODES    RECLAIM POLICY    STATUS    CLAIM
                    STORAGECLASS    REASON    AGE
pv01    50Mi        RWO                        Retain           Bound     default/po
stgres-pvc                                     31s
```

The PVC is bound, which means it has claimed the PV. The capacity is 50 MB, which is the PV capacity. The PVC requested only 40 MB.

The PV shows it has been claimed. The access mode and storage available in the PV matched the request in the PVC.

Figure 5.13   PVs are just units of storage in the cluster; you claim them for your app with a PVC.

This is a static provisioning approach, where the PV needs to be explicitly created so Kubernetes can bind to it. If there is no matching PV when you create a PVC, the claim is still created, but it's not usable. It will stay in the system waiting for a PV to be created that meets its requirements.

> **TRY IT NOW**   The PV in your cluster is already bound to a claim, so it can't be used again. Create another PVC that will remain unbound.

```
# create a PVC that doesn't match any available PVs:
kubectl apply -f todo-list/postgres-persistentVolumeClaim-too-big.yaml

# check claims:
kubectl get pvc
```

You can see in figure 5.14 that the new PVC is in the Pending status. It will remain that way until a PV appears in the cluster with at least 100 MB capacity, which is the storage request in this claim.

A PVC needs to be bound before a Pod can use it. If you deploy a Pod that references an unbound PVC, the Pod will stay in the Pending state until the PVC is bound,

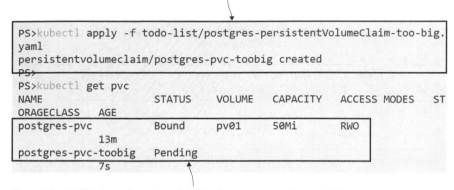

Deploys a PVC that requests 100 MB of storage. There are no available PVs in the cluster that can satisfy the claim.

```
PS>kubectl apply -f todo-list/postgres-persistentVolumeClaim-too-big.
yaml
persistentvolumeclaim/postgres-pvc-toobig created
PS>
PS>kubectl get pvc
NAME                     STATUS    VOLUME    CAPACITY   ACCESS MODES    ST
ORAGECLASS    AGE
postgres-pvc             Bound     pv01      50Mi       RWO
              13m
postgres-pvc-toobig      Pending
              7s
```

The original PVC is bound to the only PV in the system, so the new PVC cannot be bound. It will stay in the pending state until a PV becomes available.

Figure 5.14   With static provisioning, a PVC will be unusable until there is a PV it can bind to.

and so your app will never run until it has the storage it needs. The first PVC we created has been bound, so it can be used, but by only one Pod. The access mode of the claim is ReadWriteOnce, which means the volume is writable but can be mounted by only one Pod. Listing 5.7 shows an abbreviated Pod spec for a Postgres database, using the PVC for storage.

Listing 5.7   todo-db.yaml, a Pod spec consuming a PVC

```
spec:
  containers:
    - name: db
      image: postgres:11.6-alpine
      volumeMounts:
        - name: data
          mountPath: /var/lib/postgresql/data
  volumes:
    - name: data
      persistentVolumeClaim:          # Volume uses a PVC
        claimName: postgres-pvc        # PVC to use
```

Now we have all the pieces in place to deploy a Postgres database Pod using a volume, which may or may not be backed by distributed storage. The application designer owns the Pod spec and the PVC and isn't concerned about the PV—that's dependent on the infrastructure of the Kubernetes cluster and could be managed by a different team. In our lab environment, we own it all. We need to take one more step: create the directory path on the node that the volume expects to use.

TRY IT NOW   You probably won't have access to log on to the nodes in a real Kubernetes cluster, so we'll cheat here by running a sleep Pod, which has a HostPath mount to the node's root, and create the directory using the mount.

```
# run the sleep Pod, which has access to the node's disk:
kubectl apply -f sleep/sleep-with-hostPath.yaml

# wait for the Pod to be ready:
kubectl wait --for=condition=Ready pod -l app=sleep

# create the directory path on the node, which the PV expects:
kubectl exec deploy/sleep -- mkdir -p /node-root/volumes/pv01
```

Figure 5.15 shows the sleep Pod running with root permissions, so it can create the directory on the node, even though I don't have access to the node directly.

```
PS>kubectl apply -f sleep/sleep-with-hostPath.yaml
deployment.apps/sleep configured
PS>
PS>kubectl exec deploy/sleep -- mkdir -p /node-root/volumes/pv01
```

This is the path on the host that the PV expects to use. We can create it using a Pod that has access to the node's filesystem.

Figure 5.15   In this example, the HostPath is an alternative way to access the PV source on the node.

Everything is in place now to run the to-do list app with persistent storage. Normally, you won't need to go through as many steps as this, because you'll know the capabilities your cluster provides. I don't know what your cluster can do, however, so these exercises work on any cluster, and they've been a useful introduction to all the storage resources. Figure 5.16 shows what we've deployed so far, along with the database we're about to deploy.

Let's run the database. When the Postgres container is created, it mounts the volume in the Pod, which is backed by the PVC. This new database container connects to an empty volume, so when it starts up, it will initialize the database, creating the write-ahead log (WAL), which is the main data file. The Postgres Pod doesn't know it, but the PVC is backed by a local volume on the node, where we also have a sleep Pod running, which we can use to look at the Postgres files.

The database uses a PVC. It states its storage requirements but not the volume implementation.

The sleep Pod uses a `HostPath` volume, which gives us another way to work with the PV storage volume.

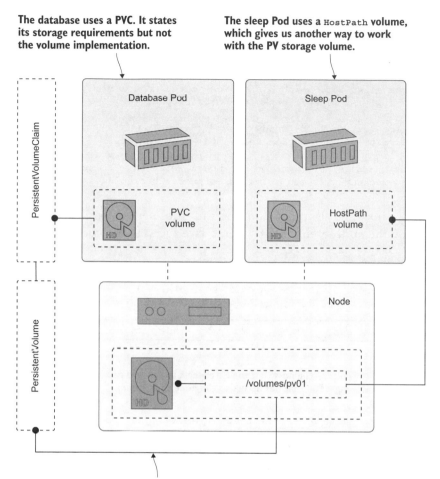

The PV uses a local volume, which happens to map to the same source as the `HostPath`. Typically, the PV would be backed by distributed storage.

Figure 5.16   Just a little bit complicated—mapping a PV and a `HostPath` to the same storage location

TRY IT NOW   Deploy the database, and give it time to initialize the data files, and then check what's been written in the volume using the sleep Pod.

```
# deploy the database:
kubectl apply -f todo-list/postgres/

# wait for Postgres to initialize:
sleep 30

# check the database logs:
kubectl logs -l app=todo-db --tail 1
```

```
# check the data files in the volume:
kubectl exec deploy/sleep -- sh -c 'ls -l /node-root/volumes/pv01 |
  grep wal'
```

My output in figure 5.17 shows the database server starting correctly and waiting for connections, having written all its data files to the volume.

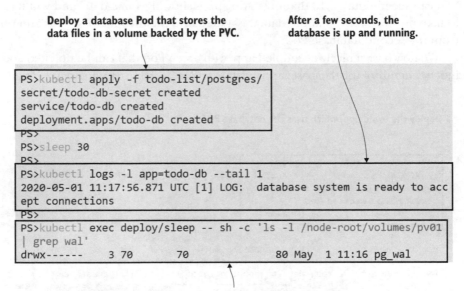

Deploy a database Pod that stores the data files in a volume backed by the PVC.

After a few seconds, the database is up and running.

```
PS>kubectl apply -f todo-list/postgres/
secret/todo-db-secret created
service/todo-db created
deployment.apps/todo-db created
PS>
PS>sleep 30
PS>
PS>kubectl logs -l app=todo-db --tail 1
2020-05-01 11:17:56.871 UTC [1] LOG:  database system is ready to acc
ept connections
PS>
PS>kubectl exec deploy/sleep -- sh -c 'ls -l /node-root/volumes/pv01
| grep wal'
drwx------    3 70      70              80 May  1 11:16 pg_wal
```

The sleep Pod has access to the same path on the host, where we can see the database files have been created.

Figure 5.17　The database container writes to the local data path, but that's actually a mount for the PVC.

The last thing to do is run the app, test it, and confirm the data still exists if the database Pod is replaced.

> **TRY IT NOW**　Run the web Pod for the to-do app, which connects to the Postgres database.

```
# deploy the web app components:
kubectl apply -f todo-list/web/

# wait for the web Pod:
kubectl wait --for=condition=Ready pod -l app=todo-web

# get the app URL from the Service:
kubectl get svc todo-web -o
  jsonpath='http://{.status.loadBalancer.ingress[0].*}:8081/new'

# browse to the app, and add a new item
```

```
# delete the database Pod:
kubectl delete pod -l app=todo-db

# check the contents of the volume on the node:
kubectl exec deploy/sleep -- ls -l /node-root/volumes/pv01/pg_wal

# check that your item is still in the to-do list
```

You can see in figure 5.18 that my to-do app is showing some data, and you'll just have to take my word for it that the data was added into the first database Pod and reloaded from the second database Pod.

We now have a nicely decoupled app, with a web Pod that can be updated and scaled independently of the database, and a database Pod, which uses persistent storage outside

Deploy the to-do app, which uses the database Pod.

```
PS>kubectl apply -f todo-list/web/
configmap/todo-web-config created
secret/todo-web-secret created
service/todo-web created
deployment.apps/todo-web created
PS>
PS>kubectl wait --for-condition=Ready pod -l app=todo-web
pod/todo-web-fb77d6775-75vgb condition met
PS>
PS>kubectl get svc todo-web -o jsonpath='http://{.status.loadBalancer.ingress[0]
.*}:8081/new'
http://localhost:8081/new
PS>
PS>
PS>
PS>
PS>
PS>
PS>
PS>
PS>
PS>kubectl delete pod -l app=todo-db
pod "todo-db-868cd8cf58-gxnd7" deleted
PS>
PS>kubectl exec deploy/sleep -- ls -l /node-root/volumes/pv01/pg_wal
total 16384
-rw-------    1 70       70        16777216 May   4 14:44 000000010000000000000000
1
drwx------    2 70       70              40 May   4 14:42 archive_status
```

Delete the database Pod. The replacement uses the same PVC and the same PV, so the original data is still there.

My to-do item lives in a local volume on my node, but to use distributed storage, all I need to change is the PV spec.

Figure 5.18   The storage abstractions mean the database gets persistent storage just by mounting a PVC.

of the Pod life cycle. This exercise used a local volume as the backing store for the persistent data, but the only change you'd need to make for a production deployment is to replace the volume spec in the PV with a distributed volume supported by your cluster.

Whether you should run a relational database in Kubernetes is a question we'll address at the end of the chapter, but before we do that, we'll look at the real deal with storage: having the cluster dynamically provision volumes based on an abstracted storage class.

5.4 *Dynamic volume provisioning and storage classes*

So far we've used a static provisioning workflow. We explicitly created the PV and then created the PVC, which Kubernetes bound to the PV. That works for all Kubernetes clusters and might be the preferred workflow in organizations where access to storage is strictly controlled, but most Kubernetes platforms support a simpler alternative with dynamic provisioning.

In the dynamic provisioning workflow, you just create the PVC, and the PV that backs it is created on demand by the cluster. Clusters can be configured with multiple storage classes that reflect the different volume capabilities on offer as well as a default storage class. PVCs can specify the name of the storage class they want, or if they want to use the default class, then they omit the storage class field in the claim spec, as shown in listing 5.8.

> **Listing 5.8 postgres-persistentVolumeClaim-dynamic.yaml, dynamic PVC**

```
apiVersion: v1
kind: PersistentVolumeClaim
metadata:
  name: postgres-pvc-dynamic
spec:
  accessModes:
    - ReadWriteOnce
  resources:
    requests:
      storage: 100Mi
      # There is no storageClassName field, so this uses the default class.
```

You can deploy this PVC to your cluster without creating a PV—but I can't tell you what will happen, because that depends on the setup of your cluster. If your Kubernetes platform supports dynamic provisioning with a default storage class, then you'll see a PV is created and bound to the claim, and that PV will use whatever volume type your cluster has set for the default.

TRY IT NOW Deploy a PVC, and see if it is dynamically provisioned.

```
# deploy the PVC from listing 5.8:
kubectl apply -f todo-list/postgres-persistentVolumeClaim-dynamic.yaml

# check claims and volumes:
kubectl get pvc
kubectl get pv
```

```
# delete the claim:
kubectl delete pvc postgres-pvc-dynamic

# check volumes again:
kubectl get pv
```

What happens when you run the exercise? Docker Desktop uses a `HostPath` volume in the default storage class for dynamically provisioned PVs; AKS uses Azure Files; K3s uses `HostPath` but with a different configuration from Docker Desktop, which means you won't see the PV because it is created only when a Pod that uses the PVC is created. Figure 5.19 shows my output from Docker Desktop. The PV is created and bound to the PVC, and when the PVC is deleted, the PV is removed, too.

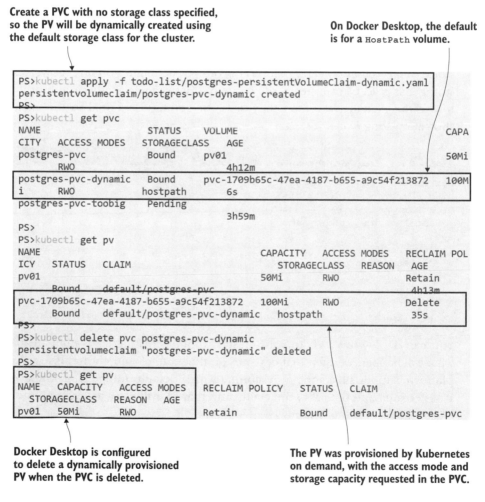

Create a PVC with no storage class specified, so the PV will be dynamically created using the default storage class for the cluster.

On Docker Desktop, the default is for a `HostPath` **volume.**

Docker Desktop is configured to delete a dynamically provisioned PV when the PVC is deleted.

The PV was provisioned by Kubernetes on demand, with the access mode and storage capacity requested in the PVC.

Figure 5.19 Docker Desktop has one set of behaviors for the default storage class; other platforms differ.

Storage classes provide a lot of flexibility. You create them as standard Kubernetes resources, and in the spec, you define exactly how the storage class works with the following three fields:

- `provisioner`—the component that creates PVs on demand. Different platforms have different provisioners, for example, the provisioner in the default AKS storage class integrates with Azure Files to create new file shares.
- `reclaimPolicy`—defines what to do with dynamically created volumes when the claim is deleted. The underlying volume can be deleted, too, or it can be retained.
- `volumeBindingMode`—determines whether the PV is created as soon as the PVC is created or not until a Pod that uses the PVC is created.

Combining those properties lets you put together a choice of storage classes in your cluster, so applications can request the properties they need—everything from fast local storage to highly available clustered storage—without ever specifying the exact details of a volume or volume type. I can't give you a storage class YAML that I can be sure will work on your cluster, because clusters don't all have the same provisioners available. Instead we'll create a new storage class by cloning your default class.

TRY IT NOW Fetching the default storage class and cloning it contains some nasty details, so I've wrapped those steps in a script. You can check the script contents if you're curious, but you may need to have a lie-down afterward.

```
# list the storage classes in the cluster:
kubectl get storageclass

# clone the default on Windows:
Set-ExecutionPolicy Bypass -Scope Process -Force;
  ./cloneDefaultStorageClass.ps1

# OR on Mac/Linux:
chmod +x cloneDefaultStorageClass.sh && ./cloneDefaultStorageClass.sh

# list storage classes:
kubectl get sc
```

The output you see from listing the storage classes shows what your cluster has configured. After running the script, you should have a new class called `kiamol`, which has the same setup as the default storage class. My output from Docker Desktop is shown in figure 5.20.

Now you have a custom storage class that your apps can request in a PVC. This is a much more intuitive and flexible way to manage storage, especially in a cloud platform where dynamic provisioning is simple and fast. Listing 5.9 shows a PVC spec requesting the new storage class.

Storage classes have a provisioner, which is the component that integrates your cluster with the storage systems it can use.

This script gets the details of the default storage class and creates a clone called `kiamol`.

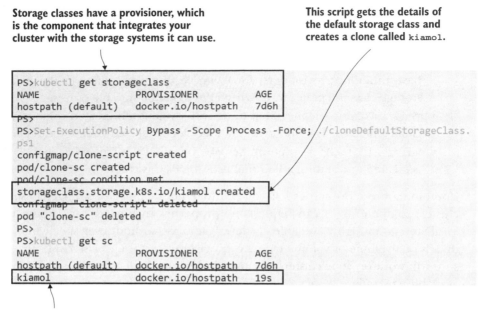

```
PS>kubectl get storageclass
NAME                PROVISIONER           AGE
hostpath (default)  docker.io/hostpath    7d6h
PS>
PS>Set-ExecutionPolicy Bypass -Scope Process -Force; ./cloneDefaultStorageClass.
ps1
configmap/clone-script created
pod/clone-sc created
pod/clone-sc condition met
storageclass.storage.k8s.io/kiamol created
configmap "clone-script" deleted
pod "clone-sc" deleted
PS>
PS>kubectl get sc
NAME                PROVISIONER           AGE
hostpath (default)  docker.io/hostpath    7d6h
kiamol              docker.io/hostpath    19s
```

Here's the new storage class. In a production cluster in the cloud, you might already have multiple storage classes with different capabilities.

Figure 5.20   Cloning the default storage class to create a custom class you can use in PVC specs

Listing 5.9   postgres-persistentVolumeClaim-storageClass.yaml

```
spec:
  accessModes:
    - ReadWriteOnce
  storageClassName: kiamol        # The storage class is the abstraction.
  resources:
    requests:
      storage: 100Mi
```

The storage classes in a production cluster will have more meaningful names, but we all now have a storage class with the same name in our clusters, so we can update the Postgres database to use that explicit class.

TRY IT NOW   Create the new PVC, and update the database Pod spec to use it.

```
# create a new PVC using the custom storage class:
kubectl apply -f storageClass/postgres-persistentVolumeClaim-
    storageClass.yaml

# update the database to use the new PVC:
kubectl apply -f storageClass/todo-db.yaml
```

```
# check the storage:
kubectl get pvc
kubectl get pv

# check the Pods:
kubectl get pods -l app=todo-db

# refresh the list in your to-do app
```

This exercise switches the database Pod to use the new dynamically provisioned PVC, as shown in my output in figure 5.21. The new PVC is backed by a new volume, so it will start empty and you'll lose your previous data. The previous volume still exists, so you could deploy another update to your database Pod, revert it back to the old PVC, and see your items.

Updates the Postgres database Pod to use a new PVC that specifies the `kiamol` storage class

That uses the same provisioner as the default to create and bind a PV on demand.

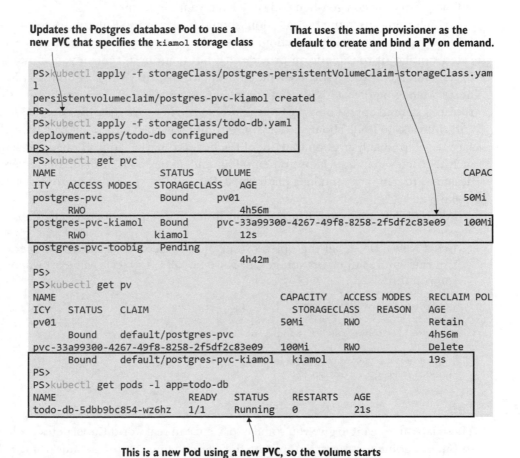

```
PS>kubectl apply -f storageClass/postgres-persistentVolumeClaim-storageClass.yaml
persistentvolumeclaim/postgres-pvc-kiamol created
PS>
PS>kubectl apply -f storageClass/todo-db.yaml
deployment.apps/todo-db configured
PS>
PS>kubectl get pvc
NAME                    STATUS    VOLUME                                      CAPAC
ITY    ACCESS MODES    STORAGECLASS    AGE
postgres-pvc            Bound     pv01                                        50Mi
       RWO                             4h56m
postgres-pvc-kiamol     Bound     pvc-33a99300-4267-49f8-8258-2f5df2c83e09    100Mi
       RWO             kiamol          12s
postgres-pvc-toobig     Pending
                                       4h42m
PS>
PS>kubectl get pv
NAME                                                CAPACITY  ACCESS MODES  RECLAIM POL
ICY    STATUS    CLAIM                               STORAGECLASS  REASON  AGE
pv01                                                50Mi      RWO           Retain
       Bound     default/postgres-pvc                                      4h56m
pvc-33a99300-4267-49f8-8258-2f5df2c83e09  100Mi     RWO           Delete
       Bound     default/postgres-pvc-kiamol  kiamol                       19s
PS>
PS>kubectl get pods -l app=todo-db
NAME                         READY  STATUS    RESTARTS  AGE
todo-db-5dbb9bc854-wz6hz     1/1    Running   0         21s
```

This is a new Pod using a new PVC, so the volume starts off empty, and the database will initialize with new files.

Figure 5.21 Using storage classes greatly simplifies your app spec; you just name the class in your PVC.

5.5 *Understanding storage choices in Kubernetes*

So that's storage in Kubernetes. In your usual work, you'll define PersistentVolume-Claims for your Pods and specify the size and storage class you need, which could be a custom value like FastLocal or Replicated. We took a long journey to get there in this chapter, because it's important to understand what actually happens when you claim storage, what other resources are involved, and how you can configure them.

We also covered volume types, and that's an area you'll need to research more to understand what options are available on your Kubernetes platform and what capabilities they provide. If you're in a cloud environment, you should have the luxury of multiple clusterwide storage options, but remember that storage costs, and fast storage costs a lot. You need to understand that you can create a PVC using a fast storage class that could be configured to retain the underlying volume, and that means you'll still be paying for storage when you've deleted your deployment.

Which brings us to the big question: should you even use Kubernetes to run stateful apps like databases? The functionality is all there to give you highly available, replicated storage (if your platform provides it), but that doesn't mean you should rush to decommission your Oracle estate and replace it with MySQL running in Kubernetes. Managing data adds a lot of complexity to your Kubernetes applications, and running stateful apps is only part of the problem. There are data backups, snapshots, and rollbacks to think about, and if you're running in the cloud, a managed database service will probably give you that out of the box. But having your whole stack defined in Kubernetes manifests is pretty tempting, and some modern database servers are designed to run in a container platform; TiDB and CockroachDB are options worth looking at.

All that's left now is to tidy up your lab cluster before we move on to the lab.

TRY IT NOW Delete all the objects from the manifests used in this chapter. You can ignore any errors you get, because not all the objects will exist when you run this.

```
# delete deployments, PVCs, PVs, and Services:
kubectl delete -f pi/v1 -f sleep/ -f storageClass/ -f todo-list/web -f
   todo-list/postgres -f todo-list/

# delete the custom storage class:
kubectl delete sc kiamol
```

5.6 *Lab*

These labs are meant to give you some experience in real-world Kubernetes problems, so I'm not going to ask you to replicate the exercise to clone the default storage class. Instead we have a new deployment of the to-do app, which has a couple of issues. We're using a proxy in front of the web Pod to improve performance and a local database file inside the web Pod because this is just a development deployment. We need some persistent storage configured at the proxy layer and the web layer, so you can remove Pods and deployments, and the data still persists.

- Start by deploying the app manifests in the `ch05/lab/todo-list` folder; that creates the Services and Deployments for the proxy and web components.
- Find the URL for the LoadBalancer, and try using the app. You'll find it doesn't respond, and you'll need to dig into the logs to find out what's wrong.
- Your task is to configure persistent storage for the proxy cache files and for the database file in the web Pod. You should be able to find the mount targets from the log entries and the Pod spec.
- When you have the app running, you should be able to add some data, delete all your Pods, refresh the browser, and see that your data is still there.
- You can use any volume type or storage class that you like. This is a good opportunity to explore what your platform provides.

My solution is on GitHub as usual for you to check if you need to: https://github .com/sixeyed/kiamol/blob/master/ch05/lab/README.md.

Scaling applications across multiple Pods with controllers

The basic idea for scaling applications is simple: run more Pods. Kubernetes abstracts networking and storage away from the compute layer, so you can run many Pods, which are copies of the same app, and just plug them into the same abstractions. Kubernetes calls those Pods replicas, and in a multinode cluster, they'll be distributed across many nodes. This gives you all the benefits of scale: greater capacity to handle load and high availability in case of failure—all in a platform that can scale up and down in seconds.

Kubernetes also provides some alternative scaling options to meet different application requirements, and we'll work through them all in this chapter. The one you'll use most often is the Deployment controller, which is actually the simplest, but we'll spend time on the others, too, so you understand how to scale different types of applications in your cluster.

6.1   How Kubernetes runs apps at scale

The Pod is the unit of compute in Kubernetes, and you learned in chapter 2 that you don't usually run Pods directly; instead, you define another resource to manage them for you. That resource is a controller, and we've used Deployment controllers ever since. A controller spec includes a Pod template, which it uses to create and replace Pods. It can use that same template to create many replicas of a Pod.

Deployments are probably the resource you'll use most in Kubernetes, and you've already had lots of experience with them. Now it's time to dig a bit deeper and learn that Deployments don't actually manage Pods directly—that's done by another resource called a ReplicaSet. Figure 6.1 shows the relationship among Deployment, ReplicaSet, and Pods.

122

ReplicaSets manage Pods. Change the scale of a ReplicaSet, and it will add or remove Pods. If Pods disappear, the ReplicaSet replaces them.

Pods manage containers. If a container exits, the Pod replaces it.

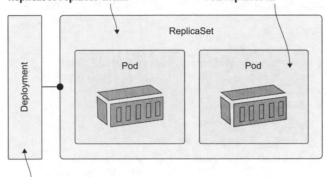

Deployments manage ReplicaSets. It's another layer of abstraction, which makes for smooth application updates.

Figure 6.1   Every software problem can be solved by adding another layer of abstraction.

You'll use a Deployment to describe your app in most cases; the Deployment is a controller that manages ReplicaSets, and the ReplicaSet is a controller that manages Pods. You can create a ReplicaSet directly rather than using a Deployment, and we'll do that for the first few exercises, just to see how scaling works. The YAML for a ReplicaSet is almost the same as for a Deployment; it needs a selector to find the resources it owns and a Pod template to create resources. Listing 6.1 shows an abbreviated spec.

> **Listing 6.1   whoami.yaml, a ReplicaSet without a Deployment**

```
apiVersion: apps/v1
kind: ReplicaSet         # The spec is almost identical to a Deployment.
metadata:
  name: whoami-web
spec:
  replicas: 1
  selector:              # The selector for the ReplicaSet to find its Pods
    matchLabels:
      app: whoami-web
  template:              # The usual Pod spec follows.
```

The only things different in this spec from the Deployment definitions we've used are the object type ReplicaSet and the `replicas` field, which states how many Pods to run. This spec uses a single replica, which means Kubernetes will run a single Pod.

TRY IT NOW   Deploy the ReplicaSet, along with a LoadBalancer Service, which uses the same label selector as the ReplicaSet to send traffic to the Pods.

```
# switch to this chapter's exercises:
cd ch06
```

```
# deploy the ReplicaSet and Service:
kubectl apply -f whoami/

# check the resource:
kubectl get replicaset whoami-web

# make an HTTP GET call to the Service:
curl $(kubectl get svc whoami-web -o
  jsonpath='http://{.status.loadBalancer.ingress[0].*}:8088')

# delete all the Pods:
kubectl delete pods -l app=whoami-web

# repeat the HTTP call:
curl $(kubectl get svc whoami-web -o
  jsonpath='http://{.status.loadBalancer.ingress[0].*}:8088')

# show the detail about the ReplicaSet:
kubectl describe rs whoami-web
```

You can see my output in figure 6.2. There's nothing new here; the ReplicaSet owns a single Pod, and when you delete that Pod, the ReplicaSet replaces it. I've removed the kubectl describe output in the final command, but if you run that, you'll see it ends with a list of events, where the ReplicaSet writes activity logs on how it created Pods.

The ReplicaSet replaces deleted Pods because it constantly runs a control loop, checking that the number of objects it owns matches the number of replicas it should have. You use the same mechanism when you scale up your application—you update the ReplicaSet spec to set a new number of replicas, and then the control loop sees that it needs more and creates them from the same Pod template.

TRY IT NOW Scale up the application by deploying an updated ReplicaSet definition that specifies three replicas.

```
# deploy the update:
kubectl apply -f whoami/update/whoami-replicas-3.yaml

#check Pods:
kubectl get pods -l app=whoami-web

# delete all the Pods:
kubectl delete pods -l app=whoami-web

# check again:
kubectl get pods -l app=whoami-web

# repeat this HTTP call a few times:
curl $(kubectl get svc whoami-web -o
  jsonpath='http://{.status.loadBalancer.ingress[0].*}:8088')
```

The ReplicaSet shows the desired and current status for the number of Pods it manages.

This app just returns the hostname in an HTTP response, which is the Pod name in Kubernetes.

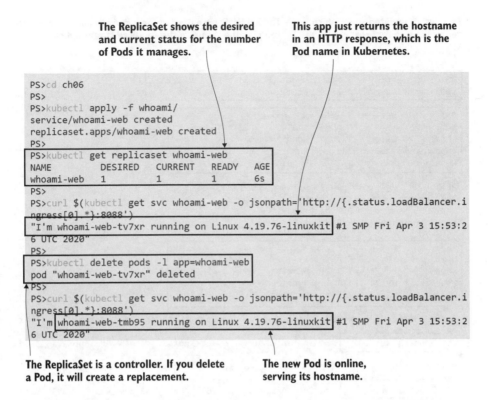

```
PS>cd ch06
PS>
PS>kubectl apply -f whoami/
service/whoami-web created
replicaset.apps/whoami-web created
PS>
PS>kubectl get replicaset whoami-web
NAME          DESIRED   CURRENT   READY   AGE
whoami-web    1         1         1       6s
PS>
PS>curl $(kubectl get svc whoami-web -o jsonpath='http://{.status.loadBalancer.i
ngress[0].*}:8088')
"I'm whoami-web-tv7xr running on Linux 4.19.76-linuxkit #1 SMP Fri Apr 3 15:53:2
6 UTC 2020"
PS>
PS>kubectl delete pods -l app=whoami-web
pod "whoami-web-tv7xr" deleted
PS>
PS>curl $(kubectl get svc whoami-web -o jsonpath='http://{.status.loadBalancer.i
ngress[0].*}:8088')
"I'm whoami-web-tmb95 running on Linux 4.19.76-linuxkit #1 SMP Fri Apr 3 15:53:2
6 UTC 2020"
```

The ReplicaSet is a controller. If you delete a Pod, it will create a replacement.

The new Pod is online, serving its hostname.

Figure 6.2 Working with a ReplicaSet is just like working with a Deployment: it creates and manages Pods.

My output, shown in figure 6.3, raises a couple of questions: How does Kubernetes manage to scale the app so quickly, and how do the HTTP responses come from different Pods?

The first is simple to answer: this is a single-node cluster, so every Pod will run on the same node, and that node has already pulled the Docker image for the app. When you scale up in a production cluster, it's likely that new Pods will be scheduled to run on nodes that don't have the image locally, and they'll need to pull the image before they can run the Pod. The speed at which you can scale is bounded by the speed at which your images can be pulled, which is why you need to invest time in optimizing your images.

As to how we can make an HTTP request to the same Kubernetes Service and get responses from different Pods, that's all down to the loose coupling between Services and Pods. When you scaled up the ReplicaSet, there were suddenly multiple Pods that matched the Service's label selector, and when that happens, Kubernetes load-balances

Deploys an updated spec, which requires three replicas

The ReplicaSet creates two new Pods to join the original, bringing the set up to the required three replicas.

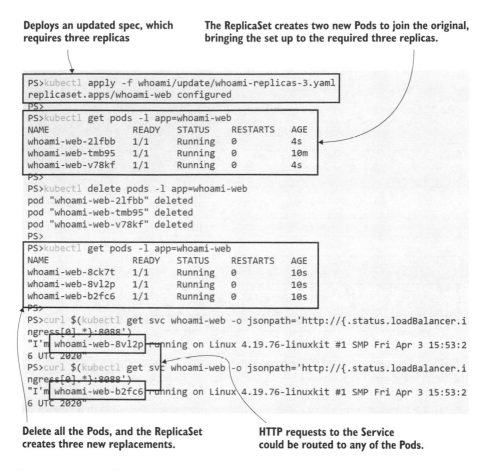

```
PS>kubectl apply -f whoami/update/whoami-replicas-3.yaml
replicaset.apps/whoami-web configured
PS>
PS>kubectl get pods -l app=whoami-web
NAME               READY   STATUS    RESTARTS   AGE
whoami-web-2lfbb   1/1     Running   0          4s
whoami-web-tmb95   1/1     Running   0          10m
whoami-web-v78kf   1/1     Running   0          4s
PS>
PS>kubectl delete pods -l app=whoami-web
pod "whoami-web-2lfbb" deleted
pod "whoami-web-tmb95" deleted
pod "whoami-web-v78kf" deleted
PS>
PS>kubectl get pods -l app=whoami-web
NAME               READY   STATUS    RESTARTS   AGE
whoami-web-8ck7t   1/1     Running   0          10s
whoami-web-8vl2p   1/1     Running   0          10s
whoami-web-b2fc6   1/1     Running   0          10s
PS>
PS>curl $(kubectl get svc whoami-web -o jsonpath='http://{.status.loadBalancer.i
ngress[0].*}:8088')
 "I'm whoami-web-8vl2p running on Linux 4.19.76-linuxkit #1 SMP Fri Apr 3 15:53:2
6 UTC 2020"
PS>curl $(kubectl get svc whoami-web -o jsonpath='http://{.status.loadBalancer.i
ngress[0].*}:8088')
 "I'm whoami-web-b2fc6 running on Linux 4.19.76-linuxkit #1 SMP Fri Apr 3 15:53:2
6 UTC 2020"
```

Delete all the Pods, and the ReplicaSet creates three new replacements.

HTTP requests to the Service could be routed to any of the Pods.

Figure 6.3   Scaling ReplicaSets is fast, and at scale, a Service can distribute requests to many Pods.

requests across the Pods. Figure 6.4 shows how the same label selector maintains the relationship between ReplicaSet and Pods and between Service and Pods.

The abstraction between networking and compute is what makes scaling so easy in Kubernetes. You may be experiencing a warm glow about now—suddenly all the complexity starts to fit into place, and you see how the separation between resources is the enabler for some very powerful features. This is the core of scaling: you run as many Pods as you need, and they all sit behind one Service. When consumers access the Service, Kubernetes distributes the load between Pods.

Load balancing is a feature of all the Service types in Kubernetes. We've deployed a LoadBalancer Service in these exercises, and that receives traffic into the cluster and sends it to the Pods. It also creates a ClusterIP for other Pods to use, and when Pods communicate within the cluster, they also benefit from load balancing.

The label selector of the Service matches the
label selector of the ReplicaSet, so the Service
registers an endpoint for every Pod.

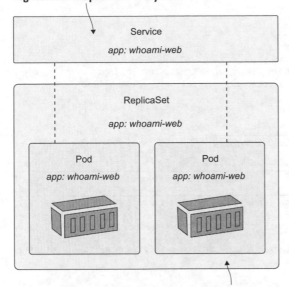

The ReplicaSet uses the label selector to identify its
Pods, and it applies the label when it creates Pods.
Scaling the ReplicaSet also affects the endpoints
in the Service.

Figure 6.4 A Service with the same
label selector as a ReplicaSet will use
all of its Pods.

TRY IT NOW Deploy a new Pod, and use it to call the who-am-I Service internally, using the ClusterIP, which Kubernetes resolves from the service name.

```
# run a sleep Pod:
kubectl apply -f sleep.yaml

# check the details of the who-am-I Service:
kubectl get svc whoami-web

# run a DNS lookup for the Service in the sleep Pod:
kubectl exec deploy/sleep -- sh -c 'nslookup whoami-web | grep
   "^[^*]"'

# make some HTTP calls:
kubectl exec deploy/sleep -- sh -c 'for i in 1 2 3; do curl -w \\n -s
   http://whoami-web:8088; done;'
```

As shown in figure 6.5, the behavior for a Pod consuming an internal Service is the
same as for external consumers, and requests are load-balanced across the Pods.
When you run this exercise, you may see the requests distributed exactly equally, or
you may see some Pods responding more than once, depending on the vagaries of
the network.

Run a sleep Pod so we can see how
the Service works inside the cluster.

In a DNS lookup, the IP address is
the Service ClusterIP, as we'd expect.

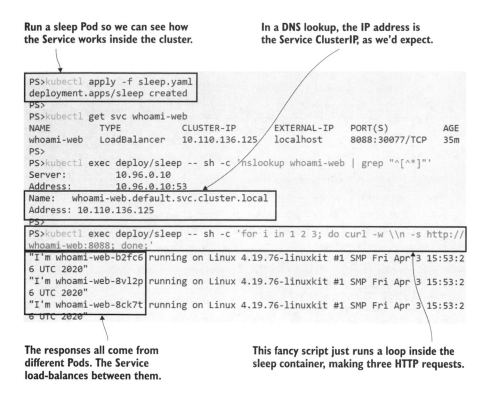

```
PS>kubectl apply -f sleep.yaml
deployment.apps/sleep created
PS>
PS>kubectl get svc whoami-web
NAME         TYPE           CLUSTER-IP       EXTERNAL-IP   PORT(S)        AGE
whoami-web   LoadBalancer   10.110.136.125   localhost     8088:30077/TCP 35m
PS>
PS>kubectl exec deploy/sleep -- sh -c 'nslookup whoami-web | grep "^[^*]"'
Server:      10.96.0.10
Address:     10.96.0.10:53
Name:    whoami-web.default.svc.cluster.local
Address: 10.110.136.125
PS>
PS>kubectl exec deploy/sleep -- sh -c 'for i in 1 2 3; do curl -w \\n -s http://
whoami-web:8088; done;'
"I'm whoami-web-b2fc6 running on Linux 4.19.76-linuxkit #1 SMP Fri Apr 3 15:53:2
6 UTC 2020"
"I'm whoami-web-8vl2p running on Linux 4.19.76-linuxkit #1 SMP Fri Apr 3 15:53:2
6 UTC 2020"
"I'm whoami-web-8ck7t running on Linux 4.19.76-linuxkit #1 SMP Fri Apr 3 15:53:2
6 UTC 2020"
```

The responses all come from
different Pods. The Service
load-balances between them.

This fancy script just runs a loop inside the
sleep container, making three HTTP requests.

Figure 6.5   **The world inside the cluster: Pod-to-Pod networking also benefits from Service
load balancing.**

In chapter 3, we covered Services and how the ClusterIP address is an abstraction
from the Pod's IP address, so when a Pod is replaced, the application is still accessible
using the same Service address. Now you see that the Service can be an abstraction
across many Pods, and the same networking layer that routes traffic to a Pod on any
node can load-balance across multiple Pods.

6.2   *Scaling for load with Deployments and ReplicaSets*

ReplicaSets make it incredibly easy to scale your app: you can scale up or down in seconds just by changing the number of replicas in the spec. It's perfect for stateless components that run in small, lean containers, and that's why applications built for
Kubernetes typically use a distributed architecture, breaking down functionality across
many pieces, which can be individually updated and scaled.

Deployments add a useful management layer on top of ReplicaSets. Now that we
know how they work, we won't be using ReplicaSets directly anymore—Deployments
should be your first choice for defining applications. We won't explore all the features of Deployments until we get to application upgrades and rollbacks in chapter 9,

but it's useful to understand exactly what the extra abstraction gives you. Figure 6.6 shows this.

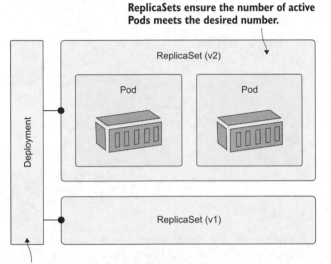

ReplicaSets ensure the number of active Pods meets the desired number.

Deployments can manage multiple ReplicaSets. In this case, the v2 update means the v1 ReplicaSet has been scaled down to zero nodes.

Figure 6.6   Zero is a valid number of desired replicas; Deployments scale down old ReplicaSets to zero.

A Deployment is a controller for ReplicaSets, and to run at scale, you include the same `replicas` field in the Deployment spec, and that is passed to the ReplicaSet. Listing 6.2 shows the abbreviated YAML for the Pi web application, which explicitly sets two replicas.

Listing 6.2   web.yaml, a Deployment to run multiple replicas

```
apiVersion: apps/v1
kind: Deployment
metadata:
  name: pi-web
spec:
  replicas: 2              # The replicas field is optional; it defaults to 1.
selector:
  matchLabels:
    app: pi-web
  template:                # The Pod spec follows.
```

The label selector for the Deployment needs to match the labels defined in the Pod template, and those labels are used to express the chain of ownership from Pod to

ReplicaSet to Deployment. When you scale a Deployment, it updates the existing Replica-Set to set the new number of replicas, but if you change the Pod spec in the Deployment, it replaces the ReplicaSet and scales the previous one down to zero. That gives the Deployment a lot of control over how it manages the update and how it deals with any problems.

TRY IT NOW   Create a Deployment and Service for the Pi web application, and make some updates to see how the ReplicaSets are managed.

```
# deploy the Pi app:
kubectl apply -f pi/web/

# check the ReplicaSet:
kubectl get rs -l app=pi-web

# scale up to more replicas:
kubectl apply -f pi/web/update/web-replicas-3.yaml

# check the RS:
kubectl get rs -l app=pi-web

# deploy a changed Pod spec with enhanced logging:
kubectl apply -f pi/web/update/web-logging-level.yaml

# check ReplicaSets again:
kubectl get rs -l app=pi-web
```

This exercise shows that the ReplicaSet is still the scale mechanism: when you increase or decrease the number of replicas in your Deployment, it just updates the ReplicaSet. The Deployment is the, well, deployment mechanism, and it manages application updates through multiple ReplicaSets. My output, which appears in figure 6.7, shows how the Deployment waits for the new ReplicaSet to be fully operational before completely scaling down the old one.

You can use the kubectl scale command as a shortcut for scaling controllers. You should use it sparingly because it's an imperative way to work, and it's much better to use declarative YAML files, so that the state of your apps in production always exactly matches the spec stored in source control. But if your app is underperforming and the automated deployment takes 90 seconds, it's a quick way to scale—as long as you remember to update the YAML file, too.

TRY IT NOW   Scale up the Pi application using kubectl directly, and then see what happens with the ReplicaSets when another full deployment happens.

```
# we need to scale the Pi app fast:
kubectl scale --replicas=4 deploy/pi-web

# check which ReplicaSet makes the change:
kubectl get rs -l app=pi-web

# now we can revert back to the original logging level:
kubectl apply -f pi/web/update/web-replicas-3.yaml
```

```
# but that will undo the scale we set manually:
kubectl get rs -l app=pi-web

# check the Pods:
kubectl get pods -l app=pi-web
```

**This Deployment creates a
ReplicaSet with two replicas.**

**Updating the Deployment with an increased
replica count just scales the existing ReplicaSet.**

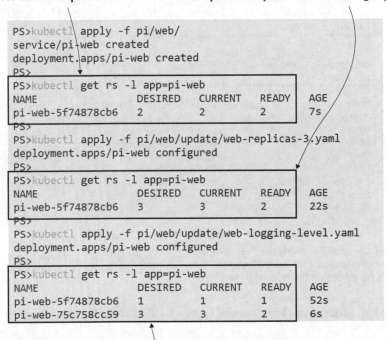

```
PS>kubectl apply -f pi/web/
service/pi-web created
deployment.apps/pi-web created
PS>
PS>kubectl get rs -l app=pi-web
NAME                    DESIRED    CURRENT    READY    AGE
pi-web-5f74878cb6       2          2          2        7s
PS>
PS>kubectl apply -f pi/web/update/web-replicas-3.yaml
deployment.apps/pi-web configured
PS>
PS>kubectl get rs -l app=pi-web
NAME                    DESIRED    CURRENT    READY    AGE
pi-web-5f74878cb6       3          3          2        22s
PS>
PS>kubectl apply -f pi/web/update/web-logging-level.yaml
deployment.apps/pi-web configured
PS>
PS>kubectl get rs -l app=pi-web
NAME                    DESIRED    CURRENT    READY    AGE
pi-web-5f74878cb6       1          1          1        52s
pi-web-75c758cc59       3          3          2        6s
```

**The next update alters the Pod spec, so the original ReplicaSet's Pods
are no longer a match. The Deployment creates a new ReplicaSet and
scales down the old one as the new Pods become ready.**

**Figure 6.7   Deployments manage ReplicaSets to keep the desired number of Pods available
during updates.**

You'll see two things when you apply the updated YAML: the app scales back down to
three replicas, and the Deployment does that by scaling the new ReplicaSet down to zero
Pods and scaling the old ReplicaSet back up to three Pods. Figure 6.8 shows that the
updated Deployment results in three new Pods being created.

It shouldn't be a surprise that the Deployment update overwrote the manual scale
level; the YAML definition is the desired state, and Kubernetes does not attempt to
retain any part of the current spec if the two differ. It might be more of a surprise that

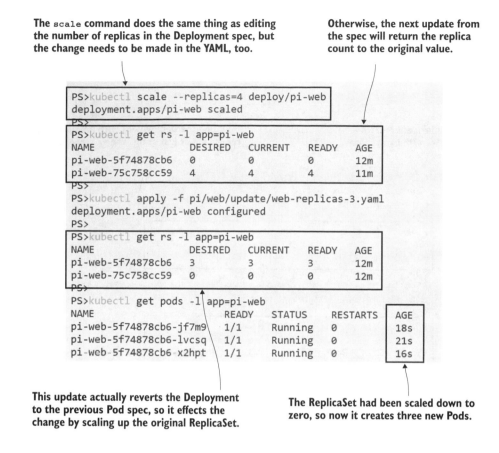

The `scale` command does the same thing as editing the number of replicas in the Deployment spec, but the change needs to be made in the YAML, too.

Otherwise, the next update from the spec will return the replica count to the original value.

This update actually reverts the Deployment to the previous Pod spec, so it effects the change by scaling up the original ReplicaSet.

The ReplicaSet had been scaled down to zero, so now it creates three new Pods.

Figure 6.8   Deployments know the spec for their ReplicaSets and can roll back by scaling an old ReplicaSet.

the Deployment reused the old ReplicaSet instead of creating a new one, but that's a more efficient way for Kubernetes to work, and it's possible because of more labels.

Pods created from Deployments have a generated name that looks random but actually isn't. The Pod name contains a hash of the template in the Pod spec for the Deployment, so if you make a change to the spec that matches a previous Deployment, then it will have the same template hash as a scaled-down ReplicaSet, and the Deployment can find that ReplicaSet and scale it up again to effect the change. The Pod template hash is stored in a label.

TRY IT NOW   Check out the labels for the Pi Pods and ReplicaSets to see the template hash.

```
# list ReplicaSets with labels:
kubectl get rs -l app=pi-web --show-labels
```

```
# list Pods with labels:
kubectl get po -l app-pi-web --show-labels
```

Figure 6.9 shows that the template hash is included in the object name, but this is just for convenience—Kubernetes uses the labels for management.

The ReplicaSet has the app label specified in the YAML file and also a hash for the Pod spec template, which is used by the Deployment.

```
PS>kubectl get rs -l app=pi-web --show-labels
NAME                    DESIRED    CURRENT    READY    AGE    LABELS
pi-web-5f74878cb6       3          3          3        32m    app=pi-web,pod-template-ha
sh=5f74878cb6
pi-web-75c758cc59       0          0          0        31m    app=pi-web,pod-template-ha
sh=75c758cc59
PS>
PS>kubectl get po -l app=pi-web --show-labels
NAME                    READY      STATUS     RESTARTS    AGE    LABELS
pi-web-5f74878cb6-jf7m9 1/1        Running    0           19m    app=pi-web,pod-temp
late-hash=5f74878cb6
pi-web-5f74878cb6-lvcsq 1/1        Running    0           19m    app=pi-web,pod-temp
late-hash=5f74878cb6
pi-web-5f74878cb6-x2hpt 1/1        Running    0           19m    app=pi-web,pod-temp
late-hash=5f74878cb6
```

The Pods have the same template hash label. The hash is also used in the name for the generated objects, the ReplicaSet and Pods.

Figure 6.9 Object names generated by Kubernetes aren't just random—they include the template hash.

Knowing the internals of how a Deployment is related to its Pods will help you understand how changes are rolled out and clear up any confusion when you see lots of ReplicaSets with desired Pod counts of zero. But the interaction between the compute layer in the Pods and the network layer in the Services works in the same way.

In a typical distributed application, you'll have different scale requirements for each component, and you'll make use of Services to achieve multiple layers of load balancing between them. The Pi application we've deployed so far has only a ClusterIP Service—it's not a public-facing component. The public component is a proxy (actually, it's a reverse proxy because it handles incoming traffic rather than outgoing traffic), and that uses a LoadBalancer Service. We can run both the web component and the proxy at scale and achieve load balancing from the client to the proxy Pods and from the proxy to the application Pods.

TRY IT NOW Create the proxy Deployment, which runs with two replicas, along with a Service and ConfigMap, which sets up the integration with the Pi web app.

```
# deploy the proxy resources:
kubectl apply -f pi/proxy/
```

```
# get the URL to the proxied app:
kubectl get svc whoami-web -o
    jsonpath='http://{.status.loadBalancer.ingress[0].*}:8080/?dp=10000'

# browse to the app, and try a few different values for 'dp' in the URL
```

If you open the developer tools in your browser and look at the network requests, you can find the response headers sent by the proxy. These include the hostname of the proxy server—which is actually the Pod name—and the web page itself includes the name of the web application Pod that generated the response. My output, which appears in figure 6.10, shows a response that came from the proxy cache.

There are two layers of load-balancing in this app: into the proxy Pods and into the web Pods.

The response contains the name of the Pod that originally handled the request.

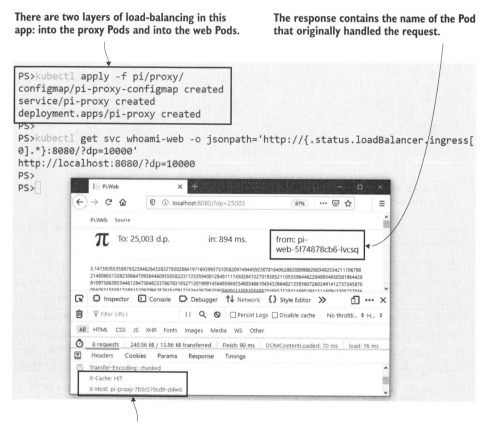

The HTTP headers also include the name of the proxy Pod that sent the response. This was a cache hit, which means the proxy already had the response cached and didn't call a web Pod.

Figure 6.10   The Pi responses include the name of the Pod that sent them, so you can see the load balancing at work.

This configuration is a simple one, which makes it easy to scale. The Pod spec for the proxy uses two volumes: a ConfigMap to load the proxy configuration file and an

EmptyDir to store the cached responses. ConfigMaps are read-only, so one ConfigMap can be shared by all the proxy Pods. EmptyDir volumes are writable, but they're unique to the Pod, so each proxy gets its own volume to use for cache files. Figure 6.11 shows the setup.

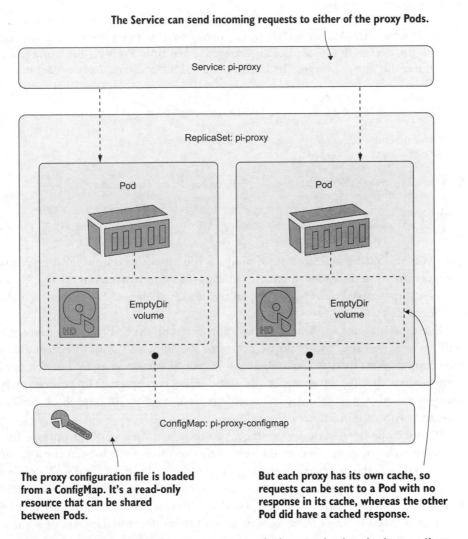

The Service can send incoming requests to either of the proxy Pods.

The proxy configuration file is loaded from a ConfigMap. It's a read-only resource that can be shared between Pods.

But each proxy has its own cache, so requests can be sent to a Pod with no response in its cache, whereas the other Pod did have a cached response.

Figure 6.11   Running Pods at scale—some types of volume can be shared, whereas others are unique to the Pod.

This architecture presents a problem, which you'll see if you request Pi to a high number of decimal places and keep refreshing the browser. The first request will be slow because it is computed by the web app; subsequent responses will be fast, because they come from the proxy cache, but soon your request will go to a different proxy Pod that doesn't have that response in its cache, so the page will load slowly again.

It would be nice to fix this by using shared storage, so every proxy Pod had access to the same cache. Doing so will bring us back to the tricky area of distributed storage that we thought we'd left behind in chapter 5, but let's start with a simple approach and see where it gets us.

TRY IT NOW   Deploy an update to the proxy spec, which uses a `HostPath` volume for cache files instead of an `EmptyDir`. Multiple Pods on the same node will use the same volume, which means they'll have a shared proxy cache.

```
# deploy the updated spec:
kubectl apply -f pi/proxy/update/nginx-hostPath.yaml

# check the Pods—the new spec adds a third replica:
kubectl get po -l app=pi-proxy

# browse back to the Pi app, and refresh it a few times

# check the proxy logs:
kubectl logs -l app=pi-proxy --tail 1
```

Now you should be able to refresh away to your heart's content, and responses will always come from the cache, no matter which proxy Pod you are directed to. Figure 6.12 shows all my proxy Pods responding to requests, which are shared between them by the Service.

For most stateful applications, this approach wouldn't work. Apps that write data tend to assume they have exclusive access to the files, and if another instance of the same app tries to use the same file location, you'd get unexpected but disappointing results—like the app crashing or the data being corrupted. The reverse proxy I'm using is called Nginx; it's unusually lenient here, and it will happily share its cache directory with other instances of itself.

If your apps need scale and storage, you have a couple of other options for using different types of controller. In the rest of this chapter, we'll look at the DaemonSet; the final type is the StatefulSet, which gets complicated quickly, and we'll come to it in chapter 8 where it gets most of the chapter to itself. DaemonSets and StatefulSets are both Pod controllers, and although you'll use them a lot less frequently than Deployments, you need to know what you can do with them because they enable some powerful patterns.

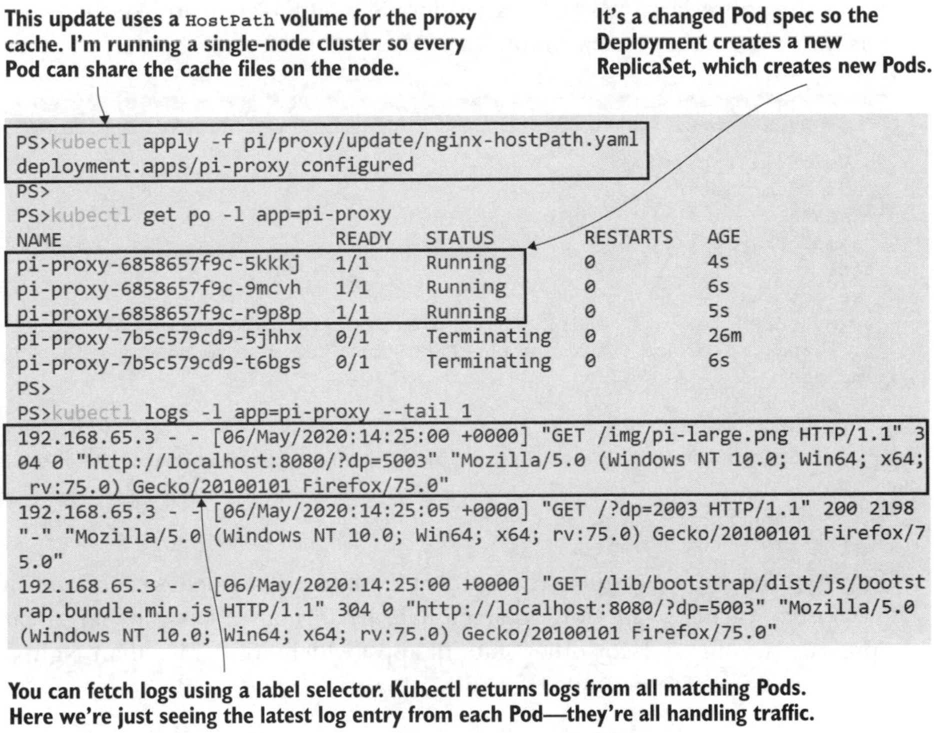

This update uses a `HostPath` volume for the proxy cache. I'm running a single-node cluster so every Pod can share the cache files on the node.

It's a changed Pod spec so the Deployment creates a new ReplicaSet, which creates new Pods.

```
PS>kubectl apply -f pi/proxy/update/nginx-hostPath.yaml
deployment.apps/pi-proxy configured
PS>
PS>kubectl get po -l app=pi-proxy
NAME                      READY   STATUS        RESTARTS   AGE
pi-proxy-6858657f9c-5kkkj  1/1    Running       0          4s
pi-proxy-6858657f9c-9mcvh  1/1    Running       0          6s
pi-proxy-6858657f9c-r9p8p  1/1    Running       0          5s
pi-proxy-7b5c579cd9-5jhhx  0/1    Terminating   0          26m
pi-proxy-7b5c579cd9-t6bgs  0/1    Terminating   0          6s
PS>
PS>kubectl logs -l app=pi-proxy --tail 1
192.168.65.3 - - [06/May/2020:14:25:00 +0000] "GET /img/pi-large.png HTTP/1.1" 3
04 0 "http://localhost:8080/?dp=5003" "Mozilla/5.0 (Windows NT 10.0; Win64; x64;
 rv:75.0) Gecko/20100101 Firefox/75.0"
192.168.65.3 - - [06/May/2020:14:25:05 +0000] "GET /?dp=2003 HTTP/1.1" 200 2198
"-" "Mozilla/5.0 (Windows NT 10.0; Win64; x64; rv:75.0) Gecko/20100101 Firefox/7
5.0"
192.168.65.3 - - [06/May/2020:14:25:00 +0000] "GET /lib/bootstrap/dist/js/bootst
rap.bundle.min.js HTTP/1.1" 304 0 "http://localhost:8080/?dp=5003" "Mozilla/5.0
(Windows NT 10.0; Win64; x64; rv:75.0) Gecko/20100101 Firefox/75.0"
```

You can fetch logs using a label selector. Kubectl returns logs from all matching Pods. Here we're just seeing the latest log entry from each Pod—they're all handling traffic.

Figure 6.12   At scale, you can see all the Pod logs with kubectl, using a label selector.

6.3   Scaling for high availability with DaemonSets

The DaemonSet takes its name from the Linux daemon, which is usually a system process that runs constantly as a single instance in the background (the equivalent of a Windows Service in the Windows world). In Kubernetes, the DaemonSet runs a single replica of a Pod on every node in the cluster, or on a subset of nodes, if you add a selector in the spec.

DaemonSets are common for infrastructure-level concerns, where you might want to grab information from every node and send it on to a central collector. A Pod runs on each node, grabbing just the data for that node. You don't need to worry about any resource conflicts, because there will be only one Pod on the node. We'll use Daemon-Sets later in this book to collect logs from Pods, and metrics about the node's activity.

You can also use them in your own designs when you want high availability without the load requirements for many replicas on each node. A reverse proxy is a good example: a single Nginx Pod can handle many thousands of concurrent connections, so you don't necessarily need a lot of them, but you may want to be sure there's one running on every node, so a local Pod can respond wherever the traffic lands. Listing 6.3

shows the abbreviated YAML for a DaemonSet—it looks much like the other controllers but without the replica count.

```
apiVersion: apps/v1
kind: DaemonSet
metadata:
  name: pi-proxy
spec:
  selector:
    matchLabels:       # DaemonSets use the same label selector mechanism.
      app: pi-proxy     # Finds the Pods that the set owns
template:
  metadata:
    labels:
      app: pi-proxy     # Labels applied to the Pods must match the selector.
spec:
# Pod spec follows
```

This spec for the proxy still uses a `HostPath` volume. That means each Pod will have its own proxy cache, so we don't get ultimate performance from a shared cache. This approach would work for other stateful apps, which are fussier than Nginx, because there's no issue with multiple instances using the same data files.

> **TRY IT NOW**   You can't convert from one type of controller to another, but we can make the change from Deployment to DaemonSet without breaking the app.

```
# deploy the DaemonSet:
kubectl apply -f pi/proxy/daemonset/nginx-ds.yaml

# check the endpoints used in the proxy service:
kubectl get endpoints pi-proxy

# delete the Deployment:
kubectl delete deploy pi-proxy

# check the DaemonSet:
kubectl get daemonset pi-proxy

# check the Pods:
kubectl get po -l app=pi-proxy

# refresh your latest Pi calculation on the browser
```

Figure 6.13 shows my output. Creating the DaemonSet before removing the Deployment means there are always Pods available to receive requests from the Service. Deleting the Deployment first would make the app unavailable until the DaemonSet started. If you check the HTTP response headers, you should also see that your

Creating the DaemonSet while the Deployment still exists. The DaemonSet's Pod
is added to the endpoints for the Service, so all four Pods can receive traffic.

```
PS>kubectl apply -f pi/proxy/daemonset/nginx-ds.yaml
daemonset.apps/pi-proxy created
PS>
PS>kubectl get endpoints pi-proxy
NAME        ENDPOINTS                                          AGE
pi-proxy    10.1.2.46:80,10.1.2.47:80,10.1.2.48:80 + 1 more... 81m
PS>
PS>kubectl delete deploy pi-proxy
deployment.apps "pi-proxy" deleted
PS>
PS>kubectl get daemonset pi-proxy
NAME        DESIRED    CURRENT    READY    UP-TO-DATE    AVAILABLE    NODE SELECTOR
AGE
pi-proxy    1          1          1        1            1            <none>
32s
PS>
PS>kubectl get po -l app=pi-proxy
NAME                         READY    STATUS        RESTARTS    AGE
pi-proxy-6858657f9c-5kkkj    0/1      Terminating   0           55m
pi-proxy-6858657f9c-9mcvh    0/1      Terminating   0           55m
pi-proxy-6858657f9c-r9p8p    0/1      Terminating   0           55m
pi-proxy-rwhwt               1/1      Running       0           38s
```

Deleting the Deployment means its Pods get removed, but there have been
Pods available to serve traffic throughout the change to the DaemonSet.

Figure 6.13   You need to plan the order of the deployment for a big change to keep your app online.

request came from the proxy cache, because the new DaemonSet Pod uses the same
HostPath volume as the Deployment Pods.

I'm using a single-node cluster, so my DaemonSet runs a single Pod; with more
nodes, I'd have one Pod on each node. The control loop watches for nodes joining
the cluster, and any new nodes will be scheduled to start a replica Pod as soon as they
join. The controller also watches the Pod status, so if a Pod is removed, then a replacement starts up.

TRY IT NOW   Manually delete the proxy Pod. The DaemonSet will start a
replacement.

```
# check the status of the DaemonSet:
kubectl get ds pi-proxy

# delete its Pod:
kubectl delete po -l app=pi-proxy

# check the Pods:
kubectl get po -l app=pi-proxy
```

If you refresh your browser while the Pod is being deleted, you'll see it doesn't respond until the DaemonSet has started a replacement. This is because you're using a single-node lab cluster. Services send traffic only to running Pods, so in a multinode environment, the request would go to a node that still had a healthy Pod. Figure 6.14 shows my output.

```
PS>kubectl get daemonset pi-proxy
NAME          DESIRED   CURRENT   READY   UP-TO-DATE   AVAILABLE   NODE SELECTOR
AGE
pi-proxy      1         1         1       1            1           <none>
17m
PS>
┌─────────────────────────────────────────────────────────────┐
│ PS>kubectl delete po -l app=pi-proxy                         │
│ pod "pi-proxy-wq7bt" deleted                                 │
│ PS>                                                          │
│ PS>kubectl get po -l app=pi-proxy                            │
│ NAME             READY   STATUS    RESTARTS   AGE            │
│ pi-proxy-tcdrx   1/1     Running   0          4s             │
└─────────────────────────────────────────────────────────────┘
```

DaemonSets have different rules than Deployments for creating replicas, but they are still Pod controllers and will replace any Pods that are lost.

Figure 6.14   DaemonSets watch nodes and Pods to ensure the desired replica count is always met.

Situations where you need a DaemonSet are often a bit more nuanced than just wanting to run a Pod on every node. In this proxy example, your production cluster might have only a subset of nodes that can receive traffic from the internet, so you'd want to run proxy Pods only on those nodes. You can achieve that with labels, adding whatever arbitrary label you'd like to identify your nodes and then selecting that label in the Pod spec. Listing 6.4 shows this with a `nodeSelector` field.

Listing 6.4   nginx-ds-nodeSelector.yaml, a DaemonSet with node selection

```
# This is the Pod spec within the template field of the DaemonSet.
spec:
  containers:
    # ...
  volumes:
    # ...
  nodeSelector:       # Pods will run only on certain nodes.
    kiamol: ch06      # Selected with the label kiamol=ch06
```

The DaemonSet controller doesn't just watch to see nodes joining the cluster; it looks at all nodes to see if they match the requirements in the Pod spec. When you deploy this change, you're telling the DaemonSet to run on only nodes that have the label `kiamol` set to the value of `ch06`. There will be no matching nodes in your cluster, so the DaemonSet will scale down to zero.

TRY IT NOW   Update the DaemonSet to include the node selector from listing 6.4. Now there are no nodes that match the requirements, so the existing
Pod will be removed. Then label a node, and a new Pod will be scheduled.

```
# update the DaemonSet spec:
kubectl apply -f pi/proxy/daemonset/nginx-ds-nodeSelector.yaml

# check the DS:
kubectl get ds pi-proxy

# check the Pods:
kubectl get po -l app=pi-proxy

# now label a node in your cluster so it matches the selector:
kubectl label node $(kubectl get nodes -o
  jsonpath='{.items[0].metadata.name}') kiamol=ch06 --overwrite

# check the Pods again:
kubectl get ds pi-proxy
```

You can see the control loop for the DaemonSet in action in figure 6.15. When the
node selector is applied, no nodes meet the selector, so the desired replica count for
the DaemonSet drops to zero. The existing Pod is one too many for the desired count,
so it is removed. Then, when the node is labeled, there's a match for the selector, and
the desired count increases to one, so a new Pod is created.

**The new DaemonSet spec includes a node selector that no
nodes in my cluster match, so the set is scaled down to zero.**

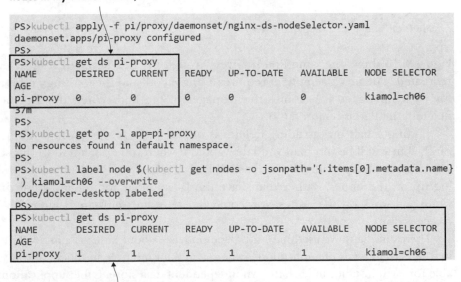

**When I label a node, there's now one match for the
node selector, and the DaemonSet scales up to one.**

Figure 6.15   DaemonSets watch nodes and their labels, as well as the current Pod status.

DaemonSets have a different control loop from ReplicaSets because their logic needs to watch node activity as well as Pod counts, but fundamentally, they are both controllers that manage Pods. All controllers are responsible for the life cycle of their managed objects, but the links can be broken. We'll use the DaemonSet in one more exercise to show how Pods can be set free from their controllers.

TRY IT NOW Kubectl has a cascade option on the delete command, which you can use to delete a controller without deleting its managed objects. Doing so leaves orphaned Pods behind, which can be adopted by another controller if they are a match for their previous owner.

```
# delete the DaemonSet, but leave the Pod alone:
kubectl delete ds pi-proxy --cascade=false

# check the Pod:
kubectl get po -l app=pi-proxy

# recreate the DS:
kubectl apply -f pi/proxy/daemonset/nginx-ds-nodeSelector.yaml

# check the DS and Pod:
kubectl get ds pi-proxy

kubectl get po -l app=pi-proxy

# delete the DS again, without the cascade option:
kubectl delete ds pi-proxy

# check the Pods:
kubectl get po -l app=pi-proxy
```

Figure 6.16 shows the same Pod survives through the DaemonSet being deleted and recreated. The new DaemonSet requires a single Pod, and the existing Pod is a match for its template, so it becomes the manager of the Pod. When this DaemonSet is deleted, the Pod is removed too.

Putting a halt on cascading deletes is one of those features you're going to use rarely, but you'll be very glad you knew about it when you do need it. In this scenario, you might be happy with all your existing Pods but have some maintenance tasks coming up on the nodes. Rather than have the DaemonSet adding and removing Pods while you work on the nodes, you could delete it and reinstate it after the maintenance is done.

The example we've used here for DaemonSets is about high availability, but it's limited to certain types of application—where you want multiple instances and it's acceptable for each instance to have its own independent data store. Other applications where you need high availability might need to keep data synchronized between instances, and for those, you can use StatefulSets. Don't skip on to chapter 8 yet, though, because you'll learn some neat patterns in chapter 7 that help with stateful apps, too.

Cascading deletes are the default, but you
can specify not to cascade, so deleting a
controller won't delete its Pods.

The labels on the Pod still match the DaemonSet's
selector, so when the DaemonSet is recreated, it
adopts the existing Pod.

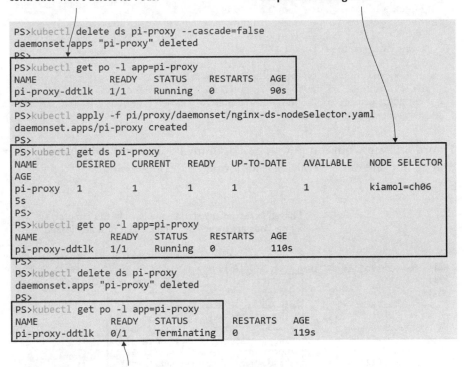

```
PS>kubectl delete ds pi-proxy --cascade=false
daemonset.apps "pi-proxy" deleted
PS>
PS>kubectl get po -l app=pi-proxy
NAME             READY    STATUS       RESTARTS    AGE
pi-proxy-ddtlk   1/1      Running      0           90s
PS>
PS>kubectl apply -f pi/proxy/daemonset/nginx-ds-nodeSelector.yaml
daemonset.apps/pi-proxy created
PS>
PS>kubectl get ds pi-proxy
NAME         DESIRED    CURRENT    READY    UP-TO-DATE    AVAILABLE    NODE SELECTOR
AGE
pi-proxy     1          1          1        1             1            kiamol=ch06
5s
PS>
PS>kubectl get po -l app=pi-proxy
NAME             READY    STATUS       RESTARTS    AGE
pi-proxy-ddtlk   1/1      Running      0           110s
PS>
PS>kubectl delete ds pi-proxy
daemonset.apps "pi-proxy" deleted
PS>
PS>kubectl get po -l app=pi-proxy
NAME             READY    STATUS                RESTARTS    AGE
pi-proxy-ddtlk   0/1      Terminating           0           119s
```

Adopting the Pod means the DaemonSet owns it again, so when the DaemonSet
is deleted with the default cascade behavior, the Pod is deleted, too.

**Figure 6.16   Orphaned Pods have lost their controller, so they're not part of a highly available
set anymore.**

StatefulSets, DaemonSets, ReplicaSets, and Deployments are the tools you use to model your apps, and they should give you enough flexibility to run pretty much anything in Kubernetes. We'll finish this chapter with a quick look at how Kubernetes actually manages objects that own other objects, and then we'll review how far we've come in this first section of the book.

6.4   *Understanding object ownership in Kubernetes*

Controllers use a label selector to find objects that they manage, and the objects themselves keep a record of their owner in a metadata field. When you delete a controller, its managed objects still exist but not for long. Kubernetes runs a garbage collector process that looks for objects whose owner has been deleted, and it deletes them, too. Object ownership can model a hierarchy: Pods are owned by ReplicaSets, and ReplicaSets are owned by Deployments.

TRY IT NOW   Look at the owner reference in the metadata fields for all Pods and ReplicaSets.

```
# check which objects own the Pods:
kubectl get po -o custom-columns=NAME:'{.metadata.name}',
    OWNER:'{.metadata.ownerReferences[0].name}',OWNER_KIND:'{.metadata.
    ownerReferences[0].kind}'

# check which objects own the ReplicaSets:
kubectl get rs -o custom-columns=NAME:'{.metadata.name}',
    OWNER:'{.metadata.ownerReferences[0].name}',OWNER_KIND:'{.metadata.
    ownerReferences[0].kind}'
```

Figure 6.17 shows my output, where all of my Pods are owned by some other object, and all but one of my ReplicaSets are owned by a Deployment.

I haven't created any standalone Pods in this chapter, so all my Pods are owned by a DaemonSet or a ReplicaSet.

```
PS>kubectl get po -o custom-columns=NAME:'{.metadata.name}',OWNER:'{.metadata.ow
nerReferences[0].name}',OWNER KIND:'{.metadata.ownerReferences[0].kind}'
NAME                       OWNER              OWNER_KIND
pi-proxy-5x2cp             pi-proxy           DaemonSet
pi-web-5f74878cb6-jf7m9    pi-web-5f74878cb6  ReplicaSet
pi-web-5f74878cb6-lvcsq    pi-web-5f74878cb6  ReplicaSet
pi-web-5f74878cb6-x2hpt    pi-web-5f74878cb6  ReplicaSet
sleep-b8f5f69-5dvjw        sleep-b8f5f69      ReplicaSet
whoami-web-8ck7t           whoami-web         ReplicaSet
whoami-web-8vl2p           whoami-web         ReplicaSet
whoami-web-b2fc6           whoami-web         ReplicaSet
PS>
PS>kubectl get rs -o custom-columns=NAME:'{.metadata.name}',OWNER:'{.metadata.ow
nerReferences[0].name}',OWNER KIND:'{.metadata.ownerReferences[0].kind}'
NAME                   OWNER      OWNER_KIND
pi-web-5f74878cb6      pi-web     Deployment
pi-web-75c758cc59      pi-web     Deployment
sleep-b8f5f69          sleep      Deployment
whoami-web             <none>     <none>
```

I did create one standalone ReplicaSet that has no owner, but all the others are owned by Deployments.

Figure 6.17   Objects know who their owners are—you can find this in the object metadata.

Kubernetes does a good job of managing relationships, but you need to remember that controllers track their dependents using the label selector alone, so if you fiddle with labels, you could break that relationship. The default delete behavior is what you want most of the time, but you can stop cascading deletes using kubectl and delete only the controller—that removes the owner reference in the metadata for the dependents, so they don't get picked up by the garbage collector.

We're going to finish up with a look at the architecture for the latest version of the Pi app, which we've deployed in this chapter. Figure 6.18 shows it in all its glory.

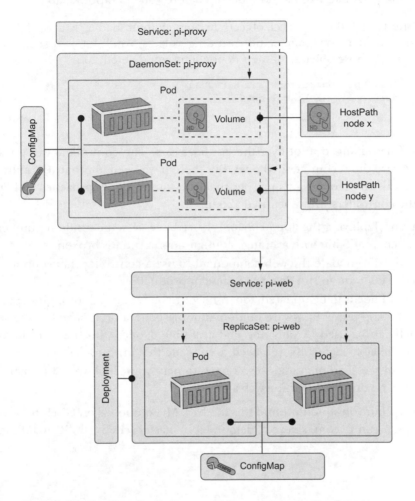

Figure 6.18 The Pi application: no annotations necessary—the diagram should be crystal clear.

Quite a lot is going on in this diagram: it's a simple app, but the deployment is complex because it uses lots of Kubernetes features to get high availability, scale, and flexibility. By now you should be comfortable with all those Kubernetes resources, and you should understand how they fit together and when to use them. Around 150 lines of YAML define the application, but those YAML files are all you need to run this app on your laptop or on a 50-node cluster in the cloud. When someone new joins the project, if they have solid Kubernetes experience—or if they've read the first six chapters of this book—they can be productive straight away.

That's all for the first section. My apologies if you had to take a few extended lunchtimes this week, but now you have all the fundamentals of Kubernetes, with best practices built in. All we need to do is tidy up before you attempt the lab.

TRY IT NOW   All the top-level objects in this chapter had a `kiamol` label applied. Now that you understand cascading deletes, you'll know that when you delete all those objects, all their dependents get deleted, too.

```
# remove all the controllers and Services:
kubectl delete all -l kiamol=ch06
```

6.5   *Lab*

Kubernetes has changed a lot over the last few years. The controllers we've used in this chapter are the recommended ones, but there have been alternatives in the past. Your job in this lab is to take an app spec that uses some older approaches and update it to use the controllers you've learned about.

- Start by deploying the app in `ch06/lab/numbers`—it's the random-number app from chapter 3 but with a strange configuration. And it's broken.
- You need to update the web component to use a controller that supports high load. We'll want to run dozens of these in production.
- The API needs to be updated, too. It needs to be replicated for high availability, but the app uses a hardware random-number generator attached to the server, which can be used by only one Pod at a time. Nodes with the right hardware have the label `rng=hw` (you'll need to simulate that in your cluster).
- This isn't a clean upgrade, so you need to plan your deployment to make sure there's no downtime for the web app.

Sounds scary, but you shouldn't find this too bad. My solution is on GitHub for you to check: https://github.com/sixeyed/kiamol/blob/master/ch06/lab/README.md.

Week 2

Kubernetes in the real world

When you start using Kubernetes for real, you soon find that not all applications fit the simple patterns. This section introduces more advanced features to get you ready for that. You'll learn how multiple containers can work together to make legacy apps behave like new ones, and how Kubernetes can provide a stable environment for stateful applications. You'll also get experience managing applications—configuring the upgrade process, packaging and distributing apps with Helm, and understanding the developer workflow.

7

Extending
applications with
multicontainer Pods

We met Pods in chapter 2, when you learned that you can run many containers in one Pod, but you didn't actually do it. In this chapter, you're going to see how it works and understand the patterns it enables. This is the first of the more advanced topics in this part of the book, but it's not a complicated subject—it just helps to have all the background knowledge from the previous chapters. Conceptually, it's quite simple: one Pod runs many containers, which is typically your app container plus some helper containers. It's what you can do with those helpers that makes this feature so interesting.

Containers in a Pod share the same virtual environment, so when one container takes an action, other containers can see it and react to it. They can even modify the intended action without the original container knowing. This behavior lets you model your application so that the app container is very simple—it just focuses on its work, and it has helpers that take care of integrating the app with other components and with the Kubernetes platform. It's a great way to add a consistent management API to all your apps, whether new or legacy.

7.1 How containers communicate in a Pod

The Pod is a virtual environment that creates a shared networking and filesystem space for one or more containers. The containers are isolated units; they have their own processes and environment variables, and they can use different images with different technology stacks. The Pod is a single unit, so when it is allocated to run on a node, all the Pod containers run on the same node. You can have one container running Python and another running Java, but you can't have some Linux

149

and some Windows containers in the same Pod (yet), because Linux containers need to run on a Linux node and Windows containers on a Windows node.

Containers in a Pod share the network, so each container has the same IP address—the IP address of the Pod. Multiple containers can receive external traffic, but they need to listen on different ports, and containers within the Pod can communicate using the localhost address. Each container has its own filesystem, but it can mount volumes from the Pod, so containers can exchange information by sharing the same mounts. Figure 7.1 shows the layout of a Pod with two containers.

One Pod can host many containers, using the same or different Docker images. Containers in the Pod can communicate using the localhost address.

The Pod is a single network space—it has one IP address, and the containers in the Pod can listen for traffic on different ports.

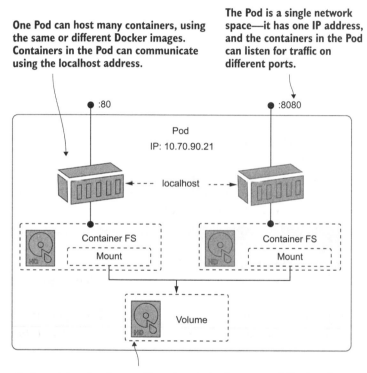

Each container has its own filesystem, but volumes are defined at the Pod level and can be mounted into multiple containers to share data.

Figure 7.1   The Pod is a shared network and storage environment for many containers.

That's all the theory we need for now, and as we go through the chapter, you'll be surprised at some of the smart things you can do just with shared networking and disk. We'll start with some simple exercises in this section to explore the Pod environment. Listing 7.1 shows the multicontainer Pod spec for a Deployment. Two containers are defined that happen to use the same image, and they both mount an `EmptyDir` volume, which is defined in the Pod.

Listing 7.1 sleep-with-file-reader.yaml, a simple multicontainer Pod spec

```
spec:
  containers:                        # The containers field is an array.
    - name: sleep
      image: kiamol/ch03-sleep
      volumeMounts:
        - name: data
          mountPath: /data-rw        # Mounts a volume as writable
    - name: file-reader              # Containers need different names.
      image: kiamol/ch03-sleep       # But containers can use the same or
                                     # different images.

      volumeMounts:
        - name: data
          mountPath: /data-ro
          readOnly: true             # Mounts the same volume as read-only
  volumes:
    - name: data                     # Volumes can be mounted by many
      containers.
        emptyDir: {}
```

This is a single Pod spec that runs two containers. When you deploy it, you'll see that there are some differences in how you work with multicontainer Pods.

TRY IT NOW   Deploy listing 7.1, and run a Pod with two containers.

```
# switch to the chapter folder:
cd ch07

# deploy the Pod spec:
kubectl apply -f sleep/sleep-with-file-reader.yaml

# get the detailed Pod information:
kubectl get pod -l app=sleep -o wide

# show the container names:
kubectl get pod -l app=sleep -o
  jsonpath='{.items[0].status.containerStatuses[*].name}'

# check the Pod logs—this will fail:
kubectl logs -l app=sleep
```

My output, which appears in figure 7.2, shows the Pod has two containers with a single IP address, which both run on the same node. You can see the details of the Pod as a single unit, but you can't print the logs at a Pod level; you need to specify a container from which to fetch the logs.

Both of the containers in that exercise use the sleep image, so they're not doing anything, but the containers keep running, and the Pod stays available to work with. The containers both mount the EmptyDir volume from the Pod, so that's a shared part of the filesystem, and you can use it in both containers.

The Ready column shows this Pod should have two containers running, and they are both up.

The wide output shows additional information, confirming that the Pod has a single IP address and runs on a single node.

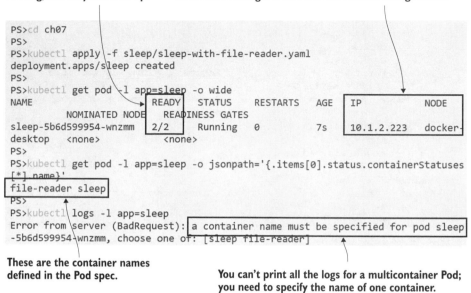

These are the container names defined in the Pod spec.

You can't print all the logs for a multicontainer Pod; you need to specify the name of one container.

Figure 7.2   **You always work with a Pod as a single unit, except when you need to specify a container.**

TRY IT NOW   One container mounts the volume as read-write and the other one as read-only. You can write files in one container and read them in the other.

```
# write a file to the shared volume using one container:
kubectl exec deploy/sleep -c sleep -- sh -c 'echo ${HOSTNAME} > /data-
    rw/hostname.txt'

# read the file using the same container:
kubectl exec deploy/sleep -c sleep -- cat /data-rw/hostname.txt

# read the file using the other container:
kubectl exec deploy/sleep -c file-reader -- cat /data-ro/hostname.txt

# try to add to the file to the read-only container—this will fail:
kubectl exec deploy/sleep -c file-reader -- sh -c 'echo more >> /data-
    ro/hostname.txt'
```

You'll see when you run this exercise that the first container can write data into the shared volume, and the second container can read it, but it can't write data itself. That's because the volume mount is defined as read-only for the second container in this Pod spec. It's not a generic Pod limitation; mounts can be defined as writable for multiple containers if you need that. Figure 7.3 shows my output.

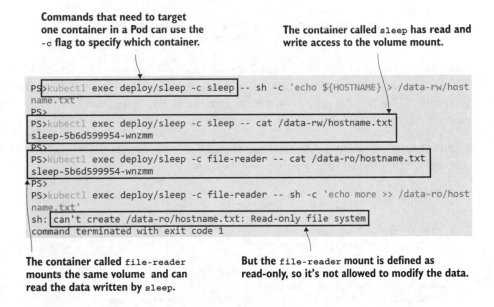

Commands that need to target one container in a Pod can use the -c flag to specify which container.

The container called `sleep` has read and write access to the volume mount.

The container called `file-reader` mounts the same volume and can read the data written by `sleep`.

But the `file-reader` mount is defined as read-only, so it's not allowed to modify the data.

Figure 7.3　Containers can mount the same Pod volume to share data but with different access levels.

A good old empty directory volume shows its worth again here; it's a simple scratch pad that all the Pod containers can access. Volumes are defined at the Pod level and mounted at the container level, which means you can use any type of volume or PVC and make it available for many containers to use. Decoupling the volume definition from the volume mount also allows selective sharing, so one container may be able to see Secrets whereas the others can't.

The other shared space is the network, where containers can listen on different ports and provide independent pieces of functionality. This is useful if your app container is doing some background work but doesn't have any features to report on progress. Another container in the same Pod can provide a REST API, which reports on what the app container is doing.

Listing 7.2 shows a simplified version of this process. This is an update to the sleep deployment that replaces the file-sharing container with a new container spec that runs a simple HTTP server.

> Listing 7.2　**sleep-with-server.yaml, running a web server in a second container**

```
spec:
  containers:
    - name: sleep
      image: kiamol/ch03-sleep    # The same container spec as listing 7.1
    - name: server
      image: kiamol/ch03-sleep    # The second container is different.
      command: ['sh', '-c', "while true; do echo -e 'HTTP/1.1 ...'"]
```

```
  ports:
    - containerPort: 8080      # Including the port just documents
                               # which port the application uses.
```

Now the Pod will run with the original app container—the sleep container, which isn't really doing anything—and a server container, which provides an HTTP endpoint on port 8080. The two containers share the same network space, so the sleep container can access the server using the localhost address.

TRY IT NOW   Update the sleep Deployment using the file from listing 7.2, and confirm that the server container is accessible.

```
# deploy the update:
kubectl apply -f sleep/sleep-with-server.yaml

# check the Pod status:
kubectl get pods -l app=sleep

# list the container names in the new Pod:
kubectl get pod -l app=sleep -o
    jsonpath='{.items[0].status.containerStatuses[*].name}'

# make a network call between the containers:
kubectl exec deploy/sleep -c sleep -- wget -q -O - localhost:8080

# check the server container logs:
kubectl logs -l app=sleep -c server
```

You can see my output in figure 7.4. Although these are separate containers, at the network level they function as though they were different processes running on the same machine, using the local address for communication.

It's not just within the Pod that the network is shared. The Pod has an IP address on the cluster, and if any containers in the Pod are listening on ports, then other Pods can access them. You can create a Service that routes traffic to the Pod on a specific port, and whichever container is listening on that port will receive the request.

TRY IT NOW   Use a kubectl command to expose the Pod port—this is a quick way to create a Service without writing YAML—and then test that the HTTP server is accessible externally.

```
# create a Service targeting the server container port:
kubectl expose -f sleep/sleep-with-server.yaml --type LoadBalancer --
    port 8020 --target-port 8080

# get the URL for your service:
kubectl get svc sleep -o
    jsonpath='http://{.status.loadBalancer.ingress[0].*}:8020'
# open the URL in your browser

# check the server container logs:
kubectl logs -l app=sleep -c server
```

The container spec is different in this update, so the Pod is replaced.

Both containers in the old Pod are stopped, and the two containers in the new Pod are started.

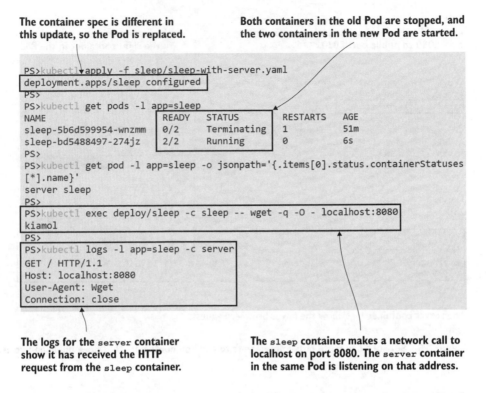

```
PS>kubectl apply -f sleep/sleep-with-server.yaml
deployment.apps/sleep configured
PS>
PS>kubectl get pods -l app=sleep
NAME                          READY   STATUS        RESTARTS   AGE
sleep-5b6d599954-wnzmm        0/2     Terminating   1          51m
sleep-bd5488497-274jz         2/2     Running       0          6s
PS>
PS>kubectl get pod -l app=sleep -o jsonpath='{.items[0].status.containerStatuses
[*].name}'
server sleep
PS>
PS>kubectl exec deploy/sleep -c sleep -- wget -q -O - localhost:8080
kiamol
PS>
PS>kubectl logs -l app=sleep -c server
GET / HTTP/1.1
Host: localhost:8080
User-Agent: Wget
Connection: close
```

The logs for the `server` container show it has received the HTTP request from the `sleep` container.

The `sleep` container makes a network call to localhost on port 8080. The `server` container in the same Pod is listening on that address.

Figure 7.4 Network communication between containers in the same Pod is over localhost.

Figure 7.5 shows my output. From the outside world, it's just network traffic going to a Service, which gets routed to a Pod. The Pod is running multiple containers, but that's a detail that is hidden from the consumer.

You should be getting a feel for how powerful running multiple containers in a Pod is, and in the rest of the chapter, we'll put the ideas to work in real-world scenarios. There's one thing that needs to be stressed, though: a Pod is not a replacement for a VM, so don't think you can run all the components of an app in one Pod. You might be tempted to model an app like that, with a web server container and an API container running in the same Pod—don't. A Pod is a single unit, and it should be used for a single component of your app. Additional containers can be used to support the app container, but you shouldn't be running different apps in the same Pod. Doing so ruins your ability to update, scale, and manage those components independently.

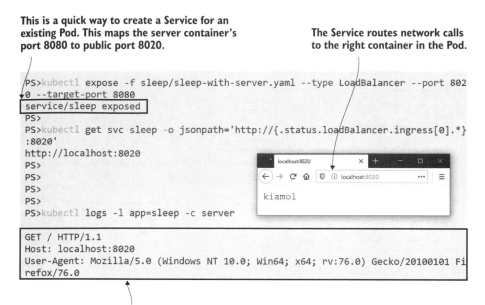

This is a quick way to create a Service for an existing Pod. This maps the server container's port 8080 to public port 8020.

The Service routes network calls to the right container in the Pod.

The server container logs show the latest browser request.

Figure 7.5   Services can route network requests to any Pod containers that have published ports.

7.2   Setting up applications with init containers

So far we've run Pods with multiple containers where all the containers run in parallel: they start together, and the Pod isn't considered to be ready until all the containers are ready. You'll hear that referred to as the *sidecar pattern*, which reinforces the idea that additional containers (the sidecars) play a supporting role to the application container (the motorcycle). There's another pattern that Kubernetes supports when you need a container to run before the app container to set up part of the environment. This is called an *init container.*

Init containers work differently from sidecars. You can have multiple init containers defined for the Pod, and they run in sequence, in the order in which they're written in the Pod spec. Each init container needs to complete successfully before the next one starts, and all must complete successfully before the Pod containers are started. Figure 7.6 shows the startup sequence for a Pod with init containers.

All containers can access volumes defined in the Pod, so the major use case is for an init container to write data that prepares the environment for the application container. Listing 7.3 shows a simple extension to the HTTP server in the sleep Pod from the previous exercise. An init container runs and generates an HTML file, which it writes in a mount for an EmptyDir volume. The server container responds to HTTP requests by sending the contents of that file.

Init containers run in sequence—each needs to complete successfully before the next one starts. They share the Pod environment with app containers.

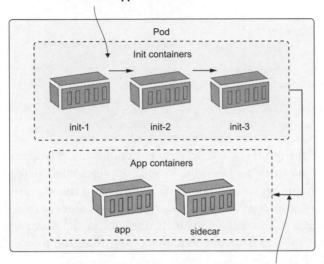

App containers start in parallel once all init containers have completed. All app containers need to be ready before the Pod is considered to be ready.

Figure 7.6   Init containers are useful for startup tasks to prepare the Pod for the app containers.

Listing 7.3   sleep-with-html-server.yaml, an init container in the Pod spec

```
spec:                                 # Pod spec in the Deployment template
  initContainers:                     # Init containers have their own array,
   - name: init-html                  # and they run in sequence.
     image: kiamol/ch03-sleep
     command: ['sh', '-c', "echo '<!DOCTYPE html...' > /data/index.html"]
     volumeMounts:
    - name: data
      mountPath: /data                # Init containers can mount Pod volumes.
```

This example uses the same sleep image for the init container, but it can be any image. You might use an init container to set up the application environment using tools that you don't want to be present in the running application. An init container can use a Docker image with the Git command line installed and clone a repository into the shared filesystem. The app container can access to the files without you having to set up the Git client in your app image.

TRY IT NOW   Deploy the update from listing 7.3, and see how init containers work.

```
# apply the updated spec with the init container:
kubectl apply -f sleep/sleep-with-html-server.yaml
```

```
# check the Pod containers:
kubectl get pod -l app=sleep -o
    jsonpath='{.items[0].status.containerStatuses[*].name}'

# check the init containers:
kubectl get pod -l app=sleep -o
    jsonpath='{.items[0].status.initContainerStatuses[*].name}'

# check logs from the init container—there are none:
kubectl logs -l app=sleep -c init-html

# check that the file is available in the sidecar:
kubectl exec deploy/sleep -c server -- ls -l /data-ro
```

You'll pick up a few things from this exercise. App containers are guaranteed not to run until init containers complete successfully, so your app can safely make assumptions about the environment that the init container prepares. In this case, the HTML file is sure to exist before the server container starts. Init containers are a different part of the Pod spec, but some management features work in the same way as app containers—you can read the logs from init containers even after they have exited. My output appears in figure 7.7.

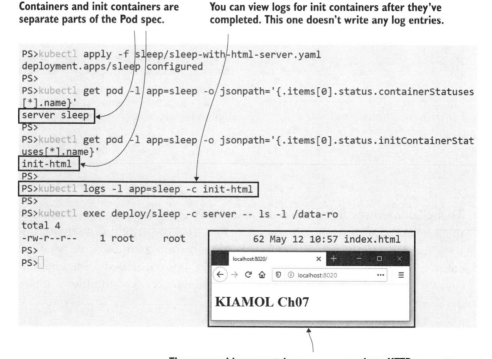

Containers and init containers are separate parts of the Pod spec.

You can view logs for init containers after they've completed. This one doesn't write any log entries.

```
PS>kubectl apply -f sleep/sleep-with-html-server.yaml
deployment.apps/sleep configured
PS>
PS>kubectl get pod -l app=sleep -o jsonpath='{.items[0].status.containerStatuses
[*].name}'
server sleep
PS>
PS>kubectl get pod -l app=sleep -o jsonpath='{.items[0].status.initContainerStat
uses[*].name}'
init-html
PS>
PS>kubectl logs -l app=sleep -c init-html
PS>
PS>kubectl exec deploy/sleep -c server -- ls -l /data-ro
total 4
-rw-r--r--    1 root     root            62 May 12 10:57 index.html
PS>
PS>
```

localhost:8020

localhost:8020

KIAMOL Ch07

The server sidecar container now responds to HTTP requests with the HTML file generated by the init container.

Figure 7.7   Init containers are useful for preparing the Pod environment for app and sidecar containers.

That still isn't a very real-world example, though, so let's do something better. We covered app configuration in chapter 4 and saw how to use environment variables, Config-Maps, and Secrets to build up a hierarchy of configuration settings. That's great if your app supports it, but many older apps don't have that flexibility; they expect to find a single config file in one place, and they don't go looking anywhere else. Let's look at an app like that.

TRY IT NOW This chapter has a new demo app, because if I'm getting bored with looking at Pi, then you must be, too. This one isn't much more fun, but at least it's different. It just writes a timestamp to a log file every few seconds. It has an old-style configuration framework, so we can't use any of the configuration techniques we've learned so far.

```
# run the app, which uses a single config file:
kubectl apply -f timecheck/timecheck.yaml

# check the container logs—there won't be any:
kubectl logs -l app=timecheck

# check the log file inside the container:
kubectl exec deploy/timecheck -- cat /logs/timecheck.log

# check the config setup:
kubectl exec deploy/timecheck -- cat /config/appsettings.json
```

You can see my output in figure 7.8. A limited configuration framework isn't the only reason this app isn't a good citizen in a container platform—there are no logs

This version of the app doesn't write log entries where Kubernetes can find them.

Instead they're written in a file in the container filesystem.

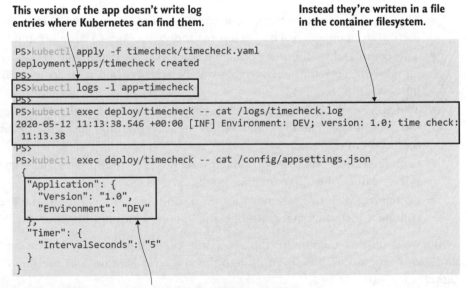

```
PS>kubectl apply -f timecheck/timecheck.yaml
deployment.apps/timecheck created
PS>
PS>kubectl logs -l app=timecheck
PS>
PS>kubectl exec deploy/timecheck -- cat /logs/timecheck.log
2020-05-12 11:13:38.546 +00:00 [INF] Environment: DEV; version: 1.0; time check:
 11:13.38
PS>
PS>kubectl exec deploy/timecheck -- cat /config/appsettings.json
{
"Application": {
  "Version": "1.0",
  "Environment": "DEV"
},
 "Timer": {
  "IntervalSeconds": "5"
 }
}
```

The log entries use settings from the config file, including the environment name and the app version.

Figure 7.8 Older apps that use a single configuration source can't benefit from a configuration hierarchy.

in the Pod, either—but we can address all the problems with additional containers in the Pod.

An init container is a perfect tool to bring this app into line with the configuration approach we want to use for all our apps. We can store the settings in ConfigMaps, Secrets, and environment variables, and use an init container to read from all the different inputs, merge the contents, and write the output to the single file location that the app uses. Listing 7.4 shows the init container in the Pod spec.

> **Listing 7.4   timecheck-with-config.yaml, an init container that writes configuration**

```
spec:
  initContainers:
  - name: init-config
    image: kiamol/ch03-sleep      # This image has the jq tool.
    command: ['sh', '-c', "cat /config-in/appsettings.json | jq --arg
    APP_ENV \"$APP_ENVIRONMENT\" '.Application.Environment=$APP_ENV' >
    /config-out/appsettings.json"]
    env:
      - name: APP_ENVIRONMENT      # All containers have their own environment
        value: TEST                # variables—they're not shared in the Pod.
    volumeMounts:
      - name: config-map           # Mounts a ConfigMap volume to read
        mountPath: /config-in
      - name: config-dir
        mountPath: /config-out     # Mounts an EmptyDir volume to write to
```

There are a few things to note before we update the deployment:

- The init container uses the jq tool, which the app doesn't need. The containers use different images, each with just the tools necessary to run that step.
- The command in the init container reads from a `ConfigMap` volume mount, merges the environment variable values, and writes out to an `EmptyDir` volume mount.
- The app container mounts the `EmptyDir` volume to the path where the config file needs to be. The file generated by the init container hides the default configuration in the app image.
- Containers don't share environment variables. The settings are specified for the init container; the app container doesn't see those.
- Containers map the volumes they need. Both containers mount the `EmptyDir` volume, which they share, but only the init container mounts the `ConfigMap`.

When we apply this update, the app's behavior will change in line with the `ConfigMap` and environment variables, even though the app container doesn't use them as configuration sources.

TRY IT NOW Update the timecheck app using listing 7.4 so the app container is configured from multiple sources.

```
# apply the ConfigMap and the new Deployment spec:
kubectl apply -f timecheck/timecheck-configMap.yaml -f
  timecheck/timecheck-with-config.yaml

# wait for the containers to start:
kubectl wait --for=condition=ContainersReady pod -l
  app=timecheck,version=v2

# check the log file in the new app container:
kubectl exec deploy/timecheck -- cat /logs/timecheck.log

# see the config file built by the init container:
kubectl exec deploy/timecheck -- cat /config/appsettings.json
```

You'll see when you run this that the app works with the new configuration, and the only change for the application container spec is that the config directory is mounted from the EmptyDir volume. My output is shown in figure 7.9.

This approach works because the config file is loaded from a dedicated directory. Remember that a volume mount overwrites a directory from the image, if it already exists. If the app loaded a config file from the same directory as the app binaries, you

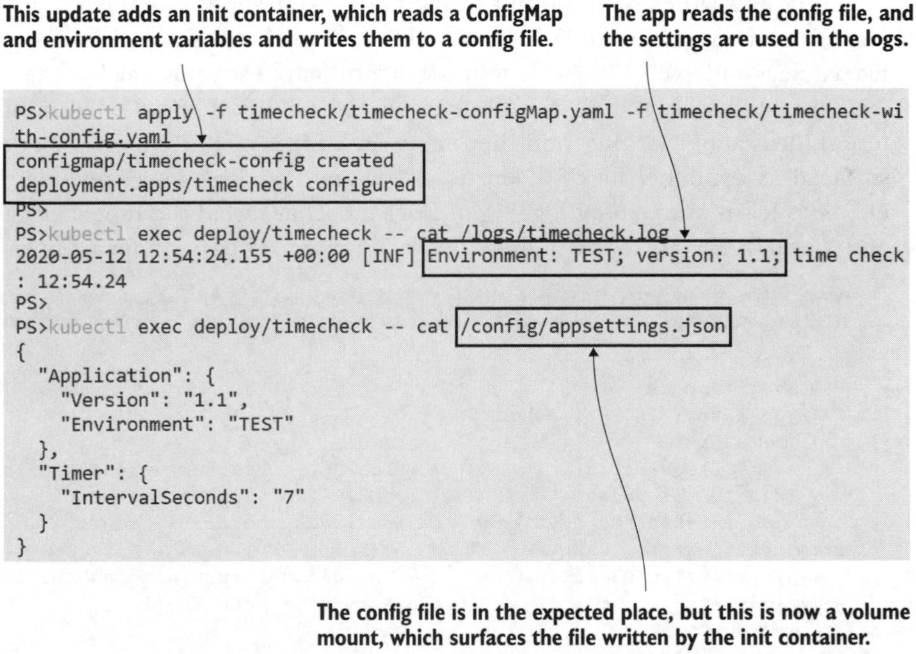

This update adds an init container, which reads a ConfigMap and environment variables and writes them to a config file.

The app reads the config file, and the settings are used in the logs.

```
PS>kubectl apply -f timecheck/timecheck-configMap.yaml -f timecheck/timecheck-wi
th-config.yaml
configmap/timecheck-config created
deployment.apps/timecheck configured
PS>
PS>kubectl exec deploy/timecheck -- cat /logs/timecheck.log
2020-05-12 12:54:24.155 +00:00 [INF] Environment: TEST; version: 1.1; time check
: 12:54.24
PS>
PS>kubectl exec deploy/timecheck -- cat /config/appsettings.json
{
  "Application": {
    "Version": "1.1",
    "Environment": "TEST"
  },
  "Timer": {
    "IntervalSeconds": "7"
  }
}
```

The config file is in the expected place, but this is now a volume mount, which surfaces the file written by the init container.

Figure 7.9 Init containers can change app behavior without changes to the app code or Docker image.

couldn't do this because the `EmptyDir` mount would overwrite the whole app folder. In that scenario, you would need an additional step in the app container startup to copy the config file from the mount into the application directory.

Applying a standard configuration approach to nonstandard apps is a great use for init containers, but older apps still won't play nicely in a modern platform, and that's where sidecar containers can help.

7.3 *Applying consistency with adapter containers*

Moving apps to Kubernetes is a great opportunity to add a layer of consistency across all your apps, so you deploy and manage them the same way using the same tools, no matter what the app is doing, or what technology stack it uses, or when it was developed. My fellow Docker Captain, Sune Keller, has talked about the service hotel (https://bit.ly/376rBcF) concept they use at Alm Brand. Their container platform offers a set of guarantees for "customers" (like high availability and security), provided they adhere to the rules (like pulling the configuration from the platform and writing logs out to it).

Not all apps know about the rules, and some of them can't be applied by the platform from the outside, but sidecar containers run alongside the app container so they have a privileged position. You can use them as *adapters*, which understand some aspect of how the app works and adapts it to how the platform wants it to work. Logging is a classic example.

Every app writes some output to log entries—or should; otherwise, it would be entirely unmanageable, and you should refuse to work with it. Modern app platforms like Node.js and .NET Core write to the standard output stream, which is where Docker fetches container logs and where Kubernetes gets the Pod logs. Older apps have different ideas about logging, and they may write to files or other targets that never get surfaced as container logs, so you never see any Pod logs (see Appendix D in the ebook to learn more about logging in Docker). That's what the timecheck app does, and we can fix it with a very simple sidecar container. The spec appears in listing 7.5.

> **Listing 7.5   timecheck-with-logging.yaml, using a sidecar container to expose logs**

```
containers:
  - name: timecheck
    image: kiamol/ch07-timecheck
    volumeMounts:
      - name: logs-dir                    # The app container writes the log file
        mountPath: /logs                  # to an EmptyDir volume mount.
      # Abbreviated—the full spec also includes the config mount.
  - name: logger
    image: kiamol/ch03-sleep              # The sidecar just watches the log file.
    command: ['sh', '-c', 'tail -f /logs-ro/timecheck.log']
    volumeMounts:
      - name: logs-dir
        mountPath: /logs-ro               # Uses the same volume as the app
        readOnly: true
```

All the sidecar does is mount the log volume (go `EmptyDir`!) and use the standard Linux `tail` command to read from the log file. The `-f` option means the command will follow the file; effectively, it just sits and watches for new writes, and when any lines are written to the file, they're echoed to standard out. It's a relay that adapts the app's actual logging implementation to the expectations of Kubernetes.

> **TRY IT NOW**   Apply the update from listing 7.5, and check the app logs are available.

```
# add the sidecar logging container:
kubectl apply -f timecheck/timecheck-with-logging.yaml

# wait for the containers to start:
kubectl wait --for=condition=ContainersReady pod -l
  app=timecheck,version=v3

# check the Pods:
kubectl get pods -l app=timecheck

# check the containers in the Pod:
kubectl get pod -l app=timecheck -o
  jsonpath='{.items[0].status.containerStatuses[*].name}'

# now you can see the app logs in the Pod:
kubectl logs -l app=timecheck -c logger
```

There's some inefficiency here because the app container writes logs to a file and then the logging container reads them back out again. There will be a small time lag and potentially a lot of wasted disk, but the Pod will be replaced in the next app update, and all the space used in the volume will be reclaimed. The benefit is that this Pod now behaves like every other Pod, making application logs available to Kubernetes but without any changes needed to the app itself, as is shown in figure 7.10.

Receiving configuration from the platform and writing logs to the platform are pretty much the fundamentals for any application, but as your platform matures, you'll have more expectations for standard behavior. You'll want to be able to test that the application inside the container is healthy, and you'll also want to be able to pull metrics from the app to see what it's doing and how hard it's working.

Sidecars can help there, too, either by running custom containers, which provide information tailored to the app, or by having standard health and metrics container images, which you apply to all your Pod specs. We'll round off the exercises using the timecheck app and add those features that make it a good citizen for Kubernetes. We'll cheat, though, with some more static HTTP server containers, which you can see in listing 7.6.

The original Pod had a single app container—the init container isn't included as a running container. The replacement has two.

Those are the timecheck app container and the logging sidecar.

```
PS>kubectl apply -f timecheck/timecheck-with-logging.yaml
deployment.apps/timecheck configured
PS>
PS>kubectl get pods -l app=timecheck
NAME                         READY   STATUS        RESTARTS   AGE
timecheck-674dddcb7f-h9257   2/2     Running       0          6s
timecheck-779f995658-q9cs4   1/1     Terminating   0          54m
PS>
PS>kubectl get pod -l app=timecheck -o jsonpath='{.items[0].status.containerStat
uses[*].name}'
logger timecheck
PS>
PS>kubectl logs -l app=timecheck -c logger
2020-05-12 13:48:37.065 +00:00 [INF] Environment: TEST; version: 1.1; time check
: 13:48.37
```

The sidecar is a log adapter—the entries written to the filesystem in the app container are now available from the Pod.

Figure 7.10   Adapters bring a layer of consistency to Pods, making old apps behave like new apps.

Listing 7.6   timecheck-good-citizen.yaml, more sidecars to extend the app

```
containers:                  # The previous app and logging containers are the same.
  - name: timecheck
# ...
  - name: logger
# ...

  - name: healthz      # A new sidecar that exposes a healthcheck API
    image: kiamol/ch03-sleep    # This is just a static response.
    command: ['sh', '-c', "while true; do echo -e 'HTTP/1.1 200 OK\nContent-
    Type: application/json\nContent-Length: 17\n\n{\"status\": \"OK\"}' | nc
    -l -p 8080; done"]
    ports:
      - containerPort: 8080      # Available at port 8080 in the Pod

  - name: metrics                # Another sidecar, which adds a metrics API
    image: kiamol/ch03-sleep    # The content is static again.
    command: ['sh', '-c', "while true; do echo -e 'HTTP/1.1 200 OK\nContent-
    Type: text/plain\nContent-Length: 104\n\n# HELP timechecks_total The
    total number timechecks.\n# TYPE timechecks_total
    counter\ntimechecks_total 6' | nc -l -p 8081; done"]
```

```
ports:
 - containerPort: 8081        # The content is avaialable on a different
                              # port.
```

The full YAML file also includes a ClusterIP Service, which publishes on port 8080 for the health endpoint and port 8081 for the metrics endpoint. In a production cluster, these would be used by other components to collect monitoring stats. The Deployment is an extension of the previous releases, so the app uses an init container for configuration and has a logging sidecar along with the new sidecars.

> **TRY IT NOW** Deploy the update, and check the new management endpoints for the health and performance of the app.

```
# apply the update:
kubectl apply -f timecheck/timecheck-good-citizen.yaml

# wait for all the containers to be ready:
kubectl wait --for=condition=ContainersReady pod -l
  app=timecheck,version=v4

# check the running containers:
kubectl get pod -l app=timecheck -o
  jsonpath='{.items[0].status.containerStatuses[*].name}'

# use the sleep container to check the timecheck app health:
kubectl exec deploy/sleep -c sleep -- wget -q -O - http://timecheck:8080

# check its metrics:
kubectl exec deploy/sleep -c sleep -- wget -q -O - http://timecheck:8081
```

When you run the exercise, you'll see everything works as expected, as shown in figure 7.11. You may also see the updates weren't as speedy as you're used to, with the new Pod taking longer to start up and the old Pod taking longer to terminate. The additional startup time is from having the init container, the app container, and all the sidecars—they all need to be ready before the new Pod is considered ready. The additional termination time is because the replaced Pod also had multiple containers, which are each given a grace period for the container process to shut down.

The update has to start multiple containers in the new Pod and terminate multiple containers in the old Pod, so it takes longer than for a single-container Pod.

The new Pod has four active containers: the app container and three sidecars.

```
PS>kubectl apply -f timecheck/timecheck-good-citizen.yaml
service/timecheck created
deployment.apps/timecheck configured
PS>
PS>kubectl wait --for=condition=ContainersReady pod -l app=timecheck,version=v4
pod/timecheck-54b49f688-76f7l condition met
PS>
PS>kubectl get pod -l app=timecheck -o jsonpath='{.items[0].status.containerStat
uses[*].name}'
healthz logger metrics timecheck
PS>
PS>kubectl exec deploy/sleep -c sleep -- wget -q -O - http://timecheck:8080
{"status": "OK"}
PS>
PS>kubectl exec deploy/sleep -c sleep -- wget -q -O - http://timecheck:8081
# HELP timechecks_total The total number timechecks.
# TYPE timechecks_total counter
timechecks_total 6
```

Port 8081 returns (fake) metrics. These can be used to monitor what the app is doing.

Port 8080 is a simple health check, which returns a (fake) JSON response. This can be used to check if the app is healthy.

Figure 7.11   Multiple adapter sidecars give the app a consistent management API.

There is an overhead to running all these sidecar containers as adapters. You've seen that it increases deployment times, but it also increases the ongoing compute requirements of the app—even storage and basic sidecars, which just tail log files and serve simple HTTP responses, all use memory and compute cycles. But if you want to move existing apps to Kubernetes that don't have those features, it's an acceptable approach to get all your apps behaving in the same way, as shown in figure 7.12.

In the previous exercise, we used an old sleep Pod we had lying around to call the new HTTP endpoints for the timecheck app. Remember that Kubernetes has a flat networking model, where Pods can send traffic to any other Pods via a Service. You may want more control over the network communication in your app, and you can do that with sidecars, too, by running a proxy container that manages the outgoing traffic from your app container.

Both Pods have the same behavior, viewed from outside. They ingest
ConfigMaps to configure the app, they write log entries out from the
Pod, and they have HTTP endpoints for metrics and health.

In the old app, all those features are provided by additional containers.

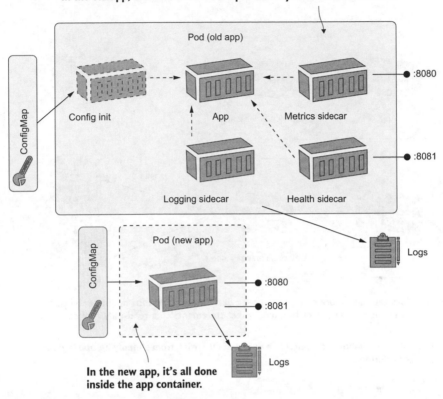

Figure 7.12   A consistent management API makes it easy to work with Pods—it doesn't
matter how the API is provided inside the Pod.

7.4   *Abstracting connections with ambassador containers*

The ambassador pattern lets you control and simplify outgoing connections from
your application: your app makes network requests to the localhost address, which are
picked up and performed by the ambassador. You can make use of a generic ambassador container, or one that is specific to your application components, in several situations. Figure 7.13 shows some examples. The logic in the ambassador might be geared
to improving performance or increasing reliability or security.

Taking control of the network away from the application is hugely powerful. A proxy
container can do service discovery, load balancing, retries, and even layer encryption
onto an unencrypted channel. Perhaps you've heard of the service mesh architecture,

App containers send service requests to localhost addresses, where they get picked up by the ambassador container.

An HTTP ambassador could be a simple proxy that abstracts the details of the actual connection from the app.

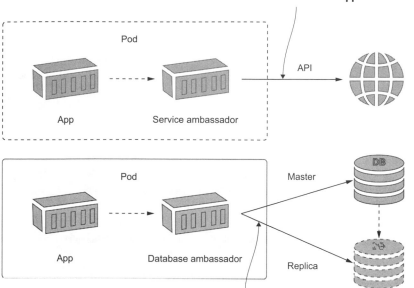

Ambassadors can have more complex logic—a database ambassador might send update statements to the master server but send select statements to a read-only replica.

Figure 7.13   The ambassador pattern has lots of potential, from simplifying app logic to increasing performance.

using technologies like Linkerd and Istio—they're all powered by proxy sidecar containers in a variation of the ambassador pattern.

We won't use a service mesh architecture here because that would take us well past lunchtime and on into the night, but we'll get a flavor of what it can do with a simplified example. The starting point is the random-number app we've used before. There's a web app running in a Pod, which consumes an API running in another Pod. The API is the only component the web app uses, so ideally we would restrict network calls to any other address, but in the initial deployment that doesn't happen.

TRY IT NOW   Run the random-number app, and verify that the web app container can use any network address.

```
# deploy the app and Services:
kubectl apply -f numbers/

# find the URL for your app:
kubectl get svc numbers-web -o
  jsonpath='http://{.status.loadBalancer.ingress[0].*}:8090'
```

```
# browse and get yourself a nice random number

# check that the web app has access to other endpoints:
kubectl exec deploy/numbers-web -c web -- wget -q -O -
   http://timecheck:8080
```

The web Pod can reach the API using the ClusterIP Service and the domain name numbers-api, but it can also access any other address, which could be a URL on the public internet or another ClusterIP Service. Figure 7.14 shows the app can read the health endpoint of the timecheck app—that should be a private endpoint, and it might expose information that is useful to someone up to no good.

The web application gets its numbers from a call to the API, running in another Pod.

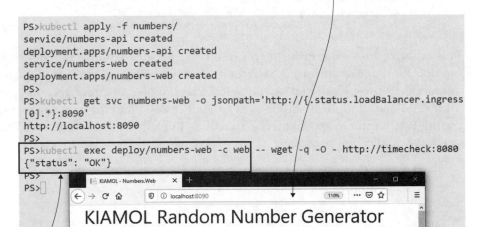

But the web container can access any network address. If it were compromised, attackers could use it to explore other apps in the cluster.

Figure 7.14   Kubernetes doesn't have any default restrictions on outgoing connections from Pod containers.

You have a lot of options for restricting network access besides using a proxy sidecar, but the ambassador pattern comes with some additional features that make it worth considering. Listing 7.7 shows an update to the web app spec, using a simple proxy container as an ambassador.

Listing 7.7   web-with-proxy.yaml, using a proxy as an ambassador

```
containers:
  - name: web
    image: kiamol/ch03-numbers-web
    env:
      - name: http_proxy                     # Sets the container to use the proxy
        value: http://localhost:1080         # so traffic goes to the ambassador
      - name: RngApi__Url
        value: http://localhost/api          # Uses a localhost address for the API
  - name: proxy
    image: kiamol/ch07-simple-proxy          # This is a basic HTTP proxy.
      env:
        - name: Proxy__Port                   # Routes network requests from the app
          value: "1080"                       # using the configured URI mapping
        - name: Proxy__Request__UriMap__Source
          value: http://localhost/api
        - name: Proxy__Request__UriMap__Target
          value: http://numbers-api/sixeyed/kiamol/master/ch03/numbers/rng
```

This example shows the major pieces of the ambassador pattern: the app container uses localhost addresses for any services it consumes, and it's configured to route all network calls through the proxy container. The proxy is a custom app that logs network calls, maps localhost addresses to real addresses, and blocks any addresses that are not listed in the map. All that becomes functionality in the Pod, but it's transparent to the application container.

TRY IT NOW   Update the random-number app, and confirm the network is now locked down.

```
# apply the update from listing 7.5:
kubectl apply -f numbers/update/web-with-proxy.yaml

# refresh your browser, and get a new number

# check the proxy container logs:
kubectl logs -l app=numbers-web -c proxy

# try to read the health of the timecheck app:
kubectl exec deploy/numbers-web -c web -- wget -q -O -
  http://timecheck:8080

# check proxy logs again:
kubectl logs -l app=numbers-web -c proxy
```

Now the web app is decoupled even further from the API, because it doesn't even know the URL of the API—that's set in the ambassador, which can be configured independently of the app. The web app is also restricted to using a single address for outgoing requests, and all of those calls are logged by the proxy, as you see in figure 7.15.

The ambassador for this web app proxies HTTP calls outside of the Pod, but the ambassador pattern is wider than that. It plugs into the network at the transport layer,

The web container routes all traffic through the proxy, which maps the
requested address to the actual address and logs the connection request.

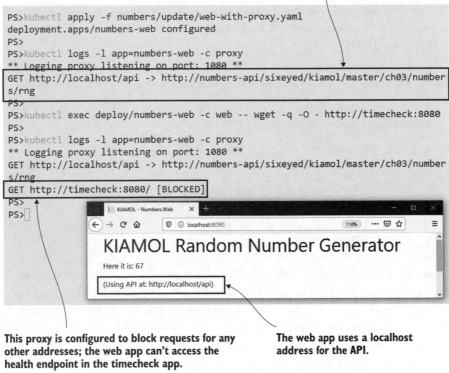

```
PS>kubectl apply -f numbers/update/web-with-proxy.yaml
deployment.apps/numbers-web configured
PS>
PS>kubectl logs -l app=numbers-web -c proxy
** Logging proxy listening on port: 1080 **
GET http://localhost/api -> http://numbers-api/sixeyed/kiamol/master/ch03/number
s/rng
PS>
PS>kubectl exec deploy/numbers-web -c web -- wget -q -O - http://timecheck:8080
PS>
PS>kubectl logs -l app=numbers-web -c proxy
** Logging proxy listening on port: 1080 **
GET http://localhost/api -> http://numbers-api/sixeyed/kiamol/master/ch03/number
s/rng
GET http://timecheck:8080/ [BLOCKED]
PS>
PS>
```

KIAMOL - Numbers.Web

← → C ⌂   localhost:8090   110%   ··· ♡ ☆   ≡

KIAMOL Random Number Generator

Here it is: 67

(Using API at: http://localhost/api)

This proxy is configured to block requests for any
other addresses; the web app can't access the
health endpoint in the timecheck app.

The web app uses a localhost
address for the API.

Figure 7.15   All network access is via the ambassador, which can implement its own access rules.

so it can work on any kind of traffic. A database ambassador can make some smart
choices, like sending queries to a read-only database replica and using only the master
database for writes. That's going to improve performance and scale, while keeping
complex logic out of the application.

We'll round out the chapter by taking a closer look at what it means to use the Pod
as a shared environment for many containers.

7.5   *Understanding the Pod environment*

The Pod is a boundary around one or more containers, just like the container is a
boundary around one or more processes. Pods create layers of virtualization without
adding overhead, so they're flexible and efficient. The cost of that flexibility is—as
always—complexity, and you need to be aware of some nuances to working with multicontainer Pods.

The main thing to understand is that the Pod is still the single unit of compute,
even if lots of containers are running inside it. Pods aren't ready until all the containers

in the Pod are ready, and Services send traffic only to Pods that are ready. Adding side-cars and init containers adds to the failure modes for your application.

TRY IT NOW   You can break your application if an init container fails. This update to the numbers app won't be successful because the init container is misconfigured.

```
# apply the update:
kubectl apply -f numbers/update/web-v2-broken-init-container.yaml

# check the new Pod:
kubectl get po -l app=numbers-web,version=v2

# check the logs for the new init container:
kubectl logs -l app=numbers-web,version=v2 -c init-version

# check the status of the Deployment:
kubectl get deploy numbers-web

# check the status of the ReplicaSets:
kubectl get rs -l app=numbers-web
```

You can see in this exercise that the failed init container effectively prevents the application from updating. The new Pod never enters the running state and won't receive traffic from the Service. The Deployment never scales down the old ReplicaSet because the new one doesn't reach the required level of availability, but the basic details of the Deployment look like the update has worked, as shown in figure 7.16.

The same situation will happen if a sidecar container fails on startup—the Pod doesn't have all of its containers running so the Pod itself isn't ready. Any deployment checks you have in place need to be extended for multicontainer Pods to ensure all init containers run to completion and all Pod containers are running. You need to be aware of the following restart conditions, too:

- If a Pod with init containers is replaced, then the new Pod runs all the init containers again. You must ensure your init logic can be run repeatedly.
- If you deploy a change to the init container image(s) for a Pod, that restarts the Pod. Init containers all execute again, and app containers are replaced.
- If you deploy a Pod spec change to the app container image(s), the app containers are replaced, but the init containers are not executed again.
- If an application container exits, then the Pod re-creates it. Until the container is replaced, the Pod is not fully running and won't receive Service traffic.

The Pod is a single compute environment, but when you add multiple moving parts inside that environment, you need to test all the failure scenarios and make sure your app behaves as you expect.

There's one last part of the Pod environment that we haven't covered: the compute layer. Pod containers have a shared network and can share parts of the filesystem, but they can't access each other's processes—the container boundary still provides

This update has a broken init container spec. Kubernetes restarts the container, but it will never run successfully, so the app containers won't start, and the Pod will never be ready.

The logs from the failed init container are still available.

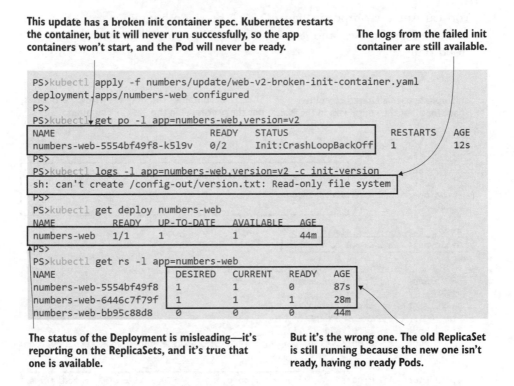

```
PS>kubectl apply -f numbers/update/web-v2-broken-init-container.yaml
deployment.apps/numbers-web configured
PS>
PS>kubectl get po -l app=numbers-web,version=v2
NAME                             READY   STATUS                 RESTARTS   AGE
numbers-web-5554bf49f8-k5l9v     0/2     Init:CrashLoopBackOff  1          12s
PS>
PS>kubectl logs -l app=numbers-web,version=v2 -c init-version
sh: can't create /config-out/version.txt: Read-only file system
PS>
PS>kubectl get deploy numbers-web
NAME          READY   UP-TO-DATE   AVAILABLE   AGE
numbers-web   1/1     1            1           44m
PS>
PS>kubectl get rs -l app=numbers-web
NAME                    DESIRED   CURRENT   READY   AGE
numbers-web-5554bf49f8  1         1         0       87s
numbers-web-6446c7f79f  1         1         1       28m
numbers-web-bb95c88d8   0         0         0       44m
```

The status of the Deployment is misleading—it's reporting on the ReplicaSets, and it's true that one is available.

But it's the wrong one. The old ReplicaSet is still running because the new one isn't ready, having no ready Pods.

Figure 7.16 Adding more containers to your Pod spec adds more opportunities for the Pod to fail

compute isolation. That's the default behavior, but in some cases, you want your sidecar to have access to the processes in the application container, either for interprocess communication or so the sidecar can fetch metrics about the app process.

You can enable this access with a simple setting in the Pod spec: `shareProcess-Namespace: true`. That means every container in the Pod shares the same compute space and can see each other's processes.

TRY IT NOW Deploy an update to the sleep Pod so the containers use a shared compute space and can access each other's processes.

```
# check the processes in the current container:
kubectl exec deploy/sleep -c sleep -- ps

# apply the update:
kubectl apply -f sleep/sleep-with-server-shared.yaml

# wait for the new containers:
kubectl wait --for=condition=ContainersReady pod -l
  app=sleep,version=shared

# check the processes again:
kubectl exec deploy/sleep -c sleep -- ps
```

You can see my output in figure 7.17. The sleep container can see all the server container's processes, and it could happily kill them all and leave the Pod in a confused state.

This update uses a shared compute   **The `sleep` container can only see its own processes,**
space for all of the containers in the Pod. **not the processes in the `server` container.**

```
PS>kubectl exec deploy/sleep -c sleep -- ps
PID   USER    TIME  COMMAND
    1 root    0:00  /bin/sh -c trap : TERM INT; (while true; do sleep 1000; don
e) & wait
   44 root    0:00  sleep 1000
   45 root    0:00  ps
PS>
PS>kubectl apply -f sleep/sleep-with-server-shared.yaml
deployment.apps/sleep configured
PS>
PS>kubectl wait --for=condition=ContainersReady pod -l app=sleep,version=shared
pod/sleep-7594f96c7c-xqgn5 condition met
PS>
PS>kubectl exec deploy/sleep -c sleep -- ps
PID   USER    TIME  COMMAND
    1 root    0:00  /pause
    6 root    0:00  /bin/sh -c trap : TERM INT; (while true; do sleep 1000; don
e) & wait
   18 root    0:00  sleep 1000
   19 root    0:00  sh -c while true; do echo -e 'HTTP/1.1 200 OK Content-Type:
text/plain Content-Length: 7  kiamol' | nc -l -p 8080; done
   25 root    0:00  nc -l -p 8080
   31 root    0:00  ps
```

**Now the `sleep` container can see the `nc` process, which
is the HTTP server running in the sidecar container.**

Figure 7.17 You can configure a Pod so all containers can see all processes—use with care.

That's all for multicontainer Pods. You've seen in this chapter that you can use init containers to prepare the environment for your application container and run sidecar containers to add features to your app, all without changing the app code or the Docker image. There are some caveats to using multiple containers, but it's a pattern you'll use often to extend your applications. Just remember that the Pod should be one logical component: I don't want to see you running Nginx, WordPress, and MySQL in a single Pod just because you can. Let's tidy up now and get ready for the lab.

TRY IT NOW   Remove everything matching this chapter's label.

```
kubectl delete all -l kiamol=ch07
```

7.6   *Lab*

It's back to the Pi app for this lab. The Docker image `kiamol/ch05-pi` can actually be used in different ways, and to run it as a web app, you need to override the startup command in the container spec. We've done that in the YAML files in previous chapters, but now we've been asked to use a standard approach to setting up the pod. Here are the requirements and some hints:

- The app container needs to use a standard startup command that all Pods in our platform are using. It should run `/init/startup.sh`.
- The Pod should use port 80 for the app container.
- The Pod should also publish port 8080 for an HTTP server, which returns the version number of the app,
- The app container image doesn't contain a startup script, so you'll need to use something that can create that script and make it executable for the app container to run.
- The app doesn't publish a version API on port 8080 (or anywhere else), so you'll need something that can provide that (it can just be any static text).

The starting point is the YAML in `ch07/lab/pi`, which is broken at the moment. You'll need to do some investigation into how the app ran in previous chapters and apply the techniques we've learned in this chapter. You have plenty of ways to approach this one, and you'll find my sample solution in the usual place: https://github.com/sixeyed/kiamol/blob/master/ch07/lab/README.md.

Running
data-heavy apps
with StatefulSets and Jobs

"Data heavy" isn't a very scientific term, but this chapter is about running a class of application that isn't just stateful but is also demanding about how it uses state. Databases are one example of this class. They need to run across multiple instances for high availability, each instance needs a local data store for fast access, and those independent data stores need to be kept in sync. The data has its own availability requirements, and you'll need to run backups periodically to guard against terminal failure or corruption. Other data-intensive applications, like message queues and distributed caches, have similar requirements.

You can run those kinds of app in Kubernetes, but you need to design around an inherent conflict: Kubernetes is a dynamic environment, and data-heavy apps typically expect to run in a stable environment. Clustered applications, which expect to find peers at a known network address, won't work nicely in a ReplicaSet, and backup jobs, which expect to read from a disk drive, won't work well with PersistentVolumeClaims. You need to model your app differently if it has strict data requirements, and we'll cover how to do that in this chapter with some more advanced controllers: StatefulSets, Jobs, and CronJobs.

8.1   How Kubernetes models stability with StatefulSets

A StatefulSet is a Pod controller with predictable management features: it lets you run applications at scale within a stable framework. When you deploy a ReplicaSet, it creates Pods with random names, which are not individually addressable over the domain name system (DNS), and it starts them in parallel. When you deploy a StatefulSet, it creates Pods with predictable names, which can be individually accessed over DNS, and starts them in order; the first Pod needs to be up and running before the second Pod is created.

Clustered applications are a great candidate for StatefulSets. Typically they're designed with a primary instance and one or more secondaries, which gives them high availability. You might be able to scale the secondaries, but they all need to reach the primary and then use it to synchronize their own data. You can't model that with a Deployment because in the ReplicaSet, there is no way to identify a single Pod as the primary, so you'd end up with bizarre and unpredictable conditions with multiple primaries or zero primaries.

Figure 8.1 shows an example of that, which could be used to run the Postgres database we've used in previous chapters for the to-do list application, but it uses a StatefulSet to achieve replicated data and high availability.

The Pod runs a script at startup, which checks to see if it is Pod 0. If it is, the Pod sets itself up as the primary instance of the app.

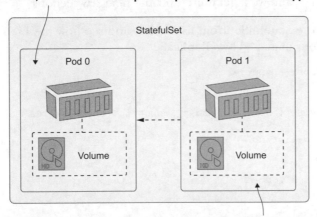

The next Pod doesn't start until Pod 0 is running. The same startup script tells Pod 1 it is not the primary, so it sets itself up as a secondary and synchronizes data from Pod 0.

Figure 8.1   In a StatefulSet, each Pod can have its own copy of data replicated from the first Pod.

The setup for this is quite involved, and we'll spend a couple of sections getting there in stages, so you learn how all the pieces of a working StatefulSet fit together. It's a pattern that is useful for more than just databases—many older applications were designed for a static runtime environment and made assumptions about stability that don't hold true in Kubernetes. StatefulSets allow you to model that stability, and if your goal is to move your existing apps to Kubernetes, then they may be something you use early in that journey.

Let's start with a simple StatefulSet that shows the basics. Listing 8.1 shows that StatefulSets have pretty much the same specs as other Pod controllers, except that they also need to include the name of a Service.

Listing 8.1   todo-db.yaml, a simple StatefulSet

```
apiVersion: apps/v1
kind: StatefulSet
metadata:
  name: todo-db
spec:
  selector:                 # StatefulSets use the same selector mechanism.
    matchLabels:
      app: todo-db
  serviceName: todo-db      # StatefulSets must be linked to a Service.
  replicas: 2
  template:
    # pod spec...
```

When you deploy this YAML file, you'll get a StatefulSet running two Postgres pods, but don't get too excited—they're just two separate database servers that happen to be managed by the same controller. There's more work needed to get two Pods to be a replicated database cluster, and we'll get there over the next few sections.

TRY IT NOW   Deploy the StatefulSet from listing 8.1, and see how the Pods it creates compare to Pods managed by a ReplicaSet.

```
# switch to the chapter's source:
cd ch08

# deploy the StatefulSet, Service, and a Secret for the Postgres
# password:
kubectl apply -f todo-list/db/

# check the StatefulSet:
kubectl get statefulset todo-db

# check the Pods:
kubectl get pods -l app=todo-db

# find the hostname of Pod 0:
kubectl exec pod/todo-db-0 -- hostname

# check the logs of Pod 1:
kubectl logs todo-db-1 --tail 1
```

You can see from figure 8.2 that a StatefulSet works in a very different way from a ReplicaSet or a DaemonSet. The Pods have a predictable name, which is the Stateful-Set name followed by the index of the Pod, so you can manage the Pods using their names instead of having to use a label selector.

The Pods are still managed by the controller, but in a more predictable way than with a ReplicaSet. Pods are created in order from zero up to n; if you scale down the set, the controller will remove them in the reverse order, starting from n and working down. If you delete a Pod, the controller will create a replacement. It will have the same name and configuration as the original, but it will be a new Pod.

StatefulSets are Pod controllers, but they work in a predictable way: the Pods
are started in order, and the Pod name contains the index of the Pod in the set.

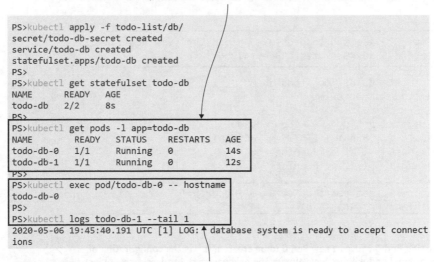

```
PS>kubectl apply -f todo-list/db/
secret/todo-db-secret created
service/todo-db created
statefulset.apps/todo-db created
PS>
PS>kubectl get statefulset todo-db
NAME      READY   AGE
todo-db   2/2     8s
PS>
PS>kubectl get pods -l app=todo-db
NAME        READY   STATUS    RESTARTS   AGE
todo-db-0   1/1     Running   0          14s
todo-db-1   1/1     Running   0          12s
PS>
PS>kubectl exec pod/todo-db-0 -- hostname
todo-db-0
PS>
PS>kubectl logs todo-db-1 --tail 1
2020-05-06 19:45:40.191 UTC [1] LOG: database system is ready to accept connect
ions
```

This is a stable environment; the logic inside the Pod can confirm it is the first Pod
in the set, and operators can use the predictable Pod names to work with them.

**Figure 8.2   A StatefulSet can create the environment for a clustered application, but the
app needs to configure itself.**

TRY IT NOW   Delete Pod 0 of the StatefulSet, and see that Pod 0 comes back
again.

```
# check the internal ID of Pod 0:
kubectl get pod todo-db-0 -o jsonpath='{.metadata.uid}'

# delete the Pod:
kubectl delete pod todo-db-0

# check Pods:
kubectl get pods -l app=todo-db

# check that the new Pod is a new Pod:
kubectl get pod todo-db-0 -o jsonpath='{.metadata.uid}'
```

You can see in figure 8.3 that a StatefulSet provides a stable environment for the app.
Pod 0 is replaced with an identical Pod 0, but that doesn't trigger a whole new set; the
original Pod 1 remains. Ordering is applied only for creation and scaling, not for
replacing missing Pods.

The StatefulSet is only the first part of modeling a stable environment. You can get
DNS names for each Pod linking the StatefulSet to a service, and that means you can configure Pods to initialize themselves by working with other replicas at known addresses.

Every Kubernetes object has an internal ID: the UID. You don't often use them, but they're useful when objects are replaced by different objects with the same name.

```
PS>kubectl get pod todo-db-0 -o jsonpath='{.metadata.uid}'
071ec8fd-5056-49e8-9feb-d83dc91412b6
PS>
PS>kubectl delete pod todo-db-0
pod "todo-db-0" deleted
PS>
PS>kubectl get pods -l app=todo-db
NAME        READY    STATUS     RESTARTS    AGE
todo-db-0   1/1      Running    0           4s
todo-db-1   1/1      Running    0           11m
PS>
PS>kubectl get pod todo-db-0 -o jsonpath='{.metadata.uid}'
cb813fad-0082-4623-a7b1-0b2c844ae1d8
```

Deleting Pod 0 causes a new Pod 0 to be created. It has the configuration of the original and will use any volumes the original used, but it is a new object.

Figure 8.3   StatefulSets replace missing replicas exactly as they were.

8.2   *Bootstrapping Pods with init containers in StatefulSets*

The Kubernetes API composes objects from other objects: the Pod template in a StatefulSet definition is the same object type you use in the template for a Deployment and in a bare Pod definition. That means all the Pod features are available for StatefulSets even though the Pods themselves are managed in a different way. We learned about init containers in chapter 7, and they're a perfect tool for the complicated initialization steps you often need in clustered applications.

Listing 8.2 shows the first init container for an update to the Postgres deployment. Multiple init containers in this Pod spec run in sequence, and because the Pods also start in sequence, you can guarantee that the first init container in Pod 1 won't run until Pod 0 is fully initialized and ready.

Listing 8.2   todo-db.yaml, the replicated Postgres setup with initialization

```
initContainers:
  - name: wait-service
    image: kiamol/ch03-sleep
    envFrom:                          # env file for sharing between containers
      - configMapRef:
        name: todo-db-env
    command: ['/scripts/wait-service.sh']
    volumeMounts:
      - name: scripts                 # Volume loads scripts from ConfigMap.
        mountPath: "/scripts"
```

The script that runs in this init container has two functions: if it's running in Pod 0, it just prints a log to confirm that this is the database primary, and then the container exits; if it's running in any other Pod, it makes a DNS lookup call to the primary, to make sure it's accessible before continuing. The next init container will start the replication process, so this one makes sure everything is in place.

The exact steps in this example are specific to Postgres, but the pattern is the same for many clustered and replicated applications—MySQL, Elasticsearch, RabbitMQ, and NATS all have broadly similar requirements. Figure 8.4 shows how you can model that pattern using init containers in a StatefulSet.

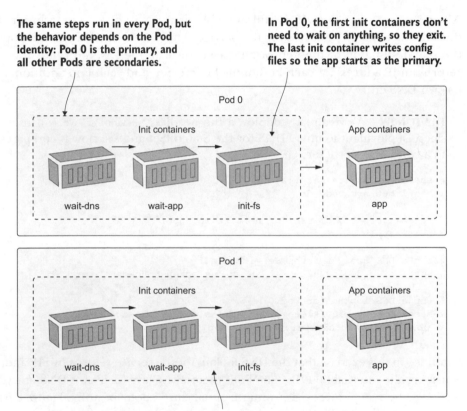

The same steps run in every Pod, but the behavior depends on the Pod identity: Pod 0 is the primary, and all other Pods are secondaries.

In Pod 0, the first init containers don't need to wait on anything, so they exit. The last init container writes config files so the app starts as the primary.

In Pod 1, the init containers first make sure that Pod 0 is reachable from DNS and that the primary is ready. Then the secondary config files are written, and the app starts.

Figure 8.4   The stable environment of a StatefulSet gives guarantees you can use in initialization.

You define DNS names for the individual Pods in a StatefulSet by identifying a Service in the spec, but it needs to be a special configuration of headless Service. Listing 8.3 shows how the database Service is configured with no ClusterIP address and with a selector for the Pods.

Listing 8.3   todo-db-service.yaml, a headless Service for a StatefulSet

```
apiVersion: v1
kind: Service
metadata:
  name: todo-db
spec:
  selector:
    app: todo-db        # The Pod selector matches the StatefulSet.
  clusterIP: None       # The service will not get its own IP address.
  ports:
    # ports follow
```

A Service with no ClusterIP is still available as a DNS entry in the cluster, but it doesn't use a fixed IP address for the Service. There's no virtual IP that is routed to the real destination by the networking layer. Instead, the DNS entry for the service returns an IP address for each Pod in the StatefulSet, and each Pod additionally gets its own DNS entry.

> **TRY IT NOW**   We've already deployed the headless Service, so we can use a sleep Deployment to query DNS for the StatefulSet and see how it compares to a typical ClusterIP service.

```
# show the Service details:
kubectl get svc todo-db

# run a sleep Pod to use for network lookups:
kubectl apply -f sleep/sleep.yaml

# run a DNS query for the Service name:
kubectl exec deploy/sleep -- sh -c 'nslookup todo-db | grep "^[^*]"'

# run a DNS lookup for Pod 0:
kubectl exec deploy/sleep -- sh -c 'nslookup todo-db-0.todo-
   db.default.svc.cluster.local | grep "^[^*]"'
```

You'll see in this exercise that the DNS lookup for the service returns two IP addresses, which are the internal Pod IPs. The Pods themselves have their own DNS entry in the format pod-name.service-name with the usual cluster domain suffix. Figure 8.5 shows my output.

Predictable startup order and individually addressable Pods are the foundation for initializing a clustered app in a StatefulSet. The details will differ wildly between applications, but broadly, the startup logic for the Pod will be something like this: if I am Pod 0, then I'm the primary, so I do all the primary setup stuff; otherwise, I'm a secondary, so I'll give the primary some time to get set up, check that everything's working, and then synchronize using the Pod 0 address.

The actual setup for Postgres is quite involved, so I'll skip over it here. It uses scripts in ConfigMaps with init containers to set up the primary and secondaries. I use

This Service doesn't have its own virtual IP address like a typical ClusterIP service.

It still has a DNS entry, but the lookup returns the IP addresses for all of the Pods.

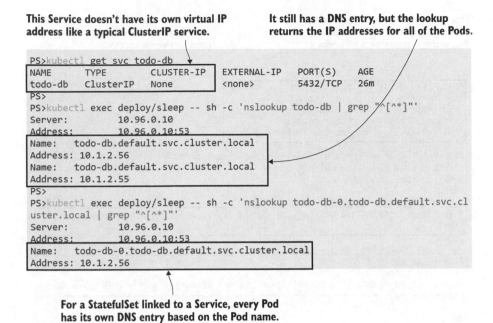

For a StatefulSet linked to a Service, every Pod has its own DNS entry based on the Pod name.

Figure 8.5   StatefulSets give each Pod its own DNS entry, so they are individually addressable.

various techniques we've covered in the book so far in the spec for the StatefulSet, which is worth exploring, but the details of the scripts are all specific to Postgres.

TRY IT NOW   Update the database to make it a replicated setup. There are configuration files and startup scripts in ConfigMaps, and the StatefulSet is updated to use them in init containers.

```
# deploy the replicated StatefulSet setup:
kubectl apply -f todo-list/db/replicated/

# wait for the Pods to spin up
kubectl wait --for=condition=Ready pod -l app=todo-db

# check the logs of Pod 0—the primary:
kubectl logs todo-db-0 --tail 1

# and of Pod 1—the secondary:
kubectl logs todo-db-1 --tail 2
```

Postgres uses an active-passive model for replication, so the primary is used for database reads and writes, and the secondaries sync data from the primary and can be used by clients, but only for read access. Figure 8.6 shows how the init containers recognize the role for each Pod and initialize them.

This deployment uses init containers, running scripts to establish if the Pod is the primary or a secondary.

Pod 0 has set itself up as the primary, and it's available for clients to use for read and write access.

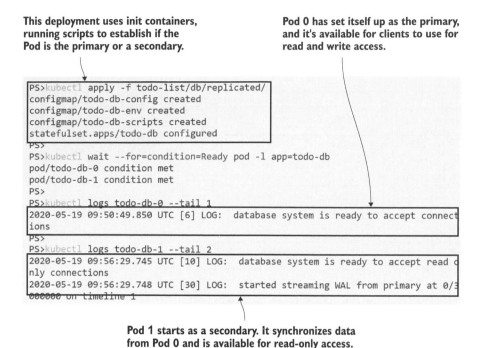

```
PS>kubectl apply -f todo-list/db/replicated/
configmap/todo-db-config created
configmap/todo-db-env created
configmap/todo-db-scripts created
statefulset.apps/todo-db configured
PS>
PS>kubectl wait --for=condition=Ready pod -l app=todo-db
pod/todo-db-0 condition met
pod/todo-db-1 condition met
PS>
PS>kubectl logs todo-db-0 --tail 1
2020-05-19 09:50:49.850 UTC [6] LOG:   database system is ready to accept connect
ions
PS>
PS>kubectl logs todo-db-1 --tail 2
2020-05-19 09:56:29.745 UTC [10] LOG:   database system is ready to accept read o
nly connections
2020-05-19 09:56:29.748 UTC [30] LOG:   started streaming WAL from primary at 0/3
000000 on timeline 1
```

Pod 1 starts as a secondary. It synchronizes data from Pod 0 and is available for read-only access.

Figure 8.6   Pods are replicas, but they can have different behavior, using init containers to choose a role.

Most of the complexity in initializing replicated apps like this is around modelling the workflow, which is specific to the app. The init container scripts here use the pg_isready tool to verify that the primary is ready to receive connections and the pb_basebackup tool to start the replication. Those implementation details are abstracted away from operators managing the system. They can add more replicas by scaling up the Stateful-Set, like with any other replication controller.

> **TRY IT NOW**   Scale up the database to add another replica, and confirm that the new Pod also starts as a secondary.

```
# add another replica:
kubectl scale --replicas=3 statefulset/todo-db

# wait for Pod 2 to spin up
kubectl wait --for=condition=Ready pod -l app=todo-db

# check that the new Pod sets itself up as another secondary:
kubectl logs todo-db-2 --tail 2
```

I wouldn't call this an enterprise-grade production setup, but it's a good starting point where a real Postgres expert could take over. You now have a functional, replicated

Postgres database cluster with a primary and two secondaries—Postgres calls them *standbys*. As you can see in figure 8.7, all the standbys start in the same way, syncing data from the primary, and they can all be used by clients for read-only access.

The StatefulSet spec hides all of the complexity of the underlying app, so scaling up is simple.

```
PS>kubectl scale --replicas=3 statefulset/todo-db
statefulset.apps/todo-db scaled
PS>
PS>kubectl wait --for=condition=Ready pod -l app=todo-db
pod/todo-db-0 condition met
pod/todo-db-1 condition met
pod/todo-db-2 condition met
PS>
PS>kubectl logs todo-db-2 --tail 2
2020-05-19 09:59:53.022 UTC [10] LOG:  database system is ready to accept read o
nly connections
2020-05-19 09:59:53.025 UTC [30] LOG:  started streaming WAL from primary at 0/5
000000 on timeline 1
```

**Any Pods that aren't Pod 0 will initialize themselves as secondaries.
We can scale up to add as many secondaries as we need.**

Figure 8.7   Using individually addressable Pods means secondaries can always find the primary.

One obvious part is missing here—the actual storage of the data. The setup we have isn't really usable because it doesn't have any volumes for storage, so each database container writes data in its own writable layer, not in a persistent volume. StatefulSets have a neat way of defining volume requirements: you can include a set of Persistent Volume Claim (PVC) templates in the spec.

8.3 *Requesting storage with volume claim templates*

Volumes are part of the standard Pod spec, and you can load ConfigMaps and Secrets into the Pods for a StatefulSet. You can even include a PVC and mount it into the app container, but that gives you volumes that are shared among all the Pods. That's fine for read-only configuration settings where you want every Pod to have the same data, but if you mount a standard PVC for data storage, then every Pod will try to write to the same volume.

You actually want each Pod to have its own PVC, and Kubernetes provides that for StatefulSets with the `volumeClaimTemplates` field in the spec. Volume claim templates can include a storage class as well as capacity and access mode requirements. When you deploy a StatefulSet with volume claim templates, it creates a PVC for each Pod, and they're linked, so if Pod 0 is replaced, the new Pod 0 will attach to the PVC used by the previous Pod 0.

Listing 8.4 shows a simple sleep spec that uses volume claim templates. As we learned in chapter 5, different Kubernetes platforms offer different storage classes, and I can't be sure what your cluster provides. This spec omits the storage class, which means the volume will be dynamically provisioned using your cluster's default storage class.

Listing 8.4   sleep-with-pvc.yaml, a StatefulSet with volume claim templates

```
spec:
  selector:
    # pod selector...
  serviceName:
    # headless service name...
  replicas: 2
  template:
    # pod template...

  volumeClaimTemplates:
    - metadata:
        name: data          # The name to use for volume mounts in the Pod
      spec:                  # This is a standard PVC spec.
        accessModes:
          - ReadWriteOnce
        resources:
          requests:
            storage: 5Mi
```

We'll use this exercise to see how volume claim templates in StatefulSets work in a simple environment before adding them as the storage layer for our database cluster.

TRY IT NOW   Deploy the StatefulSet from listing 8.4, and explore the PVCs it creates.

```
# deploy the StatefulSet with volume claim templates:
kubectl apply -f sleep/sleep-with-pvc.yaml

# check that the PVCs are created:
kubectl get pvc

# write some data to the PVC mount in Pod 0:
kubectl exec sleep-with-pvc-0 -- sh -c 'echo Pod 0 > /data/pod.txt'

# confirm Pod 0 can read the data:
kubectl exec sleep-with-pvc-0 -- cat /data/pod.txt

# confirm Pod 1 can't—this will fail:
kubectl exec sleep-with-pvc-1 -- cat /data/pod.txt
```

You'll see that each Pod in the set gets a PVC created dynamically, which in turn creates a PersistentVolume using the default storage class (or the requested storage class, if I had included one in the spec). The PVCs all have the same configuration, and they use the same stable approach as Pods in the StatefulSet: they have a predictable name, and, as you see in figure 8.8, each Pod has its own PVC, giving the replicas independent storage.

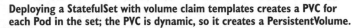

**Deploying a StatefulSet with volume claim templates creates a PVC for
each Pod in the set; the PVC is dynamic, so it creates a PersistentVolume.**

```
PS>kubectl apply -f sleep/sleep-with-pvc.yaml
service/sleep-with-pvc created
statefulset.apps/sleep-with-pvc created
PS>
PS>kubectl get pvc
NAME                    STATUS   VOLUME                                        CAPA
CITY    ACCESS MODES    STORAGECLASS   AGE
data-sleep-with-pvc-0   Bound    pvc-15f602b0-88e8-4a36-9d15-16c199983b02      5Mi
        RWO             hostpath       5s
data-sleep-with-pvc-1   Bound    pvc-cc969eba-e7b6-4ed6-9d22-bee6fd5cd617      5Mi
        RWO             hostpath       1s
PS>
PS>kubectl exec sleep-with-pvc-0 -- sh -c 'echo Pod 0 > /data/pod.txt'
PS>
PS>kubectl exec sleep-with-pvc-0 -- cat /data/pod.txt
Pod 0
PS>
PS>kubectl exec sleep-with-pvc-1 -- cat /data/pod.txt
cat: can't open '/data/pod.txt': No such file or directory
command terminated with exit code 1
```

**Pods have the same volume mount in the spec, but each
PVC is linked to one Pod, so they mount their own volumes.**

Figure 8.8 Volume claim templates dynamically create storage for Pods in StatefulSets.

The link between the Pod and its PVC is maintained when Pods are replaced, which is what really gives StatefulSets the power to run data-heavy applications. When you roll out an update to your app, the new Pod 0 will attach to the PVC from the previous Pod 0, and the new app container will have access to the exact same state as the replaced app container.

TRY IT NOW Trigger a Pod replacement by removing Pod 0. It will be replaced with another Pod 0 that attaches to the same PVC.

```
# delete the Pod:
kubectl delete pod sleep-with-pvc-0

# check that the replacement gets created:
kubectl get pods -l app=sleep-with-pvc

# check that the new Pod 0 can see the old data:
kubectl exec sleep-with-pvc-0 -- cat /data/pod.txt
```

This simple example makes this clear—you can see in figure 8.9 that the new Pod 0 has access to all the data from the original Pod. In a production cluster, you would specify a storage class that uses a volume type that any node can access, so replacement Pods can run on any node, and the app container can still mount the PVC.

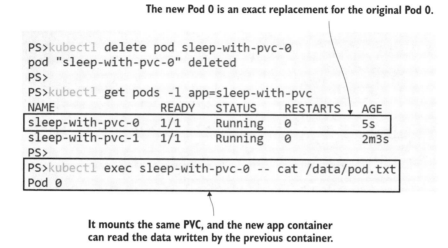

Figure 8.9   Stability in a StatefulSet extends to preserving the PVC link between Pod replacements.

Volume claim templates are the final piece we need to add to the Postgres deployment to model a fully reliable database. StatefulSets are intended to present a stable environment for your app, so they're less flexible than other controllers when it comes to updates—you can't update an existing StatefulSet and make a fundamental change, like adding volume claims. You need to make sure your design meets the app requirements for a StatefulSet because it's hard to maintain service levels during big changes.

TRY IT NOW   We'll update the Postgres deployment, but first we need to remove the existing StatefulSet.

```
# apply the update with volume claim templates—this will fail:
kubectl apply -f todo-list/db/replicated/update/todo-db-pvc.yaml

# delete the existing set:
kubectl delete statefulset todo-db

# create a new one with volume claims:
kubectl apply -f todo-list/db/replicated/update/todo-db-pvc.yaml

# check the volume claims:
kubectl get pvc -l app=todo-db
```

When you run this exercise, you should see clearly how the StatefulSet preserves order and waits for each Pod to be running before it starts the next Pod. PVCs are created for each Pod in sequence, too, as you can see from my output, shown in figure 8.10.

You can't make significant changes to an existing StatefulSet—it's meant to be a stable environment.

```
PS>kubectl apply -f todo-list/db/replicated/update/todo-db-pvc.yaml
The StatefulSet "todo-db" is invalid: spec: Forbidden: updates to statefulset sp
ec for fields other than 'replicas', 'template', and 'updateStrategy' are forbid
den
PS>
PS>kubectl delete statefulset todo-db
statefulset.apps "todo-db" deleted
PS>
PS>kubectl apply -f todo-list/db/replicated/update/todo-db-pvc.yaml
statefulset.apps/todo-db created
PS>
PS>kubectl get pvc -l app=todo-db
NAME              STATUS    VOLUME                                      CAPACITY
ACCESS MODES      STORAGECLASS    AGE
data-todo-db-0    Bound     pvc-8421f65a-a8cf-4007-8226-e725d69de206    50Mi
RWO               hostpath        59s
data-todo-db-1    Bound     pvc-341556e-ea74-4421-acf2-44adbd1c5039     50Mi
RWO               hostpath        16s
```

Deploying a StatefulSet with volume claim templates creates a PVC for each Pod. They're created in order like the Pods, so Pod 1's PVC isn't created until Pod 0 is up and running.

Figure 8.10   PVCs are created and allocated to the Postgres Pods.

It feels like we've spent a long time on StatefulSets, but it's a topic you should understand well so you're not taken by surprise when someone asks you to move their database to Kubernetes (which they will). StatefulSets come with a good deal of complexity, and you'll avoid using them most of the time. But if you are looking to migrate existing apps to Kubernetes, StatefulSets could be the difference between being able to run everything on the same platform or having to keep a handful of VMs just to run one or two apps.

We'll finish the section with an exercise to show the power of our clustered database. The Postgres secondary replicates all the data from the primary, and it can be used by clients for read-only access. If we had a serious production issue with our to-do list app that was causing it to lose data, we have the option to switch to read-only mode and use the secondary while we investigate the problem. That keeps the app running safely with minimal functionality, which is definitely preferable to taking it offline.

TRY IT NOW   Run the to-do web app and enter some items. In the default configuration, it connects to the Postgres primary in Pod 0 of the StatefulSet. Then we'll switch the app configuration to put it into read-only mode. This makes it connect to the read-only Postgres standby in Pod 1, which has replicated all the data from Pod 0.

```
# deploy the web app:
kubectl apply -f todo-list/web/

# get the URL for the app:
kubectl get svc todo-web -o
    jsonpath='http://{.status.loadBalancer.ingress[0].*}:8081/new'

# browse and add a new item

# switch to read-only mode, using the database secondary:
kubectl apply -f todo-list/web/update/todo-web-readonly.yaml

# refresh the app—the /new page is read-only;
# browse to /list and you'll see your original data

# check that there are no clients using the primary in Pod 0:
kubectl exec -it todo-db-0 -- sh -c "psql -U postgres -t -c 'SELECT
    datname, query FROM pq_stat_activity WHERE datid > 0'"

# check that the web app really is using the secondary in Pod 1:
kubectl exec -it todo-db-1 -- sh -c "psql -U postgres -t -c 'SELECT
    datname, query FROM pg_stat_activity WHERE datid > 0'"
```

You can see my output in figure 8.11, with some tiny screenshots to show the app running in read-only mode but still with access to all the data.

Postgres has existed as a SQL database engine since 1996—it predates Kubernetes by almost 25 years. Using a StatefulSet, you can model an application environment that suits Postgres and other clustered applications like it, providing stable networking, storage, and initialization in the dynamic world of containers.

8.4   *Running maintenance tasks with Jobs and CronJobs*

Data-intensive apps need replicated data with storage aligned to compute, and they usually also need some independent nurturing of the storage layer. Data backups and reconciliation are well suited to another type of Pod controller: the Job. Kubernetes Jobs are defined with a Pod spec, and they run the Pod as a batch job, ensuring it runs to completion.

Jobs aren't just for stateful apps; they're a great way to bring a standard approach to any batch-processing problems, where you can hand off all the scheduling and monitoring and retry logic to the cluster. You can run any container image in the Pod for a Job, but it should start a process that ends; otherwise, your jobs will keep running forever. Listing 8.5 shows a Job spec that runs the Pi application in batch mode.

Starts the web app—this configuration uses the Pod 0 address for the database StatefulSet for read/write access.

Browse to the new item page where you can add data.

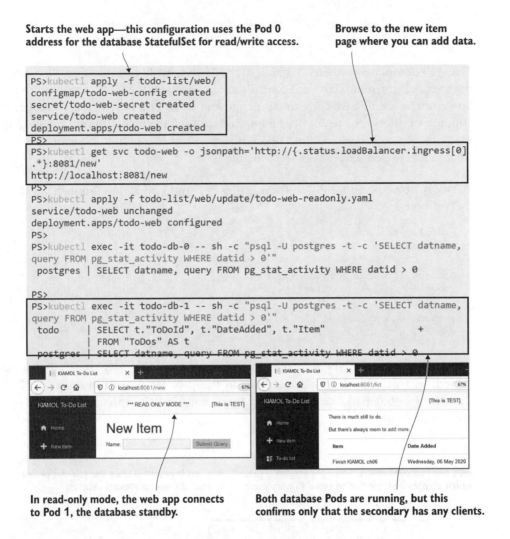

```
PS>kubectl apply -f todo-list/web/
configmap/todo-web-config created
secret/todo-web-secret created
service/todo-web created
deployment.apps/todo-web created
PS>
PS>kubectl get svc todo-web -o jsonpath='http://{.status.loadBalancer.ingress[0]
.*}:8081/new'
http://localhost:8081/new
PS>
PS>kubectl apply -f todo-list/web/update/todo-web-readonly.yaml
service/todo-web unchanged
deployment.apps/todo-web configured
PS>
PS>kubectl exec -it todo-db-0 -- sh -c "psql -U postgres -t -c 'SELECT datname,
query FROM pg_stat_activity WHERE datid > 0'"
 postgres | SELECT datname, query FROM pg_stat_activity WHERE datid > 0

PS>
PS>kubectl exec -it todo-db-1 -- sh -c "psql -U postgres -t -c 'SELECT datname,
query FROM pg_stat_activity WHERE datid > 0'"
 todo     | SELECT t."ToDoId", t."DateAdded", t."Item"          +
          | FROM "ToDos" AS t
 postgres | SELECT datname, query FROM pg_stat_activity WHERE datid > 0
```

In read-only mode, the web app connects to Pod 1, the database standby.

Both database Pods are running, but this confirms only that the secondary has any clients.

Figure 8.11 Switching an app to read-only mode is a useful option if there's a data issue

Listing 8.5 pi-job.yaml, a simple Job to calculate Pi

```
apiVersion: batch/v1
kind: Job                          # Job is the object type.
metadata:
  name: pi-job
spec:
  template:
    spec:                          # The standard Pod spec
      containers:
        - name: pi                 # The container should run and exit.
          image: kiamol/ch05-pi
```

```
command: ["dotnet", "Pi.Web.dll", "-m", "console", "-dp", "50"]
restartPolicy: Never          # If the container fails, replace the Pod.
```

The Job template contains a standard Pod spec, with the addition of a required `restartPolicy` field. That field controls the behavior of the Job in response to failure. You can choose to have Kubernetes restart the same Pod with a new container if the run fails or always create a replacement Pod, potentially on a different node. In a normal run of the Job where the Pod completes successfully, the Job and the Pod are retained so the container logs are available.

TRY IT NOW   Run the Pi Job from listing 8.5, and check the output from the Pod.

```
# deploy the Job:
kubectl apply -f pi/pi-job.yaml

# check the logs for the Pod:
kubectl logs -l job-name=pi-job

# check the status of the Job:
kubectl get job pi-job
```

Jobs add their own labels to the Pods they create. The `job-name` label is always added, so you can navigate to Pods from the Job. My output in figure 8.12 shows that the Job has had one successful completion and the calculation result is available in the logs.

Jobs are Pod controllers. This spec creates a Job,   **The Pod is retained after the Job completes,**
which creates a single Pod to run a Pi calculation.   **so you can see its logs and status.**

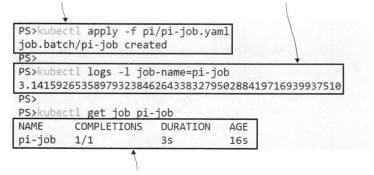

Jobs can be configured to run multiple Pods. This
is set for a single run, which has completed.

Figure 8.12   Jobs create Pods, make sure they complete, and then leave them in the cluster.

It's always useful to have different options for computing Pi, but this is just a simple example. You can use any container image in the Pod spec so you can run any kind of batch process with a Job. You might have a set of input items that need the same work done on them; you can create one Job for the whole set, which creates a Pod for each item, and Kubernetes distributes the work all throughout the cluster. The Job spec supports this with the following two optional fields:

- `completions`—specifies how many times the Job should run. If your Job is processing a work queue, then the app container needs to understand how to fetch the next item to work on. The Job itself just ensures that it runs a number of Pods equal to the desired number of completions.
- `parallelism`—specifies how many Pods to run in parallel for a Job with multiple completions set. This setting lets you tweak the speed of running the Job, balancing that with the compute requirements on the cluster.

One last Pi example for this chapter: a new Job spec that runs multiple Pods in parallel, each computing Pi to a random number of decimal places. This spec uses an init container to generate the number of decimal places to use, and the app container reads that input using a shared `EmptyDir` mount. This is a nice approach because the app container doesn't need to be modified to work in a parallel environment. You could extend this with an init container that fetched a work item from a queue, so the app itself wouldn't need to be aware of the queue.

TRY IT NOW Run an alternative Pi Job that uses parallelism and shows that multiple Pods from the same spec can process different workloads.

```
# deploy the new Job:
kubectl apply -f pi/pi-job-random.yaml

# check the Pod status:
kubectl get pods -l job-name=pi-job-random

# check the Job status:
kubectl get job pi-job-random

# list the Pod output:
kubectl logs -l job-name=pi-job-random
```

This exercise may take a while to run, depending on your hardware and the number of decimal places it generates. You'll see all the Pods running in parallel, working on their own calculations. The final output will be three sets of Pi, probably to thousands of decimal places. I've abbreviated my results, shown in figure 8.13.

Jobs are a great tool to have in your pocket. They're perfect for anything compute intensive or IO intensive, where you want to make sure a process completes but don't mind when. You can even submit Jobs from your own application—a web app running

This Job manages multiple Pods. It's
configured to run three completions,
with a parallelism value of three.

All three Pods start simultaneously.
On a multinode cluster, these would
be distributed across nodes.

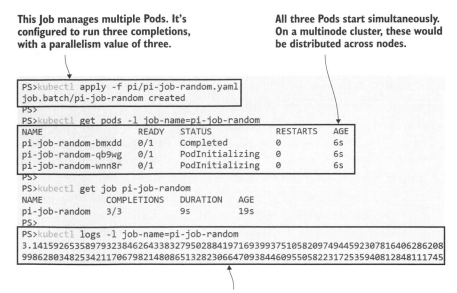

```
PS>kubectl apply -f pi/pi-job-random.yaml
job.batch/pi-job-random created
PS>
PS>kubectl get pods -l job-name=pi-job-random
NAME                   READY   STATUS          RESTARTS   AGE
pi-job-random-bmxdd    0/1     Completed       0          6s
pi-job-random-qb9wg    0/1     PodInitializing 0          6s
pi-job-random-wnn8r    0/1     PodInitializing 0          6s
PS>
PS>kubectl get job pi-job-random
NAME            COMPLETIONS   DURATION   AGE
pi-job-random   3/3           9s         19s
PS>
PS>kubectl logs -l job-name=pi-job-random
3.14159265358979323846264338327950288419716939937510582097494459230781640628620899862803482534211706798214808651328230664709384460955058223172535940812848111745
```

When the Job completes, you can see the output from all of the Pods in their logs. These
are calculating Pi to a random number of decimal places, so the output is quite large.

**Figure 8.13   Jobs can run multiple Pods from the same spec that each process different
workloads.**

in Kubernetes has access to the Kubernetes API server, and it can create Jobs to run
work for users.

The real power of Jobs is that they run in the context of the cluster, so they have all
the cluster resources available to them. Back to the Postgres example, we can run a
database-backup process in a Job, and the Pod it runs can access the Pods in the Stateful-
Set or the PVCs, depending on what it needs to do. That takes care of the nurturing
aspect of these data-intensive apps, but those Jobs need to be run regularly, which is
where the CronJob comes in. The CronJob is a Job controller, which creates Jobs on a
regular schedule. Figure 8.14 shows the workflow.

CronJob specs include a Job spec, so you can do anything in a CronJob that you
can do in a Job, including running multiple completions in parallel. The schedule for
running the Job uses the Linux Cron format, which lets you express everything from
simple "every minute" or "every day" schedules to more complex "at 4 a.m. and 6 a.m.
every Sunday" routines. Listing 8.6 shows part of the CronJob spec for running database backups.

CronJobs control Jobs, and Jobs control Pods. The relationship
is similar to Deployments and ReplicaSets.

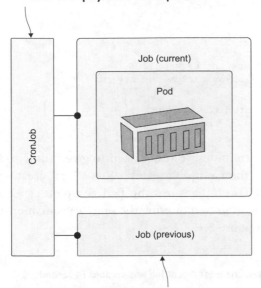

Jobs and Pods are retained after completion
and need to be manually cleaned up.

**Figure 8.14   CronJobs are the ultimate
owner of the Job Pods, so everything can
be removed with cascading deletes.**

Listing 8.6   todo-db-backup-cronjob.yaml, a CronJob for database backups

```
apiVersion: batch/v1beta1
kind: CronJob
metadata:
  name: todo-db-backup
spec:
  schedule: "*/2 * * * *"        # Creates a Job every 2 minutes
  concurrencyPolicy: Forbid      # Prevents overlap so a new Job won't be
  jobTemplate:                   # created if the previous one is running
    spec:
      # job template...
```

The full spec uses the Postgres Docker image, with a command to run the pg_dump
backup tool. The Pod loads environment variables and passwords from the same Config-
Maps and Secrets that the StatefulSet uses, so there's no duplication in the config file.
It also uses its own PVC as the storage location to write the backup files.

TRY IT NOW   Create a CronJob from the spec in listing 8.6 to run a database
backup Job every two minutes.

```
# deploy the CronJob and target PVC for backup files:
kubectl apply -f todo-list/db/backup/
```

```
# wait for the Job to run—this is a good time to make tea:
sleep 150

# check the CronJob status:
kubectl get cronjob todo-db-backup

# now run a sleep Pod that mounts the backup PVC:
kubectl apply -f sleep/sleep-with-db-backup-mount.yaml

# check if the CronJob Pod created the backup:
kubectl exec deploy/sleep -- ls -l /backup
```

The CronJob is set to run every two minutes, so you'll need to give it time to fire up during this exercise. On schedule, the CronJob creates a Job, which creates a Pod, which runs the `backup` command. The Job ensures the Pod completes successfully. You can confirm the backup file is written by mounting the same PVC in another Pod. You can see it all works correctly in figure 8.15.

This CronJob is set to run every two minutes. The most recent Job was created 74 seconds ago.

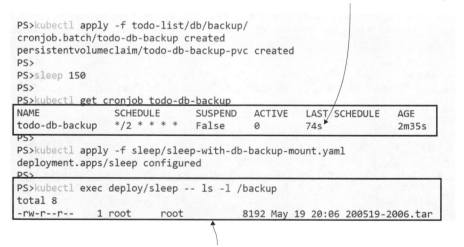

Running a Pod that mounts the same PVC the backup Job uses—the `tar` file was created by the backup Pod, by connecting to one of the Postgres read-only replicas.

Figure 8.15   CronJobs run Pods, which can access other Kubernetes objects. This one connects to a database Pod.

CronJobs don't perform an automatic cleanup for Pods and Jobs. The time-to-live (TTL) controller does this, but it's an alpha-grade feature that isn't available in many Kubernetes platforms. Without it you need to manually delete the child objects when you're sure you no longer need them. You can also move CronJobs to a suspended state, which means the object spec still exists in the cluster, but it doesn't run until the CronJob is activated again.

TRY IT NOW   Suspend the CronJob so it doesn't keep creating backup Jobs, and then explore the status of the CronJob and its Jobs.

```
# update the CronJob, and set it to suspend:
kubectl apply -f todo-list/db/backup/update/todo-db-backup-cronjob-
    suspend.yaml

# check the CronJob:
kubectl get cronjob todo-db-backup

# find the Jobs owned by the CronJob:
kubectl get jobs -o jsonpath="{.items[?(@.metadata.ownerReferences[0]
    .name=='todo-db-backup')].metadata.name}"
```

If you explore the object hierarchy, you'll see that CronJobs don't follow the standard controller model, with a label selector to identify the Jobs it owns. You can add your own labels in the Job template for the CronJob, but if you don't do that, you need to identify Jobs where the owner reference is the CronJob, as shown in figure 8.16.

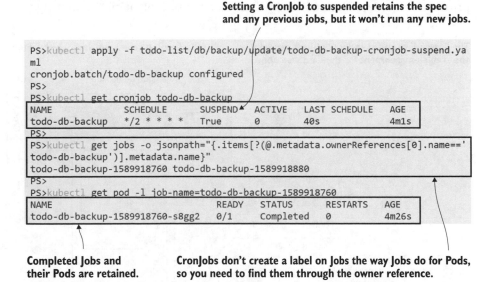

Setting a CronJob to suspended retains the spec and any previous jobs, but it won't run any new jobs.

Completed Jobs and their Pods are retained.

CronJobs don't create a label on Jobs the way Jobs do for Pods, so you need to find them through the owner reference.

Figure 8.16   CronJobs don't use a label selector to model ownership, because they don't keep track of Jobs.

As you start to make more use of Jobs and CronJobs, you'll realize that the simplicity of the spec masks some complexity in the process and presents some interesting failure modes. Kubernetes does its best to make sure your batch jobs start when you want them to and run to completion, which means your containers need to be resilient. Completing a Job might mean restarting a Pod with a new container or replacing the Pod on a new node, and for CronJobs, multiple Pods could be running if the process takes longer than the schedule interval. Your container logic needs to allow for all those scenarios.

Now you know how to run data-heavy apps in Kubernetes, with StatefulSets to model a stable runtime environment and initialize the app, and CronJobs to process data backups and other regular maintenance work. We'll close out the chapter thinking about whether this is really a good idea.

8.5   *Choosing your platform for stateful apps*

The great promise of Kubernetes is that it gives you a single platform that can run all your apps, on any infrastructure. It's hugely appealing to think that you can model all the aspects of any application in a chunk of YAML, deploy it with some kubectl commands, and know it will run in the same way on any cluster, taking advantage of all the extended features the platform offers. But data is precious and usually irreplaceable, so you need to think carefully before you decide that Kubernetes is the place to run data-heavy apps.

Figure 8.17 shows the full setup we've built in this chapter to run an almost-production-grade SQL database in Kubernetes. Just look at all the moving parts—do

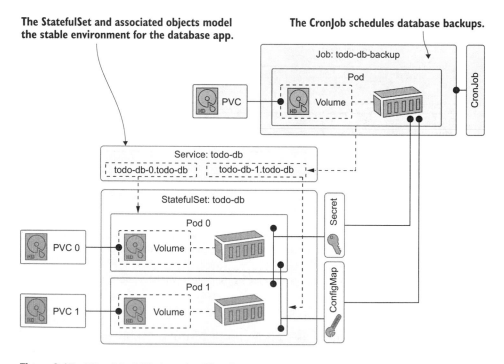

Figure 8.17   Yikes! And this is a simplification that doesn't show volumes or init containers.

you really want to manage all that? And how much time will you need to invest just testing this setup with your own data sizes: validating that the replicas are syncing correctly, verifying the backups can be restored, running chaos experiments to be sure that failures are handled in the way you expect?

Compare that to a managed database in the cloud. Azure, AWS, and GCP all offer managed services for Postgres, MySQL, and SQL Server, as well as their own custom cloud-scale databases. The cloud provider takes care of scale and high availability, including features for backups to cloud storage and more advanced options like threat detection. An alternative architecture just uses Kubernetes for compute and plugs in to managed cloud services for data and communication.

Which is the better option? Well, I'm a consultant by day, and I know the only real answer is: "It depends." If you're running in the cloud, then I think you need a very good reason *not* to use managed services in production, where data is critical. In non-production environments, it often makes sense to run equivalent services in Kubernetes instead, so you run a containerized database and message queue in your development and test environments for lower costs and ease of deployment and swap out to managed versions in production. Kubernetes makes a swap like that very simple, with all the Pod and Service configuration options.

In the data center, the picture is a little different. If you're already invested in running Kubernetes on your own infrastructure, you're taking on a lot of management, and it might make sense to maximize utilization of your clusters and use them for everything. If you choose to go that way, Kubernetes gives you the tools to migrate data-heavy apps into the cluster and run them with the levels of availability and scale that you need. Just don't underestimate the complexity of getting there.

We're done with StatefulSets and Jobs now, so we can clean up before going on to the lab.

TRY IT NOW All the top-level objects are labeled, so we can remove everything with cascading deletes.

```
# delete all the owning objects:
kubectl delete all -l kiamol=ch08

# delete the PVCs
kubectl delete pvc -l kiamol=ch08
```

8.6 Lab

So, how much of your lunchtime do you have left for this lab? Can you model a MySQL database from scratch, with backups? Probably not, but don't worry—this lab isn't as involved as that. The goal is just to give you some experience working with StatefulSets and PVCs, so we'll use a much simpler app. You're going to run the Nginx web server in a StatefulSet, where each Pod writes log files to a PVC of its own, and then you'll run a Job that prints the size of each Pod's log file. The basic pieces are there for you, so it's about applying some of the techniques from the chapter.

- The starting point is the Nginx spec in `ch08/lab/nginx`, which runs a single Pod writing logs to an `EmptyDir` volume.
- The Pod spec needs to be migrated to a StatefulSet definition, which is configured to run with three Pods and provide separate storage for each of them.
- When you have the StatefulSet working, you should be able to make calls to your Service and see the log files being written in the Pods.
- Then you can complete the Job spec in the file `disk-calc-job.yaml`, adding the volume mounts so it can read the log files from the Nginx Pods.

It's not as bad as it looks, and it will get you thinking about storage and Jobs. My solution is on GitHub for you to check in the usual place: https://github.com/sixeyed/kiamol/blob/master/ch08/lab/README.md.

Managing
app releases with
rollouts and rollbacks

You'll update existing apps far more often than you'll deploy something new. Containerized apps inherit multiple release cadences from the base images they use; official images on Docker Hub for operating systems, platform SDKs, and runtimes typically have a new release every month. You should have a process to rebuild your images and release updates whenever those dependencies get updated, because they could contain critical security patches. Key to that process is being able to roll out an update safely and give yourself options to pause and roll back the update if it goes wrong. Kubernetes has those scenarios covered for Deployments, DaemonSets, and StatefulSets.

A single update approach doesn't work for every type of application, so Kubernetes provides different update strategies for the controllers and options to tune how the strategies work. We'll explore all those options in this chapter. If you're thinking of skipping this one because you're not excited by the thought of 6,000 words on application updates, I'd recommend sticking with it. Updates are the biggest cause of application downtime, but you can reduce the risk significantly if you understand the tools Kubernetes gives you. And I'll try to inject a little excitement along the way.

9.1 How Kubernetes manages rollouts

We'll start with Deployments—actually, you've already done plenty of Deployment updates. Every time we've applied a change to an existing Deployment (something we do 10 times a chapter), Kubernetes has implemented that with a *rollout*. In a rollout, the Deployment creates a new ReplicaSet and scales it up to the desired number of replicas, while scaling down the previous ReplicaSet to zero replicas. Figure 9.1 shows an update in progress.

The Deployment requires three replicas. It is part-way through an update with two version 2 Pods and one version 1 Pod, manged with separate ReplicaSets.

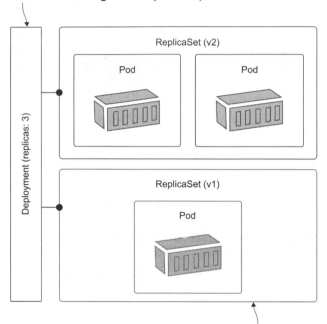

When the update is complete, the version 2 ReplicaSet will have three Pods, and the version 1 ReplicaSet will scale down to zero, but the empty ReplicaSet is retained.

Figure 9.1   Deployments control multiple ReplicaSets so they can manage rolling updates.

Rollouts aren't triggered from every change to a Deployment, only from a change to the Pod spec. If you make a change that the Deployment can manage with the current ReplicaSet, like updating the number of replicas, that's done without a rollout.

TRY IT NOW   Deploy a simple app with two replicas, then update it to increase scale, and see how the ReplicaSet is managed.

```
# change to the exercise directory:
cd ch09

# deploy a simple web app:
kubectl apply -f vweb/

# check the ReplicaSets:
kubectl get rs -l app=vweb
```

```
# now increase the scale:
kubectl apply -f vweb/update/vweb-v1-scale.yaml

# check the ReplicaSets:
kubectl get rs -l app=vweb

# check the deployment history:
kubectl rollout history deploy/vweb
```

The kubectl rollout command has options to view and manage rollouts. You can see from my output in figure 9.2 that there's only one rollout in this exercise, which was the initial deployment that created the ReplicaSet. The scale update changed only the existing ReplicaSet, so there was no second rollout.

This Deployment requires two Pods, which it manages through the ReplicaSet.

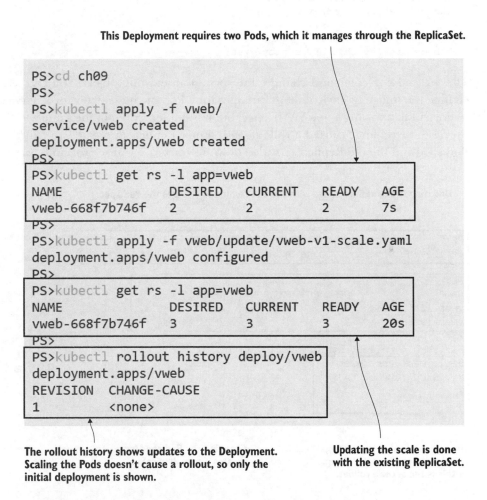

The rollout history shows updates to the Deployment. Scaling the Pods doesn't cause a rollout, so only the initial deployment is shown.

Updating the scale is done with the existing ReplicaSet.

Figure 9.2 Deployments manage changes through rollouts but only if the Pod spec changes.

Your ongoing application updates will center on deploying new Pods running an updated version of your container image. You should manage that with an update to your YAML specs, but kubectl provides a quick alternative with the set command. Using this command is an imperative way to update an existing Deployment, and you should view it the same as the scale command—it's a useful hack to get out of a sticky situation, but it needs to be followed up with an update to the YAML files.

> **TRY IT NOW**   Use kubectl to update the image version for the Deployment. This is a change to the Pod spec, so it will trigger a new rollout.

```
# update the image for the web app:
kubectl set image deployment/vweb web=kiamol/ch09-vweb:v2

# check the ReplicaSets again:
kubectl get rs -l app=vweb

# check the rollouts:
kubectl rollout history deploy/vweb
```

The kubectl set command changes the spec of an existing object. You can use it to change the image or environment variables for a Pod or the selector for a Service. It's a shortcut to applying a new YAML spec, but it is implemented in the same way. In this exercise, the change caused a rollout, with a new ReplicaSet created to run the new Pod spec and the old ReplicaSet scaled down to zero. You can see this in figure 9.3.

Updating the container image with the `set` command changes the Pod spec.

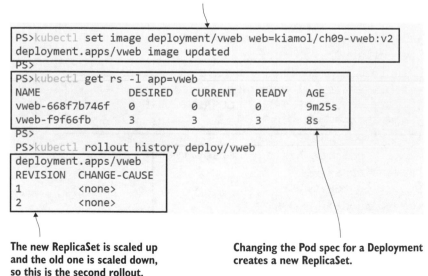

The new ReplicaSet is scaled up and the old one is scaled down, so this is the second rollout.

Changing the Pod spec for a Deployment creates a new ReplicaSet.

Figure 9.3   Imperative updates go through the same rollout process, but now your YAML is out of sync.

Kubernetes uses the same concept of rollouts for the other Pod controllers, Daemon-Sets and StatefulSets. They're an odd part of the API because they don't map directly to an object (you don't create a resource with the kind "rollout"), but they're an important management tool to work with your releases. You can use rollouts to track release history and to revert back to previous releases.

9.2 Updating Deployments with rollouts and rollbacks

If you look again at figure 9.3, you'll see the rollout history is pretty unhelpful. There's a revision number recorded for each rollout but nothing else. It's not clear what caused the change or which ReplicaSet relates to which revision. It's good to include a version number (or a Git commit ID) as a label for the Pods, and then the Deployment adds that label to the ReplicaSet, too, which makes it easier to trace updates.

> **TRY IT NOW** Apply an update to the Deployment, which uses the same Docker image but changes the version label for the Pod. That's a change to the Pod spec, so it will create a new rollout.

```
# apply the change using the record flag:
kubectl apply -f vweb/update/vweb-v11.yaml --record

# check the ReplicaSets and their labels:
kubectl get rs -l app=vweb --show-labels

# check the current rollout status:
kubectl rollout status deploy/vweb

# check the rollout history:
kubectl rollout history deploy/vweb

# show the rollout revision for the ReplicaSets:
kubectl get rs -l app=vweb -o=custom-columns=NAME:.metadata.name,
    REPLICAS:.status.replicas,REVISION:.metadata.annotations.deployment
    \.kubernetes\.io/revision
```

My output appears in figure 9.4. Adding the `record` flag saves the kubectl command as a detail to the rollout, which can be helpful if your YAML files have identifying names. Often they won't because you'll be deploying a whole folder, so the version number label in the Pod spec is a useful addition. Then, however, you need some awkward JSONPath to find the link between a rollout revision and a ReplicaSet.

As your Kubernetes maturity increases, you'll want to have a standard set of labels that you include in all your object specs. Labels and selectors are a core feature, and you'll use them all the time to find and manage objects. Application name, component name, and version are good labels to start with, but it's important to distinguish between the labels you include for your convenience and the labels that Kubernetes uses to map object relationships.

Listing 9.1 shows the Pod labels and the selector for the Deployment in the previous exercise. The app label is used in the selector, which the Deployment uses to find

The `record` flag saves the details of the kubectl command for the rollout.

The Pod specs include a version label, which the Deployment adds to the ReplicaSet labels.

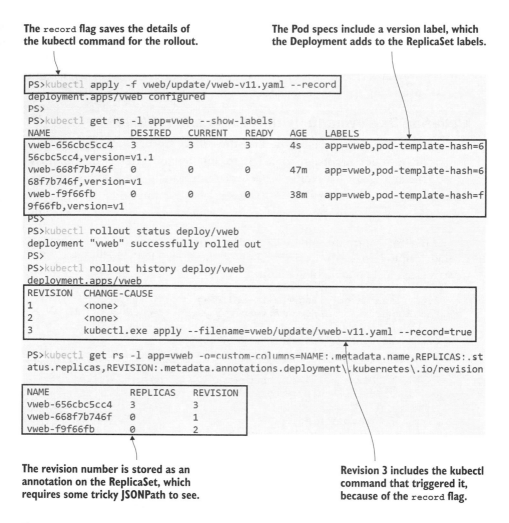

```
PS>kubectl apply -f vweb/update/vweb-v11.yaml --record
deployment.apps/vweb configured
PS>
PS>kubectl get rs -l app=vweb --show-labels
NAME                  DESIRED    CURRENT    READY    AGE    LABELS
vweb-656cbc5cc4       3          3          3        4s     app=vweb,pod-template-hash=6
56cbc5cc4,version=v1.1
vweb-668f7b746f       0          0          0        47m    app=vweb,pod-template-hash=6
68f7b746f,version=v1
vweb-f9f66fb          0          0          0        38m    app=vweb,pod-template-hash=f
9f66fb,version=v1
PS>
PS>kubectl rollout status deploy/vweb
deployment "vweb" successfully rolled out
PS>
PS>kubectl rollout history deploy/vweb
deployment.apps/vweb
REVISION   CHANGE-CAUSE
1          <none>
2          <none>
3          kubectl.exe apply --filename=vweb/update/vweb-v11.yaml --record=true

PS>kubectl get rs -l app=vweb -o=custom-columns=NAME:.metadata.name,REPLICAS:.st
atus.replicas,REVISION:.metadata.annotations.deployment\.kubernetes\.io/revision

NAME                  REPLICAS    REVISION
vweb-656cbc5cc4       3           3
vweb-668f7b746f       0           1
vweb-f9f66fb          0           2
```

The revision number is stored as an annotation on the ReplicaSet, which requires some tricky JSONPath to see.

Revision 3 includes the kubectl command that triggered it, because of the `record` flag.

Figure 9.4   Kubernetes uses labels for key information, and extra detail is stored in annotations.

its Pods. The Pod also contains a `version` label for our convenience, but that's not part of the selector. If it were, then the Deployment would be linked to one version, because you can't change the selector once a Deployment is created.

Listing 9.1   vweb-v11.yaml, a Deployment with additional labels in the Pod spec

```
spec:
  replicas: 3
  selector:
    matchLabels:
      app: vweb          # The app name is used as the selector.
  template:
```

```
metadata:
  labels:
    app: vweb
    version: v1.1     # The Pod spec also includes a version label.
```

You need to plan your selectors carefully up front, but you should add whatever labels you need to your Pod spec to make your updates manageable. Deployments retain multiple ReplicaSets (10 is the default), and the Pod template hash in the name makes them hard to work with directly, even after just a few updates. Let's see what the app we've deployed actually does and then look at the ReplicaSets in another rollout.

> **TRY IT NOW**   Make an HTTP call to the web Service to see the response, then start another update and check the response again.

```
# we'll use the app URL a lot, so save it to a local file:
kubectl get svc vweb -o
  jsonpath='http://{.status.loadBalancer.ingress[0].*}:8090/v.txt' >
  url.txt

# then use the contents of the file to make an HTTP request:
curl $(cat url.txt)

# deploy the v2 update:
kubectl apply -f vweb/update/vweb-v2.yaml --record

# check the response again:
curl $(cat url.txt)

# check the ReplicaSet details:
kubectl get rs -l app=vweb --show-labels
```

You'll see in this exercise that ReplicaSets aren't easy objects to manage, which is where standardized labels come in. It's easy to see which version of the app is active by checking the labels for the ReplicaSet which has all the desired replicas—as you see in figure 9.5—but labels are just text fields, so you need process safeguards to make sure they're reliable.

Rollouts do help to abstract away the details of the ReplicaSets, but their main use is to manage releases. We've seen the rollout history from kubectl, and you can also run commands to pause an ongoing rollout or roll back a deployment to an earlier revision. A simple command will roll back to the previous deployment, but if you want to roll back to a specific version, you need some more JSONPath trickery to find the revision you want. We'll see that now and use a very handy feature of kubectl that tells you what will happen when you run a command, without actually executing it.

> **TRY IT NOW**   Check the rollout history and try rolling back to v1 of the app.

```
# look at the revisions:
kubectl rollout history deploy/vweb
```

Using some kubectl magic to write the app URL to a file, and then calling the app by
reading that URL from the file. Version 1 of the app returns the response "v1."

```
PS>kubectl get svc vweb -o jsonpath='http://{.status.loadBalancer.ingress[0].*}:
8090/v.txt' > url.txt
PS>
PS>curl $(cat url.txt)
v1
PS>
```

```
PS>kubectl apply -f vweb/update/vweb-v2.yaml --record
deployment.apps/vweb configured
PS>
PS>curl $(cat url.txt)
v2
```

```
PS>
PS>kubectl get rs -l app=vweb --show-labels
NAME                  DESIRED   CURRENT   READY   AGE     LABELS
vweb-656cbc5cc4       0         0         0       39m     app=vweb,pod-template-hash
=656cbc5cc4,version=v1.1
vweb-668f7b746f       0         0         0       86m     app=vweb,pod-template-hash
=668f7b746f,version=v1
vweb-7659d9d47f       3         3         3       2m28s   app=vweb,pod-template-hash
=7659d9d47f,version=v2
vweb-f9f66fb          0         0         0       77m     app=vweb,pod-template-hash
=f9f66fb,version=v1
```

This updates the
app to version 2,
which returns the
response "v2."

Which is which? ReplicaSets are shown in name order, which is by the Pod
template hash. In this case, the active ReplicaSet is third in the list, and
without the version label, we wouldn't know what those Pods are running.

Figure 9.5   Kubernetes manages rollouts for you, but it helps if you add labels to see what's what.

```
# list ReplicaSets with their revisions:
kubectl get rs -l app=vweb -o=custom-
    columns=NAME:.metadata.name,REPLICAS:.status.replicas,VERSION:.meta
    data.labels.version,REVISION:.metadata.annotations.deployment\.kube
    rnetes\.io/revision

# see what would happen with a rollback:
kubectl rollout undo deploy/vweb --dry-run

# then start a rollback to revision 2:
kubectl rollout undo deploy/vweb --to-revision=2

# check the app—this should surprise you:
curl $(cat url.txt)
```

Hands up if you ran that exercise and got confused when you saw the final output
shown in figure 9.6 (this is the exciting part of the chapter). My hand is up, and I
already knew what was going to happen. This is why you need a consistent release

There are four revisions of the app:
the initial rollout and three updates.

You can print custom columns from the ReplicaSet
to see the revisions matched to the version labels.

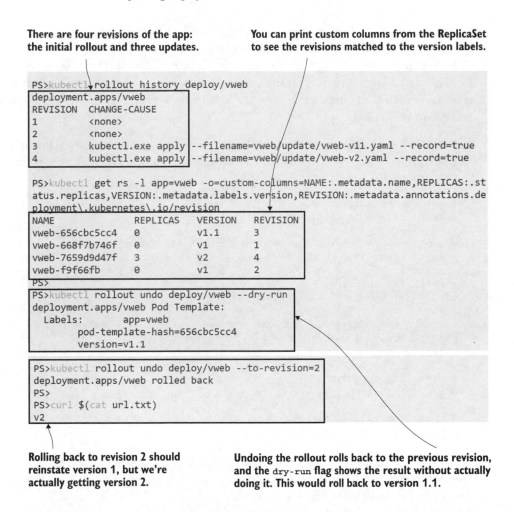

```
PS>kubectl rollout history deploy/vweb
deployment.apps/vweb
REVISION   CHANGE-CAUSE
1          <none>
2          <none>
3          kubectl.exe apply --filename=vweb/update/vweb-v11.yaml --record=true
4          kubectl.exe apply --filename=vweb/update/vweb-v2.yaml --record=true

PS>kubectl get rs -l app=vweb -o=custom-columns=NAME:.metadata.name,REPLICAS:.st
atus.replicas,VERSION:.metadata.labels.version,REVISION:.metadata.annotations.de
ployment\.kubernetes\.io/revision
NAME               REPLICAS   VERSION   REVISION
vweb-656cbc5cc4    0          v1.1      3
vweb-668f7b746f    0          v1        1
vweb-7659d9d47f    3          v2        4
vweb-f9f66fb       0          v1        2
PS>
PS>kubectl rollout undo deploy/vweb --dry-run
deployment.apps/vweb Pod Template:
  Labels:       app=vweb
        pod-template-hash=656cbc5cc4
        version=v1.1

PS>kubectl rollout undo deploy/vweb --to-revision=2
deployment.apps/vweb rolled back
PS>
PS>curl $(cat url.txt)
v2
```

Rolling back to revision 2 should
reinstate version 1, but we're
actually getting version 2.

Undoing the rollout rolls back to the previous revision,
and the dry-run flag shows the result without actually
doing it. This would roll back to version 1.1.

Figure 9.6   Labels are a key management feature, but they're set by humans so they're fallible.

process, preferably one that is fully automated, because as soon as you start mixing approaches, you get confusing results. I rolled back to revision 2, and that should have reverted back to v1 of the app, judging by the labels on the ReplicaSets. But revision 2 was actually from the kubectl set image exercise in section 9.1, so the container image is v2, but the ReplicaSet label is v1.

You see that the moving parts of the release process are fairly simple: Deployments create and reuse ReplicaSets, scaling them up and down as required, and changes to ReplicaSets are recorded as rollouts. Kubernetes gives you control of the key factors in the rollout strategy, but before we move on to that, we're going to look at releases which also involve a configuration change, because that adds another complicating factor.

In chapter 4, I talked about different approaches to updating the content of Config-Maps and Secrets, and the choice you make impacts your ability to roll back cleanly. The first approach is to say that configuration is mutable, so a release might include a ConfigMap change, which is an update to an existing ConfigMap object. But if your release is *only* a configuration change, then you have no record of that as a rollout and no option to roll back.

TRY IT NOW   Remove the existing Deployment so we have a clean history, then deploy a new version that uses a ConfigMap, and see what happens when you update the same ConfigMap.

```
# remove the existing app:
kubectl delete deploy vweb

# deploy a new version that stores content in config:
kubectl apply -f vweb/update/vweb-v3-with-configMap.yaml --record

# check the response:
curl $(cat url.txt)

# update the ConfigMap, and wait for the change to propagate:
kubectl apply -f vweb/update/vweb-configMap-v31.yaml --record
sleep 120

# check the app again:
curl $(cat url.txt)

# check the rollout history:
kubectl rollout history deploy/vweb
```

As you see in figure 9.7, the update to the ConfigMap changes the behavior of the app, but it's not a change to the Deployment, so there is no revision to roll back to if the configuration change causes an issue.

This is the hot reload approach, which works nicely if your apps support it, precisely because a configuration-only change doesn't require a rollout. The existing Pods and containers keep running, so there's no risk of service interruption. The cost is the loss of the rollback option, and you'll have to decide whether that's more important than a hot reload.

Your alternative is to consider all ConfigMaps and Secrets as immutable, so you include some versioning scheme in the object name and never update a config object once it's created. Instead you create a new config object with a new name and release it along with an update to your Deployment, which references the new config object.

TRY IT NOW   Deploy a new version of the app with an immutable config, so you can compare the release process.

```
# remove the old Deployment:
kubectl delete deploy vweb
```

```
# create a new Deployment using an immutable config:
kubectl apply -f vweb/update/vweb-v4-with-configMap.yaml --record

# check the output:
curl $(cat url.txt)

# release a new ConfigMap and updated Deployment:
kubectl apply -f vweb/update/vweb-v41-with-configMap.yaml --record

# check the output again:
curl $(cat url.txt)

# the update is a full rollout:
kubectl rollout history deploy/vweb

# so you can rollback:
kubectl rollout undo deploy/vweb
curl $(cat url.txt)
```

The new Deployment uses a ConfigMap for the response content to the HTTP request.

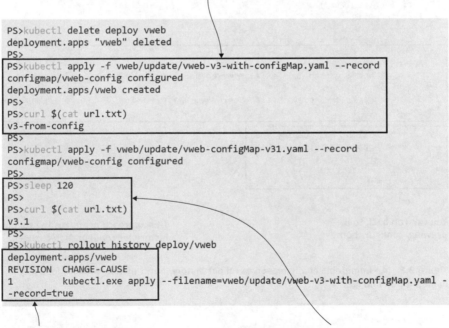

```
PS>kubectl delete deploy vweb
deployment.apps "vweb" deleted
PS>
PS>kubectl apply -f vweb/update/vweb-v3-with-configMap.yaml --record
configmap/vweb-config configured
deployment.apps/vweb created
PS>
PS>curl $(cat url.txt)
v3-from-config
PS>
PS>kubectl apply -f vweb/update/vweb-configMap-v31.yaml --record
configmap/vweb-config configured
PS>
PS>sleep 120
PS>
PS>curl $(cat url.txt)
v3.1
PS>
PS>kubectl rollout history deploy/vweb
deployment.apps/vweb
REVISION   CHANGE-CAUSE
1          kubectl.exe apply --filename=vweb/update/vweb-v3-with-configMap.yaml -
-record=true
```

The app's behavior is different, but there was no change to the Deployment, so there's no option to roll back.

The app reloads configuration when the ConfigMap file changes, but Kubernetes caches the content, so it can take two minutes to take effect.

Figure 9.7 Configuration updates might change app behavior but without recording a rollout.

Figure 9.8 shows my output, where the config update is accompanied by a Deployment update, which preserves the rollout history and enables the rollback.

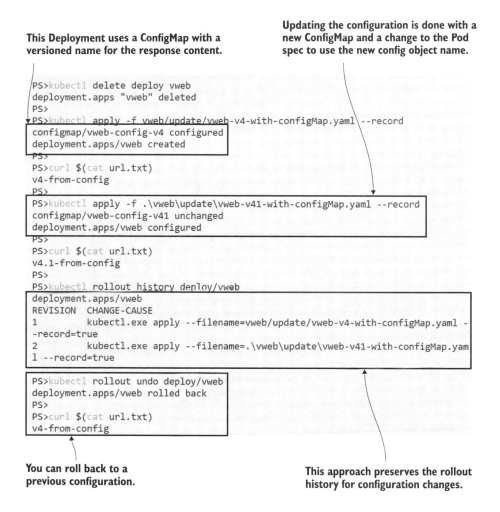

This Deployment uses a ConfigMap with a versioned name for the response content.

Updating the configuration is done with a new ConfigMap and a change to the Pod spec to use the new config object name.

```
PS>kubectl delete deploy vweb
deployment.apps "vweb" deleted
PS>
PS>kubectl apply -f vweb/update/vweb-v4-with-configMap.yaml --record
configmap/vweb-config-v4 configured
deployment.apps/vweb created
PS>
PS>curl $(cat url.txt)
v4-from-config
PS>
PS>kubectl apply -f .\vweb\update\vweb-v41-with-configMap.yaml --record
configmap/vweb-config-v41 unchanged
deployment.apps/vweb configured
PS>
PS>curl $(cat url.txt)
v4.1-from-config
PS>
PS>kubectl rollout history deploy/vweb
deployment.apps/vweb
REVISION   CHANGE-CAUSE
1          kubectl.exe apply --filename=vweb/update/vweb-v4-with-configMap.yaml -
-record=true
2          kubectl.exe apply --filename=.\vweb\update\vweb-v41-with-configMap.yam
l --record=true

PS>kubectl rollout undo deploy/vweb
deployment.apps/vweb rolled back
PS>
PS>curl $(cat url.txt)
v4-from-config
```

You can roll back to a previous configuration.

This approach preserves the rollout history for configuration changes.

Figure 9.8   An immutable config preserves rollout history, but it means a rollout for every configuration change.

Kubernetes doesn't really care which approach you take, and your choice will partly depend on who owns the configuration in your organization. If the project team also owns deployment and configuration, then you might prefer mutable config objects to simplify the release process and the number of objects to manage. If a separate team owns the configuration, then the immutable approach will be better because they can deploy new config objects ahead of the release. The scale of your apps will affect the decision, too: at a high scale, you may prefer to reduce the number of app deployments and rely on mutable configuration.

There's a cultural impact to this decision, because it frames how application releases are perceived—as everyday events that are no big deal, or as something slightly scary that is to be avoided as much as possible. In the container world, releases should be trivial events that you're happy to do with minimal ceremony as soon as they're needed. Testing and tweaking your release strategy will go a long way to giving you that confidence.

9.3 *Configuring rolling updates for Deployments*

Deployments support two update strategies: RollingUpdate is the default and the one we've used so far, and the other is Recreate. You know how rolling updates work—by scaling down the old ReplicaSet while scaling up the new ReplicaSet, which provides service continuity and the ability to stagger the update over a longer period. The Recreate strategy gives you neither of those. It still uses ReplicaSets to implement changes, but it scales down the previous set to zero before scaling up the replacement. Listing 9.2 shows the Recreate strategy in a Deployment spec. It's just one setting, but it has a significant impact.

> **Listing 9.2 vweb-recreate-v2.yaml, a Deployment using the recreate update strategy**

```
apiVersion: apps/v1
kind: Deployment
metadata:
  name: vweb
spec:
  replicas: 3
  strategy:                       # This is the update strategy.
    type: Recreate                # Recreate is the alternative to the
                                  # default strategy, RollingUpdate.
  # selector & Pod spec follow
```

When you deploy this, you'll see it's just a normal app with a Deployment, a ReplicaSet, and some Pods. If you look at the details of the Deployment, you'll see it uses the Recreate update strategy, but that has an effect only when the Deployment is updated.

> **TRY IT NOW** Deploy the app from listing 9.2, and explore the objects. This is just like a normal Deployment.

```
# delete the existing app:
kubectl delete deploy vweb

# deploy with the Recreate strategy:
kubectl apply -f vweb-strategies/vweb-recreate-v2.yaml

# check the ReplicaSets:
kubectl get rs -l app=vweb
```

```
# test the app:
curl $(cat url.txt)

# look at the details of the Deployment:
kubectl describe deploy vweb
```

As shown in Figure 9.9, this is a new deployment of the same old web app, using version 2 of the container image. There are three Pods, they're all running, and the app works as expected—so far so good.

This Deployment uses the Recreate update strategy, but until you update it, the behavior is the same as a standard Deployment.

```
PS>kubectl delete deploy vweb
deployment.apps "vweb" deleted
PS>
PS>kubectl apply -f vweb-strategies/vweb-recreate-v2.yaml
deployment.apps/vweb created
PS>
PS>kubectl get rs -l app=vweb
NAME                DESIRED   CURRENT   READY   AGE
vweb-7659d9d47f     3         3         3       6s
PS>
PS>curl $(cat url.txt)
v2
PS>kubectl describe deploy vweb
Name:               vweb
Namespace:          default
CreationTimestamp:  Fri, 22 May 2020 20:32:15 +0100
Labels:             kiamol=ch09
Annotations:        deployment.kubernetes.io/revision: 1

Replicas:           3 desired | 3 updated | 3 total | 3 available | 0 unavailabl
e
StrategyType:       Recreate
```

This abbreviated output shows the current revision and the update strategy of the Deployment.

Same old app, running version 2 of the container image

Figure 9.9 The Recreate update strategy doesn't affect behavior until you release an update.

This configuration is dangerous, though, and one you should use only if different versions of your app can't coexist—something like a database schema update, where you need to be sure that only one version of your app connects to the database. Even in that case, you have better options, but if you have a scenario that definitely needs this approach, then you'd better be sure you test all your updates before you go live. If you deploy an update where the new Pods fail, you won't know that until your old Pods have all been terminated, and your app will be completely unavailable.

TRY IT NOW Version 3 of the web app is ready to deploy. It's broken, as you'll see when the app goes offline because no Pods are running.

```
# deploy the updated Pod spec:
kubectl apply -f vweb-strategies/vweb-recreate-v3.yaml

# check the status, with a time limit for updates:
kubectl rollout status deploy/vweb --timeout=2s

# check the ReplicaSets:
kubectl get rs -l app=vweb

# check the Pods:
kubectl get pods -l app=vweb

# test the app-this will fail:
curl $(cat url.txt)
```

You'll see in this exercise that Kubernetes happily takes your app offline, because that's what you've requested. The Recreate strategy creates a new ReplicaSet with the updated Pod template, then scales down the previous ReplicaSet to zero and scales up the new ReplicaSet to three. The new image is broken, so the new Pods fail, and there's nothing to respond to requests, as you see in figure 9.10.

This update will fail because the new container image is broken.

Checking the status will wait for the rollout to complete, but it never will in this case, so the timeout just waits for two seconds.

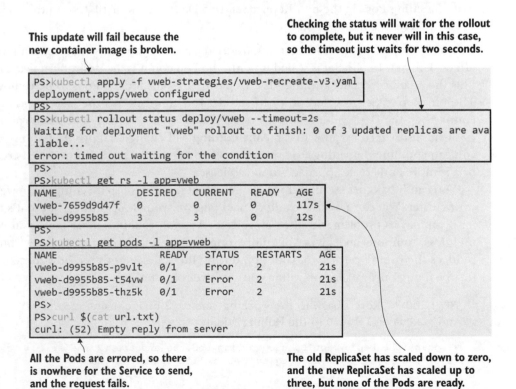

All the Pods are errored, so there is nowhere for the Service to send, and the request fails.

The old ReplicaSet has scaled down to zero, and the new ReplicaSet has scaled up to three, but none of the Pods are ready.

Figure 9.10 The Recreate strategy happily takes down your app if the new Pod spec is broken.

Now that you've seen it, you should probably try to forget about the Recreate strategy. In some scenarios, it might seem attractive, but when it does, you should still consider alternative options, even if it means looking again at your architecture. The wholesale takedown of your application is going to cause downtime, and probably more downtime than you plan for.

Rolling updates are the default because they guard against downtime, but even then, the default behavior is quite aggressive. For a production release, you'll want to tune a few settings that set the speed of the release and how it gets monitored. As part of the rolling update spec, you can add options that control how quickly the new ReplicaSet is scaled up and how quickly the old ReplicaSet is scaled down, using the following two values:

- maxUnavailable is the accelerator for scaling down the old ReplicaSet. It defines how many Pods can be unavailable during the update, relative to the desired Pod count. You can think of it as the batch size for terminating Pods in the old ReplicaSet. In a Deployment of 10 Pods, setting this to 30% means three Pods will be terminated immediately.
- maxSurge is the accelerator for scaling up the new ReplicaSet. It defines how many extra Pods can exist, over the desired replica count, like the batch size for creating Pods in the new ReplicaSet. In a Deployment of 10, setting this to 40% will create four new Pods.

Nice and simple, except both settings are used during a rollout, so you have a seesaw effect. The new ReplicaSet is scaled up until the Pod count is the desired replica count plus the maxSurge value, and then the Deployment waits for old Pods to be removed. The old ReplicaSet is scaled down to the desired count minus the maxUnavailable count, then the Deployment waits for new Pods to reach the ready state. You can't set both values to zero because that means nothing will change. Figure 9.11 shows how you can combine the settings to prefer a create-then-remove, or a remove-then-create, or a remove-and-create approach to new releases.

You can tweak these settings for a faster rollout if you have spare compute power in your cluster. You can also create additional Pods over your scale setting, but that's riskier if you have a problem with the new release. A slower rollout is more conservative: it uses less compute and gives you more opportunity to discover any issues, but it reduces the overall capacity of your app during the release. Let's see how these look, first by fixing our broken app with a conservative rollout.

TRY IT NOW   Revert back to the working version 2 image, using maxSurge=1 and maxUnavailable=0 in the RollingUpdate strategy.

```
# update the Deployment to use rolling updates and the v2 image:
kubectl apply -f vweb-strategies/vweb-rollingUpdate-v2.yaml

# check the Pods for the app:
kubectl get po -l app=vweb
```

```
# check the rollout status:
kubectl rollout status deploy/vweb

# check the ReplicaSets:
kubectl get rs -l app=vweb

# test the app:
curl $(cat url.txt)
```

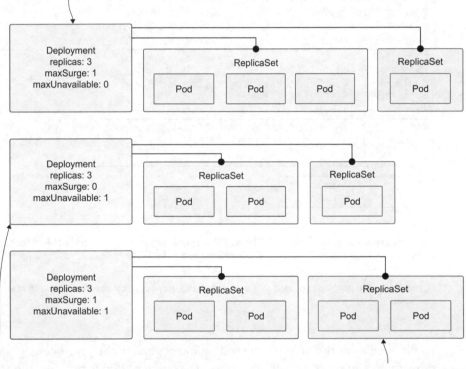

`maxSurge` is set to 1, so the Deployment can expand to four replicas, one above the desired count. `maxUnavailable` is set to 0, so a new Pod is created before an old one is terminated.

`maxSurge` is 0, so there will be a maximum of three Pods. `maxUnavailable` is set to 1, so an old Pod is terminated before a new Pod is created.

`maxSurge` and `maxUnavailable` are both set to 1, so an old Pod is terminated, and two new Pods can be created.

Figure 9.11 Deployment updates in progress, using different rollout options

In this exercise, the new Deployment spec changed the Pod image back to version 2, and it also changed the update strategy to a rolling update. You can see in figure 9.12 that the strategy change is made first, and then the Pod update is made in line with the new strategy, creating one new Pod at a time.

This spec changes the update strategy and the container image. The strategy
change is made first, and the Pods are updated using the new strategy.

`maxSurge` is set to 1, so the Deployment can have four Pods. One old Pod
is terminating, so there are four active Pods, two from each ReplicaSet.

```
PS>kubectl apply -f vweb-strategies/vweb-rollingUpdate-v2.yaml
deployment.apps/vweb configured
PS>kubectl get po -l app=vweb
NAME                   READY   STATUS             RESTARTS   AGE
vweb-7659d9d47f-5hc72  1/1     Running            0          2s
vweb-7659d9d47f-fkzn4  0/1     ContainerCreating  0          1s
vweb-d9955b85-p9vlt    0/1     CrashLoopBackOff   30         47h
vweb-d9955b85-t54vw    0/1     CrashLoopBackOff   30         47h
vweb-d9955b85-thz5k    0/1     Terminating        30         47h
PS>
PS>kubectl rollout status deploy/vweb
deployment "vweb" successfully rolled out
PS>
PS>kubectl get rs -l app=vweb
NAME             DESIRED   CURRENT   READY   AGE
vweb-7659d9d47f  3         3         3       47h
vweb-d9955b85    0         0         0       47h
PS>
PS>curl $(cat url.txt)
v2
```

The Pods are working correctly,
so the app is back online.

The new Pod spec is the same as the original Pod spec, so the
Deployment reuses the first ReplicaSet, scaling it up to 3.

Figure 9.12 **Deployment updates will use an existing ReplicaSet if the Pod template matches the
new spec.**

You'll need to work fast to see the rollout in progress in the previous exercise, because
this simple app starts quickly, and as soon as one new Pod is running, the rollout continues with another new Pod. You can control the pace of the rollout with the following two fields in the Deployment spec:

- `minReadySeconds` adds a delay where the Deployment waits to make sure new
  Pods are stable. It specifies the number of seconds the Pod should be up with
  no containers crashing before it's considered to be successful. The default is
  zero, which is why new Pods are created quickly during rollouts.
- `progressDeadlineSeconds` specifies the amount of time a Deployment update
  can run before it's considered as failing to progress. The default is 600 seconds, so if an update is not completed within 10 minutes, it's flagged as not
  progressing.

Monitoring how long the release takes sounds useful, but as of Kubernetes 1.19, exceeding the deadline doesn't actually affect the rollout—it just sets a flag on the Deployment. Kubernetes doesn't have an automatic rollback feature for failed rollouts, but when that feature does come, it will be triggered by this flag. Waiting and checking a Pod for failed containers is a fairly blunt tool, but it's better than having no checks at all, and you should consider having minReadySeconds specified in all your Deployments.

These safety measures are useful to add to your Deployment, but they don't really help with our web app because the new Pods always fail. We can make this Deployment safe and keep the app online using a rolling update. The next version 3 update sets both maxUnavailable and maxSurge to 1. Doing so has the same effect as the default values (each 25%), but it's clearer to use exact values in the spec, and Pod counts are easier to work with than percentages in small deployments.

> **TRY IT NOW** Deploy the version 3 update again. It will still fail, but by using a RollingUpdate strategy, it doesn't take the app offline.

```
# update to the failing container image:
kubectl apply -f vweb-strategies/vweb-rollingUpdate-v3.yaml

# check the Pods:
kubectl get po -l app=vweb

# check the rollout:
kubectl rollout status deploy/vweb

# see the scale in the ReplicaSets:
kubectl get rs -l app=vweb

# test the app:
curl $(cat url.txt)
```

When you run this exercise, you'll see the update never completes, and the Deployment is stuck with two ReplicaSets having a desired Pod count of two, as shown in figure 9.13. The old ReplicaSet won't scale down any further because the Deployment has maxUnavailable set to 1; it has already been scaled down by 1 and no new Pods will become ready to continue the rollout. The new ReplicaSet won't scale up anymore because maxSurge is set to 1, and the total Pod count for the Deployment has been reached.

If you check back on the new Pods in a few minutes, you'll see they're in the state CrashLoopBackoff. Kubernetes keeps restarting failed Pods by creating replacement containers, but it adds a pause between each restart so it doesn't choke the CPU on the node. That pause is the backoff time, and it increases exponentially—10 seconds for the first restart, then 20 seconds, and then 40 seconds, up to a maximum of 5 minutes. These version 3 Pods will never restart successfully, but Kubernetes will keep trying.

Deployments are the controllers you use the most, and it's worth spending time working through the update strategy and timing settings to be sure you understand

This rolling update has `maxSurge` **and** `maxUnavailable` **both set to 1, so the initial batch terminates one old version 2 Pod and creates two new version 3 Pods.**

The update is set with a progress deadline of 120 seconds. The `status` **command waits until the rollout hits that deadline.**

```
PS>kubectl apply -f vweb-strategies/vweb-rollingUpdate-v3.yaml
deployment.apps/vweb configured
PS>
PS>kubectl get po -l app=vweb
NAME                      READY    STATUS        RESTARTS    AGE
vweb-7659d9d47f-5t78g     1/1      Running       0           5m58s
vweb-7659d9d47f-k986n     0/1      Terminating   0           5m58s
vweb-7659d9d47f-tslh7     1/1      Running       0           5m58s
vweb-d9955b85-769g2       0/1      Error         0           2s
vweb-d9955b85-s86bj       0/1      Error         0           2s
PS>
PS>kubectl rollout status deploy/vweb
Waiting for deployment "vweb" rollout to finish: 2 out of 3 new replicas have be
en updated...
error: deployment "vweb" exceeded its progress deadline
PS>
PS>kubectl get rs -l app=vweb
NAME                 DESIRED    CURRENT    READY    AGE
vweb-7659d9d47f      2          2          2        2d
vweb-d9955b85        2          2          0        2d
PS>
PS>curl $(cat url.txt)
v2
```

The app is still running at reduced capacity, using the version 2 Pods.

The update won't progress because the new Pods have failed. Kubernetes doesn't have automatic rollbacks, so this is the final state.

Figure 9.13   Failed updates don't automatically roll back or pause; they just keep trying.

the impact for your apps. DaemonSets and StatefulSets also have rolling update functionality, and because they have different ways of managing their Pods, they have different approaches to rollouts, too.

9.4   *Rolling updates in DaemonSets and StatefulSets*

DaemonSets and StatefulSets have two update strategies available. The default is RollingUpdate, which we'll explore in this section. The alternative is OnDelete, which is for situations when you need close control over when each Pod is updated. You deploy the update, and the controller watches Pods, but it doesn't terminate any existing Pods. It waits until they are deleted by another process, and then it replaces them with Pods from the new spec.

This isn't quite as pointless as it sounds, when you think about the use cases for these controllers. You may have a StatefulSet where each Pod needs to have flushed data to disk before it's removed, and you can have an automated process to do that. You may have a DaemonSet where each Pod needs to be disconnected from a hardware component, so it's free for the next Pod to use. These are rare cases, but the OnDelete strategy lets you take ownership of when Pods are deleted and still have Kubernetes automatically create replacements.

We'll focus on rolling updates in this section, and for that we'll deploy a version of the to-do list app, which runs the database in a StatefulSet, the web app in a Deployment, and a reverse proxy for the web app in a DaemonSet.

TRY IT NOW The to-do app runs across six Pods, so start by clearing the existing apps to make room. Then deploy the app, and test that it works correctly.

```
# remove all of this chapter's apps:
kubectl delete all -l kiamol=ch09

# deploy the to-do app, database, and proxy:
kubectl apply -f todo-list/db/ -f todo-list/web/ -f todo-list/proxy/

# get the app URL:
kubectl get svc todo-proxy -o
   jsonpath='http://{.status.loadBalancer.ingress[0].*}:8091'

# browse to the app, add an item, and check that it's in the list
```

This is just setting us up for the updates. You should now have a working app where you can add items and see the list. My output is shown in figure 9.14.

The current state of the to-do app: a StatefulSet for the database, Deployment for the website, DaemonSet for the proxy, and associated ConfigMaps and Secrets.

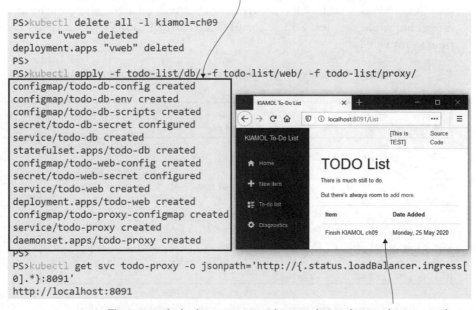

The app works in the same way, and now we're ready to make some updates.

Figure 9.14 Running the to-do app with a gratuitous variety of controllers

The first update is for the DaemonSet, where we'll be rolling out a new version of the Nginx proxy image. DaemonSets run a single Pod on all (or some) of the nodes in the cluster, and with a rolling update, you have no surge option. During the update, nodes will never run two Pods, so this is always a delete-then-remove strategy. You can add the `maxUnavailable` setting to control how many nodes are updated in parallel, but if you take down multiple Pods, you'll be running at reduced capacity until the replacements are ready.

We'll update the proxy using a `maxUnavailable` setting of 1, and a `minReadySeconds` setting of 90. On a single-node lab cluster, the delay won't have any effect—there's only one Pod on one node to replace. On a larger cluster, it would mean replacing one Pod at a time and waiting 90 seconds for the Pod to prove it's stable before moving on to the next.

TRY IT NOW   Start the rolling update of the DaemonSet. On a single-node cluster, a short outage will occur while the replacement Pod starts.

```
# deploy the DaemonSet update:
kubectl apply -f todo-list/proxy/update/nginx-rollingUpdate.yaml

# watch the Pod update:
kubectl get po -l app=todo-proxy --watch

# Press ctrl-c when the update completes
```

The `watch` flag in kubectl is useful for monitoring changes—it keeps looking at an object and prints an update line whenever the state changes. In this exercise you'll see that the old Pod is terminated before the new one is created, which means the app has downtime while the new Pod starts up. Figure 9.15 shows I had one second of downtime in my release.

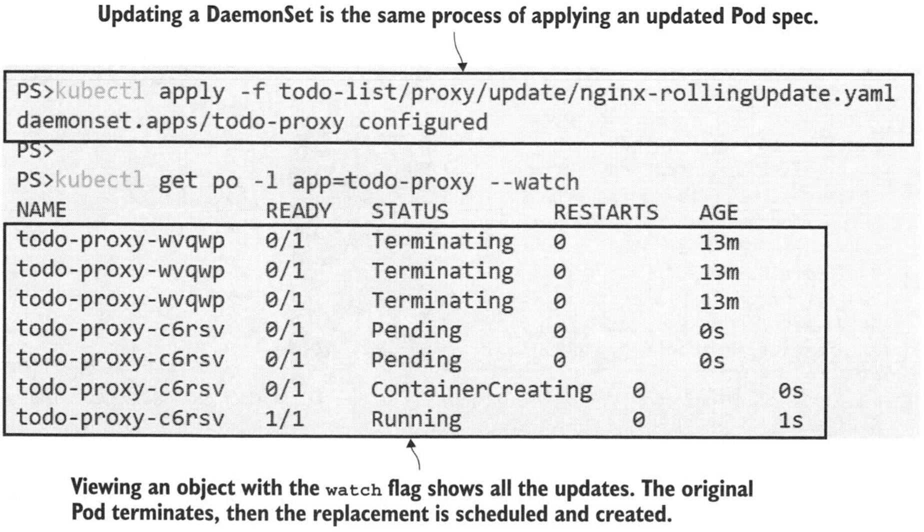

Updating a DaemonSet is the same process of applying an updated Pod spec.

```
PS>kubectl apply -f todo-list/proxy/update/nginx-rollingUpdate.yaml
daemonset.apps/todo-proxy configured
PS>
PS>kubectl get po -l app=todo-proxy --watch
NAME                READY   STATUS             RESTARTS   AGE
todo-proxy-wvqwp    0/1     Terminating        0          13m
todo-proxy-wvqwp    0/1     Terminating        0          13m
todo-proxy-wvqwp    0/1     Terminating        0          13m
todo-proxy-c6rsv    0/1     Pending            0          0s
todo-proxy-c6rsv    0/1     Pending            0          0s
todo-proxy-c6rsv    0/1     ContainerCreating  0          0s
todo-proxy-c6rsv    1/1     Running            0          1s
```

Viewing an object with the `watch` flag shows all the updates. The original Pod terminates, then the replacement is scheduled and created.

Figure 9.15   DaemonSets update by removing the existing Pod before creating a replacement.

A multinode cluster wouldn't have any downtime because the Service sends traffic only to Pods that are ready, and only one Pod at a time gets updated, so the other Pods are always available. You will have reduced capacity, though, and if you tune a faster rollout with a higher `maxUnavailable` setting, that means a greater reduction in capacity as more Pods are updated in parallel. That's the only setting you have for DaemonSets, so it's a simple choice between manually controlling the update by deleting Pods or having Kubernetes roll out the update by a specified number of Pods in parallel.

StatefulSets are more interesting, although they have only one option to configure the rollout. Pods are managed in order by the StatefulSet, which also applies to updates—the rollout proceeds backward from the last Pod in the set down to the first. That's especially useful for clustered applications where Pod 0 is the primary, because it validates the update on the secondaries first.

There is no `maxSurge` or `maxUnavailable` setting for StatefulSets. The update is always by one Pod at a time. Your configuration option is to define how many Pods should be updated in total, using the `partition` setting. This setting defines the cut-off point where the rollout stops, and it's useful for performing a staged rollout of a stateful app. If you have five replicas in your set and your spec includes partition=3, then only Pod 4 and Pod 3 will be updated; Pods 0, 1, and 2 are left running the previous spec.

> **TRY IT NOW**   Deploy a partitioned update to the database image in the Stateful-Set, which stops after Pod 1, so Pod 0 doesn't get updated.

```
# deploy the update:
kubectl apply -f todo-list/db/update/todo-db-rollingUpdate-
   partition.yaml

# check the rollout status:
kubectl rollout status statefulset/todo-db

# list the Pods, showing the image name and start time:
kubectl get pods -l app=todo-db -o=custom-columns=NAME:.metadata.name,
   IMAGE:.spec.containers[0].image,START_TIME:.status.startTime

# switch the web app to read-only mode, so it uses the secondary
# database:
kubectl apply -f todo-list/web/update/todo-web-readonly.yaml

# test the app—the data is there, but now it's read-only
```

This exercise is a partitioned update that rolls out a new version of the Postgres container image, but only to the secondary Pods, which is a single Pod in this case, as shown in figure 9.16. When you use the app in read-only mode, you'll see that it connects to the updated secondary, which still contains the replicated data from the previous Pod.

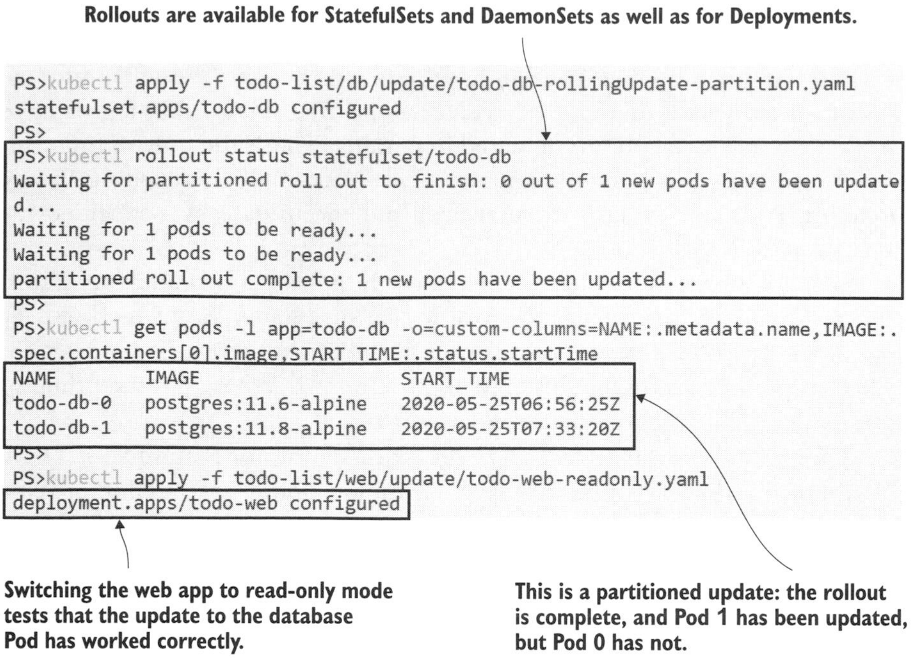

Rollouts are available for StatefulSets and DaemonSets as well as for Deployments.

```
PS>kubectl apply -f todo-list/db/update/todo-db-rollingUpdate-partition.yaml
statefulset.apps/todo-db configured
PS>
PS>kubectl rollout status statefulset/todo-db
Waiting for partitioned roll out to finish: 0 out of 1 new pods have been update
d...
Waiting for 1 pods to be ready...
Waiting for 1 pods to be ready...
partitioned roll out complete: 1 new pods have been updated...
PS>
PS>kubectl get pods -l app=todo-db -o=custom-columns=NAME:.metadata.name,IMAGE:.
spec.containers[0].image,START TIME:.status.startTime
NAME          IMAGE                  START_TIME
todo-db-0     postgres:11.6-alpine   2020-05-25T06:56:25Z
todo-db-1     postgres:11.8-alpine   2020-05-25T07:33:20Z
PS>
PS>kubectl apply -f todo-list/web/update/todo-web-readonly.yaml
deployment.apps/todo-web configured
```

Switching the web app to read-only mode tests that the update to the database Pod has worked correctly.

This is a partitioned update: the rollout is complete, and Pod 1 has been updated, but Pod 0 has not.

Figure 9.16 Partitioned updates to StatefulSets let you update secondaries and leave the primary unchanged.

This rollout is complete, even though the Pods in the set are running from different specs. For a data-heavy application in a StatefulSet, you may have a suite of verification jobs that you need to run on each updated Pod before you're happy to continue the rollout, and a partitioned update lets you do that. You can manually control the pace of the release by running successive updates with decreasing partition values, until you remove the partition altogether in the final update to finish the set.

TRY IT NOW Deploy the update to the database primary. This spec is the same as the previous exercise but with the partition setting removed.

```
# apply the update:
kubectl apply -f todo-list/db/update/todo-db-rollingUpdate.yaml

# check its progress:
kubectl rollout status statefulset/todo-db

# Pods should now all have the same spec:
kubectl get pods -l app=todo-db -o=custom-
  columns=NAME:.metadata.name,IMAGE:.spec.containers[0].image,START
  _TIME:.status.startTime
```

```
# reset the web app back to read-write mode:
kubectl apply -f todo-list/web/todo-web.yaml

# test that the app works and is connected to the updated primary Pod
```

You can see my output in figure 9.17, where the full update has completed and the primary is using the same updated version of Postgres as the secondary. If you've done updates to replicated databases before, you'll know that this is about as simple as it gets—unless you're using a managed database service, of course.

The final stage in the StatefulSet update—with no partition setting, the rollout will update Pod 0.

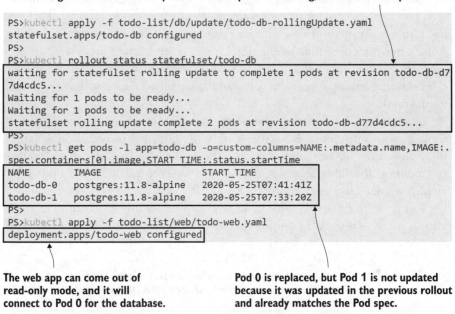

The web app can come out of read-only mode, and it will connect to Pod 0 for the database.

Pod 0 is replaced, but Pod 1 is not updated because it was updated in the previous rollout and already matches the Pod spec.

Figure 9.17 Completing the StatefulSet rollout, with an update that is not partitioned

Rolling updates are the default for Deployments, DaemonSets, and StatefulSets, and they all work in broadly the same way: gradually replacing Pods running the previous application spec with Pods running the new spec. The actual details differ because the controllers work in different ways and have different goals, but they impose the same requirement on your app: it needs to work correctly when multiple versions are live. That's not always possible, and there are alternative ways to deploy app updates in Kubernetes.

9.5   *Understanding release strategies*

Take the example of a web application. A rolling update is great because it lets each Pod close gracefully when all its client requests are dealt with, and the rollout can be as fast or as conservative as you like. The practical side of the rollout is simple, but you have to consider the user experience (UX) side, too.

Application updates might well change the UX—with a different design, new features, or an updated workflow. Any changes like that will be pretty strange for the user if they see the new version during a rollout, then refresh and find themselves with the old version, because the requests have been served by Pods running different versions of the app.

The strategies to deal with that go beyond the RollingUpdate spec in your controllers. You can set cookies in your web app to link a client to a particular UX, and then use a more advanced traffic routing system to ensure users keep seeing the new version. When we cover that in chapter 15, you'll see it introduces several more moving parts. For cases where that method is too complex or doesn't solve the problem of dual running multiple versions, you can manage the release yourself with a blue-green deployment.

Blue-green deployments are a simple concept: you have both the old and new versions of your app deployed at the same time, but only one version is active. You can flip a switch to choose which version is the active one. In Kubernetes, you can do that by updating the label selector in a Service to send traffic to the Pods in a different Deployment, as shown in figure 9.18.

You need to have the capacity in your cluster to run two complete copies of your app. If it's a web or API component, then the new version should be using minimal

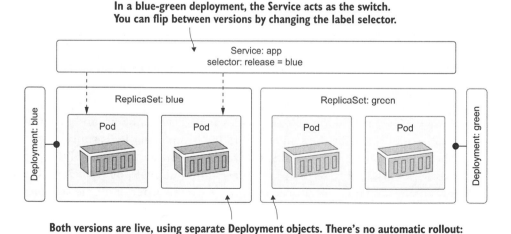

In a blue-green deployment, the Service acts as the switch.
You can flip between versions by changing the label selector.

Both versions are live, using separate Deployment objects. There's no automatic rollout: the update is done in advance, and the release happens when the traffic is switched.

Figure 9.18   You run multiple versions of the app in a blue-green deployment, but only one is live.

memory and CPU because it's not receiving any traffic. You switch between versions by updating the label selector for the Service, so the update is practically instant because all the Pods are running and ready to receive traffic. You can flip back and forth easily, so you can roll back a problem release without waiting for ReplicaSets to scale up and down.

Blue-green deployments are less sophisticated than rolling updates, but they're simpler because of that. They can be a better fit for organizations moving to Kubernetes who have a history of big-bang deployments, but they're a compute-intensive approach that requires multiple steps and doesn't preserve the rollout history of your app. You should look to rolling updates as your preferred deployment strategy, but blue-green deployments are a good stepping-stone to use while you gain confidence.

That's all on rolling updates for now, but we will return to the concepts when we cover topics in production readiness, network ingress, and monitoring. We just need to tidy up the cluster now before going on to the lab.

TRY IT NOW Remove all the objects created for this chapter.

```
kubectl delete all -l kiamol=ch09
kubectl delete cm -l kiamol=ch09
kubectl delete pvc -l kiamol=ch09
```

9.6 *Lab*

We learned the theory of blue-green deployments in the previous section, and now in the lab, you're going to make it happen. Working through this lab will help make it clear how selectors relate Pods to other objects and give you experience working with the alternative to rolling updates.

- The starting point is version 1 of the web app, which you can deploy from the lab/v1 folder.
- You need to create a blue-green deployment for version 2 of the app. The spec will be similar to the version 1 spec but using the :v2 container image.
- When you deploy your update, you should be able to flip between the version 1 and version 2 release just by changing the Service and without any updates to Pods.

This is good practice in copying YAML files and trying to work out which fields you need to change. You can find my solution on GitHub: https://github.com/sixeyed/kiamol/blob/master/ch09/lab/README.md.

Packaging and managing apps with Helm

As vast as Kubernetes is, it doesn't solve every problem by itself; a large ecosystem exists to fill the gaps. One of these gaps is packaging and distributing apps, and the solution is Helm. You can use Helm to group a set of Kubernetes YAML files into one artifact and share that on a public or private repository. Anyone with access to the repository can install the app with a single Helm command. That command might deploy a whole set of related Kubernetes resources including ConfigMaps, Deployments, and Services, and you can customize the configuration as part of the installation.

People use Helm in different ways. Some teams use Helm only to install and manage third-party apps from public repositories. Other teams use Helm for their own applications, packaging and publishing them to private repositories. In this chapter, you'll learn how to do both, and you'll leave with your own idea of how Helm might fit in your organization. You don't need to learn Helm to be effective with Kubernetes, but it's widely used so it's something you should be familiar with. The project is governed by the Cloud Native Computing Foundation (CNCF)—the same foundation that stewards Kubernetes—which a reliable indicator of maturity and longevity.

10.1 What Helm adds to Kubernetes

Kubernetes apps are modeled in a sprawl of YAML files at design time and managed using sets of labels at run time. There's no native concept of an "application" in Kubernetes, which clearly groups together a set of related resources, and that's one of the problems Helm solves. It's a command-line tool that interacts with repository servers to find and download application packages and, with your Kubernetes cluster, to install and manage applications.

Helm is another layer of abstraction, this time at the application level. When you install an application with Helm, it creates a set of resources in your Kubernetes cluster—and they're standard Kubernetes resources. The Helm packaging format extends Kubernetes YAML files, so a Helm package is really just a set of Kubernetes manifests stored along with some metadata. We'll start by using Helm to deploy one of the sample apps from previous chapters, but first we need to install Helm.

TRY IT NOW Helm is a cross-platform tool that runs on Windows, macOS, and Linux. You can find the latest installation instructions here: https://helm.sh/ docs/intro/install. This exercise assumes you already have a package manager like Homebrew or Chocolatey installed. If not, you'll need to refer to the Helm site for the full installation instructions.

```
# on Windows, using Chocolatey:
choco install -y kubernetes-helm

# on Mac, using Homebrew:
brew install helm

# on Linux, using the Helm install script:
curl https://raw.githubusercontent.com/helm/helm/master/scripts/get-
   helm-3 | bash

# check that Helm is working:
helm version
```

The installation steps in this exercise may not work on your system, in which case, you'll need to stop here and head to the Helm installation docs. We can't go much further until you have Helm installed and you see successful output from the `version` command, like that shown in figure 10.1.

Helm is a client-side tool. Previous versions of Helm required a server component to be deployed in your Kubernetes cluster, but that was changed in the major update to Helm 3. The Helm CLI uses the same connection information that kubectl uses to connect to your Kubernetes cluster, so you don't need any extra configuration to install an app. You do need to configure a package repository, however. Helm repositories are similar to container image registries like Docker Hub, but the server publishes an index of all available packages; Helm caches a local copy of your repository indexes, which you can use to search packages.

TRY IT NOW Add the Helm repository for the book, sync it, and search for an app.

```
# add a repository, using a local name to refer to a remote server:
helm repo add kiamol https://kiamol.net

# update the local repository cache:
helm repo update

# search for an app in the repo cache:
helm search repo vweb --versions
```

**Helm is an open source project published on GitHub. It's available
through package managers. I'm using Chocolatey on Windows.**

```
PS>choco install -y --limit-output kubernetes-helm
Installing the following packages:
kubernetes-helm
By installing you accept licenses for the packages.
Progress: Downloading kubernetes-helm 3.2.3... 100%

 The install of kubernetes-helm was successful.
  Software installed to 'C:\ProgramData\chocolatey\lib\kubernetes-helm\tools'

Chocolatey installed 1/1 packages.
 See the log for details (C:\ProgramData\chocolatey\logs\chocolatey.log).
PS>
PS>
PS>helm version
version.BuildInfo{Version:"v3.2.3", GitCommit:"8f832046e258e2cb800894579b1b3b50c
2d83492", GitTreeState:"clean", GoVersion:"go1.13.12"}
```

**Helm is a command-line utility. Make sure you're running
version 3—it's a significant upgrade from previous versions.**

Figure 10.1   There are lots of options to install Helm; using a package manager is easiest.

The Kiamol repository is a public server, and you can see in this exercise that there are
two versions of the package called vweb. My output appears in figure 10.2.

**There are lots of public Helm repositories,
and you can run your own repository server.
This is the repository for the book.**

**Updating the repository downloads
the package index to a local cache.**

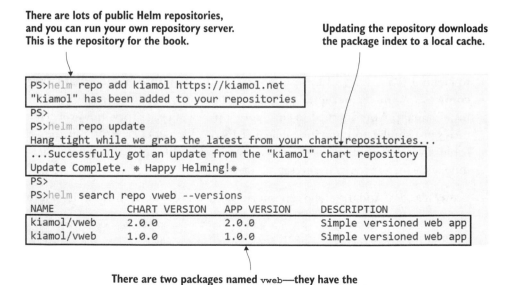

```
PS>helm repo add kiamol https://kiamol.net
"kiamol" has been added to your repositories
PS>
PS>helm repo update
Hang tight while we grab the latest from your chart repositories...
...Successfully got an update from the "kiamol" chart repository
Update Complete. ⚓ Happy Helming!⚓
PS>
PS>helm search repo vweb --versions
NAME            CHART VERSION   APP VERSION     DESCRIPTION
kiamol/vweb     2.0.0           2.0.0           Simple versioned web app
kiamol/vweb     1.0.0           1.0.0           Simple versioned web app
```

There are two packages named vweb**—they have the
same name and description but different version numbers.**

Figure 10.2   Syncing a local copy of the Kiamol Helm repository and searching for packages

You're getting a feel for Helm, but it's time for some theory so we can use the correct concepts and their correct names before we go any further. An application package in Helm is called a *chart*; charts can be developed and deployed locally or published to a *repository*. When you install a chart, that's called a *release*; every release has a name, and you can install multiple instances of the same chart in your cluster as separate, named releases.

Charts contain Kubernetes YAML manifests, and the manifests typically contain parameterized values so users can install the same chart with different configuration settings—the number of replicas to run or the application logging level could be parameter values. Each chart also contains a default set of values, and they can be inspected using the command line. Figure 10.3 shows the file structure of a Helm chart.

Charts are packaged as compressed archives, named with the chart name and version. The archive contains a folder, which is the name of the chart.

The chart file contains metadata, including name, version, and description.

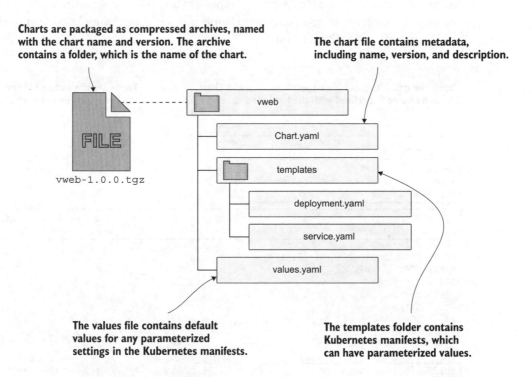

vweb-1.0.0.tgz

The values file contains default values for any parameterized settings in the Kubernetes manifests.

The templates folder contains Kubernetes manifests, which can have parameterized values.

Figure 10.3   Helm charts contain all the Kubernetes YAML for the app, plus some metadata.

The vweb charts package contains the simple web app we used to demonstrate updates and rollbacks in chapter 9. Each chart contains a spec for a Service and a Deployment, with some parameterized values and default settings. You can use the Helm command line to inspect all the available values before installing the chart and then override the defaults with custom values when you install a release.

TRY IT NOW   Check the values available in version 1 of the vweb chart, and then install a release using custom values.

```
# inspect the default values stored in the chart:
helm show values kiamol/vweb --version 1.0.0

# install the chart, overriding the default values:
helm install --set servicePort=8010 --set replicaCount=1 ch10-vweb
  kiamol/vweb --version 1.0.0

# check the releases you have installed:
helm ls
```

In this exercise, you can see that the chart has default values for the Service port and the number of replicas in the Deployment. My output is shown in figure 10.4. You use the set argument with helm install to specify your own values, and when the install completes, you have an app running in Kubernetes without using kubectl and without any direct use of YAML manifests.

Shows the default values for a specific version of a chart.
The chart name is prefixed with the local repo name, `kiamol`.

These are the settings in the
`values.yaml` file in the chart.

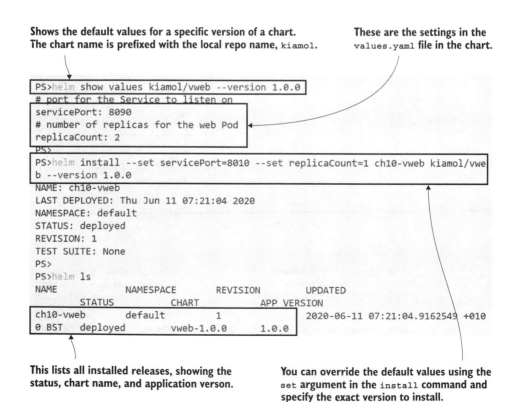

```
PS>helm show values kiamol/vweb --version 1.0.0
# port for the Service to listen on
servicePort: 8090
# number of replicas for the web Pod
replicaCount: 2
PS>
PS>helm install --set servicePort=8010 --set replicaCount=1 ch10-vweb kiamol/vwe
b --version 1.0.0
NAME: ch10-vweb
LAST DEPLOYED: Thu Jun 11 07:21:04 2020
NAMESPACE: default
STATUS: deployed
REVISION: 1
TEST SUITE: None
PS>
PS>helm ls
NAME            NAMESPACE       REVISION        UPDATED
      STATUS          CHART           APP VERSION
ch10-vweb       default         1               2020-06-11 07:21:04.9162549 +010
0 BST   deployed        vweb-1.0.0      1.0.0
```

This lists all installed releases, showing the
status, chart name, and application verson.

You can override the default values using the
set argument in the `install` command and
specify the exact version to install.

Figure 10.4   Installing an app with Helm—this creates Kubernetes resources, without using kubectl.

Helm has a set of features for working with repositories and charts and for installing, updating, and rolling back releases, but it's not intended for ongoing management of applications. The Helm command line isn't a replacement for kubectl—you use them together. Now that the release is installed, you can work with the Kubernetes resources in the usual way, and you can also return to Helm if you need to modify settings.

> **TRY IT NOW**   Check the resources Helm has deployed using kubectl, and then return to Helm to scale up the Deployment and check that the app is working correctly.

```
# show the details of the Deployment:
kubectl get deploy -l app.kubernetes.io/instance=ch10-vweb --show-
   labels

# update the release to increase the replica count:
helm upgrade --set servicePort=8010 --set replicaCount=3 ch10-vweb
   kiamol/vweb --version 1.0.0

# check the ReplicaSet:
kubectl get rs -l app.kubernetes.io/instance=ch10-vweb

# get the URL for the app:
kubectl get svc ch10-vweb -o
   jsonpath='http://{.status.loadBalancer.ingress[0].*}:8010'

# browse to the app URL
```

Let's look at a couple of things from that exercise. The first is that the labels are a lot more verbose than the standard "app" and "version" labels you've seen so far. That's because this is a public chart on a public repository, so I'm using the recommended label names from the Kubernetes Configuration Best Practices guide—that's my choice, not a requirement of Helm. The second is that the Helm upgrade command specifies the Service port again, although it's only the replica count I want to modify. This is because Helm uses the default values unless you specify them, so if the port isn't included in the upgrade command, it would be changed to the default value. You can see my output in figure 10.5.

This is the consumer side of the Helm workflow. You can search repositories for applications, discover the configuration values available for an app, and then install and upgrade the application, all from the Helm command line. It's package management for apps built to run in Kubernetes. In the next section you'll learn how to package and publish your own apps, which is the producer side of the workflow.

10.2 Packaging your own apps with Helm

Helm charts are folders or zipped archives that contain Kubernetes manifests. You create your own charts by taking your application manifests, identifying any values you want to be parameterized, and replacing the actual value with a templated variable.

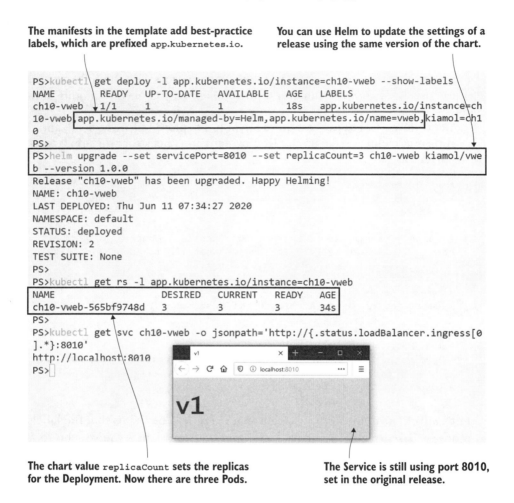

The manifests in the template add best-practice labels, which are prefixed app.kubernetes.io.

You can use Helm to update the settings of a release using the same version of the chart.

The chart value replicaCount sets the replicas for the Deployment. Now there are three Pods.

The Service is still using port 8010, set in the original release.

Figure 10.5   You don't use Helm to manage apps, but you can use it to update the configuration.

Listing 10.1 shows the beginning of a templated Deployment spec, which uses values set by Helm for the resource name and the label value.

Listing 10.1   web-ping-deployment.yaml, a templated Kubernetes manifest

```
apiVersion: apps/v1
kind: Deployment                              # This much is standard Kubernetes YAML.

metadata:
  name: {{ .Release.Name }}                   # Contains the name of the release
  labels:
    kiamol: {{ .Values.kiamolChapter }}       # Contains the "kiamolChapter"
                                              # value
```

The double-brace syntax is for templated values—everything from the opening {{ to the closing }} is replaced at install time, and Helm sends the processed YAML to Kubernetes. Multiple sources can be used as the input to replace templated values. The snippet in listing 10.1 uses the Release object to get the name of the release and the Values object to get a parameter value called `kiamolChapter`. The Release object is populated with information from the `install` or `upgrade` command, and the Values object is populated from defaults in the chart and any settings the user has overridden. Templates can also access static details about the chart and runtime details about the capabilities of the Kubernetes cluster.

Helm is very particular about the file structure in a chart. You can use the `helm create` command to generate the boilerplate structure for a new chart. The top level is a folder whose name has to match the chart name you want to use, and that folder must have at least the following three items:

- A `Chart.yaml` file that specifies the chart metadata, including the name and version
- A `values.yaml` file that sets the default values for parameters
- A `templates` folder that contains the templated Kubernetes manifests

Listing 10.1 is from a file called `web-ping-deployment.yaml` in the `web-ping/templates` folder in this chapter's source. The `web-ping` folder contains all the files needed for a valid chart, and Helm can validate the chart contents and install a release from the chart folder.

> **TRY IT NOW** When you're developing charts, you don't need to package them in zip archives; you can work with the chart folder.

```
# switch to this chapter's source:
cd ch10

# validate the chart contents:
helm lint web-ping

# install a release from the chart folder:
helm install wp1 web-ping/

# check the installed releases:
helm ls
```

The `lint` command is only for working with local charts, but the `install` command is the same for local charts and for charts stored in a repository. Local charts can be folders or zipped archives, and you'll see in this exercise that installing a release from a local chart is the same experience as installing from a repository. My output in figure 10.6 shows I now have two releases installed: one from the vweb chart and one from the web-ping chart.

The web-ping application is a basic utility that checks whether a website is up by making HTTP requests to a domain name on a regular schedule. Right now, you have

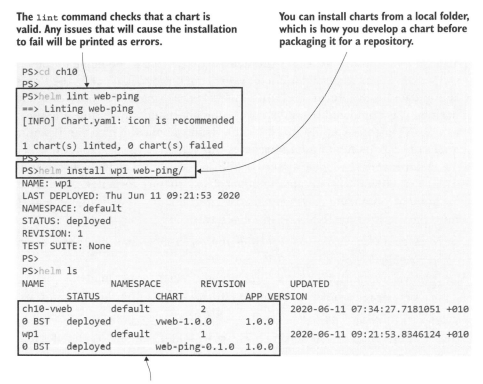

The `lint` **command checks that a chart is valid. Any issues that will cause the installation to fail will be printed as errors.**

You can install charts from a local folder, which is how you develop a chart before packaging it for a repository.

```
PS>cd ch10
PS>
PS>helm lint web-ping
==> Linting web-ping
[INFO] Chart.yaml: icon is recommended

1 chart(s) linted, 0 chart(s) failed
PS>
PS>helm install wp1 web-ping/
NAME: wp1
LAST DEPLOYED: Thu Jun 11 09:21:53 2020
NAMESPACE: default
STATUS: deployed
REVISION: 1
TEST SUITE: None
PS>
PS>helm ls
NAME            NAMESPACE       REVISION      UPDATED
        STATUS          CHART         APP VERSION
ch10-vweb       default         2             2020-06-11 07:34:27.7181051 +010
0 BST   deployed        vweb-1.0.0    1.0.0
wp1             default         1             2020-06-11 09:21:53.8346124 +010
0 BST   deployed        web-ping-0.1.0 1.0.0
```

The chart metadata in the folder contains a version number, so all charts are versioned in the same way whether the source is a local folder or a remote repository.

Figure 10.6   Installing and upgrading from a local folder lets you iterate quickly on chart development.

a Pod running, which is sending requests to my blog every 30 seconds. My blog runs on Kubernetes, so I'm sure it will be able to handle that. The app uses environment variables to configure the URL to use and the schedule interval, and those are templated in the manifest for Helm. Listing 10.2 shows the Pod spec with the templated variables.

Listing 10.2   web-ping-deployment.yaml, templated container environment

```
spec:
  containers:
    - name: app
      image: kiamol/ch10-web-ping
      env:
        - name: TARGET
          value: {{ .Values.targetUrl }}
        - name: INTERVAL
          value: {{ .Values.pingIntervalMilliseconds | quote }}
```

Helm has a rich set of templating functions you can use to manipulate the values that get set in the YAML. The quote function in listing 10.2 wraps the provided value in quotation marks, if it doesn't already have them. You can include looping and branching logic in your templates, calculate strings and numbers, and even query the Kubernetes API to find details from other objects. We won't get into that much detail, but it's important to remember that Helm lets you generate sophisticated templates that can do pretty much anything.

You need to think carefully about the parts of your spec that need to be templated. One of the big benefits of Helm over standard manifest deployments is that you can run multiple instances of the same app from a single chart. You can't do that with kubectl because the manifests contain resource names that need to be unique. If you deploy the same set of YAML multiple times, Kubernetes will just update the same resources. If you template all the unique parts of the spec—like resource names and label selectors—then you can run many copies of the same app with Helm.

> **TRY IT NOW** Deploy a second release of the web-ping app, using the same chart folder but specifying a different URL to ping.

```
# check the available settings for the chart:
helm show values web-ping/

# install a new release named wp2, using a different target:
helm install --set targetUrl=kiamol.net wp2 web-ping/

# wait a minute or so for the pings to fire, then check the logs:
kubectl logs -l app=web-ping --tail 1
```

You'll see in this exercise that I need to do some optimization on my blog—it returns in around 500 ms whereas the Kiamol website returns in 100 ms. More important, you can see two instances of the app running: two Deployments managing two sets of Pods with different container specs. My output is shown in figure 10.7.

It should be clear now that the Helm workflow for installing and managing apps is different from the kubectl workflow, but you also need to understand that the two are *incompatible.* You can't deploy the app by running kubectl apply in the templates folder for the chart, because the templated variables are not valid YAML, and the command will fail. If you adopt Helm, you need to choose between using Helm for every environment, which is likely to slow down the developer workflow, or using plain Kubernetes manifests for development and Helm for other environments, which means you'll have multiple copies of your YAML.

Remember that Helm is about distribution and discovery as much as it's about installation. The additional friction that Helm brings is the price of being able to simplify complex applications down to a few variables and share them on a repository. A repository is really just an index file with a list of chart versions that can be stored on any web server (the Kiamol repository uses GitHub pages, and you can see the whole contents at https://kiamol.net/index.yaml).

These values in the chart are used in environment variables in the Deployment template, so they set the configuration of the app.

```
PS>helm show values web-ping/
# targetUrl - URL of the website to ping
targetUrl: blog.sixeyed.com
# httpMethod - HTTP method to use for pings
httpMethod: HEAD
# pingIntervalMilliseconds - interval between pings in ms
pingIntervalMilliseconds: 30000
# chapter where this exercise is used
kiamolChapter: ch10
PS>
PS>helm install --set targetUrl=kiamol.net wp2 web-ping/
NAME: wp2
LAST DEPLOYED: Thu Jun 11 10:46:58 2020
NAMESPACE: default
STATUS: deployed
REVISION: 1
TEST SUITE: None
PS>
PS>kubectl logs -l app=web-ping --tail 1
Got response status: 200 at 1591869361199; duration: 507ms
Got response status: 200 at 1591869360941; duration: 113ms
```

Both instances of the app are busy pinging different websites and logging the response times. The Pods in different Deployments have the same `app` label.

Installing the same chart with a different name deploys a completely separate release.

Figure 10.7   You can't install multiple instances of an app with plain manifests, but you can with Helm.

You can use any server technology to host your repository, but for the rest of this section, we'll use a dedicated repository server called ChartMuseum, which is a popular open source option. You can run ChartMuseum as a private Helm repository in your own organization, and it's easy to set up because you can install it with a Helm chart.

TRY IT NOW   The ChartMuseum chart is on the official Helm repository, conventionally called "stable." Add that repository, and you can install a release to run your own repository locally.

```
# add the official Helm repository:
helm repo add stable https://kubernetes-charts.storage.googleapis.com

# install ChartMuseum—the repo flag fetches details from
# the repository so you don't need to update your local cache:
```

```
helm install --set service.type=LoadBalancer --set
  service.externalPort=8008 --set env.open.DISABLE_API=false repo
  stable/chartmuseum --version 2.13.0 --wait

# get the URL for your local ChartMuseum app:
kubectl get svc repo-chartmuseum -o
  jsonpath='http://{.status.loadBalancer.ingress[0].*}:8008'

# add it as a repository called local:
helm repo add local $(kubectl get svc repo-chartmuseum -o
  jsonpath='http://{.status.loadBalancer.ingress[0].*}:8008')
```

Now you have three repositories registered with Helm: the Kiamol repository, the stable Kubernetes repository (which is a curated set of charts, similar to the official images in Docker Hub), and your own local repository. You can see my output in figure 10.8, which is abridged to reduce the output from the Helm `install` command.

Add the official Helm chart repository, which hosts the ChartMuseum chart.

Install ChartMuseum with settings to use a LoadBalancer Service on port 8008, and enable the application API.

```
PS>helm repo add stable https://kubernetes-charts.storage.googleapis.com
"stable" has been added to your repositories
PS>
PS>helm install --set service.type=LoadBalancer --set service.externalPort=8008
--set env.open.DISABLE_API=false repo stable/chartmuseum --version 2.13.0
NAME: repo
LAST DEPLOYED: Thu Jun 11 12:04:31 2020
NAMESPACE: default
STATUS: deployed
REVISION: 1
TEST SUITE: None
NOTES:
** Please be patient while the chart is being deployed **

PS>kubectl get svc repo-chartmuseum -o jsonpath='http://{.status.loadBalancer.in
gress[0].*}:8008'
http://localhost:8008
PS>
PS>helm repo add local $(kubectl get svc repo-chartmuseum -o jsonpath='http://{.
status.loadBalancer.ingress[0].*}:8008')
"local" has been added to your repositories
```

Use the URL to add your local ChartMuseum repository to Helm.

When the install completes, check the URL for the Service.

Figure 10.8   Running your own Helm repository is as simple as installing a chart from a Helm repository.

Charts need to be packaged before they can be published to a repository, and publishing is usually a three-stage process: package the chart into a zip archive, upload the archive to a server, and update the repository index to add the new chart. Chart-Museum takes care of the last step for you, so you just need to package and upload the chart for the repository index to be automatically updated.

TRY IT NOW   Use Helm to create the zip archive for the chart, and use `curl` to upload it to your ChartMuseum repository. Check the repository—you'll see your chart has been indexed.

```
# package the local chart:
helm package web-ping

# *on Windows 10* remove the PowerShell alias to use the real curl:
Remove-Item Alias:curl -ErrorAction Ignore

# upload the chart zip archive to ChartMuseum:
curl --data-binary "@web-ping-0.1.0.tgz" $(kubectl get svc repo-
  chartmuseum -o
  jsonpath='http://{.status.loadBalancer.ingress[0].*}:8008/api/chart
  s')

# check that ChartMuseum has updated its index:
curl $(kubectl get svc repo-chartmuseum -o jsonpath='http://{.status
  .loadBalancer.ingress[0].*}:8008/index.yaml')
```

Helm uses compressed archives to make charts easy to distribute, and the files are tiny—they contain the Kubernetes manifests and the metadata and values, but they don't contain any large binaries. Pod specs in the chart specify container images to use, but the images themselves are not part of the chart—they're pulled from Docker Hub or your own image registry when you install a release. You can see in figure 10.9 that ChartMusem generates the repository index when you upload a chart and adds the new chart details.

You can use ChartMuseum or another repository server in your organization to share internal applications or to push charts as part of your continuous integration process before making release candidates available on your public repository. The local repository you have is running only in your lab environment, but it's published using a LoadBalancer Service, so anyone with network access can install the web-ping app from it.

TRY IT NOW   Install yet another version of the web-ping app, this time using the chart from your local repository and providing a values file instead of specifying each setting in the `install` command.

```
# update your repository cache:
helm repo update

# verify that Helm can find your chart:
helm search repo web-ping

# check the local values file:
cat web-ping-values.yaml
```

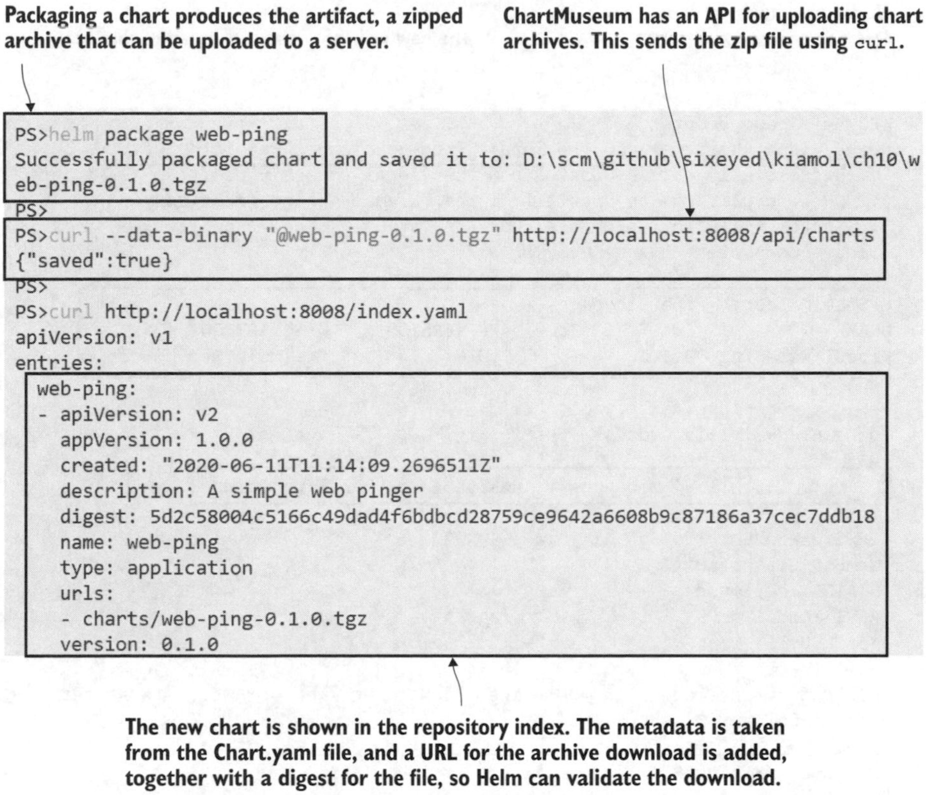

Packaging a chart produces the artifact, a zipped
archive that can be uploaded to a server.

ChartMuseum has an API for uploading chart
archives. This sends the zIp file using `curl`.

```
PS>helm package web-ping
Successfully packaged chart and saved it to: D:\scm\github\sixeyed\kiamol\ch10\w
eb-ping-0.1.0.tgz
PS>
PS>curl --data-binary "@web-ping-0.1.0.tgz" http://localhost:8008/api/charts
{"saved":true}
PS>
PS>curl http://localhost:8008/index.yaml
apiVersion: v1
entries:
web-ping:
- apiVersion: v2
  appVersion: 1.0.0
  created: "2020-06-11T11:14:09.2696511Z"
  description: A simple web pinger
  digest: 5d2c58004c5166c49dad4f6bdbcd28759ce9642a6608b9c87186a37cec7ddb18
  name: web-ping
  type: application
  urls:
  - charts/web-ping-0.1.0.tgz
  version: 0.1.0
```

The new chart is shown in the repository index. The metadata is taken
from the Chart.yaml file, and a URL for the archive download is added,
together with a digest for the file, so Helm can validate the download.

Figure 10.9   You can run ChartMuseum as a private repository to easily share charts between
teams.

```
# install from the repository using the values file:
helm install -f web-ping-values.yaml wp3 local/web-ping

# list all the Pods running the web-ping apps:
kubectl get pod -l app=web-ping -o custom-
    columns='NAME:.metadata.name,ENV:.spec.containers[0].env[*].value'
```

In this exercise, you saw another way to install a Helm release with custom settings—
using a local values file. That's a good practice, because you can store the settings for
different environments in different files, and you mitigate the risk that an update
reverts back to a default value when a setting isn't provided. My output is shown in figure 10.10.

You also saw in the previous exercise that you can install a chart from a repository without specifying a version. That's not such a good practice, because it installs
the latest version, which is a moving target. It's better to always explicitly state the
chart version. Helm requires you to use semantic versioning so chart consumers

Updating your local repository cache lets you search for charts.

The new web-ping chart is listed in the local repository.

```
PS>helm repo update
Hang tight while we grab the latest from your chart repositories...
...Successfully got an update from the "local" chart repository
...Successfully got an update from the "kiamol" chart repository
...Successfully got an update from the "stable" chart repository
Update Complete. * Happy Helming!*
PS>
PS>helm search repo web-ping
NAME            CHART VERSION   APP VERSION     DESCRIPTION
local/web-ping  0.1.0           1.0.0           A simple web pinger
PS>
PS>cat web-ping-values.yaml
pingIntervalMilliseconds: 15000
PS>
PS>helm install -f web-ping-values.yaml wp3 local/web-ping
NAME: wp3
LAST DEPLOYED: Thu Jun 11 13:49:51 2020
NAMESPACE: default
STATUS: deployed
REVISION: 1
TEST SUITE: None
PS>
PS>kubectl get pod -l app=web-ping -o custom-columns='NAME:.metadata.name,ENV:.s
pec.containers[0].env[*].value'
NAME                    ENV
wp1-658b698fb-qc285     blog.sixeyed.com,HEAD,30000
wp2-77b6545bf5-krsqn    kiamol.net,HEAD,30000
wp3-58998db649-7p7z5    blog.sixeyed.com,HEAD,15000
```

Each release of the app uses the same chart with different values, and those values set environment variables in the Pod container.

Installation with a values file is a better practice than using `set` arguments, because you can use the same file for upgrades.

Figure 10.10   Installing charts from your local repository is the same as installing from any remote repository.

know whether the package they're about to upgrade is a beta release or if it has break-ing changes.

You can do far more with charts than I'm going to cover here. They can include tests, which are Kubernetes Job specs that run after installation to verify the deploy-ment; they can have hooks, which let you run Jobs at specific points in the installation workflow; and they can be signed and shipped with a signature for provenance. In the next section, I'm going to cover one more feature you use in authoring templates, and it's an important one—building charts that are dependent on other charts.

10.3 *Modeling dependencies in charts*

Helm lets you design your app so it works in different environments, and that raises an interesting problem for dependencies. A dependency might be required in some environments but not in others. Maybe you have a web app that really needs a caching reverse proxy to improve performance. In some environments, you'll want to deploy the proxy along with the app, and in others, you'll already have a shared proxy so you just want to deploy the web app itself. Helm supports these with conditional dependencies.

Listing 10.3 shows a chart manifest for the Pi web application we've been using since chapter 5. It has two dependencies—one from the Kiamol repository, and one from the local filesystem—and they are separate charts.

> **Listing 10.3   chart.yaml, a chart that includes optional dependencies**

```
apiVersion: v2          # The version of the Helm spec
name: pi                # Chart name
version: 0.1.0          # Chart version
dependencies:           # Other charts this chart is dependent on
  - name: vweb
    version: 2.0.0
    repository: https://kiamol.net    # A dependency from a repository
    condition: vweb.enabled           # Installed only if required
  - name: proxy
    version: 0.1.0
    repository: file://../proxy        # A dependency from a local folder
    condition: proxy.enabled           # Installed only if required
```

You need to keep your charts flexible when you model dependencies. The *parent chart* (the Pi app, in this case) may require the *subchart* (the proxy and vweb charts), but subcharts themselves need to be standalone. You should template the Kubernetes manifests in a subchart to make it generically useful. If it's something that is useful in only one application, then it should be part of that application chart and not a subchart.

My proxy is generically useful; it's just a caching reverse proxy, which can use any HTTP server as the content source. The chart uses a templated value for the name of the server to proxy, so although it's primarily intended for the Pi app, it can be used to proxy any Kubernetes Service. We can verify that by installing a release that proxies an existing app in the cluster.

> **TRY IT NOW**   Install the proxy chart on its own, using it as a reverse proxy for the vweb app we installed earlier in the chapter.

```
# install a release from the local chart folder:
helm install --set upstreamToProxy=ch10-vweb:8010 vweb-proxy proxy/

# get the URL for the new proxy service:
kubectl get svc vweb-proxy-proxy -o
  jsonpath='http://{.status.loadBalancer.ingress[0].*}:8080'

# browse to the URL
```

The proxy chart in that exercise is completely independent of the Pi app; it's being used to proxy the web app I deployed with Helm from the Kiamol repository. You can see in figure 10.11 that it works as a caching proxy for any HTTP server.

The proxy chart is used as a subchart for the Pi application, but it can also be installed as a standalone chart. The value here filters into a ConfigMap and sets the proxy to load content from the vweb app.

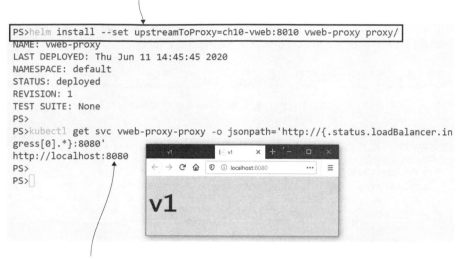

```
PS>helm install --set upstreamToProxy=ch10-vweb:8010 vweb-proxy proxy/
NAME: vweb-proxy
LAST DEPLOYED: Thu Jun 11 14:45:45 2020
NAMESPACE: default
STATUS: deployed
REVISION: 1
TEST SUITE: None
PS>
PS>kubectl get svc vweb-proxy-proxy -o jsonpath='http://{.status.loadBalancer.in
gress[0].*}:8080'
http://localhost:8080
PS>
PS>
```

The proxy uses a LoadBalancer Service listening on port 8080. When you browse to that URL, you'll see the vweb app, with the content served by the proxy.

Figure 10.11 The proxy subchart is built to be useful as a chart in its own right—it can proxy any app.

To use the proxy as a dependency, you need to add it in the dependency list in a parent chart, so it becomes a subchart. Then you can specify values for the subchart settings in the parent chart, by prefixing the setting name with the dependency name—the setting `upstreamToProxy` in the proxy chart is referenced as `proxy.upstreamToProxy` in the Pi chart. Listing 10.4 shows the default values file for the Pi app, which includes settings for the app itself and for the proxy dependency.

Listing 10.4 values.yaml, the default settings for the Pi chart

```
replicaCount: 2                # Number of app Pods to run
serviceType: LoadBalancer      # Type of the Pi Service

proxy:                         # Settings for the reverse proxy
  enabled: false               # Whether to deploy the proxy
  upstreamToProxy: "{{ .Release.Name }}-web"    # Server to proxy
  servicePort: 8030            # Port of the proxy Service
  replicaCount: 2              # Number of proxy Pods to run
```

These values deploy the app itself without the proxy, using a LoadBalancer Service for the Pi Pods. The setting `proxy.enabled` is specified as the condition for the proxy dependency in the Pi chart, so the entire subchart is skipped unless the install settings override the default. The full values file also sets the `vweb.enabled` value to false—that dependency is there only to demonstrate that subcharts can be sourced from repositories, so the default is not to deploy that chart, either.

There's one extra detail to call out here. The name of the Service for the Pi app is templated in the chart, using the release name. That's important to enable multiple installs of the same chart, but it adds complexity to the default values for the proxy subchart. The name of the server to proxy needs to match the Pi Service name, so the values file uses the same templated value as the Service name, and that links the proxy to the Service in the same release.

Charts need to have their dependencies available before you can install or package them, and you use the Helm command line to do that. Building dependencies will populate them into the chart's charts folder, either by downloading the archive from a repository or packaging a local folder into an archive.

TRY IT NOW Build the dependencies for the Pi chart, which downloads the remote chart, packages the local chart, and adds them to the chart folder.

```
# build dependencies:
helm dependency build pi

# check that the dependencies have been downloaded:
ls ./pi/charts
```

Figure 10.12 shows why versioning is so important for Helm charts. Chart packages are versioned using the version number in the chart metadata. Parent charts are packaged with their dependencies, at the specified version. If I update the proxy chart without updating the version number, my Pi chart will be out of sync because version 0.1.0 of the proxy chart in the Pi package is different from the latest version 0.1.0. You should consider Helm charts to be immutable and always publish changes by publishing a new package version.

This principle of conditional dependencies is how you could manage a much more complex application like the to-do app from chapter 8. The Postgres database deployment would be a subchart, which users could skip altogether for environments where they want to use an external database. Or you could even have multiple conditional dependencies, allowing users to deploy a simple Postgres Deployment for dev environments, use a highly available StatefulSet for test environments, and plug into a managed Postgres service in production.

The Pi app is simpler than that, and we can choose whether to deploy it on its own or with a proxy. This chart uses a templated value for the type of the Pi Service, but that could be computed in the template instead by setting it to LoadBalancer if the proxy is not deployed and ClusterIP if the proxy is deployed.

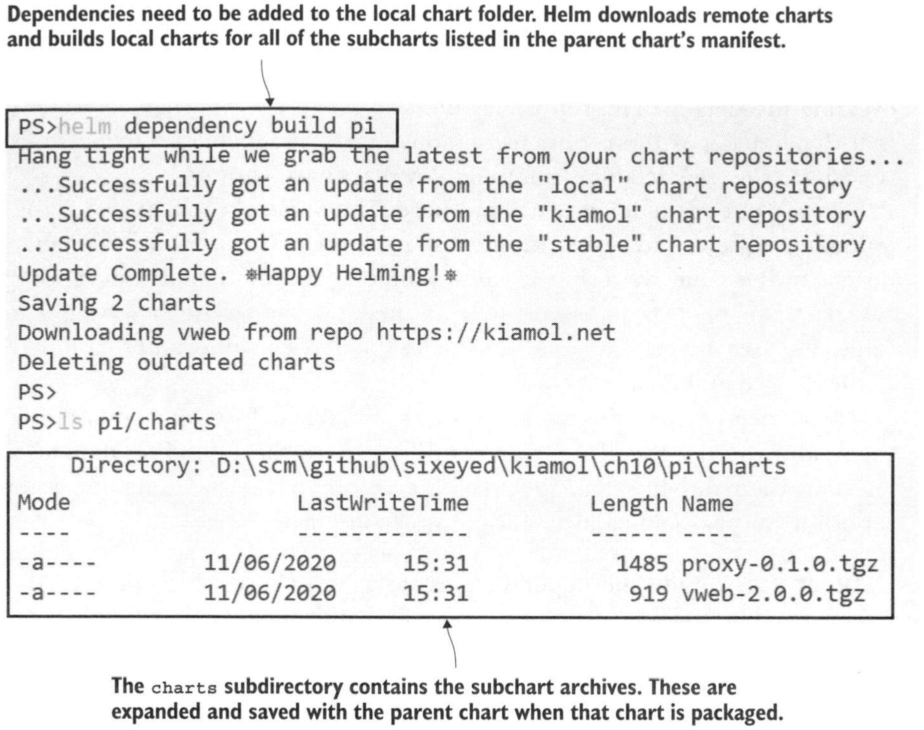

Dependencies need to be added to the local chart folder. Helm downloads remote charts
and builds local charts for all of the subcharts listed in the parent chart's manifest.

```
PS>helm dependency build pi
Hang tight while we grab the latest from your chart repositories...
...Successfully got an update from the "local" chart repository
...Successfully got an update from the "kiamol" chart repository
...Successfully got an update from the "stable" chart repository
Update Complete. *Happy Helming!*
Saving 2 charts
Downloading vweb from repo https://kiamol.net
Deleting outdated charts
PS>
PS>ls pi/charts


    Directory: D:\scm\github\sixeyed\kiamol\ch10\pi\charts

Mode                LastWriteTime         Length Name
----                -------------         ------ ----
-a----        11/06/2020     15:31          1485 proxy-0.1.0.tgz
-a----        11/06/2020     15:31           919 vweb-2.0.0.tgz
```

The `charts` subdirectory contains the subchart archives. These are
expanded and saved with the parent chart when that chart is packaged.

Figure 10.12   Helm bundles dependencies into the parent chart, and they are distributed as
one package.

TRY IT NOW   Deploy the Pi app with the proxy subchart enabled. Use Helm's
dry-run feature to check the default deployment, and then use custom settings for the actual install.

```
# print the YAML Helm would deploy with default values:
helm install pi1 ./pi --dry-run

# install with custom settings to add the proxy:
helm install --set serviceType=ClusterIP --set proxy.enabled=true pi2
  ./pi

# get the URL for the proxied app:
kubectl get svc pi2-proxy -o
  jsonpath='http://{.status.loadBalancer.ingress[0].*}:8030'

# browse to it
```

You'll see in this exercise that the dry-run flag is quite useful: it applies values to the templates and writes out all the YAML for the resources it would install, without deploying anything. Then in the actual installation, setting a couple of flags deploys an additional chart that is integrated with the main chart, so the application works as a single unit. My Pi calculation appears in figure 10.13.

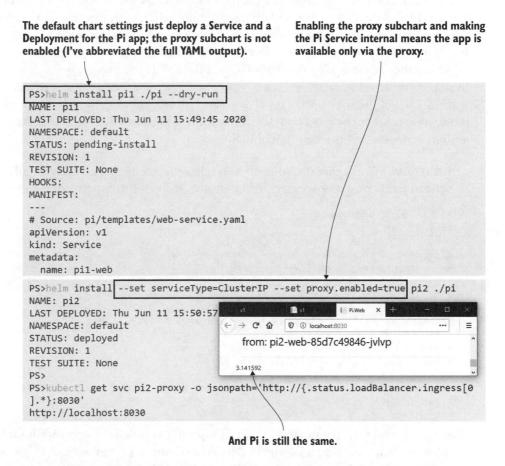

The default chart settings just deploy a Service and a Deployment for the Pi app; the proxy subchart is not enabled (I've abbreviated the full YAML output).

Enabling the proxy subchart and making the Pi Service internal means the app is available only via the proxy.

And Pi is still the same.

Figure 10.13   Installing a chart with an optional subchart by overriding default settings

There's a whole lot of Helm that I haven't made room for in this chapter, because there's a level of complexity you need to dive into only if you bet big on Helm and plan to use it extensively. If that's you, you'll find Helm has the power to cover you. How's this for an example: you can generate a hash from the contents of a ConfigMap template and use that as a label in a Deployment template, so every time the configuration changes, the Deployment label changes too, and upgrading your configuration triggers a Pod rollout.

That's neat, but it's not for everybody, so in the next section, we'll return to a simple demo app and look at how Helm smooths the upgrade and rollback process.

10.4   *Upgrading and rolling back Helm releases*

Upgrading an app with Helm doesn't do anything special; it just sends the updated specs to Kubernetes, which rolls out changes in the usual way. If you want to configure the specifics of the rollout, you still do that in the YAML files in the chart, using the settings we explored in chapter 9. What Helm brings to upgrades is a consistent approach for all types of resources and the ability to easily roll back to previous versions.

One other advantage you get with Helm is the ability to safely try out a new version by deploying an additional instance to your cluster. I started this chapter by deploying version 1.0.0 of the vweb app in my cluster, and it's still running happily. Version 2.0.0 is available now, but before I upgrade the running app, I can use Helm to install a separate release and test the new functionality.

> **TRY IT NOW**   Check that the original vweb release is still there, and then install a version 2 release alongside, specifying settings to keep the app private.

```
# list all releases:
helm ls -q

# check the values for the new chart version:
helm show values kiamol/vweb --version 2.0.0

# deploy a new release using an internal Service type:
helm install --set servicePort=8020 --set replicaCount=1 --set
  serviceType=ClusterIP ch10-vweb-v2 kiamol/vweb --version 2.0.0

# use a port-forward so you can test the app:
kubectl port-forward svc/ch10-vweb-v2 8020:8020

# browse to localhost:8020, then exit the port-forward with Ctrl-C or
# Cmd-C
```

This exercise uses the parameters the chart supports to install the app without making it publicly available, using a ClusterIP Service type and a port-forward so the app is accessible only to the current user. The original app is unchanged, and I have a chance to smoke-test the new Deployment in the target cluster. Figure 10.14 shows the new version running.

Now I'm happy that the 2.0.0 version is good, I can use the Helm upgrade command to upgrade my actual release. I want to make sure I deploy with the same values I set in the previous release, and Helm has features to show the current values and to reuse custom values in the upgrade.

> **TRY IT NOW**   Remove the temporary version 2 release, and upgrade the version 1 release to the version 2 chart reusing the same values set on the current release.

```
# remove the test release:
helm uninstall ch10-vweb-v2
```

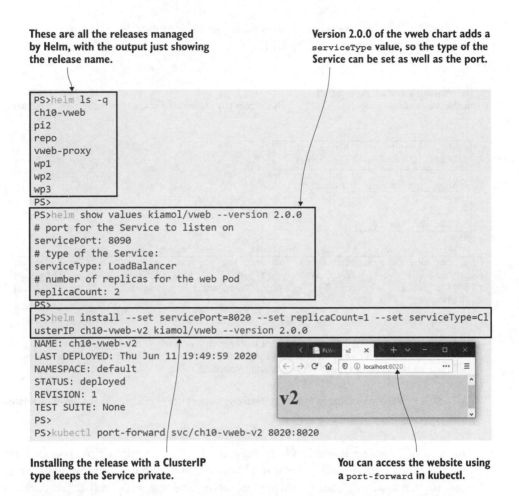

These are all the releases managed by Helm, with the output just showing the release name.

Version 2.0.0 of the vweb chart adds a `serviceType` value, so the type of the Service can be set as well as the port.

```
PS>helm ls -q
ch10-vweb
pi2
repo
vweb-proxy
wp1
wp2
wp3
PS>
PS>helm show values kiamol/vweb --version 2.0.0
# port for the Service to listen on
servicePort: 8090
# type of the Service:
serviceType: LoadBalancer
# number of replicas for the web Pod
replicaCount: 2
PS>
PS>helm install --set servicePort=8020 --set replicaCount=1 --set serviceType=Cl
usterIP ch10-vweb-v2 kiamol/vweb --version 2.0.0
NAME: ch10-vweb-v2
LAST DEPLOYED: Thu Jun 11 19:49:59 2020
NAMESPACE: default
STATUS: deployed
REVISION: 1
TEST SUITE: None
PS>
PS>kubectl port-forward svc/ch10-vweb-v2 8020:8020
```

Installing the release with a ClusterIP type keeps the Service private.

You can access the website using a `port-forward` in kubectl.

Figure 10.14 Charts that deploy Services typically let you set the type, so you can keep them private.

```
# check the values used in the current version 1 release:
helm get values ch10-vweb

# upgrade to version 2 using the same values—this will fail:
helm upgrade --reuse-values --atomic ch10-vweb kiamol/vweb --version
   2.0.0
```

Oh dear. This is a particularly nasty issue that will take some tracking down to understand. The reuse-values flag tells Helm to reuse all the values set for the current release on the new release, but the version 2.0.0 chart includes another value, the type of the Service, which wasn't set in the current release because it didn't exist. The net result is that the Service type is blank, which defaults to ClusterIP in Kubernetes, and the update fails because that clashes with the existing Service spec. You can see this hinted at in the output in figure 10.15.

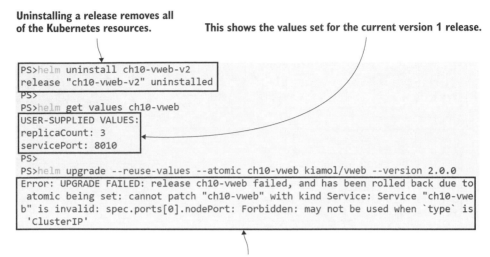

Uninstalling a release removes all of the Kubernetes resources.

This shows the values set for the current version 1 release.

```
PS>helm uninstall ch10-vweb-v2
release "ch10-vweb-v2" uninstalled
PS>
PS>helm get values ch10-vweb
USER-SUPPLIED VALUES:
replicaCount: 3
servicePort: 8010
PS>
PS>helm upgrade --reuse-values --atomic ch10-vweb kiamol/vweb --version 2.0.0
Error: UPGRADE FAILED: release ch10-vweb failed, and has been rolled back due to
 atomic being set: cannot patch "ch10-vweb" with kind Service: Service "ch10-vwe
b" is invalid: spec.ports[0].nodePort: Forbidden: may not be used when `type` is
 'ClusterIP'
```

Trying to reuse the same values for the version 2 upgrade fails because version 2 introduces a new setting. The defaults in the chart are ignored when you reuse values, so the serviceType is left blank, and the update fails.

Figure 10.15   An invalid upgrade fails, and Helm can automatically roll back to the previous release.

This sort of problem is where Helm's abstraction layer really helps. You can get the same issue with a standard kubectl deployment, but if one resource update fails, you need to check through all the other resources and manually roll them back. Helm does that automatically with the atomic flag. It waits for all the resource updates to complete, and if any of them fails, it rolls back every other resource to the previous state. Check the history of the release, and you can see that Helm has automatically rolled back to version 1.0.0.

> **TRY IT NOW**   Recall from chapter 9 that Kubernetes doesn't give you much information on the history of a rollout—compare that to the detail you get from Helm.

```
# show the history of the vweb release:
helm history ch10-vweb
```

That command gets an exercise all to itself, because there's a wealth of information that you just don't get in the history for a standard Kubernetes rollout. Figure 10.16 shows all four revisions of the release: the first install, a successful upgrade, a failed upgrade, and an automatic rollback.

Helm's history shows what action was taken and what the status was.

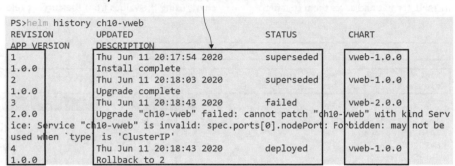

```
PS>helm history ch10-vweb
REVISION        UPDATED                        STATUS        CHART
APP VERSION     DESCRIPTION
1               Thu Jun 11 20:17:54 2020       superseded    vweb-1.0.0
1.0.0           Install complete
2               Thu Jun 11 20:18:03 2020       superseded    vweb-1.0.0
1.0.0           Upgrade complete
3               Thu Jun 11 20:18:43 2020       failed        vweb-2.0.0
2.0.0           Upgrade "ch10-vweb" failed: cannot patch "ch10-vweb" with kind Serv
ice: Service "ch10-vweb" is invalid: spec.ports[0].nodePort: Forbidden: may not be
used when `type` is 'ClusterIP'
4               Thu Jun 11 20:18:43 2020       deployed      vweb-1.0.0
1.0.0           Rollback to 2
```

It also shows the revision of the release and the versions of the chart and the application.
The app version is from the chart metadata, and it may be different from the chart version.

Figure 10.16   The release history clearly links application and chart versions to revisions.

To fix the failed update, I can manually set all the values in the `upgrade` command or use a values file with the same settings that are currently deployed. I don't have that values file, but I can save the output of the `get values` command to a file and use that in the upgrade, which gives me all my previous settings plus the defaults in the chart for any new settings.

TRY IT NOW   Upgrade to version 2 again, this time saving the current version 1 values to a file and using that in the `upgrade` command.

```
# save the values of the current release to a YAML file:
helm get values ch10-vweb -o yaml > vweb-values.yaml

# upgrade to version 2 using the values file and the atomic flag:
helm upgrade -f vweb-values.yaml --atomic ch10-vweb kiamol/vweb
   --version 2.0.0

# check the Service and ReplicaSet configuration:
kubectl get svc,rs -l app.kubernetes.io/instance=ch10-vweb
```

This upgrade succeeds, so the atomic rollback doesn't kick in. The upgrade is actually effected by the Deployment, which scales up the replacement ReplicaSet and scales down the current ReplicaSet in the usual way. Figure 10.17 shows that the configuration values set in the previous release have been retained, the Service is listening on port 8010, and three Pods are running.

All that's left is to try out a rollback, which is syntactically similar to a rollback in kubectl, but Helm makes it much easier to track down the revision you want to use. You've already seen the meaningful release history in figure 10.16, and you can also use Helm to check the values set for a particular revision. If I want to roll back the web

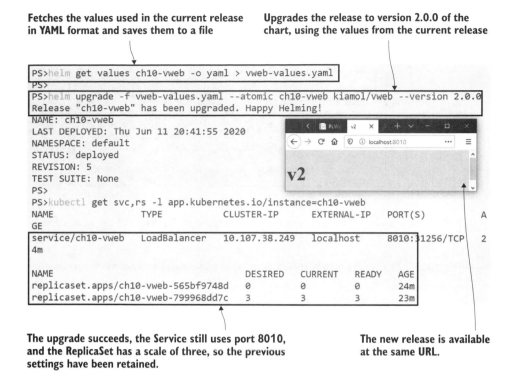

Fetches the values used in the current release in YAML format and saves them to a file

Upgrades the release to version 2.0.0 of the chart, using the values from the current release

```
PS>helm get values ch10-vweb -o yaml > vweb-values.yaml
PS>
PS>helm upgrade -f vweb-values.yaml --atomic ch10-vweb kiamol/vweb --version 2.0.0
Release "ch10-vweb" has been upgraded. Happy Helming!
NAME: ch10-vweb
LAST DEPLOYED: Thu Jun 11 20:41:55 2020
NAMESPACE: default
STATUS: deployed
REVISION: 5
TEST SUITE: None
PS>
PS>kubectl get svc,rs -l app.kubernetes.io/instance=ch10-vweb
NAME                 TYPE           CLUSTER-IP      EXTERNAL-IP    PORT(S)          A
GE
service/ch10-vweb    LoadBalancer   10.107.38.249   localhost      8010:31256/TCP   2
4m

NAME                                      DESIRED   CURRENT   READY   AGE
replicaset.apps/ch10-vweb-565bf9748d      0         0         0       24m
replicaset.apps/ch10-vweb-799968dd7c      3         3         3       23m
```

The upgrade succeeds, the Service still uses port 8010, and the ReplicaSet has a scale of three, so the previous settings have been retained.

The new release is available at the same URL.

Figure 10.17　The upgrade succeeds by exporting the release settings to a file and using them again.

application to version 1.0.0 but preserve the values I set in revision 2, I can check those values first.

TRY IT NOW　Roll back to the second revision, which was version 1.0.0 of the app upgraded to use three replicas.

```
# confirm the values used in revision 2:
helm get values ch10-vweb --revision 2

# roll back to that revision:
helm rollback ch10-vweb 2

# check the latest two revisions:
helm history ch10-vweb --max 2 -o yaml
```

You can see my output in figure 10.18, where the rollback is successful and the history shows that the latest revision is 6, which is actually a rollback to revision 2.

　The simplicity of this example is good for focusing on the upgrade and rollback workflow, and highlighting some of the quirks, but it hides the power of Helm for major upgrades. A Helm release is an abstraction of an application, and different

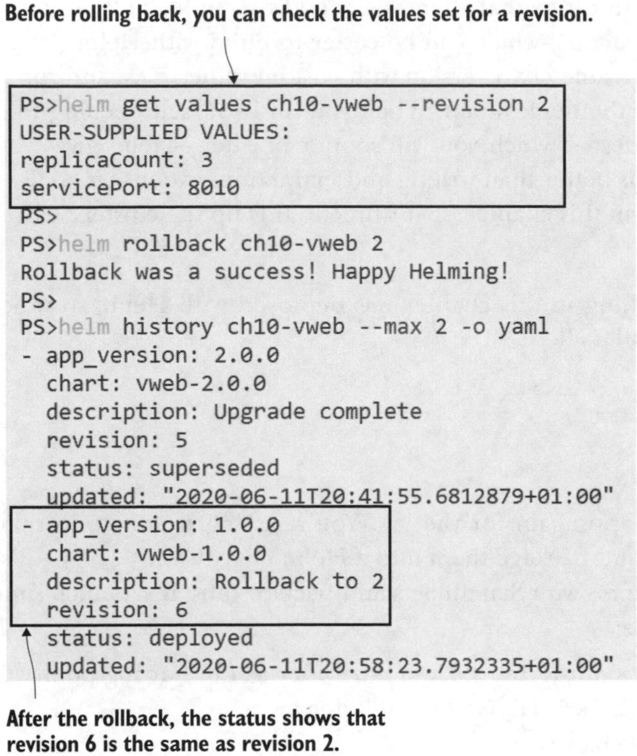

Before rolling back, you can check the values set for a revision.

```
PS>helm get values ch10-vweb --revision 2
USER-SUPPLIED VALUES:
replicaCount: 3
servicePort: 8010
PS>
PS>helm rollback ch10-vweb 2
Rollback was a success! Happy Helming!
PS>
PS>helm history ch10-vweb --max 2 -o yaml
- app_version: 2.0.0
  chart: vweb-2.0.0
  description: Upgrade complete
  revision: 5
  status: superseded
  updated: "2020-06-11T20:41:55.6812879+01:00"
- app_version: 1.0.0
  chart: vweb-1.0.0
  description: Rollback to 2
  revision: 6
  status: deployed
  updated: "2020-06-11T20:58:23.7932335+01:00"
```

After the rollback, the status shows that revision 6 is the same as revision 2.

Figure 10.18 Helm makes it easy to check exactly what you're rolling back to.

versions of the application might be modeled in different ways. A chart might use a ReplicationController in an early release, then change to a ReplicaSet and then a Deployment; as long as the user-facing parts remain the same, the internal workings become an implementation detail.

10.5 Understanding where Helm fits in

Helm adds a lot of value to Kubernetes, but it's invasive—once you template your manifests, there's no going back. Everyone on the team has to switch to Helm, or you have to commit to having multiple sets of manifests: pure Kubernetes for the development team and Helm for every other environment. You really don't want two sets of manifests getting out of sync, but equally, Kubernetes itself is plenty to learn without adding Helm on top.

Whether Helm fits in for you depends very much on the type of applications you're packaging and the way your teams work. If your app is composed of 50+ microservices, then development teams might work on only a subset of the full app, running it natively or with Docker and Docker Compose, and a separate team owns the full Kubernetes deployment. In that environment, a move to Helm will reduce friction rather than increasing it, centralizing hundreds of YAML files into manageable charts.

A couple of other indicators that Helm is a good fit include a fully automated continuous deployment process—which can be easier to build with Helm—running test environments from the same chart version with custom values files, and running verification jobs as part of the deployment. When you find yourself needing to template your Kubernetes manifests—which you will sooner or later—Helm gives you a standard approach, which is better than writing and maintaining your own tools.

That's all for Helm in this chapter, so it's time to tidy up the cluster before moving on to the lab.

TRY IT NOW   Everything in this chapter was deployed with Helm, so we can use Helm to uninstall it all.

```
# uninstall all the releases:
helm uninstall $(helm ls -q)
```

10.6   *Lab*

It's back to the to-do app again for the lab. You're going to take a working set of Kubernetes manifests and package them into a Helm chart. Don't worry—it's not the full-on app from chapter 8 with StatefulSets and backup Jobs; it's a much simpler version. Here are the goals:

- Use the manifests in the lab/todo-list folder as the starting point (there are hints in the YAML for what needs templating).
- Create the Helm chart structure.
- Template the resource names and any other values that need to be templated so the app can run as multiple releases.
- Add parameters for configuration settings to support running the app as different environments.
- Your chart should run as the Test configuration when installed with default values.
- Your chart should run as the Dev configuration when installed using the lab/ dev-values.yaml values file.

If you're planning on making use of Helm, you should really find time for this lab, because it contains the exact set of tasks you'll need to do when you package apps in Helm. My solution is on GitHub for you to check in the usual place: https://github .com/sixeyed/kiamol/blob/master/ch10/lab/README.md.

Happy Helming!

11

App development— Developer workflows and CI/CD

This is the final chapter on Kubernetes in the real world, and the focus here is the practicality of developing and delivering software to run on Kubernetes. Whether you identify as a developer or you're on the ops side working with developers, the move to containers impacts the way you work, the tools you use, and the amount of time and effort from making a code change to seeing it running in development and test environments. In this chapter, we'll examine how Kubernetes affects both the *inner loop*—the developer workflow on the local machine—and the *outer loop*—the CI/CD workflow that pushes changes to test and production.

How you use Kubernetes in your organization will be quite different from how you've used it so far in this book, because you'll use shared resources like clusters and image registries. As we explore delivery workflows in this chapter, we'll also cover lots of small details that can trip you up as you make the change to the real world—things like using private registries and maintaining isolation on a shared cluster. The main focus of the chapter is to help you understand the choice between a Docker-centric workflow and something more like a Platform-as-a-Service (PaaS) running on Kubernetes.

11.1 *The Docker developer workflow*

Developers love Docker. It was voted the number one most-wanted platform and the number two "most loved" in Stack Overflow's annual survey two years in a row. Docker makes some parts of the developer workflow incredibly easy but at a cost: the Docker artifacts become central to the project, and that has an impact on the inner loop. You can run the app in a local environment using the same technologies as production but only if you accept a different way of working. If you're not familiar with building apps using containers, appendix A in the ebook covers that in detail; it's the chapter "Packaging Applications from Source Code into Docker Images" from *Learn Docker in a Month of Lunches* (Manning, 2020).

In this section, we'll walk through the developer workflow where Docker and Kubernetes are used in every environment, and where developers have their own dedicated cluster. You'll need to have Docker running if you want to follow along with the exercises, so if your lab environment is Docker Desktop or K3s, then you're good to go. The first thing we'll look at is developer onboarding—joining a new project and getting up to speed as quickly as possible.

TRY IT NOW   This chapter offers a whole new demo app—a simple bulletin board where you can post details of upcoming events. It's written in Node.js, but you don't need to have Node.js installed to get up and running with the Docker workflow.

```
# switch to this chapter's folder in the source code:
cd ch11

# build the app:
docker-compose -f bulletin-board/docker-compose.yml build

# run the app:
docker-compose -f bulletin-board/docker-compose.yml up -d

# check the running  containers:
docker ps

# browse to the app at http://localhost:8010/
```

This is just about the simplest way you can get started as a developer on a new project. The only software you need installed is Docker, and then you grab a copy of the code, and off you go. You can see my output in figure 11.1. I don't have Node.js installed on my machine, and it doesn't matter whether you do or what version you have; your results will be the same.

Behind the magic are two things: a Dockerfile, which has all the steps to build and package the Node.js component, and a Docker Compose file, which specifies all the components and the path to their Dockerfiles. There's only one component in this app, but there could be a dozen—all using different technologies—and the workflow would be the same. But this isn't how we're going to run the app in production, so if we want to use the same technology stack, we can switch to running the app in Kubernetes locally, just using Docker for the build.

TRY IT NOW   Simple Kubernetes manifests for running the app using the local image are in the source folder. Remove the Compose version of the app, and deploy it to Kubernetes instead.

```
# stop the app in Compose:
docker-compose -f bulletin-board/docker-compose.yml down
```

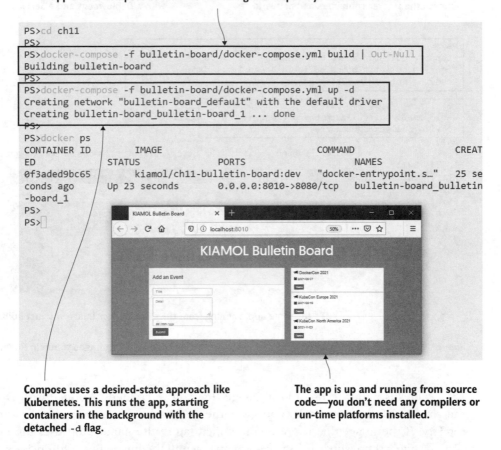

The Docker Compose file contains the path to the Dockerfile, so you can build the app with a Compose command. I'm hiding the output—you'll see a lot more.

```
PS>cd ch11
PS>
PS>docker-compose -f bulletin-board/docker-compose.yml build | Out-Null
Building bulletin-board
PS>
PS>docker-compose -f bulletin-board/docker-compose.yml up -d
Creating network "bulletin-board_default" with the default driver
Creating bulletin-board_bulletin-board_1 ... done
PS>
PS>docker ps
CONTAINER ID     IMAGE                              COMMAND              CREAT
ED            STATUS          PORTS               NAMES
0f3aded9bc65     kiamol/ch11-bulletin-board:dev     "docker-entrypoint.s…"   25 se
conds ago    Up 23 seconds   0.0.0.0:8010->8080/tcp   bulletin-board_bulletin
-board_1
PS>
PS>
```

Compose uses a desired-state approach like Kubernetes. This runs the app, starting containers in the background with the detached -d flag.

The app is up and running from source code—you don't need any compilers or run-time platforms installed.

Figure 11.1 Developer onboarding is a breeze with Docker and Compose—if there are no problems.

```
# deploy in Kubernetes:
kubectl apply -f bulletin-board/kubernetes/

# get the new URL:
kubectl get svc bulletin-board -o
   jsonpath='http://{.status.loadBalancer.ingress[0].*}:8011'

# browse
```

This workflow is still pretty simple, although we now have three container artifacts to work with: the Dockerfile, the Compose file, and the Kubernetes manifest. I have my own Kubernetes cluster, and with that I can run the app exactly as it will run in production. My output in figure 11.2 shows it's the same app, using the same local image, built with Docker Compose in the previous exercise.

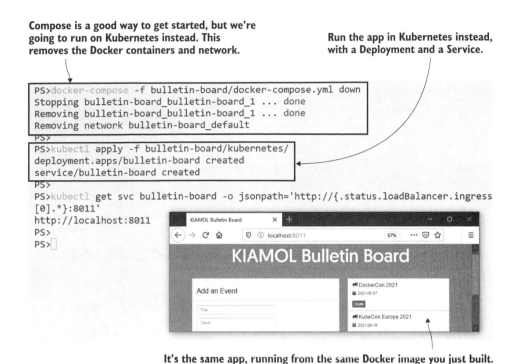

Figure 11.2   You can mix Docker and Kubernetes using Compose to build images to run in Pods.

Kubernetes is happy to use a local image that you've created or pulled with Docker, but you must follow some rules about whether it uses the local image or pulls it from a registry. If the image doesn't have an explicit tag in the name (and uses the default :latest tag), then Kubernetes will always try to pull the image first. Otherwise, Kubernetes will use the local image if it exists in the image cache on the node. You can override the rules by specifying an image pull policy. Listing 11.1 shows the Pod spec for the bulletin board app, which includes an explicit policy.

Listing 11.1   bb-deployment.yaml, specifying image pull policies

```
spec:                              # This is the Pod spec within the Deployment.
  containers:
    - name: bulletin-board
      image: kiamol/ch11-bulletin-board:dev
      imagePullPolicy: IfNotPresent   # Prefer the local image if it exists
```

That's the sort of detail that can be a nasty stumbling block in the developer workflow. The Pod spec might be configured so the registry image is preferred, and then you can rebuild your own local image as much as you like and never see any changes, because Kubernetes will always use the remote image. Similar complications exist around image versions, because an image can be replaced with another version using the same name and tag. That doesn't play well with the Kubernetes desired state approach, because if you deploy an update with an unchanged Pod spec, nothing happens, even if the image contents have changed.

Back to our demo app. Your first task on the project is to add some more detail to the events list, which is an easy code change for you. Testing your change is more challenging, because you can repeat the Docker Compose command to rebuild the image, but if you repeat the kubectl command to deploy the changes, you'll see that nothing happens. If you're into containers, you can do some investigation to understand the problem and delete the Pod to force a replacement, but if you're not, then your workflow is already broken.

> **TRY IT NOW** You don't really need to make a code change—a new file has the changes in it. Just replace the code file and rebuild the image, then delete the Pod to see the new app version running in the replacement Pod.

```
# remove the original code file:
rm bulletin-board/src/backend/events.js

# replace it with an updated version:
cp bulletin-board/src/backend/events-update.js bulletin-
   board/src/backend/events.js

# rebuild the image using Compose:
docker-compose -f bulletin-board/docker-compose.yml build

# try to redeploy using kubectl:
kubectl apply -f bulletin-board/kubernetes/

# delete the existing Pod to recreate it:
kubectl delete pod -l app=bulletin-board
```

You can see my output in figure 11.3. The updated application is running in the screenshot, but only after the Pod was manually deleted and then recreated by the Deployment controller, using the latest image version.

If you chose a Docker-centric workflow, then this is just one of the complications that will slow down and frustrate the development teams (debugging and making live app updates are the next ones they'll hit). Container technologies are not easy topics to learn as you go—they really need some dedicated time to understand the principles, and not everyone on every team will want to make that investment.

The alternative is to centralize all the container technologies in a single team that provides a CI/CD pipeline that development teams can plug into to deploy their apps. The pipeline takes care of packaging container images and deploying to the cluster, so the development teams don't need to bring Docker and Kubernetes into their own work.

This updates the app to include a description in the event display.

Building the app replaces the container image but uses the same image name.

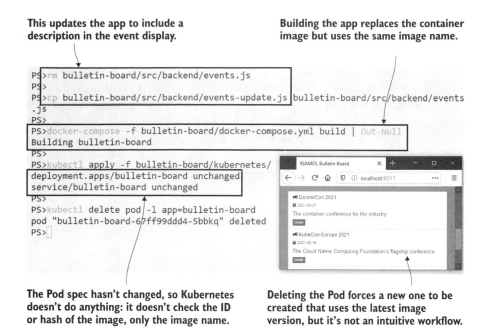

The Pod spec hasn't changed, so Kubernetes doesn't do anything: it doesn't check the ID or hash of the image, only the image name.

Deleting the Pod forces a new one to be created that uses the latest image version, but it's not an intuitive workflow.

Figure 11.3   Docker images are mutable, but renaming images doesn't trigger an update in Kubernetes.

11.2   *The Kubernetes-as-a-Service developer workflow*

A Platform-as-a-Service experience running on top of Kubernetes is an attractive option for a lot of organizations. You can run a single cluster for all your test environments that also hosts the CI/CD service to take care of the messy details about running in containers. All of the Docker artifacts are removed from the developer workflow so developers work on components directly, running Node.js and everything else they need on their machines, and they don't use containers locally.

This method moves containers to the outer loop—when developers push changes to source control, that triggers a build, which creates the container images, pushes them to a registry, and deploys the new version to a test environment in the cluster. You get all the benefits of running in a container platform, without the friction containers bring to development. Figure 11.4 shows how that looks with one set of technology options.

The promise of this approach is that you get to run your app on Kubernetes without affecting the developer workflow or requiring every team member to skill up on Docker and Compose. It can work well in organizations where development teams work on small components and a separate team assembles all the pieces into a working system, because only the assembly team needs the container skills. You can also remove Docker entirely, which is useful if your cluster uses a different container runtime. If you

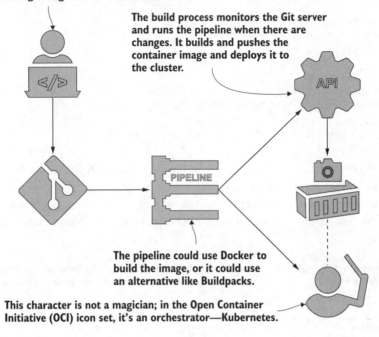

Developers work without containers,
pushing changes to the Git server.

The build process monitors the Git server
and runs the pipeline when there are
changes. It builds and pushes the
container image and deploys it to
the cluster.

The pipeline could use Docker to
build the image, or it could use
an alternative like Buildpacks.

This character is not a magician; in the Open Container
Initiative (OCI) icon set, it's an orchestrator—Kubernetes.

Figure 11.4   Using containers in the outer loop lets developers focus on code.

want to build container images without Docker, however, you need to replace it with a lot of other moving pieces. You'll end up with more complexity overall, but it will be centralized in the delivery pipelines and not the projects.

   We'll walk through an example of that in this chapter, but to manage the complexity, we'll do it in stages, starting with the view from inside the build service. To keep it simple, we'll run our own Git server so we can push changes and trigger builds all from our lab cluster.

   TRY IT NOW   Gogs is a simple but powerful Git server that is published as an image on Docker Hub. It's a great way to run a private Git server in your organization or to quickly spin up a backup if your online service goes offline. Run Gogs in your cluster to push a local copy of the book's source code.

```
# deploy the Git server:
kubectl apply -f infrastructure/gogs.yaml

# wait for it to spin up:
kubectl wait --for=condition=ContainersReady pod -l app=gogs

# add your local Git server to the book's repository—
# this grabs the URL from the Service to use as the target:
```

```
git remote add gogs $(kubectl get svc gogs -o jsonpath=
   'http://{.status.loadBalancer.ingress[0].*}:3000/kiamol/kiamol.git')

# push the code to your server—authenticate with
# username kiamol and password kiamol
git push gogs

# find the server URL:
kubectl get svc gogs -o
   jsonpath='http://{.status.loadBalancer.ingress[0].*}:3000'

# browse and sign in with the same kiamol credentials
```

Figure 11.5 shows my output. You don't need to run your own Git server for this workflow; it works in the same way using GitHub or any other source control system, but doing this makes for an easily reproducible environment—the Gogs setup for the chapter is preconfigured with a user account, so you can get up and running quickly.

Gogs is a powerful, lightweight open source Git server.

Adding the local Git server as a "remote" means you can push the book's source code to your own server.

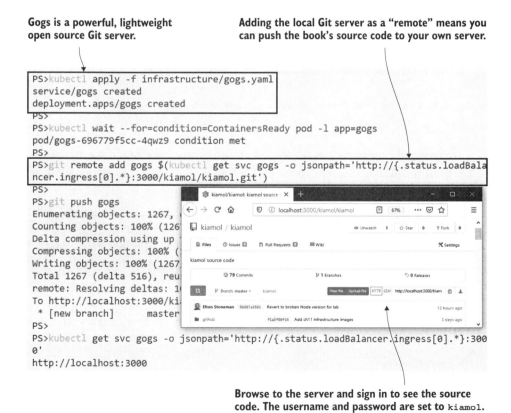

Browse to the server and sign in to see the source code. The username and password are set to `kiamol`.

Figure 11.5 Running your own Git server in Kubernetes is easy with Gogs.

Now we have a local source control server into which we can plug the other components. Next is a system that can build container images. To make this portable so it runs on any cluster, we need something that doesn't require Docker, because the cluster might use a different container runtime. We have a few options, but one of the best is BuildKit, an open source project from the Docker team. BuildKit started as a replacement for the image-building component inside the Docker Engine, and it has a pluggable architecture, so you can build images with or without Dockerfiles. You can run BuildKit as a server, so other components in the toolchain can use it to build images.

TRY IT NOW   Run BuildKit as a server inside the cluster, and confirm it has all the tools it needs to build container images without Docker.

```
# deploy BuildKit:
kubectl apply -f infrastructure/buildkitd.yaml

# wait for it to spin up:
kubectl wait --for=condition=ContainersReady pod -l app=buildkitd

# verify that Git and BuildKit are available:
kubectl exec deploy/buildkitd -- sh -c 'git version && buildctl
   --version'

# check that Docker isn't installed—this command will fail:
kubectl exec deploy/buildkitd -- sh -c 'docker version'
```

You can see my output in figure 11.6, where the BuildKit Pod is running from an image with BuildKit and the Git client installed but not Docker. It's important to realize

BuildKit is an open source tool for building container images from Dockerfiles or other inputs.

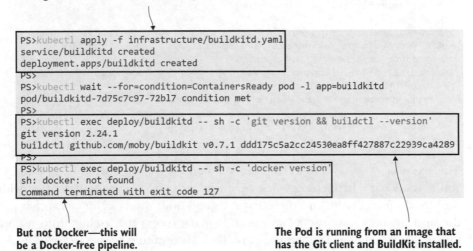

But not Docker—this will be a Docker-free pipeline.

The Pod is running from an image that has the Git client and BuildKit installed.

Figure 11.6   BuildKit running as a container image-building service, without requiring Docker

that BuildKit is completely standalone—it doesn't connect to the container runtime in Kubernetes to build images; that's all going to happen within the Pod.

We need to set up a few more pieces before we can see the full PaaS workflow, but we have enough in place now to see how the build part of it works. We're targeting a Docker-free approach here, so we're going to ignore the Dockerfile we used in the last section and build the app into a container image directly from source code. How so? By using a CNCF project called Buildpacks, a technology pioneered by Heroku to power their PaaS product.

Buildpacks use the same concept as multistage Dockerfiles: running the build tools inside a container to compile the app and then packaging the compiled app on top of another container image that has the application runtime. You can do that with a tool called Pack, which you run over the source code for your app. Pack works out what language you're using, matches it to a Buildpack, and then packages your app into an image—no Dockerfile required. Right now Pack runs only with Docker, but we're not using Docker, so we can use an alternative to integrate Buildpacks with BuildKit.

TRY IT NOW   We're going to step inside the build process to manually run a build that we'll go on to automate later in the chapter. Connect to the Build-Kit Pod, pull the book's code from your local Git server, and build it using Buildpacks instead of the Dockerfile.

```
# connect to a session on the BuildKit Pod:
kubectl exec -it deploy/buildkitd -- sh

# clone the source code from your Gogs server:
cd ~
git clone http://gogs:3000/kiamol/kiamol.git

# switch to the app directory:
cd kiamol/ch11/bulletin-board/

# build the app using BuildKit; the options tell BuildKit
# to use Buildpacks instead of a Dockerfile as input and to
# produce an image as the output:
buildctl build --frontend=gateway.v0  --opt source=kiamol/buildkit-
    buildpacks  --local context=src --output
    type=image,name=kiamol/ch11-bulletin-board:buildkit

# leave the session when the build completes
exit
```

This exercise takes a while to run, but keep an eye on the output from BuildKit, and you'll see what's happening—first, it downloads the component that provides the Buildpacks integration, and then that runs and finds this is a Node.js app; it packages the app into a compressed archive and then exports the archive into a container image that has the Node.js runtime installed. My output is shown in figure 11.7.

You can't run a container from that image on the BuildKit Pod because it doesn't have a container runtime configured, but BuildKit is able to push images to a registry

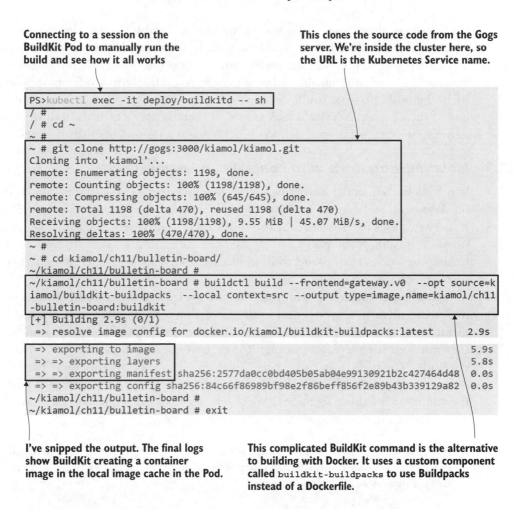

Figure 11.7 Building container images without Docker and Dockerfiles adds a lot of complexity.

after building, and that's what we'll do in the complete workflow. So far, we've seen that you can build and package your apps to run in containers without Dockerfiles or Docker, which is pretty impressive, but it comes at a cost.

The biggest issue is the complexity of the build process and the maturity of all the pieces. BuildKit is a stable tool, but it isn't anywhere near as well used as the standard Docker build engine. Buildpacks are a promising approach, but the dependency on Docker means they don't work well in a Docker-free environment like a managed Kubernetes cluster in the cloud. The component we're using to bridge them is a tool written by Tõnis Tiigi, a maintainer on the BuildKit project. It's really just a proof of concept to plug Buildpacks into BuildKit; it works well enough to demonstrate the workflow, but it's not something you would want to rely on to build apps for production.

There are alternatives. GitLab is a product that combines a Git server with a build pipeline that uses Buildpacks, and Jenkins X is a native build server for Kubernetes. They are complex products themselves, and you need to be aware that if you want to remove Docker from your developer workflow, you'll be trading it for more complexity in the build process. You'll be able to decide whether the result is worth it by the end of this chapter. Next we'll look at how you can isolate workloads in Kubernetes, so a single cluster can run your delivery pipelines and all your test environments.

11.3 *Isolating workloads with contexts and namespaces*

Way back in chapter 3, I introduced Kubernetes namespaces—and very quickly moved on. You need to be aware of them to make sense of the fully qualified DNS names Kubernetes uses for Services, but you don't need to use them until you start dividing up your cluster. Namespaces are a grouping mechanism—every Kubernetes object belongs to a namespace—and you can use multiple namespaces to create virtual clusters from one real cluster.

Namespaces are very flexible, and organizations use them in different ways. You might use them in a production cluster to divide it up for different products or to divide up a nonproduction cluster for different environments—integration test, system test, and user testing. You might even have a development cluster where each developer has their own namespace, so they don't need to run their own cluster. Namespaces are a boundary where you can apply security and resource restrictions, so they support all these scenarios. We'll use a dedicated namespace in our CI/CD deployment, but we'll start with a simple walkthrough.

> **TRY IT NOW** Kubectl is namespace aware. You can explicitly create a namespace, and then deploy and query resources using the `namespace` flag—this creates a simple sleep Deployment.

```
# create a new namespace:
kubectl create namespace kiamol-ch11-test

# deploy a sleep Pod in the new namespace:
kubectl apply -f sleep.yaml --namespace kiamol-ch11-test

# list sleep Pods—this won't return anything:
kubectl get pods -l app=sleep

# now list the Pods in the namespace:
kubectl get pods -l app=sleep -n kiamol-ch11-test
```

My output is shown in figure 11.8, where you can see that namespaces are an essential part of resource metadata. You need to explicitly specify the namespace to work with an object in kubectl. The only reason we've avoided this for the first 10 chapters is that every cluster has a namespace called `default`, which is used if you don't specify a namespace, and that's where we've created and used everything so far.

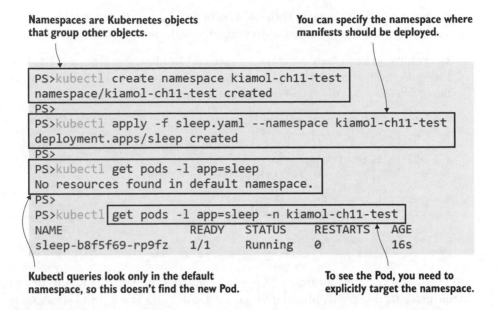

Namespaces are Kubernetes objects that group other objects.

You can specify the namespace where manifests should be deployed.

Kubectl queries look only in the default namespace, so this doesn't find the new Pod.

To see the Pod, you need to explicitly target the namespace.

Figure 11.8 Namespaces isolate workloads—you can use them to represent different environments.

Objects within a namespace are isolated, so you can deploy the same apps with the same object names in different namespaces. Resources can't see resources in other namespaces. Kubernetes networking is flat, so Pods in different namespaces can communicate through Services, but a controller looks for Pods only in its own namespace. Namespaces are ordinary Kubernetes resources, too. Listing 11.2 shows a namespace spec in YAML, along with the metadata for another sleep Deployment that uses the new namespace.

Listing 11.2   sleep-uat.yaml, a manifest that creates and targets a namespace

```
apiVersion: v1
kind: Namespace        # Namespace specs need only a name.
metadata:
  name: kiamol-ch11-uat
---
apiVersion: apps/v1
kind: Deployment
metadata:                        # The target namespace is part of the
  name: sleep                    # object metadata. The namespace needs
  namespace: kiamol-ch11-uat     # to exist, or the deployment fails.

  # The Pod spec follows.
```

The Deployment and Pod specs in that YAML file use the same names as the objects you deployed in the previous exercise, but because the controller is set to use a different namespace, all the objects it creates will be in that namespace, too. When you deploy this manifest, you'll see the new objects created without any naming collisions.

TRY IT NOW   Create a new UAT namespace and Deployment from the YAML in listing 11.2. The controller uses the same name, and you can see objects across namespaces using kubectl. Deleting a namespace deletes all its resources.

```
# create the namespace and Deployment:
kubectl apply -f sleep-uat.yaml

# list the sleep Deployments in all namespaces:
kubectl get deploy -l app=sleep --all-namespaces

# delete the new UAT namespace:
kubectl delete namespace kiamol-ch11-uat

# list Deployments again:
kubectl get deploy -l app=sleep --all-namespaces
```

You can see my output in figure 11.9. The original sleep Deployment didn't specify a namespace in the YAML file, and we created it in the kiamol-ch11-test namespace by specifying that in the kubectl command. The second sleep Deployment specified the kiamol-ch11-uat namespace in the YAML, so it was created there without needing a kubectl namespace flag.

This manifest contains a namespace and a Deployment configured to use the new namespace.

Querying objects with the all-namespaces flag shows results across all namespaces. There are two Deployments with the same name running in different namespaces.

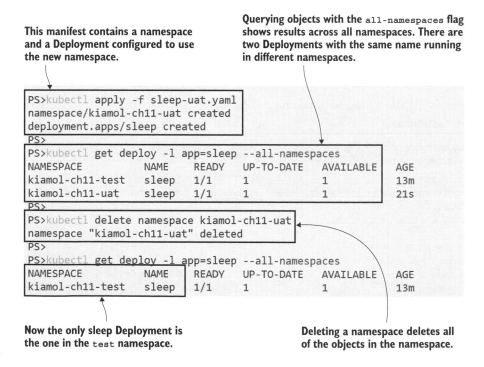

Now the only sleep Deployment is the one in the test namespace.

Deleting a namespace deletes all of the objects in the namespace.

Figure 11.9   Namespaces are a useful abstraction for managing groups of objects.

In a shared cluster environment, you might regularly use different namespaces—deploying apps in your own development namespace and then looking at logs in the test namespace. Switching between them using kubectl flags is time consuming and error prone, and kubectl provides an easier way with *contexts*. A context defines the connection details for a Kubernetes cluster and sets the default namespace to use in kubectl commands. Your lab environment will already have a context set up, and you can modify that to switch namespaces.

> **TRY IT NOW**   Show your configured contexts, and update the current one to set the default namespace to the test namespace.

```
# list all contexts:
kubectl config get-contexts

# update the default namespace for the current context:
kubectl config set-context --current --namespace=kiamol-ch11-test

# list the Pods in the default namespace:
kubectl get pods
```

You can see in figure 11.10 that setting the namespace for the context sets the default namespace for all kubectl commands. Any queries that don't specify a namespace and any `create` commands where the YAML doesn't specify a namespace will now all use the test namespace. You can create multiple contexts, all using the same cluster but different namespaces, and switch between them with the kubectl `use-context` command.

The other important use for contexts is to switch between clusters. When you set up Docker Desktop or K3s, they create a context for your local cluster—the details all live in a configuration file, which is stored in the `.kube` directory in your home folder. Managed

Contexts show the cluster name and the default namespace. A blank namespace uses the default, called `default`. The asterisk shows the currently active context.

```
PS>kubectl config get-contexts
CURRENT   NAME                    CLUSTER             AUTHINFO            NAMESPACE
*         docker-desktop          docker-desktop      docker-desktop
          docker-for-desktop      docker-desktop      docker-desktop
PS>
PS>kubectl config set-context --current --namespace=kiamol-ch11-test
Context "docker-desktop" modified.
PS>
PS>kubectl get pods
NAME                    READY     STATUS     RESTARTS    AGE
sleep-b8f5f69-rp9fz     1/1       Running    0           39m
```

Now queries are restricted to the `kiamol-ch11-test` namespace, so the sleep Pod is shown.

Updating the context lets you set a different default namespace.

Figure 11.10   Contexts are an easy way to switch between namespaces and clusters.

Kubernetes services usually have a feature to add a cluster to your config file, so you can work with remote clusters from your local machine. The remote API server will be secured using TLS, and your kubectl configuration will use a client certificate to identify you as the user. You can see those security details by viewing the configuration.

TRY IT NOW   Reset your context to use the default namespace, and then print out the details of the client configuration.

```
# setting the namespace to blank resets the default:
kubectl config set-context --current --namespace=

# printing out the config file shows your cluster connection:
kubectl config view
```

Figure 11.11 shows my output, with a local connection to my Docker Desktop cluster using TLS certificates—which aren't shown by kubectl—to authenticate the connection.

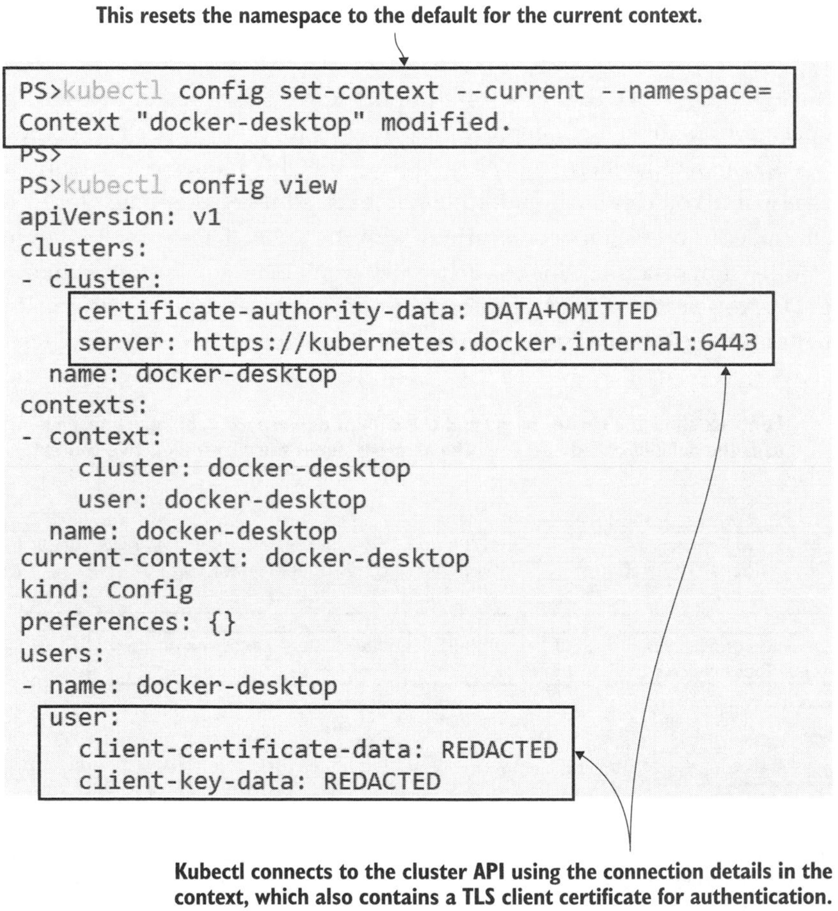

This resets the namespace to the default for the current context.

```
PS>kubectl config set-context --current --namespace=
Context "docker-desktop" modified.
PS>
PS>kubectl config view
apiVersion: v1
clusters:
- cluster:
    certificate-authority-data: DATA+OMITTED
    server: https://kubernetes.docker.internal:6443
  name: docker-desktop
contexts:
- context:
    cluster: docker-desktop
    user: docker-desktop
  name: docker-desktop
current-context: docker-desktop
kind: Config
preferences: {}
users:
- name: docker-desktop
  user:
    client-certificate-data: REDACTED
    client-key-data: REDACTED
```

Kubectl connects to the cluster API using the connection details in the context, which also contains a TLS client certificate for authentication.

Figure 11.11   Contexts contain the connection details for the cluster, which could be local or remote.

Kubectl can also use a token to authenticate with the Kubernetes API server, and Pods are provided with a token they can use as a Secret, so apps running in Kubernetes can connect to the Kubernetes API to query or deploy objects. That's a long way to getting where we want to go next: we'll run a build server in a Pod that triggers a build when the source code changes in Git, builds the image using BuildKit, and deploys it to Kubernetes in the test namespace.

11.4 *Continuous delivery in Kubernetes without Docker*

Actually, we're not quite there yet, because the build process needs to push the image to a registry, so Kubernetes can pull it to run Pod containers. Real clusters have multiple nodes, and each of them needs to be able to access the image registry. That's been easy so far because we've used public images on Docker Hub, but in your own builds, you'll push to a private repository first. Kubernetes supports pulling private images by storing registry credentials in a special type of Secret object.

You'll need to have an account set up on an image registry to follow along with this section—Docker Hub is fine, or you can create a private registry on the cloud using Azure Container Registry (ACR) or Amazon Elastic Container Registry (ECR). If you're running your cluster in the cloud, it makes sense to use that cloud's registry to reduce download times, but all registries use the same API as Docker Hub, so they're interchangeable.

TRY IT NOW Create a Secret to store registry credentials. To make it easier to follow along, there's a script to collect the credentials into local variables. Don't worry—the scripts don't email your credentials to me. . .

```
# collect the details—on Windows:
. .\set-registry-variables.ps1

# OR on Linux/Mac:
. ./set-registry-variables.sh

# create the Secret using the details from the script:
kubectl create secret docker-registry registry-creds --docker-
    server=$REGISTRY_SERVER --docker-username=$REGISTRY_USER --docker-
    password=$REGISTRY_PASSWORD

# show the Secret details:
kubectl get secret registry-creds
```

My output appears in figure 11.12. I'm using Docker Hub, which lets you create temporary access tokens that you can use in the same way as a password for your account. When I'm done with this chapter, I'll revoke the access token—that's a nice security feature in Hub.

Okay, now we're ready. We have a Docker-less build server running in the Build-Kit Pod, a local Git server we can use to quickly iterate over the build process, and a registry Secret stored in the cluster. We can use all of those pieces with an automation

This script collects registry authentication details into variables, which you can use in later commands.

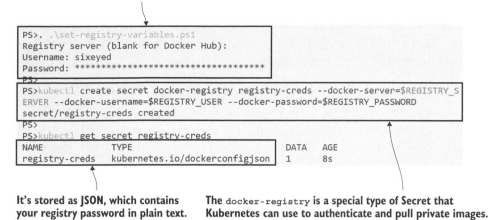

It's stored as JSON, which contains your registry password in plain text.

The `docker-registry` is a special type of Secret that Kubernetes can use to authenticate and pull private images.

Figure 11.12   Your organization may use a private image registry—you need a Secret to authenticate.

server to run the build pipeline, and we'll be using Jenkins for that. Jenkins has a long legacy as a build server, and it's very popular, but you don't need to be a Jenkins guru to set up this build, because I have it already configured in a custom Docker Hub image.

The Jenkins image for this chapter has the BuildKit and kubectl command lines installed, and the Pod is set up to surface credentials in the right places. The registry Secret you created in the previous exercise is mounted in the Pod container, so BuildKit can use it to authenticate to the registry when it pushes the image. Kubectl is configured to connect to the local API server in the cluster using the token Kubernetes provides in another Secret. Deploy the Jenkins server, and check that everything is correctly configured.

TRY IT NOW   Jenkins gets everything it needs from Kubernetes Secrets, using a startup script in the container image. Start by deploying Jenkins and confirming it can connect to Kubernetes.

```
# deploy Jenkins:
kubectl apply -f infrastructure/jenkins.yaml

# wait for the Pod to spin up:
kubectl wait --for=condition=ContainersReady pod -l app=jenkins

# check that kubectl can connect to the cluster:
kubectl exec deploy/jenkins -- sh -c 'kubectl version --short'

# check that the registry Secret is mounted:
kubectl exec deploy/jenkins -- sh -c 'ls -l /root/.docker'
```

In this exercise, you'll see kubectl report the version of your own Kubernetes lab cluster—that confirms the Jenkins Pod container is set up correctly to authenticate to Kubernetes, so it can deploy applications to the same cluster where it is running. My output is shown in figure 11.13.

The Jenkins manifest mounts the Docker registry Secret, and Kubernetes provides its own API token Secret. A startup script in the image configures all of the authentication.

Kubectl shows the version of the command-line client and the version of the cluster it's connected to. Running this in the Jenkins Pod shows it can connect to the Kubernetes API.

```
PS>kubectl apply -f infrastructure/jenkins.yaml
service/jenkins created
deployment.apps/jenkins created
PS>
PS>kubectl wait --for=condition=ContainersReady pod -l app=jenkins
pod/jenkins-888fb995-6g48p condition met
PS>
PS>kubectl exec deploy/jenkins -- sh -c 'kubectl version --short'
Client Version: v1.18.4
Server Version: v1.16.6-beta.0
PS>
PS>kubectl exec deploy/jenkins -- sh -c 'ls -l /root/.docker'
total 0
lrwxrwxrwx 1 root root 18 Jun 22 13:46 config.json -> ..data/config.json
```

The Docker registry Secret is mounted to the path where BuildKit looks for authentication. If you print the file contents, you'll see your registry password in plain text, which is why I haven't.

Figure 11.13 Jenkins runs the pipeline, so it needs authentication details for Kubernetes and the registry.

Everything is in place now for Jenkins to fetch application code from the Gogs Git server, connect to the BuildKit server to build the container image using Buildpacks and push it to the registry, and deploy the latest application version to the test namespace. That work is already set up using a Jenkins pipeline, but the pipeline steps just use simple build scripts in the application folder. Listing 11.3 shows the build stage, which packages and pushes the image.

Listing 11.3   build.sh, the build script using BuildKit

```
buildctl --addr tcp://buildkitd:1234 \      # The command runs on Jenkins,
  build \                                    # but it uses the BuildKit server.
  --frontend=gateway.v0 \
  --opt source=kiamol/buildkit-buildpacks \    # Uses Buildpacks as input
  --local context=src \
  --output type=image,name=${REGISTRY_SERVER}/${REGISTRY_USER}/bulletin-board:
    ${BUILD_NUMBER}-kiamol,push=true  # Pushes the output to the registry
```

The script is an extension of the simpler BuildKit command you ran in section 11.2, when you were pretending to be the build server. The `buildctl` command uses the same integration component for Buildpacks, so there's no Dockerfile in here. This command runs inside the Jenkins Pod, so it specifies an address for the BuildKit server, which is running in a separate Pod behind the Service called `buildkitd`. No Docker here, either. The variables in the image name are all set by Jenkins, but they're standard environment variables, so there's no dependency on Jenkins in the build scripts.

When this stage of the pipeline completes, the image will have been built and pushed to the registry. The next stage is to deploy the updated application, which is in a separate script, shown in listing 11.4. You don't need to run this yourself—it's all in the Jenkins pipeline.

> **Listing 11.4   run.sh, the deployment script using Helm**

```
helm upgrade --install  --atomic \     # Upgrades or installs the release
  --set registryServer=${REGISTRY_SERVER}, \    # Sets the values for the
        registryUser=${REGISTRY_USER}, \        # image tag, referencing
        imageBuildNumber=${BUILD_NUMBER} \      # the new image version
  --namespace kiamol-ch11-test \       # Deploys to the test namespace
  bulletin-board \
  helm/bulletin-board
```

The deployment uses Helm with a chart that has values for the parts of the image name. They're set from the same variables used in the build stage, which are compiled from the Docker registry Secret and the build number in Jenkins. In my case, the first build pushes an image to Docker Hub named `sixeyed/bulletin-board:1-kiamol` and installs a Helm release using that image. To run the build in your cluster and push to your registry, you just need to log in to Jenkins and enable the build—the pipeline itself is already set up.

> **TRY IT NOW**   Jenkins is running and configured, but the pipeline job isn't enabled. Log in to enable the job, and you will see the pipeline execute and the app deployed to the cluster.

```
# get the URL for Jenkins:
kubectl get svc jenkins -o
  jsonpath='http://{.status.loadBalancer.ingress[0].*}:8080/job/kiamol'

# browse and login with username kiamol and password kiamol;
# if Jenkins is still setting itself up you'll see a wait screen

# click enable for the Kiamol job and wait . . .

# when the pipeline completes, check the deployment:
kubectl get pods -n kiamol-ch11-test -l
  app.kubernetes.io/name=bulletin-board -o=custom-
  columns=NAME:.metadata.name,IMAGE:.spec.containers[0].image
```

```
# find the URL of the test app:
kubectl get svc -n kiamol-ch11-test bulletin-board -o
    jsonpath='http://{.status.loadBalancer.ingress[0].*}:8012'

# browse
```

The build should be fast because it's using the same BuildKit server that has already cached the images for the Buildpack build from section 11.2. When the build has completed, you can browse to the application deployed by Helm in the test namespace and see the app running—mine is shown in figure 11.14.

Browse to Jenkins, and log in with credentials kiamol/kiamol to enable the pipeline project.

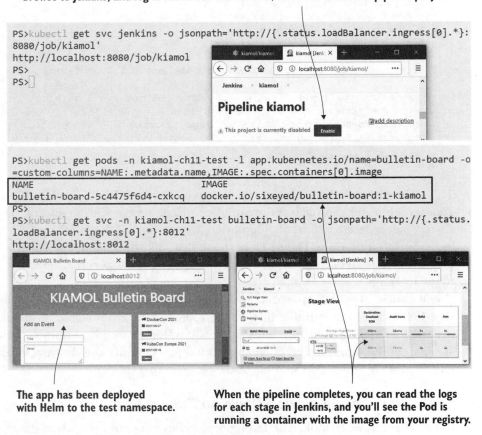

The app has been deployed with Helm to the test namespace.

When the pipeline completes, you can read the logs for each stage in Jenkins, and you'll see the Pod is running a container with the image from your registry.

Figure 11.14   The pipeline in action, built and deployed to Kubernetes without Docker or Dockerfiles

So far so good. We're playing the ops role, so we understand all the moving parts in the delivery of this app—we would own the pipeline in the Jenkinsfile and the application specs in the Helm chart. Lots of small fiddly details are in there, like the templated image name and the image pull Secret in the Deployment YAML, but from the developer's point of view, that's all hidden.

The developer's view is that you can work on the app using your local environment, push changes, and see them running at the test URL, without worrying what happens in between. We can see that workflow now. You made an application change earlier to add event descriptions to the site, and to deploy that, all you need to do is push the changes to your local Git server and wait for the Jenkins build to complete.

TRY IT NOW   Push your code change to your Gogs server; Jenkins will see the change within one minute and start a new build. That will push a new image version to your registry and update the Helm release to use that version.

```
# add your code change, and push it to Git:
git add bulletin-board/src/backend/events.js
git commit -m 'Add event descriptions'
git push gogs

# browse back to Jenkins, and wait for the new build to finish

# check that the application Pod is using the new image version:
kubectl get pods -n kiamol-ch11-test -l
  app.kubernetes.io/name=bulletin-board -o=custom-
  columns=NAME:.metadata.name,IMAGE:.spec.containers[0].image

# browse back to the app
```

This is the `git push` PaaS workflow applied to Kubernetes. We're dealing with a simple app here, but the approach is the same for a large system with many components: a shared namespace could be the deployment target for all the latest versions, pushed by many different teams. Figure 11.15 shows an application update in Kubernetes triggered from a push of code, with no requirement for developers to use Docker, Kubernetes, or Helm.

Of course, the PaaS approach and the Docker approach are not mutually exclusive. If your cluster is running on Docker, you can take advantage of a simpler build process for Docker-based apps but still support a Docker-free PaaS approach for other apps, all in the same cluster. Each approach offers benefits and drawbacks, and we'll end by looking at how you should choose between them.

11.5 *Evaluating developer workflows on Kubernetes*

In this chapter, we've looked at developer workflows at extreme ends of the spectrum, from teams who fully embrace containers and want to make them front and center in every environment, to teams who don't want to add any ceremony to their development process, want to keep working natively, and leave all the container bits to the CI/CD pipeline. There are plenty of places in between, and the likelihood is that you'll build an approach to suit your organization, your application architectures, and your Kubernetes platform.

Committing a change and pushing it to the local Git server triggers a new build in Jenkins.

When the build completes, the app is running from the updated version, which includes the event description.

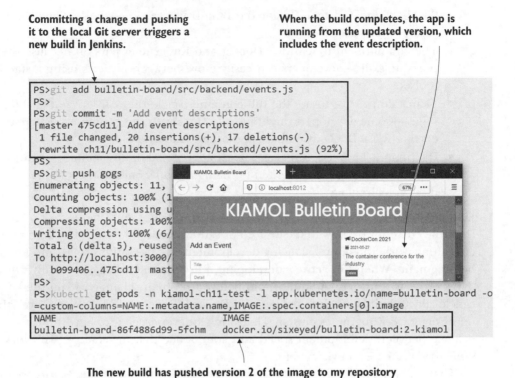

The new build has pushed version 2 of the image to my repository on Docker Hub, and the Helm update is using that version.

Figure 11.15 It's PaaS on your own Kubernetes cluster—a lot of complexity is hidden from the developer.

The decision is as much about culture as about technology. Do you want every team to level up on container knowledge, or do you want to centralize that knowledge in a service team and leave the developer teams to focus on delivering software? Although I'd love to see copies of *Learn Docker in a Month of Lunches* and *Learn Kubernetes in a Month of Lunches* on every desk, skilling up on containers does require a pretty big commitment. Here are the major advantages I see in keeping Docker and Kubernetes visible in your projects:

- The PaaS approach is complicated and bespoke—you'll be plugging together lots of different technologies with different maturity levels and support structures.
- The Docker approach is flexible—you can add any dependencies and setup you need in a Dockerfile, whereas PaaS approaches are more prescriptive, so they won't fit every app.
- PaaS technologies don't have the optimizations you can get when you fine-tune your Docker images; the bulletin board image from the Docker workflow is

95 MB compared to 1 GB for the Buildpacks version—that's a much smaller surface area to secure.

- The commitment to learning Docker and Kubernetes pays off because they're portable skills—developers can easily move between projects using a standard toolset.

- Teams don't have to use the full container stack; they can opt out at different stages—some developers might just use Docker to run containers, whereas others might use Docker Compose and others Kubernetes.

- Distributed knowledge makes for a better collaborative culture—centralized service teams might be resented for being the only ones who get to play with all the fun technology.

Ultimately, it's a decision for your organization and teams, and the pain of migrating from the current workflow to the desired workflow needs to be considered. In my own consulting work, I'm often balancing development and operations roles, and I tend to be pragmatic. When I'm actively developing, I use native tooling (I typically work on .NET projects using Visual Studio), but before I push any changes, I run the CI process locally to build container images with Docker Compose and then spin everything up in my local Kubernetes cluster. That won't fit every scenario, but I find it a good balance between development speed and confidence that my changes will work the same way in the next environment.

That's all for the developer workflow, so we can tidy up the cluster before we move on. Leave your build components running (Gogs, BuildKit, and Jenkins)—you'll need them for the lab.

TRY IT NOW   Remove the bulletin board deployments.

```
# uninstall the Helm release from the pipeline:
helm -n kiamol-ch11-test uninstall bulletin-board

# delete the manual deployment:
kubectl delete all -l app=bulletin-board
```

11.6 *Lab*

This lab is a bit nasty, so I'll apologize in advance—but I want you to see that going down the PaaS path with a custom set of tools has danger in store. The bulletin board app for this chapter used a very old version of the Node runtime, version 10.5.0, and in the lab, that needs updating to a more recent version. There's a new source code folder for the lab that uses Node 10.6.0, and your job is to set up a pipeline to build that version, and then find out why it fails and fix it. There are a few hints that follow because the goal isn't for you to learn Jenkins but to see how to debug failing pipelines:

- Start by creating a new item from the Jenkins home page: choose the option to copy an existing job, and copy the `kiamol` job; call the new job anything you like.

- In the new job configuration in the Pipeline tab, change the path to the pipeline file to the new source code folder: `ch11/lab/bulletin-board/Jenkinsfile`.
- Build the job, and look through the logs to find out why it failed.
- You'll need to make a change in the lab source folder and push it to Gogs to fix the build

My sample solution is on GitHub with some screenshots for the Jenkins setup to help you: https://github.com/sixeyed/kiamol/blob/master/ch11/lab/README.md.

Week 3

Preparing for production

Kubernetes runs your applications for you, but that doesn't mean you get a production experience for free. This section teaches you about all the day-2 operations concepts, so you'll be well prepared when you put your applications live. You'll learn about health checks that keep your apps online, centralized collection of logs and application metrics, and how to configure Kubernetes to route traffic to your containers. We'll also cover some core security subjects, so you can understand what it takes to keep your applications safe.

Empowering
self-healing apps

Kubernetes models your application with abstractions over the compute and networking layers. The abstractions allow Kubernetes to control network traffic and container lifetimes, so it can take corrective action if parts of your app fail. If you have enough detail in your specifications, the cluster can find and fix temporary problems and keep applications online. These are self-healing applications, which ride out any transient issues without needing a human to guide them. In this chapter, you'll learn how to model that in your own apps, using container probes to test for health and imposing resource limits so apps don't soak up too much compute.

There are limits to Kubernetes's healing powers, and you'll learn those in this chapter, too. We're mainly going to look at how you keep your apps running without manual administration, but we'll also look again at application updates. Updates are the most likely cause of downtime, and we'll look at some additional features of Helm that can keep your apps healthy during update cycles.

12.1 Routing traffic to healthy Pods using readiness probes

Kubernetes knows if your Pod container is running, but it doesn't know if the application inside the container is healthy. Every app will have its own idea of what "healthy" means—it might be a 200 OK response to an HTTP request—and Kubernetes provides a generic mechanism for testing health using *container probes*. Docker images can have healthchecks configured, but Kubernetes ignores them in favor of its own probes. Probes are defined in the Pod spec, and they execute on a fixed schedule, testing some aspect of the application and returning an indicator to say if the app is still healthy.

If the probe response says the container is unhealthy, Kubernetes will take action, and the action it takes depends on the type of probe. *Readiness probes* take action at the network level, managing the routing for components that listen for network requests. If the Pod container is unhealthy, the Pod is taken out of the ready state and removed from the list of active Pods for a Service. Figure 12.1 shows how that looks for a Deployment with multiple replicas, where one Pod is unhealthy.

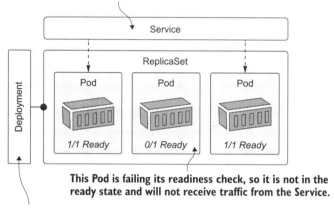

The Service has a list of endpoints where it sends traffic, built from the label selector. But Pods are included only if they are in the ready state.

This Pod is failing its readiness check, so it is not in the ready state and will not receive traffic from the Service.

The Deployment and ReplicaSet manage the Pods, but they will not replace a Pod that is not ready.

Figure 12.1　The list of endpoints for a Service excludes Pods that are not ready to receive traffic.

Readiness probes are a great way to manage temporary load issues. Some Pods might be overloaded, returning a 503 status code to every request. If the readiness probe checks for a 200 response and those Pods return 503, they will be removed from the Service and will stop receiving requests. Kubernetes keeps running the probe after it has failed, so if the overloaded Pod has a chance to recover while it's resting, the probe will succeed again, and the Pod will be enlisted back into the Service.

The random-number generator we've used in this book has a couple of features we can use to see how this works. The API can run in a mode where it fails after a certain number of requests, and it has an HTTP endpoint that returns whether it is healthy or in a failed state. We'll start by running it without a readiness probe so we can understand the problem.

TRY IT NOW Run the API with multiple replicas, and see what happens when the application fails without any container probes to test it.

```
# switch to the chapter's directory:
cd ch12

# deploy the random-number API:
kubectl apply -f numbers/

# wait for it to be ready:
kubectl wait --for=condition=ContainersReady pod -l app=numbers-api

# check that the Pod is registered as Service endpoints:
kubectl get endpoints numbers-api

# save the URL for the API in a text file:
kubectl get svc numbers-api -o jsonpath='http://{.status.loadBalancer
    .ingress[0].*}:8013' > api-url.txt

# call the API—after returning, this app server is now unhealthy:
curl "$(cat api-url.txt)/rng"

# test the health endpoints to check:
curl "$(cat api-url.txt)/healthz"; curl "$(cat api-url.txt)/healthz"

# confirm the Pods used by the service:
kubectl get endpoints numbers-api
```

You'll see from this exercise that the Service keeps both Pods in its list of endpoints, even though one of them is unhealthy and will always return a 500 error response. My output in figure 12.2 shows two IP addresses in the endpoint list before and after the request, which causes one instance to become unhealthy.

This happens because Kubernetes doesn't know one of the Pods is unhealthy. The application in the Pod container is still running, and Kubernetes doesn't know there's a health endpoint it can use to see if the app is working correctly. You can give it that information with a readiness probe in the container spec for the Pod. Listing 12.1 shows an update to the API spec, which includes the health check.

Listing 12.1 api-with-readiness.yaml, a readiness probe for the API container
---

```
spec:                 # This is the Pod spec in the Deployment.
  containers:
    - image: kiamol/ch03-numbers-api
      readinessProbe:        # Probes are set at the container level.
        httpGet:
          path: /healthz     # This is an HTTP GET, using the health URL.
          port: 80
        periodSeconds: 5      # The probe fires every five seconds.
```

Kubernetes supports different types of container probe. This one uses an HTTP GET action, which is perfect for web applications and APIs. The probe tells Kubernetes to

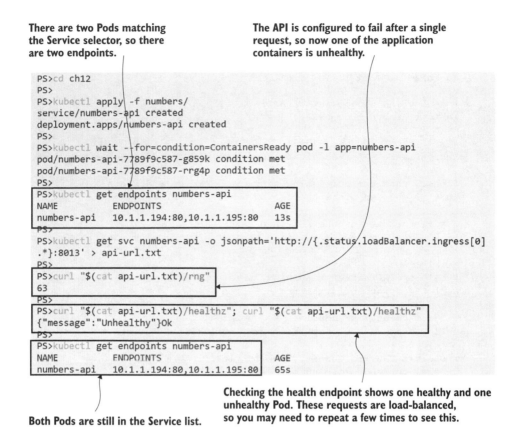

There are two Pods matching the Service selector, so there are two endpoints.

The API is configured to fail after a single request, so now one of the application containers is unhealthy.

```
PS>cd ch12
PS>
PS>kubectl apply -f numbers/
service/numbers-api created
deployment.apps/numbers-api created
PS>
PS>kubectl wait --for=condition=ContainersReady pod -l app=numbers-api
pod/numbers-api-7789f9c587-g859k condition met
pod/numbers-api-7789f9c587-rrg4p condition met
PS>
PS>kubectl get endpoints numbers-api
NAME            ENDPOINTS                      AGE
numbers-api     10.1.1.194:80,10.1.1.195:80    13s
PS>
PS>kubectl get svc numbers-api -o jsonpath='http://{.status.loadBalancer.ingress[0]
.*}:8013' > api-url.txt
PS>
PS>curl "$(cat api-url.txt)/rng"
63
PS>
PS>curl "$(cat api-url.txt)/healthz"; curl "$(cat api-url.txt)/healthz"
{"message":"Unhealthy"}Ok
PS>
PS>kubectl get endpoints numbers-api
NAME            ENDPOINTS                      AGE
numbers-api     10.1.1.194:80,10.1.1.195:80    65s
```

Both Pods are still in the Service list.

Checking the health endpoint shows one healthy and one unhealthy Pod. These requests are load-balanced, so you may need to repeat a few times to see this.

Figure 12.2   Application containers may be unhealthy, but the Pod stays in the ready state.

test the /healthz endpoint every five seconds; if the response has an HTTP status code between 200 and 399, then the probe succeeds; if any other status code is returned, it will fail. The random-number API returns a 500 code when it's unhealthy, so we can see the readiness probe in action.

TRY IT NOW   Deploy the updated spec, and verify that the Pod with the failed application is removed from the Service.

```
# deploy the updated spec from listing 12.1:
kubectl apply -f numbers/update/api-with-readiness.yaml

# wait for the replacement Pods:
kubectl wait --for=condition=ContainersReady pod -l app=numbers-
   api,version=v2

# check the endpoints:
kubectl get endpoints numbers-api
```

```
# trigger an application container to become unhealthy:
curl "$(cat api-url.txt)/rng"

# wait for the readiness probe to take effect:
sleep 10

# check the endpoints again:
kubectl get endpoints numbers-api
```

As shown in my output in figure 12.3, the readiness probe detects one of the Pods is unhealthy because the response to the HTTP request returns 500. That Pod's IP address is removed from the Service endpoint list, so it won't receive any more traffic.

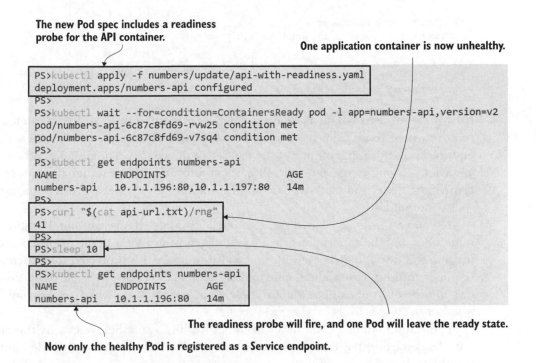

The new Pod spec includes a readiness probe for the API container.

One application container is now unhealthy.

```
PS>kubectl apply -f numbers/update/api-with-readiness.yaml
deployment.apps/numbers-api configured
PS>
PS>kubectl wait --for=condition=ContainersReady pod -l app=numbers-api,version=v2
pod/numbers-api-6c87c8fd69-rvw25 condition met
pod/numbers-api-6c87c8fd69-v7sq4 condition met
PS>
PS>kubectl get endpoints numbers-api
NAME          ENDPOINTS                         AGE
numbers-api   10.1.1.196:80,10.1.1.197:80       14m
PS>
PS>curl "$(cat api-url.txt)/rng"
41
PS>
PS>sleep 10
PS>
PS>kubectl get endpoints numbers-api
NAME          ENDPOINTS          AGE
numbers-api   10.1.1.196:80      14m
```

The readiness probe will fire, and one Pod will leave the ready state.

Now only the healthy Pod is registered as a Service endpoint.

Figure 12.3 Failing readiness probes move Pods out of the ready state so they're removed from Services.

This app is also a good example of how readiness probes on their own can be dangerous. The logic in the random-number API means once it has failed, it will always fail, so the unhealthy Pod will stay excluded from the Service, and the application will run below the expected capacity. Deployments do not replace Pods that leave the ready state when a probe fails, so we're left with two Pods running but only one receiving traffic. The situation gets much worse if the other Pod fails, too.

TRY IT NOW   Only one Pod is in the Service list. You will make a request, and that Pod goes unhealthy, too, so both Pods are removed from the Service.

```
# check the Service endpoints:
kubectl get endpoints numbers-api

# call the API, triggering it to go unhealthy:
curl "$(cat api-url.txt)/rng"

# wait for the readiness probe to fire:
sleep 10

# check the endpoints again:
kubectl get endpoints numbers-api

# check the Pod status:
kubectl get pods -l app=numbers-api

# we could reset the API... but there are no Pods ready to
# receive traffic so this will fail:
curl "$(cat api-url.txt)/reset"
```

Now we're in a fix—both Pods have failed readiness probes, and Kubernetes has removed them both from the Service endpoint list. That leaves the Service with no endpoints, so the app is offline, as you can see in figure 12.4. The situation now is that any clients trying to use the API will get a connection failure rather than an HTTP error status code, and that's true for administrators who try to reset the app using the special admin URL.

If you're thinking, "This isn't a self-healing app," you're absolutely right, but remember that the application is in a failed state anyway. Without the readiness probe, the app still doesn't work, but with the readiness probe, it's protected from incoming requests until it recovers and is able to handle them. You need to understand the failure modes of your application to know what will happen when probes fail and whether the app is likely to recover by itself.

The random-number API never becomes healthy again, but we can fix the failed state by restarting the Pod. Kubernetes will do that for you if you include another healthcheck in the container spec: a *liveness probe*.

12.2   *Restarting unhealthy Pods with liveness probes*

Liveness probes use the same healthcheck mechanism as readiness probes—the test configurations might be identical in your Pod spec—but the action for a failed probe is different. Liveness probes take action at the compute level, restarting Pods if they become unhealthy. A restart is when Kubernetes replaces the Pod container with a new one; the Pod itself isn't replaced; it continues to run on the same node but with a new container.

Listing 12.2 shows a liveness probe for the random-number API. This probe uses the same HTTP GET action to run the probe, but it has some additional configuration.

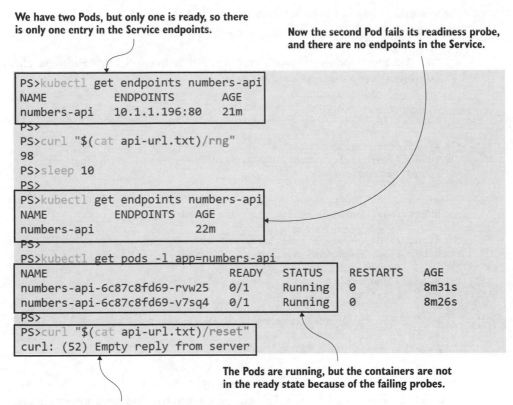

We have two Pods, but only one is ready, so there is only one entry in the Service endpoints.

Now the second Pod fails its readiness probe, and there are no endpoints in the Service.

The Pods are running, but the containers are not in the ready state because of the failing probes.

The API has a handy reset function to make it healthy again, but this request fails because there are no endpoints in the Service, so there are no Pods to send it to.

Figure 12.4   Probes are supposed to help the app, but they can remove all Pods from a Service.

Restarting a Pod is more invasive than removing it from a Service, and the extra settings help to ensure that happens only when we really need it.

Listing 12.2   api-with-readiness-and-liveness.yaml, adding a liveness probe

```
livenessProbe:
  httpGet:                        # HTTP GET actions can be used in liveness and
    path: /healthz                # readiness probes—they use the same spec.
    port: 80
  periodSeconds: 10
  initialDelaySeconds: 10   # Wait 10 seconds before running the first probe.
  failureThreshold: 2       # Allow two probes to fail before taking action.
```

This is a change to the Pod spec, so applying the update will create new replacement Pods that start off healthy. This time, when a Pod becomes unhealthy after the application fails, it will be removed from the Service thanks to the readiness probe. It will be restarted thanks to the liveness probe, and then the Pod will be added back into the Service.

TRY IT NOW   Update the API, and verify that liveness and readiness checks combined keep the application healthy.

```
# update the Pod spec from listing 12.2:
kubectl apply -f numbers/update/api-with-readiness-and-liveness.yaml

# wait for the new Pods:
kubectl wait --for=condition=ContainersReady pod -l app=numbers-
   api,version=v3

# check the Pod status:
kubectl get pods -l app=numbers-api -o wide

# check the Servivce endpoints:
kubectl get endpoints numbers-api  # two

# cause one application to become unhealthy:
curl "$(cat api-url.txt)/rng"

# wait for the probes to fire, and check the Pods again:
sleep 20
kubectl get pods -l app=numbers-api
```

In this exercise, you see the liveness probe in action, restarting the Pod when the application fails. The restart is a new Pod container, but the Pod environment is the same—it has the same IP address, and if the container mounted an `EmptyDir` volume in the Pod, it would have access to the files written by the previous container. You can see in figure 12.5 that both Pods are running and ready after the restart, so Kubernetes fixed the failure and healed the application.

Restarts aren't a permanent fix if the app keeps failing without a healthy streak, because Kubernetes won't indefinitely restart a failing Pod. For transient issues, it works well, provided the application can restart successfully in a replacement container. Probes are also useful to keep applications healthy during upgrades, because rollouts proceed only as new Pods enter the ready state, so if a readiness probe fails, that will pause the rollout.

We'll show that with the to-do list application, with specifications that include liveness and readiness checks for the web application Pod and the database. The web probes use the same HTTP GET action we've already seen, but the database doesn't have an HTTP endpoint we can use. Instead, the spec uses the other types of probe action that Kubernetes supports—the TCP socket action, which checks that a port is open and listening for incoming traffic, and the exec action, which runs a command inside the container. Listing 12.3 shows the probe setup.

The two new Pods are both running and ready;
they have readiness and liveness checks configured.

The Service endpoints are the two Pod IP addresses.

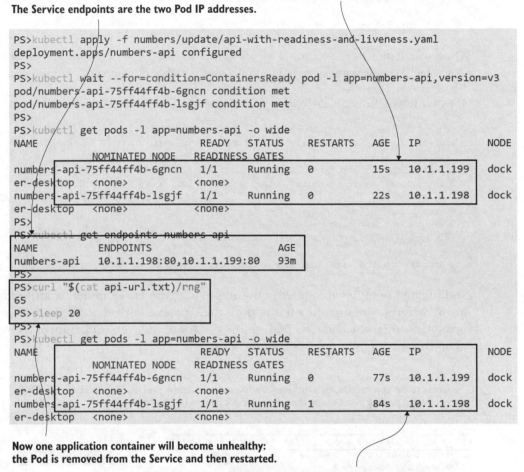

```
PS>kubectl apply -f numbers/update/api-with-readiness-and-liveness.yaml
deployment.apps/numbers-api configured
PS>
PS>kubectl wait --for=condition=ContainersReady pod -l app=numbers-api,version=v3
pod/numbers-api-75ff44ff4b-6gncn condition met
pod/numbers-api-75ff44ff4b-lsgjf condition met
PS>
PS>kubectl get pods -l app=numbers-api -o wide
NAME                           READY  STATUS   RESTARTS  AGE   IP          NODE
            NOMINATED NODE   READINESS GATES
numbers-api-75ff44ff4b-6gncn   1/1    Running  0         15s   10.1.1.199  dock
er-desktop   <none>          <none>
numbers-api-75ff44ff4b-lsgjf   1/1    Running  0         22s   10.1.1.198  dock
er-desktop   <none>          <none>
PS>
PS>kubectl get endpoints numbers-api
NAME          ENDPOINTS                        AGE
numbers-api   10.1.1.198:80,10.1.1.199:80      93m
PS>
PS>curl "$(cat api-url.txt)/rng"
65
PS>sleep 20
PS>
PS>kubectl get pods -l app=numbers-api -o wide
NAME                           READY  STATUS   RESTARTS  AGE   IP          NODE
            NOMINATED NODE   READINESS GATES
numbers-api-75ff44ff4b-6gncn   1/1    Running  0         77s   10.1.1.199  dock
er-desktop   <none>          <none>
numbers-api-75ff44ff4b-lsgjf   1/1    Running  1         84s   10.1.1.198  dock
er-desktop   <none>          <none>
```

Now one application container will become unhealthy:
the Pod is removed from the Service and then restarted.

Both Pods are running and ready again, but one has
been restarted because of the failing liveness probe.

Figure 12.5   Readiness probes and liveness probes combined help keep applications online.

Listing 12.3   todo-db.yaml, using TCP and command probes

```
spec:
  containers:
    - image: postgres:11.6-alpine
      # full spec includes environment config
      readinessProbe:
        tcpSocket:              # The readiness probe tests the
          port: 5432            # database is listening on the port.
        periodSeconds: 5
```

```
livenessProbe:              # The liveness probe runs a Postgres tool,
  exec:                     # which confirms the database is running.
    command: ["pg_isready", "-h", "localhost"]
  periodSeconds: 10
  initialDelaySeconds: 10
```

When you deploy this code, you'll see the app works in the same way as always, but now it's protected against transient failures in both the web and database components.

TRY IT NOW   Run the to-do list app with the new self-healing specification.

```
# deploy the web and database:
kubectl apply -f todo-list/db/ -f todo-list/web/

# wait for the app to be ready:
kubectl wait --for=condition=ContainersReady pod -l app=todo-web

# get the URL for the service:
kubectl get svc todo-web -o
    jsonpath='http://{.status.loadBalancer.ingress[0].*}:8081'

# browse to the app, and add a new item
```

Nothing new here, as you can see in my output in figure 12.6. But the database probes mean Postgres won't get any traffic until the database is ready, and if the Postgres server fails, then the database Pod will be restarted, with the replacement using the same data files in the EmptyDir volume in the Pod.

The latest to-do app specification includes readiness and liveness probes. The database uses TCP and command probes because the container doesn't run an HTTP server.

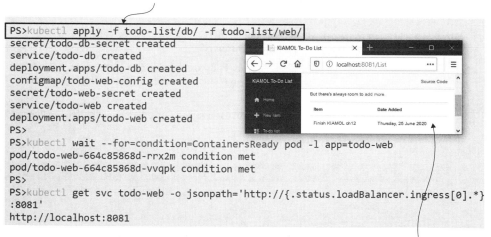

The app works in the usual way, which means all probes must be passing, and traffic is passing from the Services to the web Pods and the database Pod.

Figure 12.6   Probes are firing and returning healthy responses, so the app works in the usual way.

Container probes can also keep an application running if an update goes wrong. There's a new database spec for the to-do app that upgrades the version of Postgres, but it also overrides the container command, so it sleeps instead of starting Postgres. This is a classic left-over-from-debugging mistake: someone wanted to start a Pod with the correct configuration but without running the app so they could run a shell inside the container to check the environment, but they didn't revert their change. If the Pod didn't have any probes, the update would succeed and take down the app. The `sleep` command keeps the Pod container running, but there's no database server for the website to use. The probes stop that happening and keep the app available.

TRY IT NOW   Deploy the bad update, and verify that the failing probes in the new Pod prevent the original Pod from being removed.

```
# apply the update:
kubectl apply -f todo-list/db/update/todo-db-bad-command.yaml

# watch the Pod status changing:
kubectl get pods -l app=todo-db --watch

# refresh the app to check that it still works
# ctrl-c or cmd-c to exit the Kubectl watch
```

You can see my output in figure 12.7. The replacement database Pod is created, but it never enters the ready state because the readiness probe checks port 5342 for a process listening, and there isn't one. The Pod will keep restarting, too, because the liveness probe runs a command that checks that Postgres is ready to receive client connections. While the new Pod keeps failing, the old one is left running, and the app keeps working.

If you leave this app running for another five minutes or so and check the Pod status again, you'll see the new Pod goes into the CrashLoopBackOff status. This is how Kubernetes protects the cluster from wasting compute resources on applications that constantly fail: it adds a time delay between Pod restarts, and that delay increases with each restart. If you see a Pod in CrashLoopBackOff, it usually means the app is beyond repair.

The to-do app is in the same situation now that we first saw in chapter 9 when rollouts fail. The Deployment is managing two ReplicaSets, and its goal is to scale down the old one to zero as soon as the new one is up to capacity. But the new ReplicaSet never reaches capacity, because the probes in the new Pod constantly fail. The Deployment stays like this, hoping it can eventually finish the rollout. Kubernetes doesn't have an automatic rollback option, but Helm does, and you can extend your Helm charts to support healthy upgrades.

This update has a misconfigured Pod spec, so the container sleeps instead of running the database server, but it has the same liveness and readiness probes.

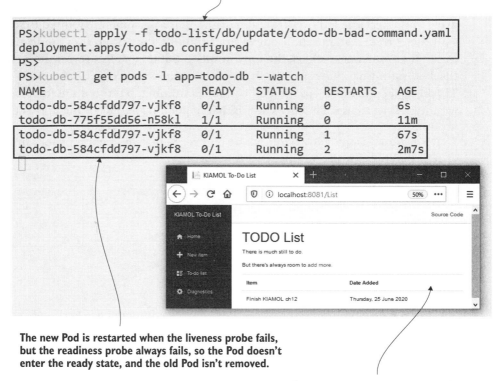

```
PS>kubectl apply -f todo-list/db/update/todo-db-bad-command.yaml
deployment.apps/todo-db configured
PS>
PS>kubectl get pods -l app=todo-db --watch
NAME                          READY   STATUS    RESTARTS   AGE
todo-db-584cfdd797-vjkf8      0/1     Running   0          6s
todo-db-775f55dd56-n58kl      1/1     Running   0          11m
todo-db-584cfdd797-vjkf8      0/1     Running   1          67s
todo-db-584cfdd797-vjkf8      0/1     Running   2          2m7s
```

The new Pod is restarted when the liveness probe fails, but the readiness probe always fails, so the Pod doesn't enter the ready state, and the old Pod isn't removed.

The app stays up throughout the failing update, using the original database Pod.

Figure 12.7   Rollouts wait for new Pods to become ready, so probes protect against failed updates.

12.3 Deploying upgrades safely with Helm

A little bit of Helm goes a long way. You learned the basics in chapter 10, and you don't need to dig too deeply into the templating functions and the dependency management to make good use of Helm for safe application upgrades. Helm supports atomic installs and upgrades, which automatically roll back if they fail, and it also has a deployment life cycle you can hook into to run validation jobs before and after installation.

The source folder for this chapter has multiple Helm charts for the to-do app, which represent different versions (normally that would be a single Helm chart that evolves with each release). The version 1 chart deploys the app using the same liveness and readiness checks we used in section 12.2; the only difference is that the database uses a PersistentVolumeClaim, so data is preserved between upgrades. We'll start by clearing down the previous exercises and installing the Helm version.

TRY IT NOW Run the to-do app using the same Pod specs but deployed using a Helm chart.

```
# remove all existing apps from the chapter:
kubectl delete all -l kiamol=ch12

# install the Helm release:
helm install --atomic todo-list todo-list/helm/v1/todo-list/

# browse to the app, and add a new item
```

Version 1 of the app is now running through Helm, and there's nothing new here except that the chart contains a file in the templates folder called NOTES.txt, which displays the helpful text you see after installation. My output is shown in figure 12.8. I haven't included an application screenshot, so you'll just have to take my word that I browsed and added an item saying "finish chapter 12."

Installing a release using Helm's atomic option means it will roll back if the deployment fails, including failing container probes.

```
PS>kubectl delete all -l kiamol=ch12
service "numbers-api" deleted
service "todo-db" deleted
service "todo-web" deleted
deployment.apps "numbers-api" deleted
deployment.apps "todo-db" deleted
deployment.apps "todo-web" deleted
PS>
PS>helm install --atomic todo-list todo-list/helm/v1/todo-list/
NAME: todo-list
LAST DEPLOYED: Thu Jun 25 10:23:13 2020
NAMESPACE: default
STATUS: deployed
REVISION: 1
TEST SUITE: None
NOTES:
Installed Kiamol to-do list 0.1.0. This is how to get the URL:
 $ kubectl get svc todo-list-web -o jsonpath='http://{.status.loadBalancer.ingress[
0].*}:8012'
PS>
PS>kubectl get svc todo-list-web -o jsonpath='http://{.status.loadBalancer.ingress[
0].*}:8012'
http://localhost:8012
```

This chart writes out notes after successful deployment, providing the kubectl command you need to run to browse to the app.

Figure 12.8 Installing apps with Helm waits for container probes to be healthy.

Version 2 of the Helm chart attempts the same database image upgrade we saw in section 12.2, complete with the misconfiguration in the command for the Postgres container. When you deploy this with Helm, the same thing happens under the hood: Kubernetes updates the Deployment, which adds a new ReplicaSet, and that Replica-Set never reaches capacity because the Pod readiness probe fails. But Helm checks the status of the rollout, and if it doesn't succeed within a specific period, it automatically rolls back.

TRY IT NOW   Upgrade the to-do app release using Helm. The upgrade fails because the Pod spec is misconfigured, and Helm rolls it back.

```
# list the current Pod status and container image:
kubectl get pods -l app=todo-list-db -o=custom-columns=NAME:.metadata
  .name,STATUS:.status.phase,IMAGE:.spec.containers[0].image

# upgrade the release with Helm—this will fail:
helm upgrade --atomic --timeout 30s todo-list todo-list/helm/v2/todo-
  list/

# list the Pods again:
kubectl get pods -l app=todo-list-db -o=custom-columns=NAME:.metadata
  .name,STATUS:.status.phase,IMAGE:.spec.containers[0].image

# browse back to the app, and refresh the list
```

If you check the Pod list a few times in that exercise, you'll see the rollback happening, as you can see in figure 12.9. At first, there's a single Pod running Postgres 11.6, and then it's joined by a new Pod running 11.8, but that's the Pod with the failing container probes. The Pod isn't ready within the Helm timeout period, so the upgrade is rolled back, and the new Pod is removed; it doesn't keep restarting and hit Crash-LoopBackOff as it did with the kubectl update.

The to-do app has been online without interruption or reduced capacity during the failed upgrade to version 2. The next version fixes the upgrade by removing the bad container command in the Pod spec, and it also adds an extra template for a Kubernetes Job, which you can run as a deployment test with Helm. Tests run on demand and not as part of the install, so they're perfect for smoke tests—automated test suites that you run to confirm that a successful release is working correctly. Listing 12.4 shows a test for the to-do database.

Listing 12.4   todo-db-test-job.yaml, a Kubernetes Job to run as a Helm test

```
apiVersion: batch/v1
kind: Job                       # This is a standard Job spec.
metadata:
  # metadata includes name and labels
  annotations:
    "helm.sh/hook": test        # Tells Helm the Job can be run in the test
spec:                           # suite for the release
  completions: 1
  backoffLimit: 0               # The Job should run once and not retry.
```

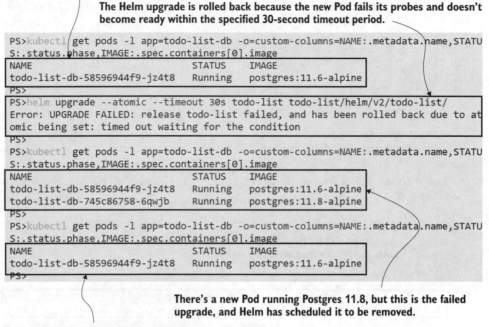

The version 1 Helm release uses Postgres 11.6.

The Helm upgrade is rolled back because the new Pod fails its probes and doesn't become ready within the specified 30-second timeout period.

```
PS>kubectl get pods -l app=todo-list-db -o=custom-columns=NAME:.metadata.name,STATU
S:.status.phase,IMAGE:.spec.containers[0].image
NAME                            STATUS    IMAGE
todo-list-db-58596944f9-jz4t8   Running   postgres:11.6-alpine
PS>
PS>helm upgrade --atomic --timeout 30s todo-list todo-list/helm/v2/todo-list/
Error: UPGRADE FAILED: release todo-list failed, and has been rolled back due to at
omic being set: timed out waiting for the condition
PS>
PS>kubectl get pods -l app=todo-list-db -o=custom-columns=NAME:.metadata.name,STATU
S:.status.phase,IMAGE:.spec.containers[0].image
NAME                            STATUS    IMAGE
todo-list-db-58596944f9-jz4t8   Running   postgres:11.6-alpine
todo-list-db-745c86758-6qwjb    Running   postgres:11.8-alpine
PS>
PS>kubectl get pods -l app=todo-list-db -o=custom-columns=NAME:.metadata.name,STATU
S:.status.phase,IMAGE:.spec.containers[0].image
NAME                            STATUS    IMAGE
todo-list-db-58596944f9-jz4t8   Running   postgres:11.6-alpine
PS>
```

There's a new Pod running Postgres 11.8, but this is the failed upgrade, and Helm has scheduled it to be removed.

Only the original Pod is still running. The upgrade failed gracefully, and the app stayed up.

Figure 12.9 The upgrade fails because the new Pod doesn't become ready, and Helm rolls back.

```
template:
  spec:                        # The container spec runs a SQL query.
    containers:
      - image: postgres:11.8-alpine
        command: ["psql", "-c", "SELECT COUNT(*) FROM \"public\".\"ToDos\""]
```

We met Jobs in chapter 8, and Helm makes good use of them. Job specs include an expectation of how many times they should run to successful completion, and Helm uses that to evaluate if the test succeeds. The version 3 upgrade should succeed, and when it completes, you can run the test Job, which runs a SQL statement to confirm the to-do database is accessible.

TRY IT NOW Upgrade to the version 3 chart, which fixes the Postgres update. Then run the test with Helm, and check the logs for the Job Pod.

```
# run the upgrade:
helm upgrade --atomic --timeout 30s todo-list todo-list/helm/v3/todo-
  list/
```

```
# list the database Pods and images:
kubectl get pods -l app=todo-list-db -o=custom-
   columns=NAME:.metadata.name,STATUS:.status.phase,IMAGE:.spec.contai
   ners[0].image,IP:.status.podIPs[].ip

# check the database Service endpoints:
kubectl get endpoints todo-list-db

# now run the test Job with Helm:
helm test todo-list

# check the output:
kubectl logs -l job-name=todo-list-db-test
```

I've snipped my output in figure 12.10, but the detail is all there—the upgrade is successful, but there are no tests as part of the upgrade command. The database is now

The version 3 chart has fixed the Postgres spec, so now the upgrade is successful.

```
PS>helm upgrade --atomic --timeout 30s todo-list todo-list/helm/v3/todo-list/
Release "todo-list" has been upgraded. Happy Helming!

PS>kubectl get pods -l app=todo-list-db -o=custom-columns=NAME:.metadata.name,STATU
S:.status.phase,IMAGE:.spec.containers[0].image,IP:.status.podIPs[].ip
NAME                             STATUS    IMAGE                IP
todo-list-db-968fff78f-592nt     Running   postgres:11.8-alpine 10.1.1.217
PS>
PS>kubectl get endpoints todo-list-db
NAME            ENDPOINTS         AGE
todo-list-db    10.1.1.217:5432   34m
PS>
PS>helm test todo-list
NAME: todo-list
LAST DEPLOYED: Thu Jun 25 10:55:01 2020
NAMESPACE: default
STATUS: deployed
REVISION: 4
TEST SUITE:      todo-list-db-test
Last Started:    Thu Jun 25 10:58:10 2020
Last Completed:  Thu Jun 25 10:58:12 2020
Phase:           Succeeded

PS>kubectl logs -l job-name=todo-list-db-test
 count
 -------
     1
```

The new database Pod is running the upgraded Postgres version, and its probes are successful, so it's listed as the Service endpoint.

The Helm test suite passes: the Job is not deleted, so the logs are available.

Figure 12.10   Running test suites on demand with Helm lets you smoke-test your app at any time.

using the upgraded version of Postgres, and when the test runs, the Job connects to the database and confirms the data is still there.

Helm manages Jobs for you. It doesn't clean up completed Jobs, so you can check the Pod status and logs if you need to, but it replaces them when you repeat the test command, so you can rerun the test suite as often as you like. There's one other use for Jobs that helps to make sure upgrades are safe, by running them before upgrades so you can check the current release is in a valid state to be upgraded.

This capability is especially useful if you support multiple versions of your app, but only with incremental upgrades, so version 1.1 needs to upgrade to version 1.2 before it can upgrade to version 2. The logic for this might involve querying the API version for different services or the schema version of a database, and Helm can run it all in a Job that has access to all the other Kubernetes objects sharing the same ConfigMaps and Secrets as the application Pods. Listing 12.5 shows a pre-upgrade test in version 4 of the to-do Helm chart.

> **Listing 12.5   todo-db-check-job.yaml, a Job that runs before a Helm upgrade**

```
apiVersion: batch/v1
kind: Job                        # The standard Job spec again
metadata:
  # metadata has name and labels
  annotations:
    "helm.sh/hook": pre-upgrade  # This runs before an upgrade and
    "helm.sh/hook-weight": "10"  # tells Helm the order in which to create
spec:                            # the object after the ConfigMap
  template:                      # that the Job requires
    spec:
      restartPolicy: Never
      containers:
        - image: postgres:11.8-alpine
          # env includes secrets
          command: ["/scripts/check-postgres-version.sh"]
          volumeMounts:
            - name: scripts              # Mounts the ConfigMap volume
              mountPath: "/scripts"
```

There are two templates for the pre-upgrade check: one is the Job spec, and the other is a ConfigMap that contains the script to run in the Job. You use annotations to control where Jobs need to run in the Helm life cycle, and this Job will run only for upgrades, not as part of a new install. The weighting annotations make sure the Config-Map is created before the Job. Life cycles and weights let you model complex validation steps in Helm, but this one is simple—it upgrades the database image but only if the release is currently running version 11.6.

TRY IT NOW   The upgrade from version 3 to version 4 isn't valid because version 3 has already upgraded the Postgres version. Run the upgrade to verify that it doesn't get deployed.

```
# run the upgrade to version 4—this will fail:
helm upgrade --atomic --timeout 30s todo-list todo-list/helm/v4/todo-
   list/

# list the Jobs:
kubectl get jobs --show-labels

# print the output of the pre-upgrade Job:
kubectl logs -l job-name=todo-list-db-check

# confirm that the database Pod is unchanged:
kubectl get pods -l app=todo-list-db -o=custom-
   columns=NAME:.metadata.name,STATUS:.status.phase,IMAGE:.spec.contai
   ners[0].image
```

In this exercise, you'll see that Helm effectively blocks the upgrade, because the pre-upgrade hook runs and the Job fails. That's all recorded in the history for the release, which will show that the latest upgrade failed and the release was rolled back to the last good revision. My output is shown in figure 12.11, and throughout this update, the app was still available.

It's good to understand what Helm brings in terms of keeping your applications healthy, because pre-upgrade validation and automatic rollbacks help to keep your application upgrades self-healing, too. Helm isn't a prerequisite for that, but if you're

This upgrade fails because the pre-upgrade Job didn't complete successfully. Helm doesn't show the output of the Job logs, but the Jobs are retained.

```
PS>helm upgrade --atomic --timeout 30s todo-list todo-list/helm/v4/todo-list/
Error: UPGRADE FAILED: release todo-list failed, and has been rolled back due to at
omic being set: pre-upgrade hooks failed: job failed: BackoffLimitExceeded
PS>
PS>kubectl get jobs --show-labels
NAME                  COMPLETIONS   DURATION   AGE    LABELS
todo-list-db-check    0/1           54s        54s    kiamol=ch12
todo-list-db-test     1/1           2s         30m    kiamol=ch12
PS>
PS>kubectl logs -l job-name=todo-list-db-check
** ERROR - Postgres not at expected version - wanted: 11.6, got: PostgreSQL 11.8 -
CANNOT UPGRADE **
PS>
PS>kubectl get pods -l app=todo-list-db -o=custom-columns=NAME:.metadata.name,STATU
S:.status.phase,IMAGE:.spec.containers[0].image
NAME                             STATUS    IMAGE
todo-list-db-968fff78f-592nt     Running   postgres:11.8-alpine
```

The logs from the failed check Job show the validation logic. This upgrade path is not supported.

The version 3 database Pod is still running, and the app is still working correctly.

Figure 12.11   Pre-upgrade Jobs in Helm charts let you validate that the release is suitable to upgrade.

not using Helm, you should consider implementing these features using kubectl in your deployment pipeline.

There's one more part of application health that we'll cover in this chapter—managing the compute resources available to your Pod containers.

12.4 Protecting apps and nodes with resource limits

Containers are a virtualized environment for your application process. Kubernetes builds that environment, and you know that Kubernetes creates the container file-system and sets up networking. The container environment also includes memory and CPU, and those can be managed by Kubernetes, too, but by default, they're not. That means Pod containers get access to all the memory and CPU on the node where they're running, which is bad for two reasons: apps can max out on memory and crash, or they can starve the node of resources so other apps can't run.

You can limit the resources available to a container in the Pod spec, and those limits are like container probes—you really shouldn't go to production without them. Apps with memory leaks can ruin your cluster very quickly, and causing a CPU spike is a nice, easy attack vector for intruders. In this section, you'll learn how to spec your Pods to prevent that, and we'll start with a new app that has a large appetite for memory.

> **TRY IT NOW** Clear down from the last exercise, and run the new app—it doesn't do anything other than allocate memory and log how much it has allocated. This Pod runs without any container limits.

```
# remove the Helm release to free up resources:
helm uninstall todo-list

# print how much memory your nodes have:
kubectl get nodes -o jsonpath='{.items[].status.allocatable.memory}'

# deploy the memory-allocating app:
kubectl apply -f memory-allocator/

# wait a few minutes, and then see how much memory it has allocated:
kubectl logs -l app=memory-allocator --tail 1
```

The memory-allocator app grabs about 10 MB of memory every five seconds, and it will keep going until it uses all the memory in your lab cluster. You can see from my output in figure 12.12 that my Docker Desktop node has access to about 25 GB of memory, and the allocator app had grabbed almost 1.5 GB when I took the screenshot.

As long as the app is running, it will keep allocating memory, so we need to get on quickly before my machine dies and I lose the edits to this chapter. Listing 12.6 shows an updated Pod spec that includes resource limits, restricting the app to 50 MB of memory.

**Kubectl can query nodes for information in the same way as other objects. My cluster
has a single node with about 25 GB of memory available for Kubernetes.**

```
PS>helm uninstall todo-list
release "todo-list" uninstalled
PS>
PS>kubectl get nodes -o jsonpath='{.items[].status.allocatable.memory}'
26109304Ki
PS>
PS>kubectl apply -f memory-allocator/
deployment.apps/memory-allocator created
PS>
PS># wait a few minutes
PS>
PS>kubectl logs -l app=memory-allocator --tail 1
Allocated ~1450MiB
```

The app in this Pod keeps allocating memory and never releases it.

**After a while, the container has allocated almost
1.5 MB of memory, and it will keep going.**

Figure 12.12 Don't run this app in production— it just keeps allocating memory until it has it all.

Listing 12.6   memory-allocator-with-limit.yaml, adding memory limits to the container

```
spec:                            # The Pod spec in the Deployment
  containers:
    - image: kiamol/ch12-memory-allocator
      resources:
        limits:                  # Resource limits constrain the compute power
          memory: 50Mi           # for the container; this limits RAM to 50 MB.
```

Resources are specified at the container level, but this is a new Pod spec, so when you
deploy the update, you'll get a new Pod. The replacement will start off with zero memory allocated, and it will start allocating 10 MB every five seconds again. Now, however,
it will hit a limit at 50 MB, and Kubernetes will take action.

TRY IT NOW   Deploy an update to the memory-allocator app with the resource
limits defined in listing 12.6. You should see the Pod is restarted, but only if
your Linux host is running without swap memory enabled. K3s doesn't have
that setup (unless you're using the Vagrant VM setup), so you won't see the
same results as Docker Desktop or a cloud Kubernetes service.

```
# appy the update:
kubectl apply -f memory-allocator/update/memory-allocator-with-
  limit.yaml

# wait for the app to allocate a chunk of memory:
sleep 20
```

```
# print the application logs:
kubectl logs -l app=memory-allocator --tail 1

# watch the status of the Pod:
kubectl get pods -l app=memory-allocator --watch
```

In this exercise, you'll see that Kubernetes enforces the memory limit: when the app tries to allocate more than 50 MB of memory, the container is replaced, and you can see the Pod enters the OOMKilled status. Exceeding the limit causes a Pod restart, so this has the same drawback as a failing liveness probe—if the replacement containers keep failing, the Pod restarts will take longer and longer as Kubernetes applies Crash-LoopBackOff, as you see in figure 12.13.

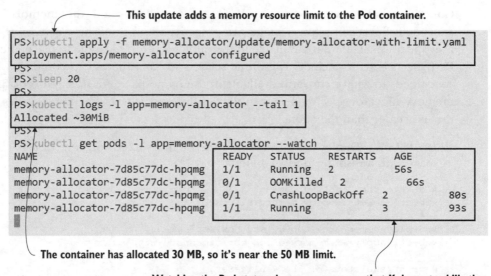

This update adds a memory resource limit to the Pod container.

```
PS>kubectl apply -f memory-allocator/update/memory-allocator-with-limit.yaml
deployment.apps/memory-allocator configured
PS>
PS>sleep 20
PS>
PS>kubectl logs -l app=memory-allocator --tail 1
Allocated ~30MiB
PS>
PS>kubectl get pods -l app=memory-allocator --watch
NAME                                  READY   STATUS            RESTARTS   AGE
memory-allocator-7d85c77dc-hpqmg      1/1     Running           2          56s
memory-allocator-7d85c77dc-hpqmg      0/1     OOMKilled         2          66s
memory-allocator-7d85c77dc-hpqmg      0/1     CrashLoopBackOff  2          80s
memory-allocator-7d85c77dc-hpqmg      1/1     Running           3          93s
```

The container has allocated 30 MB, so it's near the 50 MB limit.

Watching the Pod status change, you can see that Kubernetes kills the container when it exceeds the memory limit. The Pod restarts and flips between Running and CrashLoopBackoff status.

Figure 12.13 Memory limits are hard limits—if a container exceeds them, it gets killed and the Pod restarts.

The hard part of applying resource constraints is working out what the limits should be. You'll need to factor in some performance testing to see what your app can manage with—be aware that some application platforms will grab more than they need if they see lots of available memory. You should be generous with your initial releases and then look to bring the limits down as you get more feedback from your monitoring.

You can apply resource limits in another way, too—by specifying maximum quotas for a namespace. This method is especially useful for shared clusters where you use namespaces to divide the cluster for different teams or environments; you can enforce limits on the total amount of resources the namespace can use. Listing 12.7 shows the spec for a ResourceQuota object, which restricts the total amount of memory available to 150 MB in the namespace called `kiamol-ch12-memory`.

```
apiVersion: v1
kind: ResourceQuota                      # The ResourceQuota is applied
metadata:                                # at the specified namespace.
  name: memory-quota
  namespace: kiamol-ch12-memory
spec:
  hard:                                  # Quotas can include CPU and memory.
    limits.memory: 150Mi
```

Container limits are reactive, so Pods are restarted when the memory limit is exceeded. Because resource quotas are proactive, Pods won't be created if the limits they specify exceed what's available in the quota. If there's a quota in place, then every Pod spec needs to include a resource section so Kubernetes can compare what the spec needs to what's currently available in the namespace. An updated version of the memory-allocator spec to demonstrate that follows, where the Pod specifies a limit that is greater than the quota.

> **TRY IT NOW**   Deploy a new version of the memory allocator in its own namespace with a resource quota applied.

```
# delete the existing app:
kubectl delete deploy memory-allocator

# deploy namespace, quota, and new Deployment:
kubectl apply -f memory-allocator/namespace-with-quota/

# print the staus of the ReplicaSet:
kubectl get replicaset -n kiamol-ch12-memory

# show the events in the ReplicaSet:
kubectl describe replicaset -n kiamol-ch12-memory
```

You'll see from the output of the ReplicaSet that it has zero Pods out of a desired total of one. It can't create the Pod because it would exceed the quota for the namespace, as you can see in figure 12.14. The controller keeps trying to create the Pod, but it won't succeed unless enough quota becomes available, such as from other Pods terminating, but in this case there aren't any, so it would need to be an update to the quota.

Kubernetes can also apply CPU limits to containers and quotas, but they work in a slightly different way. Containers with a CPU limit run with a fixed amount of processing power, and they can use as much of that CPU as they like—they aren't replaced if they hit the limit. You can limit a container to one half of a CPU core, and it can run at 100% CPU while all the other cores on the node remain idle and available for other

Deploys a quota in the namespace with a 150 MB memory limit and a Pod spec that sets a 200 MB memory limit

The ReplicaSet cannot create the Pod because there is not enough memory quota in the namespace.

```
PS>kubectl delete deploy memory-allocator
deployment.apps "memory-allocator" deleted
PS>
PS>kubectl apply -f memory-allocator/namespace-with-quota/
namespace/kiamol-ch12-memory created
resourcequota/memory-quota created
deployment.apps/memory-allocator created
PS>
PS>kubectl get replicaset -n kiamol-ch12-memory
NAME                          DESIRED   CURRENT   READY   AGE
memory-allocator-579cb6f6d7   1         0         0       6s
PS>
PS>kubectl describe replicaset -n kiamol-ch12-memory
Name:           memory-allocator-579cb6f6d7
Namespace:      kiamol-ch12-memory

Conditions:
  Type             Status   Reason
  ----             ------   ------
  ReplicaFailure   True     FailedCreate
Events:
  Type      Reason        Age    From                   Message
  ----      ------        ----   ----                   -------
  Warning   FailedCreate  19s    replicaset-controller  Error creating: p
ods "memory-allocator-579cb6f6d7-782qs" is forbidden: exceeded quota: memory-quota,
 requested: limits.memory=200Mi, used: limits.memory=0, limited: limits.memory=150M
```

The events in the ReplicaSet show this is a quota issue, but the controller will keep trying to create the Pod.

Figure 12.14 Quotas with hard limits prevent Pods being created if they would exceed the quota.

containers. Calculating Pi is a compute-intensive operation, and we can see the effect of applying a CPU limit on the Pi application we've used before in the book.

TRY IT NOW Run the Pi application with and without CPU limits, and compare its performance.

```
# show the total CPU available to the nodes:
kubectl get nodes -o jsonpath='{.items[].status.allocatable.cpu}'

# deploy Pi without any CPU limits:
kubectl apply -f pi/

# get the URL for the app:
kubectl get svc pi-web -o jsonpath='http://{.status.loadBalancer
  .ingress[0].*}:8012/?dp=50000'
```

```
# browse to the URL, and see how long the calculation takes

# now update the Pod spec with a CPU limit:
kubectl apply -f pi/update/web-with-cpu-limit.yaml

# refresh the Pi app, and see how long the calculation takes
```

My output is shown in figure 12.15. Your timings will be different, depending on how much CPU is available on your node. Mine has eight cores, and with no limits, the app calculates Pi to 50,000 decimal places consistently within 3.4 seconds. After the update, the app container is limited to one quarter of one core, and the same calculation takes 14.4 seconds.

My cluster has one node with eight CPU cores available to it.

Running the Pi app with no CPU limits takes 3.3 seconds to compute Pi to 50,000 decimal places.

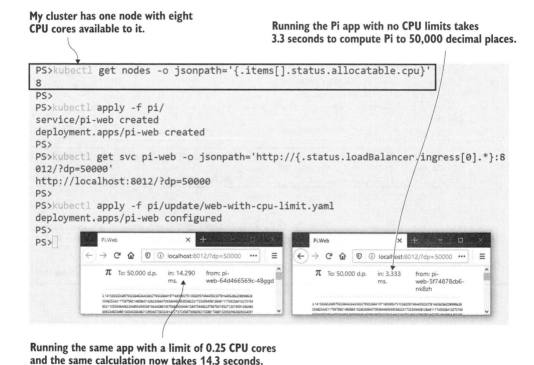

Running the same app with a limit of 0.25 CPU cores and the same calculation now takes 14.3 seconds.

Figure 12.15   Squint and you'll see that limiting CPU has an impact on calculation speed.

Kubernetes defines CPU limits using a fixed unit, where one represents a single core. You can use multiples to give your app container access to many cores or divide a single core into "millicores," where one millicore is one-thousandth of a core. Listing 12.8 shows the CPU limit applied to the Pi container from the previous exercise, where 250 millicores is one quarter of one core.

Listing 12.8   web-with-cpu-limit.yaml

```
spec:
  containers:
    - image: kiamol/ch05-pi
      command: ["dotnet", "Pi.Web.dll", "-m", "web"]
      resources:
        limits:
            cpu: 250m    # 250 millicores limits the container to 0.25 cores.
```

I'm focusing on one resource at a time so you can clearly see the impact, but typically you should include both CPU and memory limits so your apps don't surge and starve the cluster. Resource specs can also include a *requests* section, which states how much CPU and memory the container is expected to use. That helps Kubernetes decide which node should run the Pod, and we'll cover it more when we get to scheduling in chapter 18.

We'll finish this chapter with one more exercise to show how CPU limits can be applied to a quota for a namespace and what it means when the quota is exceeded. The new spec for the Pi application tries to run two replicas with 300 millicore CPU limits in a namespace that has a quota with a maximum of 500 millicores.

TRY IT NOW   Run an updated Pi application in its own namespace, which has a CPU quota applied.

```
# remove the existing app:
kubectl delete deploy pi-web

# deploy the namespace, quota, and new app spec:
kubectl apply -f pi/namespace-with-quota/

# print the ReplicaSet status:
kubectl get replicaset -n kiamol-ch12-cpu

# list the endpoints for the Service:
kubectl get endpoints pi-web -n kiamol-ch12-cpu

# show the events for the ReplicaSet:
kubectl describe replicaset -n kiamol-ch12-cpu
```

In this exercise, you can see that quotas apply across all Pods in the namespace. The ReplicaSet is running with one Pod instead of two, because the first Pod allocated 300 m CPU, which only left 200 m in the quota—not enough for the second Pod to run. Figure 12.16 shows the failure reason in the events for the ReplicaSet. The Pi app is still running but under capacity because there isn't enough CPU available.

Quotas are more for protecting your cluster than the apps themselves, but they're a good way of enforcing that all Pod specs have limits specified. If you're not dividing up your cluster with namespaces, you can still apply a quota with large CPU and memory limits to the default namespace to make sure Pod specs include limits of their own.

**Deploys the Pi app with two replicas, each set with a 300 millicore
CPU limit, into a namespace set with a 500 millicore CPU quota**

The ReplicaSet creates only one Pod.

```
PS>kubectl delete deploy pi-web
deployment.apps "pi-web" deleted
PS>
PS>kubectl apply -f pi/namespace-with-quota/
namespace/kiamol-ch12-cpu created
resourcequota/cpu-quota created
service/pi-web created
deployment.apps/pi-web created
PS>
PS>kubectl get replicaset -n kiamol-ch12-cpu
NAME                    DESIRED   CURRENT   READY   AGE
pi-web-5fc85c7d69       2         1         1       8s
PS>
PS>kubectl get endpoints pi-web -n kiamol-ch12-cpu
NAME      ENDPOINTS        AGE
pi-web    10.1.1.225:80    16s
PS>
PS>kubectl describe replicaset -n kiamol-ch12-cpu
Name:          pi-web-5fc85c7d69
Namespace:     kiamol-ch12-cpu

Conditions:
  Type             Status   Reason
  ----             ------   ------
  ReplicaFailure   True     FailedCreate
Events:
  Type      Reason           Age     From                    Message
  ----      ------           ----    ----                    -------
  Normal    SuccessfulCreate 39s     replicaset-controller   Created pod:
pi-web-5fc85c7d69-7kdss
  Warning   FailedCreate     39s     replicaset-controller   Error creatin
g: pods "pi-web-5fc85c7d69-gtcfm" is forbidden: exceeded quota: cpu-quota, requeste
d: limits.cpu=300m, used: limits.cpu=300m, limited: limits.cpu=500m
```

The Service is using the Pod.

**The controller can't create the second Pod because
there's not enough CPU quota remaining.**

Figure 12.16   Hard CPU limits in quotas are enforced to block objects from exceeding the total limit.

Resource limits, container probes, and atomic upgrades all help to keep your apps running in the face of normal failure conditions. These should be on your road map to production, but you also need to be aware that Kubernetes can't repair every kind of failure.

12.5 *Understanding the limits of self-healing apps*

Kubernetes allocates a Pod to a node, and that's the node where it will run. Pods aren't replaced unless the node goes offline, so all the repair mechanisms we've seen in this chapter work by restarting the Pod—replacing the application container. You need to make sure your app can tolerate that, especially in the multicontainer scenarios we covered in chapter 7, because init containers are executed again and sidecars are replaced when a Pod restarts.

Pod restarts are fine for most scenarios with temporary failures, but repeated failures will end up in a CrashLoopBackOff state, which can take your app offline. Kubernetes doesn't provide any configuration options for how many restarts are allowed or the backoff period, and it doesn't support replacing failed Pods with a new Pod on a different node. Those features are requested, but until they land, your nicely configured self-healing app still has the potential for all its Pods to be in a backoff state with no endpoints in the Service.

That edge case usually appears as a result of misconfigured specs or fatal problems with the application, which take more intervention than Kubernetes can manage by itself. For the typical failure states, the combination of container probes and resource limits go a long way to keeping your app running smoothly all by itself.

And that's all for self-healing apps, so we can tidy up the cluster in preparation for the lab.

TRY IT NOW   Remove the objects from this chapter.

```
# delete namespaces:
kubectl delete ns -l kiamol=ch12
kubectl delete all -l kiamol=ch12

# delete all the leftover objects:
kubectl delete secret,configmap,pvc -l kiamol=ch12
```

12.6 *Lab*

I've got a nice little capacity-planning exercise for you in this lab. The goal is to divide your cluster into three environments to run the Pi app: dev, test, and UAT. UAT should be limited to 50% of your node's total CPU, and dev and test to 25% each. Your Pi Deployment should be set with limits so it can run at least four replicas in every environment, and then you need to verify how much you can scale up to in UAT.

- Start by deploying the namespaces and Services in the lab folder.
- Then work out the CPU capacity of your node, and deploy resource quotas to limit CPU in each namespace (you'll need to write the quota specs).
- Update the Deployment spec in web.yaml to include a CPU limit that allows four replicas to run in each namespace.
- When everything's running, scale up the UAT Deployment to eight replicas, and try to find out why they don't all run.

This is a good exercise to help you understand how CPU resources get shared and to practice working with multiple namespaces. My solution is on GitHub for you to check: https://github.com/sixeyed/kiamol/blob/master/ch12/lab/README.md.

Centralizing logs with Fluentd and Elasticsearch

Applications generate lots of logs, which often aren't very useful. As you scale up your apps across multiple Pods running in a cluster, it's difficult to manage those logs using standard Kubernetes tooling. Organizations usually deploy their own logging framework, which uses a collect-and-forward model to read container logs and send them to a central store where they can be indexed, filtered, and searched. You'll learn how to do that in this chapter using the most popular technologies in this space: Fluentd and Elasticsearch. Fluentd is the collector component, and it has some nice integrations with Kubernetes; Elasticsearch is the storage component and can run either as Pods in the cluster or as an external service.

You should be aware of a couple of points before we start. The first is that this model assumes your application logs are written to the container's standard output streams so Kubernetes can find them. We covered that in chapter 7, with sample apps that wrote to standard out directly or used a logging sidecar to relay logs. The second is that the logging model in Kubernetes is very different from Docker. Appendix D in the ebook shows you how to use Fluentd with Docker, but with Kubernetes, we'll take a different approach.

13.1 How Kubernetes stores log entries

Kubernetes has a very simplistic approach to log management: it collects log entries from the container runtime and stores them as files on the node running the container. If you want to do anything more advanced, then you need to deploy your own log management system, and, fortunately, you have a world-class container platform on which to run it. The moving pieces of the logging system collect

Container logs are stored as files on the node running the Pod.	**The collector forwards logs to a central store, which has a search UI. We'll use Elasticsearch for storage and Kibana for the UI.**

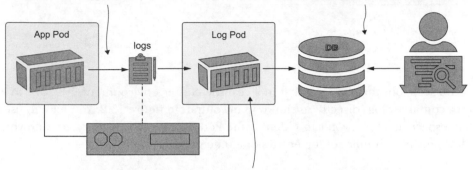

A log collector Pod runs on every node and mounts the host path where the log files are stored, so it can read them. We'll use Fluentd to collect and process logs.

Figure 13.1   Logging in Kubernetes uses a collector like Fluentd to read the log files from the node.

logs from the nodes, forward them to a centralized store, and provide a UI to search and filter them. Figure 13.1 shows the technologies we'll use in this chapter.

Nodes store log entries exactly as they come from the container, using filenames that include the namespace, Pod, and container names. The standard naming system makes it easy for the log collector to add metadata to the log entries to identify the source, and because the collector runs as a Pod itself, it can query the Kubernetes API server to get even more details. Fluentd adds Pod labels and the image tag as additional metadata, which you can use to filter or search the logs.

Deploying the log collector is straightforward. We'll start by exploring the raw log files on the node to see what we're working with. The prerequisite for any of this is to get application logs out of the container, whether the app writes those logs directly or you use a sidecar container. Start by deploying the timecheck app from chapter 7 in a couple of different configurations to generate some logs.

TRY IT NOW   Run the timecheck app using different setups in different namespaces, and then check the logs to see how you work with them natively in kubectl.

```
# switch to the chapter's folder:
cd ch13

# deploy the timecheck app in development and test namespaces:
kubectl apply -f timecheck/

# wait for the development namespace to spin up:
kubectl wait --for=condition=ContainersReady pod -l app=timecheck -n
  kiamol-ch13-dev

# check the logs:
kubectl logs -l app=timecheck --all-containers -n kiamol-ch13-dev
  --tail 1
```

```
# wait for the test namespace to spin up:
kubectl wait --for=condition=ContainersReady pod -l app=timecheck -n
  kiamol-ch13-test

# check those logs:
kubectl logs -l app=timecheck --all-containers -n kiamol-ch13-test
  --tail 1
```

You'll see from that exercise that in a realistic cluster environment, it's hard to work with container logs directly, as shown in my output in figure 13.2. You have to use one namespace at a time, you can't identify the Pod that logged the message, and you can filter only by a number of log entries or a time period.

This runs the timecheck app in two namespaces, using two Pods in the test namespace. That will produce a lot of log entries.

To read the dev logs, you need to specify a label selector and a namespace.

```
PS>cd ch13
PS>
PS>kubectl apply -f timecheck/
namespace/kiamol-ch13-dev created
deployment.apps/timecheck created
namespace/kiamol-ch13-test created
configmap/timecheck-config created
deployment.apps/timecheck created
PS>
PS>kubectl wait --for=condition=ContainersReady pod -l app=timecheck -n kiamol-ch13
-dev
pod/timecheck-555555bfd-vjzhz condition met
PS>
PS>kubectl logs -l app=timecheck --all-containers -n kiamol-ch13-dev --tail 1
2020-06-29 20:06:17.779 +00:00 [INF] Environment: DEV; version: 1.0; time check: 20
:06.17
PS>
PS>kubectl wait --for=condition=ContainersReady pod -l app=timecheck -n kiamol-ch13
-test
pod/timecheck-cf4d4f685-fz5m7 condition met
pod/timecheck-cf4d4f685-rwq4c condition met
PS>
PS>kubectl logs -l app=timecheck --all-containers -n kiamol-ch13-test --tail 1
2020-06-29 20:06:42.821 +00:00 [INF] Environment: TEST; version: 1.1; time check: 2
0:06.42
2020-06-29 20:06:33.996 +00:00 [INF] Environment: TEST; version: 1.1; time check: 2
0:06.33
```

In the test, you can see the latest log from each Pod, but there's no way to identify which Pod wrote the log. Kubectl 1.18 addresses that with a `prefix` option, but without that, it's hard to correlate the output with the app.

Figure 13.2   Kubectl is great for quickly checking logs, but it's harder with many Pods in many namespaces.

Kubectl is the simplest option for reading logs, but ultimately the log entries come from the files on each node, which means you have other options to work with logs. The source for this chapter includes a simple sleep Deployment that mounts the log path on the node as a `HostPath` volume, and you can use that to explore the log files, even if you don't have direct access to the nodes.

> **TRY IT NOW** Run a Pod with a volume mount for the host's log directory, and explore the files using the mount.

```
# run the Deployment:
kubectl apply -f sleep.yaml

# connect to a session in the Pod container:
kubectl exec -it deploy/sleep -- sh

# browse to the host log mount:
cd /var/log/containers/

# list the timecheck log files:
ls timecheck*kiamol-ch13*_logger*

# view the contents of the dev log file:
cat $(ls timecheck*kiamol-ch13-dev_logger*) | tail -n 1

# exit from the session:
exit
```

Each Pod container has a file for its log output. The timecheck app uses a sidecar container called `logger` to relay the logs from the application container, and you can see in figure 13.3 the standard naming convention Kubernetes uses for log files: `pod-name _namespace_container-name-container-id.log`. The filename has enough data to identify the source of the logs, and the content of the file is the raw JSON log output from the container runtime.

Log files are retained after a Pod restart, but most Kubernetes implementations include a log rotation system running on the nodes—outside of Kubernetes—to prevent logs from swallowing up all your disk space. Collecting and forwarding logs to a central store lets you keep them for longer and isolate log storage in one place—that also applies to logs from core Kubernetes components. The Kubernetes DNS server, API server, and network proxy all run as Pods, and you can view and collect logs from them in the same way as from application logs.

> **TRY IT NOW** Not every Kubernetes node runs the same core components, but you can use the sleep Pod to see which common components are running on your node.

```
# connect to a session in the Pod:
kubectl exec -it deploy/sleep -- sh

# browse to the host path volume:
cd /var/log/containers/
```

```
# the network proxy runs on every node:
cat $(ls kube-proxy*) | tail -n 1

# if your cluster uses Core DNS, you'll see logs here:
cat $(ls coredns*) | tail -n 1

# if your node is running the API server, you'll see these logs:
cat $(ls kube-apiserver*) | tail -n 1

# leave the session:
exit
```

This Pod spec has a volume mount to the log directory on the host node, where all the container log files are stored.

The log filenames use a standard format, including the Pod name, namespace, container name, and container ID.

```
PS>kubectl apply -f sleep.yaml
deployment.apps/sleep created
PS>
PS>kubectl exec -it deploy/sleep -- sh
/ #
/ # cd /var/log/containers/
/var/log/containers #
/var/log/containers # ls timecheck*kiamol-ch13*_logger*
timecheck-555555bfd-vjzhz_kiamol-ch13-dev_logger-0758af957fff1a7b102cfde7956964ac30
d8e636ecb33a13e6b222e59eecf74f.log
timecheck-cf4d4f685-fz5m7_kiamol-ch13-test_logger-c701156604fbbfb0ae3695b0d5e4763d1
1cd8ee8612cdbc8308585960e1d39da.log
timecheck-cf4d4f685-rwq4c_kiamol-ch13-test_logger-d71b15d0d35bdc1ce0e0625d477634c32
e0acaea9cb3231dbf88978aa1b2ff86.log
/var/log/containers #
/var/log/containers # cat $(ls timecheck*kiamol-ch13-dev_logger*) | tail -n 1
{"log":"2020-06-29 20:17:22.779 +00:00 [INF] Environment: DEV; version: 1.0; time c
heck: 20:17.22\n","stream":"stdout","time":"2020-06-29T20:17:23.682712Z"}
/var/log/containers #
/var/log/containers # exit
PS>
```

Log entries are stored as JSON with fields for the message, timestamp, and stream.

Figure 13.3   For a modern platform, Kubernetes has an old-school approach to log storage.

You might get a different output from that exercise, depending on how your lab cluster is set up. The network proxy Pod runs on every node, so you should see those logs, but you'll only see DNS logs if your cluster is using CoreDNS (which is the default DNS plugin), and you'll only see API server logs if your node is running the API server. My output from Docker Desktop is shown in figure 13.4; if you see something different, you can run ls *.log to see all the Pod log files on your node.

Now that you know how container logs are processed and stored by Kubernetes, you can see how a centralized log system makes troubleshooting so much easier. A

Core Kubernetes components run in Pods, and the container log output is stored in
the same way as application Pods, in log files on the node.

```
PS>kubectl exec -it deploy/sleep -- sh
/ #
/ # cd /var/log/containers/
/var/log/containers #
/var/log/containers # cat $(ls kube-proxy*) | tail -n 1
{"log":"I0629 19:55:09.045880       1 shared_informer.go:230] Caches are synced for
 endpoints config \n","stream":"stderr","time":"2020-06-29T19:55:09.0493553Z"}
/var/log/containers #
/var/log/containers # cat $(ls coredns*) | tail -n 1
{"log":"linux/amd64, go1.12.8, 795a3eb\n","stream":"stdout","time":"2020-06-29T19:5
5:09.2239534Z"}
/var/log/containers #
/var/log/containers # cat $(ls kube-apiserver*) | tail -n 1
{"log":"I0629 20:05:45.466396       1 controller.go:606] quota admission added eval
uator for: events.events.k8s.io\n","stream":"stderr","time":"2020-06-29T20:05:45.46
65941Z"}
/var/log/containers #
/var/log/containers # exit
```

None of these entries are very entertaining, but you should collect core
system logs as well as application logs for troubleshooting cluster issues.

Figure 13.4   Collecting and forwarding logs from the node will also include all the system Pod logs.

collector runs on every node, grabbing entries from the log files and forwarding
them. In the rest of the chapter, you'll learn how to implement that with the EFK stack:
Elasticsearch, Fluentd, and Kibana.

13.2   Collecting logs from nodes with Fluentd

Fluentd is a CNCF project, so it has a sound foundation behind it and is a mature and
popular product. Alternative log collection components exist, but Fluentd is a good
choice because it has a powerful processing pipeline to manipulate and filter log
entries as well as a pluggable architecture, so it can forward logs to different storage
systems. It also comes in two variants: the full Fluentd is fast and efficient and has
more than 1,000 plugins, but we'll be using the minimal alternative, called Fluent Bit.

Fluent Bit was originally developed as a lightweight version of Fluentd for embedded applications like IoT devices, but it has all the functionality you need for log
aggregation in a full Kubernetes cluster. Every node will run a log collector, so it
makes sense to keep the impact of that component small, and Fluent Bit happily runs
in a few tens of megabytes of memory. The Fluent Bit architecture in Kubernetes is
straightforward: a DaemonSet runs a collector Pod on every node, which uses a Host-
Path volume mount to access the log files, just like in the sleep example we've used.
Fluent Bit supports different outputs, so we'll start simple and just log to the console
in the Fluent Bit Pod.

TRY IT NOW   Deploy Fluent Bit with a configuration set up to read the time-check log files and write them to the standard output stream of the Fluent Bit container.

```
# deploy the DaemonSet and ConfigMap:
kubectl apply -f fluentbit/

# wait for Fluent Bit to start up:
kubectl wait --for=condition=ContainersReady pod -l app=fluent-bit -n
  kiamol-ch13-logging

# check the logs of the Fluent Bit Pod:
kubectl logs  -l app=fluent-bit -n kiamol-ch13-logging --tail 2
```

My output is shown in figure 13.5, where you can see the logs from the timecheck containers being surfaced in the Fluent Bit container. The Pods creating the log entries are in different namespaces, but Fluent Bit reads them from the files on the node. The content is the raw JSON plus a more precise timestamp, which Fluent Bit adds to each log entry.

Deploys the Fluent Bit log processor in its own logging namespace.

```
PS>kubectl apply -f fluentbit/
namespace/kiamol-ch13-logging created
configmap/fluent-bit-config created
daemonset.apps/fluent-bit created
PS>
PS>kubectl wait --for=condition=ContainersReady pod -l app=fluent-bit -n kiamol-ch1
3-logging
pod/fluent-bit-wwmzq condition met
PS>
PS>kubectl logs  -l app=fluent-bit -n kiamol-ch13-logging --tail 2
{"date":1593502383.721161,"log":"2020-06-30 07:33:02.957 +00:00 [INF] Environment:
DEV; version: 1.0; time check: 07:33.02\n","stream":"stdout","time":"2020-06-30T07:
33:03.7211608Z"}
{"date":1593502386.98684,"log":"2020-06-30 07:33:06.659 +00:00 [INF] Environment: T
EST; version: 1.1; time check: 07:33.06\n","stream":"stdout","time":"2020-06-30T07:
33:06.9868398Z"}
```

Fluent Bit is configured to read the timecheck log files as input and forward them to its own standard output stream. You can see log entries from both the dev and test namespaces.

Figure 13.5   A very basic Fluent Bit configuration can still aggregate log entries from multiple Pods.

There's nothing in the DaemonSet spec for Fluent Bit that you haven't already seen. I'm using a separate namespace for logging because you typically want it to run as a shared service used by all the applications running on the cluster, and a namespace is a good way to isolate all the objects. It's simple to run the Fluent Bit Pods—the complexity comes in configuring the log-processing pipeline, and we'll need to dive into that to get the most out of the logging model. Figure 13.6 shows the stages of the pipeline and how you can use them.

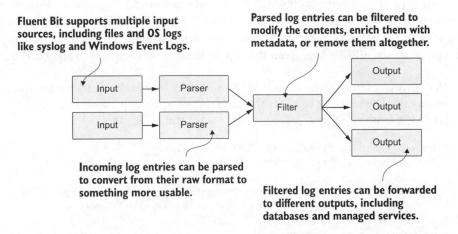

Figure 13.6   Fluent Bit's processing pipeline is super flexible and uses plugin modules for every stage.

We're currently running a simple configuration with three stages: the *input* stage reads log files, the *parser* stage deconstructs the JSON log entries, and the *output* stage writes each log as a separate line to the standard output stream in the Fluent Bit container. The JSON parser is standard for all container logs and isn't very interesting, so we'll focus on the input and output configuration in listing 13.1.

> **Listing 13.1   fluentbit-config.yaml, a simple Fluent Bit pipeline**

```
[INPUT]
    Name             tail           # Reads from the end of a file
    Tag              kube.*         # Uses a prefix for the tag
    Path             /var/log/containers/timecheck*.log
    Parser           docker         # Parses the JSON container logs
    Refresh_Interval 10        # Sets the frequency to check the file list

[OUTPUT]
    Name             stdout         # Writes to standard out
    Format           json_lines     # Formats each log as a line
    Match            kube.*         # Writes logs with a kube tag prefix
```

Fluent Bit uses *tags* to identify the source of a log entry. The tag is added at the input stage and can be used to route logs to other stages. In this configuration, the log file name is used as the tag, prefixed with kube. The match rule routes all the kube tagged entries to the output stage so every log is printed out, but the input stage reads only the timecheck log files, so those are the only log entries you see.

You don't really want to filter the input files—that's just a quick way to get started without flooding you with log entries. It's better to read all the input and then route logs based on tags, so you store only the entries you're interested in. Fluent Bit has built-in support for Kubernetes with a *filter* that can enrich log entries with metadata to identify the Pod that created it. The filter can also be configured to build a custom tag for each log that includes the namespace and Pod name; using that, you can alter the pipeline so only the logs from the test namespace are written to standard out.

TRY IT NOW   Update the Fluent Bit ConfigMap to use the Kubernetes filter, restart the DaemonSet to apply the configuration change, and then print the latest log from the timecheck app to see what the filter does.

```
# update the data pipeline configuration files:
kubectl apply -f fluentbit/update/fluentbit-config-match.yaml

# restart the DaemonSet so a new Pod gets the changed configuration:
kubectl rollout restart ds/fluent-bit -n kiamol-ch13-logging

# wait for the new logging Pod:
kubectl wait --for=condition=ContainersReady pod -l app=fluent-bit -n
  kiamol-ch13-logging

# print the last log entry:
kubectl logs  -l app=fluent-bit -n kiamol-ch13-logging --tail 1
```

You can see from my output in figure 13.7 that a lot more data is coming through Fluent Bit—the log entry is the same, but it's been enriched with the details of the source of the log. The Kubernetes filter fetches all that data from the API server, which gives you the additional context you really need when you're analyzing logs to track down issues. Seeing the image hash for the container will let you check the software version with complete certainty.

The Fluent Bit configuration for this is a little bit tricky. The Kubernetes filter works out of the box to fetch all the Pod metadata, but building a custom tag for routing needs some fiddly regular expressions. That's all in the configuration files in the ConfigMap you deployed in the previous exercise, but I'm not going to focus on it because I really dislike regular expressions. There's also no need—the setup is completely generic, so you can plug the input, filter, and parser configurations into your own cluster, and it will work for your apps without any changes.

The output configuration will be different because that's how you configure the targets. We'll look at one more feature of Fluent Bit before we plug in the log storage and search components—routing log entries to different outputs. The regular expression in the input configuration sets a custom tag for entries in the format kube.namespace.container_name.pod_name, and that can be used in matches to route logs differently based on their namespace or pod name. Listing 13.2 shows an updated output configuration with multiple destinations.

This updated configuration applies the Kubernetes filter and restricts the
output to logs from the `test` namespace.

Fluent Bit doesn't pick up configuration changes, so the Pod needs to be restarted.

```
PS>kubectl apply -f fluentbit/update/fluentbit-config-match.yaml
configmap/fluent-bit-config configured
PS>
PS>kubectl rollout restart ds/fluent-bit -n kiamol-ch13-logging
daemonset.apps/fluent-bit restarted
PS>
PS>kubectl wait --for=condition=ContainersReady pod -l app=fluent-bit -n kiamol-ch1
3-logging
pod/fluent-bit-dfv2w condition met
PS>
PS>kubectl logs  -l app=fluent-bit -n kiamol-ch13-logging --tail 1
{"date":1593505469.649095,"log":"2020-06-30 08:24:28.869 +00:00 [INF] Environment:
TEST; version: 1.1; time check: 08:24.28\n","stream":"stdout","time":"2020-06-30T08
:24:29.6490953Z","kubernetes":{"pod_name":"timecheck-cf4d4f685-rwq4c","namespace_na
me":"kiamol-ch13-test","pod_id":"9e8420f6-4cf5-4fc2-980d-7ce1870bae4d","labels":{"a
pp":"timecheck","pod-template-hash":"cf4d4f685"},"host":"docker-desktop","container
_name":"logger","docker_id":"fad628e7a3d248c9c882816191a34976525b158b9a9ca48bf86352
11336149c9","container_hash":"kiamol/ch03-sleep@sha256:f5edb5cb6df332c1bd77b33e4af1
13a3418666638065d074f8ae1abb4b5af567","container_image":"kiamol/ch03-sleep:latest"}
}
```

The timecheck app is producing the same log entries, and the Kubernetes filter enriches
them with metadata about the source, including the Pod name, the container image tag,
and the unique hash of the image.

Figure 13.7   Filters enrich log entries—the single log message now has 14 additional metadata fields.

Listing 13.2   fluentbit-config-match-multiple.yaml, routing to multiple outputs

```
[OUTPUT]
    Name      stdout                       # The standard out plugin will
    Format    json_lines                   # print only log entries where
    Match     kube.kiamol-ch13-test.*      # the namespace is test.


[OUTPUT]
    Name      counter                      # The counter prints a count of
    Match     kube.kiamol-ch13-dev.*       # logs from the dev namespace.
```

Fluent Bit supports many output plugins, from plain TCP to Postgres and cloud services like Azure Log Analytics. We've used the standard output stream so far, which
just relays log entries to the console. The counter plugin is a simple output that just
prints how many log entries have been collected. When you deploy the new configuration, you'll continue to see the log lines from the test namespace, and you'll also see a
count of log entries from the dev namespace.

TRY IT NOW   Update the configuration to use multiple outputs, and print the logs from the Fluent Bit Pod.

```
# update the configuration and restart Fluent Bit:
kubectl apply -f fluentbit/update/fluentbit-config-match-multiple.yaml

kubectl rollout restart ds/fluent-bit  n kiamol-ch13-logging

kubectl wait --for=condition=ContainersReady pod -l app=fluent-bit -n
  kiamol-ch13-logging

# print the last two log lines:
kubectl logs  -l app=fluent-bit -n kiamol-ch13-logging --tail 2
```

The counter in this exercise isn't especially useful, but it's there to show you that the complex bits in the early part of the pipeline make for easy routing later in the pipeline. Figure 13.8 shows I have different output for logs in different namespaces, and I can configure that purely using match rules in the output stages.

It should be clear how you can plug a sophisticated logging system on top of the simple log files that Kubernetes writes. The data pipeline in Fluent Bit lets you enrich log entries and route them to different outputs. If the output you want to use

This configuration update sets two outputs: standard out for logs from the `test` namespace and a simple counter for logs from the `dev` namespace.

```
PS>kubectl apply -f fluentbit/update/fluentbit-config-match-multiple.yaml
configmap/fluent-bit-config configured
PS>
PS>kubectl rollout restart ds/fluent-bit -n kiamol-ch13-logging
daemonset.apps/fluent-bit restarted
PS>
PS>kubectl wait --for=condition=ContainersReady pod -l app=fluent-bit -n kiamol-ch1
3-logging
pod/fluent-bit-psg64 condition met
PS>
PS>kubectl logs  -l app=fluent-bit -n kiamol-ch13-logging --tail 2
{"date":1593508266.990381,"log":"2020-06-30 09:11:06.659 +00:00 [INF] Environment:
TEST; version: 1.1; time check: 09:11.06\n","stream":"stdout","time":"2020-06-30T09
:11:06.9903809Z","kubernetes":{"pod_name":"timecheck-cf4d4f685-fz5m7","namespace_na
me":"kiamol-ch13-test","pod_id":"6306ef10-7337-4957-a5cb-588a694bbe51","labels":{"a
pp":"timecheck","pod-template-hash":"cf4d4f685"},"host":"docker-desktop","container
_name":"logger","docker_id":"5b995663270a1a568e5667e9ab00fdc6478693f47a87469e527e06
52614e106a","container_hash":"kiamol/ch03-sleep@sha256:f5edb5cb6df332c1bd77b33e4af1
13a3418666638065d074f8ae1abb4b5af567","container_image":"kiamol/ch03-sleep:latest"}
}
1593508267.953121,1 (total = 2266)
```

The dev logs pass through the same pipeline, so they have all the same metadata applied, but the output shows only a count of entries: 2,266. The test log entries are shown in full.

Figure 13.8   Different outputs in Fluent Bit can reshape the data—the counter just shows a count.

isn't supported by Fluent Bit, then you can switch to the parent Fluentd project, which has a larger set of plugins (including MongoDB and AWS S3)—the pipeline stages and configuration are very similar. We'll be using Elasticsearch for storage, which is perfect for high-performance search and simple to integrate with Fluent Bit.

13.3 *Shipping logs to Elasticsearch*

Elasticsearch is a production-grade open source database. It stores items as *documents* in collections called *indexes*. It's a very different storage model from a relational database because it doesn't support a fixed schema for every document in an index—each data item can have its own set of fields. That works nicely for centralized logging where the log items from different systems will have different fields. Elasticsearch runs as a single component with a REST API to insert and query data. A companion product called Kibana provides a very usable frontend to query Elasticsearch. You can run both components in Kubernetes in the same shared logging namespace as Fluent Bit.

TRY IT NOW Deploy Elasticsearch and Kibana—the storage and frontend components of the logging system.

```
# create the Elasticsearch deployment, and wait for the Pod:
kubectl apply -f elasticsearch/

kubectl wait --for=condition=ContainersReady pod -l app=elasticsearch
  -n kiamol-ch13-logging

# create the Kibana deployment, and wait for it to start:
kubectl apply -f kibana/

kubectl wait --for=condition=ContainersReady pod -l app=kibana -n
  kiamol-ch13-logging

# get the URL for Kibana:
kubectl get svc kibana -o jsonpath='http://{.status.loadBalancer
  .ingress[0].*}:5601' -n kiamol-ch13-logging
```

This basic deployment of Elasticsearch and Kibana uses a single Pod for each, as you see in figure 13.9. Logs are important, so you'll want to model for high availability in production. Kibana is a stateless component so you can increase the replica count to increase reliability. Elasticsearch works nicely as a StatefulSet across multiple Pods using persistent storage, or you can use a managed Elasticsearch service in the cloud. When you have Kibana running, you can browse to the URL. We'll be using it in the next exercise.

Fluent Bit has an Elasticsearch output plugin that creates a document for each log entry using the Elasticsearch REST API. The plugin needs to be configured with the domain name of the Elasticsearch server, and you can optionally specify the index where documents should be created. That lets you isolate log entries from different namespaces in different indexes, using multiple output stages. Listing 13.3 separates log entries from Pods in the test namespace and Kubernetes system Pods.

These Elasticsearch and Kibana Deployments use custom container images, which are much smaller than the official images. You should switch to the official images in production.

```
PS>kubectl apply -f elasticsearch/
service/elasticsearch created
deployment.apps/elasticsearch created
PS>
PS>kubectl wait --for=condition=ContainersReady pod -l app=elasticsearch -n kiamol-
ch13-logging
pod/elasticsearch-57b6f8d8fc-d7vw4 condition met
PS>
PS>kubectl apply -f kibana/
service/kibana created
deployment.apps/kibana created
PS>
PS>kubectl wait --for=condition=ContainersReady pod -l app=kibana -n kiamol-ch13-lo
gging
pod/kibana-68bbbd448-nqxz2 condition met
PS>
PS>kubectl get svc kibana -o jsonpath='http://{.status.loadBalancer.ingress[0].*}:5
601' -n kiamol-ch13-logging
http://localhost:5601
```

Kibana connects to the Elasticsearch REST API and uses port 5601 for the web UI.

Figure 13.9   Running Elasticsearch with a Service so Kibana and Fluent Bit can use the REST API.

Listing 13.3   fluentbit-config-elasticsearch.yaml, storing logs in Elasticsearch indexes

```
[OUTPUT]
    Name      es                          # Logs from the test namespace
    Match     kube.kiamol-ch13-test.*     # are routed to Elasticsearch
    Host      elasticsearch               # and created as documents in
    Index     test                        # the "test" index.

[OUTPUT]
    Name      es                          # System logs are created in
    Match     kube.kube-system.*          # the "sys" index in the same
    Host      elasticsearch               # Elasticsearch server.
    Index     sys
```

If there are log entries that don't match any output rules, they are discarded. When you deploy this updated configuration, the Kubernetes system logs and the test namespace logs are saved in Elasticsearch, but the logs from the dev namespace aren't saved.

TRY IT NOW   Update the Fluent Bit configuration to send logs to Elasticsearch, and then connect to Kibana and set up a search over the test index.

```
# deploy the updated configuration from listing 13.3
kubectl apply -f fluentbit/update/fluentbit-config-elasticsearch.yaml
```

```
# update Fluent Bit, and wait for it to restart
kubectl rollout restart ds/fluent-bit -n kiamol-ch13-logging

kubectl wait --for=condition=ContainersReady pod -l app=fluent-bit -n
  kiamol-ch13-logging

# now browse to Kibana and set up the search:
# - click Discover on the left navigation panel
# - create a new index pattern
# - enter "test" as the index pattern
# - in the next step, select @timestamp as the time filter field
# - click Create Index Pattern
# - click Discover again on the left navigation panel to see the logs
```

This process contains a few manual steps because Kibana isn't a great product to automate. My output in figure 13.10 shows the index pattern being created. When you finish that exercise, you'll have a powerful, fast, and easy-to-use search engine for all the container logs in the test namespace. The Discover tab in Kibana shows you the rate of documents stored over time—which is the rate that logs are processed—and you can drill down into each document to see the log details.

This configuration sends log entries to Elasticsearch so they can be queried using Kibana.

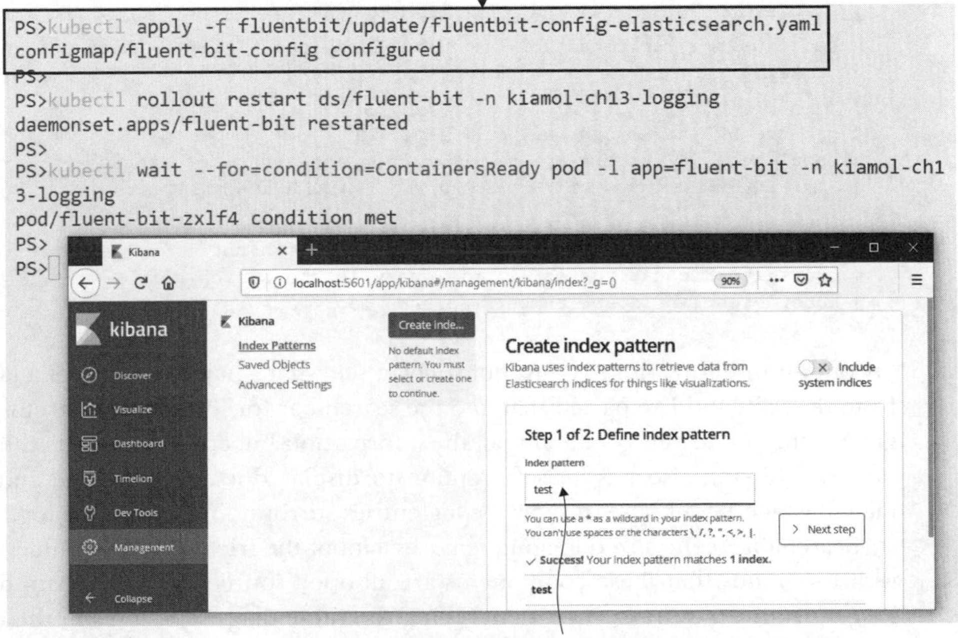

You need to manually complete the setup in Kibana, using `test` as the index pattern in this screen and selecting the `@timestamp` field in the next screen.

Figure 13.10 Setting up Fluent Bit to send logs to Elasticsearch and Kibana to search the test index

Elasticsearch and Kibana are well-established technologies but if you're new to them, now is a good time to look around the Kibana UI. You'll see a list of fields on the left of the Discover page that you can use to filter the logs. Those fields contain all the Kubernetes metadata, so you can filter by Pod name, host node, container image, and more. You can build dashboards that show headline statistics for logs split by application, which would be useful to show a sudden spike in error logs. You can also search for specific values across all documents, which is a good way to find application logs when a user gives you the ID from an error message.

I won't spend too long on Kibana, but one more exercise will show how useful it is to have a centralized logging system. We'll deploy a new application into the test namespace, and its logs will automatically get picked up by Fluent Bit and flow through to Elasticsearch without any changes to configuration. When the app shows an error to the user, we can track that down easily in Kibana.

TRY IT NOW   Deploy the random-number API we've used before—the one that crashes after the first use—along with a proxy that caches the response and almost fixes the problem. Try the API, and when you get an error, you can search for the failure ID in Kibana.

```
# deploy the API and proxy:
kubectl apply -f numbers/

# wait for the app to start up:
kubectl wait --for=condition=ContainersReady pod -l app=numbers-api -n
    kiamol-ch13-test

# get the URL to use the API via the proxy:
kubectl get svc numbers-api-proxy -o jsonpath='http://{.status
    .loadBalancer.ingress[0].*}:8080/rng' -n kiamol-ch13-test

# browse to the API, wait 30 seconds, and refresh until you get an error
# browse to Kibana, and enter this query in the search bar:
# kubernetes.labels.app:numbers-api AND log:<failure-ID-from-the-API>
```

My output in figure 13.11 is tiny, but you can see what's happening: I got a failure ID from the API, and I've pasted that into the search bar for Kibana, which returns a single match. The log entry contains all the information I need to investigate the Pod if I need to. Kibana also has a useful option to display documents before and after a match, which I could use to show the log entries surrounding the failure log.

Searchable, centralized logging removes a lot of the friction from troubleshooting, with the bonus that these components are all open source so you can run the same logging stack in every environment. Using the same diagnostic tools in the development and test environments that you use in production should help product teams understand the level of logging that's useful and improve the quality of the system logs. Good quality logging is important, but it seldom ranks highly in a product backlog,

Deploys the random-number API along with a caching proxy. The API fails
after the first call, but the proxy uses the cached response for 30 seconds.

```
PS>kubectl apply -f numbers/
service/numbers-api created
deployment.apps/numbers-api created
service/numbers-api-proxy created
configmap/numbers-api-proxy-config created
deployment.apps/numbers-api-proxy created
PS>
PS>kubectl wait --for=condition=ContainersReady pod -l app=numbers-api -n kiamol-ch
13-test
pod/numbers-api-554474cc8b-mfnmv condition met
PS>
PS>kubectl get svc numbers-api-proxy -o jsonpath='http://{.status.loadBalancer.ingr
ess[0].*}:8080/rng' -n kiamol-ch13-test
http://localhost:8080/rng
```

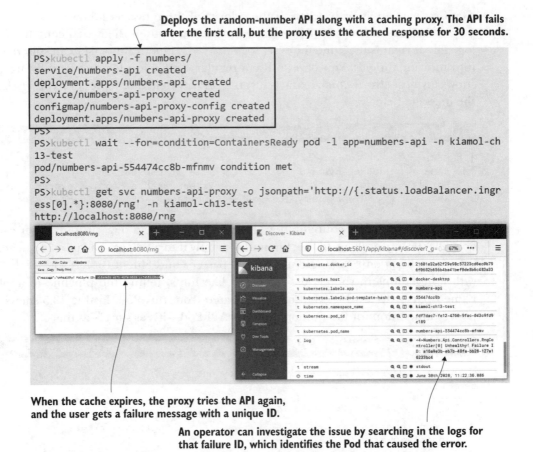

When the cache expires, the proxy tries the API again,
and the user gets a failure message with a unique ID.

An operator can investigate the issue by searching in the logs for
that failure ID, which identifies the Pod that caused the error.

Figure 13.11 The logging system in action—tracking down failures from user-facing error messages

so in some applications, you're going to be stuck with logs that aren't very useful. Fluent Bit has a couple additional features that can help there, too.

13.4 Parsing and filtering log entries

The ideal application would produce structured log data with fields for the severity of the entry and the name of the class writing the output, along with an ID for the type of event and the key data items of the event. You could use the values of those fields in your Fluent Bit pipeline to filter messages, and the fields would be surfaced in Elasticsearch so you can build more precise queries. Most systems don't produce logs like that—they just emit text—but if the text uses a known format, then Fluent Bit can parse it into fields as it passes through the pipeline.

The random-number API is a simple example. Log entries are lines of text that look like this: `<6>Microsoft.Hosting.Lifetime[0] Now listening on: http://[::]:80.`

The first part, in angle brackets, is the priority of the message, followed by the name of the class and the event ID in square brackets, and then the actual content of the log. The format is the same for every log entry, so a Fluent Bit parser can split the log into individual fields. You have to use a regular expression for that, and listing 13.4 shows my best effort, which extracts just the priority field and leaves everything else in the message field.

> **Listing 13.4   fluentbit-config-parser.yaml, a custom parser for application logs**

```
[PARSER]
    Name      dotnet-syslog               # Name of the parser
    Format    regex                       # Parses with a regular expression
    Regex     ^\<(?<priority>[0-9]+)\>*(?<message>.*)$        # Yuck
```

When you deploy this configuration, Fluent Bit will have a new custom parser called dotnet-syslog available to use, but it won't apply it to any logs. The pipeline needs to know which log entries should use custom parsers, and Fluent Bit lets you set that up with annotations in your Pods. These act like hints, telling the pipeline to apply a named parser to any logs that have originated from this Pod. Listing 13.5 shows the parser annotation for the random-number API Pod—it's as simple as that.

> **Listing 13.5   api-with-parser.yaml, Pod spec with a custom Fluent Bit parser**

```
# This is the Pod template in the Deployment spec.
template:
  metadata:                              # Labels are used for selectors and
    labels:                              # operations; annotations are often
      app: numbers-api                   # used for integration flags.
    annotations:
      fluentbit.io/parser: dotnet-syslog      # Uses the parser for Pod logs
```

Parsers can be much more effective than my custom one, and the Fluent Bit team have some sample parsers in their documentation, including one for Nginx. I'm using Nginx as a proxy for the random-number API, and in the next exercise, we'll add parsers to each component with annotations and see how structured logging makes for more targeted searching and filtering in Kibana.

TRY IT NOW   Update the Fluent Bit configuration to add parsers for the random-number app and the Nginx proxy, and then update those deployments to add annotations specifying the parser. Try the app, and check the logs in Kibana.

```
# update the pipeline configuration:
kubectl apply -f fluentbit/update/fluentbit-config-parser.yaml

# restart Fluent Bit:
kubectl rollout restart ds/fluent-bit -n kiamol-ch13-logging
kubectl wait --for=condition=ContainersReady pod -l app=fluent-bit -n
  kiamol-ch13-logging
```

```
# update the app Deployments, adding parser annotations:
kubectl apply -f numbers/update/

# wait for the API to be ready:
kubectl wait --for=condition=ContainersReady pod -l app=numbers-api -n
  kiamol-ch13-test

# use the API again, and browse to Kibana to see the logs
```

You can see in figure 13.12 that the promoted fields from the parser are available for Kibana to filter on, without me having to build up my own query. In my screenshot, I've filtered to show logs from one Pod that have a priority value of 4 (which is a warning level). When you run this yourself, you'll see that you can also filter for the API

This configuration adds parsers for the API and proxy log entries.

These Deployments include annotations so Fluent Bit uses the right parser for each Pod.

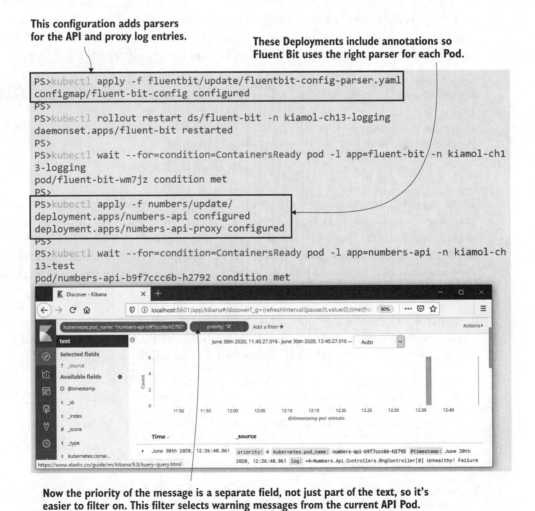

Now the priority of the message is a separate field, not just part of the text, so it's easier to filter on. This filter selects warning messages from the current API Pod.

Figure 13.12   Parsed fields from the logs are indexed, so filters and searches are faster and simpler.

proxy Pod. The log entries include fields for the HTTP request path and the response code, all parsed from Nginx text logs.

There's one final benefit of the centralized logging system with Fluent Bit: the data-processing pipeline is independent of the applications, and it can be a better place to apply filtering. That mythical ideal app would be able to increase or decrease logging levels on the fly, without an application restart. You know from chapter 4, however, that many apps need a Pod restart to pick up the latest configuration changes. That's not good when you're troubleshooting a live issue, because it means restarting the affected app if you need to increase the logging level.

Fluent Bit doesn't support live configuration reloads itself, but restarting the log collector Pods is less invasive than restarting application Pods, and Fluent Bit will pick up where it left off, so you won't miss any log entries. With this approach, you can log at a more verbose level in your applications and filter in the Fluent Bit pipeline. Listing 13.6 shows a filter that includes logs from the random-number API only if the priority field has a value of 2, 3, or 4—it filters out lower priority entries.

> **Listing 13.6   fluentbit-config-grep.yaml, filtering logs based on field values**

```
[FILTER]
    Name      grep                            # grep is a search filter.
    Match     kube.kiamol-ch13-test.api.numbers-api*
    Regex     priority [234]                  # Even I can manage this regular
                                              # expression.
```

More regular expression wrangling here, but you can see why it's important to have text log entries split into fields that the pipeline can access. The grep filter can include or exclude logs by evaluating a regular expression over a field. When you deploy this updated configuration, the API can happily write log entries at level 6, but they are dropped by Fluent Bit, and only the more important entries will make it to Elasticsearch.

> **TRY IT NOW**   Deploy the updated configuration so only high-priority logs from the random-number API are saved. Delete the API Pod, and in Kibana, you won't see any of the startup log entries, but they're still there in the Pod logs.

```
# apply the grep filter from listing 13.6:
kubectl apply -f fluentbit/update/fluentbit-config-grep.yaml

kubectl rollout restart ds/fluent-bit -n kiamol-ch13-logging

# delete the old API pod so we get a fresh set of logs:
kubectl delete pods -n kiamol-ch13-test -l app=numbers-api

kubectl wait --for=condition=ContainersReady pod -l app=numbers-api -n
    kiamol-ch13-test

# use the API, and refresh until you see a failure
```

```
# print the logs from the Pod:
kubectl logs -n kiamol-ch13-test -l app=numbers-api

# now browse to Kibana, and filter to show the API Pod logs
```

This exercise shows you how Fluent Bit can filter out logs effectively, forwarding only log entries you care about to the target output. It also shows that the lower level logging hasn't disappeared—the raw container logs are all available to see with kubectl. It's only the subsequent log processing that stops them from going to Elasticsearch. In a real troubleshooting scenario, you may be able to use Kibana to identify the Pod causing the problem and then drill down with kubectl, as shown in figure 13.13.

This configuration updates the pipeline so only high-priority logs from the API are saved.

Deleting the API Pod will create a new one with a new set of logs.

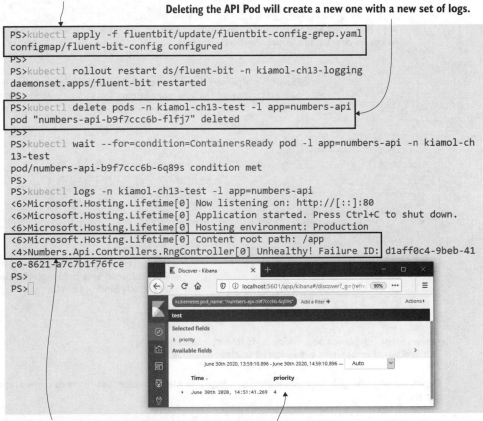

But the log entries were still created by the app, and they can be seen in the Pod logs.

I've hidden the graph here; the filter for the new API Pod shows that only the priority 4 logs have been saved; the priority 6 logs were removed in the pipeline.

Figure 13.13 Filtering log entries in Fluent Bit saves on storage, and you can easily change the filter.

There's plenty more to Fluent Bit than we've covered in these simple pipelines: you can modify log contents, throttle the rate of incoming logs, and even run custom scripts triggered by log entries. But we've covered all the main features you're likely to need, and we'll wrap up by looking at the collect-and-forward logging model compared to other options.

13.5 Understanding logging options in Kubernetes

Kubernetes has an expectation that your application logs will come from the container's standard output streams. It collects and stores all the content from those streams, and that powers the logging model we've covered in this chapter. It's a generic and flexible approach, and the technology stack we've used is reliable and performant, but there are inefficiencies along the way. Figure 13.14 shows some of the issues in getting logs from containers into searchable storage.

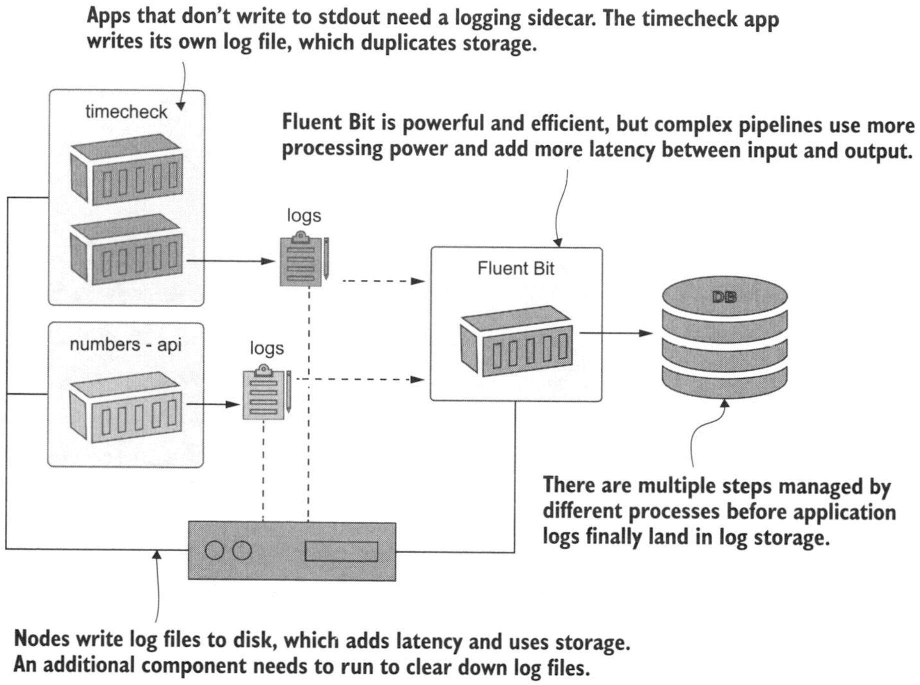

Figure 13.14   The goal is to get application logs into Elasticsearch, but it takes many steps to get there.

You can use alternative architectures that are simpler and have fewer moving pieces. You could write logs directly to Elasticsearch from your application code, or you could run a sidecar in every application Pod that reads from whatever log sink the app uses and pushes entries to Elasticsearch. That would give you a lot more control over the log data you store, without resorting to regular expressions to parse text strings. Doing this ties you to Elasticsearch (or whichever storage system you use), but that may not be a big concern if that system provides all you need.

A custom logging framework might be appealing for the first app you run on Kubernetes, but as you move more workloads to the cluster, it's going to restrict you. Requiring apps to log directly to Elasticsearch won't fit for existing apps that write to operating system logs, and you'll soon find your logging sidecar isn't flexible enough and needs tweaking for every new application. The advantage of the Fluentd/Fluent Bit model is that it's a standard approach with a community behind it; fiddling with regular expressions is much less hassle than writing and maintaining your own log collection and forwarding code.

That's all for application logs, so we can clear down the cluster to get ready for the lab.

> **TRY IT NOW** Remove this chapter's namespaces and the remaining Deployment.

```
kubectl delete ns -l kiamol=ch13
kubectl delete all -l kiamol=ch13
```

13.6 Lab

In this lab, you play the part of an operator who needs to deploy a new app into a cluster that is using the logging model from this chapter. You'll need to check the Fluent Bit configuration to find the namespace you should use for your app and then deploy the simple versioned website we've used before in the book. Here are the parts to this lab:

- Start by deploying the logging components in the lab/logging folder.
- Deploy the app from the vweb folder to the correct namespace so logs are collected, and verify you can see the logs in Kibana.
- You'll see the logs are plain text, so the next step is to update your Deployment to use the correct parser. The app runs on Nginx, and an Nginx parser is already set up for you in the Fluent Bit configuration.
- When you confirm the new logs in Kibana, you'll see several for which the status code is 304, which tells the browser to use its cached version of the page. Those logs aren't interesting, so the final task is to update the Fluent Bit configuration to filter them out.

This is a very real-world task where you'll need all the basic skills of navigating around Kubernetes to find and update all the pieces. My solution is in the usual place on GitHub for you to check: https://github.com/sixeyed/kiamol/blob/master/ch13/lab/README.md.

Monitoring applications and Kubernetes with Prometheus

Monitoring is the companion to logging: your monitoring system tells you something is wrong, and then you can dig into the logs to find out the details. Like logging, you want to have a centralized system to collect and visualize metrics about all your application components. An established approach for monitoring in Kubernetes uses another CNCF project: Prometheus, which is a server application that collects and stores metrics. In this chapter, you'll learn how to deploy a shared monitoring system in Kubernetes with dashboards that show the health of individual applications and the cluster as a whole.

Prometheus runs on many platforms, but it's particularly well suited to Kubernetes. You run Prometheus in a Pod that has access to the Kubernetes API server, and then Prometheus queries the API to find all the targets it needs to monitor. When you deploy new apps, you don't need to make any setup changes—Prometheus discovers them automatically and starts collecting metrics. Kubernetes apps are particularly well suited to Prometheus, too. You'll see in this chapter how to make good use of the sidecar pattern, so every app can provide some metrics to Prometheus, even if the application itself isn't Prometheus-ready.

14.1 How Prometheus monitors Kubernetes workloads

Metrics in Prometheus are completely generic: each component you want to monitor has an HTTP endpoint, which returns all the values that are important to that component. A web server includes metrics for the number of requests it serves, and a Kubernetes node includes metrics for how much memory is available. Prometheus doesn't care what's in the metrics; it just stores everything the component returns. What's important to Prometheus is a list of targets it needs to collect from.

Figure 14.1 shows how that works in Kubernetes, using Prometheus's built-in service discovery.

**On a regular schedule, Prometheus collects metrics from an HTTP endpoint on the Pod.
It uses the Pod's IP address, so the requests don't go via a Service.**

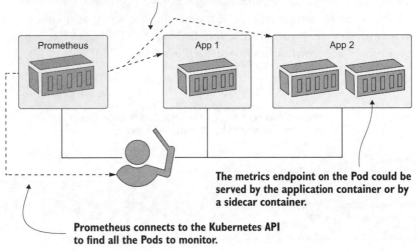

**The metrics endpoint on the Pod could be
served by the application container or by
a sidecar container.**

**Prometheus connects to the Kubernetes API
to find all the Pods to monitor.**

Figure 14.1   Prometheus uses a pull model to collect metrics, automatically finding targets.

The focus in this chapter is getting Prometheus working nicely with Kubernetes, to give you a dynamic monitoring system that keeps working as your cluster expands with more nodes running more applications. I won't go into much detail on how you add monitoring to your applications or what metrics you should record—appendix B in the ebook is the chapter "Adding Observability with Containerized Monitoring" from *Learn Docker in a Month of Lunches,* which will give you that additional detail.

We'll start by getting Prometheus up and running. The Prometheus server is a single component that takes care of service discovery and metrics collection and storage, and it has a basic web UI that you can use to check the status of the system and run simple queries.

> **TRY IT NOW**   Deploy Prometheus in a dedicated monitoring namespace, configured to find apps in a test namespace (the test namespace doesn't exist yet).

```
# switch to this chapter's folder:
cd ch14

# create the Prometheus Deployment and ConfigMap:
kubectl apply -f prometheus/

# wait for Prometheus to start:
kubectl wait --for=condition=ContainersReady pod -l app=prometheus -n
  kiamol-ch14-monitoring
```

```
# get the URL for the web UI:
kubectl get svc prometheus -o jsonpath='http://{.status.loadBalancer
  .ingress[0].*}:9090' -n kiamol-ch14-monitoring

# browse to the UI, and look at the /targets page
```

Prometheus calls metrics collection *scraping*. When you browse to the Prometheus UI, you'll see there are no scrape targets, although there is a category called `test-pods`, which lists zero targets. Figure 14.2 shows my output. The `test-pods` name comes from the Prometheus configuration you deployed in a ConfigMap, which the Pod reads from.

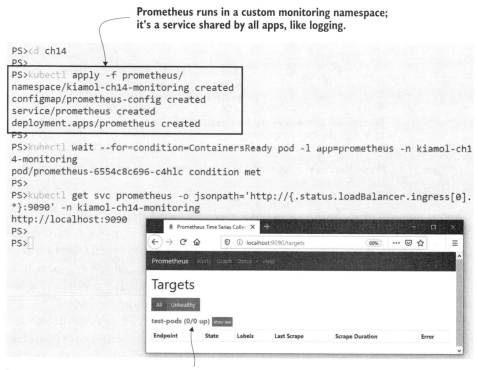

Prometheus runs in a custom monitoring namespace; it's a service shared by all apps, like logging.

Targets are the list of components from which Prometheus will scrape metrics. This configuration looks for Pods in a test namespace that doesn't exist, so there are no targets yet.

Figure 14.2　No targets yet, but Prometheus will keep checking the Kubernetes API for new Pods.

Configuring Prometheus to find targets in Kubernetes is fairly straightforward, although the terminology is confusing at first. Prometheus uses *jobs* to define a related set of targets to scrape, which could be multiple components of an application. The scrape configuration can be as simple as a static list of domain names, which Prometheus polls to grab the metrics, or it can use dynamic service discovery. Listing 14.1 shows the beginning of the `test-pods` job configuration, which uses the Kubernetes API for service discovery.

Listing 14.1   prometheus-config.yaml, scrape configuration with Kubernetes

```
scrape_configs:                      # This is the YAML inside the ConfigMap.
- job_name: 'test-pods'              # Used for test apps
  kubernetes_sd_configs:             # Finds targets from the Kubernetes API
  - role: pod                        # Searches for Pods
  relabel_configs:                   # Applies these filtering rules
  - source_labels:
      - __meta_kubernetes_namespace
    action: keep                     # Includes Pods only where the namespace
    regex: kiamol-ch14-test          # is the test namespace for this chapter
```

It's the `relabel_configs` section that needs explanation. Prometheus stores metrics with *labels*, which are key-value pairs that identify the source system and other relevant information. You'll use labels in queries to select or aggregate metrics, and you can also use them to filter or modify metrics before they are stored in Prometheus. This is *relabeling*, and conceptually, it's similar to the data pipeline in Fluent Bit—it's your chance to discard data you don't want and reshape the data you do want.

Regular expressions rear their unnecessarily complicated heads in Prometheus, too, but it's rare that you need to make changes. The pipeline you set up in the relabeling phase should be generic enough to work for all your apps. The full pipeline in the configuration file applies the following rules:

- Include Pods only from the namespace `kiamol-ch14-test`.
- Use the Pod name as the value of the Prometheus `instance` label.
- Use the app label in the Pod metadata as the value of the Prometheus `job` label.
- Use optional annotations in the Pod metadata to configure the scrape target.

This approach is convention-driven—as long as your apps are modeled to suit the rules, they'll automatically be picked up as monitoring targets. Prometheus uses the rules to find Pods that match, and for each target, it collects metrics by making an HTTP GET request to the `/metrics` path. Prometheus needs to know which network port to use, so the Pod spec needs to explicitly include the container port. That's a good practice anyway because it helps to document your application's setup. Let's deploy a simple app to the test namespace and see what Prometheus does with it.

> **TRY IT NOW** Deploy the timecheck application to the test namespace. The spec matches all the Prometheus scrape rules, so the new Pod should be found and added as a scrape target.

```
# create the test namespace and the timecheck Deployment:
kubectl apply -f timecheck/

# wait for the app to start:
kubectl wait --for=condition=ContainersReady pod -l app=timecheck -n
  kiamol-ch14-test
```

```
# refresh the target list in the Prometheus UI, and confirm the
# timecheck Pod is listed, then browse to the /graph page, select
# timecheck_total from the dropdown list, and click Execute
```

My output is shown in figure 14.3, where I've opened two browser windows so you can see what happened when the app was deployed. Prometheus saw the timecheck Pod being created, and it matched all the rules in the relabel stage, so it was added as a target. The Prometheus configuration is set to scrape targets every 30 seconds. The timecheck app has a /metrics endpoint, which returns a count for how many timecheck logs it has written. When I queried that metric in Prometheus, the app had written 22 log entries.

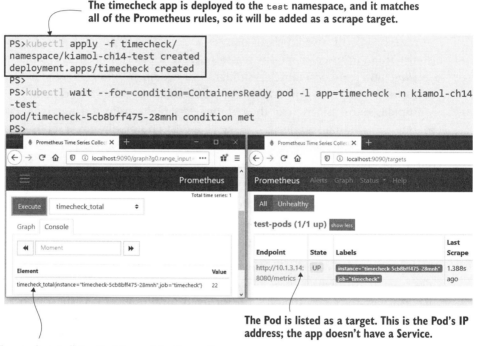

The timecheck app is deployed to the `test` namespace, and it matches all of the Prometheus rules, so it will be added as a scrape target.

```
PS>kubectl apply -f timecheck/
namespace/kiamol-ch14-test created
deployment.apps/timecheck created
PS>
PS>kubectl wait --for=condition=ContainersReady pod -l app=timecheck -n kiamol-ch14
-test
pod/timecheck-5cb8bff475-28mnh condition met
PS>
```

The Pod is listed as a target. This is the Pod's IP address; the app doesn't have a Service.

The graph page lists all of the metrics Prometheus has collected. `timecheck_total` is a counter that the timecheck app records—this is the latest value.

Figure 14.3   Deploying an app to the test namespace—Prometheus finds it and starts collecting metrics.

You should realize two important things here: the application itself needs to provide the metrics because Prometheus is just a collector, and those metrics represent the activity for one instance of the application. The timecheck app isn't a web application—it's just a background process—so there's no Service directing traffic to it. Prometheus gets the Pod IP address when it queries the Kubernetes API, and it makes the HTTP request directly to the Pod. You can configure Prometheus to query Services, too, but then you'd get a target that is a load balancer across multiple Pods, and you want Prometheus to scrape each Pod independently.

You'll use the metrics in Prometheus to power dashboards showing the overall health of your apps, and you may aggregate across all the Pods to get the headline values. You need to be able to drill down, too, to see if there are differences between the Pods. That will help you identify if some instances are performing badly, and that will feed back into your health checks. We can scale up the timecheck app to see the importance of collecting at the individual Pod level.

> **TRY IT NOW** Add another replica to the timecheck app. It's a new Pod that matches the Prometheus rules, so it will be discovered and added as another scrape target.

```
# scale the Deployment to add another Pod:
kubectl scale deploy/timecheck --replicas 2 -n kiamol-ch14-test

# wait for the new Pod to spin up:
kubectl wait --for=condition=ContainersReady pod -l app=timecheck -n
  kiamol-ch14-test

# back in Prometheus, check the target list, and in the graph page,
# execute queries for timecheck_total and dotnet_total_memory_bytes
```

You'll see in this exercise that Prometheus finds the new Pod and starts scraping it. Both Pods record the same metrics, and the Pod name is set as a label on each metric. The query for the `timecheck_total` metric now returns two results—one for each Pod—and you can see in figure 14.4 that one Pod has done a lot more work than the other.

The timecheck counter is a metric that is explicitly captured in the application code. Most languages have a Prometheus client library, which you can plug into your build. The libraries let you capture application-specific details like this, and they also collect generic information about the application run time. This is a .NET application, and the Prometheus client library records run-time details, like the amount of memory and CPU in use and the number of threads running. In the next section, we'll run a distributed application where every component exposes Prometheus metrics, and we'll see how useful an application dashboard is when it includes run-time performance as well as application details.

14.2 *Monitoring apps built with Prometheus client libraries*

Appendix B in the ebook walks through adding metrics to an app that shows a picture from NASA's Astronomy Photo of the Day (APOD) service. The components of that app are in Java, Go, and Node.js, and they each use a Prometheus client library to expose run-time and application metrics. This chapter includes Kubernetes manifests for the app that deploy to the test namespace, so all the application Pods will be discovered by Prometheus.

Adds another replica to the Deployment. This is a new Pod that matches the Prometheus rules, so it is picked up as a target.

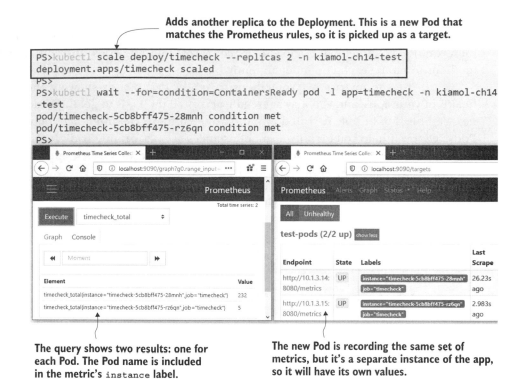

```
PS>kubectl scale deploy/timecheck --replicas 2 -n kiamol-ch14-test
deployment.apps/timecheck scaled
PS>
PS>kubectl wait --for=condition=ContainersReady pod -l app=timecheck -n kiamol-ch14
-test
pod/timecheck-5cb8bff475-28mnh condition met
pod/timecheck-5cb8bff475-rz6qn condition met
PS>
```

The query shows two results: one for each Pod. The Pod name is included in the metric's `instance` label.

The new Pod is recording the same set of metrics, but it's a separate instance of the app, so it will have its own values.

Figure 14.4   Every instance records its own metrics so you need to collect from every Pod.

TRY IT NOW   Deploy the APOD app to the test namespace, and confirm that the three components of the app are added as Prometheus targets.

```
# deploy the app:
kubectl apply -f apod/

# wait for the main component to start:
kubectl wait --for=condition=ContainersReady pod -l app=apod-api -n
  kiamol-ch14-test

# get the app URL:
kubectl get svc apod-web -o
  jsonpath='http://{.status.loadBalancer.ingress[0].*}:8014' -n
  kiamol-ch14-test

# browse to the app, and then refresh the Prometheus targets
```

You can see my output in figure 14.5, with a very pleasant image of something called Lynds Dark Nebula 1251. The application is working as expected, and Prometheus has discovered all of the new Pods. Within 30 seconds of deploying the app, you

Multiple components in the APOD app are written in different languages.
They all use a Prometheus client library to record metrics.

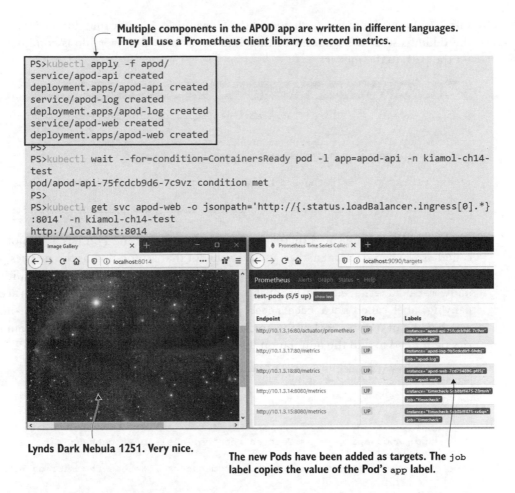

```
PS>kubectl apply -f apod/
service/apod-api created
deployment.apps/apod-api created
service/apod-log created
deployment.apps/apod-log created
service/apod-web created
deployment.apps/apod-web created
PS>
PS>kubectl wait --for=condition=ContainersReady pod -l app=apod-api -n kiamol-ch14-
test
pod/apod-api-75fcdcb9d6-7c9vz condition met
PS>
PS>kubectl get svc apod-web -o jsonpath='http://{.status.loadBalancer.ingress[0].*}
:8014' -n kiamol-ch14-test
http://localhost:8014
```

Lynds Dark Nebula 1251. Very nice.

The new Pods have been added as targets. The `job`
label copies the value of the Pod's `app` label.

Figure 14.5 The APOD components all have Services, but they are still scraped at the Pod level.

should see that the state of all of the new targets is up, which means Prometheus has
successfully scraped them.

I have two additional important things to point out in this exercise. First, the Pod
specs all include a container port, which states that the application container is listening on port 80, and that's how Prometheus finds the target to scrape. The Service for
the web UI actually listens on port 8014, but Prometheus goes directly to the Pod port.
Second, the API target isn't using the standard /metrics path, because the Java client
library uses a different path. I've used an annotation in the Pod spec to state the correct path.

Convention-based discovery is great because it removes a lot of repetitive configuration and the potential for mistakes, but not every app will fit with the conventions.
The relabeling pipeline we're using in Prometheus gives us a nice balance. The default

values will work for any apps that meet the convention, but any that don't can override the defaults with annotations. Listing 14.2 shows how the override is configured to set the path to the metrics.

```
- source_labels:    # This is a relabel configuration in the test-pods job.

   - __meta_kubernetes_pod_annotationpresent_prometheus_io_path
   - __meta_kubernetes_pod_annotation_prometheus_io_path

regex: true;(.*)    # If the Pod has an annotation named prometheus.io/path . . .

target_label: __metrics_path__   # sets the target path from the annotation.
```

This is way less complicated than it looks. The rule says: if the Pod has an annotation called prometheus.io/path, then use the value of that annotation as the metrics path. Prometheus does it all with labels, so every Pod annotation becomes a label with the name meta_kubernetes_pod_annotation_<annotation-name>, and there's an accompanying label called meta_kubernetes_pod_annotationpresent_<annotation-name>, which you can use to check if the annotation exists. Any apps that use a custom metrics path need to add the annotation. Listing 14.3 shows that for the APOD API.

```
template:                      # This is the pod spec in the Deployment.
  metadata:
    labels:
      app: apod-api        # Used as the job label in Prometheus
    annotations:
      prometheus.io/path: "/actuator/prometheus"   # Sets the metrics path
```

The complexity is centralized in the Prometheus configuration, and it's really easy for application manifests to specify overrides. The relabeling rules aren't so complex when you work with them a little more, and you're usually following exactly the same pattern. The full Prometheus configuration includes similar rules for apps to override the metrics port and to opt out of scraping altogether.

While you've been reading this, Prometheus has been busily scraping the time-check and APOD apps. Take a look at the metrics on the Graph page of the Prometheus UI to see around 200 metrics being collected. The UI is great for running queries and quickly seeing the results, but you can't use it to build a dashboard showing all the key metrics for your app in a single screen. For that you can use Grafana, another open source project in the container ecosystem, which comes recommended by the Prometheus team.

TRY IT NOW   Deploy Grafana with ConfigMaps that set up the connection to Prometheus, and include a dashboard for the APOD app.

```
# deploy Grafana in the monitoring namespace:
kubectl apply -f grafana/

# wait for it to start up:
kubectl wait --for=condition=ContainersReady pod -l app=grafana -n
  kiamol-ch14-monitoring

# get the URL for the dashboard:
kubectl get svc grafana -o
  jsonpath='http://{.status.loadBalancer.ingress[0].*}:3000/d/kb5nhJA
  Zk' -n kiamol-ch14-monitoring

# browse to the URL; log in with username kiamol and password kiamol
```

The dashboard shown in figure 14.6 is tiny, but it gives you an idea of how you can transform raw metrics into an informative view of system activity. Each visualization in

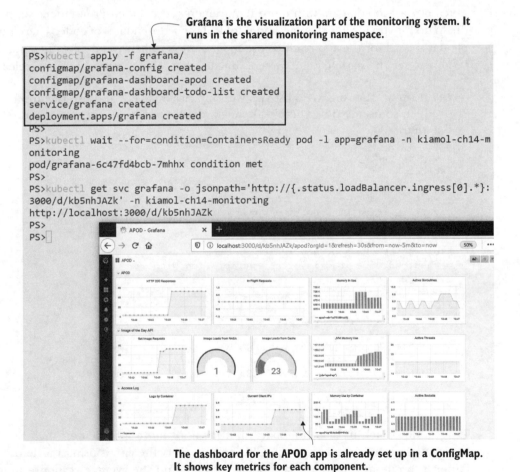

Grafana is the visualization part of the monitoring system. It runs in the shared monitoring namespace.

```
PS>kubectl apply -f grafana/
configmap/grafana-config created
configmap/grafana-dashboard-apod created
configmap/grafana-dashboard-todo-list created
service/grafana created
deployment.apps/grafana created
PS>
PS>kubectl wait --for=condition=ContainersReady pod -l app=grafana -n kiamol-ch14-m
onitoring
pod/grafana-6c47fd4bcb-7mhhx condition met
PS>
PS>kubectl get svc grafana -o jsonpath='http://{.status.loadBalancer.ingress[0].*}:
3000/d/kb5nhJAZk' -n kiamol-ch14-monitoring
http://localhost:3000/d/kb5nhJAZk
PS>
PS>
```

The dashboard for the APOD app is already set up in a ConfigMap. It shows key metrics for each component.

Figure 14.6 Application dashboards give a quick insight into performance. The graphs are all powered from Prometheus metrics.

the dashboard is powered by a Prometheus query, which Grafana runs in the background. There's a row for each component, and that includes a mixture of run-time metrics—processor and memory usage—and application metrics—HTTP requests and cache usage.

Dashboards like this will be a joint effort that cuts across the organization. The support team will set the requirements for what they need to see, and the application development and operations teams ensure the app captures the data and the dashboard shows it. Just like the logging system we looked at in chapter 13, this is a solution built from lightweight open source components, so developers can run the same monitoring system on their laptops that runs in production. That helps with performance testing and debugging in development and test.

Moving to centralized monitoring with Prometheus will require development effort, but it can be an incremental process where you start with basic metrics and add to them as teams start to come up with more requirements. I've added Prometheus support to the to-do list app for this chapter, and it took about a dozen lines of code. There's a simple dashboard for the app ready to use in Grafana, so when you deploy the app, you'll be able to see the starting point for a dashboard that will improve with future releases.

TRY IT NOW   Run the to-do list app with metrics enabled, and use the app to produce some metrics. There's already a dashboard in Grafana to visualize the metrics.

```
# deploy the app:
kubectl apply -f todo-list/

# wait for it to start:
kubectl wait --for=condition=ContainersReady pod -l app=todo-web -n
  kiamol-ch14-test

# browse to the app, and insert an item
# then run some load in with a script - on Windows:
.\loadgen.ps1

# OR on macOS/Linux:
chmod +x ./loadgen.sh && ./loadgen.sh

# get the URL for the new dashboard:
kubectl get svc grafana -o jsonpath='http://{.status.loadBalancer
  .ingress[0].*}:3000/d/Eh0VF3iGz' -n kiamol-ch14-monitoring

# browse to the dashboard
```

There's not much in that dashboard, but it's a lot more information than no dashboard at all. It tells you how much CPU and memory the app is using inside the container, the rate at which tasks are being created, and the average response time for HTTP requests. You can see my output in figure 14.7 where I've added some tasks and sent some traffic in with the load generation script.

This version of the to-do app has metrics enabled in the web component. A database and a web proxy are also deployed.

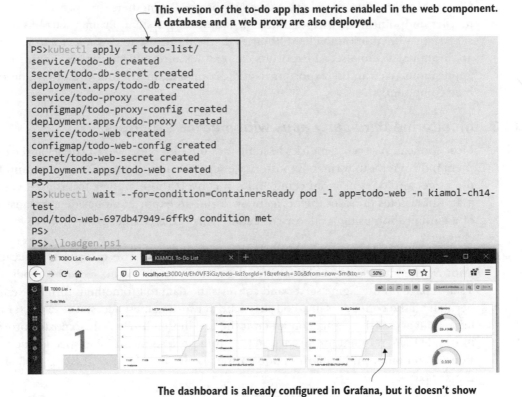

```
PS>kubectl apply -f todo-list/
service/todo-db created
secret/todo-db-secret created
deployment.apps/todo-db created
service/todo-proxy created
configmap/todo-proxy-config created
deployment.apps/todo-proxy created
service/todo-web created
configmap/todo-web-config created
secret/todo-web-secret created
deployment.apps/todo-web created
PS>
PS>kubectl wait --for=condition=ContainersReady pod -l app=todo-web -n kiamol-ch14-
test
pod/todo-web-697db47949-6ffk9 condition met
PS>
PS>.\loadgen.ps1
```

The dashboard is already configured in Grafana, but it doesn't show much, just basic application and resource usage.

Figure 14.7 A simple dashboard powered by the Prometheus client library and a few lines of code

All of those metrics are coming from the to-do application Pod. There are two other components to the app in this release: a Postgres database for storage and an Nginx proxy. Neither of those components has native support for Prometheus, so they're excluded from the target list. Otherwise, Prometheus would keep trying to scrape metrics and failing. It's the job of whoever models the application to know that a component doesn't expose metrics and to specify that it should be excluded. Listing 14.4 shows that done with a simple annotation.

Listing 14.4   proxy.yaml, a Pod spec that excludes itself from monitoring

```
template:                    # This is the Pod spec in the Deployment.
  metadata:
    labels:
      app: todo-proxy
    annotations:                             # Excludes the target in Prometheus
      prometheus.io/scrape: "false"
```

Components don't need to have native support for Prometheus and provide their own metrics endpoint to be included in your monitoring system. Prometheus has its own ecosystem—in addition to client libraries that you can use to add metrics to your own applications, a whole set of exporters can extract and publish metrics for third-party applications. We can use exporters to add the missing metrics for the proxy and database components.

14.3   *Monitoring third-party apps with metrics exporters*

Most applications record metrics in some way, but older apps won't collect and expose them in Prometheus format. Exporters are separate applications that understand how the target app does its monitoring and can convert those metrics to Prometheus format. Kubernetes provides the perfect way to run an exporter alongside every instance of an application using a sidecar container. This is the adapter pattern we covered in chapter 7.

Nginx and Postgres both have exporters available that we can run as sidecars to improve the monitoring dashboard for the to-do app. The Nginx exporter reads from a status page on the Nginx server and converts the data to Prometheus format. Remember that all the containers in a Pod share the network namespace, so the exporter container can access the Nginx container at the localhost address. The exporter provides its own HTTP endpoint for metrics on a custom port, so the full Pod spec includes the sidecar container and an annotation to specify the metrics port. Listing 14.5 shows the key parts.

> **Listing 14.5   proxy-with-exporter.yaml, adding a metrics exporter container**

```
template:                      # Pod spec in the Deployment
  metadata:
    labels:
      app: todo-proxy
    annotations:                        # The exclusion annotation is gone.
      prometheus.io/port: "9113"    # Specifies the metrics port
  spec:
    containers:
      - name: nginx
        # ... nginx spec is unchanged

      - name: exporter            # The exporter is a sidecar.
        image: nginx/nginx-prometheus-exporter:0.8.0
        ports:
          - name: metrics
            containerPort: 9113    # Specifies the metrics port
        args:                      # and loads metrics from Nginx
          - -nginx.scrape-uri=http://localhost/stub_status
```

The scrape exclusion has been removed, so when you deploy this update, Prometheus will scrape the Nginx Pod on port 9113, where the exporter is listening. All the Nginx metrics will be stored by Prometheus, and the Grafana dashboard can be updated to add a row for the proxy. We're not going to get into the Prometheus query language (PromQL) or building Grafana dashboards in this chapter—dashboards can be imported from JSON files, and there's an updated dashboard ready to be deployed.

TRY IT NOW Update the proxy Deployment to add the exporter sidecar, and load an updated dashboard into the Grafana ConfigMap.

```
# add the proxy sidecar:
kubectl apply -f todo-list/update/proxy-with-exporter.yaml

# wait for it to spin up:
kubectl wait --for=condition=ContainersReady pod -l app=todo-proxy -n
  kiamol-ch14-test

# print the logs of the exporter:
kubectl logs -l app=todo-proxy -n kiamol-ch14-test -c exporter

# update the app dashboard:
kubectl apply -f grafana/update/grafana-dashboard-todo-list-v2.yaml

# restart Grafana to load the new dashboard:
kubectl rollout restart deploy grafana -n kiamol-ch14-monitoring

# refresh the dashboard, and log in with kiamol/kiamol again
```

The Nginx exporter doesn't provide a huge amount of information, but the basic details are there. You can see in figure 14.8 that we get the number of HTTP requests and a lower-level breakdown of how Nginx handles connection requests. Even with this simple dashboard, you can see a correlation between the traffic Nginx is handling and the traffic the web app is handling, which suggests the proxy isn't caching responses and is calling the web app for every request.

It would be nice to get a bit more information from Nginx—like the breakdown of HTTP status codes in the response—but exporters can relay only the information available from the source system, which isn't much for Nginx. Other exporters provide far more detail, but you need to focus your dashboard so it shows key indicators. More than a dozen or so visualizations and the dashboard becomes overwhelming, and, if it doesn't convey useful information at a glance, then it's not doing a very good job.

There's one more component to add to the to-do list dashboard: the Postgres database. Postgres stores all sorts of useful information in tables and functions inside the database, and the exporter runs queries to power its metrics endpoint. The setup for the Postgres exporter follows the same pattern we've seen in Nginx. In this case, the sidecar is configured to access Postgres on localhost, using the same Kubernetes Secret that the Postgres container uses for the admin password. We'll make a final update to the application dashboard to show the key database metrics from the exporter.

This update adds an exporter, which makes
HTTP metrics available for the Nginx proxy.

The exporter is a sidecar that reads metrics from the Nginx
container and exposes them in Prometheus format.

```
PS>kubectl apply -f todo-list/update/proxy-with-exporter.yaml
deployment.apps/todo-proxy configured
PS>
PS>kubectl wait --for=condition=ContainersReady pod -l app=todo-proxy -n kiamol-ch1
4-test
pod/todo-proxy-78b48978b8-vmjzd condition met
PS>
PS>kubectl logs -l app=todo-proxy -n kiamol-ch14-test -c exporter
2020/07/03 10:48:58 Starting NGINX Prometheus Exporter Version= GitCommit=
2020/07/03 10:48:58 Listening on :9113
2020/07/03 10:48:58 NGINX Prometheus Exporter has successfully started
PS>
PS>kubectl apply -f grafana/update/grafana-dashboard-todo-list-v2.yaml
configmap/grafana-dashboard-todo-list configured
PS>
PS>kubectl rollout restart deploy grafana -n kiamol-ch14-monitoring
deployment.apps/grafana restarted
```

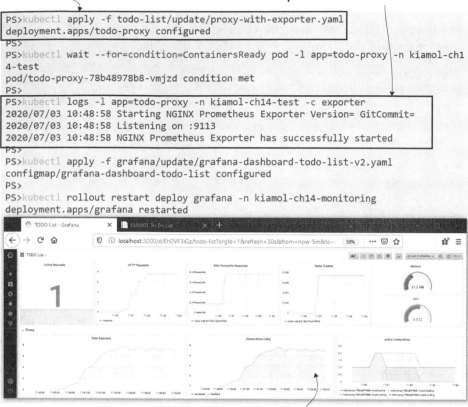

The new dashboard adds a row for the proxy, which shows incoming web requests.

Figure 14.8   Collecting proxy metrics with an exporter adds another level of detail to the dashboard.

TRY IT NOW   Update the database Deployment spec, adding the Postgres exporter as a sidecar container. Then update the to-do list dashboard with a new row to show database performance.

```
# add the exporter sidecar to Postgres:
kubectl apply -f todo-list/update/db-with-exporter.yaml

# wait for the new Pod to start:
kubectl wait --for=condition=ContainersReady pod -l app=todo-db -n
  kiamol-ch14-test

# print the logs from the exporter:
kubectl logs  l app=todo-db -n kiamol-ch14-test -c exporter
```

```
# update the dashboard and restart Grafana:
kubectl apply -f grafana/update/grafana-dashboard-todo-list-v3.yaml
kubectl rollout restart deploy grafana -n kiamol-ch14-monitoring
```

I've zoomed out and scrolled down in figure 14.9 so you can see the new visualizations, but the whole dashboard is a joy to behold in full-screen mode. A single page shows you how much traffic is coming to the proxy, how hard the app is working and what users are actually doing, and what's happening inside the database. You can get the same level of detail in your own apps with client libraries and exporters, and you're looking at just a few days' effort.

Adds an exporter sidecar for database metrics to the Postgres Pod

The exporter shares credentials with the Postgres container so it can run queries to populate the metrics endpoint (I've abbreviated the logs).

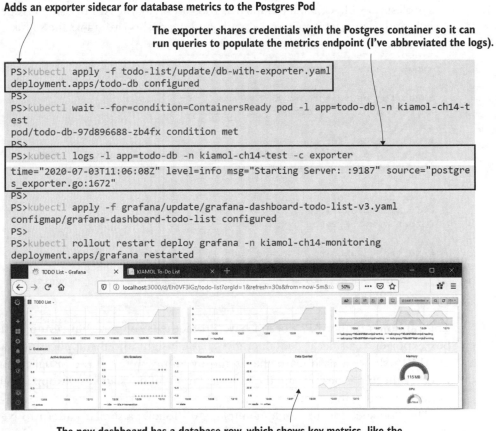

The new dashboard has a database row, which shows key metrics, like the amount of data read and the number of open connections and transactions.

Figure 14.9 The database exporter records metrics about data activity, which add detail to the dashboard.

Exporters are there to add metrics to apps that don't have Prometheus support. If your goal is to move a set of existing applications onto Kubernetes, then you may not have the luxury of a development team to add custom metrics. For those apps, you can use the Prometheus blackbox exporter, taking to the extreme the approach that some monitoring is better than none.

The blackbox exporter can run in a sidecar and make TCP or HTTP requests to your application container as well as provide a basic metrics endpoint to say whether the application is up. This approach is similar to adding container probes to your Pod spec, except that the blackbox exporter is for information only. You can run a dashboard to show the status of an app if it isn't a good fit for Kubernetes's self-healing mechanisms, like the random-number API we've used in this book.

> **TRY IT NOW**   Deploy the random-number API with a blackbox exporter and the simplest possible Grafana dashboard. You can break the API by using it repeatedly and then reset it so it works again, and the dashboard tracks the status.

```
# deploy the API to the test namespace:
kubectl apply -f numbers/

# add the new dashboard to Grafana:
kubectl apply -f grafana/update/numbers-api/

# get the URL for the API:
kubectl get svc numbers-api -o jsonpath='#app - http://{.status
  .loadBalancer.ingress[0].*}:8016/rng' -n kiamol-ch14-test

# use the API by visiting the /rng URL
# it will break after three calls;
# then visit /reset to fix it

# get the dashboard URL, and load it in Grafana:
kubectl get svc grafana -o jsonpath='# dashboard - http://{.status
  .loadBalancer.ingress[0].*}:3000/d/Tb6isdMMk' -n kiamol-ch14-
  monitoring
```

The random-number API doesn't have Prometheus support, but running the blackbox exporter as a sidecar container gives basic insight into the application status. Figure 14.10 shows a dashboard that is mostly empty, but the two visualizations show whether the app is healthy and the historical trend of the status as the app flips between unhealthy and being reset.

The Pod spec for the random-number API follows a similar pattern to Nginx and Postgres in the to-do app: the blackbox exporter is configured as an additional container and specifies the port where metrics are exposed. The Pod annotations customize the path to the metrics URL, so when Prometheus scrapes metrics from the sidecar, it calls the blackbox exporter, which checks that the API is responding to HTTP requests.

Now we have dashboards for three different apps that have different levels of detail, because the application components aren't consistent with the data they collect. But all the components have something in common: they're all running in containers

The random-number API has no Prometheus support, but it's deployed here with
a simple blackbox exporter, which reports on the HTTP status of the API container.

```
PS>kubectl apply -f numbers/
service/numbers-api created
deployment.apps/numbers-api created
PS>
PS>kubectl apply -f grafana/update/numbers-api/
configmap/grafana-dashboard-numbers-api created
deployment.apps/grafana configured
PS>
PS>kubectl get svc numbers-api -o jsonpath='# app - http://{.status.loadBalancer.in
gress[0].*}:8016/rng' -n kiamol-ch14-test
# app - http://localhost:8016/rng
PS>
PS>kubectl get svc grafana -o jsonpath='# dashboard - http://{.status.loadBalancer.
ingress[0].*}:3000/d/Tb6isdMMk' -n kiamol-ch14-monitoring
# dashboard - http://localhost:3000/d/Tb6isdMMk
```

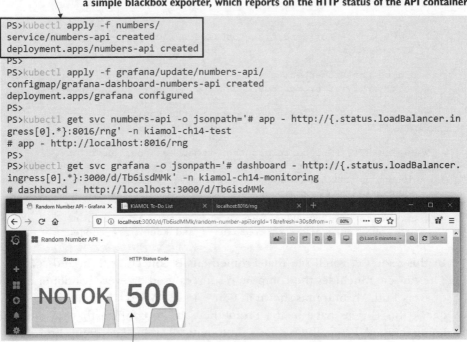

The API breaks if you use it too much, and then you can reset it. The status in Grafana
shows the app is currently broken but has had periods of working successfully.

Figure 14.10   Even a simple dashboard is useful. This shows the current and historical status of
the API.

on Kubernetes. In the next section, you'll learn how to get the next level of detail by
configuring Prometheus to collect platform metrics from the cluster itself.

14.4   *Monitoring containers and Kubernetes objects*

Prometheus integrates with Kubernetes for service discovery, but it doesn't collect any
metrics from the API. You can get metrics about Kubernetes objects and container
activity from two additional components: *cAdvisor*, a Google open source project, and
kube-state-metrics, which is part of the wider Kubernetes organization on GitHub. Both
run as containers in the cluster, but they collect data from different sources. cAdvisor
collects metrics from the container runtime, so it runs as a DaemonSet with a Pod on
each node to report on that node's containers. kube-state-metrics queries the Kubernetes API so it can run as a Deployment with a single replica on any node.

TRY IT NOW   Deploy the metric collectors for cAdvisor and kube-state-metrics,
and update the Prometheus configuration to include them as scrape targets.

```
# deploy cAdvisor and kube-state-metrics:
kubectl apply -f kube/

# wait for cAdvisor to start:
kubectl wait --for=condition=ContainersReady pod -l app=cadvisor -n
  kube-system

# update the Prometheus config:
kubectl apply -f prometheus/update/prometheus-config-kube.yaml

# wait for the ConfigMap to update in the Pod:
sleep 30

# use an HTTP POST to reload the Prometheus configuration:
curl -X POST $(kubectl get svc prometheus -o
  jsonpath='http://{.status.loadBalancer.ingress[0].*}:9090/-/reload'
  -n kiamol-ch14-monitoring)

# browse to the Prometheus UI—in the Graph page you'll see
# metrics listed covering containers and Kubernetes objects
```

In this exercise, you'll see that Prometheus is collecting thousands of new metrics. The raw data includes the compute resources used by every container and the status of every Pod. My output is shown in figure 14.11. When you run this exercise, you can check the Targets page in the Prometheus UI to confirm that the new targets are being scraped. Prometheus doesn't automatically reload configuration, so in the exercise, there's a delay to give Kubernetes time to propagate the ConfigMap update, and the `curl` command forces a configuration reload in Prometheus.

The updated Prometheus configuration you just deployed includes two new job definitions, shown in listing 14.6. kube-state-metrics is specified as a static target using the full DNS name of the Service. A single Pod collects all of the metrics so there's no load-balancing issue here. cAdvisor uses Kubernetes service discovery to find every Pod in the DaemonSet, which would present one target for each node in a multinode cluster.

> **Listing 14.6   prometheus-config-kube.yaml, new scrape targets in Prometheus**

```
- job_name: 'kube-state-metrics'        # Kubernetes metrics use a
  static_configs:                       # static configuration with DNS.
  - targets:
      - kube-state-metrics.kube-system.svc.cluster.local:8080
    - kube-state-metrics.kube-system.svc.cluster.local:8081

- job_name: 'cadvisor'                  # Container metrics use
  kubernetes_sd_configs:                # Kubernetes service discovery
  - role: pod                           # to find all the DaemonSet
  relabel_configs:                      # Pods, by namespace and label.
    - source_labels:
        - __meta_kubernetes_namespace
        - __meta_kubernetes_pod_labelpresent_app
        - __meta_kubernetes_pod_label_app
      action: keep
      regex: kube-system;true;cadvisor
```

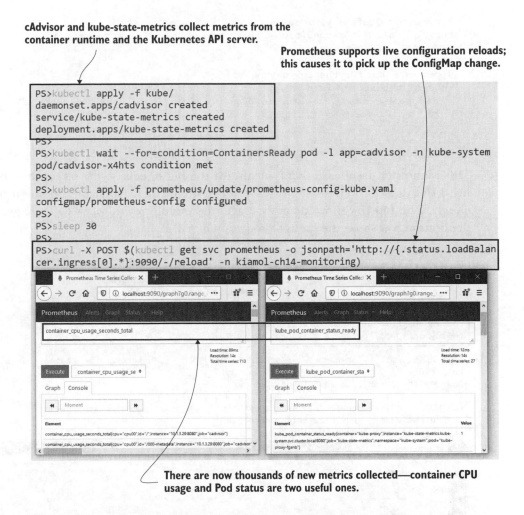

cAdvisor and kube-state-metrics collect metrics from the container runtime and the Kubernetes API server.

Prometheus supports live configuration reloads; this causes it to pick up the ConfigMap change.

```
PS>kubectl apply -f kube/
daemonset.apps/cadvisor created
service/kube-state-metrics created
deployment.apps/kube-state-metrics created
PS>
PS>kubectl wait --for=condition=ContainersReady pod -l app=cadvisor -n kube-system
pod/cadvisor-x4hts condition met
PS>
PS>kubectl apply -f prometheus/update/prometheus-config-kube.yaml
configmap/prometheus-config configured
PS>
PS>sleep 30
PS>
PS>curl -X POST $(kubectl get svc prometheus -o jsonpath='http://{.status.loadBalan
cer.ingress[0].*}:9090/-/reload' -n kiamol-ch14-monitoring)
```

There are now thousands of new metrics collected—container CPU usage and Pod status are two useful ones.

Figure 14.11 New metrics show activity at the cluster and container levels.

Now we have the opposite problem from the random-number dashboard: there's far too much information in the new metrics, so the platform dashboard will need to be highly selective if it's going to be useful. I have a sample dashboard prepared that is a good starter. It includes current resource usage and all available resource quantities for the cluster, together with some high-level breakdowns by namespace and warning indicators for the health of the nodes.

TRY IT NOW Deploy a dashboard for key cluster metrics and with an update to Grafana so it loads the new dashboard.

```
# create the dashboard ConfigMap and update Grafana:
kubectl apply -f grafana/update/kube/
```

```
# wait for Grafana to load:
kubectl wait --for=condition=ContainersReady pod -l app=grafana -n
  kiamol-ch14-monitoring

# get the URL for the new dashboard:
kubectl get svc grafana -o
  jsonpath='http://{.status.loadBalancer.ingress[0].*}:3000/d/oWe9aYx
  mk' -n kiamol-ch14-monitoring

# browse to the dashboard
```

This is another dashboard that is meant for the big screen, so the screenshot in figure 14.12 doesn't do it justice. When you run the exercise, you can examine it more closely. The top row shows memory usage, the middle row displays CPU usage, and the bottom row shows the status of Pod containers.

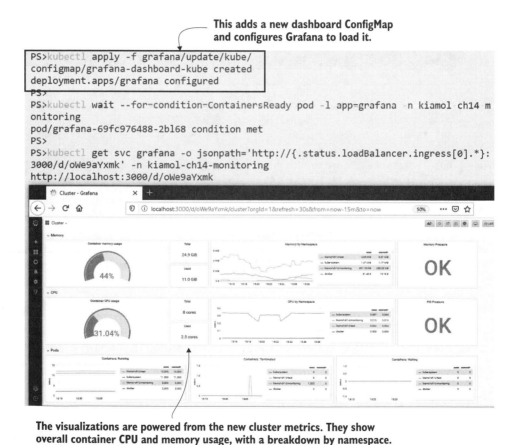

This adds a new dashboard ConfigMap and configures Grafana to load it.

The visualizations are powered from the new cluster metrics. They show overall container CPU and memory usage, with a breakdown by namespace. The bottom row shows the status of Pod containers.

Figure 14.12   Another tiny screenshot—run the exercise in your own cluster to see it full size.

A platform dashboard like this is pretty low level—it's really just showing you if your cluster is near its saturation point. The queries that power this dashboard will be more useful as alerts, warning you if resource usage is getting out of hand. Kubernetes has pressure indicators that are useful there. The memory pressure and process pressure values are shown in the dashboard, as well as a disk pressure indicator. Those values are significant because if a node comes under compute pressure, it can terminate Pod containers. Those would be good metrics to alert on because if you reach that stage, you probably need to page someone to come and nurse the cluster back to health.

Platform metrics have another use: adding detail to application dashboards where the app itself doesn't provide detailed enough metrics. The platform dashboard shows compute resource usage aggregated across the whole cluster, but cAdvisor collects it at the container level. It's the same with kube-state-metrics, where you can filter metrics for a specific workload to add platform information to the application dashboard. We'll make a final dashboard update in this chapter, adding details from the platform to the random-number app.

TRY IT NOW　Update the dashboard for the random-number API to add metrics from the platform. This is just a Grafana update; there are no changes to the app itself or to Prometheus.

```
# update the dashboard:
kubectl apply -f grafana/update/grafana-dashboard-numbers-api-v2.yaml

# restart Grafana so it reloads the dashboard:
kubectl rollout restart deploy grafana -n kiamol-ch14-monitoring

# wait for the new Pod to start:
kubectl wait --for=condition=ContainersReady pod -l app=grafana -n
  kiamol-ch14-monitoring

# browse back to the random-number API dashboard
```

As shown in figure 14.13, the dashboard is still basic, but at least we now have some detail that could help correlate any issues. If the HTTP status code shows as 503, we can quickly see if the CPU is spiking, too. If the Pod labels contain an application version (which they should), we could identify which release of the app was experiencing the problem.

There's a lot more to monitoring that I won't cover here, but now you have a solid grounding in how Kubernetes and Prometheus work together. The main pieces you're missing are collecting metrics at the server level and configuring alerts. Server metrics supply data like disk and network usage. You collect them by running exporters directly on the nodes (using the Node Exporter for Linux servers and the Windows Exporter for Windows servers), and you use service discovery to add the nodes as scrape targets. Prometheus has a sophisticated alerting system that uses PromQL queries to define alerting rules. You configure alerts so that when rules are triggered, Prometheus will send emails, create Slack messages, or send a notification through PagerDuty.

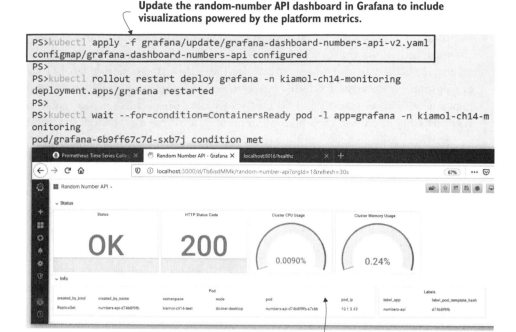

Update the random-number API dashboard in Grafana to include visualizations powered by the platform metrics.

```
PS>kubectl apply -f grafana/update/grafana-dashboard-numbers-api-v2.yaml
configmap/grafana-dashboard-numbers-api configured
PS>
PS>kubectl rollout restart deploy grafana -n kiamol-ch14-monitoring
deployment.apps/grafana restarted
PS>
PS>kubectl wait --for=condition=ContainersReady pod -l app=grafana -n kiamol-ch14-m
onitoring
pod/grafana-6b9ff67c7d-sxb7j condition met
```

Now we have CPU and memory usage for the container and details about the Pod.

Figure 14.13 Augmenting basic health stats with container and Pod metrics adds correlation.

We'll wrap up the chapter by looking at the full architecture of Prometheus in Kubernetes and digging into which pieces need custom work and where the effort needs to go.

14.5 Understanding the investment you make in monitoring

When you step outside of core Kubernetes and into the ecosystem, you need to understand whether the project you take a dependency on will still exist in five years, or one year, or by the time the chapter you're writing makes it to the printing press. I've been careful in this book to include only those ecosystem components that are open source, are heavily used, and have an established history and governance model. The monitoring architecture in figure 14.14 uses components that all meet those criteria.

I make that point because the move to Prometheus will involve development work. You need to record interesting metrics for your applications to make your dashboards truly useful. You should feel confident about making that investment because Prometheus is the most popular tool for monitoring containerized applications, and the project was the second to graduate in the CNCF—after Kubernetes itself. There's also work underway to take the Prometheus metric format into an open standard (called

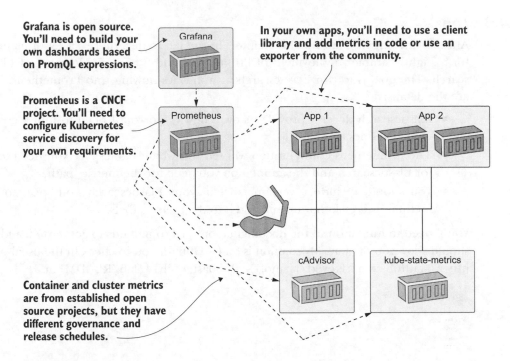

Grafana is open source. You'll need to build your own dashboards based on PromQL expressions.

In your own apps, you'll need to use a client library and add metrics in code or use an exporter from the community.

Prometheus is a CNCF project. You'll need to configure Kubernetes service discovery for your own requirements.

Container and cluster metrics are from established open source projects, but they have different governance and release schedules.

Figure 14.14 Monitoring doesn't come for free—it needs development and dependencies on open source projects.

OpenMetrics), so other tools will be able to read application metrics exposed in the Prometheus format.

What you include in those metrics will depend on the nature of your applications, but a good general approach is to follow the guidelines from Google's Site Reliability Engineering practice. It's usually pretty simple to add the four *golden signals* to your app metrics: latency, traffic, errors, and saturation. (Appendix B in the ebook walks through how those look in Prometheus.) But the real value comes when you think about application performance from the user experience perspective. A graph that shows heavy disk usage in your database doesn't tell you much, but if you can see that a high percentage of users don't complete a purchase because your website's checkout page takes too long to load, that's worth knowing.

That's all for monitoring now, so we can clear down the cluster to get ready for the lab.

TRY IT NOW Delete the namespaces for this chapter, and the objects created in the system namespace.

```
kubectl delete ns -l kiamol=ch14
kubectl delete all -n kube-system -l kiamol=ch14
```

14.6 *Lab*

Another investigative lab for this chapter. In the lab folder, there's a set of manifests for a slightly simpler deployment of Prometheus and a basic deployment of Elasticsearch. The goal is to run Elasticsearch with metrics flowing into Prometheus. Here are the details:

- Elasticsearch doesn't provide its own metrics, so you'll need to find a component that does that for you.
- The Prometheus configuration will tell you which namespace you need to use for Elasticsearch and the annotation you need for the metrics path.
- You should include a version label in your Elasticsearch Pod spec, so Prometheus will pick that up and add it to the metric labels.

You'll need to hunt around the documentation for Prometheus to get started, and that should show you the way. My solution is on GitHub for you to check in the usual place: https://github.com/sixeyed/kiamol/blob/master/ch14/lab/README.md.

Managing incoming traffic with Ingress

Services bring network traffic into Kubernetes, and you can have multiple Load-Balancer Services with different public IP addresses to make your web apps available to the world. Doing this creates a management headache because it means allocating a new IP address for every application and mapping addresses to apps with your DNS provider. Getting traffic to the right app is a routing problem, but you can manage it inside Kubernetes instead, using *Ingress*. Ingress uses a set of rules to map domain names and request paths to applications, so you can have a single IP address for your whole cluster and route all traffic internally.

Routing by domain name is an old problem that has usually been solved with a *reverse proxy*, and Kubernetes uses a pluggable architecture for Ingress. You define the routing rules as standard resources and deploy your choice of reverse proxy to receive traffic and act on the rules. All the major reverse proxies have Kubernetes support, along with a new species of container-aware reverse proxy. They all have different capabilities and working models, and in this chapter, you'll learn how you can use Ingress to host multiple apps in your cluster with two of the most popular: Nginx and Traefik.

15.1 How Kubernetes routes traffic with Ingress

We've used Nginx as a reverse proxy several times in this book already (17, by my count), but we've always used it for one application at a time. We had a reverse proxy to cache responses from the Pi app in chapter 6 and another for the random-number API in chapter 13. Ingress moves the reverse proxy into a central role, running it as a component called the *ingress controller*, but the approach is the same: the proxy receives external traffic from a LoadBalancer Service, and it fetches content from apps using ClusterIP Services. Figure 15.1 shows the architecture.

The Ingress Service is the only public-facing Service—a LoadBalancer in the cloud or a NodePort in the data center.

Application Services are all Cluster IPs. Application Pods are accessible only internally.

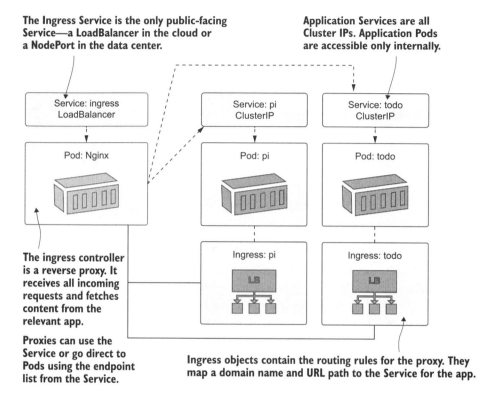

The ingress controller is a reverse proxy. It receives all incoming requests and fetches content from the relevant app.

Proxies can use the Service or go direct to Pods using the endpoint list from the Service.

Ingress objects contain the routing rules for the proxy. They map a domain name and URL path to the Service for the app.

Figure 15.1   Ingress controllers are the entry point to the cluster, routing traffic based on Ingress rules.

The important thing in this diagram is the ingress controller, which is the pluggable reverse proxy—it could be one of a dozen options including Nginx, HAProxy, Contour, and Traefik. The Ingress object stores routing rules in a generic way, and the controller feeds those rules into the proxy. Proxies have different feature sets, and the Ingress spec doesn't attempt to model every possible option, so controllers add support for those features using annotations. You'll learn in this chapter that the core functionality of routing and HTTPS support is simple to work with, but the complexity is in the ingress controller deployment and its additional features.

We'll start by running the basic Hello, World web app from way back in chapter 2, keeping it as an internal component with a ClusterIP Service and using the Nginx ingress controller to route traffic.

TRY IT NOW   Run the Hello, World app, and confirm that it's accessible only inside the cluster or externally using a port-forward in kubectl.

```
# switch to this chapter's folder:
cd ch15

# deploy the web app:
kubectl apply -f hello-kiamol/

# confirm the Service is internal to the cluster:
kubectl get svc hello-kiamol

# start a port-forward to the app:
kubectl port-forward svc/hello-kiamol 8015:80

# browse to http://localhost:8015
# then press Ctrl-C/Cmd-C to exit the port-forward
```

There's nothing new in the Deployment or Service specs for that application—no special labels or annotations, no new fields you haven't already worked with. You can see in figure 15.2 that the Service has no external IP address, and I can access the app only while I have a port-forward running.

To make the app available using Ingress rules, we need an ingress controller. Controllers manage other objects. You know that Deployments manage ReplicaSets and

This application spec deploys a ClusterIP Service, which makes the app accessible to Pods but not to the outside world.

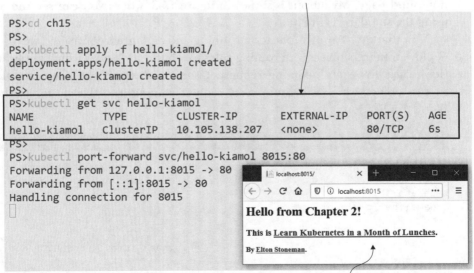

You can browse to the app only while you have a port-forward running in kubectl.

Figure 15.2   ClusterIP Services make an app available internally—it can go public with Ingress.

ReplicaSets manage Pods. Ingress controllers are slightly different; they run in standard Pods and monitor Ingress objects. When they see any changes, they update the rules in the proxy. We'll start with the Nginx ingress controller, which is part of the wider Kubernetes project. There's a production-ready Helm chart for the controller, but I'm using a much simpler deployment. Even so, there are a few security components in the manifest that we haven't covered yet, but I won't go through them now. (There are comments in the YAML if you want to investigate.)

TRY IT NOW   Deploy the Nginx ingress controller. This uses the standard HTTP and HTTPS ports in the Service, so you need to have ports 80 and 443 available on your machine.

```
# create the Deployment and Service for the Nginx ingress controller:
kubectl apply -f ingress-nginx/

# confirm the service is publicly available:
kubectl get svc -n kiamol-ingress-nginx

# get the URL for the proxy:
kubectl get svc ingress-nginx-controller -o jsonpath='http://{.status
    .loadBalancer.ingress[0].*}' -n kiamol-ingress-nginx

# browse to the URL—you'll get an error
```

When you run this exercise, you'll see a 404 error page when you browse. That proves the Service is receiving traffic and directing it to the ingress controller, but there aren't any routing rules yet so Nginx has no content to show, and it returns the default not-found page. My output is shown in figure 15.3, where you can see the Service is using the standard HTTP port.

Now that we have an application running and an ingress controller, we just need to deploy an Ingress object with routing rules to tell the controller which application Service to use for each incoming request. Listing 15.1 shows the simplest rule for an Ingress object, which will route every request coming into the cluster to the Hello, World application.

Listing 15.1   localhost.yaml, a routing rule for the Hello, World app

```
apiVersion: networking.k8s.io/v1beta1    # Beta API versions mean the spec
kind: Ingress                            # isn't final and could change.
metadata:
  name: hello-kiamol
spec:
  rules:
  - http:                                # Ingress is only for HTTP/S traffic
      paths:
      - path: /                          # Maps every incoming request
        backend:                         # to the hello-kiamol Service
          serviceName: hello-kiamol
          servicePort: 80
```

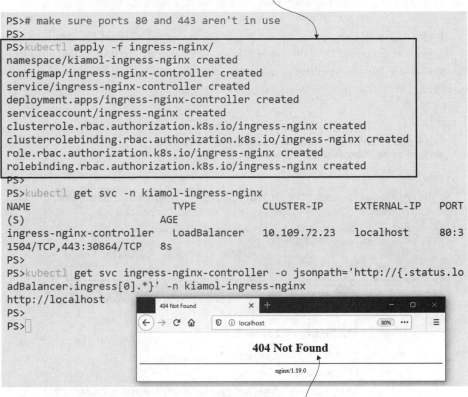

The ingress controller runs in a Deployment with a LoadBalancer Service. All the other objects are for securing access to the Kubernetes API.

```
PS># make sure ports 80 and 443 aren't in use
PS>
PS>kubectl apply -f ingress-nginx/
namespace/kiamol-ingress-nginx created
configmap/ingress-nginx-controller created
service/ingress-nginx-controller created
deployment.apps/ingress-nginx-controller created
serviceaccount/ingress-nginx created
clusterrole.rbac.authorization.k8s.io/ingress-nginx created
clusterrolebinding.rbac.authorization.k8s.io/ingress-nginx created
role.rbac.authorization.k8s.io/ingress-nginx created
rolebinding.rbac.authorization.k8s.io/ingress-nginx created
PS>
PS>kubectl get svc -n kiamol-ingress-nginx
NAME                          TYPE           CLUSTER-IP      EXTERNAL-IP    PORT
(S)                           AGE
ingress-nginx-controller      LoadBalancer   10.109.72.23    localhost      80:3
1504/TCP,443:30864/TCP        8s
PS>
PS>kubectl get svc ingress-nginx-controller -o jsonpath='http://{.status.lo
adBalancer.ingress[0].*}' -n kiamol-ingress-nginx
http://localhost
PS>
PS>
```

The Ingress Service listens on the standard HTTP and HTTPS ports. The ingress controller runs Nginx, which responds to requests. There are no Ingress rules yet, so the proxy returns a 404.

Figure 15.3 Ingress controllers receive incoming traffic, but they need routing rules to know what to do with it.

The ingress controller is watching for new and changed Ingress objects, so when you deploy any, it will add the rules to the Nginx configuration. In Nginx terms, it will set up a proxy server where the hello-kiamol Service is the upstream—the source of the content—and it will serve that content for incoming requests to the root path.

TRY IT NOW Create the Ingress rule that publishes the Hello, World app through the ingress controller.

```
# deploy the rule:
kubectl apply -f hello-kiamol/ingress/localhost.yaml
```

```
# confirm the Ingress object is created:
kubectl get ingress

# refresh your browser from the previous exercise
```

Well, that was simple—map a path to the backend Service for the application in an Ingress object, and the controller takes care of everything else. My output in figure 15.4 shows the localhost address, which previously returned a 404 error, now returns the Hello, World app in all its glory.

This Ingress object matches any host domain name and every path, so all incoming requests will use the same app.

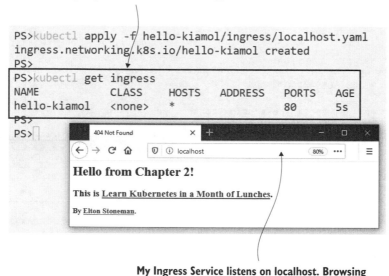

My Ingress Service listens on localhost. Browsing to any URL will show the Hello, World app.

Figure 15.4   Ingress object rules link the Ingress controller to the app Service.

Ingress is usually a centralized service in the cluster, like logging and monitoring. An admin team might deploy and manage the Ingress controller, whereas each product team owns the Ingress objects that route traffic to their apps. This process creates the potential for collisions—Ingress rules do not have to be unique, and one team's update could end up redirecting all of another team's traffic to some other app. In practice that doesn't happen because those apps will be hosted at different domains, and the Ingress rules will include a domain name to restrict their scope.

15.2   Routing HTTP traffic with Ingress rules

Ingress works only for web traffic—HTTP and HTTPS requests—because it needs to use the route specified in the request to match it to a backend service. The route in an HTTP request contains two parts: the host and the path. The host is the domain name, like `www.manning.com`, and the path is the location of the resource, like `/dotd` for the Deal of the Day page. Listing 15.2 shows an update to the Hello, World Ingress object that uses a specific host name. Now the routing rules will apply only if the incoming request is for the host `hello.kiamol.local`.

> **Listing 15.2   hello.kiamol.local.yaml, specifying a host domain for Ingress rules**

```
spec:
  rules:
  - host: hello.kiamol.local          # Restricts the scope of the
    http:                             # rules to a specific domain
      paths:
      - path: /                       # All paths in that domain will
        backend:                      # be fetched from the same Service.
          serviceName: hello-kiamol
          servicePort: 80
```

When you deploy this code, you won't be able to access the app because the domain name `hello.kiamol.local` doesn't exist. Web requests normally look up the IP address for a domain name from a public DNS server, but all computers also have their own local list in a *hosts file*. In the next exercise, you'll deploy the updated Ingress object and register the domain name in your local hosts file—you'll need admin access in your terminal session for that.

> **TRY IT NOW**   Editing the hosts file is restricted. You'll need to use the "Run as Administrator" option for your terminal session in Windows and have scripts enabled with the `Set-ExecutionPolicy` command. Be ready to enter your admin (sudo) password in Linux or macOS.

```
# add domain to hosts—on Windows:
./add-to-hosts.ps1 hello.kiamol.local ingress-nginx


# OR on Linux/macOS:
chmod +x add-to-hosts.sh && ./add-to-hosts.sh hello.kiamol.local
  ingress-nginx


# update the Ingress object, adding the host name:
kubectl apply -f hello-kiamol/ingress/hello.kiamol.local.yaml


# confirm the update:
kubectl get ingress


# browse to http://hello.kiamol.local
```

In this exercise, the existing Ingress object is updated, so there's still only one routing rule for the ingress controller to map. Now that rule is restricted to an explicit domain name. You can see in figure 15.5 that the request to `hello.kiamol.local` returns the app, and I've also browsed to the ingress controller at localhost, which returns a 404 error because there are no rules for the localhost domain.

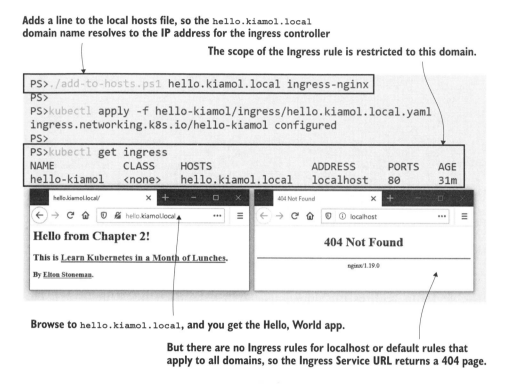

Adds a line to the local hosts file, so the `hello.kiamol.local` domain name resolves to the IP address for the ingress controller

The scope of the Ingress rule is restricted to this domain.

Browse to `hello.kiamol.local`, and you get the Hello, World app.

But there are no Ingress rules for localhost or default rules that apply to all domains, so the Ingress Service URL returns a 404 page.

Figure 15.5   You can publish apps by domain name with Ingress rules and use them locally by editing your hosts file.

Routing is an infrastructure-level concern, but like the other shared services we've seen in this section of the book, it runs in lightweight containers so you can use exactly the same setup in development, test, and production environments. That lets you run multiple apps in your nonproduction cluster with friendly domain names, without having to use different ports—the Service for the ingress controller uses the standard HTTP port for every app.

You need to fiddle with your hosts file if you want to run multiple apps with different domains in your lab environment. Typically, all the domains will resolve to 127.0.0.1, which is your machine's local address. Organizations might run their own

DNS server in a test environment, so anyone can access hello.kiamol.test from the company network, and it will resolve to the IP address of the test cluster, running in the data center. Then, in production, the DNS resolution is from a public DNS service, so hello.kiamol.net resolves to a Kubernetes cluster running in the cloud.

You can combine host names and paths in Ingress rules to present a consistent set of addresses for your application, although you could be using different components in the backend. You might have a REST API and a website running in separate Pods, and you could use Ingress rules to make the API available on a subdomain (api.rng.com) or as a path on the main domain (rng.com/api). Listing 15.3 shows Ingress rules for the simple versioned web app from chapter 9, where both versions of the app are available from one domain.

> **Listing 15.3   vweb/ingress.yaml, Ingress rules with host name and paths**

```
apiVersion: networking.k8s.io/v1beta1
kind: Ingress
metadata:
  name: vweb                              # Configures a specific feature
  annotations:                           # in Nginx
    nginx.ingress.kubernetes.io/rewrite-target: /
spec:
  rules:
  - host: vweb.kiamol.local              # All rules apply to this domain.
    http:
      paths:
      - path: /                          # Requests to the root path are
        backend:                         # proxied from the version 2 app.
          serviceName: vweb-v2
          servicePort: 80
      - path: /v1                        # Requests to the /v1 path are
        backend:                         # proxied from the version 1 app.
          serviceName: vweb-v1
          servicePort: 80
```

Modeling paths adds complexity because you're presenting a fake URL, which needs to be modified to match the real URL in the service. In this case, the ingress controller will respond to requests for http://vweb.kiamol.local/v1 and fetch the content from the vweb-v1 service. But the application doesn't have any content at /v1, so the proxy needs to rewrite the incoming URL—that's what the annotation does in listing 15.3. It's a basic example that ignores the path in the request and always uses the root path in the backend. You can't express URL rewrites with the Ingress spec, so it needs custom support from the ingress controller. A more realistic rewrite rule would use regular expressions to map the requested path to the target path.

We'll deploy this simple version to avoid any regular expressions and see how the ingress controller uses routing rules to identify the backend service and modify the request path.

TRY IT NOW   Deploy a new app with a new Ingress rule, and add a new domain to your hosts file to see the ingress controller serving multiple applications from the same domain.

```
# add the new domain name—on Windows:
./add-to-hosts.ps1 vweb.kiamol.local ingress-nginx

# OR on Linux/macOS:
./add-to-hosts.sh vweb.kiamol.local ingress-nginx

# deploy the app, Service, and Ingress:
kubectl apply -f vweb/

# confirm the Ingress domain:
kubectl get ingress

# browse to http://vweb.kiamol.local
# and http://vweb.kiamol.local/v1
```

In figure 15.6, you can see that two separate apps are made available at the same domain name, using the request path to route between different components, which are different versions of the application in this exercise.

Adds another domain name to the hosts file, which resolves to the ingress controller IP address

The new Ingress has rules for the host domain and URL path.

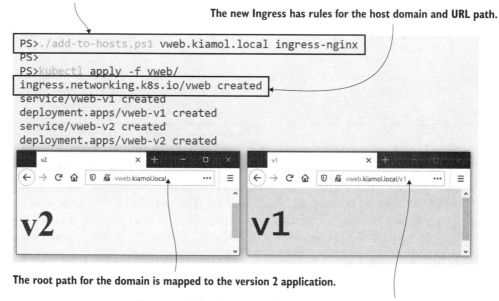

The root path for the domain is mapped to the version 2 application.

The /v1 path for the domain is mapped to the version 1 application. The proxy strips the request path and fetches content from the root path.

Figure 15.6   Ingress routing on the host name and path presents multiple apps on the same domain name.

Mapping the routing rules is the most complicated part of publishing a new app to your ingress controller, but it does give you a lot of control. The Ingress rules are the public face of your app, and you can use them to compose several components—or to restrict access to features. In this section of the book, we've seen that apps work better in Kubernetes if they have health endpoints for container probes and metrics endpoints for Prometheus to scrape, but those shouldn't be publicly available. You can use Ingress to control that, using exact path mappings, so only paths that are explicitly listed are available outside of the cluster.

Listing 15.4 shows an example of that for the to-do list app. It's abridged because the downside with this approach is that you need to specify every path you want to publish, so any paths not specified are blocked.

Listing 15.4 ingress-exact.yaml, using exact path matching to restrict access

```
rules:
  - host: todo.kiamol.local
    http:
      paths:
        - pathType: Exact        # Exact matching means only the /new
          path: /new             # path is matched—there are other
          backend:               # rules for the /list and root paths.
            serviceName: todo-web
            servicePort: 80
        - pathType: Prefix       # Prefix matching means any path that
          path: /static          # starts with /static will be mapped,
          backend:               # including subpaths like /static/app.css.
            serviceName: todo-web
            servicePort: 80
```

The to-do list app has several paths that shouldn't be available outside of the cluster—as well as `/metrics`, there's a `/config` endpoint that lists all of the application configurations and a diagnostics page. None of those paths is included in the new Ingress spec, and we can see that they're effectively blocked when the rules are applied. The PathType field is a later addition to the Ingress spec, so your Kubernetes cluster needs to be running at least version 1.18; otherwise, you'll get an error in this exercise.

TRY IT NOW Deploy the to-do list app with an Ingress spec that allows all access, and then update it with exact path matching, and confirm that the sensitive paths are no longer available.

```
# add a new domain for the app—on Windows:
./add-to-hosts.ps1 todo.kiamol.local ingress-nginx

# OR on Linux/macOS:
./add-to-hosts.sh todo.kiamol.local ingress-nginx

# deploy the app with an Ingress object that allows all paths:
kubectl apply -f todo-list/

# browse to http://todo.kiamol.local/metrics
```

```
# update the Ingress with exact paths:
kubectl apply -f todo-list/update/ingress-exact.yaml

# browse again—the app works, but metrics and diagnostics blocked
```

You'll see when you run this exercise that all of the sensitive paths are blocked when you deploy the updated Ingress rules. My output is shown in figure 15.7. It's not a perfect solution, but you can extend your ingress controller to show a friendly 404 error page instead of the Nginx default. (Docker has a nice example: try https://www .docker.com/not-real-url.) The app still shows a menu for the diagnostics page because it's not an app setting that removes the page; it's happening earlier in the process.

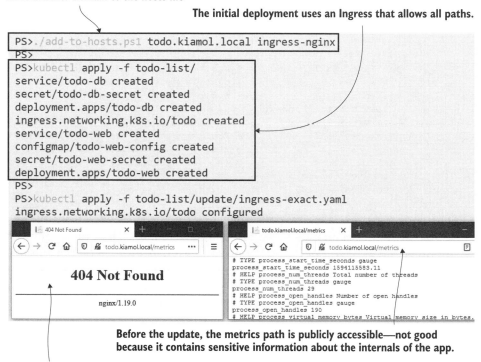

Figure 15.7   Exact path matching in Ingress rules can be used to block access to features.

The separation between Ingress rules and the ingress controller makes it easy to compare different proxy implementations and see which gives you the combination of features and usability you're happy with. But it comes with a warning because there isn't a strict ingress controller specification, and not every controller implements Ingress rules in the same way. Some controllers ignore the PathType field, so if you're relying on that to build up an access list with exact paths, you may find your site becomes access-all-areas if you switch to a different ingress controller.

Kubernetes does let you run multiple ingress controllers, and in a complex environment, you may do that to provide different sets of capabilities for different applications.

15.3 *Comparing ingress controllers*

Ingress controllers come in two categories: reverse proxies, which have been around for a long time and work at the network level, fetching content using host names; and modern proxies, which are platform-aware and can integrate with other services (cloud controllers can provision external load balancers). Choosing between them comes down to the feature set and your own technology preferences. If you have an established relationship with Nginx or HAProxy, you can continue that in Kubernetes. Or if you have an established relationship with Nginx or HAProxy, you might be glad to try a more lightweight, modern option.

Your ingress controller becomes the single public entry point for all of the apps in your cluster, so it's a good place to centralize common concerns. All controllers support SSL termination, so the proxy provides the security layer, and you get HTTPS for all of your applications. Most controllers support web application firewalls, so you can provide protection from SQL injection and other common attacks in the proxy layer. Some controllers have special powers—we've already used Nginx as a caching proxy, and you can use it for caching at the ingress level, too.

> **TRY IT NOW** Deploy the Pi application using Ingress, then update the Ingress object so the Pi app makes use of the Nginx cache in the ingress controller.

```
# add the Pi app domain to the hosts file—Windows:
./add-to-hosts.ps1 pi.kiamol.local ingress-nginx

# OR Linux/macOS:
./add-to-hosts.sh pi.kiamol.local ingress-nginx

# deploy the app and a simple Ingress:
kubectl apply -f pi/

# browse to http://pi.kiamol.local?dp=30000
# refresh and confirm the page load takes the same time

# deploy an update to the Ingress to use caching:
kubectl apply -f pi/update/ingress-with-cache.yaml

# browse to the 30K Pi calculation again—the first
# load takes a few seconds, but now a refresh will be fast
```

You'll see in this exercise that the ingress controller is a powerful component in the cluster. You can add caching to your app just by specifying new Ingress rules—no updates to the application itself and no new components to manage. The only requirement is that the HTTP responses from your app include the right caching headers, which they should anyway. Figure 15.8 shows my output, where the Pi calculation took 1.2 seconds, but the response came from the ingress controller's cache, so the page loaded pretty much instantly.

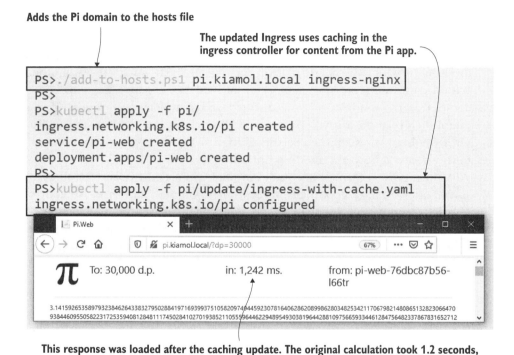

Adds the Pi domain to the hosts file

The updated Ingress uses caching in the ingress controller for content from the Pi app.

```
PS>./add-to-hosts.ps1 pi.kiamol.local ingress-nginx
PS>
PS>kubectl apply -f pi/
ingress.networking.k8s.io/pi created
service/pi-web created
deployment.apps/pi-web created
PS>
PS>kubectl apply -f pi/update/ingress-with-cache.yaml
ingress.networking.k8s.io/pi configured
```

To: 30,000 d.p.   in: 1,242 ms.   from: pi-web-76dbc87b56-l66tr

This response was loaded after the caching update. The original calculation took 1.2 seconds, but the response was cached, so repeat requests to the same page load instantly.

Figure 15.8   If your ingress controller supports response caching, that's an easy performance boost.

Not every ingress controller provides a response cache, so that's not a specific part of the Ingress spec. Any custom configuration is applied with annotations, which the controller picks up. Listing 15.5 shows the metadata for the updated cache setting you applied in the previous exercise. If you're familiar with Nginx, you'll recognize these as the proxy cache settings you would normally set in the configuration file.

> **Listing 15.5   ingress-with-cache.yaml, using the Nginx cache in the ingress controller**

```
apiVersion: networking.k8s.io/v1beta1
kind: Ingress
metadata:                      # The ingress controller looks in annotations for
  name: pi                     # custom configuration—this adds proxy caching.
```

```
annotations:
  nginx.ingress.kubernetes.io/proxy-buffering: "on"
  nginx.ingress.kubernetes.io/configuration-snippet: |
    proxy_cache static-cache;
    proxy_cache_valid 10m;
```

The configuration in an Ingress object applies to all of its rules, but if you need different features for different parts of your app, you can have multiple Ingress rules. That's true for the to-do list app, which needs some more help from the ingress controller to work properly at scale. Ingress controllers use load balancing if a Service has many Pods, but the to-do app has some cross-site forgery protection, which breaks if the request to create a new item is sent to a different app container from the one that originally rendered the new item page. Lots of apps have a restriction like this, which proxies solve using *sticky sessions.*

Sticky sessions are a mechanism for the ingress controller to send requests from the same end user to the same container, which is often a requirement for older apps where components aren't stateless. It's something to avoid where possible because it limits the cluster's potential for load balancing, so in the to-do list app, we want to restrict it to just one page. Figure 15.9 shows the Ingress rules we'll apply to get different features for different parts of the app.

The ingress controller uses load-balancing between Pods, except for the `/new` path, which uses sticky sessions, so an end user is always directed to the same Pod.

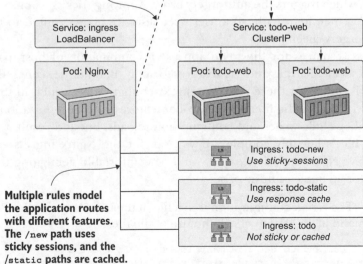

Multiple rules model the application routes with different features. The `/new` path uses sticky sessions, and the `/static` paths are cached.

Figure 15.9 A domain can be mapped with multiple Ingress rules, using different proxy features.

We can scale up the to-do app now to understand the problem and then apply the updated Ingress rules to fix it.

> **TRY IT NOW**   Scale up the to-do application to confirm that it breaks without sticky sessions, and then deploy the updated Ingress rules from figure 15.9 and confirm it all works again.

```
# scale up—the controller load-balances between the Pods:
kubectl scale deploy/todo-web --replicas 3

# wait for the new Pods to start:
kubectl wait --for=condition=ContainersReady pod -l app=todo-web

# browse to http://todo.kiamol.local/new, and add an item
# this will fail and show a 400 error page

# print the application logs to see the issue:
kubectl logs -l app=todo-web --tail 1 --since 60s

# update Ingress to add sticky sessions:
kubectl apply -f todo-list/update/ingress-sticky.yaml

# browse again, and add a new item—this time it works
```

You can see my output in figure 15.10, but unless you run the exercise yourself, you'll have to take my word for which is the "before" and which is the "after" screenshot. Scaling up the application replicas means requests from the ingress controller are load-balanced, which triggers the antiforgery error. Applying sticky sessions stops load balancing on the new item path, so a user's requests are always routed to the same Pod, and the forgery check passes.

The Ingress resources for the to-do app use a combination of host, paths, and annotations to set all the rules and the features to apply. Behind the scenes, the job of the controller is to convert those rules into proxy configuration, which in the case of Nginx means writing a config file. The controller features lots of optimizations to minimize the number of file writes and configuration reloads, but as a result, the Nginx configuration file is horribly complex. If you opt for the Nginx ingress controller because you have Nginx experience and you'd be comfortable debugging the config file, you're in for an unpleasant surprise.

> **TRY IT NOW**   The Nginx configuration is in a file in the ingress controller Pod. Run a command in the Pod to check the size of the file.

```
# run the wc command to see how many lines are in the file:
kubectl exec -n kiamol-ingress-nginx deploy/ingress-nginx-controller -
  - sh -c 'wc -l /etc/nginx/nginx.conf'
```

Figure 15.11 shows there are more than 1,700 lines in my Nginx configuration file. If you run cat instead of wc, you'll find the contents are strange, even if you're familiar

Scaling up causes a problem when you create a new item
because of antiforgery checks in the application.

Users see an unhelpful error, and the logs
record an antiforgery message.

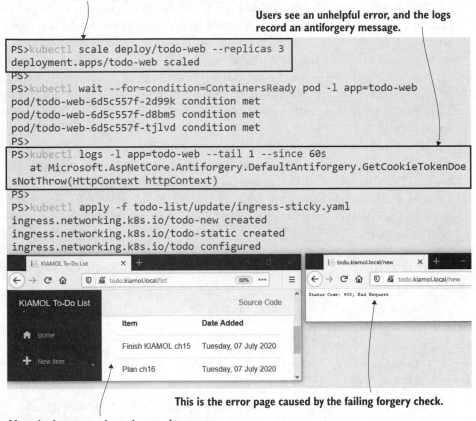

```
PS>kubectl scale deploy/todo-web --replicas 3
deployment.apps/todo-web scaled
PS>
PS>kubectl wait --for=condition=ContainersReady pod -l app=todo-web
pod/todo-web-6d5c557f-2d99k condition met
pod/todo-web-6d5c557f-d8bm5 condition met
pod/todo-web-6d5c557f-tjlvd condition met
PS>
PS>kubectl logs -l app=todo-web --tail 1 --since 60s
    at Microsoft.AspNetCore.Antiforgery.DefaultAntiforgery.GetCookieTokenDoe
sNotThrow(HttpContext httpContext)
PS>
PS>kubectl apply -f todo-list/update/ingress-sticky.yaml
ingress.networking.k8s.io/todo-new created
ingress.networking.k8s.io/todo-static created
ingress.networking.k8s.io/todo configured
```

This is the error page caused by the failing forgery check.

After the Ingress update, the new-item page
uses sticky sessions, and the app works again.

Figure 15.10 Proxy features can fix problems as well as improve performance.

The controller writes the Nginx configuration file to translate Ingress rules for the proxy.

```
PS>kubectl exec -n kiamol-ingress-nginx deploy/ingress-nginx-controller --
sh -c 'wc -l /etc/nginx/nginx.conf'
1766 /etc/nginx/nginx.conf
```

Over 1,700 lines in this config file—not going to enjoy debugging that!

Figure 15.11 The generated Nginx configuration file is not made to be human-friendly.

with Nginx. (The controller uses Lua scripts so it can update endpoints without a configuration reload.)

The ingress controller owns that complexity, but it's a critical part of your solution, and you need to be happy with how you'll troubleshoot and debug the proxy. This is when you might want to consider an alternative ingress controller that is platform aware and doesn't run from a complex configuration file. We'll look at Traefik in this chapter—it's an open source proxy that has been gaining popularity since it launched in 2015. Traefik understands containers, and it builds its routing list from the platform API, natively supporting Docker and Kubernetes, so it doesn't have a config file to maintain.

Kubernetes supports multiple Ingress controllers running in a single cluster. They'll be exposed as LoadBalancer Services, so in production, you might have different IP addresses for different ingress controllers, and you'll need to map domains to Ingress in your DNS configuration. In our lab environment, we'll be back to using different ports. We'll start by deploying Traefik with a custom port for the ingress controller Service.

TRY IT NOW   Deploy Traefik as an additional ingress controller in the cluster.

```
# create the Traefik Deployment, Service, and security resources:
kubectl apply -f ingress-traefik/

# get the URL for the Traefik UI running in the ingress controller:
kubectl get svc ingress-traefik-controller -o
    jsonpath='http://{.status.loadBalancer.ingress[0].*}:8080' -n
    kiamol-ingress-traefik

# browse to the admin UI to see the routes Traefik has mapped
```

You'll see in that exercise that Traefik has an admin UI. It shows you the routing rules the proxy is using, and as traffic passes through, it can collect and show performance metrics. It's much easier to work with than the Nginx config file. Figure 15.12 shows two *routers*, which are the incoming routes Traefik manages. If you explore the dashboard, you'll see those aren't Ingress routes; they're internal routes for Traefik's own dashboard—Traefik has not picked up any of the existing Ingress rules in the cluster.

Why hasn't Traefik built a set of routing rules for the to-do list or the Pi applications? It would if we had configured it differently, and all the existing routes would be available via the Traefik Service, but that's not how you use multiple ingress controllers because they would end up fighting over incoming requests. You run more than one controller to provide different proxy capabilities, and you need the application to choose which one to use. You do that with *ingress classes*, which are a similar concept to storage classes. Traefik has been deployed with a named ingress class, and only Ingress objects that request that class will be routed through Traefik.

**Running Traefik as an ingress controller, with a Service and
Deployment and security settings for accessing the Kubernetes API**

Traefik runs an admin UI, which you can access through the Service.

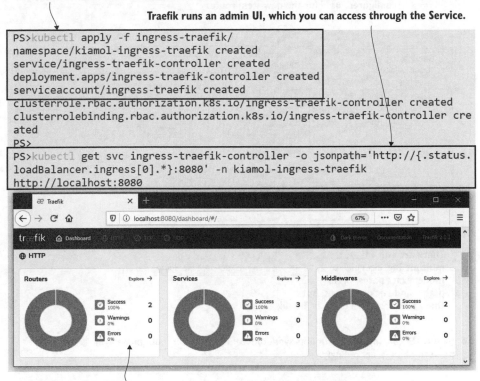

```
PS>kubectl apply -f ingress-traefik/
namespace/kiamol-ingress-traefik created
service/ingress-traefik-controller created
deployment.apps/ingress-traefik-controller created
serviceaccount/ingress-traefik created
clusterrole.rbac.authorization.k8s.io/ingress-traefik-controller created
clusterrolebinding.rbac.authorization.k8s.io/ingress-traefik-controller cre
ated
PS>
PS>kubectl get svc ingress-traefik-controller -o jsonpath='http://{.status.
loadBalancer.ingress[0].*}:8080' -n kiamol-ingress-traefik
http://localhost:8080
```

**Traefik uses its own terminology: routers are the frontend paths, services are the
backend content providers, and middlewares are features for manipulating behavior.
None of the existing Ingress rules have been applied by Traefik.**

Figure 15.12 Traefik is a container-native proxy that builds routing rules from the platform and has
a UI to display them.

The ingress class isn't the only difference between ingress controllers, and you may
need to model your routes quite differently for different proxies. Figure 15.13 shows
how the to-do app needs to be configured in Traefik. There's no response cache in
Traefik so we don't get caching for static resources, and sticky sessions are configured
at the Service level, so we need an additional Service for the new item route.

That model is significantly different from the Nginx routing in figure 15.9, so if
you do plan to run multiple ingress controllers, you need to appreciate the high risk
of misconfiguration, with teams confusing the different capabilities and approaches.
Traefik uses annotations on Ingress resources to configure the routing rules. Listing 15.6 shows a spec for the new-item path, which selects Traefik as the ingress class

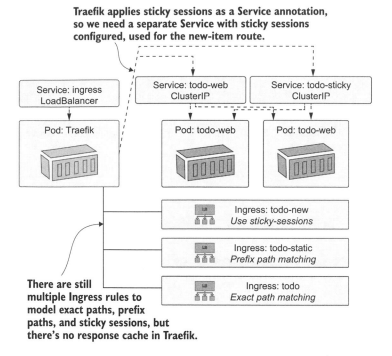

Traefik applies sticky sessions as a Service annotation, so we need a separate Service with sticky sessions configured, used for the new-item route.

There are still multiple Ingress rules to model exact paths, prefix paths, and sticky sessions, but there's no response cache in Traefik.

Figure 15.13   Ingress controllers work differently, and your route model will need to change accordingly.

and uses an annotation for exact path matching, because Traefik doesn't support the PathType field.

Listing 15.6   ingress-traefik.yaml, selecting the ingress class with Traefik annotations

```
apiVersion: networking.k8s.io/v1beta1
kind: Ingress
metadata:                                    # Annotations select the Traefik
  name: todo2-new                            # ingress class and apply exact
  annotations:                               # path matching.
    kubernetes.io/ingress.class: traefik
    traefik.ingress.kubernetes.io/router.pathmatcher: Path
spec:
  rules:
  - host: todo2.kiamol.local                 # Uses a different host so the app
    http:                                    # stays avaialable through Nginx
      paths:
      - path: /new
        backend:
          serviceName: todo-web-sticky       # Uses the Service that has sticky
          servicePort: 80                    # sessions configured for Traefik
```

We'll deploy a new set of Ingress rules using a different host name, so we can route traffic to the same set of to-do list Pods via Nginx or Traefik.

TRY IT NOW Publish the to-do app through the Traefik ingress controller, using the Ingress routes modeled in figure 15.13.

```
# add a new domain for the app—on Windows:
./add-to-hosts.ps1 todo2.kiamol.local ingress-traefik

# OR on Linux/macOS:
./add-to-hosts.sh todo2.kiamol.local ingress-traefik

# apply the new Ingress rules and sticky Service:
kubectl apply -f todo-list/update/ingress-traefik.yaml

# refresh the Traefik admin UI to confirm the new routes
# browse to http://todo2.kiamol.local:8015
```

Traefik watches for events from the Kubernetes API server and refreshes its routing list automatically. When you deploy the new Ingress objects, you'll see the paths shown as routers in the Traefik dashboard, linked to the backend Services. Figure 15.14 shows part of the routing list, together with the to-do app available through the new URL.

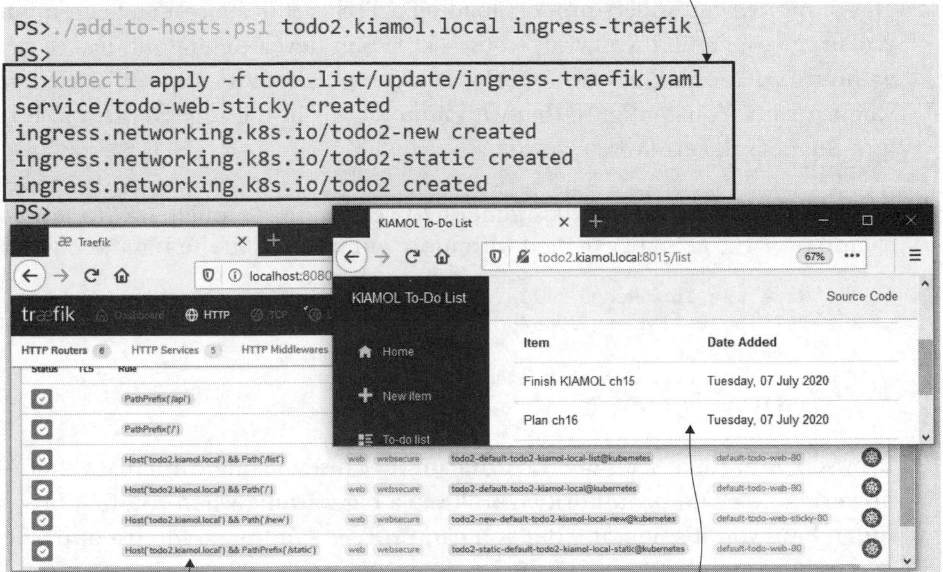

Applies new Ingress rules to make the app available through the Traefik ingress controller that are published through the LoadBalancer Service on port 8015

The router list in Traefik shows the new to-do list paths.

And the same app is available—using the same Pods—via the Traefik Ingress Service.

Figure 15.14 Ingress controllers achieve the same goals from different configuration models.

If you're evaluating ingress controllers, you should look at the ease of modeling your application paths, together with the approach to troubleshooting and the performance of the proxy. Dual-running controllers in a dedicated environment helps with that because you can isolate other factors and run comparisons using the same application components. A more realistic app will have more complex Ingress rules, and you'll want to be comfortable with how the controller implements features like rate limiting, URL rewrites, and client IP access lists.

The other major feature of Ingress is publishing apps over HTTPS without configuring certificates and security settings in your applications. This is one area that is consistent among ingress controllers, and in the next section, we'll see it with Traefik and Nginx.

15.4   *Using Ingress to secure your apps with HTTPS*

Your web apps should be published over HTTPS, but encryption needs server certificates, and certificates are sensitive data items. It's a good practice to make HTTPS an ingress concern, because it centralizes certificate management. Ingress resources can specify a TLS certificate in a Kubernetes Secret (TLS is Transport Layer Security, the encryption mechanism for HTTPS). Moving TLS away from application teams means you can have a standard approach to provisioning, securing, and renewing certificates—and you won't have to spend time explaining why packaging certificates inside a container image is a bad idea.

All ingress controllers support loading a TLS certificate from a Secret, but Traefik makes it easier still. If you want to use HTTPS in development and test environments without provisioning any Secrets, Traefik can generate its own self-signed certificate when it runs. You configure that with annotations in the Ingress rules to enable TLS and the default certificate resolver.

> **TRY IT NOW**   Using Traefik's generated certificate is a quick way to test your app over HTTPS. It's enabled with more annotations in the Ingress objects.

```
# update the Ingress to use Traefik's own certifcate:
kubectl apply -f todo-list/update/ingress-traefik-certResolver.yaml

# browse to https://todo2.kiamol.local:9443
# you'll see a warning in your browser
```

Browsers don't like self-signed certificates because anyone can create them—there's no verifiable chain of authority. You'll see a big warning when you first browse to the site, telling you it's not safe, but you can proceed, and the to-do list app will load. As shown in figure 15.15, the site is encrypted with HTTPS but with a warning so you know it's not really secure.

Your organization will probably have its own idea about certificates. If you're able to own the provisioning process, you can have a fully automated system where your cluster fetches short-lived certificates from a certificate authority (CA), installs them,

Traefik can provision TLS certificates from external issuers, or it can generate its own. This Ingress update publishes the to-do app over HTTPS using Traefik's certificates.

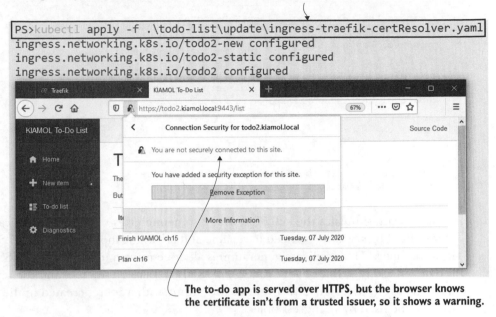

```
PS>kubectl apply -f .\todo-list\update\ingress-traefik-certResolver.yaml
ingress.networking.k8s.io/todo2-new configured
ingress.networking.k8s.io/todo2-static configured
ingress.networking.k8s.io/todo2 configured
```

The to-do app is served over HTTPS, but the browser knows the certificate isn't from a trusted issuer, so it shows a warning.

Figure 15.15   Not all HTTPS is secure—self-signed certificates are fine for development and test environments.

and renews them when required. Let's Encrypt is a great choice: it issues free certificates through an easily automated process. Traefik has native integration with Let's Encrypt; for other ingress controllers, you can use the open source cert-manager tool (https://cert-manager.io), which is a CNCF project.

Not everyone is ready for an automated provisioning process, though. Some issuers require a human to download certificate files, or your organization may create certificate files from its own certificate authority for nonproduction domains. Then you'll need to deploy the TLS certificate and key files as a Secret in the cluster. This scenario is common, so we'll walk through it in the next exercise, generating a certificate of our own.

TRY IT NOW   Run a Pod that generates a custom TLS certificate, and connect to the Pod to deploy the certificate files as a Secret. The Pod spec is configured to connect to the Kubernetes API server it's running on.

```
# run the Pod—this generates a certificate when it starts:
kubectl apply -f ./cert-generator.yaml

# connect to the Pod:
kubectl exec -it deploy/cert-generator -- sh
```

```
# inside the Pod, confirm the certificate files have been created:
ls

# rename the certificate files—Kubernetes requires specific names:
mv server-cert.pem tls.crt
mv server-key.pem tls.key

# create and label a Secret from the certificate files:
kubectl create secret tls kiamol-cert --key=tls.key --cert=tls.crt
kubectl label secret/kiamol-cert kiamol=ch15

# exit the Pod:
exit

# back on the host, confirm the Secret is there:
kubectl get secret kiamol-cert --show-labels
```

That exercise simulates the situation where someone gives you a TLS certificate as a pair of PEM files, which you need to rename and use as the input to create a TLS Secret in Kubernetes. The certificate generation is all done using a tool called OpenSSL, and the only reason for running it inside a Pod is to package up the tool and the scripts to make it easy to use. Figure 15.16 shows my output, with a Secret created in the cluster that can be used by an Ingress object.

HTTPS support is simple with an ingress controller. You add a TLS section to your Ingress spec and state the name of the Secret to use— that's it. Listing 15.7 shows an update to the Traefik ingress, which applies the new certificate to the todo2.kiamol .local host.

> **Listing 15.7   ingress-traefik-https.yaml, using the standard Ingress HTTPS feature**

```
spec:
  rules:
  - host: todo2.kiamol.local
    http:
      paths:
      - path: /new
        backend:
          serviceName: todo-web-sticky
          servicePort: 80
  tls:                                # The TLS section switches on HTTPS
    - secretName: kiamol-cert         # using the certificate in this Secret.
```

The TLS field with the Secret name is all you need, and it's portable across all ingress controllers. When you deploy the updated Ingress rules, the site will be served over HTTPS with your custom certificate. You'll still get a security warning from the browser because the certificate authority is untrusted, but if your organization has its own CA, then it will be trusted by your machine and the organization's certificates will be valid.

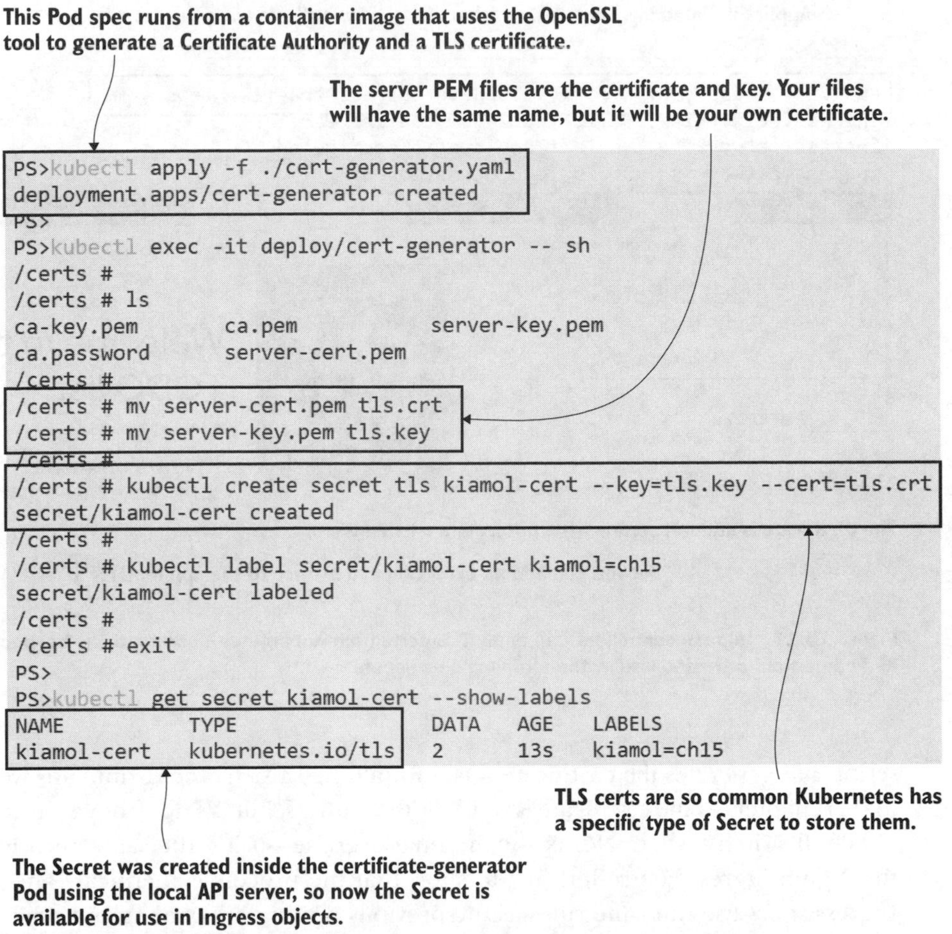

This Pod spec runs from a container image that uses the OpenSSL
tool to generate a Certificate Authority and a TLS certificate.

The server PEM files are the certificate and key. Your files
will have the same name, but it will be your own certificate.

```
PS>kubectl apply -f ./cert-generator.yaml
deployment.apps/cert-generator created
PS>
PS>kubectl exec -it deploy/cert-generator -- sh
/certs #
/certs # ls
ca-key.pem        ca.pem              server-key.pem
ca.password       server-cert.pem
/certs #
/certs # mv server-cert.pem tls.crt
/certs # mv server-key.pem tls.key
/certs #
/certs # kubectl create secret tls kiamol-cert --key=tls.key --cert=tls.crt
secret/kiamol-cert created
/certs #
/certs # kubectl label secret/kiamol-cert kiamol=ch15
secret/kiamol-cert labeled
/certs #
/certs # exit
PS>
PS>kubectl get secret kiamol-cert --show-labels
NAME            TYPE               DATA   AGE    LABELS
kiamol-cert     kubernetes.io/tls  2      13s    kiamol=ch15
```

TLS certs are so common Kubernetes has
a specific type of Secret to store them.

The Secret was created inside the certificate-generator
Pod using the local API server, so now the Secret is
available for use in Ingress objects.

Figure 15.16   If you're given PEM files from a certificate issuer, you can create them as a TLS Secret.

TRY IT NOW   Update the to-do list Ingress objects to publish HTTPS using the
Traefik ingress controller and your own TLS cert.

```
# apply the Ingress update:
kubectl apply -f todo-list/update/ingress-traefik-https.yaml

# browse to https://todo2.kiamol.local:9443
# there's still a warning, but this time it's because
# the KIAMOL CA isn't trusted
```

You can see my output in figure 15.17. I've opened the certificate details in one screen
to confirm this is my own "kiamol" certificate. I accepted the warning in the second
screen, and the to-do list traffic is now encrypted with the custom certificate. The

Applies updated Ingress rules, which use the TLS certificate from the Secret

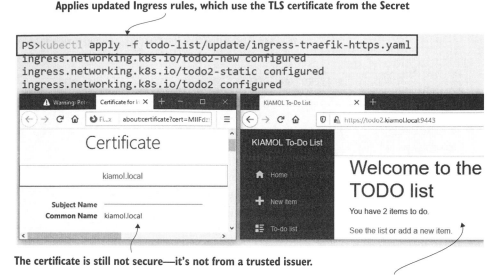

```
PS>kubectl apply -f todo-list/update/ingress-traefik-https.yaml
ingress.networking.k8s.io/todo2-new configured
ingress.networking.k8s.io/todo2-static configured
ingress.networking.k8s.io/todo2 configured
```

The certificate is still not secure—it's not from a trusted issuer.

But you can add an exception and browse to the app on HTTPS.

**Figure 15.17   Ingress controllers can apply TLS certs from Kubernetes Secrets. If the certificate
had come from a trusted issuer, the site would be secure**

script that generates the certificate sets it for all the kiamol.local domains we've used
in this chapter, so the certificate is valid for the address, but it's not from a trusted issuer.

We'll switch back to Nginx for the final exercise—using the same certificate with
the Nginx ingress controller, just to show that the process is identical. The updated
Ingress specs use the same rules as the previous Nginx deployment, but now they add
the TLS field with the same Secret name as listing 15.7.

TRY IT NOW   Update the to-do Ingress rules for Nginx, so the app is available
using HTTPS over the standard port 443, which the Nginx ingress controller
is using.

```
# update the Ingress resources:
kubectl apply -f todo-list/update/ingress-https.yaml

# browse to https://todo.kiamol.local
# accept the warnings to view the site

# confirm that the HTTP requests are redirected to HTTPS:
curl http://todo.kiamol.local
```

I cheated when I ran that exercise and added the Kiamol CA to my trusted issuer list
in the browser. You can see in figure 15.18 that the site is shown as secure, without any
warnings, which is what you'd see for an organization's own certificates. You can also

Applies TLS configuration to the Nginx Ingress rules for the to-do app

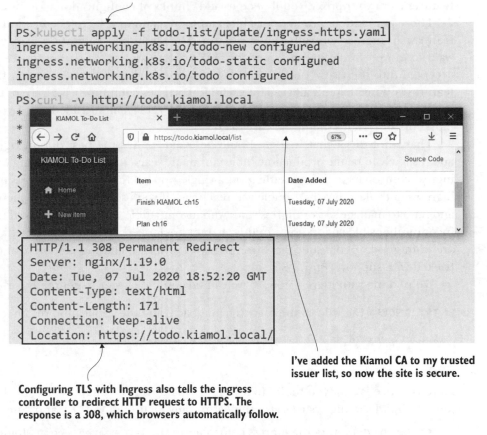

```
PS>kubectl apply -f todo-list/update/ingress-https.yaml
ingress.networking.k8s.io/todo-new configured
ingress.networking.k8s.io/todo-static configured
ingress.networking.k8s.io/todo configured
```

```
PS>curl -v http://todo.kiamol.local
```

```
< HTTP/1.1 308 Permanent Redirect
< Server: nginx/1.19.0
< Date: Tue, 07 Jul 2020 18:52:20 GMT
< Content-Type: text/html
< Content-Length: 171
< Connection: keep-alive
< Location: https://todo.kiamol.local/
```

I've added the Kiamol CA to my trusted issuer list, so now the site is secure.

Configuring TLS with Ingress also tells the ingress controller to redirect HTTP request to HTTPS. The response is a 308, which browsers automatically follow.

Figure 15.18   The TLS Ingress configuration works in the same way with the Nginx ingress controller.

see that the ingress controller redirects HTTP requests to HTTPS—the 308 redirect response in the `curl` command is taken care of by Nginx.

The HTTPS part of Ingress is solid and easy to use, and it's good to head to the end of the chapter on a high note. But using an ingress controller features a lot of complexity, and in some cases, you'll spend more time crafting your Ingress rules than you will modeling the deployment of the app.

15.5   Understanding Ingress and ingress controllers

You'll almost certainly run an ingress controller in your cluster, because it centralizes routing for domain names and moves TLS certificate management away from the applications. The Kubernetes model uses a common Ingress spec and a pluggable implementation that is very flexible, but the user experience is not straightforward.

The Ingress spec records only the most basic routing details, and to use more advanced features from your proxy, you'll need to add chunks of configuration as annotations.

Those annotations are not portable, and there is no interface specification for the features an ingress controller must support. There will be a migration project if you want to move from Nginx to Traefik or HAProxy or Contour (an open source project accepted into the CNCF on the very day I wrote this chapter), and you may find the features you need aren't all available. The Kubernetes community is aware of the limitations of Ingress and is working on a long-term replacement called the *Service API*, but as of 2021, that's still in the early stages.

That's not to say that Ingress should be avoided—it's the best option right now, and it's likely to be the production choice for many years. It's worth evaluating different ingress controllers and then settling on a single option. Kubernetes supports multiple ingress controllers, but the trouble will really start if you use different implementations and have to manage sets of Ingress rules with incompatible feature sets invoked through incomprehensible annotations. In this chapter, we looked at Nginx and Traefik, which are both good options, but there are plenty of others, including commercial options backed with support contracts.

We're done with Ingress now, so we can tidy up the cluster to get ready for the lab.

TRY IT NOW   Clear down the Ingress namespaces and the application resources.

```
kubectl delete ns,all,secret,ingress -l kiamol=ch15
```

15.6   *Lab*

Here is a nice lab for you to do, following the pattern from chapters 13 and 14. Your job is to build the Ingress rules for the Astronomy Picture of the Day app. Simple . . .

- Start by deploying the ingress controller in the `lab/ingress-nginx` folder.
- The ingress controller is restricted to look for Ingress objects in one namespace, so you'll need to figure out which one and deploy the `lab/apod/` folder to that namespace.
- The web app should be published at `www.apod.local` and the API at `api.apod.local`.
- We want to prevent distributed denial-of-service attacks, so you should use the rate-limiting feature in the ingress controller to prevent too many requests from the same IP address.
- The ingress controller uses a custom class name, so you'll need to find that, too.

This is partly about digging into the ingress controller configuration and partly about the documentation for the controller—be aware that there are two Nginx ingress controllers. We've used the one from the Kubernetes project in this chapter, but there's an alternative published by the Nginx project. My solution is ready for you to check against: https://github.com/sixeyed/kiamol/blob/master/ch15/lab/README.md.

Securing applications with policies, contexts, and admission control

16

Containers are a lightweight wrapper around application processes. They start quickly and add little overhead to your app because they use the operating system kernel of the machine on which they're running. That makes them super efficient, but at the cost of strong isolation—containers can be compromised, and a compromised container could provide unrestricted access to the server and to all the other containers running on it. Kubernetes has many features to secure your applications, but none of them are enabled by default. In this chapter, you'll learn how to use the security controls in Kubernetes and how to set up your cluster so those controls are required for all your workloads.

Securing applications in Kubernetes is about limiting what containers can do, so if an attacker exploits an app vulnerability to run commands in the container, they can't get beyond that container. We can do this by restricting network access to other containers and the Kubernetes API, restricting mounts of the host's filesystem, and limiting the operating system features the container can use. We'll cover the essential approaches, but the security space is large and evolving. This chapter is even longer than the others—you're about to learn a lot, but it will be only the start of your journey to a secure Kubernetes environment.

16.1 Securing communication with network policies

Restricting network access is one of the simplest ways to secure your applications. Kubernetes has a flat networking model, where every Pod can reach every other Pod by its IP address, and Services are accessible throughout the cluster. There's no reason why the Pi web application should access the to-do list database, or why the Hello, World web app should use the Kubernetes API, but by default, they can. You learned in chapter 15 how you can use Ingress resources to control access to HTTP routes, but that applies only to external traffic coming into the cluster. You also need to control access within the cluster, and for that, Kubernetes offers *network policies*.

Network policies work like firewall rules, blocking traffic to or from Pods at the port level. The rules are flexible and use label selectors to identify objects. You can deploy a blanket deny-all policy to stop outgoing traffic from all Pods, or you can deploy a policy that restricts incoming traffic to a Pod's metrics port so it can be accessed only from Pods in the monitoring namespace. Figure 16.1 shows how that looks in the cluster.

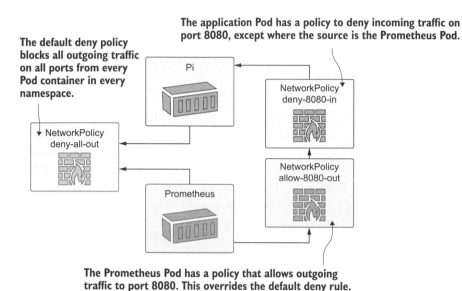

Figure 16.1   Network policy rules are granular—you can apply clusterwide defaults with Pod overrides.

NetworkPolicy objects are separate resources, which means they could be modeled outside of the application by a security team, or they could be built by the product team. Or, of course, each team might think the other team has it covered, and apps make it to production without any policies, which is a problem. We'll deploy an app that has slipped through with no policies and look at the problems it has.

TRY IT NOW   Deploy the Astronomy Picture of the Day (APOD) app, and confirm that the app components can be accessed by any Pod.

```
# switch to the chapter folder:
cd ch16

# deploy the APOD app:
kubectl apply -f apod/
```

```
# wait for it to be ready:
kubectl wait --for=condition=ContainersReady pod -l app=apod-web

# browse to the Service on port 8016 if you want to see today's
# picture

# now run a sleep Pod:
kubectl apply -f sleep.yaml

# confirm that the sleep Pod can use the API:
kubectl exec  deploy/sleep -- curl -s http://apod-api/image

# read the metrics from the access log:
kubectl exec deploy/sleep -- sh -c 'curl -s http://apod-log/metrics |
  head -n 2'
```

You can clearly see the issue in this exercise—the whole of the cluster is wide open, so from the sleep Pod, you can access the APOD API and the metrics from the access log component. Figure 16.2 shows my output. Let's be clear that there's nothing special

The APOD app is distributed across many components.
The web Pod needs to access the API and access log.

This sleep Pod doesn't need to use APOD components,
but without network policies, it can access them.

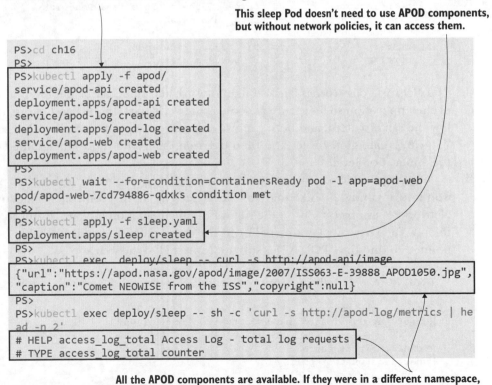

All the APOD components are available. If they were in a different namespace,
the URL would need to change, but they would still be accessible.

Figure 16.2 The downside of Kubernetes's flat networking model is that every Pod is accessible.

about the sleep Pod; it's just a simple way to demonstrate the problem. Any container in the cluster can do the same.

Pods should be isolated so they receive traffic only from the components that need to access them, and they send traffic only to components they need to access. Network policies model that with *ingress rules* (don't confuse them with Ingress resources), which restrict incoming traffic, and *egress rules*, which restrict outgoing traffic. In the APOD app, the only component that should have access to the API is the web app. Listing 16.1 shows this as an ingress rule in a NetworkPolicy object.

> **Listing 16.1   networkpolicy-api.yaml, restricting access to Pods by their labels**

```
apiVersion: networking.k8s.io/v1
kind: NetworkPolicy
metadata:
  name: apod-api
spec:
  podSelector:              # This is the Pod where the rule applies.
    matchLabels:
      app: apod-api
  ingress:                  # Rules default to deny, so this rule
  - from:                   # denies all ingress except where the
    - podSelector:          # source of the traffic is a Pod with
        matchLabels:        # the apod-web label.
          app: apod-web
    ports:                  # This restriction is by port.
    - port: api             # The port is named in the API Pod spec.
```

The NetworkPolicy spec is fairly straightforward, and rules can be deployed in advance of the application so it's secure as soon as the Pods start. Ingress and egress rules follow the same pattern, and both can use namespace selectors as well as Pod selectors. You can create global rules and then override them with more fine-grained rules at the application level.

One big problem with network policy—when you deploy the rules, they probably won't do anything. Just like Ingress objects need an ingress controller to act on them, NetworkPolicy objects rely on the network implementation in your cluster to enforce them. When you deploy this policy in the next exercise, you'll probably be disappointed to find the APOD API is still not restricted to the web app.

TRY IT NOW   Apply the network policy, and see if your cluster actually enforces it.

```
# create the policy:
kubectl apply -f apod/update/networkpolicy-api.yaml

# confirm it is there:
kubectl get networkpolicy

# try to access the API from the sleep Pod—this is not permitted
# by the policy:
kubectl exec deploy/sleep -- curl http://apod-api/image
```

You can see in figure 16.3 that the sleep Pod can access the API—the NetworkPolicy that limits ingress to the web Pods is completely ignored. I'm running this on Docker Desktop, but you'll get the same results with a default setup in K3s, AKS, or EKS.

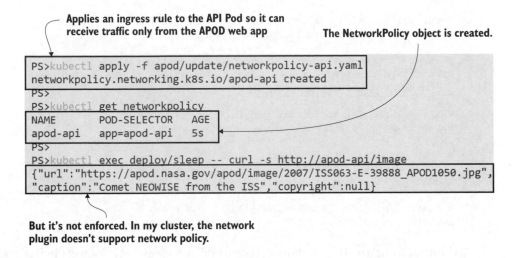

Applies an ingress rule to the API Pod so it can receive traffic only from the APOD web app

The NetworkPolicy object is created.

But it's not enforced. In my cluster, the network plugin doesn't support network policy.

Figure 16.3   The network setup in your Kubernetes cluster may not enforce network policies.

The networking layer in Kubernetes is pluggable, and not every network plugin supports NetworkPolicy enforcement. The simple networks in standard cluster deployments don't have support, so you get into this tricky situation where you can deploy all your NetworkPolicy objects, but you don't know whether they're being enforced unless you test them. Cloud platforms have different levels of support here. You can specify a network policy option when you create an AKS cluster; with EKS, you need to manually install a different network plugin after you create the cluster.

This is all very frustrating for you following along with these exercises (and me writing them), but it causes a much more dangerous disconnect for organizations using Kubernetes in production. You should look to adopt security controls early in the build cycle, so NetworkPolicy rules are applied in your development and test environments to run the app with a close-to-production configuration. A misconfigured network policy can easily break your app, but you won't know that if your nonproduction environments don't enforce policy.

If you want to see NetworkPolicy in action, the next exercise creates a custom cluster using Kind with Calico, an open source network plugin that enforces policy. You'll need Docker and the Kind command line installed for this. Be warned: **This exercise alters the Linux configuration for Docker and will make your original cluster unusable**. Docker Desktop users can fix everything with the *Reset Kubernetes* button, and Kind users can replace their old cluster with a new one, but other setups might not be so lucky. It's fine to skip these exercises and just read through my output; we'll switch back to your normal cluster in the next section.

TRY IT NOW   Create a new cluster with Kind, and deploy a custom network plugin.

```
# install the Kind command line using instructions at
# https://kind.sigs.k8s.io/docs/user/quick-start/

# create a new cluster with a custom Kind configuration:
kind create cluster --image kindest/node:v1.18.4 --name kiamol-ch16
  --config kind/kind-calico.yaml

# install the Calico network plugin:
kubectl apply -f kind/calico.yaml

# wait for Calico to spin up:
kubectl wait --for=condition=ContainersReady pod -l k8s-app=calico-
  node -n kube-system

# confirm your new cluster is ready:
kubectl get nodes
```

My output in figure 16.4 is abbreviated; you'll see many more objects being created in the Calico deployment. At the end, I have a new cluster that enforces network policy. Unfortunately, the only way to know if your cluster uses a network plugin that does enforce policy is to set up your cluster with a network plugin that you know enforces policy.

Now we can try again. This cluster is completely new, with nothing running, but, of course, Kubernetes manifests are portable, so we can quickly deploy the APOD app again and try it out. (Kind supports multiple clusters running different Kubernetes versions with different configurations, so it's a great option for test environments, but it's not as developer-friendly as Docker Desktop or K3s).

TRY IT NOW   Repeat the APOD and sleep deployments, and confirm that the network policy blocks unauthorized traffic.

```
# deploy the APOD app to the new cluster:
kubectl apply -f apod/

# wait for it to spin up:
kubectl wait --for=condition=ContainersReady pod -l app=apod-web

# deploy the sleep Pod:
kubectl apply -f sleep.yaml

# confirm the sleep Pod has access to the APOD API:
kubectl exec deploy/sleep -- curl -s http://apod-api/image

# apply the network policy:
kubectl apply -f apod/update/networkpolicy-api.yaml
```

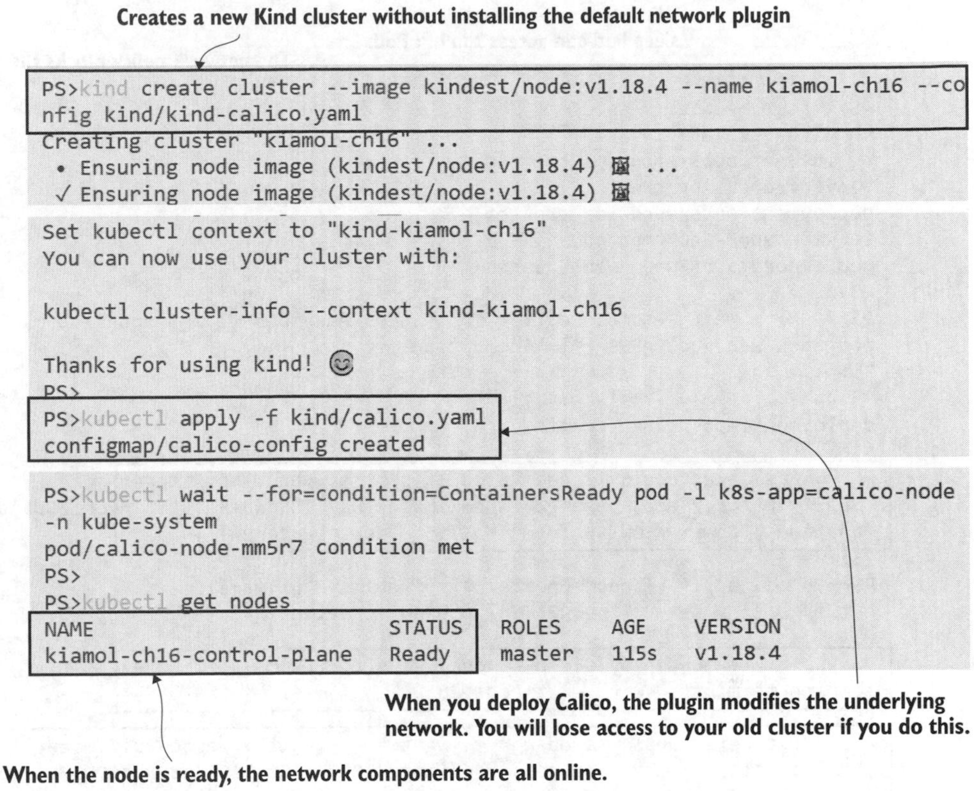

Creates a new Kind cluster without installing the default network plugin

```
PS>kind create cluster --image kindest/node:v1.18.4 --name kiamol-ch16 --co
nfig kind/kind-calico.yaml
Creating cluster "kiamol-ch16" ...
 • Ensuring node image (kindest/node:v1.18.4) 🖼 ...
 ✓ Ensuring node image (kindest/node:v1.18.4) 🖼

Set kubectl context to "kind-kiamol-ch16"
You can now use your cluster with:

kubectl cluster-info --context kind-kiamol-ch16

Thanks for using kind! 😊
PS>
PS>kubectl apply -f kind/calico.yaml
configmap/calico-config created

PS>kubectl wait --for=condition=ContainersReady pod -l k8s-app=calico-node
-n kube-system
pod/calico-node-mm5r7 condition met
PS>
PS>kubectl get nodes
NAME                        STATUS   ROLES    AGE    VERSION
kiamol-ch16-control-plane   Ready    master   115s   v1.18.4
```

When you deploy Calico, the plugin modifies the underlying network. You will lose access to your old cluster if you do this.

When the node is ready, the network components are all online.

Figure 16.4   Installing Calico gives you a cluster with network policy support—at the cost of your other cluster.

```
# confirm the sleep Pod can't access the API:
kubectl exec deploy/sleep -- curl -s http://apod-api/image

# confirm the APOD web app still can:
kubectl exec deploy/apod-web -- wget -O- -q http://apod-api/image
```

Figure 16.5 shows what we expected the first time around: only the APOD web app can access the API, and the sleep app times out when it tries to connect because the network plugin blocks the traffic.

Network policies are an important security control in Kubernetes, and they're attractive to infrastructure teams who are used to firewalls and segregated networks. But you need to understand where policies fit in your developer workflow if you do choose to adopt them. If engineers run their own clusters without enforcement and you apply policy only later in the pipeline, your environments have very different configurations, and something will get broken.

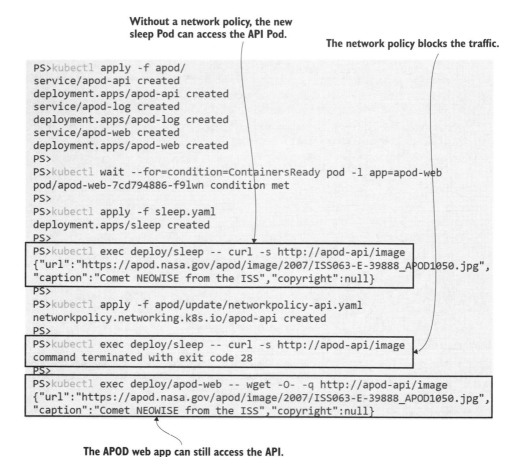

Without a network policy, the new sleep Pod can access the API Pod.

The network policy blocks the traffic.

```
PS>kubectl apply -f apod/
service/apod-api created
deployment.apps/apod-api created
service/apod-log created
deployment.apps/apod-log created
service/apod-web created
deployment.apps/apod-web created
PS>
PS>kubectl wait --for=condition=ContainersReady pod -l app=apod-web
pod/apod-web-7cd794886-f9lwn condition met
PS>
PS>kubectl apply -f sleep.yaml
deployment.apps/sleep created
PS>
PS>kubectl exec deploy/sleep -- curl -s http://apod-api/image
{"url":"https://apod.nasa.gov/apod/image/2007/ISS063-E-39888_APOD1050.jpg",
"caption":"Comet NEOWISE from the ISS","copyright":null}
PS>
PS>kubectl apply -f apod/update/networkpolicy-api.yaml
networkpolicy.networking.k8s.io/apod-api created
PS>
PS>kubectl exec deploy/sleep -- curl -s http://apod-api/image
command terminated with exit code 28
PS>
PS>kubectl exec deploy/apod-web -- wget -O- -q http://apod-api/image
{"url":"https://apod.nasa.gov/apod/image/2007/ISS063-E-39888_APOD1050.jpg",
"caption":"Comet NEOWISE from the ISS","copyright":null}
```

The APOD web app can still access the API.

Figure 16.5   Calico enforces policy so traffic to the API Pod is allowed only from the web Pod.

I've covered only the basic details of the NetworkPolicy API here, because the complexity is more in the cluster configuration than in the policy resources. If you want to explore further, there's a great GitHub repository full of network policy recipes published by Ahmet Alp Balkan, an engineer at Google: https://github.com/ahmetb/kubernetes-network-policy-recipes.

Now let's clear up the new cluster and see if your old cluster still works.

TRY IT NOW   Remove the Calico cluster, and see if the old cluster is still accessible.

```
# delete the new cluster:
kind delete cluster --name kiamol-ch16

# list your Kubernetes contexts:
kubectl config get-contexts
```

```
# switch back to your previous cluster:
kubectl config set-context <your_old_cluster_name>

# see if you can connect:
kubectl get nodes
```

Your previous cluster is probably no longer accessible because of the network changes Calico made, even though Calico isn't running now. Figure 16.6 shows me about to hit the *Reset Kubernetes* button in Docker Desktop; if you're using Kind, you'll need to delete and recreate your original cluster, and if you're using something else and it doesn't work . . . I did warn you.

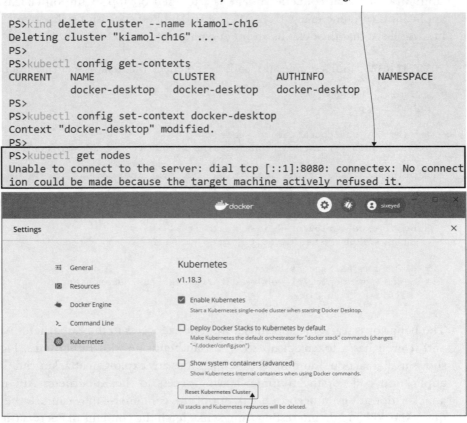

The new cluster changed the network in Docker Desktop, so my old cluster is still running, but it's unreachable.

```
PS>kind delete cluster --name kiamol-ch16
Deleting cluster "kiamol-ch16" ...
PS>
PS>kubectl config get-contexts
CURRENT   NAME             CLUSTER          AUTHINFO         NAMESPACE
          docker-desktop   docker-desktop   docker-desktop
PS>
PS>kubectl config set-context docker-desktop
Context "docker-desktop" modified.
PS>
PS>kubectl get nodes
Unable to connect to the server: dial tcp [::1]:8080: connectex: No connect
ion could be made because the target machine actively refused it.
```

Resetting the Kubernetes cluster in Docker Desktop—or
deleting and creating a new cluster in Kind—will fix it.

Figure 16.6 Calico running in a container was able to reconfigure my network and break things.

Now that we're all back to normal (hopefully), we can move on to securing containers themselves, so applications don't have privileges like reconfiguring the network stack.

16.2 Restricting container capabilities with security contexts

Container security is really about Linux security and the access model for the container user (Windows Server containers have a different user model that doesn't have the same issues). Linux containers usually run as the *root* super-admin account, and unless you explicitly configure the user, root inside the container is root on the host, too. If an attacker can break out of a container running as root, they're in charge of your server now. That's a problem for all container runtimes, but Kubernetes adds a few more problems of its own.

In the next exercise, you'll run the Pi web application with a basic Deployment configuration. That container image is packaged on top of the official .NET Core application run-time image from Microsoft. The Pod spec isn't deliberately insecure, but you'll see that the defaults aren't encouraging.

TRY IT NOW   Run a simple application, and check the default security situation.

```
# deploy the app:
kubectl apply -f pi/

# wait for the container to start:
kubectl wait --for=condition=ContainersReady pod -l app=pi-web

# print the name of the user in the Pod container:
kubectl exec deploy/pi-web -- whoami

# try to access the Kubernetes API server:
kubectl exec deploy/pi-web -- sh -c 'curl -k -s
  https://kubernetes.default | grep message'

# print the API access token:
kubectl exec deploy/pi-web -- cat /run/secrets/kubernetes.io/
  serviceaccount/token
```

The behavior is scary: the app runs as root, it has access to the Kubernetes API server, and it even has a token set up so it can authenticate with Kubernetes. Figure 16.7 shows it all in action. Running as root magnifies any exploit an attacker can find in the application code or the runtime. Having access to the Kubernetes API means an attacker doesn't even need to break out of the container—they can use the token to query the API and do interesting things, like fetch the contents of Secrets (depending on the access permissions for the Pod, which you'll learn about in chapter 17).

Kubernetes provides multiple security controls at the Pod and container levels, but they're not enabled by default because they could break your app. You can run containers as a different user, but some apps work only if they're running as root. You can

Deploys the Pi application from a simple spec, which doesn't apply any security controls

The container runs processes as root, which is a big risk if the app is compromised.

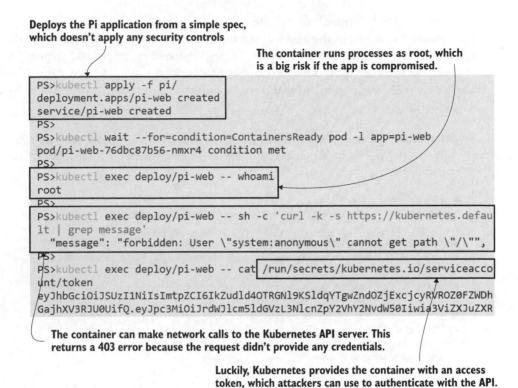

```
PS>kubectl apply -f pi/
deployment.apps/pi-web created
service/pi-web created
PS>
PS>kubectl wait --for=condition=ContainersReady pod -l app=pi-web
pod/pi-web-76dbc87b56-nmxr4 condition met
PS>
PS>kubectl exec deploy/pi-web -- whoami
root
PS>
PS>kubectl exec deploy/pi-web -- sh -c 'curl -k -s https://kubernetes.defau
lt | grep message'
  "message": "forbidden: User \"system:anonymous\" cannot get path \"/\"",
PS>
PS>kubectl exec deploy/pi-web -- cat /run/secrets/kubernetes.io/serviceacco
unt/token
eyJhbGciOiJSUzI1NiIsImtpZCI6IkZudld4OTRGNl9KSldqYTgwZndOZjExcjcyRVROZ0FZWDh
GajhXV3RJU0UifQ.eyJpc3MiOiJrdWJlcm5ldGVzL3NlcnZpY2hY2NvdW50Iiwia3ViZXJuZXR
```

The container can make network calls to the Kubernetes API server. This returns a 403 error because the request didn't provide any credentials.

Luckily, Kubernetes provides the container with an access token, which attackers can use to authenticate with the API.

Figure 16.7 If you've heard the phrase "secure by default," it wasn't said about Kubernetes.

drop Linux capabilities to restrict what the container can do, but then some app features could fail. This is where automated testing comes in, because you can increasingly tighten the security around your apps, running tests at each stage to confirm everything still works.

The main control you'll use is the SecurityContext field, which applies security at the Pod and container levels. Listing 16.2 shows a Pod SecurityContext that explicitly sets the user and the Linux group (a collection of users), so all of the containers in the Pod run as the *unknown* user rather than root.

Listing 16.2 deployment-podsecuritycontext.yaml, running as a specific user

```
spec:                      # This is the Pod spec in the Deployment.
  securityContext:         # These controls apply to all Pod containers.
    runAsUser: 65534       # Runs as the "unknown" user
    runAsGroup: 3000       # Runs with a nonexistent group
```

That's simple enough, but moving away from root has repercussions, and the Pi spec needs a few more changes. The app listens on port 80 inside the container, and Linux requires elevated permissions to listen on that port. Root has the permission, but the new user doesn't, so the app will fail to start. It needs some additional configuration in an environment variable to set the app to listen on port 5001 instead, which is valid for the new user. This is the sort of detail you need to drive out for each app or each class of application, and you'll find the requirements only when the app stops working.

TRY IT NOW   Deploy the secured Pod spec. This uses a nonroot user and an unrestricted port, but the port mapping in the Service hides that detail from consumers.

```
# add the nonroot SecurityContext:
kubectl apply -f pi/update/deployment-podsecuritycontext.yaml

# wait for the new Pod:
kubectl wait --for=condition=ContainersReady pod -l app=pi-web

# confirm the user:
kubectl exec deploy/pi-web -- whoami

# list the API token files:
kubectl exec deploy/pi-web -- ls -l /run/secrets/kubernetes.io/
   serviceaccount/token

# print out the access token:
kubectl exec deploy/pi-web -- cat /run/secrets/kubernetes.io/
   serviceaccount/token
```

Running as a nonroot user addresses the risk of an application exploit escalating into a full server takeover, but as shown in figure 16.8, it doesn't solve all the problems. The Kubernetes API token is mounted with permissions for any account to read it, so an attacker could still use the API in this setup. What they can do with the API depends on how your cluster is configured—in early versions of Kubernetes, they'd be able to do everything. The identity to access the API server is different from the Linux user, and it might have administrator rights in the cluster, even though the container process is running as a least-privilege user.

An option in the Pod spec stops Kubernetes from mounting the access token, which you should include for every app that doesn't actually need to use the Kubernetes API—which will be pretty much everything, except workloads like ingress controllers, which need to find Service endpoints. It's a safe option to set, but the next level of run-time control will need more testing and evaluation. The SecurityContext field in the container spec allows for more fine-grained control than at the Pod level. Listing 16.3 shows a set of options that work for the Pi app.

The Pod SecurityContext sets the container user to a least-privilege account.

But the token file grants read access to all users.

```
PS>kubectl apply -f pi/update/deployment-podsecuritycontext.yaml
deployment.apps/pi-web configured
PS>
PS>kubectl wait --for=condition=ContainersReady pod -l app=pi-web
pod/pi-web-74c97dbd7b-9tqkf condition met
PS>
PS>kubectl exec deploy/pi-web -- whoami
nobody
PS>
PS>kubectl exec deploy/pi-web -- ls -l /run/secrets/kubernetes.io/serviceac
count/token
lrwxrwxrwx 1 root root 12 Jul 10 10:41 /run/secrets/kubernetes.io/serviceac
count/token -> ..data/token
PS>
PS>kubectl exec deploy/pi-web -- cat /run/secrets/kubernetes.io/serviceacco
unt/token
eyJhbGciOiJSUzI1NiIsImtpZCI6IkZudld4OTRGNl9KSldqYTgwZndOZjExcjcyRVROZ0FZWDh
GajhXV3RJU0UifQ.eyJpc3MiOiJrdWJlcm5ldGVzL3NlcnZpY2VhY2NvdW50Iiwia3ViZXJuZXR
```

So, the new user could still access the Kubernetes API server.

Figure 16.8 You need an in-depth security approach to Kubernetes; one setting is not enough.

Listing 16.3 deployment-no-serviceaccount-token.yaml, tighter security policies

```
spec:
  automountServiceAccountToken: false    # Removes the API token
  securityContext:                       # Applies to all containers
    runAsUser: 65534
    runAsGroup: 3000
  containers:
    - image: kiamol/ch05-pi
      # ...
      securityContext:                   # Applies for this container
        allowPrivilegeEscalation: false  # The context settings block
        capabilities:                    # the process from escalating to
          drop:                          # higher privileges and drops
            - all                        # all additional capabilities.
```

The capabilities field lets you explicitly add and remove Linux kernel capabilities. This app works happily with all capabilities dropped, but other apps will need some added back in. One feature this app doesn't support is the readOnlyRootFilesystem option. That's a powerful one to include if your app can work with a read-only filesystem, because it means attackers can't write files, so they can't download malicious scripts or binaries. How far you take this depends on the security profile of your organization. You can mandate that all apps need to run as nonroot, with all capabilities dropped and with a read-only filesystem, but that might mean you need to rewrite most of your apps.

A pragmatic approach is to secure your existing apps as tightly as you can at the container level and make sure you have security in depth around the rest of your policies and processes. The final spec for the Pi app is not perfectly secure, but it's a big improvement on the defaults—and the application still works.

TRY IT NOW   Update the Pi app with the final security configuration.

```
# update to the Pod spec in listing 16.3:
kubectl apply -f pi/update/deployment-no-serviceaccount-token.yaml

# confirm the API token doesn't exist:
kubectl exec deploy/pi-web -- cat /run/secrets/kubernetes.io/
   serviceaccount/token

# confirm that the API server is still accessible:
kubectl exec deploy/pi-web -- sh -c 'curl -k -s
   https://kubernetes.default | grep message'

# get the URL, and check that the app still works:
kubectl get svc pi-web -o jsonpath='http://{.status.loadBalancer
   .ingress[0].*}:8031'
```

As shown in figure 16.9, the app can still reach the Kubernetes API server, but it has no access token, so an attacker would need to do more work to send valid API requests. Applying a NetworkPolicy to deny ingress to the API server would remove that option altogether.

You need to invest in adding security to your apps, but if you have a reasonably small range of application platforms, you can build up generic profiles: you might find that all your .NET apps can run as nonroot but need a writable filesystem, and all your Go apps can run with a read-only filesystem but need some Linux capabilities added. The challenge, then, is in making sure your profiles actually are applied, and Kubernetes has a nice feature for that: *admission control*.

16.3   *Blocking and modifying workloads with webhooks*

Every object you create in Kubernetes goes through a process to check if it's okay for the cluster to run that object. That process is admission control, and we saw an admission controller at work in chapter 12, trying to deploy a Pod spec that requested more resources than the namespace had available. The ResourceQuota admission controller is a built-in controller, which stops workloads from running if they exceed quotas, and Kubernetes has a plug-in system so you can add your own admission control rules.

Two other controllers add that extensibility: the ValidatingAdmissionWebhook, which works like ResourceQuota to allow or block object creation, and the MutatingAdmissionWebhook, which can actually edit object specs, so the object that is created is different from the request. Both controllers work in the same way: you create a

This spec tightens security for the app. It could do more, but the app doesn't work with all of Kubernetes's security controls.

The API token doesn't exist this time.

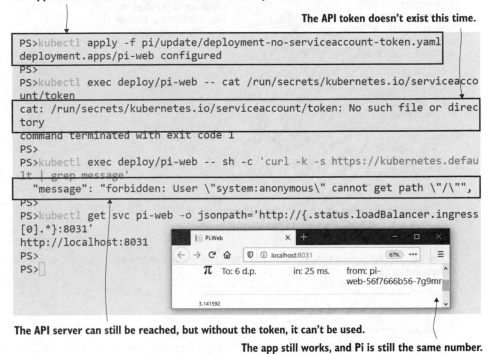

```
PS>kubectl apply -f pi/update/deployment-no-serviceaccount-token.yaml
deployment.apps/pi-web configured
PS>
PS>kubectl exec deploy/pi-web -- cat /run/secrets/kubernetes.io/serviceacco
unt/token
cat: /run/secrets/kubernetes.io/serviceaccount/token: No such file or direc
tory
command terminated with exit code 1
PS>
PS>kubectl exec deploy/pi-web -- sh -c 'curl -k -s https://kubernetes.defau
lt | grep message'
   "message": "forbidden: User \"system:anonymous\" cannot get path \"/\"",
PS>
PS>kubectl get svc pi-web -o jsonpath='http://{.status.loadBalancer.ingress
[0].*}:8031'
http://localhost:8031
PS>
PS>
```

The API server can still be reached, but without the token, it can't be used.

The app still works, and Pi is still the same number.

Figure 16.9   The secured app is the same for users but much less fun for attackers.

configuration object specifying the object life cycles you want to control and a URL for a web server that applies the rules. Figure 16.10 shows how the pieces fit together.

Admission webhooks are hugely powerful because Kubernetes calls into your own code, which can be running in any language you like and can apply whatever rules you need. In this section, we'll apply some webhooks I've written in Node.js. You won't need to edit any code, but you can see in listing 16.4 that the code isn't particularly complicated.

Listing 16.4   validate.js, custom logic for a validating webhook

```
# the incoming request has the object spec—this checks to see
# if the service token mount property is set to false;
# if not, the response stops the object from being created:

if (object.spec.hasOwnProperty("automountServiceAccountToken")) {
    admissionResponse.allowed =
    (object.spec.automountServiceAccountToken == false);
}
```

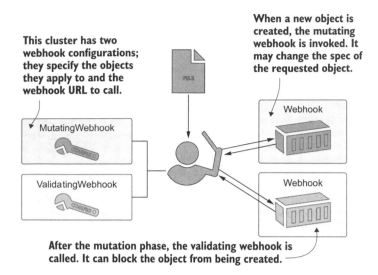

This cluster has two webhook configurations; they specify the objects they apply to and the webhook URL to call.

When a new object is created, the mutating webhook is invoked. It may change the spec of the requested object.

MutatingWebhook

ValidatingWebhook

Webhook

Webhook

After the mutation phase, the validating webhook is called. It can block the object from being created.

Figure 16.10   Admission webhooks let you apply your own rules when objects are created.

Webhook servers can run anywhere—inside or outside of the cluster—but they must be served on HTTPS. The only complication comes if you want to run webhooks inside your cluster signed by your own certificate authority (CA), because the webhook configuration needs a way to trust the CA. This is a common scenario, so we'll walk through that complexity in the next exercises.

> **TRY IT NOW**   Start by creating a certificate and deploying the webhook server to use that certificate.

```
# run the Pod to generate a certificate:
kubectl apply -f ./cert-generator.yaml

# when the container is ready, the certificate is done:
kubectl wait --for=condition=ContainersReady pod -l app=cert-generator

# the Pod has deployed the cert as a TLS Secret:
kubectl get secret -l kiamol=ch16

# deploy the webhook server, using the TLS Secret:
kubectl apply -f admission-webhook/

# print the CA certificate:
kubectl exec -it deploy/cert-generator -- cat ca.base64
```

The last command in that exercise will fill your screen with Base64-encoded text, which you'll need in the next exercise (don't worry about writing it down, though;

we'll automate all the steps). You now have the webhook server running, secured by a TLS certificate issued by a custom CA. My output appears in figure 16.11.

This tool creates a CA and a TLS certificate and deploys the certificate as a Secret in the cluster.

The webhook server is secured with HTTPS, using the TLS Secret.

```
PS>kubectl apply -f ./cert-generator.yaml
deployment.apps/cert-generator created
PS>
PS>kubectl wait --for=condition=ContainersReady pod -l app=cert-generator
pod/cert-generator-6db9bfbcc5-brdgw condition met
PS>
PS>kubectl get secret -l kiamol=ch16
NAME                       TYPE                DATA   AGE
admission-webhook-secret   kubernetes.io/tls   2      3m7s
PS>
PS>kubectl apply -f admission-webhook/
service/admission-webhook created
deployment.apps/admission-webhook created
PS>
PS>kubectl exec -it deploy/cert-generator -- cat ca.base64
LS0tLS1CRUdJTiBDRRVJUSUZJQ0FURS0tLS0tCk1JSUZnVENDQT tZ0F3SUJBZ0lVTGppb3ppIbj: 
Gdmgxb1VLdXhPNUkzb3NFRndjd0RRWUpLb1pJaHZjTkFRRUwKQ FBd1VERUxNQWtHQTFVRUJoTl 
```

Webhook configurations need to trust the CA if it's not a recognized issuer.
This file contains the CA certificate in the format Kubernetes expects.

Figure 16.11 Webhooks are potentially dangerous, so they need to be secured with HTTPS.

The Node.js app is running and has two endpoints: a validating webhook, which checks that all Pod specs have the `automountServiceAccountToken` field set to false, and a mutating webhook, which applies a container SecurityContext set with the `runAsNon-Root` flag. Those two policies are intended to work together to ensure a base level of security for all applications. Listing 16.5 shows the spec for the ValidatingWebhook-Configuration object.

Listing 16.5 validatingWebhookConfiguration.yaml, applying a webhook

```
apiVersion: admissionregistration.k8s.io/v1beta1
kind: ValidatingWebhookConfiguration
metadata:
  name: servicetokenpolicy
webhooks:
  - name: servicetokenpolicy.kiamol.net
    rules:                                      # These are the object
      - operations: [ "CREATE", "UPDATE" ]      # types and operations
        apiGroups: [""]                         # that invoke the
        apiVersions: ["v1"]                     # webhook—all Pods.
        resources: ["pods"]
```

```
clientConfig:
  service:
    name: admission-webhook          # The webhook Service to call
    namespace: default
    path: "/validate"                # URL for the webhook
  caBundle: {{ .Values.caBundle }}   # The CA certificate
```

Webhook configurations are flexible: you can set the types of operation and the types of object on which the webhook operates. You can have multiple webhooks configured for the same object—validating webhooks are all called in parallel, and any one of them can block the operation. This YAML file is part of a Helm chart that I'm using just for this config object, as an easy way to inject the CA certificate. A more advanced Helm chart would include a job to generate the certificate and deploy the webhook server along with the configurations—but then you wouldn't see how it all fits together.

> **TRY IT NOW**   Deploy the webhook configuration, passing the CA cert from the generator Pod as a value to the local Helm chart. Then try to deploy an app, which fails the policy.

```
# install the configuration object:
helm install validating-webhook admission-webhook/helm/validating-
  webhook/ --set caBundle=$(kubectl exec -it deploy/cert-generator
  -- cat ca.base64)

# confirm it's been created:
kubectl get validatingwebhookconfiguration

# try to deploy an app:
kubectl apply -f vweb/v1.yaml

# check the webhook logs:
kubectl logs -l app=admission-webhook --tail 3

# show the ReplicaSet status for the app:
kubectl get rs -l app=vweb-v1

# show the details:
kubectl describe rs -l app=vweb-v1
```

In this exercise, you can see the strength and the limitation of validating webhooks. The webhook operates at the Pod level, and it stops Pods from being created if they don't match the service token rule. But it's the ReplicaSet and the Deployment that try to create the Pod, and they don't get blocked by the admission controller, so you have to dig a bit deeper to find why the app isn't running. My output is shown in figure 16.12, where the describe command is abridged to show just the error line.

You need to think carefully about the objects and operations you want your webhook to act on. This validation could happen at the Deployment level instead, which would give a better user experience, but it would miss Pods created directly or by other types of controllers. It's also important to return a clear message in the webhook

Creates a validating webhook, using the local webhook
server and the CA certificate from the generator

The webhook is called, and the spec fails to meet the rules.

```
PS>helm install validating-webhook admission-webhook/helm/validating-webhook
/ --set caBundle=$(kubectl exec -it deploy/cert-generator -- cat ca.base64)
NAME: validating-webhook
LAST DEPLOYED: Fri Jul 10 13:19:24 2020
NAMESPACE: default
STATUS: deployed
REVISION: 1
TEST SUITE: None
PS>
PS>kubectl get validatingwebhookconfiguration
NAME                    WEBHOOKS    AGE
servicetokenpolicy      1           12s
PS>
PS>kubectl apply -f vweb/v1.yaml
service/vweb-v1 created
deployment.apps/vweb-v1 created
PS>
PS>kubectl logs -l app=admission-webhook --tail 3
info: Validating: vweb-v1-647d5657b-mxmlf; request UID: 3d736c6d-7f19-4554-9
dbc-49b0eaa6e5a0
info: - no automountServiceAccountToken
info: Validated request UID: 3d736c6d-7f19-4554-9dbc-49b0eaa6e5a0
PS>
PS>kubectl get rs -l app=vweb-v1
NAME                DESIRED    CURRENT    READY    AGE
vweb-v1-647d5657b   1          0          0        14s
PS>
PS>kubectl describe rs -l app=vweb-v1
Name:            vweb-v1-647d5657b

  Warning  FailedCreate  17s (x14 over 58s)  replicaset-controller  Error cr
eating: admission webhook "servicetokenpolicy.kiamol.net" denied the request
: automountServiceAccountToken must be set to false
```

The deployment doesn't fail, but the ReplicaSet is not up to scale.

Digging into the detail, we can see that the webhook blocked the object
creation. This is the response message from the Node.js webhook server.

Figure 16.12 Validating webhooks can block object creation, whether it was instigated by a
user or a controller.

response, so users know how to fix the issue. The ReplicaSet will just keep trying to
create the Pod and failing (it's tried 18 times on my cluster while I've been writing
this), but the failure message tells me what to do, and this one is easy to fix.

One of the problems with admission webhooks is that they score very low on discoverability. You can use kubectl to check if there are any validating webhooks configured, but that doesn't tell you anything about the actual rules, so you need to have
that documented outside of the cluster. The situation gets even more confusing with

mutating webhooks, because if they work as expected, they give users a different object from the one they tried to create. In the next exercise, you'll see that a well-intentioned mutating webhook can break applications.

> **TRY IT NOW**   Configure a mutating webhook using the same webhook server but a different URL path. This webhook adds security settings to Pod specs. Deploy another app, and you'll see the changes from the webhook stop the app from running.

```
# deploy the webhook configuration:
helm install mutating-webhook admission-webhook/helm/mutating-webhook/
    --set caBundle=$(kubectl exec -it deploy/cert-generator -- cat
    ca.base64)

# confirm it's been created:
kubectl get mutatingwebhookconfiguration

# deploy a new web app:
kubectl apply -f vweb/v2.yaml

# print the webhook server logs:
kubectl logs -l app=admission-webhook --tail 5

# show the status of the ReplicaSet:
kubectl get rs -l app=vweb-v2

# show the details:
kubectl describe pod -l app=vweb-v2
```

Oh dear. The mutating webhook adds a SecurityContext to the Pod spec with the runAsNonRoot field set to true. That flag tells Kubernetes not to run any containers in the Pod if they're configured to run as root—which this app is, because it's based on the official Nginx image, which does use root. As you can see in figure 16.13, describing the Pod tells you what the problem is, but it doesn't state that the spec has been mutated. Users will be highly confused when they check their YAML again and find no runAsNonRoot field.

The logic inside a mutating webhook is entirely up to you—you can accidentally change objects to set an invalid spec they will never deploy. It's a good idea to have a more restrictive object selector for your webhook configurations. Listing 16.5 applies to every Pod, but you can add namespace and label selectors to narrow the scope. This webhook has been built with sensible rules, and if the Pod spec already contains a runAsNonRoot value, the webhook leaves it alone, so apps can be modeled to explicitly require the root user.

Admission controller webhooks are a useful tool to know about, and they let you do some cool things. You can add sidecar containers to Pods with mutating webhooks, so you could use a label to identify all the apps that write log files and have a webhook automatically add a logging sidecar to those Pods. Webhooks can be dangerous, which

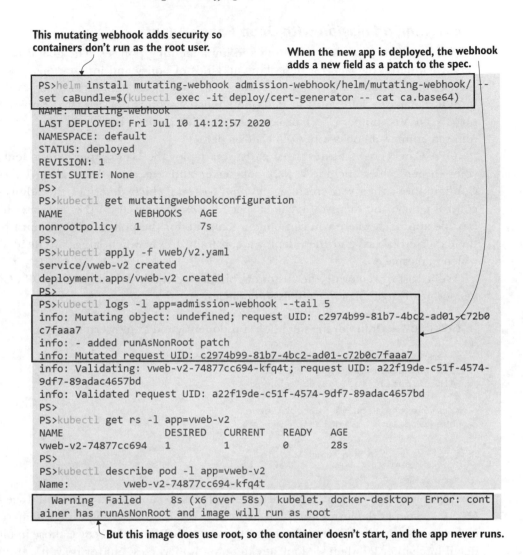

This mutating webhook adds security so containers don't run as the root user.

When the new app is deployed, the webhook adds a new field as a patch to the spec.

```
PS>helm install mutating-webhook admission-webhook/helm/mutating-webhook/ --
set caBundle=$(kubectl exec -it deploy/cert-generator -- cat ca.base64)
NAME: mutating-webhook
LAST DEPLOYED: Fri Jul 10 14:12:57 2020
NAMESPACE: default
STATUS: deployed
REVISION: 1
TEST SUITE: None
PS>
PS>kubectl get mutatingwebhookconfiguration
NAME             WEBHOOKS    AGE
nonrootpolicy    1           7s
PS>
PS>kubectl apply -f vweb/v2.yaml
service/vweb-v2 created
deployment.apps/vweb-v2 created
PS>
PS>kubectl logs -l app=admission-webhook --tail 5
info: Mutating object: undefined; request UID: c2974b99-81b7-4bc2-ad01-c72b0
c7faaa7
info: - added runAsNonRoot patch
info: Mutated request UID: c2974b99-81b7-4bc2-ad01-c72b0c7faaa7
info: Validating: vweb-v2-74877cc694-kfq4t; request UID: a22f19de-c51f-4574-
9df7-89adac4657bd
info: Validated request UID: a22f19de-c51f-4574-9df7-89adac4657bd
PS>
PS>kubectl get rs -l app=vweb-v2
NAME                 DESIRED    CURRENT    READY    AGE
vweb-v2-74877cc694   1          1          0        28s
PS>
PS>kubectl describe pod -l app=vweb-v2
Name:          vweb-v2-74877cc694-kfq4t

  Warning  Failed    8s (x6 over 58s)  kubelet, docker-desktop  Error: cont
ainer has runAsNonRoot and image will run as root
```

But this image does use root, so the container doesn't start, and the app never runs.

Figure 16.13 Mutating webhooks can cause application failures, which are difficult to debug.

is something you can mitigate with good testing and selective rules in your config objects, but they will always be invisible because the logic is hidden inside the webhook server.

In the next section, we'll look at an alternative approach that uses validating webhooks under the hood but wraps them in a management layer. *Open Policy Agent* (OPA) lets you define your rules in Kubernetes objects, which are discoverable in the cluster and don't require custom code.

16.4   *Controlling admission with Open Policy Agent*

OPA is a unified approach to writing and implementing policies. The goal is to provide a standard language for describing all kinds of policy and integrations to apply policies in different platforms. You can describe data access policies and deploy them in SQL databases, and you can describe admission control policies for Kubernetes objects. OPA is another CNCF project that provides a much cleaner alternative to custom validating webhooks with OPA Gatekeeper.

OPA Gatekeeper features three parts: you deploy the Gatekeeper components in your cluster, which include a webhook server and a generic ValidatingWebhook-Configuration; then you create a *constraint template*, which describes the admission control policy; and then you create a specific *constraint* based on the template. It's a flexible approach where you can build a template for the policy "all Pods must have the expected labels" and then deploy a constraint to say which labels are needed in which namespace.

We'll start by removing the custom webhooks we added and deploying OPA Gatekeeper, ready to apply some admission policies.

> **TRY IT NOW**   Uninstall the webhook components, and deploy Gatekeeper.

```
# remove the webhook configurations created with Helm:
helm uninstall mutating-webhook
helm uninstall validating-webhook

# remove the Node.js webhook server:
kubectl delete -f admission-webhook/

# deploy Gatekeeper:
kubectl apply -f opa/
```

I've abbreviated my output in figure 16.14—when you run the exercise, you'll see the OPA Gatekeeper deployment installs many more objects, including things we haven't come across yet called CustomResourceDefinitions (CRDs). We'll cover those in more detail in chapter 20 when we look at extending Kubernetes, but for now, it's enough to know that CRDs let you define new types of object that Kubernetes stores and manages for you.

Gatekeeper uses CRDs so you can create templates and constraints as ordinary Kubernetes objects, defined in YAML and deployed with kubectl. The template contains the generic policy definition in a language called Rego (pronounced "ray-go"). It's an expressive language that lets you evaluate the properties of some input object to check if they meet your requirements. It's another thing to learn, but Rego has some big advantages: policies are fairly easy to read, and they live in your YAML files, so they're not hidden in the code of a custom webhook; and there are lots of sample Rego policies to enforce the kind of rules we've looked at in this chapter. Listing 16.6 shows a Rego policy that requires objects to have labels.

Removes all the webhooks so we can switch to OPA and apply rules with policies

```
PS>helm uninstall mutating-webhook
release "mutating-webhook" uninstalled
PS>
PS>helm uninstall validating-webhook
release "validating-webhook" uninstalled
PS>
PS>kubectl delete -f admission-webhook/
service "admission-webhook" deleted
deployment.apps "admission-webhook" deleted
PS>
PS>kubectl apply -f opa/
namespace/gatekeeper-system created
```

```
secret/gatekeeper-webhook-server-cert created
service/gatekeeper-webhook-service created
deployment.apps/gatekeeper-audit created
deployment.apps/gatekeeper-controller-manager created
validatingwebhookconfiguration.admissionregistration.k8s.io/gatekeeper-valid
ating-webhook-configuration created
```

OPA Gatekeeper installs a lot of objects, including its own webhook server, TLS certificate, and validating webhook. There are no default policies, so this just sets up the framework.

Figure 16.14   OPA Gatekeeper takes care of all the tricky parts of running a webhook server.

Listing 16.6   requiredLabels-template.yaml, a basic Rego policy

```
# This fetches all the labels on the object and all the
# required labels from the constraint; if required labels
# are missing, that's a violation that blocks object creation.

violation[{"msg": msg, "details": {"missing_labels": missing}}] {
  provided := {label | input.review.object.metadata.labels[label]}
  required := {label | label := input.parameters.labels[_]}
  missing := required - provided
  count(missing) > 0
  msg := sprintf("you must provide labels: %v", [missing])
}
```

You deploy that policy with Gatekeeper as a constraint template, and then you deploy a constraint object that enforces the template. In this case, the template, called RequiredLabels, uses parameters to define the labels that are required. Listing 16.7 shows a specific constraint for all Pods to have app and version labels.

Listing 16.7   requiredLabels.yaml, a constraint from a Gatekeeper template

```
apiVersion: constraints.gatekeeper.sh/v1beta1
kind: RequiredLabels          # The API and Kind identify this as
metadata:                     # a Gatekeeper constraint from the
  name: requiredlabels-app    # RequiredLabels template.
```

```
spec:
  match:
    kinds:
      - apiGroups: [""]
        kinds: ["Pod"]              # The constraint applies to all Pods.
    parameters:
      labels: ["app", "version"]    # Requires two labels to be set
```

This is much easier to read, and you can deploy many constraints from the same template. The OPA approach lets you build a standard policy library, which users can apply in their application specs without needing to dig into the Rego. In the next exercise, you'll deploy the constraint from listing 16.7 with another constraint that requires all Deployments, Services, and ConfigMaps to have a `kiamol` label. Then you'll try to deploy a version of the to-do app that fails all those policies.

TRY IT NOW   Deploy required label policies with Gatekeeper, and see how they are applied.

```
# create the constraint template first:
kubectl apply -f opa/templates/requiredLabels-template.yaml

# then create the constraint:
kubectl apply -f opa/constraints/requiredLabels.yaml

# the to-do list spec doesn't meet the policies:
kubectl apply -f todo-list/

# confirm the app isn't deployed:
kubectl get all -l app=todo-web
```

You can see in figure 16.15 that this user experience is clean—the objects we're trying to create don't have the required labels, so they get blocked, and we see the message from the Rego policy in the output from kubectl.

Gatekeeper evaluates constraints using a validating webhook, and it's very obvious when failures arise in the object you're creating. It's a bit less clear when objects created by controllers fail validation, because the controller itself can be fine. We saw that in section 16.3, and because Gatekeeper uses the same validation mechanism, it has the same issue. You'll see that if you update the to-do app so the Deployment meets the label requirements but the Pod spec doesn't.

TRY IT NOW   Deploy an updated to-do list spec, which has the correct labels for all objects except the Pod.

```
# deploy the updated manifest:
kubectl apply -f todo-list/update/web-with-kiamol-labels.yaml

# show the status of the ReplicaSet:
kubectl get rs -l app=todo-web
```

The constraint template defines the rule with a set of parameters.

Constraints use the template and supply parameter values. These require different labels for different object types.

```
PS>kubectl apply -f opa/templates/requiredLabels-template.yaml
constrainttemplate.templates.gatekeeper.sh/requiredlabels created
PS>
PS>kubectl apply -f opa/constraints/requiredLabels.yaml
requiredlabels.constraints.gatekeeper.sh/requiredlabels-kiamol created
requiredlabels.constraints.gatekeeper.sh/requiredlabels-app created
PS>
PS>kubectl apply -f todo-list/
Error from server ([denied by requiredlabels-kiamol] you must provide labels
: {"kiamol"}): error when creating "todo-list\\web.yaml": admission webhook
"validation.gatekeeper.sh" denied the request: [denied by requiredlabels-kia
mol] you must provide labels: {"kiamol"}
Error from server ([denied by requiredlabels-kiamol] you must provide labels
: {"kiamol"}): error when creating "todo-list\\web.yaml": admission webhook
"validation.gatekeeper.sh" denied the request: [denied by requiredlabels-kia
mol] you must provide labels: {"kiamol"}
Error from server ([denied by requiredlabels-kiamol] you must provide labels
: {"kiamol"}): error when creating "todo-list\\web.yaml": admission webhook
"validation.gatekeeper.sh" denied the request: [denied by requiredlabels-kia
mol] you must provide labels: {"kiamol"}
PS>
PS>kubectl get all -l app=todo-web
No resources found in default namespace.
```

This to-do list spec fails all the policies. The failures are for objects that kubectl creates—the Deployment, Service, and ConfigMap—so the errors are shown in the output.

Figure 16.15 Deployment failures show a clear error message returned from the Rego policy.

```
# print the detail:
kubectl describe rs -l app=todo-web

# remove the to-do app in preparation for the next exercise:
kubectl delete -f todo-list/update/web-with-kiamol-labels.yaml
```

You'll find in this exercise that the admission policy worked, but you see the problem only when you dig into the description for the failing ReplicaSet, as in figure 16.16. That's not such a great user experience. You could fix this with a more sophisticated policy that applies at the Deployment level and checks labels in the Pod template—that could be done with extended logic in the Rego for the constraint template.

We'll finish this section with the following set of admission policies that cover some more production best practices, all of which help to make your apps more secure:

- All Pods must have container probes defined. This is for keeping your apps healthy, but a failed healthcheck could also indicate unexpected activity from an attack.

The objects kubectl creates all have the
correct labels now, so there are no errors.

But the Pod spec doesn't have all the required
labels, so the ReplicaSet can't create the Pod.

```
PS>kubectl apply -f todo-list/update/web-with-kiamol-labels.yaml
service/todo-web created
configmap/todo-web-config created
deployment.apps/todo-web created
PS>
PS>kubectl get rs -l app=todo-web
NAME                     DESIRED   CURRENT   READY   AGE
todo-web-84d79cf6b9      1         0         0       6s
PS>
PS>kubectl describe rs -l app=todo-web
Name:           todo-web-84d79cf6b9
```

```
   Warning  FailedCreate  16s (x13 over 36s)  replicaset-controller  Error cr
eating: admission webhook "validation.gatekeeper.sh" denied the request: [de
nied by requiredlabels-app] you must provide labels: {"version"}
PS>
PS>kubectl delete -f todo-list/update/web-with-kiamol-labels.yaml
service "todo-web" deleted
configmap "todo-web-config" deleted
deployment.apps "todo-web" deleted
```

The error message from Gatekeeper is clear, but it's hidden in the ReplicaSet details.

Figure 16.16   OPA Gatekeeper makes for a better process, but it's still a wrapper around validating webhooks.

- Pods can run containers only from approved image repositories. Restricting containers to a set of "golden" repositories with secured production images ensures malicious payloads can't be deployed.
- All containers must have memory and CPU limits set. This prevents a compromised container maxing out the compute resources of the node and starving all the other Pods.

These generic policies apply to pretty much every organization. You can add to them with constraints that require network policies for every app and security contexts for every Pod. As you've learned in this chapter, not all rules are universal, so you might need to be selective on how you apply those constraints. In the next exercise, you'll apply the production constraint set to a single namespace.

TRY IT NOW   Deploy a new set of constraints and a version of the to-do app where the Pod spec fails most of the policies.

```
# create templates for the production constraints:
kubectl apply -f opa/templates/production/

# create the constraints:
kubectl apply -f opa/constraints/production/
```

```
# deploy the new to-do spec:
kubectl apply -f todo-list/production/

# confirm the Pods aren't created:
kubectl get rs -n kiamol-ch16 -l app=todo-web

# show the error details:
kubectl describe rs -n kiamol-ch16 -l app=todo-web
```

Figure 16.17 shows that the Pod spec fails all the rules except one—my image repository policy allows any images from Docker Hub in the kiamol organization, so the to-do app image is valid. But there's no version label, no health probes, and no resource limits, and this spec is not fit for production.

This is a useful set of constraints that require generic security controls in Pod specs.

```
PS>kubectl apply -f opa/templates/production/
constrainttemplate.templates.gatekeeper.sh/policycontainerprobes created
constrainttemplate.templates.gatekeeper.sh/policyimagerepository created
constrainttemplate.templates.gatekeeper.sh/policyresourcelimits created
PS>
PS>kubectl apply -f opa/constraints/production/
policycontainerprobes.constraints.gatekeeper.sh/container-probes created
policyimagerepository.constraints.gatekeeper.sh/image-repository created
policyresourcelimits.constraints.gatekeeper.sh/resource-limits created
PS>
PS>kubectl apply -f todo-list/production/
namespace/kiamol-ch16 created
service/todo-web created
configmap/todo-web-config created
deployment.apps/todo-web created
PS>
PS>kubectl get rs -n kiamol-ch16 -l app=todo-web
NAME                 DESIRED   CURRENT   READY   AGE
todo-web-84d79cf6b9  1         0         0       6s
PS>
PS>kubectl describe rs -n kiamol-ch16 -l app=todo-web
Name:            todo-web-84d79cf6b9

from similar events): Error creating: admission webhook "validation.gatekeep
er.sh" denied the request: [denied by requiredlabels-app] you must provide l
abels: {"version"}
[denied by container-probes] Container <web> in your <Pod> <todo-web-84d79cf
6b9-lrh5c> has no <readinessProbe>
[denied by container-probes] Container <web> in your <Pod> <todo-web-84d79cf
6b9-lrh5c> has no <livenessProbe>
[denied by resource-limits] container <web> has no resource limits
```

The ReplicaSet is created but no Pods—the spec is missing a version label, as well as readiness and liveness probes and resource limits.

Figure 16.17 All constraints are evaluated, and you see the full list of errors in the Rego output.

Just to prove those policies are achievable and OPA Gatekeeper will actually let the to-do app run, you can apply an updated spec that meets all the rules for production. If you compare the YAML files in the production folder and the update folder, you'll see the new spec just adds the required fields to the Pod template; there are no significant changes in the app.

> **TRY IT NOW**   Apply a production-ready version of the to-do spec, and confirm the app really runs.

```
# this spec meets all production policies:
kubectl apply -f todo-list/production/update

# wait for the Pod to start:
kubectl wait --for=condition=ContainersReady pod -l app=todo-web -n
  kiamol-ch16

# confirm it's running:
kubectl get pods -n kiamol-ch16 --show-labels

# get the URL for the app and browse:
kubectl get svc todo-web -n kiamol-ch16 -o jsonpath='http://{.status
  .loadBalancer.ingress[0].*}:8019'
```

Figure 16.18 shows the app running, after the updated deployment has been permitted by OPA Gatekeeper.

Open Policy Agent is a much cleaner way to apply admission controls than custom validating webhooks, and the sample policies we've looked at are only some simple ideas to get you started. Gatekeeper doesn't have mutation functionality, but you can combine it with your own webhooks if you have a clear case to modify specs. You could use constraints to ensure every Pod spec includes an application-profile label and then mutate specs based on your profiles—setting your .NET Core apps to run as a nonroot user and switching to a read-only filesystem for all your Go apps.

Securing your apps is about closing down exploit paths, and a thorough approach includes all the tools we've covered in this chapter and more. We'll finish up with a look at a secure Kubernetes landscape.

16.5   *Understanding security in depth in Kubernetes*

Build pipelines can be compromised, container images can be modified, containers can run vulnerable software as privileged users, and attackers with access to the Kubernetes API could even take control of your cluster. You won't know your app is 100% secure until it has been replaced and you can confirm no security breaches occurred during its operation. Getting to that happy place means applying security in depth across your whole software supply chain. This chapter has focused on securing apps at run time, but you should start before that by scanning container images for known vulnerabilities.

This updated Pod spec has all the required fields to comply with production policy.

The Pod starts and has the expected app and version labels.

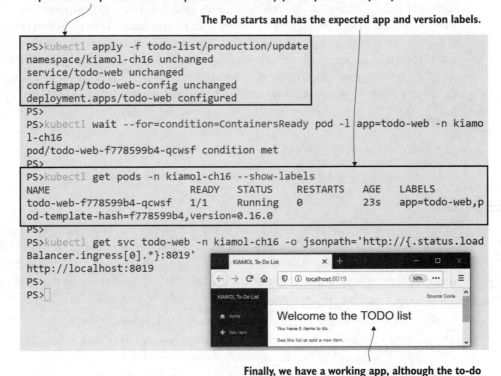

```
PS>kubectl apply -f todo-list/production/update
namespace/kiamol-ch16 unchanged
service/todo-web unchanged
configmap/todo-web-config unchanged
deployment.apps/todo-web configured
PS>
PS>kubectl wait --for=condition=ContainersReady pod -l app=todo-web -n kiamo
l-ch16
pod/todo-web-f778599b4-qcwsf condition met
PS>
PS>kubectl get pods -n kiamol-ch16 --show-labels
NAME                      READY   STATUS    RESTARTS   AGE   LABELS
todo-web-f778599b4-qcwsf  1/1     Running   0          23s   app=todo-web,p
od-template-hash=f778599b4,version=0.16.0
PS>
PS>kubectl get svc todo-web -n kiamol-ch16 -o jsonpath='http://{.status.load
Balancer.ingress[0].*}:8019'
http://localhost:8019
PS>
PS>
```

Finally, we have a working app, although the to-do list is empty, which is probably not accurate.

Figure 16.18   Constraints are powerful, but you need to make sure apps can actually comply.

Security scanners look inside an image, identify the binaries, and check them on CVE (Common Vulnerabilities and Exposures) databases. Scans tell you if known exploits are in the application stack, dependencies, or operating system tools in your image. Commercial scanners have integrations with managed registries (you can use Aqua Security with Azure Container Registry), or you can run your own (Harbor is the CNCF registry project, and it supports the open source scanners Clair and Trivy; Docker Desktop has an integration with Snyk for local scans).

You can set up a pipeline where images are pushed to a production repository only if the scan is clear. Combine that with a repository admission policy, and you can effectively ensure that containers run only if the image is safe. A secure image running in a securely configured container is still a target, though, and you should look at run-time security with a tool that monitors containers for unusual activity and can generate alerts or shut down suspicious behavior. Falco is the CNCF project for run-time security, and there are supported commercial options from Aqua and Sysdig (among others).

Overwhelmed? You should think about securing Kubernetes as a road map that starts with the techniques I've covered in this chapter. You can adopt security contexts first, then network policies, and then move on to admission control when you're clear about the rules that matter to you. Role-based access control, which we cover in chapter 17, is the next stage. Security scanning and run-time monitoring are further steps you can take if your organization has enhanced security requirements. But I won't throw anything more at you now—let's tidy up and get ready for the lab.

TRY IT NOW   Delete all the objects we created.

```
kubectl delete -f opa/constraints/ -f opa/templates/ -f
    opa/gatekeeper.yaml
kubectl delete all,ns,secret,networkpolicy -l kiamol=ch16
```

16.6 *Lab*

At the start of the chapter, I said that volume mounts for host paths are a potential attack vector, but we didn't address that in the exercises, so we'll do it in the lab. This is a perfect scenario for admission control, where Pods should be blocked if they use volumes that mount sensitive paths on the host. We'll use OPA Gatekeeper, and I've written the Rego for you, so you just need to write a constraint.

- Start by deploying `gatekeeper.yaml` in the lab folder.
- Then deploy the constraint template in `restrictedPaths-template.yaml`— you'll need to look at the spec to see how to build your constraint.
- Write and deploy a constraint that uses the template and restricts these host paths: /, /bin, and /etc. The constraint should apply only to Pods with the label `kiamol=ch16-lab`.
- Deploy `sleep.yaml` in the lab folder. Your constraint should prevent the Pod from being created because it uses restricted volume mounts.

This one is fairly straightforward, although you'll need to read about *match expressions,* which is how Gatekeeper implements label selectors. My solution is up on GitHub: https://github.com/sixeyed/kiamol/blob/master/ch16/lab/README.md.

Pure and applied Kubernetes

In this final section, you'll dig into technical topics to round off your understanding of Kubernetes. You'll learn about the architecture of Kubernetes, how you can control where your containers run, and how you can extend the platform with custom resources and new features. You'll also learn how to use role-based access control to restrict what users and applications can do in the cluster. The section ends with some guidance on where to go next in your Kubernetes journey and how to become part of the Kubernetes community.

Securing resources with role-based access control

You have complete control over your lab cluster: you can deploy workloads, read Secrets, and even delete control plane components if you want to see how quickly they return. You don't want anyone to have that much power in a production cluster, because if they have full admin control, then it's really their cluster. Their account could be compromised, and then some rogue party deletes all your apps and turns your cluster into their personal Bitcoin miner. Kubernetes supports least-privilege access with *role-based access control* (RBAC). In this chapter, you'll learn how RBAC works and some of the challenges that come with restricting access.

RBAC applies to end users working with kubectl and to internal components using the Kubernetes API with service account tokens. You need a different RBAC approach for each of those, which we'll cover in this chapter, together with the best practices. You'll also learn how Kubernetes gets the credentials for external users and how you can manage end users inside the cluster if you don't have an external authentication system. RBAC is a straightforward model but with lots of moving pieces, and it can be hard to keep track of who can do what, so we'll finish the chapter looking at management tools.

17.1 How Kubernetes secures access to resources

RBAC works by granting permissions to perform actions on resources. Every resource type can be secured, so you can set up permissions to get Pod details, list Services, and delete Secrets. You apply permissions to a subject, which could be a user, a system account, or a group, but you don't apply them directly, because that would create an unmanageable sprawl of permissions. You set permissions in a role, and you apply a role to one or more subjects with a role binding, as shown in figure 17.1.

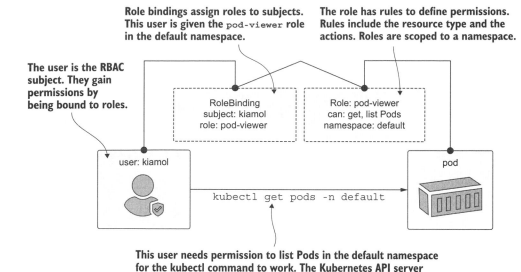

The user is the RBAC subject. They gain permissions by being bound to roles.

Role bindings assign roles to subjects. This user is given the `pod-viewer` role in the default namespace.

The role has rules to define permissions. Rules include the resource type and the actions. Roles are scoped to a namespace.

RoleBinding
subject: kiamol
role: pod-viewer

Role: pod-viewer
can: get, list Pods
namespace: default

user: kiamol

pod

`kubectl get pods -n default`

This user needs permission to list Pods in the default namespace for the kubectl command to work. The Kubernetes API server checks that the user is bound to a role that has the permission.

Figure 17.1   RBAC is a security abstraction; object permissions are granted through roles and bindings.

Some Kubernetes resources are specific to a namespace, and some are clusterwide, so the RBAC structure actually has two sets of objects to describe and allocate permissions: Role and RoleBinding objects work on namespaced objects, and ClusterRole and ClusterRoleBinding objects work on the whole cluster. RBAC is technically an optional component in Kubernetes, but it is enabled in almost all platforms now. You can check that it's enabled and see some of the default roles using standard kubectl commands.

TRY IT NOW   You can check the features in your cluster by printing the API versions it supports. Docker Desktop, K3s, and all the cloud platforms support RBAC by default.

```
# switch to this chapter's folder:
cd ch17

# PowerShell doesn't have a grep command; run this on Windows to add it:
. .\grep.ps1

# check that the API versions include RBAC:
kubectl api-versions | grep rbac

# show the admin cluster roles:
kubectl get clusterroles | grep admin
```

```
# show the details of the cluster admin:
kubectl describe clusterrole cluster-admin
```

You can see in figure 17.2 a whole lot of built-in roles are clusterwide. One is cluster-admin, and that's the role you have in your lab cluster. It has permissions for all actions (Kubernetes calls them *verbs*) on all resources, and that's why you can do anything you like. The next most powerful role is admin, which has pretty much all permissions on all objects but limited to a single namespace.

This adds a `grep` command to PowerShell—you need it only on Windows.

My cluster supports the RBAC APIs, which means RBAC is enabled.

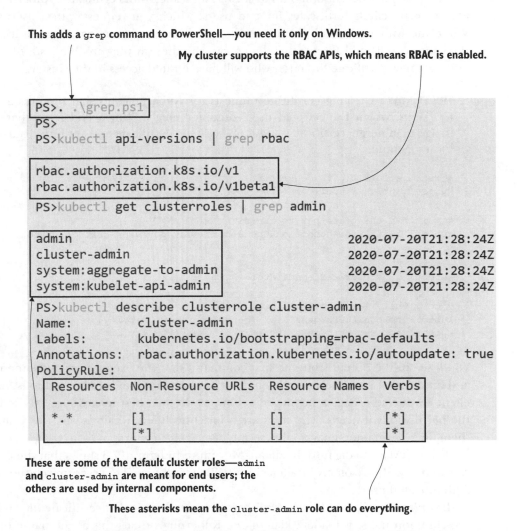

```
PS>. .\grep.ps1
PS>
PS>kubectl api-versions | grep rbac

rbac.authorization.k8s.io/v1
rbac.authorization.k8s.io/v1beta1
PS>kubectl get clusterroles | grep admin

admin                                        2020-07-20T21:28:24Z
cluster-admin                                2020-07-20T21:28:24Z
system:aggregate-to-admin                    2020-07-20T21:28:24Z
system:kubelet-api-admin                     2020-07-20T21:28:24Z
PS>kubectl describe clusterrole cluster-admin
Name:          cluster-admin
Labels:        kubernetes.io/bootstrapping=rbac-defaults
Annotations:   rbac.authorization.kubernetes.io/autoupdate: true
PolicyRule:
  Resources   Non-Resource URLs   Resource Names   Verbs
  ---------   -----------------   --------------   -----
  *.*         []                  []               [*]
              [*]                 []               [*]
```

These are some of the default cluster roles—`admin` and `cluster-admin` are meant for end users; the others are used by internal components.

These asterisks mean the `cluster-admin` role can do everything.

Figure 17.2   RBAC has a default set of roles and bindings for users and service accounts.

That's all very well, but *who* has the cluster-admin role? You don't log in to kubectl with a username and password for your own lab, and there is no user object in Kubernetes, so how does Kubernetes know who the user is? Kubernetes does not authenticate end users; it relies on external identity providers and trusts them to authenticate. In a production system, your cluster would be configured to use your organization's existing authentication system—Active Directory (AD), LDAP, and OpenID Connect (OIDC) are all options.

Cloud platforms integrate Kubernetes with their own authentication, so AKS users authenticate with Azure AD accounts. You can configure your own OIDC provider, but the setup is quite heavy, so in our lab cluster, we'll stick with certificates. Kubernetes is able to issue client certificates for end users, which you request with a username. When the Kubernetes API server sees that certificate in incoming requests, it trusts the issuer (itself) and accepts that the user is who they say they are. We'll start by generating a new certificate for a user who will have limited access in the cluster.

TRY IT NOW   Creating certificate requests for Kubernetes to sign requires a few steps, which I've scripted in a container image. Run a Pod from that image to generate certificates and then copy the certificate and key onto your local machine.

```
# run the certificate generator:
kubectl apply -f user-cert-generator.yaml

# wait for the container to start:
kubectl wait --for=condition=ContainersReady pod user-cert-generator

# print the logs:
kubectl logs user-cert-generator --tail 3

# copy the files onto your local disk:
kubectl cp user-cert-generator:/certs/user.key user.key
kubectl cp user-cert-generator:/certs/user.crt user.crt
```

You'll see in the output from the first command that the exercise creates some roles and bindings of its own. The Pod container runs a script that uses kubectl to issue the client certificate. That's a privileged action, so the manifest makes sure the Pod has the permissions it needs. The steps are a bit convoluted, which is why I've wrapped them in a container image—the script user-cert-generator/start.sh does the work, if you want to dig into the detail. My output in figure 17.3 shows that the certificate and key file are on my local machine, which is all I need to access my cluster as an authenticated user.

If you're into OpenSSL and certificates, you can decode that certificate file and see the common name is reader@kiamol.net. Kubernetes treats this as the name of the user, and that will be the subject we can use to apply RBAC. Permissions are all additive with RBAC, so subjects start with no permissions, and as role bindings are applied, they end up with the sum total of all role permissions. The RBAC model is grant-only—you can't deny permissions. The absence of a permission is the same as a deny.

This runs a script to generate a client certificate signed by Kubernetes, which can be used to authenticate to the cluster. The script needs permissions to create the certificate.

```
PS>kubectl apply -f user-cert-generator.yaml
serviceaccount/user-cert-generator created
pod/user-cert-generator created
clusterrole.rbac.authorization.k8s.io/create-approve-csr created
clusterrolebinding.rbac.authorization.k8s.io/user-cert-generator created
PS>
PS>kubectl logs user-cert-generator --tail 3
----------------
Cert generated: /certs/user.key and /certs/user.crt
----------------
PS>
PS>kubectl cp user-cert-generator:/certs/user.key user.key
tar: removing leading '/' from member names
PS>
PS>kubectl cp user-cert-generator:/certs/user.crt user.crt
tar: removing leading '/' from member names
PS>
PS>cat user.crt
-----BEGIN CERTIFICATE-----
MIIDHjCCAgagAwIBAgIQODxSHRSqLfMllfLHqJHG2DANBgkqhkiG9w0BAQsFADAV
MRMwEQYDVQQT:wprdWJlcm5ldGVzMB4XDTIwMDcyMTEwMzM1OFoXDTIxMDcyMTEw
MzM1OF  d45 MAkGA1UEBhMCVUsyDzANBgNVBAgTBkx,DTkRDTiEDMADGA1UEBxMG
```

Users need the certificate and key file to authenticate.

The certificate is a standard X.509 certificate, issued by Kubernetes.

Figure 17.3 Kubernetes can issue its own client certificates for new authenticated users.

We can set up a kubectl context with the new certificate and confirm the user starts with zero access.

> **TRY IT NOW** Create a new context in kubectl using the generated certificate as the credentials, and confirm you can use it to access the cluster.

```
# set the credentials for a new context from the client certificate:
kubectl config set-credentials reader --client-key=./user.key
  --client-certificate=./user.crt --embed-certs=true

# set the cluster for the context:
kubectl config set-context reader --user=reader --cluster $(kubectl
  config view -o jsonpath='{.clusters[0].name}')

# try to deploy a Pod using the new context—
# if your cluster is configured with authentication
# this won't work as the provider tries to authenticate:
kubectl apply -f sleep/ --context reader

# impersonate the user to confirm their permissions:
kubectl get pods --as reader@kiamol.net
```

There are two parts to a context in kubectl: the user credentials and the cluster to which to connect. In figure 17.4, you can see the user is configured with the client certificates, which are embedded into the kubectl config file. If you use client certificates like this, your config file is sensitive: if someone obtains a copy, they have all they need to connect to your cluster with one of your contexts.

Stores the client certificates as credentials in kubectl, and creates a new context using the credentials. This authenticates using the certificate issued by Kubernetes.

```
PS>kubectl config set-credentials reader --client-key=./user.key
--client-certificate=./user.crt --embed-certs=true
User "reader" set.
PS>
PS>kubectl config set-context reader --user=reader --cluster $(ku
bectl config view -o jsonpath='{.clusters[0].name}')
Context "reader" created.
PS>
PS>kubectl apply -f sleep/ --context reader
Error from server (Forbidden): error when retrieving current conf
iguration of:
Resource: "apps/v1, Resource=deployments", GroupVersionKind: "app
s/v1, Kind=Deployment"
Name: "sleep", Namespace: "default"
from server for: "sleep\\sleep.yaml": deployments.apps "sleep" is
  forbidden: User "reader@kiamol.net" cannot get resource "deploym
ents" in API group "apps" in the namespace "default"
PS>
PS>kubectl get pods --as reader@kiamol.net
Error from server (Forbidden): pods is forbidden: User "reader@ki
amol.net" cannot list resource "pods" in API group "" in the name
space "default"
```

The user is authenticated but not authorized. RBAC error messages state the user names and the permissions they lack.

Figure 17.4   Authenticated but unauthorized—users start with no RBAC roles.

The last command in the exercise uses impersonation to confirm that the new user doesn't have any permissions, but Kubernetes doesn't store users. You can use any random string for the username in the as parameter, and the output will tell you it doesn't have permissions. What Kubernetes actually looks for is any role binding where the username matches the name in the request. If there are no bindings, then there are no permissions, so the action is blocked, whether or not the username exists in the authentication system. Listing 17.1 shows a role binding we can apply to give the new user read-only access to resources in the default namespace.

Listing 17.1   reader-view-default.yaml, applying permissions with a role binding

```
apiVersion: rbac.authorization.k8s.io/v1
kind: RoleBinding
metadata:
  name: reader-view
  namespace: default                       # The scope of the binding
subjects:
- kind: User
  name: reader@kiamol.net                  # The subject is the new user
  apiGroup: rbac.authorization.k8s.io
roleRef:
  kind: ClusterRole
  name: view                               # Gives them the view role for
  apiGroup: rbac.authorization.k8s.io      # objects in the default namespace
```

This is a good way to get started with RBAC—use the predefined cluster roles, and bind them to subjects for a specified namespace. As we go through the chapter, you'll see how to build custom roles, which are great when you want explicit access permissions, but they get hard to manage at scale. Role bindings abstract the subject from the roles they have, so you can make changes to access without changing roles or objects. When you deploy the role binding from listing 17.1, the new user will be able to view resources in the default namespace.

> **TRY IT NOW**   Apply a role binding, and impersonate the new user to confirm that they have read-only access to resources.

```
# deploy a sleep Pod as your normal user:
kubectl apply -f sleep/

# deploy the role binding so the reader can view the Pod:
kubectl apply -f role-bindings/reader-view-default.yaml

# confirm the user sees Pods in the default namespace:
kubectl get pods --as reader@kiamol.net

# confirm the user is blocked from the system namespace:
kubectl get pods -n kube-system --as reader@kiamol.net

# confirm the user can't delete Pods—this will fail:
kubectl delete -f sleep/ --as reader@kiamol.net
```

You can see the view role in action in figure 17.5—the new user can list Pods but only in the default namespace. The role has no permission to delete objects, so the reader user can see Pods but not delete them.

The disconnect between users and roles feels slightly odd and can lead to problems. Kubernetes has no real integration with the authentication system, so it doesn't validate that usernames are correct or that groups exist. It's strictly authorization you configure in RBAC as far as end users are concerned. But you know from chapter 16 that you also need to secure the cluster from inside for apps that use the

Applies a role binding, giving the reader user access
to view resources in the `default` **namespace**

The user can list Pods, a permission that is in the view role.

```
PS>kubectl apply -f sleep/
deployment.apps/sleep created
PS>
PS>kubectl apply -f role-bindings/reader-view-default.yaml
rolebinding.rbac.authorization.k8s.io/reader-view created
PS>
PS>kubectl get pods --as reader@kiamol.net
NAME                        READY    STATUS      RESTARTS    AGE
sleep-85fdd4cf75-xngp7      1/1      Running     0           15s
user-cert-generator         1/1      Running     0           126m
PS>
PS>kubectl get pods -n kube-system --as reader@kiamol.net
Error from server (Forbidden): pods is forbidden: User "reader@ki
amol.net" cannot list resource "pods" in API group "" in the name
space "kube-system"
PS>
PS>kubectl delete -f sleep/ --as reader@kiamol.net
Error from server (Forbidden): error when deleting "sleep\\sleep.
yaml": deployments.apps "sleep" is forbidden: User "reader@kiamol
.net" cannot delete resource "deployments" in API group "apps" in
 the namespace "default"
```

But the role is scoped only to the default namespace,
so the user has no access to `kube-system`.

And the view role does not have permission to delete resources.

Figure 17.5   Role bindings are scoped so the permissions apply to only one namespace.

Kubernetes API, and the cluster manages both authentication and authorization for service accounts.

17.2   *Securing resource access within the cluster*

Every namespace has a default service account created automatically, and any Pods that don't specify a service account will use the default. The default service account is just like any other RBAC subject: it starts off with no permissions until you add some, and you add them using the same role bindings and cluster role bindings that you use with end user subjects. Service accounts are different because apps generally need a much more limited set of permissions, so the best practice is to create a dedicated service account for each component.

Creating a service account and setting up roles and bindings adds a lot of overhead, but remember that this is not about restricting access to resources in your application model. You can include ConfigMaps and Secrets and whatever else you need in your manifests, and they not are affected by the service account permissions at run time. RBAC for service accounts is purely about securing apps that use the Kubernetes API server—like Prometheus, which queries the API to get lists of Pods. This situation should be rare with your standard business apps, so this procedure is just about securing the special cases where you'll run into problems if you use the default service account in the same namespace for every app. We'll start this section by creating a new namespace to look at its default service account.

TRY IT NOW   Create a new namespace, and check the permissions of its service account—and fixing a bug with Docker Desktop if you use it.

```
# on Docker Desktop for Mac run this to fix the RBAC setup:
kubectl patch clusterrolebinding docker-for-desktop-binding --type=json
   --patch $'[{"op":"replace", "path":"/subjects/0/name",
   "value":"system:serviceaccounts:kube-system"}]'

# OR on Docker Desktop for Windows:
kubectl patch clusterrolebinding docker-for-desktop-binding
   --type=json --patch '[{\"op\":\"replace\", \"path\":\"/subjects/0/
   name\", \"value\":\"system:serviceaccounts:kube-system\"}]'

# create the new namespace:
kubectl apply -f namespace.yaml

# list service accounts:
kubectl get serviceaccounts -n kiamol-ch17

# check permissions for your own account:
kubectl auth can-i "*" "*"

# check permissions for the new service account:
kubectl auth can-i "*" "*" --as system:serviceaccount:kiamol-
   ch17:default

kubectl auth can-i get pods -n kiamol-ch17 --as
   system:serviceaccount:kiamol-ch17:default
```

The can-i command is a useful way to check permissions without actually affecting any objects. You can see in figure 17.6 that you can combine the command with impersonation and a namespace scope to show the permissions for another subject, which could be a user or a service account.

You saw in the exercise that new service accounts start with zero permissions, which is where the trouble starts if you use the default account for all your apps. Each app might need a set of permissions—they all get added to the default account, which soon ends up with far more power than it needs. If any of the apps using that service account are compromised, the attacker finds themselves with a bonus set of roles. The certificate generator from section 17.1 is a good example: it uses the Kubernetes API to issue client certificates, which is a privileged action. Listing 17.2 shows the cluster

Docker Desktop has an RBAC bug that gives service accounts more permissions than they should have. This fixes it.

Every namespace has a default service account, which the cluster creates automatically.

```
PS>kubectl patch clusterrolebinding docker-for-desktop-binding --
type=json --patch '[{\"op\":\"replace\", \"path\":\"/subjects/0\n
ame\", \"value\":\"system:serviceaccounts:kube-system\"}]'
clusterrolebinding.rbac.authorization.k8s.io/docker-for-desktop-b
inding patched
PS>
PS>kubectl apply -f namespace.yaml
namespace/kiamol-ch17 created
PS>
PS>kubectl get serviceaccounts -n kiamol-ch17
NAME       SECRETS   AGE
default    1         69s
PS>
PS>kubectl auth can-i "*" "*"
yes
PS>
PS>kubectl auth can-i "*" "*" --as system:serviceaccount:kiamol-c
h17:default
no
PS>
PS>kubectl auth can-i get pods -n kiamol-ch17 --as system:service
account:kiamol-ch17:default
no
```

Using `can-i` with impersonation confirms the new service account does not have cluster admin permissions.

It can't even list Pods in its own namespace.

Figure 17.6   A system controller ensures every namespace has a default service account.

role the app's service account uses to get the permissions it needs. The full manifest also contains a cluster role binding.

Listing 17.2   user-cert-generator.yaml, a custom cluster role for certificate generation

```
apiVersion: rbac.authorization.k8s.io/v1
kind: ClusterRole
metadata:
  name: create-approve-csr
rules:
- apiGroups: ["certificates.k8s.io"]          # Generating certificates
  resources: ["certificatesigningrequests"]   # needs permission to create
  verbs: ["create", "get", "list", "watch"]   # a signing request.
- apiGroups: ["certificates.k8s.io"]
  resources: ["certificatesigningrequests/approval"]
```

```
    verbs: ["update"]                                    # And to approve the request
- apiGroups:   ["certificates.k8s.io"]
    resources:   ["signers"]                             # Uses the cluster to sign
    resourceNames:   ["kubernetes.io/kube-apiserver-client"]
    verbs: ["approve"]
```

Generating certificates needs permission to create signing requests and approve them using the API Server issuer. If I was lazy, I could bind this role to the default service account on the justification that this app isn't publicly accessible, so the attack surface is small, and no other apps are using that account. But, of course, it's the default service account, and Kubernetes mounts the account token by default. If someone deploys a vulnerable web app in this same namespace, it will have permission to generate user certificates so attackers could generate their own credentials. Instead, I created a dedicated service account just for the certificate generator.

> **TRY IT NOW**   Confirm that the custom service account for the certificate generator app has permission to create certificate-signing requests, but standard service accounts don't have that permission.

```
# run a can-i check inside the certificate generator Pod:
kubectl exec user-cert-generator -- kubectl auth can-i create csr
    --all-namespaces

# use impersonation for the same check:
kubectl auth can-i create csr -A --as
    system:serviceaccount:default:user-cert-generator

# confirm the new service account doesn't have the permission:
kubectl auth can-i create csr -A --as system:serviceaccount:kiamol-
    ch17:default
```

You'll see in this exercise that only the certificate-generator service account has the certificate permissions. In fact, those are the only permissions that account has, so you can't use it to list namespaces or delete persistent volume claims or anything else. You also see in figure 17.7 that the syntax for referring to a service account is different from other resource references in Kubernetes—system:serviceaccount is the prefix, followed by the namespace and account name separated by colons.

Issuing client certificates is not a typical app requirement, but creating a separate service account for every app that uses the Kubernetes API is still a best practice. We've got two more examples in this section to show you how apps might need to use the API and how to secure them. The key thing to understand in RBAC is the scope of your bindings, to be sure you're applying permissions at the right level—typically for a single namespace. The first example of that is for a simple web app that lists Pods and lets you delete them.

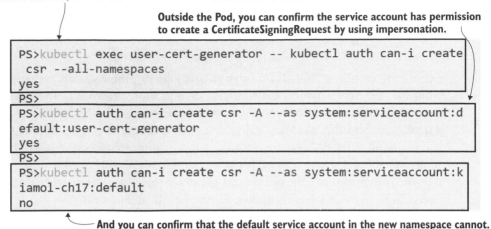

Inside the Pod, the kubectl command uses the context of a custom service account.

Outside the Pod, you can confirm the service account has permission to create a CertificateSigningRequest by using impersonation.

```
PS>kubectl exec user-cert-generator -- kubectl auth can-i create
 csr --all-namespaces
yes
PS>
PS>kubectl auth can-i create csr -A --as system:serviceaccount:d
efault:user-cert-generator
yes
PS>
PS>kubectl auth can-i create csr -A --as system:serviceaccount:k
iamol-ch17:default
no
```

And you can confirm that the default service account in the new namespace cannot.

Figure 17.7   Using separate service accounts for apps ensures the least-privilege approach.

TRY IT NOW   Run the Kube Explorer app, which lists Pods in a web UI. This deployment uses a custom service account and role for permissions.

```
# deploy the app and the RBAC rules:
kubectl apply -f kube-explorer/

# wait for the Pod:
kubectl wait --for=condition=ContainersReady pod -l app=kube-explorer

# get the URL for the app:
kubectl get svc kube-explorer -o
   jsonpath='http://{.status.loadBalancer.ingress[0].*}:8019'

# browse to the app, and confirm you can view and delete
# Pods in the default namespace; then add ?ns=kube-system
# to the URL, and you'll see an error.
```

My output is in figure 17.8, where you can see the app is happily listing and deleting Pods for the default namespace. When you switch to a different namespace, you'll see an authorization error, which comes from the Kubernetes API (it's an HTTP API so you actually get a 403 forbidden response). The app uses the service account token mounted in the Pod to authenticate, and the account has list and delete Pod permissions for only the default namespace, not for other namespaces.

Little apps like this take no time to build because most languages have a Kubernetes library, which takes care of authentication by using the token in the default path. They can be very useful for sharing a limited view of the cluster for teams who don't need kubectl access and who don't need to learn how Kubernetes works just to

The explorer app lists Pods. It has its own service account, role, and role binding to get list and delete permissions for the default namespace.

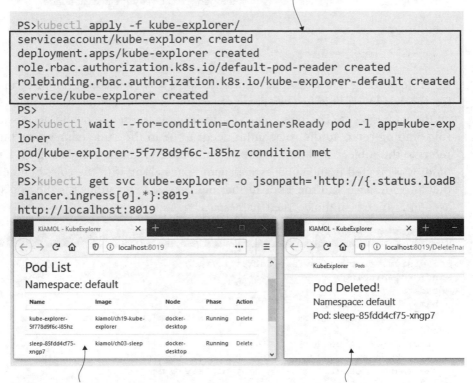

```
PS>kubectl apply -f kube-explorer/
serviceaccount/kube-explorer created
deployment.apps/kube-explorer created
role.rbac.authorization.k8s.io/default-pod-reader created
rolebinding.rbac.authorization.k8s.io/kube-explorer-default created
service/kube-explorer created
PS>
PS>kubectl wait --for=condition=ContainersReady pod -l app=kube-exp
lorer
pod/kube-explorer-5f778d9f6c-l85hz condition met
PS>
PS>kubectl get svc kube-explorer -o jsonpath='http://{.status.loadB
alancer.ingress[0].*}:8019'
http://localhost:8019
```

Browse to the app, and you'll see a list of Pods. When you click the Delete link, the Pod is deleted. Try to use a different namespace by adding `?ns=kube-system` to the URL, and you'll see a permissions error.

Figure 17.8   An app with its own service account and just enough permissions to do its job

see what's running. This app needs RBAC permissions to list Pods, show their details, and delete them. Right now, those permissions are in a role that is bound to the default namespace. To make other namespaces available, we need to add more roles and bindings.

Listing 17.3 shows the new rules that grant permission to get and list Pods in the kube-system namespace. The most important thing to take away here is that the namespace in the role metadata is not just where the role gets created, it's also the scope where the role applies. This role grants access to Pods in the kube-system namespace.

Listing 17.3   rbac-with-kube-system.yaml, applying a role to the system namespace

```
apiVersion: rbac.authorization.k8s.io/v1
kind: Role
```

```
metadata:
  name: system-pod-reader
  namespace: kube-system          # Scoped to the system namespace
rules:
- apiGroups: [""]                 # The API group of the object spec
  resources: ["pods"]             # Pods are in the core group, which
  verbs: ["get", "list"]          # is identified with an empty string.
```

The role binding that adds that role to the app's service account is in the same manifest file, but I've split it into two listings to examine them separately and make sense of all the namespaces. The namespace for the role is the scope of the permissions; the role binding refers to the role, and it needs to be in the same namespace, but it also refers to the subject, and that can be in a different namespace. In listing 17.4, the role binding is created in the kube-system namespace along with the role. Between them, they provide access to the Pods in that namespace. The subject is the app's service account, which is in the default namespace.

Listing 17.4   rbac-with-kube-system.yaml, role binding to a subject

```
apiVersion: rbac.authorization.k8s.io/v1
kind: RoleBinding
metadata:
  name: kube-explorer-system
  namespace: kube-system          # Needs to match the role
subjects:
- kind: ServiceAccount
  name: kube-explorer             # The subject can be in a
  namespace: default              # different namespace.
roleRef:
  apiGroup: rbac.authorization.k8s.io
  kind: Role
  name: system-pod-reader
```

You can see how things spiral when you have permission requirements that aren't a good fit for the standard cluster roles. In this case, permissions are different for different namespaces, so you need a set of roles and role bindings for each namespace. When you deploy these new rules, the app will be able to show system Pods. Access rules are evaluated when the API call is made, so there are no changes to the app or the service account; the new permissions take effect right away.

> **TRY IT NOW**   Add access rules for system Pods to the Kube Explorer app.

```
# apply the new role and binding
kubectl apply -f kube-explorer/update/rbac-with-kube-system.yaml

# refresh the explorer app with the path /?ns=kube-system.
# you can see the Pods now, but you can't delete them.
```

As shown in figure 17.9, the payback for managing lots of roles and bindings is that you can build very fine-grained access policies. This app can list and delete Pods in the

Grants get and list access to Pods in the system namespace

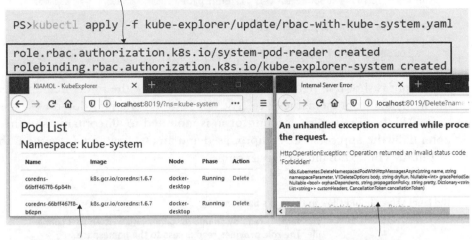

```
PS>kubectl apply -f kube-explorer/update/rbac-with-kube-system.yaml

role.rbac.authorization.k8s.io/system-pod-reader created
rolebinding.rbac.authorization.k8s.io/kube-explorer-system created
```

Now the app can display system Pods, but it doesn't have delete permissions, so the delete function fails.

Figure 17.9 RBAC rules take immediate effect when you apply or remove a binding.

default namespace, but it can only list Pods in the system namespace. No other apps can get those permissions by accident; they would need to specify the Kube Explorer service account and be deployed by someone who has access to use that account.

The last example in this section shows how apps might need to get some configuration data from the cluster that isn't in a ConfigMap or Secret. We'll use the to-do app again. This version displays a banner message on the home page, and it gets the content for the banner from the kiamol label on the namespace where the Pod is running. An init container sets up kubectl with the service account token, grabs the label value for the namespace, and writes it to a config file, which the app container picks up. It's not a very realistic scenario, but it shows you how to inject data from the cluster into app configuration.

TRY IT NOW Deploy the new to-do list app, and confirm the banner message is populated from the namespace label.

```
# print the label value on the namespace:
kubectl get ns kiamol-ch17 --show-labels

# deploy the to-do list app:
kubectl apply -f todo-list/

# wait for the Pod to start:
kubectl wait --for=condition=ContainersReady pod -l app=todo-web -n
  kiamol-ch17
```

```
# print the logs of the init container:
kubectl logs -l app=todo-web -c configurator --tail 1 -n kiamol-ch17

# get the URL, and browse to the app:
kubectl get svc todo-web -n kiamol-ch17 -o jsonpath='http://{.status
    .loadBalancer.ingress[0].*}:8020'
```

My output is shown in figure 17.10, where you can see the init container has fetched
the metadata from the namespace. The application container doesn't use the Kubernetes API, but the service account token is mounted to all containers in the Pod, so
potentially the app could be compromised and an attacker could use the Kubernetes
API in the context of the service account.

The label value should show in the app's banner.

**The value is read by an init container and written to a config
file. The role provides read access to the namespace.**

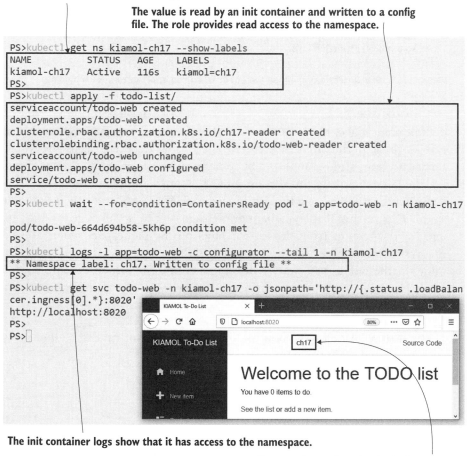

The init container logs show that it has access to the namespace.

The app shows the value in the banner.

Figure 17.10   Applications might need to access configuration data from other cluster resources.

There's not much an attacker could do if they did get access to the API from the to-do list app. The app uses a dedicated service account, and that account has a single permission: it can get the details of the namespace `kiamol-ch17`. Listing 17.5 shows how rules inside roles and cluster roles can restrict permissions to named resources.

Listing 17.5   02-rbac.yaml, rules for named resources

```
apiVersion: rbac.authorization.k8s.io/v1
kind: ClusterRole
metadata:
  name: ch17-reader
rules:
- apiGroups: [""]                    # Namespace access requires a
    resources: ["namespaces"]        # ClusterRole; this grants
    resourceNames: ["kiamol-ch17"]   # get access for one namespace.
    verbs: ["get"]
```

One drawback with RBAC is that resources need to exist before the rules can be applied, so in this case, the namespace and service account must exist before the role and role binding can be created. When you apply a folder of manifests with kubectl, it doesn't look for dependencies to create resources in the correct order. It just applies the files in filename order. That's why the RBAC manifest in listing 17.6 is called `02-rbac.yaml`, to ensure it is created after the service account and namespace exist.

We've looked at drilling down into specific permissions for individual apps, but the other major function of RBAC is to apply the same set of rules to groups of subjects. We'll move on to that next.

17.3   Binding roles to groups of users and service accounts

Role bindings and cluster role bindings can be applied to groups, and both users and service accounts can belong to groups, although they work differently. End users are authenticated outside of Kubernetes, and the API trusts the username and group information that is presented. Users can be members of multiple groups, and the group name and membership are managed by the authentication system. Service accounts are more restricted; they always belong to two groups: a group for all service accounts in the cluster, and a group for all the service accounts in a namespace.

Groups are another kind of subject for a binding, so the spec is the same, except you bind a role—or cluster role—to a group instead of a user or service account. Kubernetes doesn't validate the group name, so it's up to you to make sure the group in the binding matches the group set by the authentication system. Certificates can include group information, so we can create certificates for users who belong to different groups.

TRY IT NOW   Use the certificate generator to create some more authenticated users, this time with group membership set in the certificate, for a site reliability engineer (SRE) group and a group for testers.

```
# create two users:
kubectl apply -f user-groups/

# confirm that the SRE can't delete Pods:
kubectl exec sre-user -- kubectl auth can-i delete pods

# print the username and group in the certificate:
kubectl exec sre-user -- sh -c 'openssl x509 -text -noout -in
  /certs/user.crt | grep Subject:'

# confirm the test user can't read Pod logs:
kubectl exec test-user -- kubectl auth can-i get pod/logs

# print this certificate's details:
kubectl exec test-user -- sh -c 'openssl x509 -text -noout -in
  /certs/user.crt | grep Subject:'
```

Now you have two user certificates where the user belongs to a group representing their team: SREs and testers. No bindings exist in the cluster for either of the usernames or the groups, so the users can't do anything yet. Figure 17.11 shows that Kubernetes uses standard fields in the certificate's subject—the common name is the username and the organization is the group (multiple organizations can map to multiple groups).

The SRE user should be able to delete Pods, but they're a new user and have no permissions yet.

The O in the cert is the organization that is the `sre` group; the CN is the common name, which is the `sre1` username.

```
PS>kubectl apply -f user-groups/
pod/sre-user created
pod/test-user created
PS>
PS>kubectl exec sre-user -- kubectl auth can-i delete pods
no
command terminated with exit code 1
PS>
PS>kubectl exec sre-user -- sh -c 'openssl x509 -text -noout -in /certs/u
ser.crt | grep Subject:'
        Subject: C = UK, ST = LONDON, L = London, O = sre, CN = sre1
PS>
PS>kubectl exec test-user -- kubectl auth can-i get pod/logs
no
command terminated with exit code 1
PS>
PS>kubectl exec test-user -- sh -c 'openssl x509 -text -noout -in /certs/
user.crt | grep Subject:'
        Subject: C = UK, ST = LONDON, L = London, O = test, CN = tester1
```

The test user doesn't have permission to read logs.

In this certificate, the group is `test`, and the user is `tester1`.

Figure 17.11   Certificates can contain zero or more groups as well as the username.

We do want SREs to be able to delete Pods, and we do want testers to be able to read Pod logs. We can apply bindings at the group level to give all the users in the team the same permissions. We then move responsibility for managing group membership to the authentication system. For SREs, the simplest thing is for them to have the view role throughout the cluster so they can help diagnose issues, and the edit role for the namespaces their team manages. Those are built-in cluster roles, so we just need bindings where the subject is the SRE group. For testers, we want the very restricted set of permissions in listing 17.6.

```
apiVersion: rbac.authorization.k8s.io/v1
kind: ClusterRole
metadata:
  name: logs-reader
rules:
- apiGroups: [""]
  resources: ["pods ", "pods/log"]  # Logs are a subresource of Pods
  verbs: ["get"]                     # that need explicit permissions.
```

The full manifest from listing 17.6 includes a cluster role binding, giving this role to the test group, which effectively gives testers permission to look at any Pods and view their logs, but not to list Pods or do anything to any other resources. Some resources have subresources, which are permissioned separately, so if you have permission to get Pods, you can't read the logs unless you also have permission to get the logs subresource. When you apply the bindings for the two groups, the users will have the permissions they need.

TRY IT NOW   Empower the new users by binding the roles they need to the groups they belong to.

```
# apply the roles and bindings:
kubectl apply -f user-groups/bindings/

# confirm the SRE cannot delete in the default namespace:
kubectl exec sre-user -- kubectl auth can-i delete pods

# confirm they can delete in the ch17 namespace:
kubectl exec sre-user -- kubectl auth can-i delete pods -n kiamol-ch17

# confirm the tester can't list Pods:
kubectl exec test-user -- kubectl get pods

# confirm the tester can read the logs for a known Pod:
kubectl exec test-user -- kubectl logs test-user --tail 1
```

You can see in figure 17.12 that this works as expected: the users have the permissions they need, but we apply them at a higher level, binding roles to groups. We can change permissions without modifying users or groups. New users can arrive, and

**These roles and bindings give the groups the permissions they
need, and the users in those groups will inherit the permissions.**

**The SRE user can delete Pods only in the
namespace for the apps they work on.**

```
PS>kubectl apply -f user-groups/bindings/
clusterrolebinding.rbac.authorization.k8s.io/sre-view-cluster created
rolebinding.rbac.authorization.k8s.io/sre-edit-ch17 created
clusterrole.rbac.authorization.k8s.io/logs-reader created
clusterrolebinding.rbac.authorization.k8s.io/test-logs-cluster created
PS>
PS>kubectl exec sre-user -- kubectl auth can-i delete pods
no
command terminated with exit code 1
PS>
PS>kubectl exec sre-user -- kubectl auth can-i delete pods -n kiamol-ch17
yes
PS>
PS>kubectl exec test-user -- kubectl get pods
Error from server (Forbidden): pods is forbidden: User "tester1" cannot li
st resource "pods" in API group "" in the namespace "default"
command terminated with exit code 1
PS>
PS>kubectl exec test-user -- kubectl logs test-user --tail 1
** Using context for user: tester1; group: test
```

The tester cannot list Pods, but given a Pod name, they can read the logs.

Figure 17.12   Permissions at the group level give users what they need with an easy management
experience.

people can move between teams without any RBAC changes, as long as the authentication system is kept up to date so Kubernetes sees the current group membership in
the API call.

This is all fine in a corporate environment with Active Directory configured or a
cloud environment with integrated authentication. In smaller-scale clusters, you may
want to manage authentication within Kubernetes, but generating certificates like
we've done in this section isn't really feasible. The script creates certificates which are
valid for a year, and the group list is baked into the certificate, so it's hard to make
changes to group membership. If you want to revoke access, you need to rotate the
Kubernetes issuer certificate and distribute new certificates to every user.

A common alternative is to misuse service accounts, creating a service account for
every end user and distributing a token for authentication with kubectl. This approach
doesn't scale to hundreds of users, but it is a viable option if you don't have an external authentication system and you want secure access to Kubernetes for a small number of users. You have to take a slightly quirky approach to groups, because you can't
create a group and add a service account to it. Instead, you need to treat namespaces

as groups, create a namespace for each group you want, and put all the service accounts in that group. Figure 17.13 shows the setup.

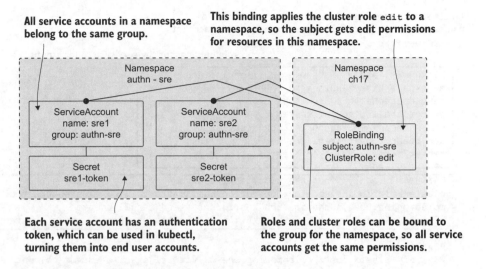

Figure 17.13   Service accounts have tokens and groups so they can be misused as user accounts.

Service accounts work as user accounts because you can manage them within the cluster, creating or removing them easily and revoking access by deleting the token. We can recreate our SRE and tester users with service accounts, using separate namespaces to represent the two groups and applying bindings to the groups.

TRY IT NOW   Create namespaces for the SRE and tester groups and a service account and token for a user in each namespace.

```
# create namespaces, service accounts, and tokens:
kubectl apply -f user-groups/service-accounts/

# apply bindings to the groups:
kubectl apply -f user-groups/service-accounts/role-bindings/

# confirm the SRE group has view access across the cluster:
kubectl get clusterrolebinding sre-sa-view-cluster -o custom-
    columns='ROLE:.roleRef.name,SUBJECT KIND:.subjects[0].kind,SUBJECT
    NAME:.subjects[0].name'
```

The new cluster role bindings apply to the service account groups, which is the namespace where the service accounts have been created. The difference between these cluster roles and the user certificate cluster roles is just the group name:

`system:serviceaccounts:kiamol-authn-sre` for SREs, which is the group for all the service accounts in the `kiamol-authn-sre` namespace, as you can see in figure 17.14.

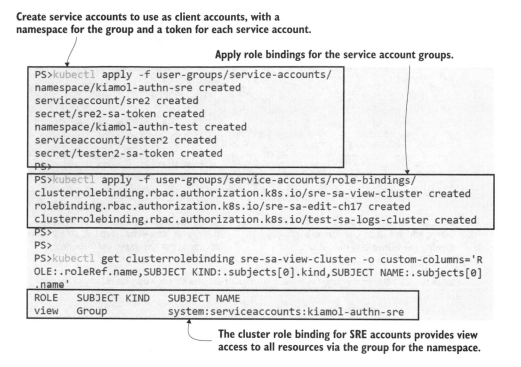

Create service accounts to use as client accounts, with a namespace for the group and a token for each service account.

Apply role bindings for the service account groups.

```
PS>kubectl apply -f user-groups/service-accounts/
namespace/kiamol-authn-sre created
serviceaccount/sre2 created
secret/sre2-sa-token created
namespace/kiamol-authn-test created
serviceaccount/tester2 created
secret/tester2-sa-token created
PS>
```

```
PS>kubectl apply -f user-groups/service-accounts/role-bindings/
clusterrolebinding.rbac.authorization.k8s.io/sre-sa-view-cluster created
rolebinding.rbac.authorization.k8s.io/sre-sa-edit-ch17 created
clusterrolebinding.rbac.authorization.k8s.io/test-sa-logs-cluster created
PS>
PS>
PS>kubectl get clusterrolebinding sre-sa-view-cluster -o custom-columns='R
OLE:.roleRef.name,SUBJECT KIND:.subjects[0].kind,SUBJECT NAME:.subjects[0]
.name'
ROLE    SUBJECT KIND    SUBJECT NAME
view    Group           system:serviceaccounts:kiamol-authn-sre
```

The cluster role binding for SRE accounts provides view access to all resources via the group for the namespace.

Figure 17.14 Faking an authentication system with service accounts, tokens, and namespaces

Service accounts use a JSON Web Token (JWT) to authenticate. This token is prepopulated in Pod volumes. Tokens are created as a Secret of type `kubernetes.io/service-account-token`, and Kubernetes ensures every service account has at least one token. You can also create your own, which makes it easy to distribute, rotate, and revoke the token. The process is simple because Kubernetes actually generates the token; you just need to create an empty Secret of the correct type, and the cluster adds the data—you did that in the previous exercise, so these accounts are ready to use.

Kubectl supports several different authentication options—certificates we've already seen as well as username and password, third-party authentication, and JWT. You can authenticate to the cluster by setting up a new context with credentials that use the token from the service account. Any kubectl commands using that context will operate as the service account, so the permissions for the service account group will apply.

TRY IT NOW   Create a new context in kubectl for the SRE service account and confirm you can access the cluster. This will work with your cluster, whatever authentication system it uses.

```
# add a Base64 command if you're using Windows:
. .\base64.ps1

# decode the Secret for the token, and save to a file:
kubectl get secret sre2-sa-token -n kiamol-authn-sre -o
  jsonpath='{.data.token}' | base64 -d > sa-token

# load new credentials into kubectl from the token file:
kubectl config set-credentials ch17-sre --token=$(cat sa-token)

# create a new context using the SRE credentials:
kubectl config set-context ch17-sre --user=ch17-sre --cluster
  $(kubectl config view -o jsonpath='{.clusters[0].name}')

# confirm you can delete Pods as the SRE account:
kubectl delete pods -n kiamol-ch17 -l app=todo-web --context ch17-sre
```

This exercise works on all clusters, even if they have third-party authentication configured, because it uses Kubernetes's own authentication for service accounts. You can see in figure 17.15 that I can issue commands as the SRE service account and that user has access to delete Pods in the kiamol-ch17 namespace.

The data in the Secret is the JWT to authenticate the service account. Decode the Base64 to get the token.

Kubectl can use the JWT as credentials to authenticate.

```
PS>. .\base64.ps1
PS>
PS>kubectl get secret sre2-sa-token -n kiamol-authn-sre -o jsonpath='{.dat
a.token}' | base64 -d > sa-token
PS>
PS>kubectl config set-credentials ch17-sre --token=$(cat sa-token)
User "ch17-sre" set.
PS>
PS>kubectl config set-context ch17-sre --user=ch17-sre --cluster $(kubectl
 config view -o jsonpath='{.clusters[0].name}')
Context "ch17-sre" created.
PS>
PS>kubectl delete pods -n kiamol-ch17 -l app=todo-web --context ch17-sre
pod "todo-web-664d694b58-p5mq5" deleted
```

Using the SRE context, kubectl authenticates as the SRE service account, which does have access to delete Pods in the ch17 namespace.

Figure 17.15   Distributing the service account token lets users authenticate as the account.

If you're into JWT, you can decode the contents of that `sa-token` file (the online tool at https://jwt.io will do it for you), and you'll see that Kubernetes is the issuer and the subject is the service account name `system:serviceaccount:kiamol-authn-sre:sre2`. RBAC permissions are the combined roles for that service account, the group for the service account namespace, and the group for all service accounts. A small note of caution here: Be very careful with the subject when you grant roles to service account groups. It's easy to accidentally make every account a cluster admin by leaving the namespace off the subject (which is the exact problem with some versions of Docker Desktop; see the history at https://github.com/docker/for-mac/issues/4774).

Now that we manage authentication within the cluster, it's easy to revoke access to a specific user by deleting the token for their service account. The token they present from kubectl no longer authenticates the service account, so they'll get unauthorized errors for every action

> **TRY IT NOW**   Stop users authenticating as the SRE service account by deleting the token.

```
# delete the access token:
kubectl delete secret sre2-sa-token -n kiamol-authn-sre

# wait for the token removal to reach controllers:
sleep 30

# now try to get Pods as the SRE account:
kubectl get pods --context ch17-sre
```

Revoking access is easy, as you can see in figure 17.16. Rotating tokens requires a bit more of a process; you can create a new token and send it to the user (securely!) and then delete the old token once the user has updated their context. Changing groups is more involved because you need to create a new service account in the namespace for the group, create and send the new token, and delete the old service account.

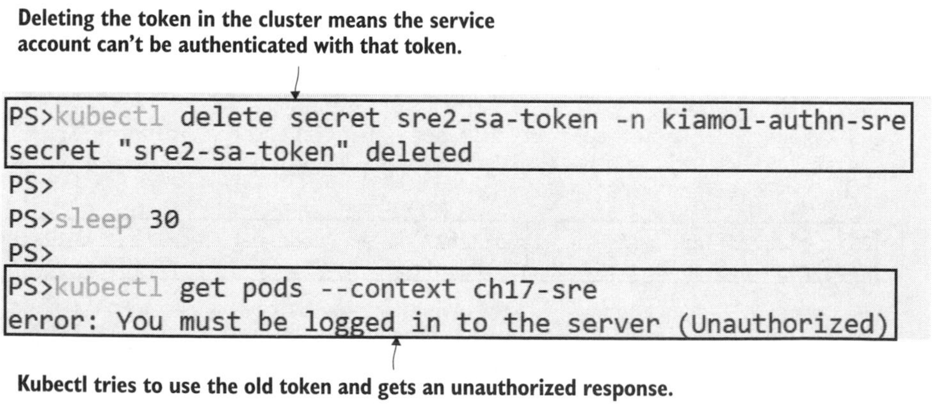

Deleting the token in the cluster means the service
account can't be authenticated with that token.

```
PS>kubectl delete secret sre2-sa-token -n kiamol-authn-sre
secret "sre2-sa-token" deleted
PS>
PS>sleep 30
PS>
PS>kubectl get pods --context ch17-sre
error: You must be logged in to the server (Unauthorized)
```

Kubectl tries to use the old token and gets an unauthorized response.

Figure 17.16   You can remove access without removing service accounts by deleting tokens.

Service accounts for users is a simple approach to securing your cluster, if you can live with the limitations. It might be a reasonable way to get started, but you should understand your road map, which will most likely be to use OpenID Connect (OIDC) for authentication and bind your RBAC rules to OIDC username and group claims.

When you have your authentication system wired up and your RBAC rules set, you still have a challenge. Kubernetes doesn't have a great set of tools for auditing permissions, so in the next section, we'll look at third-party options for verifying permissions.

17.4 *Discovering and auditing permissions with plugins*

The kubectl can-i command is useful for checking if a user can perform a function, but that's the only tool you get for validating permissions, and it doesn't really go far enough. You often want to approach it the other way around and ask who can perform a function or print out a matrix of access permissions or search for an RBAC subject and see their roles. Kubectl has a plugin system to support additional commands, as well as plugins to satisfy all these different ways to approach RBAC.

The best way to add kubectl plugins is with Krew, the plugin manager. You can install Krew directly on your machine, but the installation isn't super-smooth, and you might not want plugins installed on that machine (if you do, the install documentation is here https://krew.sigs.k8s.io/docs/user-guide/setup/install). I've prepped a container image with Krew already installed—you can use that image to try out plugins in a safe way. The first one we'll look at is who-can, which is like the reverse of can-i.

> **TRY IT NOW**   Start the Krew Pod, and connect to install and use the who-can plugin.

```
# run a Pod with kubectl and Krew already installed:
kubectl apply -f rbac-tools/

# wait for the Pod:
kubectl wait --for=condition=ContainersReady pod -l app=rbac-tools

# connect to the container:
kubectl exec -it deploy/rbac-tools -- sh

# install the who-can plugin:
kubectl krew install who-can

# list who has access to the todo-list ConfigMap:
kubectl who-can get configmap todo-web-config
```

Any binary can be a kubectl plugin, but Krew simplifies the setup and adds some process by curating useful plugins. (Krew is a Kubernetes Special Interest Group project.) Plugins operate in the context of your authenticated user, so you need to be sure they don't do anything they shouldn't. The who-can plugin from this exercise is published by Aqua Security, and as you see in figure 17.17, it works by traversing RBAC roles to find matching permissions and then prints the subjects who have bindings for those roles.

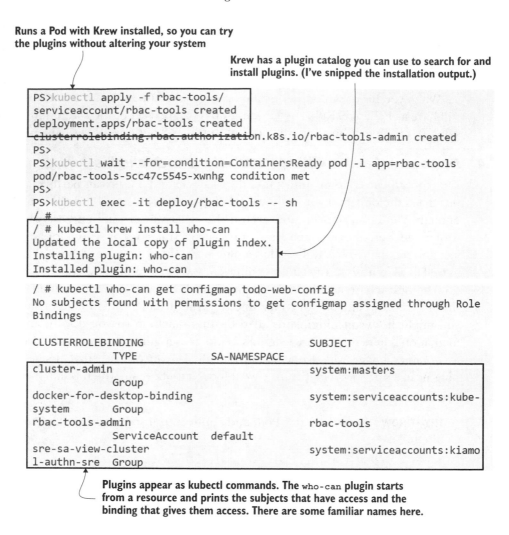

Runs a Pod with Krew installed, so you can try the plugins without altering your system

Krew has a plugin catalog you can use to search for and install plugins. (I've snipped the installation output.)

```
PS>kubectl apply -f rbac-tools/
serviceaccount/rbac-tools created
deployment.apps/rbac-tools created
clusterrolebinding.rbac.authorization.k8s.io/rbac-tools-admin created
PS>
PS>kubectl wait --for=condition=ContainersReady pod -l app=rbac-tools
pod/rbac-tools-5cc47c5545-xwnhg condition met
PS>
PS>kubectl exec -it deploy/rbac-tools -- sh
/ #
/ # kubectl krew install who-can
Updated the local copy of plugin index.
Installing plugin: who-can
Installed plugin: who-can

/ # kubectl who-can get configmap todo-web-config
No subjects found with permissions to get configmap assigned through Role
Bindings

CLUSTERROLEBINDING                                  SUBJECT
                TYPE          SA-NAMESPACE
cluster-admin                                       system:masters
                Group
docker-for-desktop-binding                          system:serviceaccounts:kube-
system          Group
rbac-tools-admin                                    rbac-tools
                ServiceAccount   default
sre-sa-view-cluster                                 system:serviceaccounts:kiamo
l-authn-sre    Group
```

Plugins appear as kubectl commands. The who-can plugin starts from a resource and prints the subjects that have access and the binding that gives them access. There are some familiar names here.

Figure 17.17   Plugins add new features to kubectl: who-can is a useful tool for RBAC queries.

We'll look at two more plugins that fill gaps in RBAC auditing. The next is access-matrix, which operates on a resource type or a specific resource and prints all the access rules for that object, showing who can do what. This is the most useful tool for ongoing auditing, where you could run a scheduled job that collects a set of access matrices and confirms no unexpected permissions have been set.

TRY IT NOW   Install the access-matrix plugin, and print the matrices for different resources.

```
# install the plugin:
kubectl krew install access-matrix
```

```
# print the matrix for Pods:
kubectl access-matrix for pods -n default

# the print the matrix for the to-do list ConfigMap:
kubectl access-matrix for configmap todo-web-config -n default
```

The default output from `access-matrix` prints nice icons, as you see in figure 17.18, but you can configure plain ASCII output in the command line. My output is heavily snipped because the full permissions list includes all the controllers and other system components. The access matrix for a ConfigMap is more manageable, and you can see the SRE groups created in section 17.3 have list permission, so they can see this object, but the `rbac-tools` service account has full update and delete permissions. That's because I was lazy for this exercise and gave the account the `cluster-admin` role instead of building a custom role with just the permissions the plugins need.

The `access-matrix` plugin lists who can perform actions on a resource.

I've snipped the output for Pods, but you can see lots of system components. You know how Deployments work, so it makes sense that Deployments can list Pods and ReplicaSets can create and delete them.

```
/ # kubectl krew install access-matrix
Updated the local copy of plugin index.
Installing plugin: access-matrix
Installed plugin: access-matrix
```

```
/ # kubectl access-matrix for pods -n default
```

NAME	KIND	SA-NAMESPACE	LIST	CREATE	UPDATE	DELETE
deployment-controller	ServiceAccount	kube-system	✓	✗	✓	✗
replicaset-controller	ServiceAccount	kube-system	✓	✓	✗	✓
sre	Group		✓	✗	✗	✗
statefulset-controller	ServiceAccount	kube-system	✓	✓	✓	✓
system:kube-controller-manager	User		✓	✗	✗	✗
system:kube-scheduler	User		✓	✗	✗	✗
system:masters	Group		✓	✓	✓	✓
system:serviceaccounts:kiamol-authn-sre	Group		✓	✗	✗	✗
system:serviceaccounts:kube-system	Group		✓	✓	✓	✓

```
/ # kubectl access-matrix for configmap todo-web-config -n default
```

NAME	KIND	SA-NAMESPACE	LIST	CREATE	UPDATE	DELETE
generic-garbage-collector	ServiceAccount	kube-system	✓	✗	✓	✓
horizontal-pod-autoscaler	ServiceAccount	kube-system	✓	✗	✗	✗
namespace-controller	ServiceAccount	kube-system	✓	✗	✗	✓
rbac-tools	ServiceAccount	default	✓	✓	✓	✓
resourcequota-controller	ServiceAccount	kube-system	✓	✗	✗	✗
sre	Group		✓	✗	✗	✗
system:kube-controller-manager	User		✓	✗	✗	✗
system:masters	Group		✓	✓	✓	✓
system:serviceaccounts:kiamol-authn-sre	Group		✓	✗	✗	✗

A ConfigMap also has lots of system components in the list, together with the SRE groups I created and the service account for this `rbac-tools` Pod. That account doesn't need all these permissions.

Figure 17.18 The `access-matrix` plugin shows who can do what with different resources.

The last plugin we'll look at is `rbac-lookup`, which is useful for searching RBAC subjects. It finds matches in users, service accounts, and groups and shows you the roles that are bound to the subject. It's a good one for checking RBAC from the user perspective, when you want to confirm that a subject has the correct roles assigned.

> **TRY IT NOW**   Install the `rbac-lookup` plugin, and search for SRE and test subjects.

```
# install the plugin:
kubectl krew install rbac-lookup

# search for SRE:
kubectl rbac-lookup sre

# search for test:
kubectl rbac-lookup test
```

One thing no plugin can do is give you the consolidated permissions for a user and all the groups they belong to, because Kubernetes has no idea about group membership. RBAC works by getting the consolidated permissions when a user is presented with the list of their groups, but outside of an incoming request, there is no link between users and groups. That's different with service accounts because they always belong to known groups—you can see the SRE groups in figure 17.19. There's no way to find which users belong to the SRE user group, but you can list all the service accounts in the `kiamol-authn-sre` namespace to see who belongs to the service account group.

The `rbac-lookup` plugin searches for subjects and prints their roles.

There are two SRE group subjects: one for users, and one for service accounts. Both have the same cluster and namespace roles.

```
/ # kubectl krew install rbac-lookup
Updated the local copy of plugin index.
Installing plugin: rbac-lookup
Installed plugin: rbac-lookup
```

```
/ # kubectl rbac-lookup sre
SUBJECT                                      SCOPE          ROLE
sre                                          cluster-wide   ClusterRole/view
sre                                          kiamol-ch17    ClusterRole/edit
system:serviceaccounts:kiamol-authn-sre      kiamol-ch17    ClusterRole/edit
system:serviceaccounts:kiamol-authn-sre      cluster-wide   ClusterRole/view
/ #
/ # kubectl rbac-lookup test
SUBJECT                                      SCOPE          ROLE
system:serviceaccounts:kiamol-authn-test     cluster-wide   ClusterRole/logs-reader
test                                         cluster-wide   ClusterRole/logs-reader
```

There are also two test group subjects. Both have the custom `logs-reader` role applied for the whole cluster.

Figure 17.19   Searching for RBAC subjects and printing the roles to which they're bound

It's worth exploring the Krew catalog to find more plugins that can help your daily workflow. This section focused on the established plugins that help with RBAC; they're popular and have been around for a long time, but there are plenty more gems to find. That's it for the practical work in this chapter. We'll finish up looking at how RBAC affects your workloads and guidance for implementing access controls.

17.5 *Planning your RBAC strategy*

RBAC gives you a consistent way to secure Kubernetes for external users and apps running in the cluster. The mechanics of roles and bindings are the same for both types of subject, but they need very different approaches. Users are authenticated by a separate, trusted system that asserts the username and groups the user belongs to. Guidance here is to start with the predefined cluster roles—view, edit, and admin—and apply them to groups. The cluster admin role should be strictly guarded and used only if you really need it, preferably restricting it to service accounts for automated processes.

Think about using namespaces as a security boundary so you can limit scope further. If your authentication system has group information that identifies someone's team and their function on that team, that might be enough to map bindings to a role and a product namespace. Be wary of clusterwide roles because they can be used to gain elevated access. If a user can read Secrets in any namespace, they can potentially grab the JWT token for a privileged service account and get admin access to that namespace.

Service accounts should be used sparingly and only by apps that need access to the Kubernetes API server. You can disable automounting the token in Pods as a property of the default service account, so Pods never see the token unless they actively request it. Remember that RBAC is not about restricting access at deployment time. Pods don't need a service account configured to use a ConfigMap that is mounted as a volume. You need service accounts only for apps that use the Kubernetes API, and in those cases, each app should have a dedicated service account with just enough permissions for the app to do what it needs, preferably with named resources.

Applying RBAC isn't the end of the story. As your security profile matures, you'll want to add auditing to ensure policies don't get subverted and admission controllers to ensure new apps have the required security controls. We won't cover that here; just be aware that securing your cluster is about using multiple approaches to gain security in depth.

Okay, time to clear down the cluster before you move on to the lab.

TRY IT NOW Remove all of the chapter's resources.

```
kubectl delete all,ns,rolebinding,clusterrolebinding,role
  ,clusterrole,serviceaccount -l kiamol=ch17
```

17.6 Lab

The Kube Explorer app you ran in section 17.2 can also display service accounts, but it needs some more permissions to do that. There's a new set of manifests for the app in the lab folder that give it permissions to access Pods in the default namespace. Your task for this lab is to add roles and bindings so the app can do the following things:

- Display and delete Pods in the `kiamol-ch17-lab` namespace
- Display service accounts in the `default` namespace
- Display service accounts in the `kiamol-ch17-lab` namespace

Look closely at how the existing RBAC rules are set up—that should make this one straightforward. Just remember how namespaces in the bindings affect scope. My solution is available for you to check: https://github.com/sixeyed/kiamol/blob/master/ch17/lab/README.md.

Deploying Kubernetes: Multinode and multiarchitecture clusters

You can do an awful lot with Kubernetes without understanding the architecture of the cluster and how all the pieces fit together—you already have in the previous 17 chapters. But that additional knowledge will help you understand what high availability looks like in Kubernetes and what you need to think about if you want to run your own cluster. The best way to learn about all of the Kubernetes components is to install a cluster from scratch, and that's what you'll do in this chapter. The exercises start with plain virtual machines and walk you through a basic Kubernetes setup for a multinode cluster, which you can use to run some of the sample apps you're familiar with from the book.

Every app we've run so far has used Linux containers built for Intel 64-bit processors, but Kubernetes is a multiarchitecture platform. A single cluster can have nodes with different operating systems and different types of CPU, so you can run a variety of workloads. In this chapter, you'll also add a Windows Server node to your cluster and run some Windows applications. That part is optional, but if you're not a Windows user, it's worth following through those exercises to see how Kubernetes uses the same modeling language for different architectures, with just a few tweaks to the manifests.

18.1 What's inside a Kubernetes cluster?

You'll need some different tools to follow along in this chapter and some virtual machine images, which will take a while to download. You can start the installation now, and by the time we've finished looking at the architecture of Kubernetes, you should be ready to go.

TRY IT NOW   You'll use Vagrant, a free open source tool for VM management, to run the virtual machines. You also need to have a VM runtime; you can use VirtualBox, Hyper-V (on Windows), or Parallels (on macOS) for these machines. Install Vagrant, and then download the base VM images you'll use for your cluster.

```
# install Vagrant-
# browse to https://www.vagrantup.com to download
# OR on Windows you can use: choco install vagrant
# OR on macOS you can use: brew cask install vagrant

# Vagrant packages VM images into "boxes"
# download a Linux box—this will ask you to choose a provider,
# and you should select your VM runtime:
vagrant box add bento/ubuntu-20.04

# if you want to add Windows, download a Windows box:
vagrant box add kiamol/windows-2019
```

Okay, while that's happening, it's time to learn about the architecture of Kubernetes. You know that a cluster is composed of one or more servers called nodes, but those nodes can play different roles. There's the Kubernetes *control plane*, which is the management side of the cluster (previously called master nodes), and then *nodes*, which run your workloads (these were once called minions). At a high level, the control plane is the thing that receives your kubectl deployment requests, and it actions them by scheduling Pods on the nodes. Figure 18.1 shows the cluster at the user-experience level.

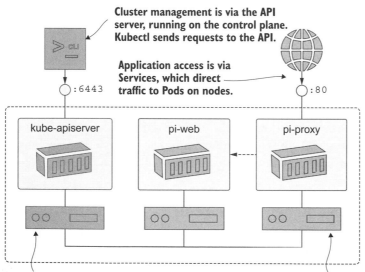

Cluster management is via the API server, running on the control plane. Kubectl sends requests to the API.

Application access is via Services, which direct traffic to Pods on nodes.

:6443   :80

kube-apiserver   pi-web   pi-proxy

The control plane node runs the API server, along with DNS and core system controllers.

Standard nodes run only application workloads. They are in communication with the control plane, receiving requests to run Pods and sending health reports.

Figure 18.1   From the user perspective, this is one cluster with management and application endpoints.

In a managed Kubernetes platform in the cloud, the control plane is taken care of for you, so you only need to worry about your own nodes (in AKS, the control plane is completely abstracted so you see—and pay for—only worker nodes). That's one reason why a managed platform is so attractive—the control plane contains multiple components, and you need to manage those if you run your own environment. The following components are all critical for the cluster to function:

- The *API server* is the management interface. It's a REST API on an HTTPS endpoint, which you connect to with kubectl and which Pods can use internally. It runs in the kube-apiserver Pod, and it can be scaled up for high availability.
- The *scheduler* watches for new Pod requests and selects a node to run them. It runs in the kube-scheduler Pod, but it's a pluggable component—you can deploy your own custom scheduler.
- The *controller manager* runs core controllers, which are internal components, not visible controllers like Deployments. The kube-controller-manager Pod runs controllers that observe node availability and manage Service endpoints.
- *etcd* is the Kubernetes data store where all cluster data is stored. It's a distributed key-value database, which replicates data across many instances.

You need to run multiple control plane nodes for high availability. Use an odd number to support failures, so if the manager node goes down, the remaining nodes can vote for a new manager. Each control plane node runs an instance of all of these components, as shown in figure 18.2. The API server is load-balanced, and the backend

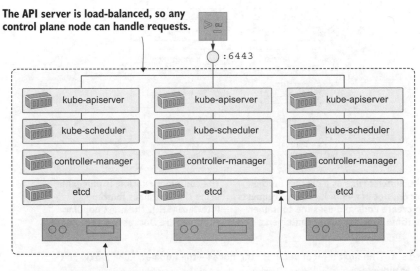

The API server is load-balanced, so any control plane node can handle requests.

Each control plane node runs its own copy of all the key components, all in Pods. The control plane can tolerate the loss of individual nodes.

The etcd data store is replicated, so all nodes have the same state. The API server on each node uses its local etcd instance.

Figure 18.2   Production clusters need multiple control plane nodes for high availability.

data is replicated, so any control plane node can work on a request, and it will be processed in the same way.

Your downloads should be nearly done now, so we'll look at just one more level of detail—the components running on each node. Nodes are responsible for creating Pods and ensuring their containers keep running and for connecting Pods to the Kubernetes network.

- The *kubelet* is a background agent that runs on the server—not in a Pod or in a container. It receives requests to create Pods and manages the Pod life cycle and also sends heartbeats to the API server confirming the node is healthy.
- The *kube-proxy* is the network component that routes traffic between Pods or from Pods to the outside world. It runs as a DaemonSet, with a Pod on each node managing that node's traffic.
- The *container runtime*, used by the kubelet to manage Pod containers. Typically Docker, containerd, or CRI-O, this is pluggable with any runtime that supports CRI (the Container Runtime Interface).

Figure 18.3 shows the internal components on each node, and these all run on the control plane nodes, too.

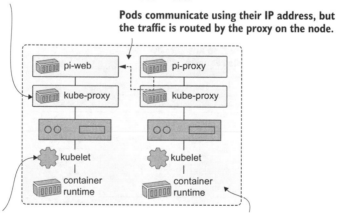

Every node runs a proxy server. It runs as a normal Pod, but it takes care of all the network traffic between Pods.

Pods communicate using their IP address, but the traffic is routed by the proxy on the node.

The kubelet runs as a process on the server, not in a Pod. It receives requests to create Pods and uses the container runtime to manage Pod containers.

The container runtime is pluggable, using the Container Runtime Interface (CRI). The most popular runtimes are Docker and containerd.

Figure 18.3 The next level of detail for the nodes—the kubelet, kube-proxy, and container runtime

You can see that Kubernetes is a complex platform with lots of moving pieces. These are just the core components; there's also Pod networking, DNS, and, in the cloud, a separate cloud controller manager, which integrates with cloud services. You can deploy and manage your own Kubernetes cluster with 100% open source components, but you need to be aware of the complexity you're taking on. And that's more than enough theory—let's go build a cluster.

18.2 *Initializing the control plane*

Most of the work in deploying Kubernetes is taken care of by a tool called kubeadm. It's an administration command line that can initialize a new control plane, join nodes to the cluster, and upgrade the Kubernetes version. Before you get to kubeadm, you need to install several dependencies. In a production environment, you'd have these already installed in your VM image, but to show you how it works, we'll start from scratch.

> **TRY IT NOW** Run a Linux VM, which will be the control plane node and install all of the Kubernetes dependencies. If you're using Hyper-V on Windows, you'll need to run your shell as administrator.

```
# switch to this chapter's source:
cd ch18

# use Vagrant to start a new VM—depending on your VM runtime,
# you'll get prompts asking you to choose a network and to
# provide your credentials to mount folders from your machine:
vagrant up kiamol-control

# connect to the VM:
vagrant ssh kiamol-control

# this folder maps the ch18 source folder:
cd /vagrant/setup

# make the install script executable, and run it:
sudo chmod +x linux-setup.sh && sudo ./linux-setup.sh

# confirm Docker has been installed:
which docker

# confirm all the Kubernetes tools have been installed:
ls /usr/bin/kube*
```

Figure 18.4 gives you the highlights—creating the VM, running the setup script, and verifying all the tools are there. If you inspect the linux-setup.sh script in this chapter's source, you'll see that it installs Docker and the Kubernetes tools and sets a couple of memory and network configurations for the server.

Now this machine is ready to become a Kubernetes control plane node. After all the build-up to get here, the next exercise will be an anticlimax: you need to run only a single command to initialize the cluster and get all the control plane components running. Keep an eye on the output, and you'll see all the pieces you learned about in section 18.1 starting up.

Vagrant is a tool for managing VMs. The chapter source has a Vagrantfile, which defines the VMs for the cluster, and this starts the VM, which will be the control plane node.

Vagrant shares your local folder with the VM, so you may be asked for credentials.

```
PS>cd /ch18
PS>
PS>vagrant up kiamol-control
Bringing machine 'kiamol-control' up with 'hyperv' provider...
==> kiamol-control: Verifying Hyper-V is enabled...
==> kiamol-control: Verifying Hyper-V is accessible...
==> kiamol-control: Importing a Hyper-V instance

    kiamol-control: Username (user[@domain]): elton
    kiamol-control: Password (will be hidden):

Vagrant requires administrator access to create SMB shares and
may request access to complete setup of configured shares.
==> kiamol-control: Setting hostname...
==> kiamol-control: Mounting SMB shared folders...
    kiamol-control: D:/scm/github/sixeyed/kiamol/ch18 => /vagrant
vagrant@kiamol-control:~$ cd /vagrant/setup
vagrant@kiamol-control:/vagrant/setup$ sudo chmod +x linux-setup.sh && sudo
./linux-setup.sh
Get:1 http://security.ubuntu.com/ubuntu focal-security InRelease [107 kB]

vagrant@kiamol-control:/vagrant/setup$ which docker
/usr/bin/docker
vagrant@kiamol-control:/vagrant/setup$ ls /usr/bin/kube*
/usr/bin/kubeadm  /usr/bin/kubectl  /usr/bin/kubelet
vagrant@kiamol-control:/vagrant/setup$ 
```

The setup script installs all the Kubernetes dependencies: Docker, the kubelet, kubectl, and kubeadm.

Confirms the prerequisites are all installed

Figure 18.4   Kubeadm is the tool that sets up the cluster, but it needs the container runtime and kubelet.

TRY IT NOW   Use kubeadm to initialize a new cluster with a fixed set of network addresses for Pods and Services.

```
# initialize a new cluster:
sudo kubeadm init --pod-network-cidr="10.244.0.0/16" --service-
  cidr="10.96.0.0/12" --apiserver-advertise-address=$(cat /tmp/ip.txt)

# create a folder for the kubectl config file:
mkdir ~/.kube

# copy the admin configuration to your folder:
sudo cp /etc/kubernetes/admin.conf ~/.kube/config

# make the file readable so kubectl can access it:
sudo chmod +r ~/.kube/config
```

```
# confirm you have a Kubernetes cluster:
kubectl get nodes
```

The output from initializing the cluster tells you what to do next, including the command you'll run on other nodes to join the cluster (you'll need that for later exercises, so be sure to copy it into a text file somewhere). The command also generates a config file, which you can use to manage the cluster with kubectl. You can see in figure 18.5 that the cluster exists with a single control plane node, but the node isn't in the Ready status.

Kubeadm runs a series of checks to confirm your machine is suitable. The install script from the previous exercise set everything up so the checks all pass.

```
vagrant@kiamol-control:/vagrant/setup$ sudo kubeadm init --pod-network-cidr=
"10.244.0.0/16" --service-cidr="10.96.0.0/12"
W0713 10:59:57.286462   19160 configset.go:202] WARNING: kubeadm cannot vali
date component configs for API groups [kubelet.config.k8s.io kubeproxy.confi
g.k8s.io]
[init] Using Kubernetes version: v1.18.5
[preflight] Running pre-flight checks
```

```
Then you can join any number of worker nodes by running the following on eac
h as root:
```

```
kubeadm join 172.21.120.227:6443 --token zc9m76.8l4573wyjf9vokg3 \
    --discovery-token-ca-cert-hash sha256:2c520ea15a99bd68b74d04f40056996dff
5b6ed1e76dfaeb0211c6db18ba0393
vagrant@kiamol-control:/vagrant/setup$
vagrant@kiamol-control:/vagrant/setup$ mkdir ~/.kube
vagrant@kiamol-control:/vagrant/setup$
vagrant@kiamol-control:/vagrant/setup$ sudo cp /etc/kubernetes/admin.conf ~/
.kube/config
vagrant@kiamol-control:/vagrant/setup$
vagrant@kiamol-control:/vagrant/setup$ sudo chmod +r ~/.kube/config
vagrant@kiamol-control:/vagrant/setup$
vagrant@kiamol-control:/vagrant/setup$ kubectl get nodes
NAME             STATUS     ROLES     AGE      VERSION
kiamol-control   NotReady   master    4m10s    v1.18.5
```

The output of the `init` command is a `join` command. Your own command will have a different IP address, token, and CA hash. You'll need to copy it for later.

The cluster is created! It has a control plane node, but it's not ready to use yet.

Figure 18.5   Initializing the cluster is simple: kubeadm starts all the control plane components.

The cluster isn't ready because it doesn't have a Pod network installed. You know from chapter 16 that Kubernetes has a network plugin model, and different plugins have different capabilities. We used Calico in that chapter to demonstrate network policy enforcement, and in this chapter, we'll use flannel (another open source option), because it has the most mature support for clusters with mixed architectures. You install flannel in the same way as Calico: with a Kubernetes manifest you apply on the control plane node.

TRY IT NOW   Add a network plugin to your new cluster, using a ready-made flannel manifest.

```
# deploy flannel:
kubectl apply -f flannel.yaml

# wait for the DNS Pods to start:
kubectl -n kube-system wait --for=condition=ContainersReady pod -l
  k8s-app=kube-dns

# print the node status:
kubectl get nodes

# leave the control plane VM:
exit
```

Kubeadm deploys the DNS server for the cluster as Pods in the kube-system name-space, but those Pods can't start until the network plugin is running. As soon as flan-nel is deployed, the DNS Pods start and the node is ready. My output in figure 18.6

Flannel is a network plugin with great cross-platform support. It runs a Pod on each node using DaemonSets for different architectures, supporting everything from Raspberry Pi to IBM mainframes.

```
vagrant@kiamol-control:/vagrant/setup$ kubectl apply -f flannel.yaml
podsecuritypolicy.policy/psp.flannel.unprivileged created
clusterrole.rbac.authorization.k8s.io/flannel created
clusterrolebinding.rbac.authorization.k8s.io/flannel created
serviceaccount/flannel created
configmap/kube-flannel-cfg created
daemonset.apps/kube-flannel-ds-amd64 created
daemonset.apps/kube-flannel-ds-arm64 created
daemonset.apps/kube-flannel-ds-arm created
daemonset.apps/kube-flannel-ds-ppc64le created
daemonset.apps/kube-flannel-ds-s390x created
vagrant@kiamol-control:/vagrant/setup$
vagrant@kiamol-control:/vagrant/setup$ kubectl -n kube-system wait --for=con
dition=ContainersReady pod -l k8s-app=kube-dns
pod/coredns-66bff467f8-kcbw5 condition met
pod/coredns-66bff467f8-l9f85 condition met
vagrant@kiamol-control:/vagrant/setup$
vagrant@kiamol-control:/vagrant/setup$ kubectl get nodes
NAME            STATUS    ROLES    AGE    VERSION
kiamol-control  Ready     master   16m    v1.18.5
```

DNS relies on the Pod network, so when DNS is running, the network must be operational.

And now the control plane node is ready.

Figure 18.6   Kubeadm doesn't deploy a Pod network; flannel is a good multiarchitecture option.

shows the multiarchitecture support in flannel. If you want to add an IBM mainframe to your Kubernetes cluster, you can do that.

And that's all you need for the control plane. I've glossed over the network setup—the IP address ranges in the kubeadm command use the configuration flannel expects—but you'll need to plan that out so it works with your own network. And I skipped over the other 25 options for kubeadm, but you'll want to research them if you're serious about managing your own cluster. Right now, you have a simple single-node cluster. You can't use it for application workloads yet because the default setup restricts the control plane nodes, so they run only system workloads. Next we'll add another node and run some apps.

18.3 Adding nodes and running Linux workloads

The output of the kubeadm initialization gives you the command you need to run on other servers to join them to the cluster. New Linux nodes require the same setup as the control plane node, with a container runtime and all the Kubernetes tools. In the next exercise, you'll create another VM and install the prerequisites using the same setup script you used for the control plane.

> **TRY IT NOW**   Create a second VM with Vagrant, and install the prerequisites for it to join the Kubernetes cluster.

```
# start the node VM:
vagrant up kiamol-node

# connect to the VM:
vagrant ssh kiamol-node

# run the setup script:
sudo /vagrant/setup/linux-setup.sh
```

Figure 18.7 is pretty much the same as figure 18.5 except for the machine name, so you can see that the setup script should really be part of the VM provisioning. That way, when you spin up a new machine with Vagrant (or Terraform or whatever tool works for your infrastructure), it will have all the prerequisites and will be ready to join the cluster.

Now you can double the size of your Kubernetes cluster by joining a new node. The output of the kubeadm `init` command contains everything you need—a CA certificate hash so the new node can trust the control plane and a `join` token so the control plane allows the new server to join. The `join` token is sensitive, and you need to distribute it securely to stop rogue nodes from joining your cluster. Any machine with network access to the control plane and the token could potentially join. Your new VM is in the same virtual network as the control plane VM, so all you need to do is run the `join` command.

Starts a second VM, which will join the cluster as a node

**Nodes need the same prerequisites as the
control plane, so we run the same setup script.**

```
PS>vagrant up kiamol-node
Bringing machine 'kiamol-node' up with 'hyperv' provider...
==> kiamol-node: Verifying Hyper-V is enabled...
==> kiamol-node: Verifying Hyper-V is accessible...
==> kiamol-node: Importing a Hyper-V instance
vagrant@kiamol-node:~$ sudo /vagrant/setup/linux-setup.sh
Hit:1 http://archive.ubuntu.com/ubuntu focal InRelease
Get:2 http://archive.ubuntu.com/ubuntu focal-updates InRelease [107 kB]
Setting up kubelet (1.18.5-00) ...
Created symlink /etc/systemd/system/multi-user.target.wants/kubelet.service
→ /lib/systemd/system/kubelet.service.
Setting up kubeadm (1.18.5-00) ...
Processing triggers for man-db (2.9.1-1) ...
net.bridge.bridge-nf-call-iptables = 1
vagrant@kiamol-node:~$ 
```

**Kubeadm, the kubelet, and Docker are all installed, so this VM is ready. The setup should be
automated in the VM provisioning stage if you're doing this for real.**

Figure 18.7   Installing required dependencies—nodes need the same initial setup as the control plane.

TRY IT NOW   Join the cluster using kubeadm and the `join` command from the
control plane.

```
# you'll need to use your own join command;
# the control plane IP address, token, and CA hash
# will be different—this just shows you how it looks:

sudo kubeadm join 172.21.125.229:6443
--token 3sqpc7.a19sx21toelnar5i
--discovery-token-ca-cert-hash
  sha256:ed01ef0e33f7ecd56f1d39b5db0fbaa56811ac055f43adb37688a2a2d9cc
  86b9

# if your token has expired, run this on the control plane node:
kubeadm token create --print-join-command
```

In this exercise, you'll see logs from the kubelet about TLS bootstrapping. The control plane generates TLS certificates for new nodes so the kubelet can authenticate with the API server. You can customize the kubeadm install to provide your own certificate authority, but that's another layer of detail (including certificate renewal and external CAs) that we won't cover here. Figure 18.8 shows my new node successfully joining the cluster with the simple default setup.

The new node runs its own subset of the components already running on the control plane. The kubelet runs as a background process outside of Kubernetes,

The `join` **token and CA hash are security controls around nodes joining the cluster. The token has a short life span, but you need to treat it as sensitive information.**

```
vagrant@kiamol-node:~$ sudo kubeadm join 172.21.120.227:6443 --token 5wbq7j.
bew48gsfy0maa2bo --discovery-token-ca-cert-hash sha256:2c520ea15a99bd68b74d0
4f40056996dff5b6ed1e76dfaeb0211c6db18ba0393
```
```
W0713 11:47:53.750388    18304 join.go:346] [preflight] WARNING: JoinControlP
ane.controlPlane settings will be ignored when control-plane flag is not set
.
[preflight] Running pre-flight checks
```
```
[kubelet-start] Starting the kubelet
[kubelet-start] Waiting for the kubelet to perform the TLS Bootstrap...

This node has joined the cluster:
* Certificate signing request was sent to apiserver and a response was recei
ved.
* The Kubelet was informed of the new secure connection details.

Run 'kubectl get nodes' on the control-plane to see this node join the clust
er.
```

Communication between nodes is secured. The control plane generates a client certificate for the kubelet to authenticate with the API server.

Figure 18.8 Joining a node to the cluster sets up secure communication to the control plane.

communicating with Docker, which also runs as a background process. It runs two more components in Pods: the network proxy and the network plugin. All the other components—DNS, the controller manager, and the API server—are specific to control plane nodes and won't run on standard nodes. Switch back to the control plane node, and you can see the Pods.

> **TRY IT NOW** Kubectl is set up only on the control plane, although you can share the config file to connect from another machine. Switch back to that control plane node to see all the cluster resources.

```
# connect to the control plane node:
vagrant ssh kiamol-control

# print the node status:
kubectl get nodes

# list all the Pods on the new node:
kubectl get pods --all-namespaces --field-selector
   spec.nodeName=kiamol-node
```

My output is shown in figure 18.9. You should see the same, unless the flannel Pod is still starting up, in which case, the new node won't be ready yet.

You're good to deploy an app now, but you need to be aware of the limitations in this cluster. There is no default storage class set up and no volume provisioners, so you

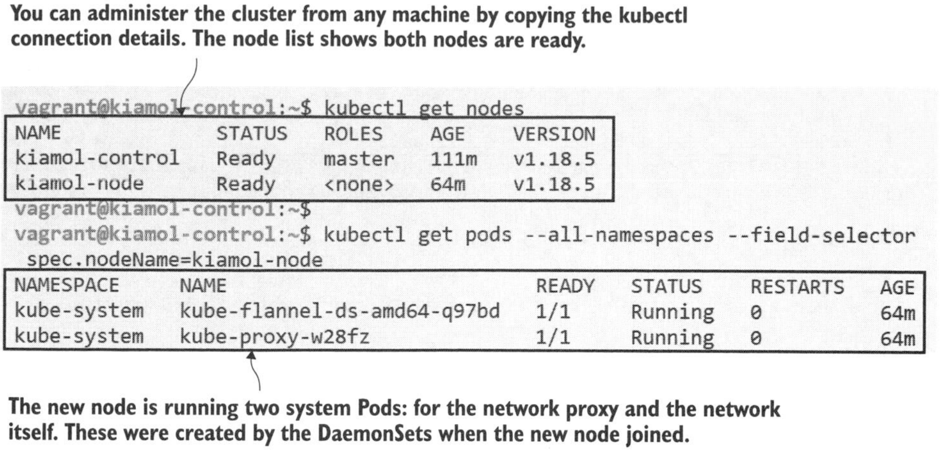

You can administer the cluster from any machine by copying the kubectl
connection details. The node list shows both nodes are ready.

```
vagrant@kiamol-control:~$ kubectl get nodes
NAME            STATUS   ROLES    AGE    VERSION
kiamol-control  Ready    master   111m   v1.18.5
kiamol-node     Ready    <none>   64m    v1.18.5
vagrant@kiamol-control:~$
vagrant@kiamol-control:~$ kubectl get pods --all-namespaces --field-selector
  spec.nodeName=kiamol-node
NAMESPACE     NAME                         READY   STATUS    RESTARTS   AGE
kube-system   kube-flannel-ds-amd64-q97bd  1/1     Running   0          64m
kube-system   kube-proxy-w28fz             1/1     Running   0          64m
```

The new node is running two system Pods: for the network proxy and the network
itself. These were created by the DaemonSets when the new node joined.

Figure 18.9   DaemonSets run a Pod on every node; the new Pod runs system components when
it joins.

won't be able to deploy dynamic PersistentVolumeClaims (which we covered in chapter 6), and you're stuck using `HostPath` volumes. There's also no load balancer integration so you can't use LoadBalancer services. In the datacenter, you could use network file system (NFS) shares for distributed storage, and a project called MetalLB for load balancer support. That's all too much for this chapter, so we'll stick to simple apps with no storage requirements and use NodePort Services to get traffic into the cluster.

NodePorts are a much simpler type of Service: they work in the same way as other Services to distribute traffic to Pods, but they listen for incoming traffic on a specific port on the node. Every node listens on the same port, so any server can receive a request and route it to the correct Pod, even if that Pod is running on a different node. You can use NodePorts in on-premises clusters if you have an existing load balancer, but NodePorts are restricted to certain port ranges, so your load balancer will need to do some port mapping. Listing 18.1 shows a NodePort Service spec for the Astronomy Picture of the Day web application.

Listing 18.1   web.yaml, a Service exposed as a NodePort

```
apiVersion: v1
kind: Service
metadata:
  name: apod-web
spec:
  type: NodePort        # Every node will listen on the port.
  ports:
    - port: 8016        # The internal ClusterIP port
      targetPort: web   # The container port to send to
      nodePort: 30000   # The port the node listens on—
```

```
selector:              # it must be >= 30000, a security restriction.
  app: apod-web
```

The APOD application contains three components, and the Service type is the only difference between this spec and the others we've deployed. When you run the app, you might expect Kubernetes to distribute Pods all around the cluster, but remember that control plane nodes are isolated from user workloads by default.

TRY IT NOW Deploy the app to your new cluster, and see where the Pods are scheduled to run.

```
# deploy the manifests in the usual way:
kubectl apply -f /vagrant/apod/

# print the Pod status:
kubectl get pods -o wide
```

You can see in figure 18.10 that every Pod is scheduled to run on the same node. That's a new VM with none of the container images for the book available, so it will download them from Docker Hub. The Pods will be in the ContainerCreating status while that happens. The largest image for this app is just over 200 MB, so it shouldn't take too long to start up.

If this is the first time you've used a different Kubernetes cluster from your normal lab environment, then it's now that you see how powerful Kubernetes is. This is a

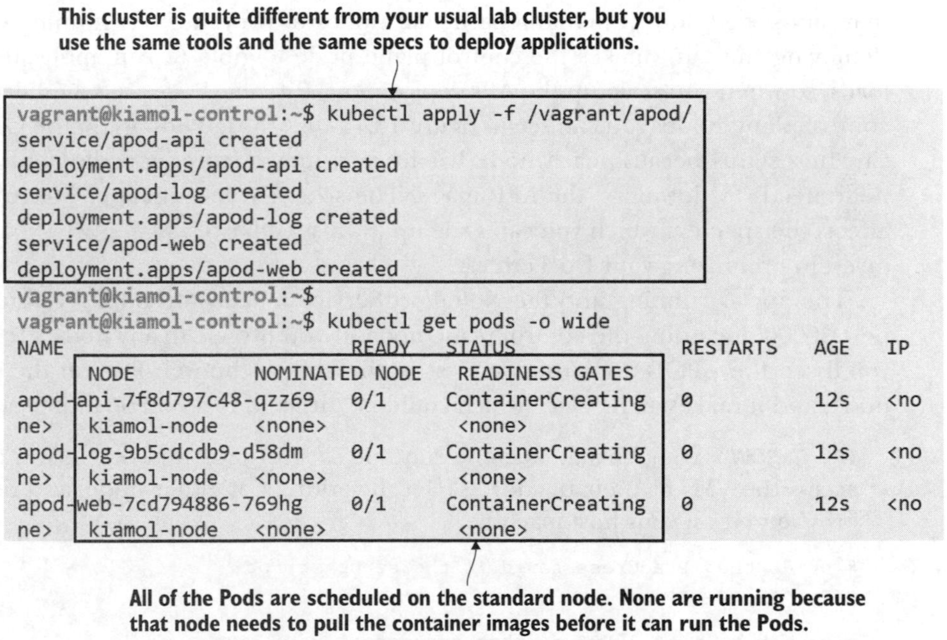

This cluster is quite different from your usual lab cluster, but you
use the same tools and the same specs to deploy applications.

```
vagrant@kiamol-control:~$ kubectl apply -f /vagrant/apod/
service/apod-api created
deployment.apps/apod-api created
service/apod-log created
deployment.apps/apod-log created
service/apod-web created
deployment.apps/apod-web created
vagrant@kiamol-control:~$
vagrant@kiamol-control:~$ kubectl get pods -o wide
NAME                        READY   STATUS             RESTARTS   AGE   IP
         NODE          NOMINATED NODE   READINESS GATES
apod-api-7f8d797c48-qzz69   0/1     ContainerCreating   0         12s   <no
ne>      kiamol-node   <none>           <none>
apod-log-9b5cdcdb9-d58dm    0/1     ContainerCreating   0         12s   <no
ne>      kiamol-node   <none>           <none>
apod-web-7cd794886-769hg    0/1     ContainerCreating   0         12s   <no
ne>      kiamol-node   <none>           <none>
```

All of the Pods are scheduled on the standard node. None are running because
that node needs to pull the container images before it can run the Pods.

Figure 18.10 The user experience is mostly the same for all Kubernetes clusters.

completely different setup, probably using a different version of Kubernetes, maybe a different container runtime, and a different host operating system. With one change to the spec, you can deploy and manage the APOD app in exactly the same way you previously did. You could take any of the exercises from this book and deploy them here, but you'd have to make changes to Services and volumes so they use valid types for the new cluster.

Kubernetes stops control plane nodes from running application workloads to make sure they aren't starved of compute resources. If your control plane node is maxing CPU while calculating Pi to one million decimal places, there's nothing left for the API server and DNS Pods, and your cluster becomes unusable. You should leave that safety guard in place for real clusters, but in a lab setup, you can relax it to get the most out of your servers.

TRY IT NOW   Kubernetes uses taints to classify nodes, and the `master` taint prevents application workloads running. Remove that taint, and scale up the app to see new Pods being scheduled on the control plane node.

```
# remove the master taint from all nodes:
kubectl taint nodes --all node-role.kubernetes.io/master-

# scale up, adding two more APOD API Pods:
kubectl scale deploy apod-api --replicas=3

# print the Pods to see where they're scheduled:
kubectl get pods -l app=apod-api -o wide
```

You'll learn all about taints and scheduling in chapter 19; for now, it's enough to know that taints are a way of marking particular nodes to prevent Pods running on them. Removing the taint makes the control plane node eligible to run application workloads, so when you scale up the API deployment, the new Pods are scheduled on the control plane node. You can see in figure 18.11 that those Pods are in the Container-Creating status because each node has its own image store, and the control plane node needs to download the API image. The size of your container images directly affects the speed at which you can scale up in this scenario, which is why you need to invest in optimizing your Dockerfiles.

The app is running and the NodePort Service means all nodes are listening on port 30000, including the control plane node. If you browse to any node's IP address, you'll see the APOD app. Your request is directed to the web Pod on the standard node, and it makes an API call, which could be directed to a Pod on either node.

TRY IT NOW   Your Virtual Machine runtime sets up your network so you can access the VMs by their IP address. Get the address of either node, and then browse to it on your host machine.

```
# print the IP address saved in the setup script:
cat /tmp/ip.txt

# browse to port 30000 on that address—if your VM
# provider uses a complicated network stack, you may
# not be able to reach the VM externally :(
```

Removing the master taint makes the control plane node eligible to run application Pods. The second node produces the error line because it doesn't have the taint.

```
vagrant@kiamol-control:~$ kubectl taint nodes --all node-role.kubernetes.io/
master-
node/kiamol-control untainted
error: taint "node-role.kubernetes.io/master" not found
vagrant@kiamol-control:~$
vagrant@kiamol-control:~$ kubectl scale deploy apod-api --replicas=3
deployment.apps/apod-api scaled
vagrant@kiamol-control:~$
vagrant@kiamol-control:~$ kubectl get pods -l app=apod-api -o wide
NAME                      READY    STATUS            RESTARTS  AGE  IP
                  NODE          NOMINATED NODE   READINESS GATES
apod-api-7f8d797c48-gvj24  0/1     ContainerCreating  0        5s   <no
ne>              kiamol-control  <none>           <none>
apod-api-7f8d797c48-qzz69  1/1     Running            0        17m  10.
244.1.2          kiamol-node     <none>           <none>
apod-api-7f8d797c48-rzxhp  0/1     ContainerCreating  0        5s   <no
ne>              kiamol-control  <none>           <none>
```

The two new Pods are scheduled on the control plane node. They won't start until that node has pulled the container image from Docker Hub.

Figure 18.11 You can run application Pods on the control plane nodes, but you shouldn't do so in production.

My output appears in figure 18.12. The picture I saw when I was working through the exercises was much more striking, but I didn't grab a screenshot, so we've got this comet instead.

Building your own Kubernetes cluster isn't all that complicated if you're happy to keep it simple, with NodePorts, HostPaths, and maybe NFS volumes. If you want to, you can extend this cluster and add more nodes; the Vagrant setup includes machine definitions for `kiamol-node2` and `kiamol-node3`, so you can repeat the first two exercises in this section with those VM names to build a four-node cluster. But that just gives you a boring all-Linux cluster. One of the great benefits of Kubernetes is that it can run all sorts of apps. Next, we'll see how to add a different architecture to the cluster—a Windows server—so we can run all-Windows or hybrid Linux-Windows apps.

18.4 *Adding Windows nodes and running hybrid workloads*

The Kubernetes website itself says *Windows applications constitute a large portion of the services and applications that run in many organizations,* so bear that in mind if you're thinking of skipping this section. I won't go into a lot of detail about Windows containers and the differences from Linux (for that, you can read my book *Docker on Windows;* Packt Publishing, 2019)—just the basics so you can see how Windows apps fit in Kubernetes.

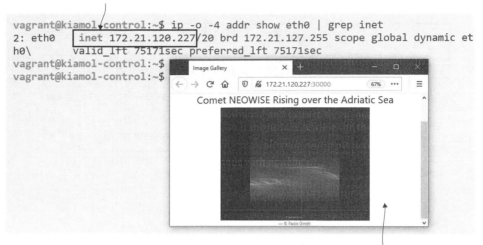

Both nodes are listening on port 30000 for the APOD web app Service. I can browse using the IP address of either node.

The control plane node forwards traffic to the Pod on the second node, and that Pod accesses the APOD API, which is load-balanced across Pods on both nodes.

Figure 18.12   NodePort and ClusterIP Services span the Pod network so traffic can be routed to any node.

Container images are built for a specific architecture: a combination of operating system and CPU. Containers use the kernel of the machine they're running on, so that has to match the architecture of the image. You can build a Docker image on a Raspberry Pi, but you can't run it on your laptop because the Pi uses an Arm CPU and your laptop uses Intel. It's the same with the operating system—you can build an image on a Windows machine to run a Windows app, but you can't run that in a container on a Linux server. Kubernetes supports different types of workload by having nodes with different architectures in the same cluster.

You have some restrictions as to how diverse your cluster can be, but the diagram in figure 18.13 is something you can genuinely build. The control plane is Linux only, but the kubelet and proxy are cross platform. AWS has Arm-powered servers, which are almost half the price of Intel equivalents, and you can use them as nodes in EKS. If you have a large application suite with some apps that work in Linux on Arm, some that need Linux on Intel, and some that are Windows, you can run and manage them all in one cluster.

Let's get to it and add a Windows node to your cluster. The approach is the same as adding a Linux node—spin up a new VM, add a container runtime and the Kubernetes tools, and join it to the cluster. Windows Server 2019 is the minimum version supported in Kubernetes, and Docker is the only container runtime available at the time of writing—containerd support for Windows is in progress.

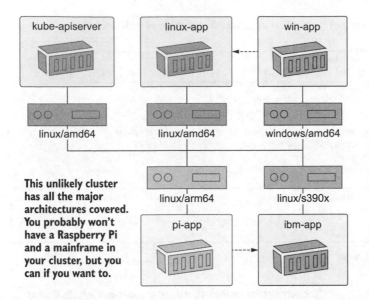

This unlikely cluster has all the major architectures covered. You probably won't have a Raspberry Pi and a mainframe in your cluster, but you can if you want to.

Figure 18.13 Who hasn't got a spare Raspberry Pi and IBM Z mainframe gathering dust?

TRY IT NOW Create a Windows VM, and install the Kubernetes prerequisites. Folder-sharing in Vagrant doesn't always work for Windows, so you'll download the setup script from the book's source on GitHub.

```
# spin up a Windows Server 2019 machine:
vagrant up kiamol-node-win

# connect—you need the password, which is vagrant
vagrant ssh kiamol-node-win

# switch to PowerShell:
powershell

# download the setup script:
curl.exe -s -O windows-setup.ps1
   https://raw.githubusercontent.com/sixeyed/kiamol/master/ch18/setup/
   windows-setup.ps1

# run the script—this reboots the VM when it finishes:
./windows-setup.ps1
```

The Windows setup needs to enable an operating system feature and install Docker; the script reboots the VM when that's done. You can see in figure 18.14 that my session is back to the normal command line.

This is only the first part of the setup, because the control plane needs to be configured for Windows support. The standard deployment of flannel and the kube proxy doesn't create a DaemonSet for Windows nodes, so we need to set that up as an additional step. The new DaemonSets use Windows container images in the spec, and the Pods are configured to work with the Windows server to set up networking.

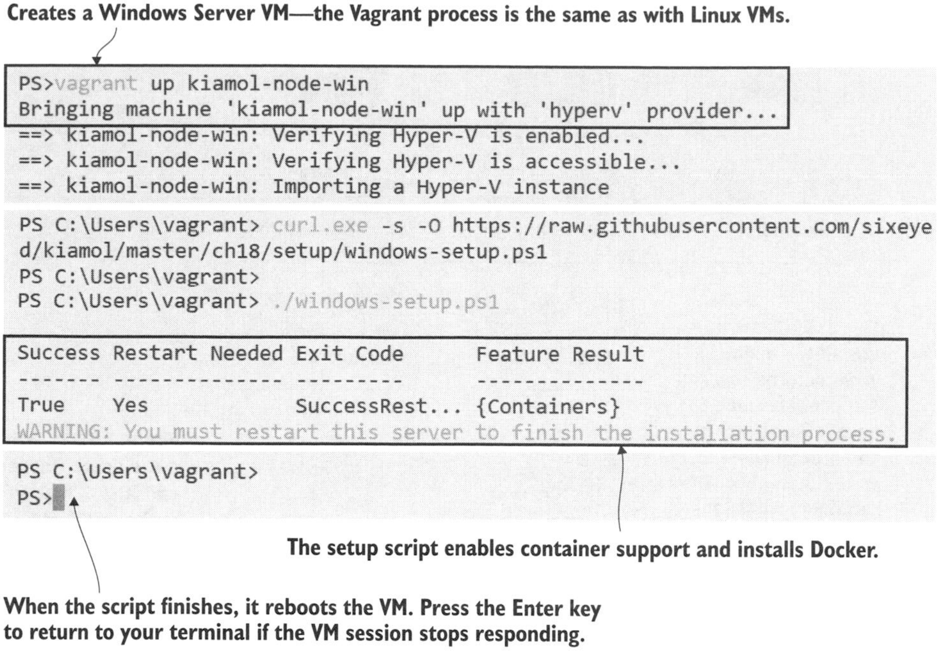

Creates a Windows Server VM—the Vagrant process is the same as with Linux VMs.

```
PS>vagrant up kiamol-node-win
Bringing machine 'kiamol-node-win' up with 'hyperv' provider...
==> kiamol-node-win: Verifying Hyper-V is enabled...
==> kiamol-node-win: Verifying Hyper-V is accessible...
==> kiamol-node-win: Importing a Hyper-V instance

PS C:\Users\vagrant> curl.exe -s -O https://raw.githubusercontent.com/sixeye
d/kiamol/master/ch18/setup/windows-setup.ps1
PS C:\Users\vagrant>
PS C:\Users\vagrant> ./windows-setup.ps1

Success Restart Needed Exit Code       Feature Result
------- -------------- ---------       --------------
True    Yes            SuccessRest...  {Containers}
WARNING: You must restart this server to finish the installation process.

PS C:\Users\vagrant>
PS>
```

The setup script enables container support and installs Docker.

**When the script finishes, it reboots the VM. Press the Enter key
to return to your terminal if the VM session stops responding.**

Figure 18.14   The first stage in adding a Windows node is installing the container runtime.

TRY IT NOW   Deploy the new system components for the Windows node.

```
# connect to the control plane:
vagrant ssh kiamol-control

# create the Windows proxy:
kubectl apply -f /vagrant/setup/kube-proxy.yml

# create the Windows network:
kubectl apply -f /vagrant/setup/flannel-overlay.yml

# confirm that the new DaemonSets are there:
kubectl get ds -n kube-system
```

Again, this is something you would add to the initial cluster setup if you're serious about running your own hybrid cluster. I've kept it as a separate step so you can see what needs to change to add Windows support—which you can do with an existing cluster, provided it's running Kubernetes 1.14 or greater. My output in figure 18.15 shows the new Windows-specific DaemonSets, with a desired count of zero because the Windows node hasn't joined yet.

Join the Windows node. It will have Pods scheduled for the proxy and the network components, so it will download the images and start containers. One difference is

Creates configuration and DaemonSets to run the system components on Windows nodes

```
vagrant@kiamol-control:~$ kubectl apply -f /vagrant/setup/kube-proxy.yml
configmap/kube-proxy-windows created
daemonset.apps/kube-proxy-windows created
vagrant@kiamol-control:~$
vagrant@kiamol-control:~$ kubectl apply -f /vagrant/setup/flannel-overlay.ym
l
configmap/kube-flannel-windows-cfg created
daemonset.apps/kube-flannel-ds-windows-amd64 created
vagrant@kiamol-control:~$
vagrant@kiamol-control:~$ kubectl get ds -n kube-system
NAME                             DESIRED   CURRENT   READY   UP-TO-DATE   AVA
ILABLE    NODE SELECTOR          AGE
kube-flannel-ds-amd64            2         2         2       2            2
         <none>                 4h3m
kube-flannel-ds-windows-amd64    0         0         0       0            0
         <none>                 34s
kube-proxy                       2         2         2       2            2
         kubernetes.io/os=linux 4h19m
kube-proxy-windows               0         0         0       0            0
         kubernetes.io/os=windows 41s
```

There are two desired nodes for the Linux proxy, but none for the Windows proxy or the Windows flannel network (I've snipped the other architectures from the output). As soon as the Windows node joins, the new DaemonSets will schedule Pods.

Figure 18.15 Updating the control plane to schedule system components on Windows nodes

that Windows containers are more restricted than Linux containers, so the flannel setup is slightly different. The Kubernetes Special Interest Group (SIG) for Windows publishes a helper script to set up flannel and the kubelet. I have a snapshot of that script in the source folder for this chapter, which matches the Kubernetes version we're running; after this second setup script, the node is ready to join.

TRY IT NOW Add the remaining dependencies to the Windows node, and join it to the cluster.

```
# connect to the Windows node:
vagrant ssh kiamol-node-win

# run PowerShell:
powershell

# download the second setup script:
curl.exe -s -o PrepareNode.ps1 https://raw.githubusercontent.com/sixeyed/
   kiamol/master/ch18/setup/PrepareNode.ps1

# run the script:
.\PrepareNode.ps1
```

```
# run the join command—remember to use your command; this
# is just a reminder of how the command looks:
kubeadm join 172.21.120.227:6443
--token 5wbq7j.bew48gsfy0maa2bo
--discovery-token-ca-cert-hash
   sha256:2c520ea15a99bd68b74d04f40056996dff5b6ed1e76dfaeb0211c6db18ba0393
```

The happy message "this node has joined the cluster" that you see in figure 18.16 is a bit ahead of itself. The new node needs to download the proxy and network images. The flannel image is 5 GB, so it will take a few minutes before the Windows node is ready.

This script downloads kubeadm and sets up flannel and the kubelet on the Windows node.

There's lots of output, so I've trimmed it here. When the script finishes, you can run your kubeadm `join` command.

```
PS C:\Users\vagrant> curl.exe -s -o PrepareNode.ps1 https://raw.githubuserco
ntent.com/sixeyed/ kiamol/master/ch18/setup/PrepareNode.ps1
PS C:\Users\vagrant>
PS C:\Users\vagrant> .\PrepareNode.ps1
Using Kubernetes version: v1.18.5

Action                 : Allow
Direction              : Inbound
DisplayGroup           :
DisplayName            : kubelet

PS C:\Users\vagrant> kubeadm join 172.21.120.227:6443 --token 5wbq7j.bew48gs
fy0maa2bo      --discovery-token-ca-cert-hash sha256:2c520ea15a99bd68b74d04f4
0056996dff5b6ed1e76dfaeb0211c6db18ba0393
W0713 15:38:40.229522    1760 join.go:346] [preflight] WARNING: JoinControlP
ane.controlPlane settings will be ignored when control-plane flag is not set
.
[preflight] Running pre-flight checks

This node has joined the cluster:
* Certificate signing request was sent to apiserver and a response was recei
ved.
* The Kubelet was informed of the new secure connection details.

Run 'kubectl get nodes' on the control-plane to see this node join the clust
er.
```

The joining process is the same as in a Linux node, with the preflight checks and the TLS bootstrap. The Windows server is a Kubernetes node now, but it needs to download the system images before it's ready to run workloads.

Figure 18.16   Joining the Windows node uses the same kubeadm command as the Linux node.

While that's downloading, we'll look at modeling applications to run on different architectures. Kubernetes doesn't automatically work out which nodes are suitable for which Pods—this isn't easy to do from the image name alone. Instead, you add a selector in your Pod spec to specify the architecture the Pod needs. Listing 18.2 shows a selector that sets the Pod to run on a Windows node.

> **Listing 18.2   api.yaml, using a node selector to request a specific operating system**

```
spec:                                        # Pod spec in the Deployment
  containers:
    - name: api
      image: kiamol/ch03-numbers-api:windows  # A Windows-specific image
  nodeSelector:
    kubernetes.io/os: windows                # Selects nodes with Windows OS
```

That's it. Remember that Pods run on a single node, so if you have multiple containers in your Pod spec, they all need to use the same architecture. It's a good practice to include a node selector for every Pod if you're running a multiarchitecture cluster to ensure Pods always end up where they should. You can include an operating system, CPU architecture, or both.

The listing in 18.2 is for a Windows version of the random-number API, which also has a Linux version of the website to go with it. The web spec includes a node selector for the Linux OS. You can deploy the app, and the Pods will run on different nodes, but the website still accesses the API Pod in the usual way through a ClusterIP Service, even though it's running on Windows.

> **TRY IT NOW**   This is a hybrid application, with one Windows and one Linux component. Both use the same YAML format, and in the specs, only the node selectors show they need to run on different architectures.

```
# connect to the control plane:
vagrant ssh kiamol-control

# wait for all the nodes to be ready:
kubectl -n kube-system wait --for=condition=Ready node --all

# deploy the hybrid app:
kubectl apply -f /vagrant/numbers

# wait for the Windows Pod to be ready:
kubectl wait --for=condition=ContainersReady pod -l
  app=numbers,component=api

# confirm where the Pods are running:
kubectl get pods -o wide -l app=numbers

# browse to port 30001 on any node to use the app
```

It's a shame the demo app in figure 18.17 is so basic, because this capability has taken many years and a ton of effort from the Kubernetes community and the engineering teams at Microsoft and Docker.

By day, I work as a consultant helping companies adopt container technologies, and the pattern here is exactly what many organizations want to do with their Windows

Ensures the Windows node has loaded system components and is ready to run workloads

The web Deployment uses a Linux node selector, and the API Deployment uses a Windows node selector.

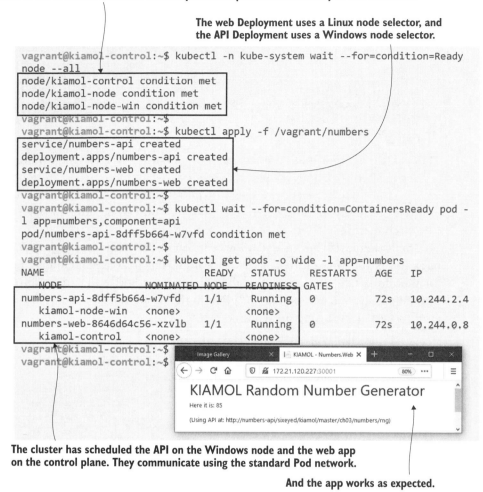

```
vagrant@kiamol-control:~$ kubectl -n kube-system wait --for=condition=Ready
node --all
node/kiamol-control condition met
node/kiamol-node condition met
node/kiamol-node-win condition met
vagrant@kiamol-control:~$
vagrant@kiamol-control:~$ kubectl apply -f /vagrant/numbers
service/numbers-api created
deployment.apps/numbers-api created
service/numbers-web created
deployment.apps/numbers-web created
vagrant@kiamol-control:~$
vagrant@kiamol-control:~$ kubectl wait --for=condition=ContainersReady pod -
l app=numbers,component=api
pod/numbers-api-8dff5b664-w7vfd condition met
vagrant@kiamol-control:~$
vagrant@kiamol-control:~$ kubectl get pods -o wide -l app=numbers
NAME                          READY   STATUS     RESTARTS   AGE    IP
   NODE                NOMINATED NODE   READINESS GATES
numbers-api-8dff5b664-w7vfd   1/1     Running    0          72s    10.244.2.4
   kiamol-node-win     <none>           <none>
numbers-web-8646d64c56-xzvlb  1/1     Running    0          72s    10.244.0.8
   kiamol-control      <none>           <none>
vagrant@kiamol-control:~$
vagrant@kiamol-control:~$
```

KIAMOL - Numbers.Web

172.21.120.227:30001   80%

KIAMOL Random Number Generator

Here it is: 85

(Using API at: http://numbers-api/sixeyed/kiamol/master/ch03/numbers/rng)

The cluster has scheduled the API on the Windows node and the web app on the control plane. They communicate using the standard Pod network.

And the app works as expected.

Figure 18.17   A world-class container orchestrator running a hybrid app to generate one random number

apps—move them to Kubernetes without any changes, and then gradually break up the monolithic architecture with new components running in lightweight Linux containers. It's a pragmatic and low-risk approach to modernizing applications that takes full advantage of all the features of Kubernetes, and it gives you an easy migration to the cloud.

Way back in chapter 1, I said that Kubernetes runs your applications, but it doesn't really care what those applications are. We'll prove that with one last deployment to the cluster: the Windows Pet Shop app. Microsoft built this demo app in 2008 to showcase the latest features of .NET. It uses technologies and approaches that have long since been replaced, but the source code is still out there, and I've packaged it up to run in Windows containers and published the images on Docker Hub. This exercise shows you that you really can run decade-old applications in Kubernetes without any changes to the code.

> **TRY IT NOW** Deploy a legacy Windows app. This one downloads more large container images, so it will take a while to start.

```
# on the control plane, deploy the Petshop app:
kubectl apply -f /vagrant/petshop/

# wait for all the Pods to start—it might need more than five minutes:
kubectl wait --for=condition=ContainersReady pod -l app=petshop --
    timeout=5m
kubectl get pods -o wide -l app=petshop

# browse to port 30002 on any node to see the app
```

There you have it. Figure 18.18 could be faked—but it's not—and you can run this all yourself to prove it. (I will admit it took me two attempts—my Windows VM lost network connectivity the first time around, which is most likely a Hyper-V issue.) The Pet Shop is an app that last had a code change 12 years ago, now running in the latest version of Kubernetes.

That's as far as we'll go with this cluster. If you want to add more Windows nodes, you can repeat the setup and join exercises from this section for two more machines defined in Vagrant: `kiamol-node-win2` and `kiamol-node-win3`. You'll just about squeeze the control plane node, three Linux nodes, and three Windows nodes onto your machine if you have a least 16 GB of memory. We'll finish up with a look at the considerations for multinode Kubernetes clusters and the future of multiarchitecture.

18.5 *Understanding Kubernetes at scale*

Whether you diligently followed the exercises in this chapter or just skimmed through, you now have a good idea of how complex it is to set up and manage a Kubernetes cluster, and you'll understand why I recommend Docker Desktop or K3s for your lab environment. Deploying a multinode cluster is a great learning exercise to see how all the pieces fit together, but it's not something I'd recommend for production.

Kubernetes is all about high availability and scale, and the more nodes you have, the more complex it becomes to manage. You need multiple control plane nodes for high availability; if you lose the control plane, your apps keep running on the nodes, but you can't manage them with kubectl, and they're no longer self-healing. The control plane stores all its data in etcd. For better redundancy you can run etcd outside of the cluster. For a performance improvement, you can run an additional etcd database just to store the events Kubernetes records for objects. It's all starting to look complicated, and we're still dealing with only a single cluster, not high availability across multiple clusters.

The Pet Shop app is all Windows. Windows apps can use all the
usual Kubernetes features, like Services, Secrets, and ConfigMaps.

The node needs to download and extract three images, which is a
few extra gigabytes, so it might take a while for the app to start.

```
vagrant@kiamol-control:~$ kubectl apply -f /vagrant/petshop/
secret/petshop-connection-string-secret created
service/petshop-db created
deployment.apps/petshop-db created
service/petshop-web created
deployment.apps/petshop-web created
service/petshop-webservice created
deployment.apps/petshop-webservice created
vagrant@kiamol-control:~$
vagrant@kiamol-control:~$ kubectl wait --for=condition=ContainersReady pod -
l app=petshop --timeout=5m
pod/petshop-db-b4b77968b-xhmnt condition met
pod/petshop-web-57fc985779-wfxll condition met
pod/petshop-webservice-5fd74d9fdf-h8rtm condition met
vagrant@kiamol-control:~$
vagrant@kiamol-control:~$ kubectl get pods -o wide -l app=petshop
NAME
                NODE
petshop-db-b4b77968b-xhmnt
244.2.8   kiamol-node-win
petshop-web-57fc985779-wfxll
244.2.9   kiamol-node-win
petshop-webservice-5fd74d9fd
244.2.7   kiamol-node-win
vagrant@kiamol-control:~$
vagrant@kiamol-control:~$
```

All Pods are running on the Windows node.   Welcome to the world of animals, 2008 style.

Figure 18.18 I bet there hasn't been a screenshot of the Pet Shop in a book for a long time.

You can build Kubernetes clusters that run at huge scale: the latest release supports up to 5,000 nodes and 150,000 Pods in a single cluster. In practice, you're likely to hit performance issues with etcd or your network plugin when you get to around 500 nodes, and then you'll need to look at scaling parts of the control plane independently. The good news is that you can run a cluster with hundreds of worker nodes managed by a control plane with just three nodes, provided those nodes are fairly powerful. The bad news is you need to manage all that, and you'll need to decide if you're better off with one large cluster or multiple smaller clusters.

The other side of scale is being able to run as much of your application catalog as possible on a single platform. You saw in this chapter that you can run a multiarchitecture cluster by adding Windows nodes—Arm and IBM nodes work in the same way—which means you can run pretty much anything in Kubernetes. Older applications bring their own challenges, but one of the big advantages of Kubernetes is that you don't need to rewrite those apps. Breaking down monolithic apps into a more cloud-native architecture offers benefits, but that can be part of a longer-term program, which starts with moving apps to Kubernetes as is.

We're out of room to continue the discussion. You should leave your cluster running for the lab, but when you're done, come back to this final exercise to clear it down.

TRY IT NOW You have a few options for closing down your cluster—choose one after you've had a go at the lab.

```
# suspend the VMs—this preserves state so the VMs
# still consume disk or memory:
vagrant suspend

# OR stop the VMs—you can start them again, but they might
# get new IP addresses, and then your cluster won't be accessible:
vagrant halt

# Or, if you're really done with the cluster, delete everything:
vagrant destroy
```

18.6 Lab

Here's an easy lab for this chapter, but it will need some research. Time passes after you deploy your cluster, and at some point, the nodes will need maintenance work. Kubernetes lets you safely take a node out of the cluster—moving its Pods to another node—and then bring it back online when you're done. Let's do that for the Linux node in the cluster. Just one hint: you can do it all with kubectl.

This is a useful lab to work through because temporarily removing a node from service is something you'll want to do whichever platform you're using. My solution is on GitHub for you in the usual place: https://github.com/sixeyed/kiamol/blob/master/ch18/lab/README.md.

Controlling
workload placement
and automatic scaling

Kubernetes decides where to run your workloads, spreading them around the cluster to get the best use of your servers and the highest availability for your apps. Deciding which node is going to run a new Pod is the job of the scheduler, one of the control plane components. The scheduler uses all the information it can get to choose a node. It looks at the compute capacity of the server and the resources used by existing Pods. It also uses policies that you can hook into in your application specs to have more control over where Pods will run. In this chapter, you'll learn how to direct Pods to specific nodes and how to schedule the placement of Pods in relation to other Pods.

We'll also cover two other sides of workload placement in this chapter: automatic scaling and Pod eviction. Autoscaling lets you specify the minimum and maximum number of replicas for your app, along with some metric for Kubernetes to measure how hard your app is working. If the Pods are overworked, the cluster scales up automatically, adding more replicas, and scales down again when the load reduces. Eviction is the extreme scenario where nodes are maxing out resources, and Kubernetes removes Pods to keep the server stable. We'll cover some intricate details, but it's important to understand the principles to get the right balance of a healthy cluster and high-performing apps.

19.1 How Kubernetes schedules workloads

When you create a new Pod, it goes into the pending state until it's allocated to a node. The scheduler sees the new Pod and tries to find the best node to run it on. The scheduling process consists of two parts: first is *filtering*, which excludes any

472

unsuitable nodes, and then *scoring*, to rank the remaining nodes and choose the best option. Figure 19.1 shows a simplified example.

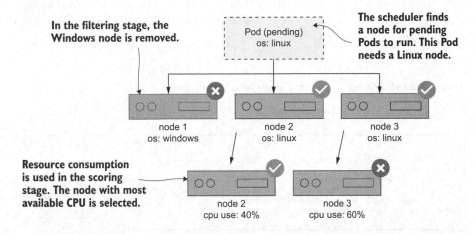

Figure 19.1   The scheduler selects nodes on their suitability and their current workload.

You've already seen the filtering stage in action in chapter 17, when you learned that the control plane node is isolated from application workloads. That's done with a taint, which is a way of flagging a node to say it isn't suitable for general work. The master taint is applied to control plane nodes by default, but taints are really a specialized type of label, and you can add your own taints to nodes. Taints have a key-value pair just like a label, and they also have an effect, which tells the scheduler how to treat this node. You'll use taints to identify nodes that are different from the rest. In the next exercise, we'll add a taint to record the type of disk a node has.

> **TRY IT NOW**   Run a simple sleep app, and then add a taint to your node to see how it affects the workload.

```
# switch to the chapter's source:
cd ch19

# print the taints already on the nodes:
kubectl get nodes -o=jsonpath='{range
  .items[*]}{.metadata.name}{.spec.taints[*].key}{end}'

# deploy the sleep app:
kubectl apply -f sleep/sleep.yaml

# add a taint to all nodes:
kubectl taint nodes --all kiamol-disk=hdd:NoSchedule

# confirm that the sleep Pod is still running:
kubectl get pods -l app=sleep
```

The key-value part of a taint is arbitrary, and you can use it to record whatever aspect of the node you care about—maybe some nodes have less memory or a slower network card. The effect of this taint is `NoSchedule`, which means workloads won't be scheduled on this node unless they explicitly *tolerate* the taint. As shown in figure 19.2, applying a `NoSchedule` taint doesn't impact existing workloads—the sleep Pod is still running after the node has been tainted.

Lists nodes and their taints—I have a single node with no taints.

```
PS>cd ch19
PS>
PS>kubectl get nodes -o=jsonpath='{range .items[*]}{.metadata.name}{.spec.ta
ints[*].key}{end}'
docker-desktop
PS>
PS>kubectl apply -f sleep/sleep.yaml
deployment.apps/sleep created
PS>
PS>kubectl taint nodes --all kiamol-disk=hdd:NoSchedule
node/docker-desktop tainted
PS>
PS>kubectl get pods -l app=sleep
NAME                      READY   STATUS    RESTARTS   AGE
sleep-85fdd4cf75-xqg8j    1/1     Running   0          16s
```

Tainting a node is like adding a label, but with an effect that impacts scheduling.

Adding a NoSchedule taint doesn't affect existing workloads—the sleep Pod is still running.

Figure 19.2   Pods need a toleration to run on a tainted node, unless they were running before the taint.

Now with the taint in place, the node will be filtered out by the scheduler for all new Pods, unless the Pod spec has a toleration for the taint. Tolerations say the workload acknowledges the taint and is happy to work with it. In this example, we've flagged nodes with spinning disks, which are probably lower performers than nodes with solid-state disks. Listing 19.1 includes a toleration to say this Pod is happy to run on these slower nodes.

Listing 19.1   sleep2-with-tolerations.yaml, tolerating a tainted node

```
spec:                           # The Pod spec in a Deployment
  containers:
    - name: sleep
      image: kiamol/ch03-sleep
  tolerations:                  # Lists taints this Pod is happy with
    - kcy: "kiamol disk"        # The key, value, and effect all need
      operator: "Equal"         # to match the taint on the node.
```

```
value: "hdd"
effect: "NoSchedule"
```

We tainted every node in this exercise so the scheduler will filter them all out for a new Pod request, unless the spec contains a toleration. Pods that can't be scheduled stay in the pending state until something changes—a new node joins without the taint, or the taint is removed from an existing node, or the Pod spec changes. As soon as a change happens and the scheduler can find a suitable placement, the Pod will be scheduled to run.

TRY IT NOW   Try deploying a copy of the sleep app without a toleration. It will stay as pending. Update it to add the toleration, and it will run.

```
# create a Pod without a toleration:
kubectl apply -f sleep/sleep2.yaml

# confirm the Pod is pending:
kubectl get po -l app=sleep2

# add the toleration from listing 19.1:
kubectl apply -f sleep/update/sleep2-with-tolerations.yaml
kubectl get po -l app=sleep2
```

This exercise used a Deployment, so the toleration actually was added to a new Pod, and the new Pod was scheduled—you can see that in figure 19.3. But if you create a

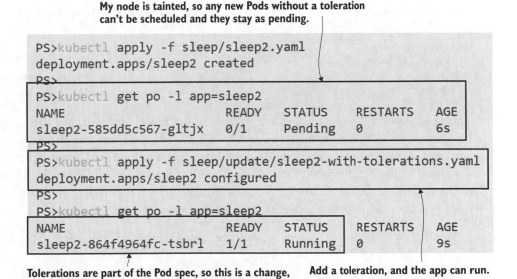

My node is tainted, so any new Pods without a toleration can't be scheduled and they stay as pending.

```
PS>kubectl apply -f sleep/sleep2.yaml
deployment.apps/sleep2 created
PS>
PS>kubectl get po -l app=sleep2
NAME                      READY   STATUS    RESTARTS   AGE
sleep2-585dd5c567-gltjx   0/1     Pending   0          6s
PS>
PS>kubectl apply -f sleep/update/sleep2-with-tolerations.yaml
deployment.apps/sleep2 configured
PS>
PS>kubectl get po -l app=sleep2
NAME                      READY   STATUS    RESTARTS   AGE
sleep2-864f4964fc-tsbrl   1/1     Running   0          9s
```

Tolerations are part of the Pod spec, so this is a change, and the Deployment creates a new ReplicaSet. The Pod can start because it tolerates the tainted node.

Add a toleration, and the app can run.

Figure 19.3   If the Pod's toleration matches the node's taint, then it can run on that node.

plain Pod without the toleration, it will go into the pending state, and when you add the toleration, that same Pod will be scheduled; the scheduler keeps trying to find a node for any unscheduled Pods.

The `NoSchedule` effect is a hard taint—it's in the scheduler's filtering stage, so Pods won't run on tainted nodes unless they have a toleration. A softer alternative is `PreferNoSchedule`, which moves the restriction to the scoring stage. Tainted nodes aren't filtered out, but they score lower than a node that doesn't have the taint. A `PreferNoSchedule` taint means Pods shouldn't run on that node unless they have a toleration for it, except when there are no other suitable nodes.

It's important to understand that taints and tolerations are for expressing something negative about the node, which means it suits only certain Pods; it's not a positive association between a node and a Pod. A Pod with a toleration might run on a tainted node, or it might not, so tolerations are not a good mechanism for ensuring Pods run on *only* certain nodes. You might need that for something like PCI compliance, where financial apps should run only on nodes that have been hardened. For that, you need to use a `NodeSelector`, which filters out nodes based on their labels— we used that in chapter 17 to make sure Pods ran on the correct CPU architecture. Listing 19.2 shows that different types of scheduler hints work together.

> **Listing 19.2**   **sleep2-with-nodeSelector.yaml, a toleration and a node selector**

```
spec:
  containers:
    - name: sleep
      image: kiamol/ch03-sleep
  tolerations:                          # The Pod tolerates nodes
    - key: "kiamol-disk"                # with the hdd taint.
      operator: "Equal"
      value: "hdd"
      effect: "NoSchedule"
  nodeSelector:                         # The Pod will run only on nodes
    kubernetes.io/arch: zxSpectrum      # that match this CPU type.
```

This spec says the Pod will tolerate a node with the hard disk taint, but the architecture has to be a ZX Spectrum. You won't have a ZX Spectrum in your cluster, so when you deploy this, the new Pod won't be scheduled. I've chosen that CPU not just out of nostalgia, but to highlight that these labels are just key-value pairs with no validation in them. The os and `arch` labels are set by Kubernetes on the nodes, but in your Pod spec, you can use incorrect values by mistake and your Pods stay pending.

> **TRY IT NOW**   Deploy the sleep app update from listing 19.2, and see if there's a matching node on your cluster.

```
# show the node's labels:
kubectl get nodes --show-labels

# update the Deployment with an incorrect node selector:
kubectl apply -f sleep/update/sleep2-with-nodeSelector.yaml
```

```
# print the Pod status:
kubectl get pods -l app=sleep2
```

You can see in my output in figure 19.4 why we're using a Deployment for this app. The new Pod goes into the pending state, and it will stay there until you add a ZX Spectrum to your cluster (which would mean building an eight-bit version of the kubelet and a container runtime). The app is still up because the Deployment won't scale down the old ReplicaSet until the replacement is at the desired capacity.

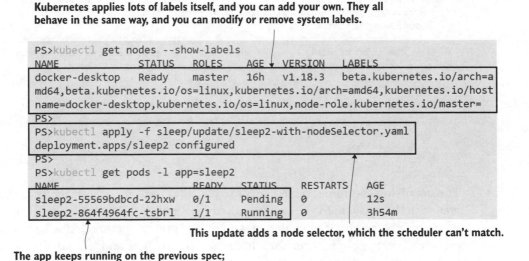

Kubernetes applies lots of labels itself, and you can add your own. They all behave in the same way, and you can modify or remove system labels.

This update adds a node selector, which the scheduler can't match.

The app keeps running on the previous spec; the new spec Pod will stay pending.

Figure 19.4   Pods that can't be scheduled don't interrupt the app if it's running in a Deployment.

Node selectors ensure that apps run only on nodes with specific label values, but you usually want some more flexibility than a straight equality match. A finer level of control comes with *affinity* and *antiaffinity*.

19.2   *Directing Pod placement with affinity and antiaffinity*

Kubernetes applies a standard set of labels to nodes, but standards change over time. The system-provided labels are prefixed with a namespace, and the namespace is versioned in the same way that the API for object specs is versioned. New clusters use `kubernetes.io` as the label prefix, but older versions use `beta.kubernetes.io`. The beta tag indicates that a feature isn't stable and the specification might change, but features can stay in beta through multiple Kubernetes versions. If you want Pods restricted to a certain architecture, you need to allow for the beta namespace to make your spec portable across different versions of Kubernetes.

Affinity provides a rich way of expressing preferences or requirements to the scheduler. You can claim an affinity to certain nodes to ensure Pods land on those nodes. Affinity uses a node selector but with a match expression rather than a simple equality check. Match expressions support multiple clauses, so you can build much more complex requirements. Listing 19.3 uses affinity to say the Pod should run on a 64-bit Intel node, in a way which works for new and old clusters.

> **Listing 19.3   sleep2-with-nodeAffinity-required.yaml, a Pod with node affinity**

```
affinity:                              # Affinity expresses a requirement
  nodeAffinity:                        # or a preference for nodes.
    requiredDuringSchedulingIgnoredDuringExecution:
      nodeSelectorTerms:
        - matchExpressions:            # Match expressions work on
          - key: kubernetes.io/arch    # labels, and you can supply
            operator: In               # a list of values that
            values:                    # should match or not match.
              - amd64
        - matchExpressions:            # Multiple match expressions
          - key: beta.kubernetes.io/arch # work as a logical OR.
            operator: In
            values:
              - amd64
```

The terrifying-sounding `requiredDuringSchedulingIgnoredDuringExecution` just means that this is a hard rule for the scheduler but it won't affect any existing Pods—they won't be removed once they're scheduled, even if the node labels change. The two match expressions cover the either/or case for new and old label namespaces, replacing the simpler node selector in listing 19.2. The full spec for listing 19.3 contains the hard-disk toleration, so when you deploy this, the sleep app will stop waiting for a ZX Spectrum to join the cluster and will run on your Intel node.

> **TRY IT NOW**   Update the sleep app. You should have one of the two architecture labels on your node, so the new Pod will run and replace the existing one.

```
# deploy the spec from listing 19.3:
kubectl apply -f sleep/update/sleep2-with-nodeAffinity-required.yaml

# confirm that the new Pod runs:
kubectl get po -l app=sleep2
```

Figure 19.5 should hold no surprises for you: it just shows the new affinity rules being put in place. Now the scheduler can find a node that suits the requirements so the Pod runs.

I have one more example of node affinity because the syntax is a bit fiddly, but it's good to know what you can do with it. Node affinity is a clean way to express scheduling requirements that combine hard rules and soft preferences, and you can do more than you can with tolerations and plain node selectors. Listing 19.4 is an abbreviation

The new affinity rules replace the node selector, and now there is a match.

```
PS>kubectl apply -f sleep/update/sleep2-with-nodeAffinity-required.yaml
deployment.apps/sleep2 configured
PS>
PS>kubectl get pods -l app=sleep2
NAME                     READY   STATUS    RESTARTS   AGE
sleep2-6c89f6f7b6-59cqr  1/1     Running   0          8s
```

The new Pod runs and replaces the previous Pod and the pending Pod.

Figure 19.5   Affinity allows for a more complex set of node-selector rules.

of a spec that says to the scheduler: Pods must run on an Intel node, and it must be Windows or Linux, but preferably Linux.

Listing 19.4   sleep2-with-nodeAffinity-preferred.yaml, requirements and preferences

```
affinity:
  nodeAffinity:
    requiredDuringSchedulingIgnoredDuringExecution:
      nodeSelectorTerms:
        - matchExpressions:
          - key: kubernetes.io/arch      # This rule requires
            operator: In                 # an Intel CPU.
            values:
              - amd64
          - key: kubernetes.io/os
            operator: In
            values:                      # And either Linux
              - linux                    # or Windows OS
              - windows
    preferredDuringSchedulingIgnoredDuringExecution:
      - weight: 1
        preference:                      # But the preference
        matchExpressions:                # is for Linux.
        - key: kubernetes.io/os
          operator: In
          values:
            - linux
```

This process is great if you have a multiarchitecture cluster that is Linux heavy, with just a few Windows nodes to run older applications. You can build multiarchitecture Docker images, so the same image tag works on Linux and Windows (or Arm or any of the other OS and architecture combinations), so one container spec is good for multiple systems. Pods with this spec will prefer Linux nodes, but if the Linux nodes are saturated and there's capacity on the Windows nodes, then we'll use that capacity and run Windows Pods instead.

The affinity syntax is a little unwieldy because it's so generic. In the *required* rules, multiple match expressions work as a logical AND, and multiple selectors work as an OR. In the *preferred* rules, multiple match expressions are an AND, and you use multiple preferences to describe an OR. The full spec of listing 19.4 includes OR logic to cover multiple namespaces; we won't run it because the output is the same as the previous exercise, but it's a good one to refer back to if you're struggling to express your affinity. Figure 19.6 shows how the rules look.

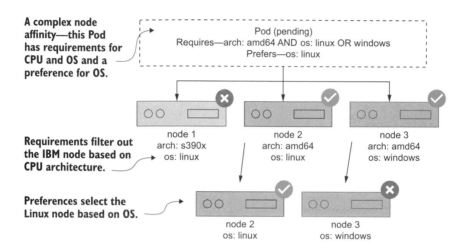

A complex node affinity—this Pod has requirements for CPU and OS and a preference for OS.

Requirements filter out the IBM node based on CPU architecture.

Preferences select the Linux node based on OS.

Figure 19.6   You can express affinity rules with multiple conditions using different node labels.

You should have a good grasp of affinity because you can use it with more than just nodes: Pods can express an affinity to other Pods so they are scheduled on the same node, or an antiaffinity so they are scheduled on a different node. This capability supports two common use cases. The first is where you want Pods for different components to be colocated to reduce network latency between them. The second is where you want replicas of the same component to be spread around the cluster to increase redundancy. Listing 19.5 shows the first scenario in the random-number web app.

Listing 19.5   web.yaml, Pod affinity to colocate components

```
affinity:                                   # Affinity rules for Pods use
  podAffinity:                              # the same spec as node affinity.
    requiredDuringSchedulingIgnoredDuringExecution:
      - labelSelector:
          matchExpressions:                 # This looks for the app and
            - key: app                      # component labels to match.
              operator: In
              values:
                - numbers
```

```
        - key: component
          operator: In
          values:
            - api
topologyKey: "kubernetes.io/hostname"
```

Pod affinity follows the same spec as node affinity, and you can include both if you really want to confuse your team. Listing 19.4 is a required rule, so Pods will be left pending if the scheduler can't fulfill it. The match expressions work as a label selector, so this says the Pod must be scheduled on a node that is already running a Pod with the labels app=numbers and component=api. That's colocation, so a web Pod will always have a local API pod, which just leaves the *topology key* to describe, and that will need its own paragraph.

Topology describes the physical layout of your cluster—where the nodes are located—which is set in node labels at different levels of detail. The hostname label is always present and is unique for the node; clusters can add their own detail. Cloud providers usually add region and zone labels, which state where the server is located; on-premises clusters might add datacenter and rack labels. A topology key sets the level where the affinity applies: hostname effectively means put the Pods on the same node, and zone would mean put the Pod on any node in the same zone as the other Pod. Hostname is a good enough topology key to see affinity in action, and you can do it on a single node.

> **TRY IT NOW** Deploy the random-number app with Pod affinity to ensure the web and API Pods run on the same node.

```
# remove the taint we applied to simplify things:
kubectl taint nodes --all kiamol-disk=hdd:NoSchedule-

# deploy the random-number app:
kubectl apply -f numbers/

# confirm that both Pods are scheduled on the same node:
kubectl get pods -l app=numbers -o wide
```

You can see in figure 19.7 that this works as expected—I only have one node, and, of course, both Pods are scheduled there. In a larger cluster, the web Pod would stay pending until the API Pod is scheduled, and then it would follow the API Pod to the same node. If that node didn't have the capacity to run the web Pod, it would stay as pending because this rule is required (a preferred rule would allow the Pod to run on a node without an API Pod).

Antiaffinity uses the same syntax, and you can use it to keep Pods away from nodes or other Pods. Antiaffinity is useful in components that run at scale for high availability—think back to the Postgres database in chapter 8. The app used a StatefulSet with multiple replicas, but the Pods themselves might all end up on the same node. That defeats the whole purpose of using replicas, because if the node goes down, it takes all

Using the `taint` command with a minus sign at the end removes a taint.

The web Pod spec expresses an affinity to the API Pod.

```
PS>kubectl taint nodes --all kiamol-disk=hdd:NoSchedule-
node/docker-desktop untainted
PS>
PS>kubectl apply -f numbers/
service/numbers-api created
deployment.apps/numbers-api created
service/numbers-web created
deployment.apps/numbers-web created
PS>
PS>kubectl get pods -l app=numbers -o wide
NAME                          READY   STATUS    RESTARTS   AGE   IP
  NODE               NOMINATED NODE   READINESS GATES
numbers-api-7f759884bd-rscjl  1/1     Running   0          5s    10.1.0.76
  docker-desktop   <none>           <none>
numbers-web-657ccf9b66-8jg89  1/1     Running   0          5s    10.1.0.77
  docker-desktop   <none>           <none>
```

**Both Pods are scheduled on the same node—you get the
same result on a single-node cluster or a 100-node cluster.**

Figure 19.7   Pod affinity controls workload placement in relation to existing workloads.

the database replicas with it. Antiaffinity can be used to express the rule: Keep me away from other Pods like me, which will spread Pods across different nodes. We won't go back to the StatefulSet; we'll keep it simple and deploy that rule for the random-number API and see what happens when we scale up.

TRY IT NOW   Update the API Deployment to use Pod antiaffinity so replicas all run on different nodes. Then scale up and confirm the status.

```
# add an antiaffinity rule to the API Pod:
kubectl apply -f numbers/update/api.yaml

# print the API Pod status:
kubectl get pods -l app=numbers

#scale up the API and the web components:
kubectl scale deploy/numbers-api --replicas 3
kubectl scale deploy/numbers-web --replicas 3

# print all the web and API Pod statuses:
kubectl get pods -l app=numbers
```

You'll want to go through figure 19.8 carefully, because the results are probably not what you expected. The updated API Deployment creates a new ReplicaSet, which creates a new Pod. That Pod stays as pending, because the antiaffinity rules won't let it

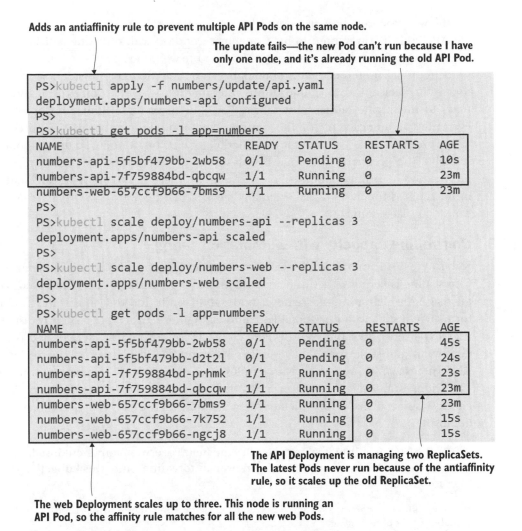

Adds an antiaffinity rule to prevent multiple API Pods on the same node.

The update fails—the new Pod can't run because I have only one node, and it's already running the old API Pod.

```
PS>kubectl apply -f numbers/update/api.yaml
deployment.apps/numbers-api configured
PS>
PS>kubectl get pods -l app=numbers
NAME                              READY   STATUS    RESTARTS   AGE
numbers-api-5f5bf479bb-2wb58      0/1     Pending   0          10s
numbers-api-7f759884bd-qbcqw      1/1     Running   0          23m
numbers-web-657ccf9b66-7bms9      1/1     Running   0          23m
PS>
PS>kubectl scale deploy/numbers-api --replicas 3
deployment.apps/numbers-api scaled
PS>
PS>kubectl scale deploy/numbers-web --replicas 3
deployment.apps/numbers-web scaled
PS>
PS>kubectl get pods -l app=numbers
NAME                              READY   STATUS    RESTARTS   AGE
numbers-api-5f5bf479bb-2wb58      0/1     Pending   0          45s
numbers-api-5f5bf479bb-d2t2l      0/1     Pending   0          24s
numbers-api-7f759884bd-prhmk      1/1     Running   0          23s
numbers-api-7f759884bd-qbcqw      1/1     Running   0          23m
numbers-web-657ccf9b66-7bms9      1/1     Running   0          23m
numbers-web-657ccf9b66-7k752      1/1     Running   0          15s
numbers-web-657ccf9b66-ngcj8      1/1     Running   0          15s
```

The API Deployment is managing two ReplicaSets. The latest Pods never run because of the antiaffinity rule, so it scales up the old ReplicaSet.

The web Deployment scales up to three. This node is running an API Pod, so the affinity rule matches for all the new web Pods.

Figure 19.8   Node antiaffinity gives unexpected results on a single-node cluster.

run on the same node as the existing API Pod—the one it's trying to replace. When the API Deployment is scaled up, another replica does run, so we have two API Pods on the same node—but this is the previous ReplicaSet, which doesn't include the antiaffinity rule. The Deployment is trying to honor the request for three replicas between the two ReplicaSets, and because the new Pods don't come online, it scales another replica of the old Pod.

How about the web Pods—did you expect to see three of them running? Well, three are running, whether or not you expected it. Affinity and antiaffinity rules check only for the existence of Pods by their labels, not the count of Pods. The affinity rule for the web Pod says it needs to run where there's an API Pod, not where there's a single API Pod. If you wanted to have only one web Pod with only one API Pod, you'd need an antiaffinity rule for other web Pods in the web Pod spec.

Scheduling preferences get complex because the scheduler considers so many factors in the decision. Your simple affinity rules might not work as you expect, and you'll need to investigate taints, node labels, Pod labels, resource limits, and quotas—or even the scheduler log file on the control plane node. Remember that required rules will prevent your Pod running if the scheduler can't find a node, so think about having a backup preferred rule. This topic is one of the more intricate ones in this chapter; next, we're going to look at how we can get Kubernetes to automatically schedule more replicas for us, and that's actually more straightforward than trying to control workload placement.

19.3 *Controlling capacity with automatic scaling*

Kubernetes can automatically scale your applications by adding or removing Pods. This scaling is *horizontal* because it makes use of your existing nodes; there is also cluster scaling, which adds and removes nodes, but you'll find that mostly in cloud platforms. We'll stick with horizontal Pod autoscaling here, which has a slightly disjointed user experience like the NetworkPolicy objects we covered in chapter 16. You can deploy an autoscale spec that describes how you would like your Pods scaled, but Kubernetes won't do anything with it unless it can check the load of the existing Pods. The wider Kubernetes project provides the metrics-server component for basic load checks—some distributions include it by default; for others, you need to manually deploy it.

TRY IT NOW Confirm if your cluster has the metrics-server component installed, and if not, deploy it, the metrics power autoscaling, and the kubectl top command.

```
# top shows resource usage if you have metrics-server installed:
kubectl top nodes

# if you get an error about "heapster,"
# you need to install metrics-server:
kubectl apply -f metrics-server/

# wait for it to spin up:
kubectl wait --for=condition=ContainersReady pod -l k8s-app=metrics-
   server -n kube-system

# it takes a minute or so for collection to start:
sleep 60

# print the metric-server Pod logs:
kubectl logs -n kube-system -l k8s-app=metrics-server --tail 2

# look at node usage again:
kubectl top nodes
```

Metrics-server is an additional component. If you don't have it installed, you won't get results from the `top` **command.**

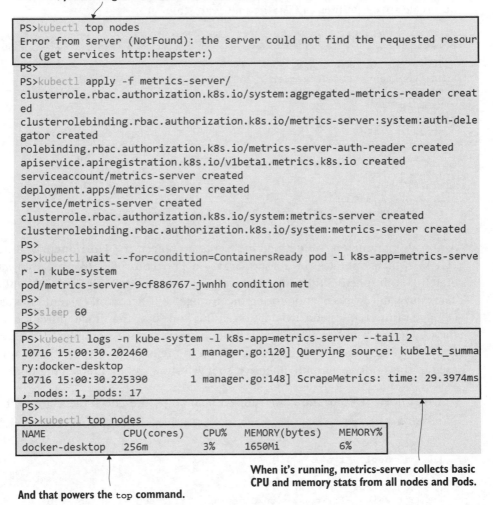

```
PS>kubectl top nodes
Error from server (NotFound): the server could not find the requested resour
ce (get services http:heapster:)
PS>
PS>kubectl apply -f metrics-server/
clusterrole.rbac.authorization.k8s.io/system:aggregated-metrics-reader creat
ed
clusterrolebinding.rbac.authorization.k8s.io/metrics-server:system:auth-dele
gator created
rolebinding.rbac.authorization.k8s.io/metrics-server-auth-reader created
apiservice.apiregistration.k8s.io/v1beta1.metrics.k8s.io created
serviceaccount/metrics-server created
deployment.apps/metrics-server created
service/metrics-server created
clusterrole.rbac.authorization.k8s.io/system:metrics-server created
clusterrolebinding.rbac.authorization.k8s.io/system:metrics-server created
PS>
PS>kubectl wait --for=condition=ContainersReady pod -l k8s-app=metrics-serve
r -n kube-system
pod/metrics-server-9cf886767-jwnhh condition met
PS>
PS>sleep 60
PS>
PS>kubectl logs -n kube-system -l k8s-app=metrics-server --tail 2
I0716 15:00:30.202460       1 manager.go:120] Querying source: kubelet_summa
ry:docker-desktop
I0716 15:00:30.225390       1 manager.go:148] ScrapeMetrics: time: 29.3974ms
, nodes: 1, pods: 17
PS>
PS>kubectl top nodes
NAME            CPU(cores)    CPU%    MEMORY(bytes)    MEMORY%
docker-desktop  256m          3%      1650Mi           6%
```

When it's running, metrics-server collects basic CPU and memory stats from all nodes and Pods.

And that powers the `top` **command.**

Figure 19.9 `metrics-server` **collects CPU and memory stats, but it's an optional component.**

Figure 19.9 shows that my lab environment doesn't have `metrics-server` deployed (it's not part of Docker Desktop or Kind, but it is installed in K3s), but thankfully the remedy is much simpler than choosing a Pod network. The `metrics-server` Deployment is a single implementation: if you get a response from the kubectl `top` command, your cluster is collecting all the metrics it needs for autoscaling; if not, just deploy `metrics-server`.

Don't confuse these with the metrics we set up with Prometheus in chapter 14. The stats collected by `metrics-server` just track the basic compute resources, CPU and memory, and it returns only the current value when it's queried. It's an easy option to use for autoscaling if your workloads are CPU or memory intensive because Kubernetes knows how to use it without any extra configuration. Listing 19.6 shows a Pod autoscale spec that uses CPU as the metric to scale on.

Listing 19.6   hpa-cpu.yaml, horizontal pod autoscaling by CPU load

```
apiVersion: autoscaling/v1
kind: HorizontalPodAutoscaler            # I love this name.
metadata:
  name: pi-cpu
spec:
  scaleTargetRef:                        # The target is the controller
    apiVersion: apps/v1                  # to scale—this targets the
    kind: Deployment                     # Pi app Deployment.
    name: pi-web
  minReplicas: 1                         # Range of the replica count
  maxReplicas: 5
  targetCPUUtilizationPercentage: 75     # Target CPU usage
```

Autoscale parameters are defined in a separate object, the HorizontalPodAutoscaler (HPA), which operates on a scale target—a Pod controller like a Deployment or StatefulSet. It specifies the range of the replica count and the desired CPU utilization. The autoscaler works by monitoring the average CPU across all current Pods as a percentage of the requested CPU amount in the Pod spec. If average utilization is below the target, the number of replicas is reduced, down to the minimum. If utilization is above the target, new replicas are added, up to the maximum. The Pi web app we've used in this book is compute intensive, so it will show us how autoscaling works.

TRY IT NOW   Deploy the Pi web app with an HPA, and check the status of the Pods.

```
# deploy the manifests:
kubectl apply -f pi/

# wait for the Pod to start:
kubectl wait --for=condition=ContainersReady pod -l app=pi-web

# print the status of the autoscaler:
kubectl get hpa pi-cpu
```

Now the Pi application is running, and the spec requests 125 millicores of CPU (one-eighth of one core). Initially, there's a single replica, which is set in the Deployment spec, and now the HPA is watching to see if it needs to create more Pods. The HPA gets its data from `metrics-server`, which takes a minute or two to catch up. You can see in figure 19.10 that the current CPU utilization is unknown, but that will soon change to 0% because the Pod isn't doing any work.

This Pod spec has a 250-millicore CPU limit, which is double the requested amount. Make a request to calculate Pi to a high level of decimal places, and you'll

The HPA is configured to monitor average CPU across all the Pi Pods. It
will scale up if the average is greater than 75% of the requested CPU.

```
PS>kubectl apply -f pi/
deployment.apps/pi-web created
horizontalpodautoscaler.autoscaling/pi-cpu created
service/pi-web created
PS>
PS>kubectl wait --for=condition=ContainersReady pod -l app=pi-web
pod/pi-web-6dc54b7c66-t5s8k condition met
PS>
PS>kubectl get hpa pi-cpu
```

NAME AGE	REFERENCE	TARGETS	MINPODS	MAXPODS	REPLICAS
pi-cpu 24s	Deployment/pi-web	\<unknown\>/75%	1	5	1

It takes a minute or so before the new Pod is scraped by the
metrics-server and the stats become available to the HPA.

Figure 19.10 The HPA works with the metrics-server to collect stats and the Deployment to
manage scale.

soon max out 0.25 of a core, and the average utilization will spike toward 200%. Then
the HPA will kick in and scale up, adding new replicas to help with the load.

> **TRY IT NOW** Run a script that makes some concurrent calls to the Pi web app,
> asking for 100,000 decimal places and causing a high CPU load. Confirm that
> the HPA scales up.

```
# run the load script—on Windows:
.\loadpi.ps1

# OR on Linux/macOS:
chmod +x ./loadpi.sh && ./loadpi.sh

# give the metrics-server and HPA time to work:
sleep 60

# confirm that the Deployment has been scaled up:
kubectl get hpa pi-cpu

# print the Pod compute usage:
kubectl top pods -l app=pi-web
```

Whether the extra Pods actually do help with the load depends on your application.
In this case, whichever Pod receives the web request will process the calculation until
it completes, so new Pods don't share the existing load. You can see in figure 19.11

Generate some load to the Pi app, and the CPU will go over the
requested amount in the Pod spec, triggering the autoscaler.

Autoscaling is reactive—it takes a while for the metrics to
come through, though 30 seconds would probably be enough.

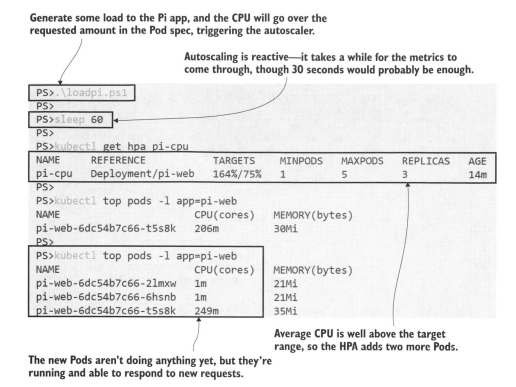

```
PS>.\loadpi.ps1
PS>
PS>sleep 60
PS>
PS>kubectl get hpa pi-cpu
NAME       REFERENCE          TARGETS     MINPODS   MAXPODS   REPLICAS   AGE
pi-cpu     Deployment/pi-web  164%/75%    1         5         3          14m
PS>
PS>kubectl top pods -l app=pi-web
NAME                          CPU(cores)   MEMORY(bytes)
pi-web-6dc54b7c66-t5s8k       206m         30Mi
PS>
PS>kubectl top pods -l app=pi-web
NAME                          CPU(cores)   MEMORY(bytes)
pi-web-6dc54b7c66-2lmxw       1m           21Mi
pi-web-6dc54b7c66-6hsnb       1m           21Mi
pi-web-6dc54b7c66-t5s8k       249m         35Mi
```

Average CPU is well above the target
range, so the HPA adds two more Pods.

The new Pods aren't doing anything yet, but they're
running and able to respond to new requests.

Figure 19.11   Autoscaling in action: the HPA triggers new Pods when CPU usage spikes.

that the original Pod is running at just about the maximum 250 millicores, and the
new Pods are doing nothing at 1 millicore. But those additional Pods increase the
capacity of the app, and they can work on any new requests that come in.

When you run this exercise, you should see similar results. The HPA will scale up
to three Pods, and before it goes any further, the app returns the Pi response, CPU utilization falls, and it doesn't need to scale up any more. The HPA adds more Pods every
15 seconds until the utilization is within target. With one Pod maxed out and two Pods
doing nothing, the average CPU falls to 66%, which is within the 75% target, so the
HPA won't add any more Pods (you can repeat the load script a few more times to
confirm it peaks to five Pods). When you stop making requests, the load will fall to 0%
again, and then the HPA waits to make sure the app stays within target for five minutes
before it scales back down to one replica.

We have several parameters here: how long to wait before scaling up or down, how
many Pods to add or remove, how quickly to add or remove Pods. None of those values can be changed in the version 1 HPA spec, but they're all exposed in the version 2
spec. The new spec is still a beta-2 feature in Kubernetes 1.18, and it's a pretty significant change. The single option to scale based on CPU has been replaced with a generic

metrics section, and the scaling behavior can be controlled. Listing 19.7 shows the new spec in an update to the Pi HPA.

Listing 19.7   hpa-cpu-v2.yaml, the extended HPA spec in version 2

```
metrics:                              # Metrics spec inside a version 2 HPA
- type: Resource
  resource:
    name: cpu                         # The resource to monitor is generic.
    target:                           # This checks for CPU, but you can use
      type: Utilization               # other metrics.
      averageUtilization: 75
  behavior:
    scaleDown:                              # This sets the parameters
      stabilizationWindowSeconds: 30        # when the HPA is scaling
      policies:                             # down—it waits for 30 seconds
      - type: Percent                       # and scales down by 50%
        value: 50                           # of the Pod count.
        periodSeconds: 15
```

I said autoscaling was more straightforward than affinity, but I really meant only version 1. The version 2 spec is complex because it supports other types of metrics, and you can use Prometheus metrics as the source for scaling decisions. You need a few more pieces to do that, so I won't go into the details, but remember it's an option. It means you can scale based on any metrics you collect, like the rate of incoming HTTP requests or the number of messages in a queue.

We're sticking with the 75% CPU target here, which uses the same metrics-server stats, but we've tuned the scale-down behavior so we'll see the number of Pods come down much more quickly once the Pi requests are processed.

TRY IT NOW   Update the HPA to use the version 2 spec; this sets a low stabilization period for scale-down events, so you'll see the Pod count fall more quickly.

```
# update the HPA settings:
kubectl apply -f pi/update/hpa-cpu-v2.yaml

# run the load script again—on Windows:
.\loadpi.ps1

# OR on macOS/Linux:
./loadpi.sh

# wait for the HPA to scale up:
sleep 60

# confirm there are more replicas:
kubectl get hpa pi-cpu # go up

# there's no more load, wait for the HPA to scale down:
sleep 60
```

```
# confirm there's only one replica:
kubectl get hpa pi-cpu

# print the Deployment status:
kubectl get deploy pi-web
```

In this exercise, you'll see the scale-up behavior works in the same way, because the version 2 defaults are the same as the version 1 defaults. The scale-down won't take so long this time, although you may see—as shown in figure 19.12—that querying the HPA status doesn't reflect the change as quickly as the Deployment itself does.

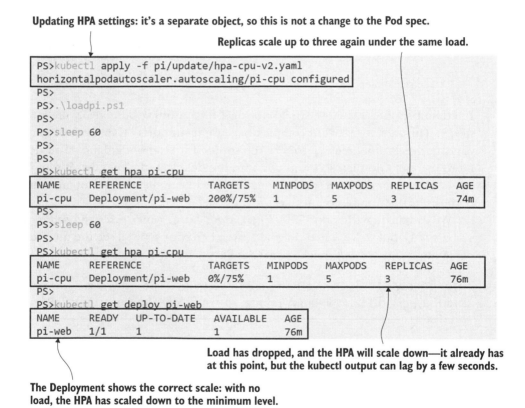

Updating HPA settings: it's a separate object, so this is not a change to the Pod spec.

Replicas scale up to three again under the same load.

Load has dropped, and the HPA will scale down—it already has at this point, but the kubectl output can lag by a few seconds.

The Deployment shows the correct scale: with no load, the HPA has scaled down to the minimum level.

Figure 19.12   The new HPA spec favors a fast scale-down, suitable for bursty workloads.

Changing the behavior lets you model how the HPA responds to scaling events. The defaults are a fairly conservative version of scale-up quickly and scale-down slowly, but you can switch it around so scaling up is more gradual and scaling down is immediate. "Immediate" isn't really true because there's a lag between the metrics being collected and made available to the HPA, but the delay will be just tens of seconds. The HPA is specific to one target, so you can have different scaling rules and rates for different parts of your app.

We've covered placing Pods and scaling up and down, and the HPA just instructs the controller to scale, so any scheduling requirements in the Pod spec apply to all Pods. The last topic on workload management is *preemption*, the process of deliberately causing Pods to fail.

19.4 *Protecting resources with preemption and priorities*

Sometimes Kubernetes realizes a node is working too hard, and it *preempts* that some Pods will fail and shuts them down in advance, giving the node time to recover. This is *eviction* and happens only under extreme circumstances, where if the cluster didn't take action, the node might become unresponsive. Evicted Pods stay on the node so you have the forensics to track down problems, but the Pod containers are stopped and removed, freeing up memory and disk. If the Pod is managed by a controller, a replacement Pod is created, which may be scheduled to run on a different node.

Preemption is what happens if you get all your resource specs, quotas, scheduling, and scaling wrong, so nodes end up running more Pods than they can manage and are starved of memory or disk. If that happens, Kubernetes considers the node to be under pressure, and it evicts Pods until the pressure situation ends. At the same time, it adds a taint to the node so no new Pods are scheduled to run on it. As the pressure situation eases, it removes the taint, and the node is able to accept new workloads.

There's no way to fake memory or disk pressure for demos or exercises, so to see how this works, we're going to need to max out your lab. It's easier to do that with memory than with disk, but it still isn't easy; the default is to start eviction when the node has less than 100 MB of memory available, which means using up nearly all of your memory. If you want to follow along with the exercises in this section, you really need to spin up a separate lab in a VM, so you can tweak the Kubernetes settings and max the memory on the VM rather than on your own machine.

> **TRY IT NOW** Start a dedicated VM using Vagrant. This setup has Kind installed and 3 GB of RAM allocated. Create a new Kind cluster with a custom kubelet configuration that lowers the memory threshold for eviction.

```
# from the kiamol source root, create a VM with Vagrant:
cd ch01/vagrant/

# create the new VM:
vagrant up

# connect to the VM:
vagrant ssh

# switch to this chapter's source inside the VM:
cd /kiamol/ch19
```

```
# create a customized Kind cluster:
kind create cluster --name kiamol-ch19--config ./kind/kiamol-ch19-
  config.yaml --image kindest/node:v1.18.8

# wait for the node to be ready:
kubectl -n kube-system wait --for=condition=Ready node --all

# print the VM's memory stats:
./kind/print-memory.sh
```

The script in this exercise uses the same logic that the kubelet uses to determine how much free memory it can access. You can see in figure 19.13 that my VM reports just under 3 GB of total memory and just under 1.5 GB free, and that's what Kubernetes sees.

This exercise uses a dedicated VM and creates a customized
Kind cluster with a low memory threshold for eviction.

```
vagrant@kiamol:~$ cd /kiamol/ch19
vagrant@kiamol:/kiamol/ch19$
vagrant@kiamol:/kiamol/ch19$ kind create cluster --name kiamol-ch19 --config
 ./kind/kiamol-ch19-config.yaml --image kindest/node:v1.15.7
Creating cluster "kiamol-ch19" ...
 ✓ Ensuring node image (kindest/node:v1.15.7) 🖼
 ✓ Preparing nodes 📦
 ✓ Writing configuration 📜
 ✓ Starting control-plane 🕹
 ✓ Installing CNI 🔌
 ✓ Installing StorageClass 💾
Set kubectl context to "kind-kiamol-ch19"

vagrant@kiamol:/kiamol/ch19$ kubectl -n kube-system wait --for=condition=Rea
dy node --all
node/kiamol-ch19-control-plane condition met
vagrant@kiamol:/kiamol/ch19$
vagrant@kiamol:/kiamol/ch19$ ./kind/print-memory.sh
----------------
Memory capacity : 2892M
Memory available: 1435M
----------------
```

This script uses the same logic as the kubelet to determine total and
available memory. Running the OS, Docker, and Kubernetes uses half
the RAM, so 1.5 GB is free for apps.

Figure 19.13   If you want to test memory pressure, it's safer to do it in a dedicated environment.

If you don't want to spin up a separate VM for these exercises, that's fine—but remember the default memory threshold is 100 MB. To force a memory pressure situation, you're going to need to allocate almost all the memory on your machine, which will probably also cause a CPU spike and make the whole thing unresponsive. You can confirm the memory limit by checking the live configuration of the kubelet; it has an HTTP endpoint you can use by proxying requests with kubectl.

TRY IT NOW Query the configuration API on the node to see the active settings for the kubelet, and confirm that the eviction level has been set.

```
# run a proxy to the Kubernetes API server:
kubectl proxy

# in a new terminal connect to the VM again:
cd ch01/vagrant/
vagrant ssh

# make a GET request to see the kubelet config:
curl -sSL "http://localhost:8001/api/v1/nodes/$(kubectl get node -o
    jsonpath={'.items[0].metadata.name'})/proxy/configz"
```

In this environment, the Kubelet is configured to trigger evictions when only 40% of memory is available on the node, as you see in figure 19.14. That's a deliberately low threshold, so we can easily trigger eviction; in a production environment, you would have it set much higher. If you use a different lab environment with no explicit setting in the kubelet, you'll be using the default 100 MB.

That's enough warnings . . . Well—one more: I trashed my Docker Desktop environment trying to force memory pressure when I was planning these exercises. Kubectl

Kubectl proxy is like a `port-forward` to get access to the Kubernetes API server.

```
vagrant@kiamol:/kiamol/ch19$ kubectl proxy
Starting to serve on 127.0.0.1:8001

    vagrant@kiamol:~$ curl -sSL "http://localhost:8001/api/v1/nodes/kia
    mol-ch19-control-plane/proxy/configz"
    {"kubeletconfig":{"staticPodPath":"/etc/kubernetes/manifests","sync
    Frequency":"1m0s","fileCheckFrequency":"20s","httpCheckFrequency":"

    evictionHard":{"memory.available":"40%"},"evictionPressureTransitio
    nPeriod":"30s","enableControllerAttachDetach":true,"makeIPTablesUti
    lChains":true,"iptablesMasqueradeBit":14,"iptablesDropBit":15,"fail
    SwapOn":false,"containerLogMaxSize":"10Mi","containerLogMaxFiles":5
    ,"configMapAndSecretChangeDetectionStrategy":"Watch","enforceNodeAl
    locatable":["pods"]}}vagrant@kiamol:~$
```

You can use it to query the configz endpoint on a node to show the kubelet configuration.
The custom config setting is to start eviction when the node has less than 40% memory available.

Figure 19.14 Low-level settings are specified in the kubelet configuration, which you can view using the proxy.

wouldn't respond, and I had to remove and reinstall everything. Let's go ahead and trigger preemption. I've built a container image that packages the Linux `stress` tool, and I have a Deployment spec for four replicas, which each allocate 300 MB of memory. That should leave the node with less than 40% of total memory available and push it into memory pressure.

TRY IT NOW   Run an app that allocates a lot of memory, and see how Kubernetes evicts Pods when the nodes are under memory pressure.

```
# the stress Pods will allocate 1.2 GB of RAM:
kubectl apply -f stress/stress.yaml

# wait for them all to start:
kubectl wait --for=condition=ContainersReady pod -l app=stress

# print the node's memory stats:
./kind/print-memory.sh

# list the Pods:
kubectl get pods -l app=stress

# remove the Deployment:
kubectl delete -f stress/stress.yaml
```

Preemption happens fast, and the transition between pressure states also happens fast. I've trimmed the output in figure 19.15 because I was too slow to run the Pod `list` command, and by the time I did, the node had evicted 23 Pods.

Why are there so many evictions? Why didn't Kubernetes just evict one Pod and leave the replacement in the pending state while the node was under memory pressure? It did. But as soon as the Pod was evicted, it freed up a bunch of memory, and the node quickly tripped out of memory pressure. Meanwhile, the Deployment created a new Pod to replace the evicted one, which ran on the no-longer-tainted node, but it immediately allocated more memory and tripped the pressure switch again for another eviction. That loop happens quickly with this app because it allocates lots of memory when it starts, but it's possible to get in the same situation with a real app if your cluster is overloaded.

Preemption events should be rare in a production environment, but if it does happen, you want to make sure your least important workloads are evicted. The kubelet decides which Pod to evict in a memory pressure situation by ranking them. That ranking looks at the amount of memory the Pod is using relative to the amount requested in the Pod spec as well as the *priority class* of the Pod. Priority classes, the last new concept for this chapter, are a simple way to classify the importance of your workloads. Listing 19.8 shows a custom priority class with a low value.

These four Pods have allocated
1.2 GB of memory between them.   The node has 26% of its memory available, which is
                                  below the 40% custom eviction threshold.

```
vagrant@kiamol:/kiamol/ch19$ kubectl apply -f stress/stress.yaml
deployment.apps/stress created
vagrant@kiamol:/kiamol/ch19$
vagrant@kiamol:/kiamol/ch19$ kubectl wait --for=condition=ContainersReady po
d -l app=stress
pod/stress-5c6fc498f-bj75f condition met
pod/stress-5c6fc498f-j8xxp condition met
pod/stress-5c6fc498f-lc7cl condition met
pod/stress-5c6fc498f-q5kgh condition met
vagrant@kiamol:/kiamol/ch19$
vagrant@kiamol:/kiamol/ch19$ ./kind/print-memory.sh

Memory capacity : 2892M
Memory available: 756M
----------------
vagrant@kiamol:/kiamol/ch19$ kubectl get pods -l app=stress
NAME                      READY   STATUS    RESTARTS   AGE
stress-5c6fc498f-2sw4d    0/1     Evicted   0          4s
stress-5c6fc498f-6pvqc    0/1     Evicted   0          4s
stress-5c6fc498f-9djbx    0/1     Evicted   0          8s
stress-5c6fc498f-bj75f    1/1     Running   0          19s
stress-5c6fc498f-jcxc8    0/1     Pending   0          3s
stress-5c6fc498f-lc7cl    1/1     Running   0          19s
stress-5c6fc498f-q5kgh    1/1     Running   0          19s
stress-5c6fc498f-rh7g2    0/1     Evicted   0          11s
stress-5c6fc498f-wm7mv    0/1     Evicted   0          5s
stress-5c6fc498f-z2vtp    0/1     Evicted   0          9s
vagrant@kiamol:/kiamol/ch19$
vagrant@kiamol:/kiamol/ch19$ kubectl delete -f stress/stress.yaml
deployment.apps "stress" deleted
```

Three of the original Pods are still running, and one was evicted. Then the node had enough
memory to run another Pod, which immediately tripped it into memory pressure and got
evicted again. And repeat.

Figure 19.15   Lots of Pods. Resource-hungry Pods can cause an eviction/creation loop.

Listing 19.8   low.yaml, a class for low-priority workloads

```
apiVersion: scheduling.k8s.io/v1
kind: PriorityClass
metadata:
  name: kiamol-low     # The Pod spec uses this name to state its priority.
value: 100             # Priority is an integer up to 1 billion.
globalDefault: true
description: "Low priority—OK to be evicted"
```

The numeric value is what decides the priority: bigger means more important. Kubernetes doesn't have any default priority classes, so you need to map your own if you want to safeguard the more important workloads. You attach a priority to a workload by adding the `PriorityClassName` field to the Pod spec. In the final exercise, we'll deploy two versions of the stress app: one with high priority and one with low priority. When the memory pressure hits, we'll see the low-priority Pods get evicted.

> **TRY IT NOW**   Run the stress exercise again but this time with two Deployments, each running two Pods. The memory allocation is the same, but the Pods have different priorities.

```
# create the custom priority classes:
kubectl apply -f priority-classes/

# deploy apps with high and low priorities:
kubectl apply -f stress/with-priorities/

# wait for the Pods to run:
kubectl wait --for=condition=ContainersReady pod -l app=stress
wait

# print the memory stats:
./kind/print-memory.sh

# confirm that the node is under memory pressure:
kubectl describe node | grep MemoryPressure


# print the Pod list:
kubectl get pods -l app=stress
```

That all worked beautifully when I ran the exercise, and you can see the output in figure 19.16. The node can manage only three Pods without tripping into memory pressure, and the evicted fourth Pod is always from the low-priority spec; the high-priority Pods keep running.

It's not just the priority class that keeps the high-priority Pods running. All of the Pods use more memory than they request, so they're all eligible to be evicted. That's when priority is taken into account. If all eligible Pods have the same priority (or no priority), Kubernetes makes the choice based on how much more memory is being used than requested, so it evicts the highest offenders. It's important to include resource requests in your Pod specs as well as limits, but a priority class is a useful protection for the more important workloads.

That was a wide-ranging tour around the major aspects of workload management. They're all features you'll use in production, and we'll finish the chapter reviewing what they give you and how they work together.

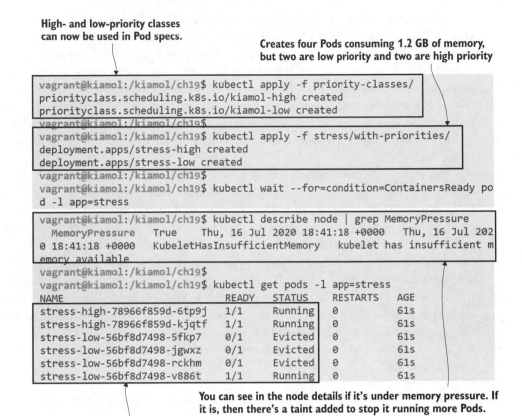

High- and low-priority classes can now be used in Pod specs.

Creates four Pods consuming 1.2 GB of memory, but two are low priority and two are high priority

```
vagrant@kiamol:/kiamol/ch19$ kubectl apply -f priority-classes/
priorityclass.scheduling.k8s.io/kiamol-high created
priorityclass.scheduling.k8s.io/kiamol-low created
vagrant@kiamol:/kiamol/ch19$
vagrant@kiamol:/kiamol/ch19$ kubectl apply -f stress/with-priorities/
deployment.apps/stress-high created
deployment.apps/stress-low created
vagrant@kiamol:/kiamol/ch19$
vagrant@kiamol:/kiamol/ch19$ kubectl wait --for=condition=ContainersReady po
d -l app=stress
vagrant@kiamol:/kiamol/ch19$ kubectl describe node | grep MemoryPressure
  MemoryPressure    True    Thu, 16 Jul 2020 18:41:18 +0000    Thu, 16 Jul 202
0 18:41:18 +0000    KubeletHasInsufficientMemory    kubelet has insufficient m
emory available
vagrant@kiamol:/kiamol/ch19$
vagrant@kiamol:/kiamol/ch19$ kubectl get pods -l app=stress
NAME                            READY   STATUS     RESTARTS   AGE
stress-high-78966f859d-6tp9j    1/1     Running    0          61s
stress-high-78966f859d-kjqtf    1/1     Running    0          61s
stress-low-56bf8d7498-5fkp7     0/1     Evicted    0          61s
stress-low-56bf8d7498-jgwxz     0/1     Evicted    0          61s
stress-low-56bf8d7498-rckhm     0/1     Evicted    0          61s
stress-low-56bf8d7498-v886t     1/1     Running    0          61s
```

You can see in the node details if it's under memory pressure. If it is, then there's a taint added to stop it running more Pods.

There's still an eviction/creation loop, but the low-priority Pods are always evicted.

Figure 19.16   Adding a priority class is a simple safeguard to protect key Pods from eviction.

19.5   *Understanding the controls for managing workloads*

Scheduling, autoscaling, and eviction are all advanced topics with even more nuances than we've covered here. You'll certainly use them in your Kubernetes journey, and it's worth bringing some controls in early on. They address different problems in managing your apps, but they all impact each other, so you need to use them carefully.

Affinity is the feature you'll use the most in large clusters. Node affinity lets you segregate workloads with stricter isolation than you get with namespaces alone, and Pod affinity lets you model the availability requirements of your apps. You can combine Pod affinity with node topology to ensure replicas run across different failure domains, so the loss of one rack or zone doesn't bring down your app because other Pods are running in a different zone. Remember that required affinity is a hard rule for the scheduler: if you require Pods to be in different zones and you have only three zones, replica number four will forever stay pending.

Autoscaling is a great feature and easy to use if your app is CPU bound. Then you can use the default `metrics-server` and the simple version 1 HPA, making sure you have CPU requests in your Pod specs. Things get more complex if you want to scale based on higher-level metrics, but that's definitely worth investigating. Having your app scale automatically when key service levels are being missed is a major benefit of Kubernetes and something to work toward when you're established in production. Scaling just increases or decreases the number of replicas, so if you have affinity rules in your spec, you need to make sure they can be met at the maximum scale level.

Preemption is Kubernetes's safety mechanism for dealing with nodes that run short on memory or disk. CPU is different because Pods can be throttled to reclaim CPU without stopping containers. Kubernetes relieves memory or disk pressure by evicting Pods, which is something you should rarely see if your cluster and apps are right-sized. You should include resource requests in your Pod specs so the worst offenders can be evicted, and consider priority classes if you have some workloads that are more important than others. If you do get in a preemption situation, you need to investigate quickly to make sure the node doesn't keep flipping in and out of pressure, constantly adding and then evicting Pods (we added node pressure indicators to the cluster dashboard in chapter 14 for this reason).

That's all for workload management. Time to clear down the cluster(s) to make way for the lab.

TRY IT NOW   Clean up your main lab environment; if you created a custom environment, it can be removed.

```
# remove objects on your main cluster:
kubectl delete all,priorityclass,hpa -l kiamol=ch19

# if you deployed the metrics-server in section 19.3, remove it:
kubectl delete -f metrics-server/

# if you created a new VM in section 19.4, it can go too:
cd ch01/vagrant/
vagrant destroy
```

19.6 Lab

We're going into production with the Pi app! Your job for this lab is to add to the spec so we can control the workload. This is the setup we need:

- The app has to run in the EU region because of data sovereignty concerns.
- It should autoscale based on target CPU utilization of 50%.
- There must be between two and five replicas running.
- The load should preferably be spread around multiple nodes in the EU region.

You'll find examples in this chapter's exercises for all these, except one, and you might need to check the API docs to see how to build up the last rule. Remember that node topology is done with labels, and you can add any labels you want to your nodes. My solution is in the usual place: https://github.com/sixeyed/kiamol/blob/master/ch19/lab/README.md.

Extending Kubernetes with custom resources and Operators

At the heart of Kubernetes is a highly available database and a REST API with a consistent way of working with objects. When you create a Pod through the API, the definition is stored in the database, and a controller is notified and knows that it needs to allocate the Pod to a node to get it running. It's a generic pattern where different controllers work on different types of objects, and it's extensible, so you can add your own resource definitions and your own custom controllers to act on those resources. This may sound like an obscure topic, but it's very common for products to extend Kubernetes to make the product itself easier to use. It's also a straightforward way to customize Kubernetes to make it work better in your organization.

Custom resources and controllers can hide a lot of the complexity in an application, and in this chapter, you'll see how to define and work with them. The definition part is simple, but controllers need custom code. We won't focus on the code, but we'll have some examples of customizations so you can see what they can do. We'll also cover the Operator pattern in this chapter, which is a way of using custom resources and controllers to automate the deployment and the ongoing operational tasks of an application.

20.1 How to extend Kubernetes with custom resources

Kubectl commands map closely to the Kubernetes REST API. When you run `kubectl get`, it makes a request to the API to get a resource or a list of resources. A standard set of actions are available for all resources, and you know from the RBAC rules covered in chapter 17 that they're defined as verbs: `create`, `get`, `list`, `watch`, and `delete`. When you define a custom resource in Kubernetes, it receives automatic support for all of those actions in the API; Kubernetes clients understand

500

custom resources, too, so you can work with them using kubectl just like any other object. Figure 20.1 shows how the cluster supports custom resources.

The CustomResourceDefinition adds a new resource type to Kubernetes. You create it in the usual way by applying a YAML spec.

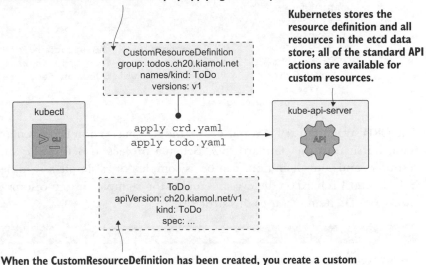

Kubernetes stores the resource definition and all resources in the etcd data store; all of the standard API actions are available for custom resources.

When the CustomResourceDefinition has been created, you create a custom resource with a spec that matches the API version and kind in the definition.

Figure 20.1   Kubernetes is extensible with custom resources, which work just like standard resources.

You define standard Kubernetes objects in YAML by specifying the kind of resource and all the fields in the spec—Pod specs have a container list, and container specs have an image name and a set of ports. Kubernetes stores those fields in a schema, so it knows the structure of the resource and can validate new objects. This is where the API version field comes in—version 1 of the HorizontalPodAutoscaler resource has a different structure from v2beta2. Custom resources have a known structure, too, and you create your own schema in a CustomResourceDefinition (CRD) object. Listing 20.1 shows a simple CRD for recording to-do items as Kubernetes objects.

Listing 20.1   todo-crd.yaml, a CRD for storing to-do items in Kubernetes

```
apiVersion: apiextensions.k8s.io/v1
kind: CustomResourceDefinition
metadata:                              # The name of the CRD needs to match
  name: todos.ch20.kiamol.net         # the names in the resource spec.
spec:
  group: ch20.kiamol.net      # Classifies a set of CRDs
  scope: Namespaced           # Can be clusterwide or namespaced
  names:                      # The names are how you refer to
    plural: todos             # custom resources in YAML and kubectl.
```

```
        singular: todo
      kind: ToDo
    versions:                        # You have multiple versions.
      - name: v1                     # Each version has a schema.
        served: true                 # Makes resources available in the API
        storage: true                # Saves resources in etcd
        schema:
          openAPIV3Schema:
            type: object
            properties:
              spec:                  # The schema sets the structure of the
                type: object         # custom resource—ToDo objects have a
                properties:          # spec field, which has an item field.
                  item:
                    type: string
```

The CRD structure itself is verbose, and the schema section is particularly awkward to read, but it uses the standard JSONSchema project to define the structure of the resource, and your definitions can be as complex or as simple as you need. The CRD in listing 20.1 is hard on the eyes but makes for a simple custom resource. Listing 20.2 shows a ToDo item that uses this structure.

Listing 20.2   todo-ch20.yaml, a ToDo custom resource

```
apiVersion: "ch20.kiamol.net/v1"   # Group name and version of the CRD
kind: ToDo                         # The resource type
metadata:                          # Standard metadata
  name: ch20
spec:
  item: "Finish KIAMOL Ch20"       # The spec needs to match the CRD schema.
```

This looks just like a normal Kubernetes YAML, which is the whole point of CRDs—to store your own resources in Kubernetes and make them feel like standard objects. The API version identifies that as a custom resource from this chapter of the book, and it's version 1. The metadata is standard metadata, so it can include labels and annotations, and the spec is the custom structure defined in the CRD. That's enough YAML now—let's put this into practice and use Kubernetes as our to-do list app.

TRY IT NOW   Deploy a custom resource definition and some resources to see how you work with them using kubectl.

```
# switch to this chapter's source:
cd ch20

# deploy the CRD:
kubectl apply -f todo-custom/

# print CRD details:
kubectl get crd -l kiamol=ch20

# create some custom resources:
kubectl apply -f todo-custom/items/
```

```
# list all the resources:
kubectl get todos
```

You can see in figure 20.2 that you work with custom resources just like any other resource. Once the CRD is deployed, the API now supports the ToDo object, and you can create items by applying YAML. Kubectl is the tool for managing custom resources, and now the get, describe, and delete commands work in the same way for ToDo objects as for Pods.

Deploying the CRD creates the object structure; there are no custom resouces yet.

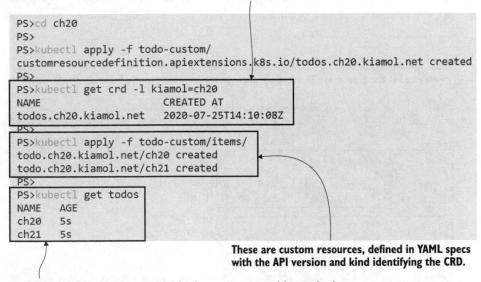

These are custom resources, defined in YAML specs with the API version and kind identifying the CRD.

You interact with custom resources in the same way as with standard resources, using kubectl commands to get, describe, and delete them.

Figure 20.2 CRDs and custom resources are described in YAML and deployed with kubectl.

The CRD specification is rich and lets you build lots of logic around your resources, including validation rules, subresources, and multiple versions. We won't get into that level of detail, but you can be confident that custom resources are a mature feature in Kubernetes with all the functionality you need to manage an evolving set of object definitions. The purpose of CRDs is to provide a simplified user experience, and we can make a small change to the ToDo CRD to make it more usable.

TRY IT NOW An update to the CRD spec makes the kubectl output more useful. This update doesn't affect the custom resources; it just adds to the columns that are printed.

```
# update the CRD, adding output columns:
kubectl apply -f todo-custom/update/
```

```
# list the to-do resources again:
kubectl get todos

# delete one of the resources:
kubectl delete todo ch21

# show the detail of the other resource:
kubectl describe todo ch20
```

This exercise updated the CRD with additional printer columns, so the API returns extra information in the get request. You can see in figure 20.3 that this is now a fully featured to-do list application. It even lets you delete items, so it's better than the to-do web app we've been running in this book.

CRDs can include custom output columns, so kubectl shows more useful output when you list the resources. This update displays the key information for each item.

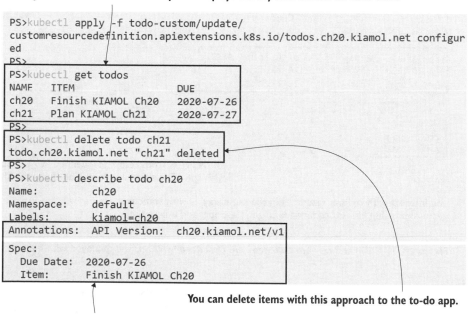

You can delete items with this approach to the to-do app.

Describing a custom resource shows the usual wealth of detail, including the API version of the CRD and the field values of the resource.

Figure 20.3   A fully functional to-do app powered by Kubernetes with no custom code!

This is fine for a simple demo, and we could get distracted writing a custom controller that watches these resources, adds items to your Google calendar, and sends email reminders when they're due, but we're not going to do that. It's not a good use of custom resources because the objects we're storing and the actions they trigger have nothing to do with Kubernetes; we're not integrating with other objects or extending what the cluster can do—we're just using Kubernetes as a massively overspecified content management system. We can do better than that, and we'll start by clearing up the ToDo resources.

> **TRY IT NOW**   Remove the to-do CRD, and confirm the custom resources are deleted, too.

```
# list the CRDs registered in your cluster:
kubectl get crds

# delete the to-do item CRD:
kubectl delete crd todos.ch20.kiamol.net

# try to list the to-do items:
kubectl get todos
```

You can see in this exercise and in figure 20.4 that custom resources can't exist without a CRD—Kubernetes won't store any unknown objects. Deleting the CRD deletes all of its resources, so if you make use of custom resources, you need to make sure your RBAC permissions around the CRD itself are tight.

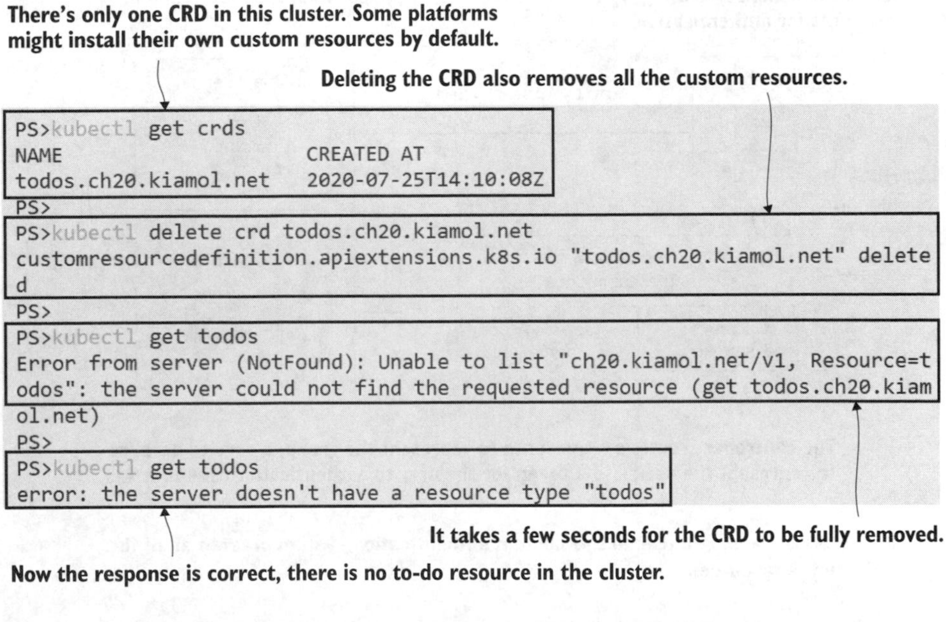

There's only one CRD in this cluster. Some platforms might install their own custom resources by default.

Deleting the CRD also removes all the custom resources.

```
PS>kubectl get crds
NAME                         CREATED AT
todos.ch20.kiamol.net        2020-07-25T14:10:08Z
PS>
PS>kubectl delete crd todos.ch20.kiamol.net
customresourcedefinition.apiextensions.k8s.io "todos.ch20.kiamol.net" delete
d
PS>
PS>kubectl get todos
Error from server (NotFound): Unable to list "ch20.kiamol.net/v1, Resource=t
odos": the server could not find the requested resource (get todos.ch20.kiam
ol.net)
PS>
PS>kubectl get todos
error: the server doesn't have a resource type "todos"
```

It takes a few seconds for the CRD to be fully removed.

Now the response is correct, there is no to-do resource in the cluster.

Figure 20.4   Custom resources are removed when the CRD that defines them is removed.

We'll go on to add a different CRD and pair it with a custom controller to add a user authentication system to Kubernetes.

20.2 *Triggering workflows with custom controllers*

You know from chapter 17 that production Kubernetes clusters are usually integrated with an external identity provider to authenticate users. Smaller organizations often use Service Accounts as end user accounts, which means you don't need an external system. You do, however, need to manage namespaces for groups and deal with creating accounts and tokens. It's a situation where Kubernetes has all the pieces for you, but you'll need to do a fair amount of work to put them together. That's exactly when you should think about custom resources and custom controllers.

The custom resource here is a *user*, and the main workflows are adding and deleting users. A simple user CRD needs to store just a name and a group, maybe with contact details, too. You can add and remove users with kubectl. When that happens, the workflow is processed by a custom controller. The controller is just an application that runs in a Pod and connects to the Kubernetes API. It watches for changes to user objects, and then it creates or deletes the necessary resources: namespaces, service accounts, and tokens. Figure 20.5 shows the add workflow, and the delete workflow is effectively the reverse.

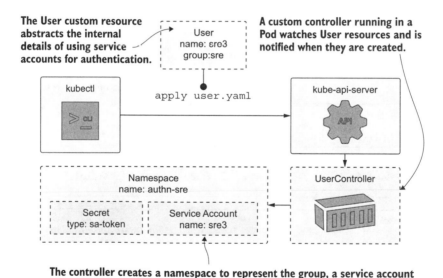

The controller creates a namespace to represent the group, a service account to represent the user, and a token for the user to authenticate with kubectl.

Figure 20.5 Adding a user in the custom authentication system creates all of the Kubernetes resources.

We'll start by deploying the user CRD and some users. The CRD is difficult to read because of the schema, but there's nothing new in it, so we'll skip the listing (it's the file user-crd.yaml, if you want to walk through it). The user resources themselves are simple. Listing 20.3 shows a user in the SRE team.

Listing 20.3 user-crd.yaml, spec for a user resource

```
apiVersion: "ch20.kiamol.net/v1"    # This is the same group and version
kind: User                          # as the other CRDs in this chapter.
metadata:
  name: sre3
spec:                               # Records the user details
  email: sre3@kiamol.net
  group: sre
```

You need to be aware that CRDs take a few seconds to register in the API server, so you can't usually deploy a folder of CRDs and custom resources in one go because the CRD often isn't ready in time. You need to deploy the CRD first, and then you can deploy the resources. We'll do that now with the SRE user and a test user.

TRY IT NOW Create the CRD for users and some user resources.

```
# deploy the CRD first:
kubectl apply -f users/crd/

# deploy the users:
kubectl apply -f users/

# print the user list:
kubectl get users
```

My output in figure 20.6 shows the user experience works well. The CRD needs to be deployed only once, and then you can add as many users as you like using simple YAML like that in listing 20.3. Now custom user objects are stored in Kubernetes, but there's no controller running, so nothing will happen yet.

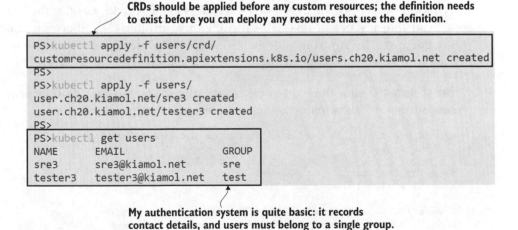

CRDs should be applied before any custom resources; the definition needs to exist before you can deploy any resources that use the definition.

```
PS>kubectl apply -f users/crd/
customresourcedefinition.apiextensions.k8s.io/users.ch20.kiamol.net created
PS>
PS>kubectl apply -f users/
user.ch20.kiamol.net/sre3 created
user.ch20.kiamol.net/tester3 created
PS>
PS>kubectl get users
NAME        EMAIL                   GROUP
sre3        sre3@kiamol.net         sre
tester3     tester3@kiamol.net      test
```

My authentication system is quite basic: it records contact details, and users must belong to a single group.

Figure 20.6 Creating the CRD and some users—this doesn't trigger anything without a controller.

Custom controllers are usually written in Go. A few packages take care of the boiler-plate wiring up that you need to do. Kubernetes API clients exist in all the major languages, though, and my user controller is written in .NET. I don't want to throw a pile of source code at you, but you should realize a couple of things about building custom controllers. Listing 20.4 is some C# code that is part of the add-user workflow (the full file is in the source code for this chapter).

Listing 20.4   UserAddedHandler.cs, using the Kubernetes API with a client library

```
// lists service accounts in a namespace, using a
// field selector to search for an account by name:
var accounts = _client.ListNamespacedServiceAccount(
        groupNamespaceName,
        fieldSelector: $"metadata.name={serviceAccountName}");

// if there's no match then we need to create the account:
if (!serviceAccounts.Items.Any())
{
  var serviceAccount = new V1ServiceAccount
  {
    // set up the spec of the service account
  };

  // create the resource:
  _client.CreateNamespacedServiceAccount(
        serviceAccount,
        groupNamespaceName);
}
```

The first thing you'll notice is that working with the Kubernetes API feels natural because all of the operations are effectively the same thing you do in kubectl but with different syntax, so writing a controller is not very difficult. The second thing is that you typically build Kubernetes resources in code, so you need to translate the YAML in your head into a series of objects—so writing a controller is cumbersome. Luckily, you've got me to do it for you, and when you deploy the user controller, it will be notified about the new users straight away, and it will run the add-user workflow.

TRY IT NOW   Deploy the custom controller, and verify that the add-user process is triggered and creates all the authentication resources.

```
# on Windows, you'll need to run this so you can decode Secrets:
. .\base64.ps1

# deploy the custom controller:
kubectl apply -f user-controller/

# wait for it to spin up:
kubectl wait --for=condition=ContainersReady pod -l app=user-controller

# check the controller logs:
kubectl logs -l app=user-controller
```

```
# print the Secret, which is the user's token:
kubectl get secret tester3-token -n kiamol-ch20-authn-test -o
    jsonpath='{.data.token}' | base64 -d
```

You see in that exercise that the controller automatically performs all the actions we did manually in section 17.3—creating a namespace for the group, creating a service account in the namespace, and requesting a new token. Actually, it does more than that, because it checks if any of those resources exist first and creates them only if it needs to. Figure 20.7 shows the outcome is a service account, which can be secured by applying RBAC rules to the group (which is the namespace), and a token, which can be distributed to the user for them to store in their kubectl context.

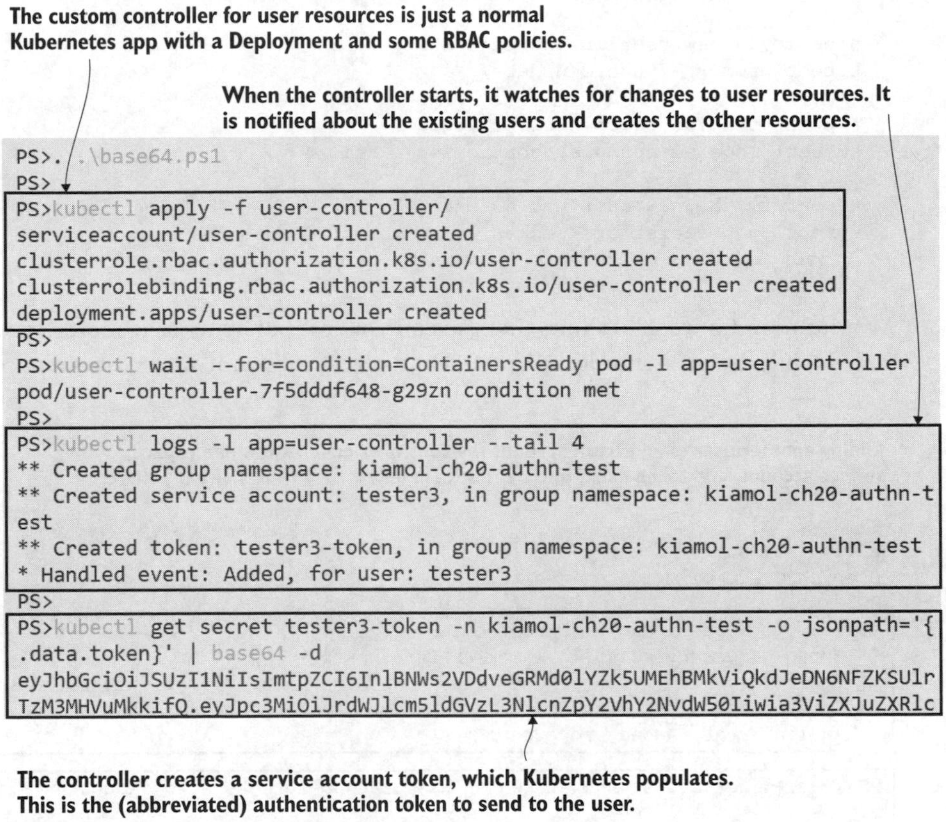

The custom controller for user resources is just a normal
Kubernetes app with a Deployment and some RBAC policies.

When the controller starts, it watches for changes to user resources. It
is notified about the existing users and creates the other resources.

```
PS>.\base64.ps1
PS>

PS>kubectl apply -f user-controller/
serviceaccount/user-controller created
clusterrole.rbac.authorization.k8s.io/user-controller created
clusterrolebinding.rbac.authorization.k8s.io/user-controller created
deployment.apps/user-controller created

PS>
PS>kubectl wait --for=condition=ContainersReady pod -l app=user-controller
pod/user-controller-7f5dddf648-g29zn condition met

PS>
PS>kubectl logs -l app=user-controller --tail 4
** Created group namespace: kiamol-ch20-authn-test
** Created service account: tester3, in group namespace: kiamol-ch20-authn-t
est
** Created token: tester3-token, in group namespace: kiamol-ch20-authn-test
* Handled event: Added, for user: tester3

PS>
PS>kubectl get secret tester3-token -n kiamol-ch20-authn-test -o jsonpath='{
.data.token}' | base64 -d
eyJhbGciOiJSUzI1NiIsImtpZCI6InlBNWs2VDdveGRMd0lYZk5UMEhBMkViQkdJeDN6NFZKSU1r
TzM3MHVuMkkifQ.eyJpc3MiOiJrdWJlcm5ldGVzL3NlcnZpY2VhY2NvdW50Iiwia3ViZXJuZXRlc
```

The controller creates a service account token, which Kubernetes populates.
This is the (abbreviated) authentication token to send to the user.

Figure 20.7 The controller automates the onboarding process, except for distributing credentials.

Please don't use this controller as your production authentication system; it's just a quick sample of how CRDs work with custom controllers to extend your Kubernetes experience. The code doesn't deal with updates to objects, and the design allows only one group per user, but you can see that the basis for managing authentication within Kubernetes is all there. You could have a source code repository with all of your user YAMLs and group RBAC rules and deploy that as part of provisioning any new cluster.

The basic role of any controller is to implement a control loop, constantly watching for changes to objects and performing whatever tasks are needed to get the actual state of the system into the desired state specified in the object. They do that by watching resources for changes—just like using the watch parameter in kubectl. The watch is an endless loop, and it is notified when objects are created, updated, or deleted. The user controller added the users it found when it started up, and it's still running in the background, waiting for you to add another user.

TRY IT NOW   The controller is watching for new users. Create another user resource, and confirm that the controller does its stuff.

```
# deploy a new user in the same SRE group:
kubectl apply -f users/update/

# print the latest controller logs:
kubectl logs -l app=user-controller --tail 4

# confirm the new user has a token:
kubectl get secret sre4-token -n kiamol-ch20-authn-sre -o
  jsonpath='{.data.token}' | base64 -d
```

My output in figure 20.8 shows that the controller is behaving as it should; the desired state is that the user should be created as a service account with a namespace for the

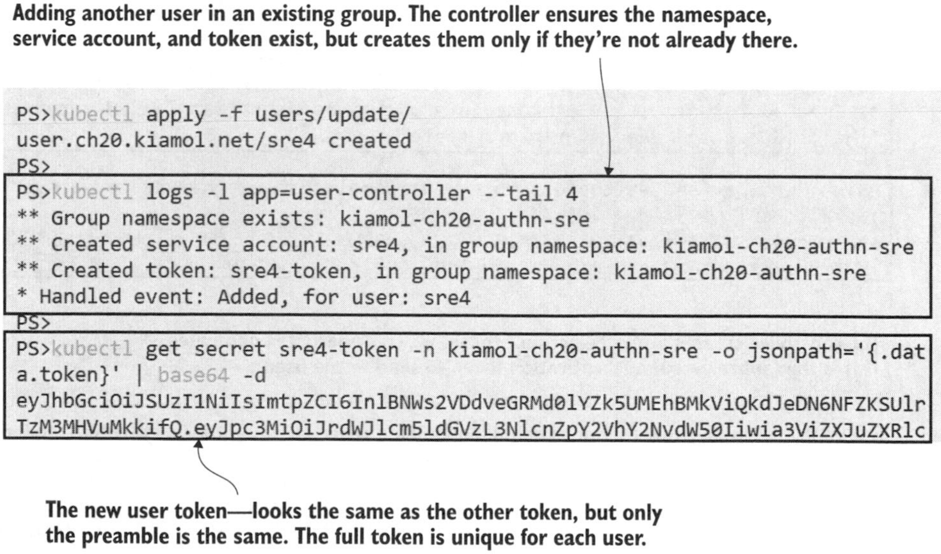

Adding another user in an existing group. The controller ensures the namespace, service account, and token exist, but creates them only if they're not already there.

```
PS>kubectl apply -f users/update/
user.ch20.kiamol.net/sre4 created
PS>
PS>kubectl logs -l app=user-controller --tail 4
** Group namespace exists: kiamol-ch20-authn-sre
** Created service account: sre4, in group namespace: kiamol-ch20-authn-sre
** Created token: sre4-token, in group namespace: kiamol-ch20-authn-sre
* Handled event: Added, for user: sre4
PS>
PS>kubectl get secret sre4-token -n kiamol-ch20-authn-sre -o jsonpath='{.dat
a.token}' | base64 -d
eyJhbGciOiJSUzI1NiIsImtpZCI6InlBNWs2VDdveGRMd0lYZk5UMEhBMkViQkdJeDN6NFZKSUlr
TzM3MHVuMkkifQ.eyJpc3MiOiJrdWJlcm5ldGVzL3NlcnZpY2VhY2NvdW50Iiwia3ViZXJuZXRlc
```

The new user token—looks the same as the other token, but only the preamble is the same. The full token is unique for each user.

Figure 20.8   The declarative desired-state approach should be used in custom controllers.

group. The namespace already exists, so the controller doesn't need to do anything there; it just creates the service account and token. Custom controllers need to work on the same principle as standard controllers: they get to the desired state no matter what the initial state is.

Custom controllers also need to own the cleanup logic, because there's a disconnect between creating a custom resource and seeing a whole bunch of extra resources being created. This is one concern with extending Kubernetes—your controller code needs to be solid to make sure any failures don't leave objects lying around that the cluster admin isn't expecting. That's particularly important for any sensitive data stored in Secrets, like the tokens created for users.

> **TRY IT NOW**   Delete the test user. Now there are no users in the group, so the namespace should be removed, too.

```
# check the authentication namespaces:
kubectl get ns -l kiamol=ch20

# delete the test user:
kubectl delete user tester3

# print the controller logs:
kubectl logs -l app=user-controller --tail 3

# confirm the tester namespace has been removed:
kubectl get ns -l kiamol=ch20
```

You can see in figure 20.9 that the controller doesn't explicitly delete the Secret, but this type of Secret is deleted by Kubernetes anyway when the service account is deleted.

Deleting a user triggers the removal process in the controller.

The service account is deleted, and then there are no more accounts in the namespace for the group, so it is deleted, too.

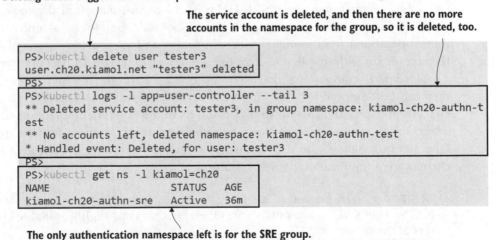

The only authentication namespace left is for the SRE group.

Figure 20.9   Controllers are notified when objects are removed so they can clean up the resources they created.

The controller does check to see if there are any more users in the group, and if not, it deletes the namespace. Woe betide you if you added any other resources in that namespace—they'll be gone now.

Custom resources are a powerful way to extend Kubernetes, especially for use cases like this where you want to provide a higher-level abstraction over stock Kubernetes objects. But those objects are just normal resources in the cluster, and your controller code needs to allow for admins coming along and deleting them, without realizing they're managed by a controller. The user controller should also watch Secrets, service accounts, and namespaces to recreate anything that is deleted outside of the controller process.

More sophisticated controllers might deploy their own RBAC rules to limit interference and would support running across multiple Pods for high availability. If you want to explore a production-grade example of CRDs and custom controllers, the cert-manager project (https://cert-manager.io) is a great example. It's a CNCF project that adds TLS certificate management to Kubernetes and can request certificates and apply them to your web apps. The next level of sophistication comes with the Operator pattern.

20.3   *Using Operators to manage third-party components*

Operators use custom resources and controllers to provide full life cycle management for an application. They're used for complex apps where a lot of operational tasks are beyond the standard Kubernetes feature set. Stateful apps are a good example—if you decide to run a database in Kubernetes, then upgrading the database server might mean putting the database into read-only mode and making a backup before the upgrade.

You can't express requirements like that with standard Kubernetes resources; you can achieve something like it with Helm install hooks, but often the logic is quite involved, and you need more control. The goal of the Operator is to implement all of those operational requirements with controllers and custom resources, abstracting the complexity with simple resources like a database object and a backup object.

Third-party components that your app relies on are much easier to work with if they can be deployed with an Operator, because it gives you an as-a-service experience, where you can focus on your app and leave the dependencies to manage themselves. In this section, we'll deploy a modified version of the to-do list web app, using Operators to manage the dependencies: a database and a message queue for asynchronous communication between components.

> **TRY IT NOW**   This version of the to-do app uses a message queue server called NATS. The NATS team publish an Operator that runs highly available clusters of queue servers.

```
# deploy the CRDs and RBAC rules for the Operator:
kubectl apply -f nats/operator/00-prereqs.yaml
```

```
# deploy the Operator itself:
kubectl apply -f nats/operator/10-deployment.yaml

# wait for it to spin up:
kubectl wait --for=condition=ContainersReady pod -l name=nats-operator

# list the CRDs to see the new NATS types:
kubectl get crd
```

NATS is a message queue that acts as a go-between for application components, so they communicate by passing messages instead of connecting to each other directly. It's a powerful and very capable technology (another CNCF project), but in a production environment, it needs to be set up carefully for high availability to make sure messages don't get lost. No one knows how to do that better than the NATS team, and they provide the Operator you've just deployed. As you see in figure 20.10, it adds a CRD for a NatsCluster object, which you can use to deploy a distributed message queue.

The NATS operator is distributed on GitHub—I've cloned the manifests in the lab folder for this exercise. The Operator runs as a Deployment, using RBAC rules for itself and the queue servers it will create.

```
PS>kubectl apply -f nats/operator/00-prereqs.yaml
serviceaccount/nats-operator created
clusterrolebinding.rbac.authorization.k8s.io/nats-operator-binding created
clusterrole.rbac.authorization.k8s.io/nats-operator created
serviceaccount/nats-server created
clusterrole.rbac.authorization.k8s.io/nats-server created
clusterrolebinding.rbac.authorization.k8s.io/nats-server-binding created
PS>
PS>kubectl apply -f nats/operator/10-deployment.yaml
deployment.apps/nats-operator created
PS>
PS>kubectl wait --for=condition=ContainersReady pod -l name=nats-operator
pod/nats-operator-59f59c5f7f-xhdwn condition met
PS>
PS>kubectl get crd
NAME                        CREATED AT
natsclusters.nats.io        2020-07-25T19:43:47Z
natsserviceroles.nats.io    2020-07-25T19:43:47Z
users.ch20.kiamol.net       2020-07-25T18:19:40Z
```

The Operator creates new CRDs when it runs. The NatsCluster resource type is the one you use to define new queue clusters.

Figure 20.10 Operators should be simple to deploy and create all the resources they need.

The updated to-do app uses a message queue to improve performance and scalability. When users save messages in the new version, the web app sends a message to the queue and then returns to the user. Another component listens for those messages and adds the item to the database. You can scale up to hundreds of web Pods without needing to scale up the database, because the queue acts as a buffer, smoothing out any peaks in traffic. The queue becomes a critical component in the app, and listing 20.5 shows just how simple it is to deploy a production-grade queue using the NATS Operator.

> **Listing 20.5   todo-list-queue.yaml, a custom resource for a message queue**

```
apiVersion: nats.io/v1alpha2      # The CRD uses an alpha version,
kind: NatsCluster                 # but it has been stable for
metadata:                         # a few years.
  name: todo-list-queue
spec:                             # The spec defines the size of
  size: 3                         # the queue cluster and NATS version.
  version: "1.3.0"
```

The NatsCluster resource contains two fields: the number of Pods to run as queue servers you want in your highly available queue cluster and the version of NATS to use. When you deploy it, the Operator creates a Service for apps to use the queue, a Service for the instances of NATS to coordinate with each other, and a set of Pods, each running NATS and configured with a Secret to run as a highly available, distributed queue.

> **TRY IT NOW**   Create the NATS cluster resource, and confirm that the Operator creates all the queue resources.

```
# deploy the queue spec from listing 20.5:
kubectl apply -f  todo-list/msgq/

# list the queues:
kubectl get nats

# list the Pods created by the Operator:
kubectl get pods -l app=nats

# list the Services:
kubectl get svc -l app=nats

# list Secrets:
kubectl get secrets -l app=nats
```

Figure 20.11 shows my NATS cluster is already up and running. The container image is just a few megabytes in size, so Pods will start quickly, even on nodes that need to pull the image. If you describe one of the Pods, you'll see the spec uses some of the best practices you've learned from this book, like container probes and Pod priority. But the Pods are not managed by a Deployment or StatefulSet; the NATS Operator is the Pod controller, which means it can use its own approach for maintaining availability.

The Operator pattern is a loose definition; there's no Operator object in Kubernetes, and it's up to the project team to decide how to design, build, and distribute

The NatsCluster defines a highly available queue in a simple custom resource.

The NATS Operator creates Pods running a clustered queue server.

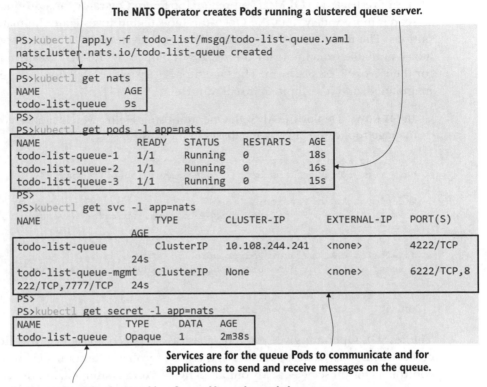

```
PS>kubectl apply -f todo-list/msgq/todo-list-queue.yaml
natscluster.nats.io/todo-list-queue created
PS>
PS>kubectl get nats
NAME                AGE
todo-list-queue     9s
PS>
PS>kubectl get pods -l app=nats
NAME                 READY   STATUS    RESTARTS   AGE
todo-list-queue-1    1/1     Running   0          18s
todo-list-queue-2    1/1     Running   0          16s
todo-list-queue-3    1/1     Running   0          15s
PS>
PS>kubectl get svc -l app=nats
NAME                    TYPE        CLUSTER-IP       EXTERNAL-IP   PORT(S)
                        AGE
todo-list-queue         ClusterIP   10.108.244.241   <none>        4222/TCP
                        24s
todo-list-queue-mgmt    ClusterIP   None             <none>        6222/TCP,8
222/TCP,7777/TCP        24s
PS>
PS>kubectl get secret -l app=nats
NAME                TYPE      DATA   AGE
todo-list-queue     Opaque    1      2m38s
```

Services are for the queue Pods to communicate and for applications to send and receive messages on the queue.

The cluster configuration is stored in a Secret. More advanced cluster specs can include authentication and authorization rules for using the queue.

Figure 20.11 Two lines of YAML in a custom resource gets you a distributed message queue.

their Operator. The NATS Operator is deployed from YAML manifests, which are released on GitHub; other projects might use Helm or a tool called the Operator Lifecycle Manager (OLM). OLM adds some consistency around Operators with a catalog to publish and distribute them, but it's one of those technologies at the fringe of the Kubernetes ecosystem that hasn't taken off so far.

You can visit the OperatorHub site (https://operatorhub.io) to see the kind of projects available through OLM. A few of them are maintained by product teams; others are published by third parties or individuals. At the time of writing, three Operators exist for the Postgres database—none of them backed by the Postgres project—and they vary wildly in capabilities and ease of use. There are no Operators for MySQL, and although there is one for MariaDB (a fork of MySQL), it's maintained by one person on GitHub—that might not be the kind of support structure you're happy with for a core component.

This is not to say that Operators are not a viable technology; it's just that the pattern isn't restricted to OLM. If you're looking for an Operator for a product, you need to search more widely than the OperatorHub site and investigate the maturity of the options. The to-do list app can use MySQL as a data store—a very good MySQL Operator is available from the team at Presslabs who operate MySQL at scale in Kubernetes for their WordPress platform. The Operator is easy to use, well documented, and well maintained, and it's simple to install with Helm.

TRY IT NOW   Deploy the MySQL Operator using Helm, which can deploy and manage replicated MySQL databases in the cluster.

```
# add the Helm repository for the Operator:
helm repo add presslabs https://presslabs.github.io/charts

# deploy a known version:
helm install mysql-operator presslabs/mysql-operator --version v0.4.0
  --atomic

# wait for the Operator Pod to spin up:
kubectl wait --for=condition=ContainersReady pod -l app=mysql-operator

# list the CRDs it installs:
kubectl get crd -l app=mysql-operator
```

The MySQL Operator gives you a database-as-a-service experience: the Helm release creates CRDs for database and database backup objects and an Operator that runs controllers for those objects. My output in figure 20.12 is snipped, but the Helm release

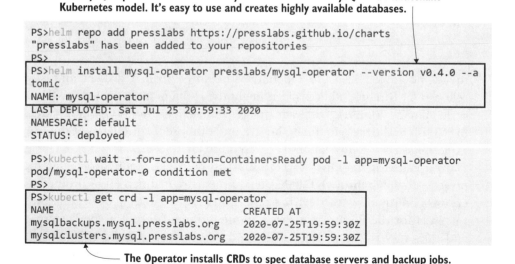

This MySQL Operator is maintained by Presslabs who run MySQL in a multitenant Kubernetes model. It's easy to use and creates highly available databases.

The Operator installs CRDs to spec database servers and backup jobs.

Figure 20.12   Complex software is easy to deploy and manage if you find a good Operator.

notes also show you how to create a database—you just need a Secret for the MySQL password and a MysqlCluster object.

You can now deploy highly available databases using a simple resource spec. Listing 20.6 shows the manifest for the to-do list database, and it also illustrates some of the limitations of custom resources. The CRD schema lets you set MySQL configuration and also customize the Pod definition the Operator generates for the database server, so you can set resource requests and limits, affinity rules, and a priority class. These Kubernetes details leak into the database object spec, so it's not purely a description of the database you need, but it's far simpler than the replicated Postgres database we set up from scratch in chapter 8.

> **Listing 20.6 todo-list-db.yaml, a replicated MySQL database using the Operator**

```
apiVersion: mysql.presslabs.org/v1alpha1
kind: MysqlCluster
metadata:
  name: todo-db
spec:
  mysqlVersion: "5.7.24"
  replicas: 2
  secretName: todo-db-secret
  podSpec:
    resources:
      limits:
        memory: 200Mi
        cpu: 200m
```

When you deploy the MysqlCluster object, the Operator creates a StatefulSet to run a replicated MySQL database and a set of Services for consumers to connect to the database. There are separate Services for the cluster as a whole and for the manager and replica nodes, so you can choose how you want your client applications to connect.

> **TRY IT NOW** Deploy the database, and confirm the expected resources are created by the Operator.

```
# create the MysqlCluster resource:
kubectl apply -f todo-list/db/

# confirm the status:
kubectl get mysql

# show the StatefulSet:
kubectl get statefulset todo-db-mysql -o wide

# show the database Services:
kubectl get svc -l app.kubernetes.io/component=database
```

You'll see when you look at the StatefulSet that the Pod runs a MySQL container and a set of sidecar containers, including the Prometheus exporter for MySQL, shown in figure 20.13. This is one of the big advantages of Operators: they model applications with best practices so you don't need to dig into the finer details yourself. If you look at the spec of one of the Pods, you'll see it has the standard Prometheus annotations we used in chapter 14, so if you have Prometheus running in your cluster, the Operator will pick up the new database Pods without any extra configuration, and you can add MySQL metrics to your dashboard.

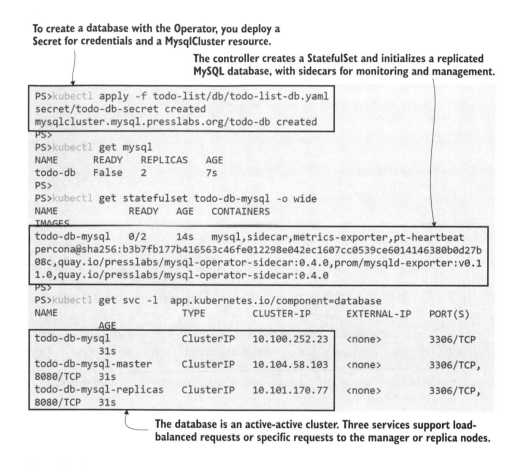

Figure 20.13   The Operator sets up an opinionated MySQL database with common best practices.

Now we have a production-grade database and message queue running, defined in just 20 lines of YAML. We could standardize on NATS and MySQL for all our apps, and the Operators would take care of multiple databases and queues. Operators are usually clusterwide, so you can still isolate application workloads in different namespaces. That's all the dependencies for the new to-do app, so we can deploy the rest of the components, the website, and the message handler, which saves data to the database.

TRY IT NOW   Deploy the application components, a website, and a message handler, which use both the queue and the database.

```
# create shared app configuration:
kubectl apply -f todo-list/config/

# deploy the web app and handler:
kubectl apply -f todo-list/save-handler/ -f todo-list/web/

# wait for the Pods to start:
kubectl wait --for=condition=ContainersReady pod -l app=todo-list

# print the app logs:
kubectl logs -l app=todo-list,component=save-handler

# browse to the app Service on port 8020, and add a new item

# print the latest logs from the message handler:
kubectl logs -l app=todo-list,component=save-handler --tail 3
```

In this exercise, you'll see the app works just the way it always has, and we've significantly reduced the amount of YAML we need to maintain, compared to our custom Postgres version. My output, shown in figure 20.14, actually hides the fact that the app doesn't quite work the way it did—now the to-do data is saved in a separate process. You'll see there's a lag between adding an item and seeing it in the list, so you'll need to refresh. Welcome to *eventual consistency*, which is a side effect of the new messaging architecture; it has nothing to do with Operators, so I'll leave you to research it, if it's a new concept for you.

It's not just ease of deployment and high availability we get from the Operators; they'll also take care of safe upgrades to the core components, and the MySQL database can be backed up to cloud storage by creating a MysqlBackup object. We won't go any further with that because we're not really running a production-grade to-do list application. In fact, the setup we have running now is probably consuming quite a lot of resources on your lab machine, so we'll clear it down before we move on.

TRY IT NOW   Remove the application, the custom resources, and the Operators.

```
# delete the app components:
kubectl delete -f todo-list/web/ -f todo-list/save-handler/ -f todo-
   list/config/

# delete the custom resources:
kubectl delete -f todo-list/db/ -f todo-list/msgq/

# uninstall the NATS Operator:
kubectl delete -f nats/operator/

# uninstall the MySQL Operator:
helm uninstall mysql-operator
```

The application manifests are simple: they focus on the app components, and dependencies are managed by Operators.

The handler connects to the queue and waits for messages.

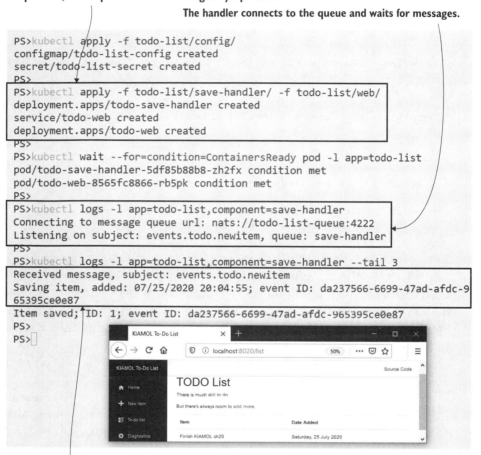

```
PS>kubectl apply -f todo-list/config/
configmap/todo-list-config created
secret/todo-list-secret created
PS>
PS>kubectl apply -f todo-list/save-handler/ -f todo-list/web/
deployment.apps/todo-save-handler created
service/todo-web created
deployment.apps/todo-web created
PS>
PS>kubectl wait --for=condition=ContainersReady pod -l app=todo-list
pod/todo-save-handler-5df85b88b8-zh2fx condition met
pod/todo-web-8565fc8866-rb5pk condition met
PS>
PS>kubectl logs -l app=todo-list,component=save-handler
Connecting to message queue url: nats://todo-list-queue:4222
Listening on subject: events.todo.newitem, queue: save-handler
PS>
PS>kubectl logs -l app=todo-list,component=save-handler --tail 3
Received message, subject: events.todo.newitem
Saving item, added: 07/25/2020 20:04:55; event ID: da237566-6699-47ad-afdc-9
65395ce0e87
Item saved; ID: 1; event ID: da237566-6699-47ad-afdc-965395ce0e87
PS>
PS>
```

The app looks the same to users, but now the save workflow goes through the message queue, which is a much more scalable architecture.

Figure 20.14   Message queues and databases are critical components, and the Operators run them with high availability.

You can see my output in figure 20.15, where uninstalling everything is just the reverse of deployment. Operators don't necessarily remove every resource they create because they might contain data you don't want to lose. Expect to see ConfigMaps, Secrets, PersistentVolumeClaims, and even CRDs hang around, even after you remove an Operator—another good reason to use separate namespaces for your apps so you can remove everything cleanly.

Removing the custom resources triggers the delete workflow in the Operators, removing all the Pods, Services, and StatefulSets.

```
PS>kubectl delete -f todo-list/web/ -f todo-list/save-handler/ -f todo-list/
config/
service "todo-web" deleted
deployment.apps "todo-web" deleted
deployment.apps "todo-save-handler" deleted
configmap "todo-list-config" deleted
secret "todo-list-secret" deleted
PS>
PS>kubectl delete -f todo-list/db/ -f todo-list/msgq/
secret "todo-db-secret" deleted
mysqlcluster.mysql.presslabs.org "todo-db" deleted
natscluster.nats.io "todo-list-queue" deleted
PS>
PS>kubectl delete -f nats/operator/
serviceaccount "nats-operator" deleted
clusterrolebinding.rbac.authorization.k8s.io "nats-operator-binding" deleted
clusterrole.rbac.authorization.k8s.io "nats-operator" deleted
serviceaccount "nats-server" deleted
clusterrole.rbac.authorization.k8s.io "nats-server" deleted
clusterrolebinding.rbac.authorization.k8s.io "nats-server-binding" deleted
deployment.apps "nats-operator" deleted
PS>
PS>helm uninstall mysql-operator
release "mysql-operator" uninstalled
```

Removing the Operators stops the controllers from running, so custom resources won't be managed, even if the Operator doesn't remove the CRD.

Figure 20.15 Operators don't necessarily clean up when they get deleted, so you'll need to manually check for leftover resources.

Operators are a neat way to manage third-party dependencies. You need to put some effort into finding an Operator that works for you, and bear in mind, many of these are open source projects that may not have a lot of momentum. Compare the Prometheus Operator (one of the best examples on OperatorHub) which has 350 contributors and new updates pretty much daily, and the MySQL Operator from Oracle, which has 18 contributors and, at the time of writing, hasn't been worked on for two years. Lots of Operators are flagged as alpha or beta software, and these are typically for critical components, so you need to be comfortable with the maturity level of anything you bring into your cluster.

But Operators are not just for third-party software; you can build your own Operator to simplify the deployment and ongoing maintenance of your own applications.

20.4   *Building Operators for your own applications*

There are two main reasons for building your own Operator. The first is for apps that have complex operational requirements, and the second is for common components that are installed as services for many projects. An Operator for the to-do app might have custom upgrade logic—updating the Service to direct traffic to an "under maintenance" page, or waiting for the message queue to be empty and then backing up the database. Any app with routine operations tasks that can be automated is a potential candidate for a custom Operator.

Building your own Operator is not a trivial task because it involves multiple custom resource types and multiple custom controllers. The complexity comes in mapping out all the scenarios, not just the workflows the Operator owns but also any additional work it needs to do to put right any interference from human operators. There's a custom Operator in this chapter's resources, but I won't focus on the code—it's an example of an as-a-service Operator for the web-ping application we used back in chapter 10. That's an app that makes GET requests to a web address on a schedule and logs the response time. At a push, I might be able to convince you that's a service many teams would use to monitor the uptime for their apps.

> **TRY IT NOW**   The web-ping Operator is deployed with YAML manifests like the NATS Operator. Install it to see how it runs and the CRDs it deploys.

```
# deploy RBAC rules and the Operator:
kubectl apply -f web-ping/operator/

# wait for it to be running:
kubectl wait --for=condition=ContainersReady pod -l app=web-ping-
    operator

# print the logs from the installer container:
kubectl logs -l app=web-ping-operator -c installer

# list new CRDs:
kubectl get crd -l operator --show-labels

# list the Pods for the Operator:
kubectl get pods -l app=web-ping-operator
```

You'll see that the Operator Pod has several roles: it installs two CRDs and runs two containers, a custom controller for each custom resource. Figure 20.16 shows that the CRDs are for a WebPinger resource, which defines the address and schedule to use, and a WebPingerArchive resource, which is for archiving the results of a WebPinger resource.

One of the goals of the Operator pattern is to keep the user experience simple, so the installation is handled inside the Operator as much as possible. That keeps the deployment spec simple and removes any potential for errors—the Operator doesn't rely on a complex manifest (with the exception of RBAC rules, which are needed in

The Operator manifest includes RBAC rules and a Deployment.

An init container in the Pod creates the CRDs.

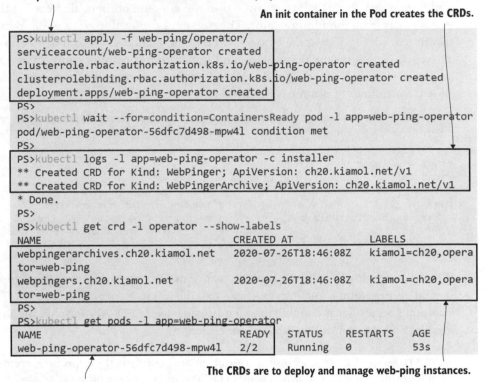

The Operator Pod runs two containers:
a custom controller for each resource type.

The CRDs are to deploy and manage web-ping instances.

Figure 20.16   The web-ping Operator has a minimal manifest and deploys other resources when it runs.

advance). The Operator spec you just deployed is shown in listing 20.7; there's an init container, which creates the CRDs, and two containers, which run the controllers.

Listing 20.7   02-wpo-deployment.yaml, the Pod spec for the Operator

```
# This is the Pod spec in the Deployment resource.
spec:
  serviceAccountName: web-ping-operator     # Uses an account set up with
  automountServiceAccountToken: true        # RBAC rules for access
  initContainers:
    - name: installer                       # Creates CRDs
      image: kiamol/ch20-wpo-installer
  containers:                               # App containers are controllers.
    - name: pinger-controller
      image: kiamol/ch20-wpo-pinger-controller
    - name: archive-controller
      image: kiamol/ch20-wpo-archive-controller
```

Not much can go wrong there. If the Operator needed ConfigMaps, Secrets, Services, and PersistentVolumeClaims, it would own the creation of them all, keeping the complexity away from the administrator. The web-ping application has a few parameters to specify the address to test, the type of HTTP request, and the interval between requests. The CRD lets users state those fields, and the custom controller running in the Operator creates a correctly configured Deployment for each instance of the app. Listing 20.8 shows a WebPinger resource configured to test my blog.

Listing 20.8   webpinger-blog.yaml, a custom resource to test a web address

```
apiVersion: "ch20.kiamol.net/v1"
kind: WebPinger
metadata:
  name: blog-sixeyed-com
spec:                               # Parameters for the app are
  target: blog.sixeyed.com          # much easier to specify in a
  method: HEAD                      # custom resource than using
  interval: "7s"                    # environment variables in a Pod.
```

When you deploy this, the Operator creates an instance of the web-ping app with a special configuration, logging responses to a file in JSON format for analysis. The Pod also includes a sidecar container, which provides an HTTP API for clearing down the log file, and that powers the archive functionality.

> **TRY IT NOW** Create a web ping resource, and confirm the Operator creates an instance of the app, which sends HTTP requests to my blog.

```
# create the custom resource:
kubectl apply -f web-ping/pingers/webpinger-blog.yaml

# print the latest logs from the Operator:
kubectl logs -l app=web-ping-operator -c pinger-controller --tail 4

# list web-ping Pods:
kubectl get po -l app=web-ping --show-labels

# print the logs from the app:
kubectl logs -l app=web-ping,target=blog.sixeyed.com -c web --tail 2

# confirm logs are also written to the JSON file:
kubectl exec deploy/wp-blog-sixeyed-com -c web -- tail /logs/web-
   ping.log -n 2
```

This is a nice and easy way to deploy simple blackbox observation of a site, and every team can include a WebPinger spec with their production deployments to keep an eye on the uptime of their app. If teams are familiar with the web-ping app, it behaves in the same way as a manual deployment with human-readable logs printing to the standard output stream. As you see in figure 20.17, the logs are also written as JSON, which is where the archive requirement comes in to protect disk space.

Creating a WebPinger resource triggers the custom controller in the
Operator, which creates a ConfigMap, Deployment, and Service.

The app runs and logs responses to the standard output stream.

```
PS>kubectl apply -f web-ping/pingers/webpinger-blog.yaml
webpinger.ch20.kiamol.net/blog-sixeyed-com created
PS>
PS>kubectl logs -l app=web-ping-operator -c pinger-controller --tail 4
** Created ConfigMap: wp-blog-sixeyed-com-config, in namespace: default
** Created Deployment: wp-blog-sixeyed-com, in namespace: default
** Created Service: wp-blog-sixeyed-com, in namespace: default
* Handled event: Added, for: blog-sixeyed-com
PS>
PS>kubectl get po -l app=web-ping --show-labels
NAME                                          READY  STATUS    RESTARTS  AGE   LA
BELS
wp-blog-sixeyed-com-5dbb59c4b6-9mmxp  2/2    Running   0         40s   ap
p=web-ping,instance=wp-blog-sixeyed-com,pod-template-hash=5dbb59c4b6,target=
blog.sixeyed.com
PS>
PS>kubectl logs -l app=web-ping,target=blog.sixeyed.com -c web --tail 2
Making request number: 28; at 1595790397497
Got response status: 200 at 1595790397941; duration: 444ms
PS>
PS>kubectl exec deploy/wp-blog-sixeyed-com -c web -- tail /logs/web-ping.log
   -n 2
{"level":"debug","message":"Making request number: 29; at 1595790404499","ti
mestamp":"2020-07-26T19:06:44.499Z"}
{"level":"debug","message":"Got response status: 200 at 1595790405097; durat
ion: 598ms","timestamp":"2020-07-26T19:06:45.097Z"}
```

The ConfigMap adds a log file output, so the app also writes logs in JSON.

Figure 20.17   The web-ping app is now easy to deploy and manage across multiple instances.

Archiving is the only operational feature provided by the web-ping Operator, and it's
simple to use: create a WebPingerArchive resource that specifies the target domain
name. The custom controller for that resource looks for a web-ping Pod that matches
the domain name and uses the API in the sidecar container to grab a snapshot of the
current log file and then clear the file down. This archive function is a good example
of the work you need to do to automate operational tasks. It's not just the CRD and
the controller; the app itself needs a sidecar to provide additional admin features.

TRY IT NOW   Test out the operational side of the web-ping app—creating an
archive of the logs for the blog requests.

```
# print the number of lines in the log file:
kubectl exec deploy/wp-blog-sixeyed-com -c web -- wc -l /logs/web-
   ping.log
```

```
# create the archive resource:
kubectl apply -f web-ping/pingers/archives/webpingerarchive-blog.yaml

# confirm that the Operator creates a Job for the archive task:
kubectl get jobs -l kiamol=ch20

# print the logs from the archive Pod:
kubectl logs -l app=web-ping-archive,target=blog.sixeyed.com --tail 2

# confirm the application log file has been cleared down:
kubectl exec deploy/wp-blog-sixeyed-com -c web -- wc -l /logs/web-
    ping.log
```

My output appears in figure 20.18. This is a contrived example, but it's a good way to
see how Operators solve complex problems without getting lost in the actual problem.
After the archive runs, the ping results are available in the Pod logs for the Job, while
the web-ping Pod is still happily chewing up my bandwidth and has an empty log file
to start filling again.

Kubernetes Operators are usually written in Go, and if you have Go, two tools take
care of a lot of the boilerplate code for you: Kubebuilder from Google and the Operator SDK, which is part of the same toolset as Operator Lifecycle Manager. My Go isn't

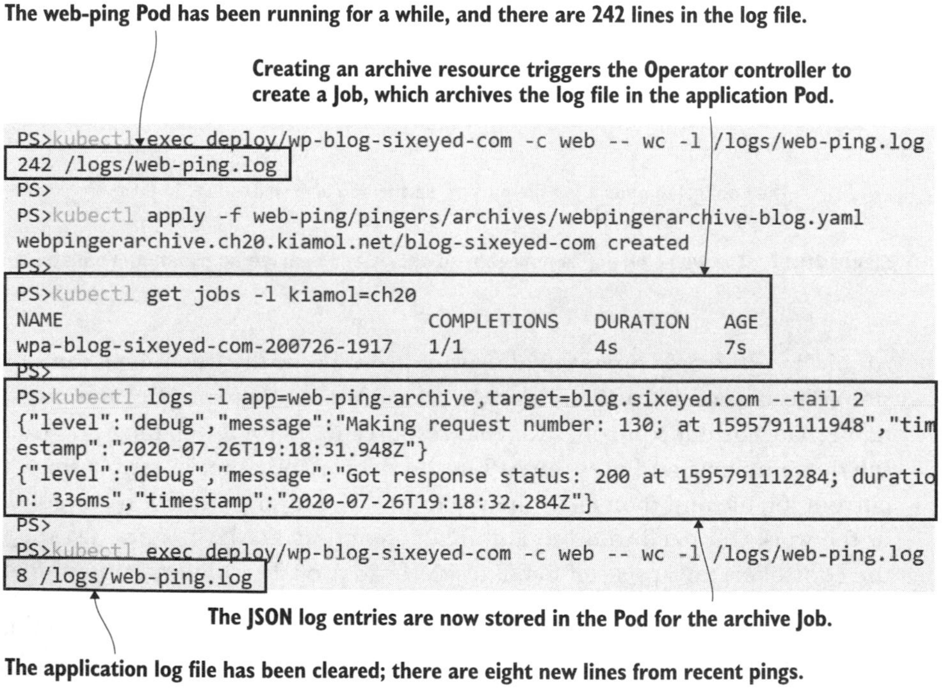

The web-ping Pod has been running for a while, and there are 242 lines in the log file.

Creating an archive resource triggers the Operator controller to
create a Job, which archives the log file in the application Pod.

```
PS>kubectl exec deploy/wp-blog-sixeyed-com -c web -- wc -l /logs/web-ping.log
242 /logs/web-ping.log
PS>
PS>kubectl apply -f web-ping/pingers/archives/webpingerarchive-blog.yaml
webpingerarchive.ch20.kiamol.net/blog-sixeyed-com created
PS>
PS>kubectl get jobs -l kiamol=ch20
NAME                                COMPLETIONS   DURATION   AGE
wpa-blog-sixeyed-com-200726-1917    1/1           4s         7s
PS>
PS>kubectl logs -l app=web-ping-archive,target=blog.sixeyed.com --tail 2
{"level":"debug","message":"Making request number: 130; at 1595791111948","tim
estamp":"2020-07-26T19:18:31.948Z"}
{"level":"debug","message":"Got response status: 200 at 1595791112284; duratio
n: 336ms","timestamp":"2020-07-26T19:18:32.284Z"}
PS>
PS>kubectl exec deploy/wp-blog-sixeyed-com -c web -- wc -l /logs/web-ping.log
8 /logs/web-ping.log
```

The JSON log entries are now stored in the Pod for the archive Job.

The application log file has been cleared; there are eight new lines from recent pings.

Figure 20.18   The archive workflow is managed by the Operator and triggered by creating another
custom resource.

really up to scratch, so my Operator is written in .NET, and it took me about a day's worth of coding to build the Operator for this section. It's good fun digging into the Kubernetes API and writing code that creates and manages resources, and building up objects in code certainly makes you appreciate YAML a whole lot more.

But it's time to stop pinging my blog. This Operator doesn't have any admission controllers to stop you from removing its CRDs, so you can delete them. That will trigger the deletion of the custom resources, and then the controllers will clean up the resources they created.

> **TRY IT NOW** Delete the Operator's CRDs. The custom resources will be deleted, triggering the removal workflows in the Operator.

```
# delete the CRDs by their labels:
kubectl delete crd -l operator=web-ping

# print the latest logs from the web-ping controller:
kubectl logs -l app=web-ping-operator -c pinger-controller --tail 4

# delete the latest logs from the archive controller:
kubectl logs -l app=web-ping-operator -c archive-controller --tail 2
```

You see in figure 20.19 that in this Operator, it's controllers all the way down. The WebPing custom controller deletes the Deployment resource, and then the system controllers delete the ReplicaSet and the Pod. The Operator doesn't try to replace or replicate Kubernetes functionality—it builds on it, using standard resources that have been used in production all around the world for many years, abstracting them to provide a simple user experience.

The Operator doesn't protect its CRDs. Deleting them deletes the custom resources.

```
PS>kubectl delete crd -l operator=web-ping
customresourcedefinition.apiextensions.k8s.io "webpingerarchives.ch20.kiamol.n
et" deleted
customresourcedefinition.apiextensions.k8s.io "webpingers.ch20.kiamol.net" del
eted
PS>
PS>kubectl logs -l app=web-ping-operator -c pinger-controller --tail 4
** Deleted Service: wp-blog-sixeyed-com, in namespace: default
** Deleted Deployment: wp-blog-sixeyed-com, in namespace: default
** Deleted ConfigMap: wp-blog-sixeyed-com-config, in namespace: default
* Handled event: Deleted, for: blog-sixeyed-com
PS>
PS>kubectl logs -l app=web-ping-operator -c archive-controller --tail 2
** Deleted Job: wpa-blog-sixeyed-com-200726-1917, in namespace: default
* Handled event: Deleted, for: blog-sixeyed-com
```

Controllers are notified of the resource deletion and remove all the resources they created.

Figure 20.19 The custom controllers in this Operator manage standard Kubernetes resources.

You need to understand how the Operator pattern works because you're sure to come across it in your Kubernetes journey, although you're more likely to use someone else's Operator than build your own. The key thing to understand is that it's a loose classification for a way of making apps simple to use and maintain, taking advantage of the extensibility of Kubernetes and making good use of the core system resources.

20.5 Understanding when to extend Kubernetes

We've covered a lot of ground in this chapter without digging too much into the detail. Extending Kubernetes is about getting the cluster to run your own code, and what happens in that code depends on the problem you're trying to solve. The patterns are generic, though, and figure 20.20 shows how all the pieces fit together with the Operator, custom resources, and custom controllers for the web-ping application.

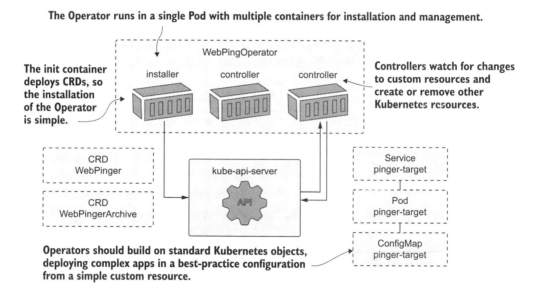

Figure 20.20   Operators and custom controllers make apps easy to manage by abstracting the complexity.

There are a few guidelines for extending Kubernetes. The first is to make sure that you really need to. Writing an Operator to save on the YAML for an app that runs a Deployment, a ConfigMap, and a Service is overkill. If your goal is to ensure the app is deployed with the proper specification, it would be better to use admission controllers. Writing and maintaining custom controllers and Operators is a chunk of work, and if you don't map out all the workflows, your app can get into an inconsistent state, and then the Operator makes maintenance harder. Admins won't enjoy manually building the spec and deploying resources that custom controllers should own.

If you do have a clear need, then start simple with CRDs and controllers, and focus on the user experience; the whole point of custom resources is to simplify complex problems. Make use of the development toolkits if you're writing in Go, and design your controllers to work with Kubernetes, building on the standard resources rather than reinventing them. It's always better to build a generic system when you have a couple of concrete examples to work from, so you know the generic approach will cover all the requirements. When you've done some complex upgrades and you know the workflows, or when you've deployed a common component multiple times and you know the variations, then it's time to design your Operator.

Third-party Operators are a great way to use somebody else's production experience to improve the reliability of your own applications. The key here is to find a good one, and that will take some investigation and experimentation with different options. Using an Operator to manage third-party components is a big dependency. You don't want to find that the project stalls and you need to reverse-engineer the Operator and take ownership yourself. The Operator Framework is the umbrella project that owns OLM and the Operator SDK, and it was added as a new CNCF project a few weeks before I wrote this chapter, so that might bring some new energy to OperatorHub.

That's all for extending Kubernetes, so we can clean up before we get to the lab.

TRY IT NOW   Clear down any remaining resources.

```
kubectl delete all,crd,secret,clusterrolebinding,clusterrole,
    serviceaccount,ns -l kiamol=ch20

kubectl delete pvc -l app=mysql-operator

kubectl delete configmap mysql-operator-leader-election
```

20.6 *Lab*

This lab will give you some experience writing a CRD and managing a custom controller. Don't worry; the controller is already written for you. In the lab folder, there's a custom resource spec for a timecheck app but no CRD, so you can't deploy it. The task is to build the CRD, deploy the controller and the resource, and verify it all works as expected. Just a couple of hints:

- The custom controller is all ready to go in the `timecheck-controller` folder.
- Your CRD names need to match the ones in the resource.
- You'll need to have a look at the logs when you deploy the controller; depending on the order in which you approach the lab, it might not work as expected.

You can check my solution on GitHub as always: https://github.com/sixeyed/kiamol/blob/master/ch20/lab/README.md.

21

Running serverless functions in Kubernetes

Welcome to the last full chapter of the book! We're going to finish on a high note, learning how to turn your Kubernetes cluster into a serverless platform. Lots of serverless platforms are in the cloud, but they're mostly bespoke systems, and you can't easily move your AWS Lambda components to Azure Functions. The extensibility of Kubernetes makes it easy to deploy a serverless runtime in the cluster, which is just as portable as all your other apps. We'll cover some open source projects in this chapter that give you a very Lambda-like experience, where you focus on the code and the platform packages and it deploys it for you. Serverless functions run as containers in Pods, so you manage them in the usual way, but the platform adds some higher-level abstractions.

Several serverless platforms exist in the Kubernetes ecosystem, and all take slightly different approaches. One of the most popular is the Knative project from Google, but it has an unusual workflow: you need to package your functions in Docker images yourself, and then Knative deploys them for you. I much prefer the code-first approach, where you bring your code and the platform runs it in a container; that fits the goal of a simple workflow for serverless functions. In this chapter, we'll use Kubeless, another popular platform, and we'll also see how to abstract the serverless platform itself with the Serverless project.

21.1 How serverless platforms work in Kubernetes

What does serverless mean in the context of Kubernetes? You obviously have servers involved because they're the nodes in your cluster. It's really about removing all the ceremony between writing code and having it running in a Pod—cutting out all the overhead in compiling the app, building a container image, designing the deployment, and crafting YAML specs. AWS Lambda and Azure Functions have a command-line interface (CLI) where you upload your code file and the function starts running somewhere in the cloud. Serverless for Kubernetes gives you the same work-flow, but you know where your function is running: in a Pod in your own cluster.

The Kubeless workflow is particularly neat: you take your source code file and deploy it as a function using the Kubeless CLI. There are no additional artifacts to describe your function, and the CLI creates a custom resource with all the details and the source code. The Kubeless controller acts on the function resource and creates a Pod to run the function. You can trigger the function manually through the CLI, or you can create a permanent trigger so the function listens for HTTP requests, sub-scribes to a message queue, or runs on a schedule. Figure 21.1 shows the architecture of a Kubeless function.

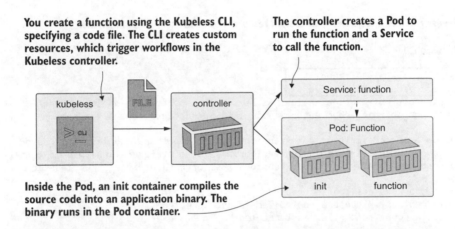

You create a function using the Kubeless CLI, specifying a code file. The CLI creates custom resources, which trigger workflows in the Kubeless controller.

The controller creates a Pod to run the function and a Service to call the function.

Inside the Pod, an init container compiles the source code into an application binary. The binary runs in the Pod container.

Figure 21.1 The serverless function with Kubeless turns your code into a running Pod.

This workflow means you run one command to get a code file running in a Pod and another command if you want to expose it over HTTP. It's perfect for webhooks, inte-gration components, and simple APIs. Other serverless platforms support Kubernetes and work in similar ways: Nuclio, OpenWhisk, and Fn Project all take your code, pack-age it into a container to run, and support multiple triggers to invoke the function. They use standard resources, like Pods and Services, and standard patterns, like ingress controllers and message queues. In this chapter, you'll use Kubeless to add new features to an existing app without changing the app itself. We'll start simple with a Hello, Kiamol example.

TRY IT NOW Start by deploying Kubeless in your cluster. There's a snapshot of the most recent release in this chapter's folder.

```
# switch to this chapter's source:
cd ch21
```

```
# deploy the CRDs and controllers:
kubectl apply -f kubeless/

# wait for the controller to start:
kubectl wait --for=condition=ContainersReady pod -l kubeless=controller
  -n kubeless

# list the CRDs:
kubectl get crd
```

You can see in figure 21.2 that Kubeless uses the techniques you learned in chapter 20: CustomResourceDefinitions for the HTTP and schedule triggers, and for serverless functions themselves. A controller monitors all those resources and turns functions into Pods, HTTP triggers into Ingress rules, and scheduled triggers into CronJobs.

Kubeless extends Kubernetes with custom resources to define serverless functions.

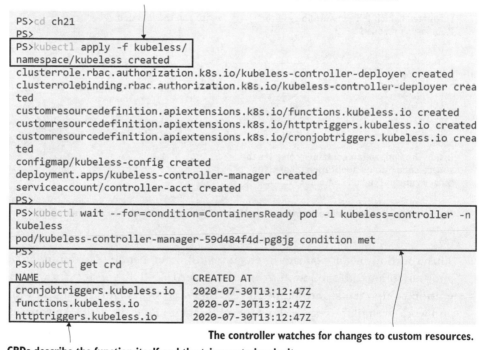

The controller watches for changes to custom resources.

CRDs describe the function itself and the triggers to invoke it.

Figure 21.2   The Kubeless architecture adds new resources to provide the serverless abstraction.

You can create Kubeless custom resources yourself, which fits neatly if your function code is all in source control and you already have a CI/CD process that uses kubectl. The Kubeless CLI is an easier option: you run simple commands, and it creates the resources for you. The CLI is a single binary you can install on macOS, Linux, or Windows. You've installed enough software already, though, so we'll run Kubeless in a Pod that has the CLI installed and kubectl configured to work with your cluster.

TRY IT NOW Run the Kubeless CLI in a Pod, and confirm it can connect to your cluster.

```
# create a Pod with the Kubeless CLI installed:
kubectl apply -f kubeless-cli.yaml

# wait for it to start:
kubectl wait --for=condition=ContainersReady pod kubeless-cli

# connect to a session in the Pod:
kubectl exec -it kubeless-cli -- sh

# print the Kubeless setup:
kubeless get-server-config

# stay connected to the Pod for the next exercise
```

Kubeless supports a lot of languages, as you see in figure 21.3, from common ones like Java, .NET, and Python, to interesting newcomers like Ballerina and Vert.x (which itself supports multiple JVM variants like Java, Kotlin, and Groovy). If any of those fit with your tech stack, you can deploy functions with Kubeless—it's a great way to evaluate new versions of your runtime or try out new languages.

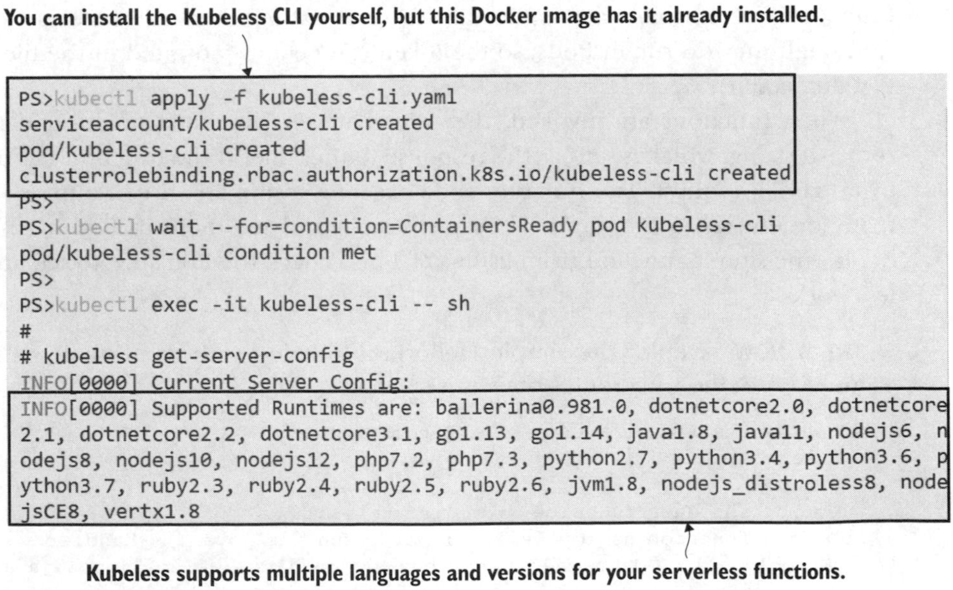

You can install the Kubeless CLI yourself, but this Docker image has it already installed.

```
PS>kubectl apply -f kubeless-cli.yaml
serviceaccount/kubeless-cli created
pod/kubeless-cli created
clusterrolebinding.rbac.authorization.k8s.io/kubeless-cli created
PS>
PS>kubectl wait --for=condition=ContainersReady pod kubeless-cli
pod/kubeless-cli condition met
PS>
PS>kubectl exec -it kubeless-cli -- sh
#
# kubeless get-server-config
INFO[0000] Current Server Config:
INFO[0000] Supported Runtimes are: ballerina0.981.0, dotnetcore2.0, dotnetcore
2.1, dotnetcore2.2, dotnetcore3.1, go1.13, go1.14, java1.8, java11, nodejs6, n
odejs8, nodejs10, nodejs12, php7.2, php7.3, python2.7, python3.4, python3.6, p
ython3.7, ruby2.3, ruby2.4, ruby2.5, ruby2.6, jvm1.8, nodejs_distroless8, node
jsCE8, vertx1.8
```

Kubeless supports multiple languages and versions for your serverless functions.

Figure 21.3 Serverless functions can be written in all the major languages with Kubeless.

Serverless functions are meant to do a single focused task, and the source code should usually be a single file, but Kubeless does let you deploy larger projects. It understands the dependency management systems for all the runtimes, and it will fetch dependencies as part of the deployment. You can upload a zip archive containing a whole project structure when you create a new function, or you can upload a single file. Listing 21.1 shows a simple hello function in Java. Don't worry about the source code too much—this example is just to show you that there's a standard approach to writing a Kubeless function, no matter what language you use.

> **Listing 21.1   hello-kiamol.java, a simple Java serverless function**

```
# the code is in a normal Java class:
public class Kiamol {

    # this is the method that Kubeless invokes:
    public String hello(io.kubeless.Event event, io.kubeless.Context context)
     {

        # it just returns a string:
        return "Hello from chapter 21!";
    }
}
```

Every function receives two fields: one with details about the event, including the type of trigger and any data sent by the caller, and one with the context of the function itself, including the runtime and the timeout set for the function to complete. There's no service account token to authenticate with the Kubernetes API server, and your functions will normally be application features rather than Kubernetes extensions (although they do run in Pods, so the token can be automounted in the filesystem if you do need it).

When functions are invoked, they do whatever they need to do, and they can return a string, which is sent as the response to the caller if the function was triggered by an HTTP request. The function code executes inside a Pod container so you can write log entries to the standard output stream and see them in Pod logs. You can deploy the simple function from listing 21.1 and check the Pod spec to see how Kubeless works.

TRY IT NOW   Deploy the simple Hello Java function with the Kubeless CLI, and look at the Kubernetes objects it creates.

```
# inside the Pod is a copy of the book's code:
cd /kiamol/ch21

# deploy the Java function from listing 21.1:
kubeless function deploy hello-kiamol --runtime java11 --handler
  Kiamol.hello --from-file functions/hello-kiamol/hello-kiamol.java

# list all functions:
kubeless function ls
```

```
# list Pods and ConfigMaps for the function:
kubectl get pods -l function=hello-kiamol
kubectl get cm -l function=hello-kiamol

# print the details, showing the build steps:
kubectl describe pod -l function=hello-kiamol | grep INFO | tail -n 5
```

Figure 21.4 ends with the logs from the init container in the Pod. Kubeless has a nice way of packaging apps without needing to build and push a container image. Every supported runtime has an init container image that has all the build tools for the runtime—in this case, it's the Java JDK and Maven for dependency management. The

Deploying a serverless function in Kubeless requires just a single command, which identifies the language runtime to use, the path to the code file, and the name of the method to call.

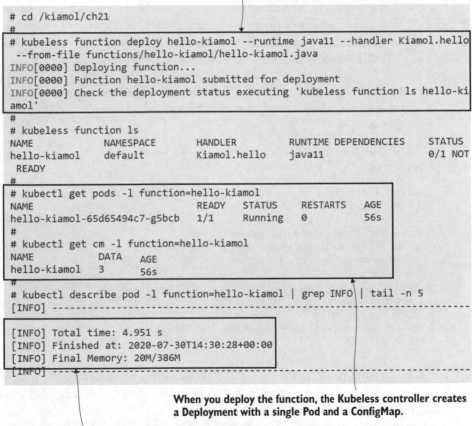

When you deploy the function, the Kubeless controller creates a Deployment with a single Pod and a ConfigMap.

The Pod container runs from a standard Java image, with an init container that compiles the code using the Java Development Kit. This output is from Maven, a Java build system.

Figure 21.4   Kubeless makes good use of init containers to compile functions without building images.

init container loads the function source code from a ConfigMap volume, builds the application, and copies the output to an `EmptyDir` volume. The app container runs from an image with the language runtime and launches the compiled application from the shared `EmptyDir` volume.

This approach means a slower startup time for functions compared to platforms that build and push an image for every function, but it removes a lot of friction for developers. It also means your cluster doesn't need to be configured with Secrets that have write permission to registries, and you don't even need to use a container runtime that can build and push images. Now you have a function running in a Pod, and you didn't need a build server or Java or Maven installed.

Function Pods have an HTTP server listening for requests. When you create a trigger, it sends requests to the Service for the Pod. You can scale and autoscale functions in the same way as standard application Pods, and requests are load-balanced by the Service in the usual way. Kubeless builds on the established Kubernetes resources and gives you an easy way to get your apps running. This function doesn't have any triggers yet, so you can't call it from outside the cluster, but you can start a proxy with kubectl and call the Service directly.

> **TRY IT NOW**   You can invoke the function with an HTTP request proxied by kubectl, or you can use the Kubeless CLI—we're still inside the Pod session for this exercise.

```
# show the Service for the function:
kubectl get svc -l function=hello-kiamol

# start a proxy to route HTTP requests to the cluster:
kubectl proxy -p 8080 &

# call the function using the proxy:
curl http://localhost:8080/api/v1/namespaces/default/services/hello-
   kiamol:http-function-port/proxy/

# but it's simpler to call it with the CLI:
kubeless function call hello-kiamol

# we're done with the Pod session for now:
exit
```

You can see in figure 21.5 that the Kubeless CLI gives you an easy way to interact with your functions, but every function is a Kubernetes app, so you can also work with it using the usual kubectl commands.

This function isn't too useful. One area where serverless functions really shine is adding new features to existing applications, without needing any changes or deployments to the main app. In the next sections, we'll use serverless functions to add some much-needed features to the beloved (or maybe not by now) to-do app.

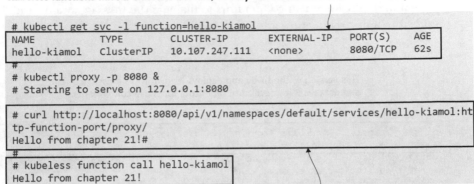

Kubeless functions have a ClusterIP Service, so they can be invoked with an HTTP request.

```
# kubectl get svc -l function=hello-kiamol
NAME          TYPE        CLUSTER-IP      EXTERNAL-IP    PORT(S)    AGE
hello-kiamol  ClusterIP   10.107.247.111  <none>         8080/TCP   62s
#
# kubectl proxy -p 8080 &
# Starting to serve on 127.0.0.1:8080

# curl http://localhost:8080/api/v1/namespaces/default/services/hello-kiamol:ht
tp-function-port/proxy/
Hello from chapter 21!#
#
# kubeless function call hello-kiamol
Hello from chapter 21!
```

You can call the function with `curl` through a kubectl proxy and see the response from the Java code.

Or you can call the function with the Kubeless CLI.

Figure 21.5   Serverless is really a deployment abstraction: Kubeless creates standard Kubernetes resources.

21.2 *Triggering functions from HTTP requests*

You learned about ingress in chapter 15. It's the usual way to route incoming requests across multiple apps running in your cluster. Ingress rules also hide the details of how a single application is put together, so different paths in the same domain name might be served by one component or by different components. You can leverage that with serverless functions to add new features that appear to be part of the main application.

We'll do that to add a new REST API for the to-do list application, building on the work we did in chapter 20. There we introduced a message queue for communication between the website and a message handler that saved new items to the database. Any component with access can post a message to the queue, so we can run a simple API in a serverless function to do that. Let's start by getting the to-do app running again.

TRY IT NOW   Deploy the to-do app using simple Deployment specs for the NATS message queue and the database.

```
# deploy all the components of the app:
kubectl apply -f todo-list/config/ -f todo-list/db/ -f todo-list/msgq/
   -f todo-list/web/ -f todo-list/save-handler/

# wait for the application Pods to start:
kubectl wait --for=condition=ContainersReady pod -l app=todo-list

# fetch the URL for the app:
kubectl get svc todo-web -o jsonpath='http://{.status.loadBalancer
   .ingress[0].*}:8021'

# browse the app to confirm it's working
```

Nothing special in figure 21.6—just the same old to-do app running. This isn't the full production deployment using Operators to manage the message queue and database, but it's the same architecture and functionality.

This version of the to-do app deploys its own NATS message queue and database; it doesn't use Operators for those components.

It's the same old app, but the messaging architecture means it will be easy to add features using serverless functions.

Figure 21.6   Serverless functions can integrate nicely with your app if it has the right architecture.

I'm going to use lots of different languages for the serverless functions in this section so you get a feel for how they work and see the similarities between runtimes. The to-do API uses Node.js, which makes use of some additional libraries to send messages to NATS. Kubeless takes care of loading dependencies in the init container when a function Pod starts; you just need to specify the dependencies in a file using the standard format for the runtime. Listing 21.2 shows the main part of the API function using the NATS library to send messages.

Listing 21.2   server.js, a serverless API in Node.js

```
# the function method receives the same event and context data:
function handler(event, context) {
```

```
# inside the function, the code builds a message:
var newItemEvent = {
  Item: {
    Item: event.data,
    DateAdded: new Date().toISOString()
  }
}

# and publishes it to the NATS queue:
nc.publish('events.todo.newitem', newItemEvent)
}
```

The Node.js function has the same structure as the Java function in listing 21.1: it receives event and context objects with details about the call. The data is the new to-do item sent by the caller, and the code builds that into a message, which it publishes to the queue. The format is the same as that the website publishes, so the message handler will receive messages from both the API and the web app and save new items to the database. Alongside the code file is a package file, which lists dependencies, so this is ready to deploy with Kubeless.

TRY IT NOW Functions with dependencies are deployed in the same way; you just need to specify the dependency file as well as the code file in the Deployment command.

```
# connect to a session in the CLI Pod:
kubectl exec -it kubeless-cli -- sh

# switch to the chapter folder:
cd /kiamol/ch21

# deploy the API function with the dependencies:
kubeless function deploy todo-api --runtime nodejs12 --handler
  server.handler --from-file functions/todo-api/server.js
  --dependencies functions/todo-api/package.json

# show the function:
kubeless function ls todo-api

# wait for the Pod to be ready:
kubectl wait --for=condition=ContainersReady pod -l function=todo-api

# call the function:
kubeless function call todo-api --data 'Finish KIAMOL ch21'

# print the function logs:
kubeless function logs todo-api | grep event

# print the message handler logs:
kubectl logs -l component=save-handler --tail 1

# leave the session, and refresh your browser
exit
```

Messaging architecture makes this sort of new functionality simple. The message handler listens for events when a new item is created and saves them to the database. It doesn't matter what the source of the event is. As shown in figure 21.7, the API function publishes a message with a random event ID, and that's the message the handler picks up. If you refresh your to-do list in the browser, you'll see the new item is there.

Functions that make use of libraries are deployed with a dependencies file. This is a Node.js app using a standard `package.json` **dependency file.**

```
PS>kubectl exec -it kubeless-cli -- sh
#
# cd /kiamol/ch21
#
# kubeless function deploy todo-api --runtime nodejs12 --handler server.handler
--from-file functions/todo-api/server.js --dependencies functions/todo-api/packa
ge.json
INFO[0000] Deploying function...
INFO[0000] Function todo-api submitted for deployment
INFO[0000] Check the deployment status executing 'kubeless function ls todo-api'

#
# kubeless function ls todo-api
NAME            NAMESPACE       HANDLER        RUNTIME       DEPENDENCIES
STATUS
todo-api        default         server.handler nodejs12      nats: 1.4.9
1/1 READY
                                                             uuid: 8.2.0

# kubectl wait --for=condition=ContainersReady pod -l function=todo-api
pod/todo-api-74984f784d-m7449 condition met
#
# kubeless function call todo-api --data 'Finish KIAMOL ch21'

# kubeless function logs todo-api | grep event
** New item published, event ID: 5409a828-6128-4a72-91ab-2278b47482ff
#
# kubectl logs -l component=save-handler --tail 1
Item saved; ID: 1; event ID: 5409a828-6128-4a72-91ab-2278b47482ff
```

Calling the function publishes a message to NATS.

The original message handler in the to-do app sees the message and creates a new item in the database.

Figure 21.7   An API for the to-do app running as a serverless function in under 20 lines of code

Serverless functions fit nicely with event-driven architectures because they can just plug into the message stream, generating or consuming different types of event. That doesn't mean messaging is a requirement, because functions can always integrate with apps at different levels. Without the message queue, the new API function could have used database integration and written a new row into the table. It's better to have higher-level integrations where you can let components own their own data, but your function code can do whatever fits with your current architecture.

Right now you have Services for the to-do web app and the API function. The next stage is to publish them both using Ingress. You can choose your URL structure when you mingle serverless functions with an existing app. In this case, I'm going to use a subdomain for the function so the app will be available at `todo.kiamol.local` and the function at `api.todo.kiamol.local`. To make that work, you'll need to deploy an ingress controller and set up some domain names in your hosts file.

TRY IT NOW Deploy an ingress controller, and add some domains to your hosts file. You'll need to run your terminal as Administrator on Windows and use sudo on Linux or macOS.

```
# run an Nginx ingress controller:
kubectl apply -f ingress-nginx/

# deploy ingress rules for the app and API:
kubectl apply -f todo-list/web/ingress/ -f functions/todo-api/ingress/

# print the ingress rules:
kubectl get ingress

# add domains to your hosts file—on Windows:
.\add-todo-to-hosts.ps1

# OR on Linux/macOS:
chmod +x ./add-todo-to-hosts.sh && ./add-todo-to-hosts.sh

# insert a new item with the API:
curl --data 'Plan KIAMOL ch22' http://api.todo.kiamol.local/todos

# browse to http://todo.kiamol.local/list
```

You'll see in that exercise that the ingress rules hide all the details about app Pods and function Pods, and consumers just use URLs, which appear to be different parts of one big application. A tiny screenshot in figure 21.8 shows two items in the list; both were added by the new API function, but they behave in the same way as if they'd been added in the website.

You can build an entire API from serverless functions using a different function for each path, but for large APIs, that's going to mean a lot of Pods, which each have their own compute requirements. Kubeless doesn't apply resource requests or limits by default, so running hundreds of function Pods is more likely to put your nodes under memory pressure than running a dozen replicas of a single API Pod. The eviction scenarios we covered in chapter 19 are more likely if you rely heavily on serverless functions, because every function will use some memory to load the language runtime.

That's not to say a serverless API isn't feasible; it just needs some additional planning. You can add a resource block to function specs if you create the custom resource

Web applications in Pods and serverless functions can be made public using Ingress rules and an ingress controller.

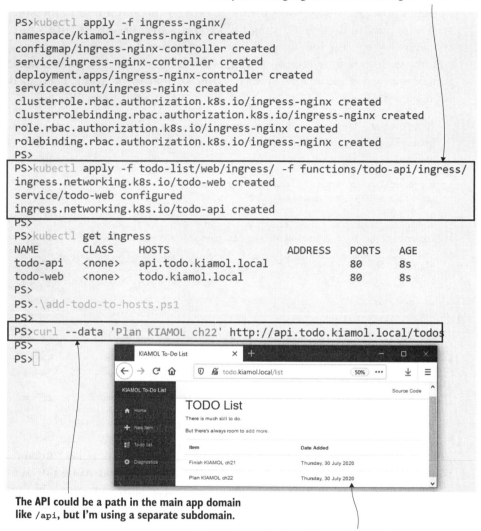

```
PS>kubectl apply -f ingress-nginx/
namespace/kiamol-ingress-nginx created
configmap/ingress-nginx-controller created
service/ingress-nginx-controller created
deployment.apps/ingress-nginx-controller created
serviceaccount/ingress-nginx created
clusterrole.rbac.authorization.k8s.io/ingress-nginx created
clusterrolebinding.rbac.authorization.k8s.io/ingress-nginx created
role.rbac.authorization.k8s.io/ingress-nginx created
rolebinding.rbac.authorization.k8s.io/ingress-nginx created
PS>
PS>kubectl apply -f todo-list/web/ingress/ -f functions/todo-api/ingress/
ingress.networking.k8s.io/todo-web created
service/todo-web configured
ingress.networking.k8s.io/todo-api created
PS>
PS>kubectl get ingress
NAME         CLASS     HOSTS                    ADDRESS     PORTS    AGE
todo-api     <none>    api.todo.kiamol.local                80       8s
todo-web     <none>    todo.kiamol.local                    80       8s
PS>
PS>.\add-todo-to-hosts.ps1
PS>
PS>curl --data 'Plan KIAMOL ch22' http://api.todo.kiamol.local/todos
PS>
PS>
```

The API could be a path in the main app domain like /api, but I'm using a separate subdomain.

Items added in the API work in the usual way.

Figure 21.8   Ingress rules hide the internal architecture, which could be one app or multiple functions.

yourself in YAML rather than using the Kubeless CLI. You'll also want to think carefully about the runtimes you use because image size affects your ability to scale quickly, and larger images provide a bigger surface area for attacks. As of Kubeless 1.0.7, the Go runtime image is under 60 MB, and the Node.js image is 10 times the size.

Now that you see how serverless functions can extend an existing application, we'll round off the to-do app with a few more features using different languages and different triggers.

21.3 *Triggering functions from events and schedules*

All serverless platforms have a similar architecture where functions can be invoked by different triggers; HTTP requests, messages arriving on a queue, and schedules are the common types of trigger. Separating the trigger from the function itself simplifies the code because the platform wires everything up for you, and you can call the same function in different ways. We can use a message queue trigger to add an auditing feature to the to-do app that logs when new items are created.

The new feature will listen for the same new-item message that the existing message handler uses to save items to the database. Queues like NATS support a publish-subscribe pattern, which means any number of subscribers can listen for the new-item messages, and they will all get a copy. Kubeless will subscribe to the queue and call the function when there are incoming events, so there's no special messaging code inside the function. The audit handler writes a log entry for every item it sees, and the function code is just the two lines of Python, shown in listing 21.3.

> **Listing 21.3   audit.py, a Python auditing function**

```
def handler(event, context):
    print(f"AUDIT @ {event['data']['Item']['DateAdded']}:
    {event['data']['Item']['Item']}")
```

There's no difference in the setup of the function; Kubeless provides the standard event and context objects, no matter what type of trigger invokes the function. The `call` command in the Kubeless CLI works in the same way, too, so you can deploy this function and verify it by sending fake data in the same format as the new-item message.

TRY IT NOW   Deploy the Python audit function, and invoke it directly with the Kubeless CLI to test it.

```
# deploy the function:
kubeless function deploy todo-audit --runtime python3.7 --handler
  audit.handler --from-file functions/todo-audit/audit.py

# wait for the function Pod to be ready:
kubectl wait --for=condition=ContainersReady pod -l function=todo-audit

# confirm the function status:
kubeless function ls todo-audit

# connect to a Kubelss CLI session:
kubectl exec -it kubeless-cli -- sh

# call the new function:
kubeless function call todo-audit --data '{"Item":{"Item":"FAKE ITEM!",
  "DateAdded":"2020-07-31T08:37:41"}}'
```

```
# print function logs:
kubeless function logs todo-audit | grep AUDIT

# leave the Pod session:
exit
```

Figure 21.9 shows this is a simple developer experience. When the function is deployed, there are no default triggers, so there's no way to invoke it except from the Kubeless CLI (or by proxying access to the function Service). Developers can quickly deploy a function and test it, iterate over the code using the `kubeless update` command, and publish a trigger to wire up the function only when they're happy with it.

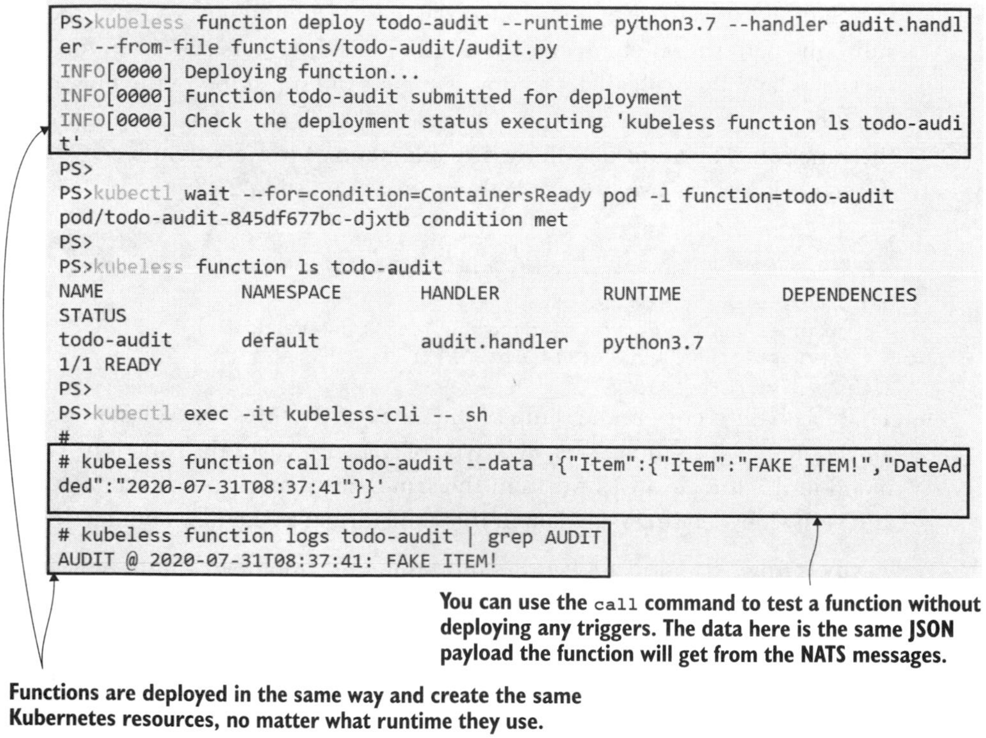

```
PS>kubeless function deploy todo-audit --runtime python3.7 --handler audit.handl
er --from-file functions/todo-audit/audit.py
INFO[0000] Deploying function...
INFO[0000] Function todo-audit submitted for deployment
INFO[0000] Check the deployment status executing 'kubeless function ls todo-audi
t'
PS>
PS>kubectl wait --for=condition=ContainersReady pod -l function=todo-audit
pod/todo-audit-845df677bc-djxtb condition met
PS>
PS>kubeless function ls todo-audit
NAME              NAMESPACE      HANDLER        RUNTIME       DEPENDENCIES
STATUS
todo-audit        default        audit.handler  python3.7
1/1 READY
PS>
PS>kubectl exec -it kubeless-cli -- sh
#
# kubeless function call todo-audit --data '{"Item":{"Item":"FAKE ITEM!","DateAd
ded":"2020-07-31T08:37:41"}}'

# kubeless function logs todo-audit | grep AUDIT
AUDIT @ 2020-07-31T08:37:41: FAKE ITEM!
```

You can use the `call` command to test a function without deploying any triggers. The data here is the same JSON payload the function will get from the NATS messages.

Functions are deployed in the same way and create the same Kubernetes resources, no matter what runtime they use.

Figure 21.9   This is the value of the serverless workflow: deployment and test with single commands.

Kubeless natively supports message triggers for the Kafka messaging system, and it has a pluggable architecture so you can add a trigger for NATS. The Kubeless project maintains that trigger (along with other plugins, like a trigger for streams of data from AWS Kinesis), and you can deploy it to create a new CRD and controller for NATS trigger resources.

TRY IT NOW   Deploy the NATS plugin for Kubeless, and add a NATS trigger to invoke the audit function when messages are published to the new-item queue.

```
# deploy the NATS trigger:
kubectl apply -f kubeless/nats-trigger/

# wait for the controller to be ready:
kubectl wait --for=condition=ContainersReady pod -l kubeless=nats-
   trigger-controller -n kubeless

# connect to a Kubeless session:
kubectl exec -it kubeless-cli -- sh

# create the trigger:
kubeless trigger nats create todo-audit --function-selector
   function=todo-audit --trigger-topic events.todo.newitem

# leave the session:
exit

# call the API function:
curl --data 'Promote DIAMOL serialization on YouTube'
   http://api.todo.kiamol.local/todos

# print the audit logs:
kubectl logs -l function=todo-audit
```

The full logs from a function Pod are quite verbose because they include entries for the HTTP requests from the container's liveness probe. My output in figure 21.10 is snipped, but you can see the new workflow in action: an item is added using the API function through its HTTP trigger, that function drops a message onto the queue, and that triggers the audit function, which writes the log entry.

This is another good example of how a flexible architecture helps you add features quickly and easily—and safely, because there's no change to the existing application. Heavily regulated industries like banking often have product backlogs that are almost entirely driven by new laws, and the ability to inject logic into existing workflows is a powerful argument for serverless. Behind the scenes, the NATS trigger controller subscribes to the event messages, and when they arrive, it invokes the function using its HTTP endpoint. That's all abstracted from the function code, which can just focus on the task.

One more example for this section will round off the main features of Kubeless: using a scheduled trigger and creating functions through YAML instead of with the CLI. The Kubeless CLI is just a wrapper that creates custom resources for you. In the `todo-mutating-handler` folder are two YAML manifests for custom resources: one for a Function and one for a CronJobTrigger. I won't echo the specs here, but if you look at the Function, you'll see it uses PHP and the source code is *inside* the custom resource spec. This approach works nicely with CI/CD pipelines because you can deploy using kubectl without needing to craft Kubeless commands.

The NATS trigger is a separate install, which adds a CRD and a new controller.

```
PS>kubectl apply -f kubeless/nats-trigger/
deployment.apps/nats-trigger-controller created
clusterrole.rbac.authorization.k8s.io/nats-controller-deployer created
clusterrolebinding.rbac.authorization.k8s.io/nats-controller-deployer created
customresourcedefinition.apiextensions.k8s.io/natstriggers.kubeless.io created
PS>
PS>kubectl wait --for=condition=ContainersReady pod -l kubeless=nats-trigger-con
troller -n kubeless
pod/nats-trigger-controller-df8995984-qt6sm condition met
PS>
PS>kubectl exec -it kubeless-cli -- sh
#
# kubeless trigger nats create todo-audit --function-selector function=todo-audi
t --trigger-topic events.todo.newitem
INFO[0000] NATS trigger todo-audit created in namespace default successfully!
#
# exit
command terminated with exit code 6
PS>
PS>curl --data 'Promote DIAMOL serialization on YouTube' http://api.todo.kiamol.
local/todos
PS>
PS>kubectl logs -l function=todo-audit
AUDIT @ 2020-07-31T08:37:41: FAKE ITEM!
AUDIT @ 2020-07-31T09:23:16.980Z: Promote DIAMOL serialization on YouTube
```

Creating a to-do item publishes a message to the queue.

The new function gets a copy of the message and writes a simple audit log. This one is about a series of videos for Manning's *Learn Docker in a Month of Lunches*, which you'll find on my YouTube channel.

Figure 21.10   Message queues decouple components; here the audit function is invoked when the API function publishes a message, without the functions communicating directly.

TRY IT NOW   Deploy the new function as a custom resource. You don't need the Kubeless CLI for this workflow, so you don't need to connect to a session in the CLI Pod.

```
# create the Kubeless resources:
kubectl apply -f functions/todo-mutating-handler/

# print all the schedule triggers:
kubectl get cronjobtriggers

# print the Kubernetes CronJobs:
kubectl get cronjobs

# wait for the Job to run:
sleep 90
```

```
# print the logs from the Job Pod:
kubectl logs -l job-name --tail 2

# refresh your to-do list in the browser
```

You'll see when you run this exercise that it adds some much-needed functionality to the to-do app to sanitize the data that comes in. The CronJob makes a function call once every minute, and the PHP script executes to clean up the data and make sure the to-do list items are useful tasks. My output appears in figure 21.11.

Kubeless functions and triggers can be created without the CLI by applying manifests with custom resources.

A scheduled trigger creates a Kubernetes CronJob that invokes the function with an HTTP request.

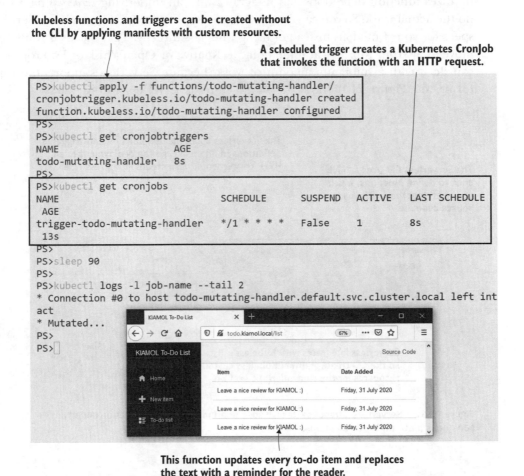

This function updates every to-do item and replaces the text with a reminder for the reader.

Figure 21.11   This handler has some unusual behavior, but it shows what you can do with functions.

Kubeless is a great way to get started with serverless and see if the functions-as-a-service model works for you. The focus on code makes Kubeless one of the better platforms for going serverless with Kubernetes, but the project hasn't been very active lately, partly because all of the main features have been stable for a while. When you bring any open source project into your organization, you need to accept the risk that it might go stale, and you'll need to spend your own engineering time helping to support it. You can mitigate that in this case by abstracting the serverless implementation using a generic project called Serverless.

21.4   *Abstracting serverless functions with Serverless*

Pay close attention to the capitalization in this section—*Serverless* is a project that standardizes function definitions and integrates with an underlying *serverless* platform to do the actual work. So you can deploy Serverless on top of Kubeless and use Serverless specs for your functions instead of using Kubeless directly. That means if you want to move away from Kubeless at some point to Knative or OpenWhisk or Fn Project, you can do it with a minimum amount of work, because Serverless supports those platforms, too. Figure 21.12 shows the architecture of Serverless with Kubeless.

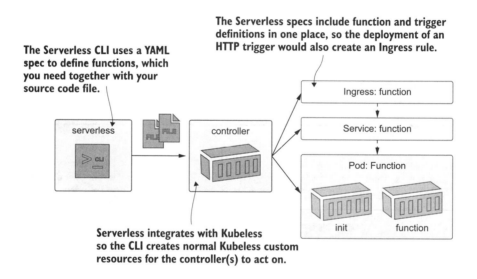

The Serverless CLI uses a YAML spec to define functions, which you need together with your source code file.

The Serverless specs include function and trigger definitions in one place, so the deployment of an HTTP trigger would also create an Ingress rule.

Serverless integrates with Kubeless so the CLI creates normal Kubeless custom resources for the controller(s) to act on.

Figure 21.12   Serverless introduces its own specification language but uses an underlying serverless platform to run functions.

Serverless isn't quite as clean as Kubeless because it adds an extra YAML specification for the function, so you can't just bring your code file and set it running. On the plus side the specification is quite simple, and it includes the function definition and the triggers in one place. Listing 21.4 shows the specification for the to-do API function. This file sits in the project folder along with the source code, and the code file itself is identical to what you deployed with Kubeless in section 21.2.

Listing 21.4   serverless.yml, a Serverless function spec

```
service: todo-api           # A service can group many functions.
provider:
  name: kubeless            # The provider is the actual platform.
  runtime: nodejs12         # You can use any runtime it supports.

  hostname: api.todo.kiamol.local   # This is used for ingress rules.

plugins:
  - serverless-kubeless
functions:                  # This is the function definition.
  todo-api:
    description: 'ToDo list - create item API'
    handler: server.handler
    events:                 # Complete with the trigger events.
      - http:
          path: /todos
```

The Serverless developer experience isn't quite as clean as Kubeless, either. Serverless uses a command-line tool, which is a Node.js package, so you need to install Node.js and then install Serverless, which downloads a ton of dependencies. I've packaged the CLI in a container image so you don't need to do that, and in this section, we'll replace the Kubeless functions with Serverless versions of the same code.

TRY IT NOW   Remove the Kubeless functions, and deploy them again using Serverless as the abstraction layer.

```
# delete the custom resources to remove functions and triggers:
kubectl delete cronjobtriggers,natstriggers,httptriggers,functions --all

# create a Pod with the Serverless CLI:
kubectl apply -f serverless-cli.yaml

# wait for it to be ready:
kubectl wait --for=condition=ContainersReady pod serverless-cli

# confirm the Serverless CLI is set up:
kubectl exec serverless-cli -- serverless --version
```

The Serverless CLI uses *providers* to adapt the generic function spec into platform components. It effectively replaces the Kubeless CLI, using the Kubeless provider and a Kubernetes client library to create custom resources, which the normal Kubeless controllers manage. Figure 21.13 shows the CLI is installed and running, but that's not quite all you need. The provider and the Kubernetes client library need to be installed in the project folder together with about 100 other dependencies.

Serverless is not a simple project, but it's extremely popular. It isn't only for serverless platforms running in Kubernetes, either. You can use it as an abstraction layer for AWS Lambda and Azure Functions, too. You can't just lift functions written for Kubeless and deploy them as Azure Functions because the platforms invoke methods in different

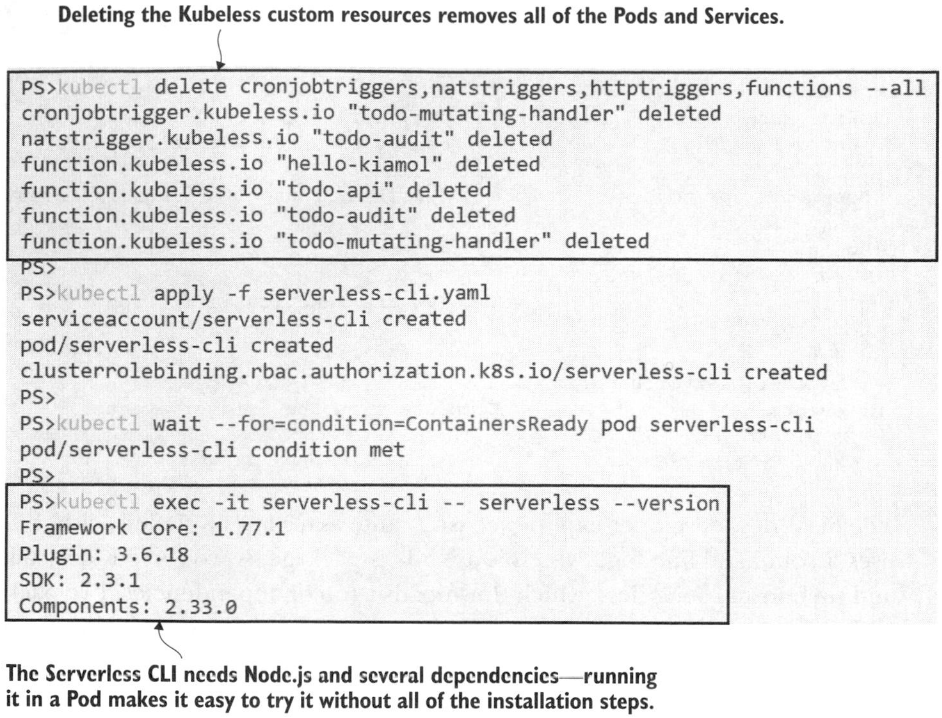

Deleting the Kubeless custom resources removes all of the Pods and Services.

```
PS>kubectl delete cronjobtriggers,natstriggers,httptriggers,functions --all
cronjobtrigger.kubeless.io "todo-mutating-handler" deleted
natstrigger.kubeless.io "todo-audit" deleted
function.kubeless.io "hello-kiamol" deleted
function.kubeless.io "todo-api" deleted
function.kubeless.io "todo-audit" deleted
function.kubeless.io "todo-mutating-handler" deleted
PS>
PS>kubectl apply -f serverless-cli.yaml
serviceaccount/serverless-cli created
pod/serverless-cli created
clusterrolebinding.rbac.authorization.k8s.io/serverless-cli created
PS>
PS>kubectl wait --for=condition=ContainersReady pod serverless-cli
pod/serverless-cli condition met
PS>
PS>kubectl exec -it serverless-cli -- serverless --version
Framework Core: 1.77.1
Plugin: 3.6.18
SDK: 2.3.1
Components: 2.33.0
```

**The Serverless CLI needs Node.js and several dependencies—running
it in a Pod makes it easy to try it without all of the installation steps.**

Figure 21.13   Serverless provides an alternative deployment experience, which will ultimately
create the same function resources with Kubeless.

ways with different parameters, but the core of the function code will be the same. Next,
we'll see how the deployment looks for the to-do API function using Serverless.

TRY IT NOW   Create the to-do API function again with the same code file but
using Serverless to define and deploy it.

```
# connect to a Serverless CLI session:
kubectl exec -it serverless-cli -- sh

# switch to the API code folder:
cd /kiamol/ch21/serverless/todo-api

# install all the deployment dependencies:
npm install

# deploy the function:
serverless deploy

# list Kubeless functions:
kubectl get functions
```

```
# confirm the Pod has been created:
kubectl get pods -l function=todo-api

# list HTTP triggers:
kubectl get httptriggers
```

You can see in figure 21.14 that the net result of installing the Serverless function using Kubeless as the provider is the same as using the Kubeless CLI or deploying custom resources directly. You must perform the setup stage for each project, but only the first time you deploy it or if you upgrade the provider, because Serverless is really just a client-side tool for deploying and managing functions.

Serverless is a client-side deployment tool: it runs on Node.js and uses libraries for the Kubeless provider and the Kubernetes API client. NPM is the Node.js package manager, which installs the libraries.

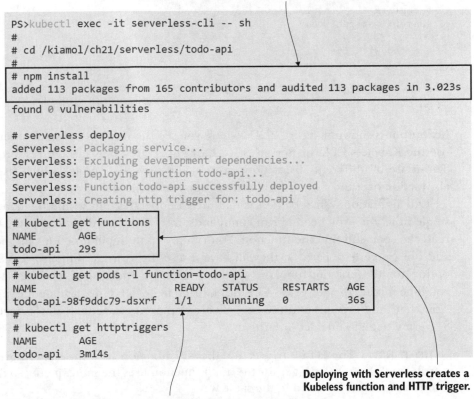

Deploying with Serverless creates a Kubeless function and HTTP trigger.

The custom resources are managed by the Kubeless controller in the usual way: the function controller creates a Pod to run the code.

Figure 21.14 Serverless is an abstraction over a serverless platform. This deployment creates a Kubeless function and trigger.

We won't deploy the mutating function because I expect you got the message in the last section, but we'll go ahead and deploy the auditing function and then confirm everything still works as expected. Serverless supports different event types to trigger functions, and the audit function spec includes a queue trigger for the NATS new-item messages.

> **TRY IT NOW**   Still in your Serverless CLI session, switch to the folder for the auditing function, and deploy it with the message queue trigger.

```
# switch to the function folder:
cd /kiamol/ch21/serverless/todo-audit

# deploy the Serverless Node.js dependencies:
npm install

# deploy the function itself:
serverless deploy

# confirm the function has been deployed:
kubectl get functions

# along with its trigger:
kubectl get natstriggers

# we're done with the CLI Pod now:
exit
```

My output is shown in figure 21.15, where you see the result is the same whether you use the Kubeless CLI, the Serverless CLI, or kubectl to apply custom resource specs. Those are all different abstractions around the serverless model, which itself is an abstraction over the standard Kubernetes application model.

One limitation with Serverless is that the CLI operates only within the context of a single function—you need to run commands in the function directory so the CLI can read the spec and find the function. You can group multiple functions in one folder and one Serverless spec, but they all have to use the same runtime, so that's not an option for the polyglot functions in this section. In practice, if you use Serverless, you'll be mixing the Serverless CLI with kubectl to get a full management experience. Now that the functions and the triggers are deployed, we actually don't need to use Serverless at all to interact with them.

> **TRY IT NOW**   The HTTP trigger for the API function uses the same ingress rule, and the NATS trigger for the audit function uses the same queue, so the end-to-end can be tested in the same way.

```
# if you're running in PowerShell, add a grep function to your session:
.\grep.ps1

# make a call to the API:
curl --data 'Sketch out volume III of the trilogy' http://api.todo
  .kiamol.local/todos
```

You need to deploy the Serverless CLI dependencies in every function folder.

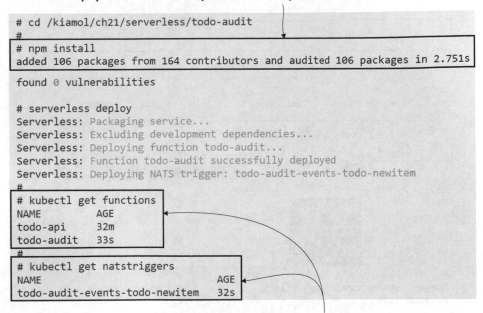

```
# cd /kiamol/ch21/serverless/todo-audit
#
# npm install
added 106 packages from 164 contributors and audited 106 packages in 2.751s

found 0 vulnerabilities

# serverless deploy
Serverless: Packaging service...
Serverless: Excluding development dependencies...
Serverless: Deploying function todo-audit...
Serverless: Function todo-audit successfully deployed
Serverless: Deploying NATS trigger: todo-audit-events-todo-newitem
#
# kubectl get functions
NAME          AGE
todo-api      32m
todo-audit    33s
#
# kubectl get natstriggers
NAME                             AGE
todo-audit-events-todo-newitem   32s
```

The Serverless spec in this folder deploys the Python audit function and the NATS trigger. The output is the same as with the Kubeless CLI.

Figure 21.15 Functions with different types of trigger are defined in the Serverless YAML spec and deployed in the same way,

```
# print the latest logs from the message handler:
kubectl logs -l component=save-handler --tail 2

# print the audit function:
kubectl logs -l function=todo-audit | grep AUDIT
```

It will be clear from this exercise and from figure 21.16 that Kubeless and Serverless layer on abstractions at the build and deploy stages, but they don't need to be used in the run stage. Functions can be delivered from single code files without a complex CI/CD pipeline and even without a container image build. The deployed components are just standard Kubernetes resources, which you can manage in the usual way. If you have centralized logging and monitoring set up in your cluster, your serverless functions integrate with them in the same way as your other applications.

That's as far as we'll go with serverless (and Serverless). It's a useful architecture, and it's good to have some experience using it with Kubernetes so you can understand how the transition from code to Pod works.

The Serverless spec for the API function uses the same host domain for the Ingress rule.

```
PS>curl --data 'Sketch out volume III of the trilogy' http://api.todo.kiamol.loc
al/todos
PS>
PS>kubectl logs -l component=save-handler --tail 2
Saving item, added: 07/31/2020 15:39:55; event ID: 71f76433-5e52-4040-bc8e-2c367
007b0b2
Item saved; ID: 5; event ID: 71f76433-5e52-4040-bc8e-2c367007b0b2
PS>
PS>kubectl logs -l function=todo-audit | grep AUDIT

AUDIT @ 2020-07-31T15:39:55.539Z: Sketch out volume III of the trilogy
```

The new item message is recorded by the audit function.

And the item is shown in the web app in the usual list.

Figure 21.16   The functions deployed with Serverless behave in the same way with the Kubeless provider.

21.5   *Understanding where serverless functions fit*

The promise of a cloud-based serverless platform is that you bring your code and you forget about the operations side—deployment is simple, and the platform keeps your code running and scales up and down with demand without any engagement from you. It's compelling for a lot of use cases, but it has the major disadvantage that the serverless components of your app are different from all the other components. The processes around serverless are minimal, but they're still needed, which leaves you with deployment pipelines, monitoring tools, and troubleshooting workflows that are different from all your other apps.

That's where serverless on Kubernetes comes in. It's a compromise because you don't get the zero-ops promise of a cloud serverless platform, and you don't get to scale at will because you need to balance compute resources with your other apps. But as you've seen in this chapter, you do get the slick developer workflow, and you do get to manage your serverless functions in the same way as your other Kubernetes deployments. It may not be something you bring into your cluster on day 2, but it's a powerful tool to have as an option.

Which just leaves the question: which tool, exactly? As of 2021, no serverless projects are under the CNCF, and the options I've mentioned in this chapter are a mixture of open source and commercial projects with pretty varied adoption and activity rates. Kubeless and Knative are the major options right now, and it's worth evaluating both, bearing in mind that the Serverless project is useful for isolating you from the underlying platform, at the cost of taking on more YAML specs. The CNCF ran a serverless working group, which morphed into CloudEvents, a generic specification for events that trigger functions and the structure of their data, which is bringing standardization to serverless platforms.

And that brings us to the end, so all that's left is to tidy up and try the lab.

TRY IT NOW Remove the Kubeless components, which will remove all the running functions, and then clean up the rest of the deployments.

```
kubectl delete -f kubeless/

kubectl delete ns,all,secret,configmap,pvc,ingress -l kiamol=ch21
```

21.6 *Lab*

I've mentioned Knative a few times in this chapter, and now it's your turn to try it out. Your task is to deploy a Knative version of the to-do list API, which is available at the same URL you used in section 21.4. The Docker image is already built, but an experienced Kubernetes user like you won't need many hints. This is your chance to navigate the Knative documentation and see if you prefer the approach to Kubeless.

- The image for your API is called `kiamol/ch21-todo-api`. You can create it as a Knative function using the Knative CLI or with a custom resource definition.
- The lab folder contains a Knative deployment and a new release of the to-do app.
- This Knative setup uses a CNCF project called Contour as the ingress controller. The IP address to access your apps is in the `envoy` Service in the `contour-external` namespace.
- Knative uses the name of the Knative Service and the Kubernetes namespace to build the ingress domain name, so you'll need to be careful how you deploy your function.

Quite a few hints actually. This one may take some investigating, but don't be disheartened—the solution is straightforward, although you'll have to align a lot of stars to get the function running as you expect. My solution is on GitHub: https://github.com/sixeyed/kiamol/blob/master/ch21/lab/README.md.

Never the end

Books in the *Month of Lunches* series traditionally finish with a chapter called "Never the end," to highlight that there's always more to learn. I think that's truer of Kubernetes than any other technology; this book turned out to be about 25% bigger than I originally intended, and still I didn't even mention every topic. I've tried to cover everything I consider important for you to have an authentic experience of using Kubernetes, and in this chapter, I'll highlight some things I didn't have time for so you can go on to explore further. I've also got some guidance on choosing a Kubernetes platform and an introduction to the community.

22.1 Further reading by chapter

The main sources of further reading are the official Kubernetes website (https://kubernetes.io), which contains documentation and guides, and the API Reference (https://kubernetes.io/docs/reference/generated/kubernetes-api/v1.20/), which has detailed descriptions of all the resources and their specifications. Those are good places to fill in some gaps from this book—and they're also the only resources you can use during the exams if you go for Kubernetes certification. As I planned each chapter, I found a topic or two that I didn't have room to include, and if you're looking to go further, here are some of the things we skipped:

- Chapter 2 introduced the YAML spec we used in every other chapter, but I didn't cover *Kustomize*. That's a tool that simplifies YAML specs. You can have a base set of specs and a set of overlays, which vary the configuration for different environments. It's powerful but simpler than the full templating experience in Helm.

- Chapter 3 introduced networking and the Service resource. A new extension called *Service Topology* gives you much finer control over load balancing between Pods. You can specify that a network connection should use a Pod on the same node as the client, or a node in the same region, to reduce network latency.

- Chapter 4 covered configuration in pretty exhaustive detail, but I skipped *projected volumes*, which are a useful way of surfacing multiple ConfigMaps and Secrets into one directory in the container filesystem—good if you want to store configuration items independently for an app that needs to see them all in the same place.

- Chapter 5 missed out on all the platform-specific volume types, which are the ones you really need to understand in production. The concepts are the same—you create a PVC and bind your Pod to it—but the underlying storage system makes a big difference. As an example, the Azure Kubernetes Service supports volumes using Azure Files or Azure Disks. Files are easier to share between nodes, but Disks offer better performance.

- Chapter 6 showed how scaling works for Deployments and DaemonSets, running many replicas of the same Pod spec. Scaling up means running more Pods, which go into the pending state to be allocated to a node by the scheduler. You can use the affinity and antiaffinity rules you learned in chapter 19 to control replica placement.

- Chapter 7 introduced multicontainer Pods. There's a new type called *ephemeral containers*, which is especially useful for debugging; it lets you run a temporary container inside an existing Pod. Ephemeral containers share the network space of the Pod and can share volumes and processes so they're great for investigating problems, particularly if your app container uses a minimal Docker image without tools like `curl` (which it should).

- Chapter 8 looked at creating a stable environment for apps with StatefulSets. In some cases, you'll want consistent Pod naming without the startup order guarantee, so Pods can start in parallel. The *Pod management policy* in the spec allows for that.

- Chapter 9 walked through rollouts and rollbacks, but you'll also want to understand *Pod disruption budgets* (PDBs). Those are separate objects that ensure a minimum number of Pods are kept available, which is an important safety control for cluster or deployment issues. PDBs take precedence over other actions, so you can't drain a node if removing its Pods would violate a PDB.

- Chapter 10 gave you an introduction to Helm with the main features covered, but an awful lot was left out. The templating language in Helm supports control flow with if and else statements and loops. You can create named templates and segments and use them multiple times in your charts, which makes complex app designs or deployment options simpler to manage.

- Chapter 11 introduced some CI/CD patterns in Kubernetes but didn't mention *GitOps*, which is an attractive new approach where the cluster watches Git repositories to check for application releases. When a release is created, the cluster deploys it automatically, so instead of an administrator having access to the cluster for app management, the cluster updates apps itself. Argo CD is the CNCF project for GitOps.

- Chapter 12 covered self-healing apps and resource limits but didn't get to *Quality of Service classes*, which is how Kubernetes provides service guarantees to Pods based on their resource specs. The classes are BestEffort, Burstable, and Guaranteed, and you should understand how they work because they affect Pod eviction.

- Chapter 13 showed you how to collect, forward, and store log entries from Pods. That includes Kubernetes components that run in Pods, like the API server and DNS plugin, but you'll also want to collect logs from the kubelet and the container runtime. How to do that is platform-dependent, but it's important get those logs into your centralized logging system too.

- Chapter 14 introduced Prometheus with a quick tour of exporters and client libraries. The Prometheus deployment was a simple one, and you should take the time to understand the *Prometheus Operator*. It's a production-grade deployment, which adds CRDs for Prometheus and Alertmanager instances and for scrape targets and alerting rules.

- Chapter 15 used Nginx and Traefik as examples of ingress controllers. You should add *Contour* to your list if you're evaluating options. It's a CNCF project that uses Envoy as the underlying proxy—a very fast and feature-rich technology.

- Chapter 16 looked at lots of security options but didn't include the *PodSecurityPolicy* resource, which lets you define rules Pods must adhere to before the cluster will run them. PodSecurityPolicies use an admission controller to block Pods that don't meet the policies you define, and they're a powerful security control, but it's a new feature and isn't available in every platform.

- Chapter 17 on RBAC didn't cover *service account projection*, which is a way for Pod specs to request a custom token with a stated expiration time and audience for the JWT. If you need a token only for an init container, you can request one that will expire after initialization. You'll also want to understand how the Kubernetes API server audits requests, and there's a useful tool on GitHub called *audit2rbac*, which can generate RBAC rules from an audit log.

- Chapter 18 gave you a flavor of installing and managing your own multinode cluster, but there is much more to understand if you plan to do that for real. *Rancher Kubernetes Engine* (RKE) is an open source product from Rancher that simplifies the installation and management of on-premises clusters. If you're looking at a hybrid environment, you can have your on-premises clusters managed in the cloud using services like *Azure Arc*.

- Chapter 19 introduced the HorizontalPodAutoscaler, but there are two other types of auto-scale. The *VerticalPodAutoscaler* is an add-on from the Kubernetes project that manages resources requests and limits based on actual usage, so

Pods scale up or down, and the cluster has an accurate resource view. *Cluster autoscaling* monitors the scheduler. If there are not enough compute resources to run pending Pods, it adds a new node in the cluster. Cloud providers typically provide cluster autoscaling.

- Chapter 20 missed an alternative option for extending Kubernetes—*API aggregation*. CRDs add new resource types to the standard API, but the aggregation layer lets you plug whole new types of functionality into the API server. It's not commonly used, but it lets you add new capabilities to your cluster, which are authenticated by Kubernetes.

- Chapter 21 introduced lots of serverless platform options, but there's another take on serverless—scaling down to zero when there's no work to be done. A CNCF project called *KEDA* (Kubernetes Event-Driven Autoscaling) covers that. It monitors event sources like message queues or Prometheus metrics and scales existing applications up or down based on incoming load. It's a nice alternative to full serverless if you want the automatic management with your existing workflow.

And I didn't mention the Kubernetes *Dashboard*. That's a web UI you run in the cluster that shows you a graphical view of your workloads and their health. You can also deploy applications and edit existing resources with the Dashboard, so if you use it, you need to be mindful of your RBAC rules and who has access to the UI.

It's up to you how much more you feel you need to dig into those additional topics. They don't feature in the book because they're not core to your Kubernetes experience, or they use new features that don't have widespread adoption. However far you decide to go, your next real task is to understand which Kubernetes platform you're going to use.

22.2 *Choosing a Kubernetes platform*

Kubernetes has a certification process for distributions and hosted platforms. If you're evaluating a platform, you should start with the certified list, which you can find on the CNCF landscape website (https://landscape.cncf.io/). Kubernetes is particularly well suited to cloud environments where you can spin up a cluster in minutes that is nicely integrated with other services from the provider. At a minimum, you should expect the following feature set, which you'll find in all the major clouds:

- Integration with LoadBalancer Services, so they're provisioned with a cloud load balancer, which spans the cluster nodes and a public IP address
- Multiple storage classes with options like SMB and SSD, so you can choose between IO performance and availability in your PersistentVolumeClaims
- Secret storage, so Secrets deployed to the cluster are actually created in a secure encrypted service, but are still accessible with the usual Secrets API
- Cluster autoscaling, so you can set minimum and maximum cluster sizes and have nodes added or removed to meet demand as your Pods scale

- Multiple authentication options, so end users can access the cluster using their cloud credentials but you can also provision access for automation systems

Your choice of cloud provider will probably be made for you if your organization has an existing relationship with one of the providers. Azure Kubernetes Service, Amazon's Elastic Kubernetes Service, and Google Kubernetes Engine are all great options. If you do have a choice, you should also consider how quickly the platform rolls out new Kubernetes versions and just how managed the service is—are the nodes fully managed, or do you need to roll out operating system patches?

When you settle on a hosted platform, you're going to need to spend some time learning how the rest of the cloud features are integrated with Kubernetes. Annotations in object metadata are often used as a bridge to include configuration settings for the cloud service that are outside the standard Kubernetes model. It's a useful way of configuring your deployments so you get exactly what you want, but you need to be aware that any customizations reduce the portability of your apps.

The situation is slightly different for on-premises deployments. You still have the certification process, and many products deliver a stock Kubernetes cluster with a bespoke management experience and a support team. Others wrap Kubernetes in their own tooling and modeling—OpenShift does that in a big way, using its own resource definitions for runtime and network abstractions and even using an alternative CLI. A wrapped distribution may offer features or processes you prefer to vanilla Kubernetes, which could make it a good choice as long as you're aware that it isn't just Kubernetes, and it may be difficult to move your apps to another platform.

Running your own open source Kubernetes cluster is definitely an option, one that is favored by startups or organizations with a large data center estate. If you're considering that route, you need to understand just how much you're taking on. Get everyone in your ops team a copy of this book, and then ask them to go on to study and pass the Certified Kubernetes Administrator exam. If they're still keen on running a cluster, go for it, but be aware that their roles are likely to transition to full-time Kubernetes administrators. It's not just a case of administering the cluster but also keeping up with the Kubernetes project itself.

22.3   *Understanding how Kubernetes is built*

Kubernetes has a quarterly release schedule, so every three months, new features are available, beta features graduate to general availability, and old features are deprecated. These are minor version updates—say, from 1.17 to 1.18. The major version is still 1, and there are no plans to jump to version 2 anytime soon. The three most recent minor versions are supported by the project, which means you should plan to upgrade your cluster at least twice a year. Patch releases occur whenever critical bugs or security issues require them; as an example, the 1.18.6 release fixed an issue where containers could fill a node's disk without triggering eviction.

Releases are all on GitHub in the `kubernetes/kubernetes` repository, and every release comes with an extensive change log. Whether you're running your own cluster or using a hosted platform, you need to know what's coming in a release before you upgrade because there are sometimes breaking changes. As features move through alpha and beta stages, the API version in the spec changes, and eventually old versions are not supported. If you have Deployment specs that use the `apps/v1beta2` API versions, you can't deploy them on Kubernetes from 1.16—you need to change the spec to use the `apps/v1` version.

Special interest groups (SIGs) own different aspects of the Kubernetes project covering releases, technical topics, and process—everything from authentication to contributor experience and Windows workloads. SIGs are public; they have regular online meetings that anyone can drop into, they have dedicated Slack channels, and all of their decisions are documented on GitHub. A technical SIG covers a wide area and is split into subprojects, which own the design and delivery of one component of Kubernetes. Overall, the Steering Committee owns the governance of the project, and committee members are elected for a two-year term.

The open structure of Kubernetes drives innovation and quality. The governance model ensures individual organizations don't have an unfair representation so they can't steer road maps in directions that suit their products. Ultimately, Kubernetes itself is stewarded by the CNCF, which is chartered to promote the technology, protect the brand, and serve the community.

22.4 *Joining the community*

That community includes you and me. If you want to see how the project evolves, the best way to start is by joining Slack at kubernetes.slack.com (you'll find me there). Every SIG has its own channel so you can follow the areas you're interested in, and general channels exist for release announcements, users, and novices. There are meetup groups all over the world with regular events, and the combined KubeCon and CloudNative-Con conferences are regional in Europe, America, and Asia. All of the Kubernetes code and documentation is open source, and you can contribute on GitHub.

And that's all from me. Thank you for reading this book, and I hope it's helped you to become comfortable and confident with Kubernetes. It can be a career-changing technology, and I hope everything you've learned here will help you on your journey.

index

Symbols

:latest tag 258

A

access-matrix plugin 442
ACR (Azure Container Registry) 271
adapter containers, applying consistency
    with 162–166
adapters 162
admission control 398
affinity and antiaffinity, directing Pod placement
    with 477–484
AKS (Azure Kubernetes Service) 5
ambassador containers, abstracting connections
    with 167–171
API aggregation 559
API server 449
APOD (Astronomy Photo of the Day) 337,
    386
app label 24, 205, 407
application manifests, defining Deployments
    in 28–32
applications
    configuring 65–91
    data-heavy 176–200
    extending 149–175
    release management 201–227
    scaling 122–146
    securing 385–414
    self-healing 283–309
apply command 29–30, 74, 81, 90
arch label 476
as parameter 422
atomic flag 250

audit2rbac tool 558
automatic scaling, controlling capacity with
    484–491
automountServiceAccountToken field 401
AWS, running single-node Kubernetes cluster
    in 12–13
Azure Container Registry (ACR) 271
Azure Kubernetes Service (AKS) 5
Azure, running single-node Kubernetes cluster
    in 12

B

beta.kubernetes.io label 477
buildkitd command 274

C

CA (certificate authority) 378, 400
cAdvisor 349
can-i command 425, 441
canonical names (CNAMEs) 55
cascade option 142
certificate authority (CA) 378, 400
Certified Kubernetes Administrator (CKA) 8
Certified Kubernetes Application Developer
    (CKAD) 8
charts, modeling dependencies in 243–247
Chart.yaml file 235
CI/CD (continuous integration/continuous
    delivery) workflow 255–279
    continuous delivery in Kubernetes without
        Docker 271–276
    Docker developer workflow 255–259
    evaluating developer workflows on
        Kubernetes 276–278

CI/CD (continuous integration/continuous delivery) workflow *(continued)*
  isolating workloads with contexts and namespaces 266–271
  Kubernetes-as-a-Service developer workflow 260–266
  lab 278–279
CKA (Certified Kubernetes Administrator) 8
CKAD (Certified Kubernetes Application Developer) 8
claims
  clusterwide data storage 105–115
  requesting storage with volume claim templates 185–190
Cloud Native Computing Foundation (CNCF) 228
cluster autoscaling 559
cluster-admin role 443
clusters 4
  overview of 447–451
  running in AWS 12–13
  running in Azure 12
  securing resources with role-based access control 424–433
  verifying 13
CNAMEs (canonical names) 55
CNCF (Cloud Native Computing Foundation) 228
Common Vulnerabilities and Exposures (CVE) databases 413
ConfigMaps
  storing and using configuration files in 69–75
  surfacing configuration data from 75–82
configuring applications 65–91
  ConfigMaps
    storing and using configuration files in 69–75
    surfacing configuration data from 75–82
  lab 91
  managing 89–90
  overview of 65–69
  Secrets, configuring sensitive data with 82–88
constraint template 406
container filesystem, data storage 92–96
container probes 283
container runtime 450
Container Runtime Interface (CRI) 19, 450
containers 15–39
  communication between 149–155
  Deployments, defining in application manifests 28–32
  extending applications with multicontainer Pods 149–175
    adapter containers 162–166
    ambassador containers 167–171

    container communication 149–155
    init containers 156–162
    lab 175
    Pod environment 171–174
  monitoring 349–354
  Pods
    running with controllers 21–28
    working with applications in 32–36
  resource management 36–38
  running and managing 15–21
contexts, isolating workloads with 266–271
Contour 558
control plane, initializing 451–455
controller manager 449
controllers
  running Pods with 21–28
  scaling applications across multiple Pods with 122–146
    lab 146
    object ownership 143–146
    overview of 122–128
    scaling for high availability 137–143
    scaling for load 128–136
  triggering workflows with customized 506–512
CrashLoopBackoff 219
CRD (CustomResourceDefinition) 406, 501
create command 28–29, 32, 65, 74, 500
CRI (Container Runtime Interface) 19, 450
CronJobs, running maintenance tasks with 190–198
curl command 240, 350, 383, 557
custom resources, extending Kubernetes with 500
CustomResourceDefinition (CRD) 406, 501
CVE (Common Vulnerabilities and Exposures) databases 413

D

DaemonSets
  rolling updates in 220–225
  scaling applications for high availability 137–143
Dashboard 559
data storage 92–121
  clusterwide data storage with persistent volumes and claims 105–115
  container filesystem 92–96
  dynamic volume provisioning and storage classes 115–119
  lab 120–121
  on node with volumes and mounts 97–104
  requesting with volume claim templates 185–190
  storage choices in Kubernetes 120

data-heavy apps 176–200
  bootstrapping Pods with init containers in
      StatefulSets 180–185
  choosing platform for stateful apps 198–199
  lab 199–200
  requesting storage with volume claim
      templates 185–190
  running maintenance tasks with Jobs and
      CronJobs 190–198
  stability modeling with StatefulSets 176–179
default namespace 61, 266, 430
delete command 36, 90, 142, 500, 503
deploying Kubernetes 447–471
  adding nodes 455–461
  adding Windows nodes 461–469
  at scale 469–471
  initializing control plane 451–455
  lab 471
  overview of clusters 447–451
  running hybrid workloads 461–469
  running Linux workloads 455–461
Deployments
  configuring rolling updates for 213–220
  defining in application manifests 28–32
  scaling applications for load 128–136
  updating with rollouts and rollbacks
      205–213
describe command 69, 83, 402, 503
development-developer workflows 255–279
  continuous delivery in Kubernetes without
      Docker 271–276
  Docker developer workflow 255–259
  evaluating developer workflows on
      Kubernetes 276–278
  isolating workloads with contexts and
      namespaces 266–271
  Kubernetes-as-a-Service developer
      workflow 260–266
  lab 278–279
DNS (Domain Name System) 42, 176
Docker
  continuous delivery in Kubernetes without
      255–259
  developer workflow 255–259
Docker Community Edition, installing 10–11
Docker Desktop, installing 9–10
Domain Name System (DNS) 42, 176
dry-run flag 246

E

ECR (Elastic Container Registry) 271
egress rules 388
EKS (Elastic Kubernetes Service) 5, 12
Elasticsearch, shipping logs to 321–325

EmptyDir volume 95–97, 99–100, 135, 150–151,
    156, 160, 163, 290, 292, 536
env 72
envFrom 72
ephemeral containers 557
etcd 449
events, triggering functions from 543–548
eventual consistency 519
exec command 35
extending applications 149–175
  abstracting connections with ambassador
      containers 167–171
  applying consistency with adapter
      containers 162–166
  container communication 149–155
  lab 175
  Pod environment 171–174
  setting up applications with init containers
      156–162
extending Kubernetes 500–529
  managing third-party components 521
  triggering workflows 506–512
  when to extend 528–529

F

filtering 318, 472
Fluentd, collecting logs from nodes with 315–321

G

get command 500, 503–504
get values command 251
git push workflow 276
GitOps 557
grep filter 328

H

headless Services 56
Helm 228–254
  deploying upgrades safely with 294–301
  indications of good fit 253–254
  lab 254
  modeling dependencies in charts 243–247
  packaging apps with 233–242
  problems solved by 228–233
  upgrading and rolling back releases 248–253
helm create command 235
helm install command 232
HorizontalPodAutoscaler (HPA) 486
HostPath volume 100–102, 104, 116, 136, 138–139,
    313, 315, 458
hosts file 363
HPA (HorizontalPodAutoscaler) 486

HTTP
routing traffic with Ingress rules 363–369
securing apps with HTTPS 378–383
triggering functions from requests 537–543

I

incoming traffic management 357–384
comparing ingress controllers 369–378
lab 384
overview of 383–384
routing HTTP traffic 363–369
securing apps with HTTPS 378–383
traffic routing in Kubernetes 357–362
Ingress 357–384
comparing ingress controllers 369–378
lab 384
overview of 383–384
routing HTTP traffic 363–369
securing apps with HTTPS 378–383
traffic routing in Kubernetes 357–362
ingress classes 374
ingress controllers
comparing 369–378
overview of 383–384
ingress rules 388
init command 455
init containers
bootstrapping Pods with 180–185
setting up applications with 156–162
inner loop 255
input stage 317
install command 235, 239
instance label 335

J

job label 335
Jobs, running maintenance tasks with 190–198
join command 455
join token 455
JWT (JSON Web Token) 438

K

K3s, installing 10–11
KEDA (Kubernetes Event-Driven
Autoscaling) 559
Kube Explorer app 428, 430–431
kubeadm command 466
kubectl apply command 237
kubectl describe output 124
kubectl get command 500
kubectl set image exercise 209
kubeless update command 544

kubelet 450
kube-proxy 450
Kubernetes
application configuration
managing 89–90
overview 65–69
choosing platform 559–560
community 561
continuous delivery in 271–276
data storage
container filesystem 92–96
storage choices 120
deploying 447–471
adding nodes 455–461
adding Windows nodes 461–469
at scale 469–471
initializing control plane 451–455
lab 471
overview of clusters 447–451
running hybrid workloads 461–469
running Linux workloads 455–461
evaluating developer workflows on 276–278
extending 500–529
building Operators for applications 522–528
lab 529
managing third-party components 512–521
triggering workflows 506–512
when to extend 528–529
with custom resources 500–505
information resources 556–559
log entry storage 310–315
logging options 330–331
monitoring
containers and objects 349–354
workloads 332–337
network traffic routing
outside Kubernetes 53–58
overview of 40–45
object ownership 143–146
overview of 4–7
Pod environment 171–174
release management
release strategies 226–227
rollout management 201–205
resource management 36–38
running and managing 15–21
scaling applications 122–128
securing access to resources 417–424
security 412–414
serverless functions 530–536
Service resolution 59–63
traffic routing 357–362
versions and releases 560–561
workload management controls 497–498
workload scheduling 472–477

Kubernetes command-line tool, installing 11
Kubernetes Event-Driven Autoscaling
    (KEDA) 559
Kubernetes-as-a-Service developer workflow
    260–266
kube-state-metrics 349
kube-system namespace 61, 429–430, 454
Kustomize 556

L

lab environment setup 8–13
    downloading source code 9
    installing Docker Community Edition and
        K3s 10–11
    installing Docker Desktop 9–10
    installing Kubernetes command-line tool 11
    running single-node Kubernetes cluster in
        AWS 12–13
    running single-node Kubernetes cluster in
        Azure 12
    verifying cluster 13
labels 335
labs xvii
    configuring applications with ConfigMaps and
        Secrets 91
    connecting Pods over network with Services
        63–64
    data storage with volumes, mounts, and
        claims 120–121
    deploying Kubernetes 471
    development-developer workflows 278–279
    extending applications with multicontainer
        Pods 175
    extending Kubernetes 529
    incoming traffic management 384
    log management 331
    monitoring 356
    packaging and managing apps with
        Helm 254
    release management with rollouts and
        rollbacks 227
    running containers in Kubernetes with Pods
        and Deployments 39
    running data-heavy apps with StatefulSets and
        Jobs 199–200
    scaling applications across multiple Pods with
        controllers 146
    securing access to resources 446
    securing applications 414
    self-healing apps 309
    serverless functions 555
    workload placement and automatic
        scaling 498–499
lint command 235

linux-setup.sh script 451
list command 494, 500
liveness probes, restarting unhealthy Pods
    288–293
log management 310–331
    collecting logs from nodes with Fluentd
        315–321
    lab 331
    logging options in Kubernetes 330–331
    parsing and filtering log entries 325–330
    shipping logs to Elasticsearch 321–325
    storage of log entries in Kubernetes 310–315
logger sidecar container 313

M

master taint 460, 473
maxSurge setting 223
maxSurge value 216, 219
maxUnavailable setting 222–223
maxUnavailable value 216, 219
metrics exporters, monitoring third-party apps
    with 344–349
metrics-server 485–486, 489, 498
minReadySeconds field 218
minReadySeconds setting 222
monitoring 332–356
    applications
        built with Prometheus client libraries
            337–344
        third-party apps with metrics exporters
            344–349
    investment in 354–355
    Kubernetes
        containers and objects 349–354
        workloads 332–337
    lab 356
mounts, data storage on node 97–104
multinode and multiarchitecture clusters
    447–471
    adding nodes 455–461
    adding Windows nodes 461–469
    initializing control plane 451–455
    lab 471
    overview of clusters 447–451
    running hybrid workloads 461–469
    running Linux workloads 455–461
    understanding Kubernetes at scale 469–471

N

namespaces 61, 266–271
Network File System (NFS) 105, 458
network policies, securing communication
    with 385–394

network traffic routing 40–64
  Kubernetes Service resolution 59–63
  lab 63–64
  outside Kubernetes 53–58
  overview of 40–45
  Pods
    routing external traffic to 49–53
    routing traffic between 45–49
NFS (Network File System) 105, 458
nodes 4, 448
  adding 455–461
  adding Windows nodes 461–469
  collecting logs from 315–321
  protecting with resource limits 301–308
NodeSelector 476
nodeSelector field 140
NoSchedule taint 474, 476

O

OIDC (OpenID Connect) 420, 441
OLM (Operator Lifecycle Manager) 515
OPA (Open Policy Agent) 405–412
Operators
  building for applications 522–528
  managing third-party components with
    512–521
os label 476
outer loop 255
output stage 317

P

PaaS (Platform-as-a-Service) 255
packaging applications, with Helm 233–242
parallelism field 193
parent chart 243
partition setting 223
PDBs (Pod disruption budgets) 557
permissions, discovering and auditing with
    plugins 441–445
Persistent Volume Claim (PVC) 107, 185
PersistentVolumes (PV) 105
Platform-as-a-Service (PaaS) 255
plugins, discovering and auditing permissions
    with 441–445
Pod disruption budgets (PDBs) 557
Pods
  bootstrapping with init containers in
    StatefulSets 180–185
  connecting over network 40–64
    Kubernetes Service resolution 59–63
    lab 63–64
    overview of network traffic routing 40–45
    routing external traffic to Pods 49–53

    routing traffic between Pods 45–49
    routing traffic outside Kubernetes
      53–58
  directing placement with affinity and
    antiaffinity 477–484
  environment overview 171–174
  extending applications with
    multicontainer 149–175
    adapter containers 162–166
    ambassador containers 167–171
    container communication 149–155
    init containers 156–162
    lab 175
  management policy 557
  restarting unhealthy 288–293
  routing traffic to healthy 283–288
  running with controllers 21–28
  scaling applications across multiple 122–146
    lab 146
    object ownership 143–146
    overview of 122–128
    scaling for high availability 137–143
    scaling for load 128–136
  working with applications in 32–36
PodSecurityPolicy 558
port-forward 248, 359
preemption, protecting resources with
    491–496
PreferNoSchedule taint 476
preferred rules 480
printenv command 71
priorities, protecting resources with 491–496
priority class 494
PriorityClassName field 496
progressDeadlineSeconds field 218
projected volumes 557
Prometheus 332–356
  investment in monitoring 354–355
  lab 356
  monitoring apps built with Prometheus
    client libraries 337–344
  monitoring containers and objects 349–354
  monitoring third-party apps with metrics
    exporters 344–349
  montioring Kubernetes workloads 332–337
Prometheus Operator 558
PromQL (Prometheus query language) 345
providers 549
provisioner field 117
PV (PersistentVolumes) 105
PVC (Persistent Volume Claim) 107, 185

Q

Quality of Service classes 558

R

Rancher Kubernetes Engine (RKE) 558
RBAC (role-based access control) 417
    binding roles to groups of users and service
        accounts 433–441
    discovering and auditing permissions with
        plugins 441–445
    lab 446
    overview of 417–424
    securing resources within clusters 424–433
    strategy for 445
rbac-lookup plugin 443
rbac-tools 443
readiness probes 284
readiness probes, routing traffic to healthy
    Pods 283–288
readOnlyRootFilesystem option 397
reclaimPolicy field 117
record flag 205
release management 201–227
    lab 227
    release strategies 226–227
    rolling updates
        configuring for Deployments 213–220
        in DaemonSets and StatefulSets 220–225
    rollout management 201–205
    rollouts and rollbacks, updating Deployments
        with 205–213
    upgrading and rolling back Helm releases
        248–253
releases 231
replicas field 123, 129
ReplicaSets, scaling applications for load
    128–136
required rules 480
requiredDuringSchedulingIgnoredDuring-
    Execution 478
resource limits, protecting apps and nodes
    with 301–308
restartPolicy field 192
reuse-values flag 249
reverse proxy 357
RKE (Rancher Kubernetes Engine) 558
role-based access control. *See* RBAC
rollout command 203
rollouts and rollbacks
    rolling updates
        configuring for Deployments 213–220
        in DaemonSets and StatefulSets 220–225
    rollout management 201–205
    updating Deployments with 205–213
    upgrading and rolling back Helm releases
        248–253
routers 374

run command 23, 28–29, 73
runAsNonRoot field 404

S

scale command 130, 204
scaling applications 122–146
    for high availability with DaemonSets 137–143
    for load with Deployments and ReplicaSets
        128–136
    lab 146
    object ownership 143–146
    overview of 122–128
scheduler 449
schedules, triggering functions from 543–548
scoring 473
scraping 334
Secrets, configuring sensitive data 82–88
securing applications 385–414
    blocking and modifying workloads 398–405
    controlling admission 406–412
    lab 414
    overview of 412–414
    restricting container capabilities 394–398
    securing communication 385–394
securing resources 417–446
    binding roles to groups of users and service
        accounts 433–441
    discovering and auditing permissions with
        plugins 441–445
    lab 446
    overview of 417–424
    strategy for 445
    within cluster 424–433
security contexts, restricting container capabilities
    with 394–398
self-healing apps 283–309
    deploying upgrades safely with Helm 294–301
    lab 309
    limits of 308–309
    protecting apps and nodes with resource
        limits 301–308
    restarting unhealthy Pods with liveness
        probes 288–293
    routing traffic to healthy Pods using readiness
        probes 283–288
serverless functions 530–555
    abstracting with Serverless 548–553
    lab 555
    overview of 530–536
    pros and cons of 554–555
    triggering from events and schedules 543–548
    triggering from HTTP requests 537–543
Serverless, abstracting serverless functions
    with 548–553

service account projection 558
service accounts, binding roles to 433–441
Service API 384
Service Topology 557
Services 40–64
    lab 63–64
    network traffic routing 40–45
    routing external traffic to Pods 49–53
    routing traffic between Pods 45–49
    routing traffic outside Kubernetes 53–58
    Service resolution 59–63
set argument 232
set command 204
Set-ExecutionPolicy command 363
shareProcessNamespace field 173
sidecar pattern 156
site reliability engineering (SRE) 8, 433
sleep command 293
source code, downloading 9
SRE (site reliability engineering) 8, 433
standbys 185
StatefulSets
    bootstrapping Pods with init containers in
        180–185
    rolling updates in 220–225
    stability modeling with 176–179
storage classes 115–119
stress tool 494
stringData field 85
subchart 243
system:serviceaccount 427

T

tail command 163
templates 185
templates folder 235
time-to-live (TTL) 196
TLS (Transport Layer Security) 378
top command 484–485
topology key 481
Transport Layer Security (TLS) 378
TTL (time-to-live) 196

U

unknown user 395
upgrade command 248, 251, 298

use-context command 269
user experience (UX) 226
UX (user experience) 226

V

values.yaml file 235
verbs 419
version label 206, 407
VerticalPodAutoscaler 558
VM (virtual machine) 9
volume claim templates, requesting storage
    with 185–190
volume mounts 75
volumeBindingMode field 117
volumeClaimTemplates field 185
volumes
    data storage
        clusterwide 105–115
        on node 97–104
    dynamic provisioning 115–119
    requesting storage with volume claim
        templates 185–190

W

watch flag 222
watch parameter 510
webhooks, blocking and modifying workloads
    with 398–405
who-can plugin 441
workflows, triggering with custom
    controllers 506–512
workload management 472–499
    automatic scaling 484–491
    controls for workload management 497–498
    directing Pod placement with affinity and
        antiaffinity 477–484
    lab 498–499
    protecting resources with preemption and
        priorities 491–496
    workload scheduling 472–477
workloads
    blocking and modifying with webhooks
        398–405
    monitoring 332–337
    running hybrid workloads 461–469
    running Linux workloads 455–461